LATIN AMERICA

An Interpretive History

LATIN AMERICA

An Interpretive History

Donald Marquand Dozer

Department of History
University of California at Santa Barbara

McGRAW-HILL BOOK COMPANY, INC.   1962

New York   San Francisco   Toronto   London

LATIN AMERICA: An Interpretive History

III

To my wife, *Alice*

Preface

The history of Latin America is one of the great epics of the modern world, lacking only its Homer and Vergil. What other area of the world can show within any five centuries of its history such action-packed drama, such fervent religiosity, such popular upsurges, such climacterics of personal achievement, such tense interplays of man and fate? Latin America is a complicated fabric, and its history is not the dead past but an ever-living reality that stretches back to the Nile Valley, the shores of ancient Greece, and the templed civilizations of Central America and the high Andes. As such it deserves at least equal status with the history of other world islands in our twentieth century.

This book attempts to get at the roots of things in Latin America and to present answers in historical perspective that are more satisfying than the usual glib newspaper clichés and brash generalizations. It undertakes to explain how Latin America has come to be what it is today. It is therefore not a factual cornucopia or detailed reference work but rather an interpretive study. It tries to make Latin American history more interesting and more meaningful than a dreary recital of the rise and fall of *caudillos*. It is intended to illuminate the problems of modern Latin America and to throw light even upon the future role of that vast area in world life, for, as Ernesto Quesada has written, "en el estudio del pasado está la enseñanza del porvenir y causas análogas pueden producir fenómenos semejantes en cualquier época" [in the study of the past is instruction for the future and analogous causes can produce similar phenomena in any epoch].

The treatment is generally chronological, covering the entire span of Latin American history from earliest times to the contemporary scene, but it avoids the country-by-country narrative which is commonly presented as the history of Latin America. One may know all that can be known about the history of Nicaragua or Argentina, for example, without understanding basic trends and forces in Latin America as a whole. The emphasis here has been placed upon the interaction of generalized forces. The purpose has been to strive constantly for high levels of comprehensiveness using individual countries only for purposes of illustration and to deal with over-all trend patterns in much the same fashion as historians of Europe seek to synthesize their story.

This book is intended to embody the results of all available modern scholarship supplemented by the author's own extensive experiences in the Latin American area. His literary collaborators, so to speak, include all the authors whose works are here cited. He owes particular appreciation to his colleague, Prof. Philip W. Powell, for his critical review of the first ten chapters and to Professors Eduardo Ruiz and John Francis Bannon, S.J., who offered suggestions on the entire manuscript while it was still in provisional form. For invaluable library assistance the author is indebted to Dr. Donald C. Davidson and his staff at the University of California, Santa Barbara, particularly Mrs. Martha H. Peterson, Mrs. Violet Shue, Miss Sheila McMurray, and Mr. Anthony Greco. Correction of minor errors in the original text has been made possible in this second printing through the suggestions of Charles A. Bacarisse, Ronald Hilton, and the Honorable Sheldon Mills.

Unless otherwise indicated, acknowledgment for the use of the maps is gratefully made to Barnes and Noble, Inc., for maps published originally in A. Curtis Wilgus, *Latin America in Maps, Historic, Geographic, Economic*, New York, 1943. Acknowledgments for the use of the other maps and for the illustrations are indicated in the appropriate credit lines.

Historians, wrote Cervantes in *Don Quixote*, ought "to be exact, truthful, and dispassionate; and neither interest nor fear, rancor nor affection should cause them to deviate from truth, whose mother is history, the rival of time, the depository of events, the witness of the past, an example and guide to the present, and the monitor of the future." In this spirit this history has been written.

Donald Marquand Dozer

Bibliographical Note

A useful companion volume to the present history is Benjamin Keen, *Readings in Latin American Civilization, 1492 to the Present* (Houghton Mifflin Company, Boston, 1955), and appropriate readings in it have been included in the suggestions for Additional Reading appended to each chapter. Other compilations of readings which can be used in connection with this history include:

Germán Arciniegas (ed.), *The Green Continent: a Comprehensive View of Latin America by Its Leading Writers*, Alfred A. Knopf, Inc., New York, 1944;

A. Curtis Wilgus, *Readings in Latin American Civilization*, Barnes & Noble, Inc., New York, 1946; and

Abel Plenn, *The Southern Americas: a New Chronicle*, Creative Age Press, Inc., New York, 1948.

The lists of Additional Readings have been intentionally kept to a minimum length. They include in general only the latest and most authoritative books and articles with occasional evaluative comment. They are not intended to constitute in total an exhaustive bibliography on Latin American history, which indeed seems unnecessary since the publication of R. A. Humphreys, *Latin American History: a Guide to the Literature in English*, Oxford University Press, New York, 1958. This outstanding critical bibliography is an indispensable tool to anyone interested in delving into the subject of Latin American history. Other bibliographical aids include Stojan Albert Bayitch, *Latin America: a Bibliographical Guide to Economy, History, Law, Politics, and Society*, University of Miami Press, Coral Gables, Florida, 1961, and the monumental work by Antonio Palau y Dulcet, *Manual del Librero Hispano-Americano: bibliografía general española e hispano-americano desde la invención de la imprenta hasta nuestros tiempos*, 2d ed., A. Palau, Barcelona, 12 vols., 1948–1959.

The references in the Additional Readings are supplemented by Appendix I, which provides a selected list of English translations of Latin American fiction. Additional titles will be found in José Manuel Topete, *A Working Bibliography of Latin American Literature*, W. B. Fraser, St. Augustine, Fla., 1952, and *A Working Bibliography of Brazilian Literature*, University of Florida Press, Gainesville, Fla., 1957. For further references to Latin American fiction readers with a competence in Spanish should consult the series

Diccionario de la Literatura Latinoamericana, published by the Department of Cultural Affairs, Pan American Union, Washington, D.C., 1958–, and Fernando Alegría, *Breve Historia de la Novela Hispanoamericana,* Gráfica Atenea, Mexico, 1959.

A few of the general histories of Latin America which are available in English have been broken down by chapters and correlated, though necessarily somewhat imperfectly, with the chapters of this history in the Additional Readings. Others have been merely listed once in the chapter list to which they seemed most pertinent but can be profitably read in connection with subsequent chapters. Further reading suggestions in both English and the languages of the Latin American countries may be found in the American Historical Association's *Guide to Historical Literature,* The Macmillan Company, New York, 1961, pages 656–696; and in the Hispanic Foundation of the Library of Congress, *Handbook of Latin American Studies,* Harvard University Press, Cambridge, Mass., 1936–1951; University of Florida Press, Gainesville, Fla., 1951–.

Statistical data on the Latin American countries may be found in the following series of annual volumes of the United Nations: *Statistical Yearbook,* Statistical Office of the United Nations, Department of Economic and Social Affairs, New York, 1948–; and the invaluable *Economic Survey of Latin America,* Economic Commission for Latin America, New York, 1948–. Other sources of data include the International Monetary Fund, *International Financial Statistics,* Washington, 1948–; and the Center of Latin American Studies, University of California, Los Angeles, *Statistical Abstract of Latin America,* 1955–. Selected basic data on the individual countries are presented in Appendix II of this history.

Contents

I

Latin America in Perspective

Latin America flashes across the newspaper headlines in the United States and Europe as a problem area. It attracts the notice of the outside world by such events as the sinking of the United States battleship *Maine* in Havana harbor in 1898, the expropriation of United Fruit Company lands by the Guatemalan government in 1952–1954, the assaults on Vice President Richard Nixon in Lima and Caracas in May, 1958, the impassioned "anti-Yanqui" speeches of Fidel Castro, and the earthquakes which shake Chile to pieces. Outsiders associate Latin America with turbulence, violence, and catastrophe. Its people are stereotyped as afflicted cyclically with siesta indolence and revolutionary destructiveness. It is usually dismissed from consideration except in times of crisis—either theirs or ours.

The story of the Latin American people has often been interpreted simply as paralleling that of the people of the United States because of the supposed common historical experiences. All the European peoples who moved into America, both North and South, were actuated, it is alleged, by much the same motives. In the New World Hispanic Americans and Anglo-Americans encountered similar environmental conditions unfamiliar to Europeans and had to adapt themselves to them. They faced similar pioneer difficulties. They founded outposts of European settlement in America in approximately the same historical epoch. In the late eighteenth and early nineteenth centuries they were inspired by the same principles of freedom and republicanism and broke with their mother countries, England, France, Spain, and Portugal. They set up independent governments at about the same time. And since independence they have had to deal with similar agricultural, industrial, and political problems. But these similarities, though striking, are likely to be deceptive. Conclusions drawn from them often degenerate into superficialities, which obscure basic differences and disagreements. They also have the effect of minimizing the uniqueness of Latin America's development, which is interesting and meaningful in itself.

Geographical Assets and Liabilities

Latin America is the name given to the land mass which lies south of the United States in the Western Hemisphere. This region includes almost 14

1

per cent of the total land area of the world and over 7 per cent of its population. Within this territory, extending from the Rio Grande and Florida on the north to Cape Horn at the southern tip of the South American continent, are situated twenty nations and several colonial dependencies of England, France, and the Netherlands. Perhaps the most conspicuous characteristic of this area is its great variety. Latin America is highly diversified as to animals, plants, terrain, climates, races, social customs, and political practices. On portions of it the taming hand of man has not yet made any considerable impression.

Here skeletons of once populous cities dead for a thousand years lie nestled among unscalable mountains or have been swallowed up by the entangling jungle. Picturesque Indians unchanged in dress and custom for centuries throng the market places or crowd the plazas on days of fiesta. Mountain-walled communities pursue their age-long life of isolation, and primitive llama trains jog lazily along mountain trails carrying precious metals for world refineries. Desert wastes alternate with fertile pampas or *llanos,* which stretch into the distance beyond the limits of human vision. Here too are great modern cities where life pulsates in time with the modern currents of art, literature, banking, and finance in the outside world, and luxurious airplanes hurry diplomats and businessmen back and forth between Latin American capitals and other world centers. The old and the new, the past and the present are strangely intermingled in the variegated lands of Latin America.

As we are accustomed to think of our own country in terms of vast distances, we find it difficult to realize that Brazil alone is larger in area than the continental United States excluding Alaska. It is almost twice as large as all of Europe west of Soviet Russia. Its mighty Amazon River, the largest stream in the world, is more than 150 miles wide at its mouth and can be navigated by ocean-going vessels for a distance of 2,300 miles, which is the approximate distance between New York and San Francisco. It drains a basin nearly as large as the United States, and its mouth is almost as close to New York by steamer as to Rio de Janeiro. But Brazil is not the only large Latin American country. Argentina is more than one-third the size of the United States and if superimposed upon North America at corresponding northern latitudes would stretch from Tampico in Mexico to Hudson Bay. Mexico is roughly equal to three states the size of Texas. Colombia is nearly nine times as large as New York State. Venezuela is equal in area to all our Atlantic seaboard states from Maine to Florida. Bolivia is ten times the area of Ohio. Chile is longer than the United States is wide. And Uruguay, the smallest nation in South America, has a greater area than all of New England. A traveler going directly by air from California to southern Argentina travels three times the distance from San Francisco to New York to reach his destination. Mexico City is almost as far by air from Buenos Aires as London is from Calcutta.

Latin America is an area of "greats"—great distances, great mountains,

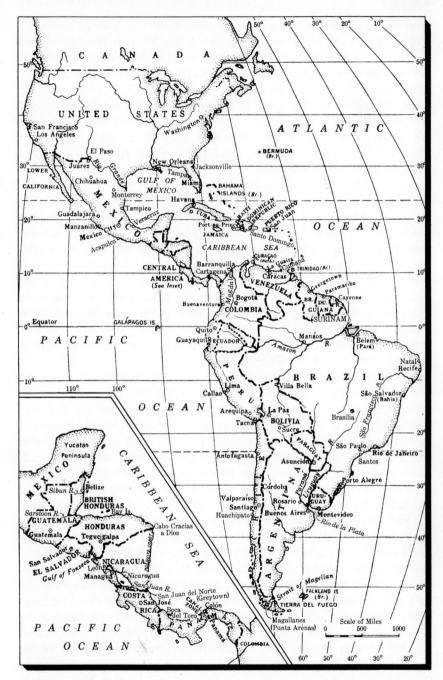

Modern Latin America.

great rivers, a great past, and a great future. Until well into the nineteenth century it was the really important part of the Western Hemisphere and exerted a larger influence on the rest of the world than did Anglo-America. It has an enormous potential for growth and progress in twentieth-century terms. Latin Americans were described by a perceptive German traveler, Baron Alexander von Humboldt, in the early nineteenth century as "ragged beggars sitting on benches of gold." Underlying most of Bolivia is a petroleum bed which is estimated to be the largest oil field in South America. It surpasses even that of Venezuela, which is the second largest national producer of petroleum in the world. Brazil has a capacity for electric power production which is the fourth largest in the world. Chile's copper reserves are more than one-third of the world's total, and her copper production is being rivaled by that of Peru. Colombia has rich salt deposits at Zipaquirá which are extraordinary for being several hundred feet thick and covering several hundred square miles. Brazil, Venezuela, and all the Andean countries of South America from Colombia to Chile have rich iron resources. Cuba's iron deposits are estimated at 3.5 billion tons. Ecuador possesses over 90,000 square miles of virgin forest rich in dyewoods, balsa wood, cinchona trees, and other valuable timber; and Brazil's forest lands in the Amazon Basin include some 1,500 different varieties of hardwoods and cover over 1 million square miles. But Latin America remains largely undeveloped. Its natural resources have scarcely been touched.[1]

Middle America and the Pacific coast of South America are strikingly devoid of large rivers and good harbors. No great river gateways lead into Latin America from the west. Indeed the entire west coast of the American continents south of the Golden Gate at San Francisco provides few natural sheltering places for ocean-going vessels. The west coast ports of Acapulco, Buenaventura, Callao, Antofagasta, and Valparaíso possess no natural roadsteads, and traders using those ports have to depend upon lighterage facilities or artificially constructed harbors. Along almost the entire west coast of South America the rivers are short and tumble precipitately into the ocean. The port cities squat precariously on narrow coastal shelves, their hinterlands blockaded by formidable mountain sentinels. The only natural harbor of any size is provided by the coastal indentation at Guayaquil. But Latin America is more fortunate in its east coast ports. Among them the breathtakingly beautiful and commodious natural harbor of Rio de Janeiro is world famous, and the La Plata estuary is capable of sheltering all the naval and merchant fleets of the world. Fortunately for the first white voyagers to Latin America the places where they made their landfalls were well supplied with natural berthing facilities for their tiny vessels—at the Ozama River mouth on the southern coast of Española, at Havana on the northwestern coast of Cuba, at Cartagena, Coro, and Cumaná on the coast of the Spanish Main, and at Veracruz on the Gulf coast of New Spain.

[1] Appendix II gives certain basic data on the Latin American countries, p. 583.

Latin America is ill-favored in many geographical and climatic aspects. Extensive deserts or areas of semiaridity in northern Mexico, the *llanos* of Colombia and Venezuela, the *caatinga* of northeastern Brazil, northwestern Argentina, and Atacama in northern Chile have repelled settlement. Mountain barriers have deflected the course of migration. Paucity of harbors and rivers along the Pacific coastal plain has rendered exploitation of the western mineral-stored interior regions difficult and has given Latin America an eastward orientation. Almost completely unconquerable by white men has been the luxuriant, savage jungle or *selva,* where the few trails lead like dark caverns into the mysterious unknown and every step makes a pool in the boggy ground. This "Green Hell" has exerted a decisive influence upon the course of settlement. In the ancient Mayan country of Yucatan and Guatemala, in the southern part of the Central American isthmus, in large parts of the Amazon River basin, and in the swamplands of the Chaco in Paraguay, the tropical forests with their "endless maze of trunks, lianas, creepers, ferns, roots, and plants that . . . twist about one another, climbing upward" have raised a menacing, impenetrable front to civilization.[2] They inexorably smother out all would-be conquerors and all evidences of their handiwork in their tentaclelike embrace. In no other setting perhaps do man's efforts seem so puny and futile. Latin America has a larger expanse of rainy tropical area than any other continent. In the Amazon Basin the heavy rainfall, which exceeds 80 inches a year, leaches away almost all surface fertility, and even the jungle trees maintain a precarious existence only by clutching a roothold in the dissolving terrain. A civilized agricultural existence here is difficult if not impossible for white men.

For a different reason the *altiplano,* which extends roughly in a northwest-southeast direction from Ecuador through Peru and Bolivia between the eastern and western ranges of the high Andean chain and south into Argentina a distance of some 2,000 miles, is inhospitable to white men and has perforce been left to its bandy-legged, ponchoed native inhabitants, descendants of the pre-Inca Quechuans and Aymarás. This tableland lying at an altitude between 11,000 and 16,000 feet above sea level is the highest plateau in the world after the great Tibetan plateau in Asia. Wind-swept, treeless, and subject to overpowering hailstorms, it produces almost nothing but dry yellow *ichu* grass, suitable as forage for the llama, alpaca, and vicuña, and potatoes which in dried form are the staple of the Indian diet. Indeed this harsh region was the original home of the "Irish" potato. Somewhat similar weather conditions, though at lower altitudes, in southern Argentina and Chile make these regions also difficult for white settlers. Here, the Chilean poetess Gabriela Mistral has written, are found "the trees of Dante's tortured forest . . . in long processions of kneeling bodies. . . . The wind does not tolerate anything in its Patagonian kingdom except the everlasting humility of the grass." Neverthe-

---

[2] Ciro Alegría, *Broad and Alien Is the World,* Holt, Rinehart and Winston, Inc., New York, 1941, p. 296.

less, on the ungrateful Strait of Magellan overlooking the island of Tierra del Fuego a white settlement has maintained itself at Punta Arenas (Magallanes) since 1843 as the southernmost town in the world.

Racial and Cultural Diversity

There is not one Latin America but many Latin Americas, differing from one another in soil, climate, population, economy, culture. Generalizations about Latin America as a whole should be avoided; they can have no more— and no less—validity than generalizations about Europe, Africa, or Asia as a whole. Like those continents Latin America must be considered as a congeries of units whose intergovernmental, interregional, and international relations have been and still are, in some cases, as complicated as those of Europe. Within the apparent unity of Hispanic-American civilization will be found a rich variety of cultures and national forms. Intelligent generalizations can therefore be made only after careful study of Brazil, Colombia, Venezuela, Costa Rica, and all the remaining countries and after due consideration of all the complicated regional factors in this area of almost infinite diversity. Modern Brazil, for example, cannot be understood without a knowledge of the interplay of forces between the north central area with its vast barren expanses inhabited by isolated groups of peasants, the northeast with its periodic droughts and floods and its unemployment and human misery, and the south with its overpopulated urban areas developing at top speed. Moreover, the Latin American people and their problems must be studied with sympathy or not at all. One of our most urgent problems is to understand what makes a Mexican a Mexican, an Argentine an Argentine, and generally what makes Latin Americans Latin Americans. How have they come to be what they are? And, further, what do they have in common with the people and policies of the United States?

The entire South American continent lies east of a line of longitude drawn through Jacksonville, Florida. It therefore is situated not south but southeast of the United States. Whereas continental United States extends over only 58 degrees of longitude, Latin America at its widest dimensions, from the westernmost tip of Mexico to the easternmost tip of Brazil, covers 82 degrees of longitude. On its eastern bulge it approaches within 1,900 miles of Africa. Latin America occupies, therefore, almost an intermediate geographical location between the Old World and the New and has been highly susceptible to influences emanating from the Old World. It is, in a much more direct sense than is the United States, the heir of Roman Europe. Its history cannot be told without reference to Roman law, the Renaissance, European encyclopedism, rationalism, romanticism, liberalism, Catholicism, socialism—even cubism, surrealism, and existentialism. Nineteen of these twenty countries, for example, still retain their linguistic and cultural allegiance to the Hispanic tradition. Latin America forms one of the most extensive Roman Catholic culture areas in the world and accounts for the fact that the peoples of the Western Hemisphere today are more than two to one Roman Catholic. The close church-state relationship that exists in many of the Latin American countries finds its counterpart in many other nations of the modern world, notably in England and Sweden.

Spain and, to a lesser extent, Portugal have projected themselves powerfully into modern Latin America. Evidence is furnished not only by the Catholicism, the prevailing languages, and the Iberian place names which are sprinkled liberally over the map but also by the tile-roofed dwellings, the cathedrals, which raise their towers over every capital plaza, the festive *carnavales* (carnivals) and *corridas de toros* (bullfights), the stylized manners of "society," and official bureaucratic techniques. Through the Iberian mother countries Moorish culture was brought to Latin America and traces of it still survive, as, for example, in the names of certain taxes and government offices and in the traditionally subordinate status of women.

After the discovery of America the newly found lands in the West became the object of interest to France and later to England and the Netherlands, which challenged Spain's claim to them by explorations and colonizations of their own. By reason of the claims thus initially laid and successfully defended through an imperial era of more than three centuries it was determined eventually that the European influences that would predominate in the area south of the United States would be Spanish and Portuguese. Until the opening of the nineteenth century the important expansions of Europe into America were made by Spain and Portugal. They were the principal carriers of European civilization to the New World. But enclaves of French, English, and Dutch culture were established and have persisted to the present time, particularly in the surviving colonial areas of those nations in Latin America.

The influence of France has been noteworthy not so much by reason of its territorial position as a Latin American government as by reason of its cultural dominance in the world of manners, fashions, and the arts. Its colonial empire in America has dwindled to French Guiana and a few sugar and rum islands in the Caribbean, of which Martinique and Guadaloupe are the most important, and its acknowledged cultural influence, though considerably bastardized, is limited to French-speaking Haiti. But its subtle influence is all-pervasive among cultured Latin Americans. Not only are Parisian books read and Parisian styles copied, but the French revolutionary tradition, embodied in the slogan *liberté, égalité, fraternité,* piques the interest of younger sons of traditional ruling elites and exerts an appeal beyond them to leaders of new social forces and mass movements.

Latin America then is deeply imbued with non-American traditions, ideas, and customs. Its history has sometimes been told as only incidental to the history of Spain, Portugal, and France, as only a projection, as it were, of their history, and a thing, therefore, scarcely worth studying in itself. Certainly an understanding of European civilizations, particularly the Spanish,

Portuguese, and French during the formative sixteenth, seventeenth, and eighteenth centuries, is essential to an understanding of modern Latin America. But the history of the Latin American peoples has also been tied up with the history of several other countries of Europe and cannot be adequately told without reference to them. So intermingled have been the European influences with the native Indian cultures that an Argentine scholar, Ricardo Rojas, has suggested the name *Eurindia* to describe the combined European-Indian civilization of Latin America.[3]

The generic term Latin America as applied to this area is, strictly speaking, not entirely accurate. It is broader and more acceptable than the occasionally used Hispanic America and Ibero-America because it gives due credit to the contributions which all countries of Europe whose languages are derived from the Latin—Spanish, Portuguese, French, and Italian—have made to the formation of modern Latin America. But it ignores the millions of Indians, descendants of the aboriginal inhabitants of the American continents, to whom the Latin-derived cultures and languages are alien, and it also ignores the Basque, Negro, German, "Syrian" or Levantine, and many other non-Latin population elements which have been and continue to be influential in the life of this area. Nevertheless the term Latin America has come to be widely used and is generally understood to apply to the continent and a half with which this book is concerned.

A conspicuous characteristic of Latin America is mixture—*mestizaje*. It is a blend of races, cultures, and even languages. Despite or rather because of all these varied elements which have entered into the making of modern Latin America it is an area which is not explicable in terms that explain other areas of the world. It must be dealt with as an area *sui generis,* having its own culture, its own racial stocks, its own traditions, its own aspirations, its own distinctive accent.

Latin America is inhabited by a polyglot population numbering almost 190 million and composed of almost all possible combinations of racial and national strains. The population of Argentina, for example, is 90 per cent European in origin, whereas that of Paraguay, adjoining it to the north, is Guaraní Indian in about the same proportion. Latin America as a whole is the largest area of Western European settlement in the world. It is also probably the largest area of African settlement. Not only Spain, Portugal, France, England, and Holland, but also Germany, Italy, Africa, and even Asia are actively present in Latin America today. Here are white Argentines and black Venezuelans who speak the language of Castile; copper-colored Paraguayans who know only their native Guaraní; black Haitians who speak French patois; black Barbadians, Trinidadians, and Panamanians who speak Oxford English; Uruguayans of Italian origin who speak Spanish; Colombian *cholos,* completely Indian in face and figure, who haggle with customers in the market in Spanish; Curaçaoans who live in Dutch colonial

[3] Ricardo Rojas, *Eurindia*, J. Roldán y Cía., Buenos Aires, 1924.

houses and speak a conglomerate idiom of French, Spanish, Dutch, and English called *papiamento;* German Chileans and Brazilians who have spoken the language of their German fatherland for four generations; Englishmen by whom Buenos Aires is always pronounced "Bonus Arez" and Managua always "Menaiguwa"; and a host of other linguistic groups. Spanish America is far from being entirely Spanish in language. Brazil is far from being entirely Portuguese in either tongue or culture. The cultural and linguistic connection between Haiti and France is tenuous in the extreme. Latin America is a crossroads of nationalities and races.

To Latin Americans race is less important than it is to certain other peoples. To them racial fusion is not only not reprobated but may even be socially encouraged. As a melting pot of races and nationalities Latin America has been active over a longer period of time and has accomplished a greater degree of amalgamation than has the United States. The general strains in that area are pure whites, pure Indians, pure Negroes; *mestizos,* called variously *ladinos, cholos,* and in Brazil *mamelucos, curibocas,* and *caboclos,* who are descendants of mixed unions of whites and Indians; *zambos* or *zambahigos* in the Caribbean area and *cafusos* in Brazil, who are of combined Indian and Negro parentage; mulattoes, who are of combined Negro and white parentage; and *pardos* in Brazil who are a mixture of all three colors. But these are the simple categories. The child of a mixed union of a *mestizo* and a white in the colonial period was called a *castizo;* of a mulatto and a white, a *morisco;* of a *morisco* and a white, a *chino;* of a *chino* and an Indian, a *salto atrás;* of a *salto atrás* and a mulatto, a *lobo;* of a *lobo* and a *chino,* a *jíbaro;* of a *jíbaro* and a mulatto, an *albarazado;* of an *albarazado* and a Negress, a *canbujo;* of a *canbujo* and an Indian, a *sanbaigo;* of a *sanbaigo* and a *lobo,* a *calpamulato;* and so on into almost infinite variety. Latin America contains almost every possible combination of colors, every mixture of mixtures. Mulattoes, for example, are characterized as *tercerones, quarterones, quinterones* and even *octorones,* depending upon the degree of color. During the colonial period Spanish law recognized approximately eighty possible racial combinations, and these have been increased since independence by mixtures with new immigrant strains.

The character of the dominant racial strain varies from country to country. A traveler visiting the ocean ports of Middle America will readily conclude that the Negro element predominates in those countries. As he proceeds south by way of the ocean ports on the Atlantic coast of South America he will find the Negro and mulatto strain dominant to the equator and below, but thereafter the port population becomes increasingly white. If our traveler goes by air and stops at capitals instead of ocean ports he will gain an entirely different impression. He will conclude now that white and *mestizo* elements prevail, for these are the populations which form the majority in the highlands, where most of the capitals are situated.

In general the blacks are most numerous in the Caribbean and along the

Atlantic coast plains of the Guianas and Brazil. The largest numbers of whites are found in the temperate-zone countries of Argentina, Uruguay, Chile, and southern Brazil. Indians predominate in those areas where they have habitually lived, namely, the Cordilleran plateaus from Bolivia north to Mexico, with offshoots in Paraguay and Venezuela. Of all the Latin American countries Haiti is the most nearly black, being more than 99 per cent either Negro or mulatto. Argentina is the most nearly white, being more nearly white than the United States. Paraguay and Bolivia have the proportionately largest number of Indians. In these last-named countries the prevalent tongues are the native Indian languages, Guaraní in Paraguay and Quechuan and Aymará in Bolivia.

The white Spanish population element in the predominantly Spanish-speaking countries of Latin America forms a cultural and in some instances also a political elite. In them the soul of Spain still lives. They trail the glory of a banished empire. They have long since sloughed off the stigma of the Black Legend (*La Leyenda Negra*), which indeed some of their *criollo* forebears helped to create—the legend of a uniquely malevolent, fanatical, and abusive stepmother Spain. They cherish and perpetuate the heritage of a European-Latin culture, which has for more than four and one-half centuries slowly fixed itself upon their countries; and if from their positions of inherited social and economic privilege they sometimes seem to be too self-contained and ungenerous it is because they take their cultural responsibilities seriously. Their Hispanism, deeply rooted in a thousand years of Mediterranean history, gives them a deep feeling for the individual person and for his natural rights, but this feeling is not associated with democracy as a rational and logical system of human relationships. Their continuing sense of being noblemen by nature helps to explain their attitude toward caste. They are guardians of gentility and maintain the tradition of gracious living. Insisting that those who have and those who know should set the standards of society, they often exert a controlling influence whether they are in official positions or not. When thrown on the defensive as they frequently are by the sheer force of opposing numbers their mental acumen, their skill in intrigue and manipulation, their traditional power position, and their close relationship with the Catholic Church usually enable them to make a quick recovery. In those countries where new articulate Indian masses and organized city workers have appeared, the Spanish elite are regarded with jealousy and hence are sources of discord; but in most countries of Latin America they are a stabilizing force. The numbers, though not the stabilizing influence, of the Spanish population element were reinforced by the influx of Spanish republican exiles after their defeat in the Spanish Civil War in 1939.

By way of contrast the Portuguese element in Brazil is more latitudinarian and relaxed. By inheritance and temperament more plastic and more adaptable than Spaniards, the Portuguese in Brazil have less of the Don Quixote in their character. They do not enjoy tilting at windmills. They accept conditions as they find them and waste little time in futile chivalric exploits. Though forming an elite in a country that has been culturally molded by Portugal the *crioulos* and their descendants were themselves considerably transformed by their new environment. Devoid of hauteur they enter freely and gaily into the life that they find around them. As a result their culture is more Brazilian than Portuguese; they do not carry the torch for alien systems or feel oppressed by the incubus of a European heritage. While showing no narrow insularity they respond to the telluric or earth forces of their own American homeland. They are cosmopolitan, conciliatory, irreverent, and, like the great body of their compatriots, optimistic of creating in Brazil a distinctive interracial American culture. Brazil, with a population of approximately sixty million in 1960, is the largest "Latin" country in the world. But its Latinism is diluted by the results of racial fusion which has been practiced there since the arrival of the first whites. Miscegenation is accepted by Brazilians as a fixed policy and has served to minimize for them many of the social and cultural problems that face other nations. The typical Brazilian is *mestiço*.

The racially mixed peoples of Latin America, generically called the *castas* or castes since colonial times, include both the black and the copper-colored peoples and all combinations of both. The Negro and mulatto population, all descendants of slaves who were imported from Africa after the early sixteenth century, are largely concentrated in the islands and hot coastal zones of Middle America, where in general, among climatic conditions similar to those in their original homeland, they perform the minimum physical labor required for a hand-to-mouth existence. If the tropics are not responsible for human indolence they at least excuse it. The swarming of the blacks in these tropical lowlands is explained in part by their congenital immunity to yellow fever, the scourge of the tropics for white men. For centuries this patient, sociable race has furnished the labor force for the sugar, rum, and tobacco industries of the Caribbean islands and for the *fazenda* economy of northeastern Brazil. They built the Panama Canal, they work the banana plantations in Central America and along the Colombian coast, and they load the ocean vessels at Puerto Barrios, Veracruz, Havana, Cartagena, and Buenaventura. Their persistent Africanism appears in the voodoo religion which they still practice in Haiti and in the fetish cult of the *candomblé* which flourishes among lower-class Negroes in coastal Brazil. They are originators of the lazy and sensuous samba dance and of calypso music, and their rhythms have been imposed upon the high-pitched, sentimental Andalusian folk songs of the Cuban *guajiros*. Though as a race they appear not to have achieved a high degree of political maturity they have produced individual leaders in Haiti, Trinidad, and Jamaica who have shown extraordinary political acumen.

The Indians, who form the numerical majority in some Latin American

countries, are believed to be as numerous today as when they were first discovered by white men. Some of them, such as the fearsome Motilone of
Venezuela, the head-hunting Jívaro of the Ecuadoran *montaña,* who shrink
the heads of their fallen foes, and the blue-dyed pigmy Choco of Panama
and Colombia, are still sunk in aboriginal barbarism. Although the art and
science of the ancient Maya perished even before the Spaniards arrived, the

Fig. 1-1. Natives of Chichicastenango in Guatemala still sacrifice to ancient Mayan
idols. (*Courtesy of Black Star, Kurt Severin.*)

culture of the common people among the Maya has survived to the present
time in peasant villages in Yucatan, Guatemala, and parts of Mexico. There
2 million people still speak Maya and perform their dances honoring the
jaguar, which was the god of all-destroying power reverenced by their pre-
Columbian ancestors. In the *altiplano* of South America the Bolivian Indians,
bronze-hued, squat, and burly, seem a part of the soil itself. They live in
huts of four mud walls covered with thatched roofs and usually containing
no furniture—no beds, chairs, tables, or rugs. They sleep on the hard earthen
floor on blankets woven with their own hands, and they know nothing of
the most elementary rules of hygiene. Uncommunicative and stoical in the
face of physical suffering they speak only the Quechua or Aymará of their
forefathers and continue in their centuries-old isolation. They live in a closed
circle based on custom, and their knowledge is limited to the circumscribed
round of community relationships. Their lives have been almost entirely un-
touched by industrialization.

The Indians are agricultural traditionalists, living close to the land as have their ancestors for a thousand years. In the *altiplano* of Bolivia, for example, they still plant potatoes with a primitive foot-plow (*chaki-taklla*), an implement of preconquest origin, which is thrust almost vertically into the earth with the foot and is then pulled down like a lever to turn up a clod of earth. Their fierce attachment to the soil makes them a powerful adjunct to nationalism. They are unaffected by changes in government, caring little which faction wins the next election or gains the presidency in the next *cuartelazo* or palace revolution. In some countries the Indian masses remain outside the effective economy of the nation and carry on their primitive business by barter without resort to a *centavo* or *peso*. Enervated by climate and poverty they usually form an inert element in the population, sustaining their energy for physical labor by chewing the narcotic leaves of the sweet coca. They are the drawers of wood and the hewers of stone, the modern copper-skinned counterparts of the pyramid builders of ancient Egypt and the medieval serfs. As agricultural laborers they form the principal racial element in the class variously called *peones, campesinos, jíbaros, cholos*. In their relations with Europeans they display a high degree of passive resistance, living in their inner world secure in the conviction that they have not really been conquered by white men. But when their grievances are exploited and they shake off their lethargy in revolt, they may precipitate social revolution. By this and also by the less violent method of intermarriage with the white invaders since the time of the *conquistadores* many of them or their *mestizo* descendants have risen to positions of great power.

All these races and racial combinations in Latin America interact upon one another and have molded one another's lives in the world's greatest experiment in racial fusion. The Iberic-Negro-Indian mixture is not notable for mechanical skills and lives at odds with the technocratic world of the twentieth century. For the inventions of the modern industrial age Latin America is dependent upon "foreigners." The foreign population groups in Latin America include, in order of estimated descending numbers, the Italians, the Germans, the English, and miscellaneous groups such as the Japanese, Chinese, Syrians, Lebanese, Scandinavians, Russians, and Poles. The Italians, numbering perhaps seven million, are concentrated in Argentina, Uruguay, and Brazil, where in general they have easily adapted themselves to Latin American life. Roughly 50 per cent of the present population of Argentina and Uruguay are of Italian extraction. The Germans, who are most numerous in southern Brazil, south central Chile, and Argentina, have tended to remain apart, cherishing the customs of the fatherland, but they display an incomparable shrewdness and alacrity in their business dealings with Latin Americans. Whereas, so the saying goes, the Frenchman will fill the hands of a prospective Latin American customer with pretty descriptive brochures of his product and the Englishman will assure him that he has come to the right company for a quality product, the German salesman says simply,

"Where shall I put it?" The English, nevertheless, have enjoyed a favored commercial position and through their intermarriage with ranking native families, as, for example, in Chile and Argentina, have acquired positions of far-reaching influence.

Citizens of the United States have not been attracted to Latin America as settlers in any considerable numbers. After the Civil War several hundred Confederates and their families voluntarily expatriated themselves from the United States and settled in Mexico, Cuba, and Brazil, where they subsequently merged themselves almost completely with the life of their new countries. In the twentieth century, communities of *Estadounidenses* or "United Statesians" in Latin American capitals contain a great many transients or residents who with their families are assigned there as representatives of business, educational, and other home establishments and who look forward to returning to the United States someday. They are therefore only sojourners in Latin America and their participation in the native life about them is consequently limited. The largest such colonies of "North Americans" are found in Mexico City and Caracas, where they number, respectively, approximately 18,000 and 7,000, their location indicating the areas of largest United States capital investment.

Other population elements in Latin America include the Japanese, who have been particularly attracted to southern Brazil and Peru, and the Chinese, who have settled in Mexico, Cuba, and Peru. Colonies of Mennonites from Canada and Soviet Russia, numbering some 12,500 persons, have settled since 1926 in Paraguay, some in the isolated Chaco region and others in the eastern part of the country. Enjoying virtual autonomy from the Paraguayan government, they operate their own schools, practice their religion, and support themselves by raising crops of cotton, peanuts, beans, and sweet potatoes. The "Syrians," a popularly named category which variously includes Levantines and Armenians, are the traders, often migratory, who contribute little but their merchandising shrewdness. In some urban communities, however, particularly in Colombia and Brazil, the Syrio-Lebanese have risen to influential positions in commerce, industry, education, and politics. Akin to them are the East Indians who have moved into Trinidad and neighboring Caribbean islands. The Jews in Latin America, approximately 650,000, are concentrated in greatest numbers, respectively, in Argentina, Brazil, Uruguay, and Chile, where they have settled almost exclusively in urban communities. Their numbers have been augmented by the influx of Jewish refugees from Europe into several parts of Latin America during and after World War II. A sprinkling of Russians, Czechoslovaks, Yugoslavs, Poles, and Belgians virtually completes the composition of Latin America in terms of national origins.

Economic Activities

In Latin America as a whole the population density amounts to only about twenty-three persons per square mile. But in an area of such vast distances and unequal geographical features, statistics on population density are meaningless or at least unimportant. More significant is the general picture of population distribution. In Middle America the greatest concentrations of population are found in Haiti, central Mexico, and the highland areas of Central America. In South America, on the other hand, the largest populations are concentrated in port cities or within 300 or 400 miles of the coast. In other words, the conspicuous characteristic of settlement here is that it is peripheral; settlers have avoided the interior of the continent and concentrated in the areas of both aboriginal and early European settlement. Population expansion into the interior, particularly into the tropics, has been discouraged not only by the climatic factor but also by the factor of cultural isolation, the one factor aggravating the other.

But more important than population distribution, at least for the future, are population trends. For the greater part of its history Latin America, whose colonization by Europeans began a full century before the colonization of that part of North America which later became the United States, far outstripped the North American temperate-zone settlements in population. While New York had only around 14,000 residents at the middle of the eighteenth century Latin America contained dozens of bustling cities with populations five and six times larger. By 1800 Latin America's peoples numbered approximately 19 million as compared with only 5.3 million in the United States, and they retained a numerical advantage until 1870 when for the first time Latin America was obliged to yield population parity to the United States. But in the decade of the 1940s Latin America again surpassed the United States, and since then its rate of net population increase has grown to be more than three times that of the United States. Largely as a result of high fertility, reduction of infant mortality, and prolonged life spans, Latin America's rate of population increase of 2.5 per cent is at least double the world average. Projections made on this basis indicate that by the year 2000 the total population of the countries south of the United States may reach 550 million, outnumbering the combined populations of the United States and Canada by as much as two to one. The probable consequences for power relationships in the Western Hemisphere can be imagined.

The effect of this high rate of population increase upon the means of subsistence also needs to be considered. Not only are the Latin American peoples expanding their numbers in almost geometrical ratio, but they are being attracted increasingly to city life. They form a ring of poverty around the cities, living in suburban shacks improvised of carton material, tin sheeting, and almost anything that comes to hand. By 1954 Latin America contained 62 cities with a population of more than 100,000, compared with 106 in the United States. Among the six largest cities in the Western Hemisphere the third, fourth, fifth, and sixth are located in Latin America—Buenos Aires, São Paulo, Rio de Janeiro, and Mexico City. This increased urban growth gives new urgency to problems of food supply, potable water, transportation, and police. In Peru the city of Ayacucho, for example, with more than 30,000 population, possessed only five telephones in 1961. Growing cities stimulate new needs. They lead to construction of factories which in turn produce an urban working class. They open up new horizons in art and literature, create new social pressures, and accentuate differences between city and country. The effects of these developments may have momentous consequences not only for the political and social life of the Latin American nations but also for the world outside.

Despite this notable growth of urban concentration Latin America remains predominantly agricultural. Both its life and its livelihood grow out of its soil. From the tiny hillside corn patch scratched with a fire-hardened stick or a wooden plow to the mechanized wheat farm of thousands of acres Latin Americans depend upon the good earth both for subsistence and for exchange. Over 60 per cent of Latin America's exports are agricultural, and the bulk of these are accounted for by nine staples—coffee, sugar, cotton, wool, meat, wheat, bananas, timber, and cacao in order of importance. Over one-third of the world's sugar is produced in Latin America, and of the total Latin American sugar exports about 80 per cent originates in Cuba.

Veneration for the land and a fierce feeling of possessiveness for it are the heritage of Latin America derived from both the Hispanic and the Indian past. The humid pampa of Argentina, its rich black topsoil ranging from 6 to 18 feet in depth and suffering almost no loss from erosion, is unmatched in the world for fertility and productiveness. Other areas of Latin America may be less ideally suited for wheat and cattle production, but they excel in other types of agriculture: coffee in Brazil, Guatemala, Colombia, and El Salvador; tropical fruits in the Central American and Caribbean countries; cacao in Ecuador; *yerba maté* in Paraguay; brazil nuts in the country for which they were named; mahogany and other tropical woods in Central America and the Amazon Basin; and rubber, sugar, cotton, rice, wine, corn, and many other products which are staples of world commerce. Irish linen is made from Argentine flax, and English beefeaters get their dyspepsia from Latin American beef. Agriculture engages the interest of one-half the total laboring population of Latin America. The *peón* or *campesino* is the typical Latin American.

But agricultural production is spotty and is inadequate even for human subsistence in certain parts of Latin America because of unfavorable climatic and geographical factors in some places, the preoccupation of the workers with mining in other places, and urban concentration in still others. From the time of the first discovery of the American hemisphere its subsoil resources, principally gold, silver, and precious stones, held out a glittering lure to white settlers and yielded in the succeeding four and one-half centuries greater quantities of precious metals than any other area of the world. In the twentieth century, different mineral products of Latin America are valued. Our commercial and industrial development puts a high premium upon iron, petroleum, tin, nitrates, tungsten, manganese, lead, and with the coming of the atomic age, thorium, plutonium, uranium, and other fissionable minerals. Since these latter are found in close association with the heavy metals, the mines of Huancavelica and Potosí may perhaps again regain the fabulous mineral preeminence which they once enjoyed. But pending this problematical development, mining engages the attention of only 1 per cent of the laboring population of Latin America and provides only 4 per cent of its gross output. Nevertheless it is of crucial importance in certain countries. In Bolivia, for example, some 60,000 miners dig the products that yield 98 per cent of the country's foreign exchange and so pay for virtually all the imports of the entire country. As a result of Bolivia's concentration upon mining only 1 per cent of the country's agricultural area is cultivated. This and other predominantly mineral areas, as, for example, northern Chile and the petroleum areas of Venezuela, depend upon imported foodstuffs for subsistence. For different reasons both Mexico and Peru also are net importers of foodstuffs.

The burgeoning population growth in Latin America emphasizes the need for industrialization as a means of absorbing additional population. In general, Latin America is as industrialized as the United States was in 1870. Industry there has traditionally been a highly individualized craftsmanship not amenable to mass techniques and assembly-line production. Mexico pioneered in heavy industry by establishing a steel mill in Monterrey early in the twentieth century by means of large government subsidies and other official encouragement. Under the exigencies and isolation imposed by World War I some countries began to enter the field of light industry, such as textiles, beer, paper, glass, soap, and matches. This process of industrialization was accelerated by World War II and continued with increasing momentum after the war, resulting in the establishment of steel mills in Brazil, Chile, and Colombia and hopes for a heavy steel industry in several other countries. By 1950 the nationally owned steel plant at Huachipato in Chile was even shipping pig iron to the United States. Latin Americans look forward to the day when they will possess the skills and the means to process their own raw materials both for internal consumption and for export. Almost two-fifths of the working population are engaged in manufacturing and its allied occupations, construction and commerce.

All these lines of activity—both the traditional ones and the newly developing ones—present unique problems. The dependence of certain Latin American countries upon one or a few exports, such as sugar from Cuba, coffee from El Salvador and Guatemala, and tin from Bolivia, has rendered

Fig. 1-2. A handicraft industry in Haiti. Women rub in the many coats of lacquer that give bowls a beautiful gloss. (*Courtesy of Vories Fisher, Chicago.*)

their entire economies highly susceptible to foreign market demands. Agriculture in many places is still primitive and needs the improvements which would come from modern skills and mechanization. Development in this field is hindered in some places and stimulated in others by the concentration of the land in large holdings. Where the *peones* who till the lands are deprived of the incentives which come from landownership, agricultural processes are usually inefficient. On the other hand, the breaking up of the *latifundios* or large landholdings and their assignment in severalty to the *peones,* as in Mexico, has deprived agriculture of the advantages which are made possible by concentration of capital and resulting large-scale operations. In general the per capita productivity of Latin American agriculture remains low.

Industrial expansion is handicapped by lack of adequate foreign capital investment, which means technical knowledge and machinery, and by the inadequacy of developed power resources and transportation facilities. After the end of World War II the question of foreign capital became the central element in the relations between Latin America and the United States. Latin Americans felt that they did not receive from either the United States government or private United States investors the amounts of capital which they needed for their economic development. Latin America is a colonial area— not literally but metaphorically—which is striving for independence. The political independence which the peoples in this area achieved in the nine-

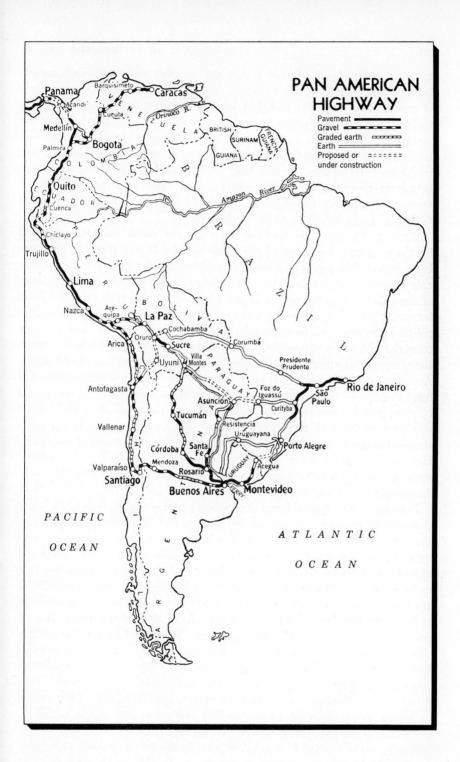

PAN AMERICAN
HIGHWAY

Pavement ━━━━━━
Gravel ▰▰▰▰
Graded earth ┅┅┅┅
Earth ══════
Proposed or ═══════
under construction

Panama
Barquisimeto
Acandí
Caracas
Cúcuta
Medellín
Orinoco R.
Palmira
Bogotá
VENEZUELA
BRITISH
GUIANA
SURINAM
FRENCH
GUIANA
COLOMBIA
Quito
ECUADOR
Cuenca
Amazon River
Chiclayo
Trujillo
B
R
Lima
A
PERU
Nazca
Are-
quipa
BOLIVIA
La Paz
Z
Oruro
Cochabamba
Arica
Sucre
Corumbá
I
Uyuni
Villa
Montes
PARAGUAY
Antofagasta
Presidente
Prudente
L
Foz do
Iguassú
Rio de Janeiro
Asunción
São
Paulo
Vallenar
Tucumán
Curityba
Resistencia
Córdoba
Santa
Fe
Uruguayana
Porto Alegre
Valparaíso
Mendoza
URUGUAY
Acegua
Santiago
Rosario
Buenos Aires
Montevideo

PACIFIC
OCEAN

ARGENTINA

ATLANTIC
OCEAN

19

teenth century signalized only a first step in their advance toward nation-hood. Their objective in the twentieth century is to achieve a larger measure of economic independence and thus, as they conceive it, full nationhood. For this purpose industrialization is considered essential. Latin America therefore wants to draw upon the technical knowledge and inventions of the industrialized nations. Its programs of economic development call for expanded and modernized transportation facilities, exploitation of its water, coal, and petroleum resources for power, expansion of light industry, and further ventures into heavy industry. All this is considered necessary to move a "colonial" Latin America into the modern age.

These aspirations have resulted from the new social ferments generated by the economic depression of the 1930s and by World War II. They are being reflected in political action, for political leaders have discovered that only by gratifying these aspirations can they remain in power. The techniques of the old-style dictator are no longer adequate to cope with pressures from increasingly literate, articulate, ambitious, and nationalistic populations. The political responses of these populations are changing slowly and in some countries almost imperceptibly, but they are tending increasingly to match the systems of popular self-government which are characteristic of the Anglo-American world. Democracy is everywhere latent in Latin America. Even the most ruthless dictator cannot indefinitely and with impunity ignore public opinion. But by means of new mass media of communication this public opinion may be both more easily molded and more successfully exploited than in the nineteenth century by special interests and scheming demagogues. Hence arises the danger of stultifying reaction, on the one hand, or radical social overturn, on the other. Violence is the daily companion of the Latin American peasant and lies close to the surface of politics.

Because of the long colonial background of the Latin Americans, their condition of continuing economic dependence, and their own adaptations to the geographical and climatic influences in their area, they cannot be judged by the criteria which are applied to other peoples of the world. They are unique and must be assessed in accordance with their own rules of conduct and their own requirements of action. Their heritage and their potentialities are different from ours. They have not adapted themselves as successfully as have the people of the United States to the nineteenth-century idea of progress, conceived largely in material terms. But judged by other standards than the progressivist ideal, they have developed modern, complicated societies highly important in themselves. They have faced the same social, political, and economic problems that other peoples have faced, but they have often solved them differently—not worse or better, but differently. They refuse to accept the tyranny of ideas, whether unitarism, federalism, socialism, communism, or any other strait-jacketing system, but yield themselves willingly to the control of a *caudillo* who demonstrates pragmatically that he possesses qualities of personal superiority. In this as in other respects

Latin Americans can be appraised and understood properly only by those foreigners who divest themselves of their own racial, national, and even in some cases, religious and moral preconceptions. As a people accustomed to emphasize spiritual values, personal dignity, and "serenity" of spirit, Latin Americans do not like to have their civilization measured solely by bushels per acre or gilt-edged investments in utilities. When they are subjected to attempts by foreigners to impose these measurements, or to apply unaccustomed forms of logic to their culture, or to impose alien technologies, they assume a defense posture. Such attempts may even produce bloody catastrophe.

Latin America cannot be said to have enjoyed the dubious dignity of being a "world island" in the Mackinder, Haushofer, or any other geopolitical sense. Throughout its history it has been a peripheral area, subject to control by the imperial and industrial nations. As such it has been indispensable to them as a feeder or tributary area. It has consequently been an area of intense economic rivalry among several world powers, and parts of it have, on certain occasions, changed hands as a result of rivalry among them. But Latin America has seldom been fought over physically by European armies, as have the other continents, Europe, Asia, and Africa. Indeed it has been singularly free from bloody international wars. From the viewpoint of global politics its importance in the twentieth century derives principally from its ability, both developed and potential, to supply raw materials. This somewhat cynical fact goes a long way toward explaining the attitudes and policies of the outside world toward Latin America, particularly after World War II. Its logistical importance in that war was due, first, to German submarine operations in the Caribbean in 1942 and 1943, which revealed the vulnerability of the southern flank of the United States and the eastern approaches to the Panama Canal to German attack; second, the existence of French and British colonial possessions in the Western Hemisphere, which, if occupied by the conquering Germans, would pose a threat to the Monroe Doctrine; and, third, its ability to supply strategic materials. In this last respect the Latin American raw-materials zone admirably reinforced the North American industrial zone to achieve victory in the war. The defense planning since World War II against another enemy than Germany for a war which will be fought with atomic weapons and over polar air routes minimizes the logistical importance of Latin America, including the Panama Canal, and stresses principally the raw-materials contribution that the Latin American area can make.

Inter-American Relations

Cooperative action for peace among the Latin American nations and for their defense against aggressors from outside the hemisphere was urged upon them by their great leader Simón Bolívar soon after the wars of independence.

This has been one of the objectives of the inter-American system which was organized on the initiative of the United States in 1889. This organization, successively called the Commercial or the International Bureau of the American Republics (1890–1910), the Pan American Union (1910–1948), and the Organization of American States (1948–   ), includes not only all the independent Latin American nations but also the United States and envisages the ultimate admission of Canada. The oldest existing international regional organization in the world, it has served as a model of peaceful international relations and as a prototype for other international systems. After World War II it was converted into a defensive alliance against aggression from outside the Western Hemisphere.

The inter-American system defines, though it does not limit, the scope of relations among all the member states. Within it many of the problems of the Latin American nations with the United States come to a focus. Their supposed affinity with republican institutions and their large commercial potentialities gave them an importance to the United States which was early manifested in the Monroe Doctrine of 1823. But thereafter in the 1840s and 1850s some of them became coveted objects of territorial acquisition to powerful interests in the United States. More than one-third of the territory of Mexico was seized by the United States. Cuba and Nicaragua were invaded by lustful filibusters from the north, and the acquisition of Caribbean islands became an obsession of President Ulysses Grant.

Latin America's commercial possibilities became newly interesting to an outreaching United States in the 1880s and served as the primary motivation of its interest there down to World War I. To these commercial relations was added during World War I and the subsequent interwar period a new concern for hemispheric defense. The cooperation of all the Latin American nations with the United States to defend the hemisphere against a victorious Germany and its allies had to be assured. The groundwork for such cooperation was laid by the Franklin Roosevelt administration in the 1930s and brought several of these nations initially and all of them eventually into World War II against the Axis Powers. Since World War II the Latin American nations have been interesting to the United States mainly as a market for capital investment and as necessary allies in the cold war and in a possible future world war. United States private investment in Latin America has increased from only 1.6 billion dollars in 1913 to approximately 6 billion dollars in 1960, exceeding the investment of United States private capital in any other major geographical area of the world. But the relations of Anglo-America and Latin America are still prejudiced by the historical heritage which goes back to the days of Henry VIII and Charles V, based on the defeat of the Spanish Armada and on the Black Legend of Spain's unparalleled cruelty in the conquest of the New World.

The responses of the Latin American peoples to the policies of the United States since World War II are susceptible of various interpretations, which will emerge later in this book. The cultivation of friendly relations between them and the United States deserves all the study and effort that it can possibly receive. To Latin America go one-fifth of our exports, and from it come roughly one-third of our imports. Investments of United States citizens are responsible for one-third of all the exports of the Latin American countries. In time of peace the products of these countries are essential to the smooth functioning of our industry and the maintenance of our standard of living. In time of war they may well be indispensable to our national survival. Our relations with them must necessarily grow out of a realistic appraisal of the facts of Latin American life. To such an appraisal a knowledge of the historical process by which the Latin American peoples have evolved into what they are today is fundamental. A study of their history will contribute to an understanding of modern Latin America and consequently, it is hoped, to the preservation of harmonious inter-American relations.

Latin America was created largely by Europe, but it has become a world entity in its own right. It cannot be dealt with any longer simply as a projection of Europe and Africa. Latin Americans realize that their European mother countries have passed their peaks of culture and influence. The Golden Age of Portugal, Spain, and France are now history. Latin America will yet reach its Golden Age. In the twentieth century Latin Americans are still striving toward self-consciousness and fulfillment, as are the peoples of Africa, Asia, and the Middle East struggling toward their place in the sun.

The Euro-African-Indian mind is different from the Anglo-American mind in traditions, customs, modes of action, thought processes, and goals. The traditionally subordinate role of the Latin Americans in relation to the United States and other foreign countries has made them sensitive to criticism and desirous of becoming more than a mere echo of foreign cultures. They are ambitious to free themselves from foreign servitudes. This they cannot easily accomplish, because for them the struggle for a livelihood and for recognition of their individual and national identity is particularly difficult in the complicated world of the twentieth century. Though they are fascinated by the inventive genius of other peoples and wish to profit from it, at the same time they fear that foreign importations may force them to cease being themselves.

Latin Americans possess a strong consciousness of their own worth both as individuals and as national communities. This is the spirit of *criollismo* or American nativism which motivated their independence movement in the first quarter of the nineteenth century. The increasing predilection of the Latin Americans for their own—their own cultures, their own values, their own earth—presages a new autochthonous development, which is big with promise for the future. To this future they have been rallied and challenged by many twentieth-century leaders, such as Alejandro Alvarez, José Enrique Rodó, Alfonso Reyes, Leopoldo Zea, José Vasconcelos, Alberto Lleras Camargo, Rómulo Betancourt, Juan Domingo Perón, Juan José Arévalo, Lázaro Cárdenas, and Fidel Castro. Under such leadership Latin Americans are struggling toward a new and more vital self-consciousness. They are seeking a clearer understanding of their own realities. To contribute to an appreciation of this contemporary travail of the Latin American mind and soul is the purpose of the succeeding chapters.

Additional Reading

Alexander, Robert J.: *Today's Latin America,* Doubleday & Company, Inc., Garden City, New York, 1962. A neat, modern introduction to Latin America for the non-specialist.

Biesanz, John and Mavis: *Costa Rican Life,* Columbia University Press, New York, 1944.

————: *The People of Panama,* Columbia University Press, New York, 1955.

Costa Eduardo, Octavio de, *The Negro in Northern Brazil: A Study in Acculturation,* Monographs of the American Ethnological Society, J. J. Augustin, Inc., Locust Valley, N.Y., 1948.

Dávila, Carlos: *We of the Americas,* Prentice-Hall, Inc., Englewood Cliffs, N.J., 1949. A challenging book by a former provisional president of Chile and secretary general of the Organization of American States arguing for a Western Hemisphere economically, politically, and militarily integrated from pole to pole.

Freyre, Gilberto: *New World in the Tropics: The Culture of Modern Brazil,* Alfred A. Knopf, Inc., New York, 1959. A provocative sociological analysis of Brazil.

James, Preston E.: *Latin America,* 3d ed., rev., The Odyssey Press, Inc., New York, 1959. The most complete descriptive account in English of the human geography of Latin America, superseding earlier studies.

Johnson, John J.: *Political Change in Latin America: the Emergence of the Middle Sectors,* Stanford University Press, Stanford, Calif., 1958.

Núñez del Prado, Oscar: "Aspects of Andean Native Life," trans. by John H. Rowe, *Kroeber Anthropological Society Papers,* Number 12, Berkeley, 1955.

Paz, Octavio: *The Labyrinth of Solitude: Life and Thought in Mexico (El Laberinto de la Soledad),* translated by Lysander Kemp, Grove Press, Inc., New York, 1961. An intellectual interpretation of Mexico.

Pierson, Donald: *Negroes in Brazil: A Study of Race Contact at Bahia,* University of Chicago Press, Chicago, 1942. A treatment of race relations broader than the subtitle indicates.

Ramos, Arthur: *The Negro in Brazil,* trans. from the Portuguese by Richard Pattee, The Associated Publishers, Washington, 1939.

————: *Las Poblaciones del Brasil,* Fondo de Cultura Económica, Mexico, 1944.

Reyes, Alfonso: *The Position of America and other Essays,* selected and trans. by Harriet de Onís, Alfred A. Knopf, Inc., New York, 1950.

Rippy, J. Fred: *Latin America and the Industrial Age,* 2d ed., G. P. Putnam's Sons, New York, 1947.

Schurz, William L., *This New World: The Civilization of Latin America,* E. P. Dutton & Co., Inc., New York, 1954.

————: *Latin America: A Descriptive Survey,* rev. ed., E. P. Dutton & Co., Inc., New York, 1949.

Tannenbaum, Frank: "Political Dilemma in Latin America," *Foreign Affairs,* vol. 38, pp. [497]–515, April, 1960.

Tavares de Sá, Hernane: *Brazilians, People of Tomorrow,* John Day, New York, 1947.

United Nations, Economic Commission for Latin America, Annual Surveys, 1948– , and various special studies.

Wythe, George: *Industry in Latin America,* 2d ed., Columbia University Press, New York, 1949. A comprehensive analysis.

Zelinsky, Wilbur: "The Historical Geography of the Negro Population of Latin America," *Journal of Negro History,* vol. 34, pp. 153–221, 1949.

II

New World, New Horizons

At the beginning of the fifteenth century geographical certitude did not extend beyond the shores of Europe. Toward the west it stopped at the Strait of Gibraltar. Europeans knew far less about the world outside their continent than we know today about the other planets in our solar system.

The Western Hemisphere was first made known to Europeans by an Italian navigator, Cristoforo Colombo or Cristóbal Colón, to give him his Spanish name. Through one of the epochal accidents of history the Great Discoverer made his explorations in the name of the king and queen of Spain. Columbus, as his name is spelled in English, was a man of the Renaissance, possessed with an idea which he took pains to represent as an idea of the ancients and whose modernity he scarcely glimpsed. But somehow the future dwelt in him. His venturings into the unknown Western Hemisphere shook the old structure of civilization to its foundations and substituted for it a new and more generous conception of the world.

Columbus's exploit was only one episode in a century of exploration which began with the discovery of the Madeira Islands in the early fifteenth century by an expedition sent out by Prince Henry the Navigator, third son of the king of Portugal, and which was climaxed by the circumnavigation of the earth in 1519–1522 by an expedition organized by Fernão de Magalhaes or, in its English form, Ferdinand Magellan, and sponsored by King Charles I of Spain. These and the intervening exploits of discovery were made possible by the new interest in the physical world, the new knowledge of topography, winds, currents, plants, and animals, and the development of new aids to ocean navigation. The discovery of the American hemisphere came about as an incident in the outreaching effort of Renaissance Europeans to broaden their horizons. Discovery was the keynote of the Renaissance—both the discovery of man and the discovery of the outer world. The westward movement across the Atlantic was only one phase of an explosive surge of Europeans into unknown areas of the entire non-European world, which opened up new lands in Africa, America, Asia, and eventually Australia and began the modern era of European colonization and imperial control. Europe thus entered upon its second great imperial epoch—the first since the Roman Empire—with no less an object than the Europeanizing of the globe.

Earlier colonization, which had peopled Europe from the shores of the

Mediterranean Sea to the Baltic Sea, had generally proceeded into adjacent territories and among peoples with an allied culture pattern living in the same climatic zone as that of the colonizers. Frontiers slowly moved forward amoebalike, much as the later English frontier in the United States advanced from the Atlantic seaboard through the Mississippi Valley into the Great Plains. But after the discovery of America a different type of expansion occurred. Colonization moved across vast oceans into noncontiguous territories, among strange peoples, and into non-European climate zones. For the first time in history Europeans came into direct, permanent contact with another numerous race widely separated from them in civilization. They began to assume the "white man's burden." Motivating this effort was an unprecedented zeal for self-aggrandizement by the sovereigns and peoples of Western Europe, whereby each of the relatively young nation-states sought to increase its trade and riches and thus to raise itself to a new eminence of power and prestige. In this effort Spain and Portugal took the lead, with the hope of edging into the trade with the Orient which had long been a monopoly of the Italian city-states.

The Europe of Columbus

In the imperial epoch which now opened, the Iberian nations were radical innovators. Lacking precedents they created their own system and should be judged by the excellence of their performance rather than by the shortcomings which may appear in historical retrospect. They embarked upon empire without a knowledge of mercantilist theory, which indeed did not exist but was developed by the British in the seventeenth century. They did not envisage an imperial system in which colonies would serve solely an economic function and would contribute only to the glorification of the mother country. Rather they were thinking in terms of national power and glory and the extension of the Christian faith, and their subjects were motivated by the lure of wealth and opportunity which the New World outside Europe offered in the sixteenth and seventeenth centuries. After the discovery and conquest of America one of their principal concerns, as evidenced in the writings of apologists of empire, such as Bartolomé de las Casas, Juan Ginés de Sepúlveda, Francisco de Vitoria, and Francisco Suárez, was to justify to the world and to themselves their right to be in the New World.

As discovery, exploration, and colonization proceeded apace into hitherto unknown areas, the world's center of gravity changed. Customary trade routes were modified, new commercial centers were established, the growth of cities on the western periphery of Europe was stimulated at the expense of the Mediterranean cities and the Hanseatic League in the Baltic, and the character and even the commodities of international trade were altered. Vast quantities of gold and silver—the media of international exchange—flowed into Europe, most of them coming from Latin America. The new foodstuffs which Latin America supplied included white potatoes, tomatoes, Indian corn or maize, peanuts, squash, pumpkins, lima and kidney beans, coconuts, yams and sweet potatoes, cocoa or cacao, pineapples, papayas, avocados, and custard apples. Other products which the New World now introduced to the Old were tobacco, vanilla, coca from which cocaine is derived, cinchona bark from which quinine is made, and rubber. Enlarged opportunities were provided in America for the production of coffee, cotton, oranges, bananas, and sugar, which, though not indigenous to America, became so easily acclimated there as soon to become staple products of the Western Hemisphere.

The Spain from which Columbus sailed westward with his tiny armada fraught with empire was in a triumphant and expansionist mood. The marriage of Ferdinand of Aragon and Isabella of Castile in 1469 and the later accession of this extraordinary and complementary pair of sovereigns to power cemented the union between the two principal kingdoms of Spain. The process of national unification was further advanced in January, 1492, by the expulsion of the Moors from Granada, their last stronghold in the Iberian peninsula, after a five-centuries-long crusade against them. This struggle, carried through to victory under the inspiration of the patron saint of the Spanish people, St. James (Santiago), laid the foundations of the Spanish nation in close conjunction with the Christian faith. Spaniards, romantic medievalists at heart, were inspired by the masculine ideal of the warrior saint, riding on horseback and clad in armor. In the course of the reconquest they acquired a religious zeal which was later to motivate them deeply in their conquest of America and which was to give Spain a preeminent place in the Catholic Reformation. Their style of living became closely associated with the church. From a certain aspect their conquest of America can be viewed as a continuation of their crusade against the Moslem crescent. They imagined themselves the spiritual saviors of America, bringing salvation in their caravels. The religious fervor of the Spanish *conquistadores* as they moved through America was indistinguishable from national fervor, and their national fervor was indistinguishable from religious fervor. They were the agents of both a missionary state and an imperial church. The union of Spain's military might with her spiritual zeal made her an irresistible conquering power.

The Spanish genius for directing the destinies of empire was created by the history and environment of the homeland. Here a warlike mode of life had become indispensable during the struggle against the Moslems. The beau ideal of Spanish manhood was the soldier, the knight. The martial virtues of physical endurance, personal heroism, and steellike temper were the first prerequisites to winning the Spanish peninsula back to Christianity from the infidels. Fighting became the profession of the knightly class, while commerce and industry were usually left to the Moslems and the Jews. And yet this military background had prevented a rigid formalization of society.

The warrior tradition encouraged and made possible a considerable mobility of classes, with the result that the social structure of Spain was perhaps more fluid than that of any other contemporary country of Europe. It included the grandees and the higher clergy at the top, the lesser *hidalgos* and *caballeros* (horsemen), and finally the lower class, which comprised the servants and industrial and agricultural laborers. At intermediate levels were distributed the *letrados*—university men trained in the law who bridged the gaps between the classes and from whose ranks came many of the *conquistadores,* as for example Fernando Cortés and Jiménez de Quesada. They became the idea men and the administrators in Spain's imperial bureaucracy. The combined influence of the *letrado* and the church advanced Spain a century ahead of her European contemporaries in juristic concepts and ensured a Spanish Empire that would be neither conquered by large armies nor kept under control by military force. It would be essentially an intellectual creation.

The Italian historian Francesco Guicciardini unsympathetically characterized his Spanish contemporaries in 1513, as follows:

> They are proud by nature and think that no other nation compares with theirs. . . . They dislike foreigners and are discourteous toward them. They are more warlike, perhaps, than any other Christian nation; agile, quick, and good at the handling of arms; they make a great point of honor, and prefer to die rather than submit to shame. . . . All Spaniards look down on trade, which they regard as degrading, and they put on airs as *hidalgos* and prefer to be soldiers or (before Ferdinand's time) highwaymen than to engage in trade or any other such occupation. . . . Spaniards are fond of show, wear fine clothes abroad, ride a stylish horse; but at home, in the house, they live in a beggarly fashion hard to believe. . . . In outward appearance they are very religious, but not so really.

In short, the Spain which sponsored Columbus's voyages was infused with a sense of high national destiny, a spirit of militarism, a trained body of lawyer-officials, and a zeal for Christian missionary effort which approached fanaticism.

The Aragon over which Ferdinand began to reign in 1479 was a well-ordered state governed as a limited monarchy and enjoying considerable privileges of local self-government. But its institutions were not to be the model for Spanish colonial administration. That model would be furnished by Castile, the rugged central tableland area of the Spanish peninsula, which when Isabella assumed royal authority over it in 1474 was racked by factional strife. The towns of Castile, which had long enjoyed large privileges under their municipal charters, were struggling against one another and against the feudal nobles, who like the towns enjoyed semiautonomous status. To control this anarchic situation the intelligent and dominating Isabella, with the support of Ferdinand, set out to establish the supremacy of the crown, thus preparing the way for the gradual extension of royal authority over all parts of Spain and giving them a political solidarity under Christian auspices which they had previously lacked. The theory underlying Spain's imperial administration, therefore, was to be royal absolutism. The Catholic sovereigns (*los Reyes Católicos*) sought to substitute centralized authority for the tradition of local autonomy which had prevailed in Spain for many centuries. The national state, incarnating the religious ideal, was to be transcendant over the individual.

As the crafty, secretive Ferdinand and the pious, serious-minded Isabella welded the now united portions of Spain into a new nation, having a combined population estimated at eight million, they unknowingly prepared the way for great overseas undertakings and created an institutional structure which provided models of political organization for the government of a world-wide imperial system. Among the institutions which they either developed or found already existing in Spain and later transferred to the New World was the *audiencia*, a judicial tribunal or royal court of appeals which represented the sovereign in the component parts of the nation. As the Spanish sovereigns conquered Moslem lands they sometimes assigned the lands to their favorite *conquistadores*, thus establishing a practice that was followed later in America. In the government of these newly conquered lands they superseded the medieval captains general by *adelantados*, who exercised both military and civil authority over the outlying jurisdictions of the nation. They also appointed, as direct representatives of the sovereign, viceroys or vice-kings to rule over Sardinia, Sicily, and Naples. They sent *visitadores* or royal judges through the kingdom to supervise the administration of justice and finance, and they subjected all royal officials to the *residencia*, which was a judicial investigation into their conduct of office. They even limited the traditional privileges of the towns by sending out *corregidores* to inspect the conduct of local administration and often by this means gained control over the *ayuntamientos* or town councils. They thus created a centralized administration which was supported by an elaborate system of checks to carry out the will of the sovereign and which was well prepared for great imperial effort. Even the Castilian language was utilized as an instrument of empire. It was thus referred to by Antonio de Nebrija in his *Gramática castellana* in 1492, which was the first grammar of a romance language published in the world.

The church in Spain was also made to serve the national ends of the Spanish crown. For this purpose Ferdinand and Isabella reorganized the Inquisition and made it an instrument to eradicate religious heresy from Spain, using informers, third-degree methods, and censorship over books, and assisted by the religious orders, the Franciscan, the Dominican, and later the Jesuit. These Catholic sovereigns exercised a strong influence over church officials and strengthened their national position at the expense of the Pope. They even secured from Pope Sixtus IV the *patronato* or control over the secular affairs of the church, including the right to make nominations to important vacant ecclesiastical sees, and after the fall of the last Moslem stronghold in the Kingdom of Granada they were given the *patronato* over the church there. Under the policy of the Catholic sovereigns, church and state in Spain were substantially united, the church remaining, however, under the nominal suzerainty of the Pope. The church in Spain thus became essentially a national church. It was more Spanish than papal. It was virtually absorbed by the Spanish nation and was made to serve the destinies of the nation.

The objective of national unity which motivated Ferdinand and Isabella impelled them eventually to order the expulsion of the unconverted Jews and Moslems from the realm, as these classes were monopolizing production and trade and threatened the power structure of the nation. These dissident religious groups were presented with the alternatives of either accepting Christianity or leaving the country. If they became Christians and later reverted to their original faith they were subject to trial and condemnation by the Inquisition. If they chose to retain their Jewish or Moslem faith they must leave Spain but were not legally permitted to migrate to Spanish lands beyond the sea. In fact, however, many of them found their way to America. For their effort to make their nation Christian, Ferdinand and Isabella received the enthusiastic plaudits of other European Christian rulers, who rejoiced that Spain thus repudiated Judaic and Moorish influences and redeemed itself as a Christian nation.

The Dawn of America

The dawn of America occurred when Columbus, the greatest navigator of the age and also its greatest promoter, headed westward from Palos in August, 1492, with his three tiny caravels. "God made me the messenger of the New Heaven and the new earth," Columbus later wrote, "and He showed me where I should find them." He had represented his enterprise to his sponsor, Queen Isabella, as a search for a westward route to the Indies; the charge that his real intent was to discover new lands is disproved by the fact that he carried letters from the Spanish sovereigns to the Grand Khan of Cathay (China), that he named the inhabitants Indians, and that until his death he never wavered in the conviction that he had reached the islands off the coast of Asia. On his first voyage he discovered the Bahama Islands, Cuba, and the adjoining island which he called Española, now Haiti and the Dominican Republic. Reporting to the treasurer of Aragon, Luis de Santangel, Columbus wrote:

> There are in that island mountains and valleys and meadows, and beautiful fat lands for planting and sowing, for raising cattle of all kinds, for cities and villages. The ports are such as you would not believe unless you saw them, as are the many broad rivers of sweet waters, most of which are gold-bearing. . . . The people all go about naked as their mothers bore them, save only that some of the women cover a single part with a green leaf, or with a cotton cloth made for the purpose. They have no iron or steel or arms, nor are they apt for such things, not because they are not well set up and beautiful, but because they are wonderfully timorous. . . . They are so guileless and generous with what they possess that you would not believe it without seeing it.

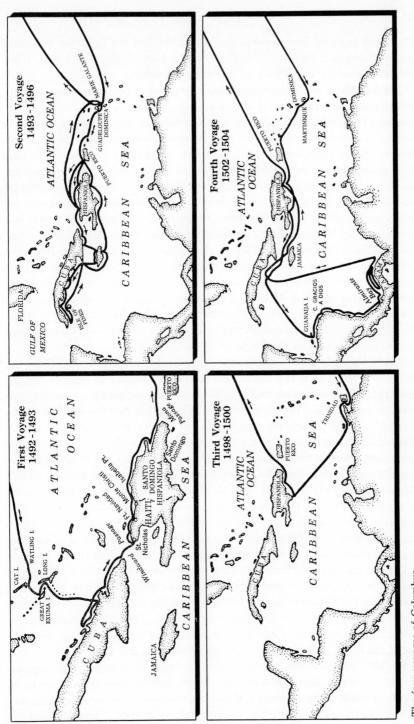

The four voyages of Columbus.

31

Thus and in many later reports the Discoverer laid the basis for the belief among Europeans that the New World was a land of plenty and that its inhabitants lived in a condition of primitive innocence.

The heartland of the pre-Columbian culture of America was the southern two-thirds of Mexico, Central America, Andean and coastal Colombia, Ecuador, and Peru, with adjacent portions of Bolivia. In this area were found the two leading centers of civilization, one in Middle America, the other in Peru-Bolivia. When Columbus arrived in the western half of the world he found there aboriginal populations who, as suggested by the most reliable archaeological and anthropological investigations, probably came originally from Asia by way of the Behring Strait and from there spread southward to become separate tribes and "nations." The Western Hemisphere, it seems certain, was not man's original home, despite the claims of certain South American scholars, presented with more patriotic fervor than substantive proof, that American prehistoric culture and perhaps even the earliest men themselves found their way from America into Europe and Africa possibly by way of a subsequently submerged continent of Atlantis. The Garden of Eden, it seems certain, was not located in the Western Hemisphere! The oldest human remains in the American hemisphere, as determined by carbon-14 dating, go back only some 30,000 years as compared with 600,000 years in Africa.

Unlike the early civilizations of the Nile, the Tigris and the Euphrates, the Indus, and the Hwang Ho, the highest native civilizations in America did not grow up along a principal river system or around an inland sea such as the Mediterranean. They were not maritime cultures but developed rather in the uplands of tropical America and in the lowlands of its coastal area, chiefly along the Atlantic seaboard. Because of the cultural similarities of the American aborigines with the Polynesian and Asiatic peoples, some writers have deduced a continuing intercontinental intercourse between them and the Orient. The religious practices, myths, pyramidal temple structures, and the cat motif in the art of some of these people suggest those of the ancient Middle East, and many carved statues of human figures that have survived in Middle America have a marked Buddha aspect. But countering the supposition of continuing contact between the American aboriginal peoples and the Oriental world is the fact that their cultures as shown in their surviving art forms reached a peak at a time when the contemporary cultures with which they might have maintained contact overseas were already using physical processes which never found their way into America. The American aborigines had at their disposal neither metal implements nor pack animals, they were unfamiliar with the use of the wheel, and they never discovered the principle of the arch.

By 1492 the American aborigines had become differentiated into approximately six major linguistic stocks in North America and three or more in South America. Some of them had not yet emerged from the Stone Age and were living in squalid barbarism when the whites arrived. These included the maritime Caribs of the Lesser Antilles and Trinidad whose principal occupation was fighting and who regularly ate their victims. Only a slightly higher cultural level had been achieved by the nomadic hunters who roamed over the rich pampas of Argentina and the great plains of central North America. Others, including the Nahuatlans, Mayas, Chibchas, Aztecs, and Incas, had reached the Bronze Age; but none of them used iron implements. Among them, the most advanced, like the Europeans, operated under laws, had established cities, were divided into social classes, had colleges of priests, were governed by reigning dynasties, maintained organized armies, and lived by national folk myths. In the Andean mountains the aboriginal peoples had reached their highest point in technological achievement and in political and religious organization. Their ceramic products, in technique, form, and ornament, excelled those of any other people ignorant of the potter's wheel. But in most respects even they were more than a thousand years behind the Europeans. They were addicted to intertribal warfare and carried on many practices which were revolting to the whites, such as head deformation, incest, human sacrifice, homosexuality, and cannibalism, in which they roasted and ate not only captives taken in warfare but even their own children.

And yet with these native peoples, all incredibly primitive in the eyes of the white newcomers, the European civilization which was imported into the New World would inevitably mingle and both cultures would be momentously modified in the process. After Columbus's discovery, the history of America, particularly Hispanic America, would be a product of the interaction of two cultures—that of Renaissance Europe and that of the Indian, as Columbus called the native peoples of the lands he discovered.

On the northern coast of Española, Columbus left a colony of forty-four of his companions at a place which he named Navidad. After he returned to Spain the first sovereign outside the Iberian peninsula to be informed of his discoveries was Pope Alexander VI, who was a Spaniard by birth. Between May and September, 1493, the Pope issued four decrees, or bulls, by which he granted to Castile lordship over all newly discovered "islands and firm land" located in "the western parts of the Ocean Sea, toward the Indies" south and west of a meridian line drawn 100 leagues west of the Cape Verde Islands and the Azores. He did not limit his grant to ecclesiastical jurisdiction but included also temporal dominion, as several previous Popes had done in disputed matters of territorial jurisdiction among the sovereigns of Europe. This assumption by the Pope of authority to assign newly discovered lands and their inhabitants to Christian sovereigns conformed to church law, which had long held that all the heathen world was subordinate to the authorities of Christendom. By means of these papal bulls the Spanish monarchs presciently requested and obligingly received papal confirmation of their new territorial claims and strengthened their position as vicegerents of the Pope in the new lands. They reinforced their temporal claims to New World sovereignty by the spiritual claims to world sovereignty by the See of St. Peter. Now, wrote the loquacious Peter Martyr, a Spanish contemporary of Columbus, "Spain spreads her wings more and more over the Indies, widens her dominions, stretches her glory and name to the antipodes."

The papal grant to Spain was immediately challenged by the Portuguese because of their active maritime interests in the Ocean Sea. It almost entirely excluded them from further exploration in that sea, failed to safeguard their southern route to India, and violated the spirit if not the provisions of the Treaty of Alçácovas of 1479–1480 in which the two nations had agreed on a partition of territories. Portugal, with a population estimated at about 1.5 million at the end of the fifteenth century, had had a headstart over Spain in maritime exploration and discovery and might have been the lucky sponsors of Columbus's expedition if King John II of Portugal to whom Columbus first appealed had not referred him to expert cosmographers who turned down his appeals. The Portuguese possessed qualifications for empire building similar to those of the Spaniards, and they were as ready for overseas enterprise when Columbus set out upon his epoch-making first voyage of discovery toward the western sun. For them the ocean and the new lands beyond it, discovered by the caravels of Prince Henry, had had a singular attraction ever since the middle of the fifteenth century. Already a colonizing and trading people they were predisposed to alliances with darker races, accustomed to work under a tropical sun, adventurous in spirit, and experienced as traders in foreign parts. Possessors of a long Christian tradition they too had fought their wars against the Moors and had finally expelled them. A centralized monarchy had been achieved there more than two centuries before Ferdinand and Isabella, and the crown had established its supremacy over both the individualistic nobles and the church. It had likewise limited the privileges of the towns, subjecting them to the same kind of administrative and fiscal supervision—by *correge-dores*—as Ferdinand and Isabella imposed upon the towns of Aragon and Castile.

King John II protested so strenuously against the Pope's grant to Castile, even threatening war, that he forced a compromise settlement upon Castile in the Treaty of Tordesillas in June, 1494, which moved the papal line of demarcation westward to a meridian drawn 370 leagues west of the Cape Verde Islands. This line, as it later appeared, entered the South American continent from the north near the present Pará at the mouth of the Amazon River, cut across the easternmost bulge of the continent, and emerged to the south near the present Santos. Portugal without having yet made or sponsored any verified voyages in the Western Hemisphere was thus given an early basis for establishing a territorial claim in the Americas, which grew later into the Portuguese colony of Brazil. Within three months of Columbus's return, Spain and Portugal therefore divided up the new lands and oceans between them, without knowing precisely what they were dividing. They appropriated practically the entire New World. Their claims to lordship over the high seas, thus asserted and presumably supported by the Pope's decrees, would, if implemented, hamper the exploring and colonizing activities of every other maritime power.

Columbus had sailed under a contract (*capitulación*) from Isabella which stipulated that he should have all the prerogatives of an admiral of Castile, that he should have the titles of hereditary viceroy, governor, and captain general of all the lands that he might discover, that he should be the source of all justice in those lands, and that he should receive a royalty of 10 per cent from the proceeds of their trade. These large privileges were probably indicative not of his standing at the court at which he had been a suitor for more than seven years but rather of the little faith that Ferdinand and Isabella placed in his enterprise. After his return from his first voyage of discovery he immediately began to plan a second expedition, primarily for colonization and development of the lands already found rather than discovery of new lands. In preparation for it he now received from the Spanish sovereigns five times the cost of the first voyage—enough to finance an expedition of seventeen ships and 1,500 men. To facilitate trade in the new lands he was instructed to erect a customs-house under royal auspices and to take with him a representative of the royal exchequer to supervise the trade.

On his second voyage starting in 1493 Columbus approached the lands of the West through the Leeward Islands, discovered Puerto Rico, which he called St. John the Baptist, and proceeded to Española, where he found only the remains of the settlement at Navidad, wiped out by the natives. At the new settlement which he now founded to the east of Navidad and which he called Isabella, he began the first experiment in royal colonization in America. But the Great Discoverer proved a failure as a colonial administrator. In his relations with his subordinates the very qualities of authoritativeness and persistence in a self-determined course which had enabled him to consummate his "Enterprise of the Indies" worked against him. Moreover, he was a foreigner placed in charge of Spanish settlers, most of whom were disdainful of manual labor and interested only in searching for gold—a "ruffianly mob," Columbus called them. Since the colonists were chronically short of food he tried to force them to work and then committed the additional mistake of requiring them to work the lands of the settlement on a communal basis. During the idleness and intrigue that resulted, he dealt harshly with his critics. He also became involved in wars with the natives, the cannibalistic Caribs. These he finally subjugated and forced to pay tribute at intervals of three months—a specified quantity of gold if they lived near the mines or an *arroba* of cotton (approximately 25 pounds) if they did not. In his report to his sovereigns Columbus proposed that settlers be sent out bringing with them cattle and beasts of burden. To meet their need for a labor force they could enslave the native population who were, he wrote, "wild people fit for any work, well-proportioned, and very intelligent, and who, when they have got rid of their cruel habits to which they have been accustomed, will be better than any other kind of slaves."

During his second stay in the Western world, extending over a period of more than two and one-half years, Columbus explored the southern shore of Cuba and discovered Jamaica. When he returned to Spain in March, 1496, he left his brother Bartholomew in charge as *adelantado* of the Indies. During Christopher's absence the Spanish headquarters at Isabella was moved to the south shore of Española and rebuilt at Santo Domingo on the Ozama River, which became the first permanent white settlement in the Western Hemisphere. There Christopher's system of communal landholding was abandoned in favor of a system of allotting land to individual farmers and giving them title to it after four years of occupancy. When Christopher returned to this settlement on his third voyage in 1498 he found that a rebellious faction, led by Francisco Roldán, had withdrawn into the interior in protest against Bartholomew's harsh discipline. He sought to restore order and unity by equally harsh methods, with the result that both he and his brother were denounced to the court as "unjust men, cruel enemies, and shedders of Spanish blood," who upon slight occasion "would rack them, hang them, and behead them." Accordingly the sensitive Columbus was replaced as governor in 1499 by Francisco Bobadilla and was, along with his two brothers, sent back to Spain in chains. Not only his failure as a colonial administrator but even his success as a discoverer now worked against him. The magnitude of his conquests, exceeding anything that his sovereigns had dreamed of, persuaded them to hedge on their commitments to him. He was pardoned by Ferdinand and Isabella, but since he had demonstrated administrative incapacity he was never given back his political authority. Henceforth he was addressed by his sovereigns only as admiral, never as viceroy or governor. He was also gradually deprived of the monopolistic control over western exploration which had been granted to him in his original contract. "If I had stolen the Indies and given them to the Moors," Columbus complained, "Spain could not have shown me greater enmity."

On his third trip to the New World Columbus saw the estuary of a large river, the Orinoco, discovered Trinidad, and sailed along the northeastern corner of South America, which, he reported to his sovereigns, constituted "another world." Here was an antipodal continent, he concluded, lying off southeast Asia. "I am convinced," he reported, "that this is the mainland and very large, of which no knowledge has been had until now." After the rejection of his political authority by the Spanish sovereigns he was permitted to make a fourth and final voyage to the hemisphere which he had discovered. On this fourth expedition in 1502–1503 he skirted the Caribbean coast of Central America from the present Honduras to Panama. But he succumbed more and more to mystical ideas, planning new crusades to recover Jerusalem and conceiving of the northern part of South America as the Garden of Eden. Burdened with geographical preconceptions, he refused to face the implications of his discovery. Saddened by the ingratitude of his sovereigns and prematurely aged by illnesses incurred in the pestilential Caribbean islands, the proud discoverer who had laid an empire at his sovereigns' feet died and was buried at Valladolid in 1506. His failure to claim the credit for discovering a new world should not deprive him of the honor of having, in fact, done so.

Successors of Columbus

Meanwhile other explorers, their appetites for adventure and wealth whetted by Columbus's success, were following in his wake and going beyond his horizons. The rapid appearance of Western European navigators in Columbus's new hemisphere after his discoveries, revealed in tantalizingly meager detail in the surviving contemporary records, suggests either that the news of his discoveries traveled through Western Europe with extraordinary speed, or, what is more probable, that the idea of western discoveries was reached independently by many minds. It was an almost self-generated product of the questing spirit of the Renaissance.

The venturesome undertakings of the first wave of Spanish pioneers were surpassed by the exploits of their successors who pushed farther and farther into unknown wildernesses, where prospects never before seen by white men burst upon their astonished eyes and hardships almost beyond endurance had to be met. And yet, compensating for the hardships suffered by the *conquistadores* in this morning of America was the excitement that came from the ploughing of strange waters, the sighting of new headlands, the discovery of broad estuaries, the encounters with exotic animals and unintelligible natives, and the naming of new places. They moved about in a strange world, and in the embraces of the sensuous Indian women they forgot their homesickness and their toilsome labors. Over the New World they patriotically sprinkled the name of their national patron, St. James, in Santiago de Cuba, Santiago de León de Caracas (Venezuela), Santiago de Nueva Estremadura (Chile), Santiago del Estero (Argentina), Santiago de la Vega (Jamaica), and a host of others. Here were original experiences; here was the hope of great riches; here also was sudden death. All was different, spine-tingling and bloodcurdling. The crown was far distant across a scarcely traversable ocean and each adventurer in America could be his own master or at least could try to be. He found himself "suddenly liberated on the edge of the world of authority." In the pell-mell quest for new empires that now began, law and order and morality were often flouted. The Spaniards who followed Columbus, wrote the *mestizo* Garcilaso de la Vega, who personally knew many of the early explorers in Peru, "after discovering the New World, were so eager to discover new lands and ever more new lands, that, although many of them were rich and prosperous, not content with what they owned, nor weary of their hardships, hungers, dangers, wounds, illnesses, bad days and worse nights spent by sea and land, undertook new conquests and greater endeavors, to achieve higher exploits which should make their names famous for eternity." [1] They were actuated by a supreme confidence in God and in themselves.

America was occupied as a series of successive frontiers, each one building

[1] Garcilaso de la Vega, *Historia general del Perú o comentarios reales de los Incas* (13 vols.), Madrid, 1800, vol. 6, p. 4.

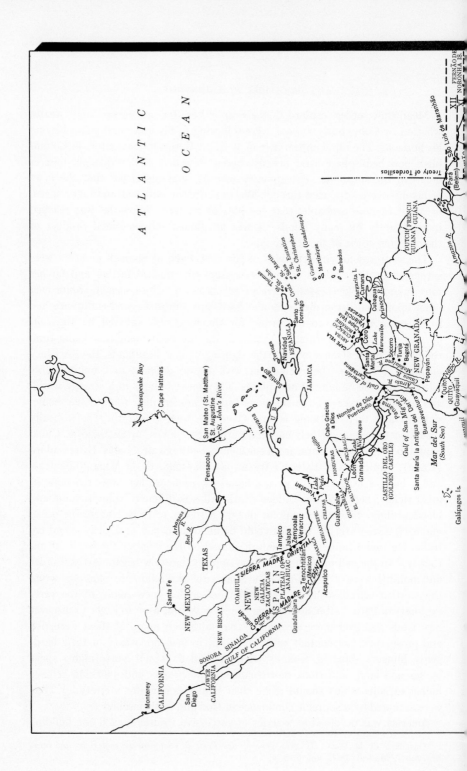

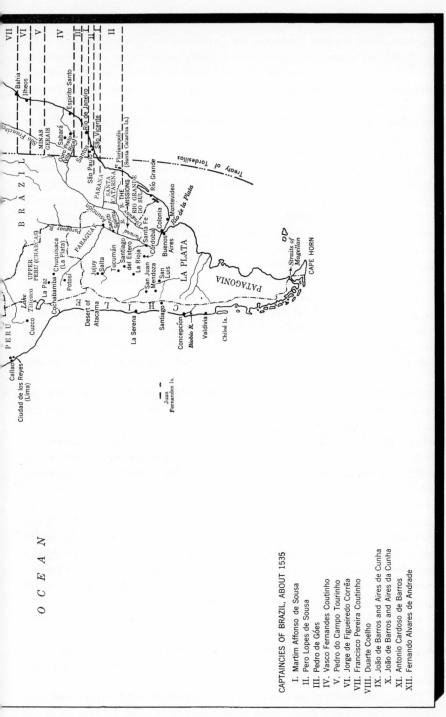

CAPTAINCIES OF BRAZIL, ABOUT 1535

  I. Martim Affonso de Sousa
  II. Pero Lopes de Sousa
  III. Pedro de Góes
  IV. Vasco Fernandes Coutinho
  V. Pedro do Campo Tourinho
  VI. Jorge de Figueiredo Corrêa
  VII. Francisco Pereira Coutinho
  VIII. Duarte Coelho
  IX. João de Barros and Aires de Cunha
  X. João de Barros and Aires da Cunha
  XI. Antonio Cardoso de Barros
  XII. Fernando Alvares de Andrade

Early settlements in America.

the next. From the first frontier in the Caribbean the Spaniards moved to the mainland and isthmus of Middle America, fanning out to the north, west, and south. The conquest of Peru, in turn, was based on Panama, and the conquest of Chile on Peru. The La Plata frontier of settlement in South America stemmed from Spain. Coastal Venezuela and Colombia were settled as off-shoots of the Spanish colonies in the Caribbean. Thus the frontier of Europe advanced in America, leaving deposits of towns and churches and Spanish officialdom as it moved inexorably on.

The occupation of these areas was a helter-skelter process, a largely direc-tionless expansion of empire. Considered as a westward movement it was finished when Vasco Núñez de Balboa sighted the Pacific Ocean at Panama in 1513, or when the *conquistadores* reached the Pacific port of Acapulco and initiated trade with the Philippines, or when Francisco Pizarro made himself master of Peru in 1531. The Spanish vanguard, pathfinders of empire, at-tracted by the temperate climate of the interior highlands, by the rich inland resources of gold, silver, and precious stones, and by the sheer numbers of Indian souls to be saved, moved in all directions—north, west, south, and even east. In this seemingly haphazard explosion of empire the conquerors over-leaped many areas of settlement which would seem rich to later generations pursuing different objectives and imbued with different interests. They were also often stopped in their advance by impassable barriers of mountain and jungle.

One of Columbus's companions on his second voyage, Alonso de Ojeda, got up an expedition of his own with the assistance of the Sevilla merchants and in 1499, accompanied by Juan de la Cosa, the famous cartographer, explored almost the entire coast of modern Venezuela, going beyond the limits of Columbus's third voyage. Between 1499 and 1502 a Florentine businessman trading in Sevilla, Amerigo Vespucci, made three voyages in the course of which he discovered the mouth of the Amazon River and explored the coast of South America from Venezuela southward beyond the Río de la Plata. His discoveries were so well publicized in Europe as opening up a New World that his first name was affixed to the new continent and eventually to the entire hemisphere of Columbus. Seldom has fame so abundantly rewarded a man for so little, though in fact it was he, rather than Columbus, who first claimed to have discovered a new world. During the same period one of Columbus's old companions, Vicente Yáñes Pinzón, traced almost the same course, and Rodrigo de Bastidas explored the coasts of Venezuela and Colom-bia, which constituted the so-called "Spanish Main," or *Tierra Firme,* as the Spanish called it. By 1501, therefore, the Spanish had explored the entire northeastern coast of the South American continent from Panama to the modern Natal.

Portuguese explorers also, who prior to Columbus's first voyage had been pioneering in voyages to the south along the African coast, became interested in westward voyages after Columbus's discovery, conceiving that they might now reach India more easily by sailing westward than by rounding Africa. In early 1500 a Portuguese expedition of twelve ships en route to India under Pedro Alvares Cabral made a landfall at Pôrto Seguro on the coast of Brazil. This landfall, whether made by accident or design, strengthened Portugal's territorial claims in the Western Hemisphere, already recognized by the Pope's bulls and by the Treaty of Tordesillas. Indeed Cabral's discovery may have been not a new discovery at all but only a rediscovery of lands of which the Portuguese had knowledge even prior to the Treaty of Tordesillas. But this is only a supposition, espoused warmly by certain Portuguese investigators but resting only upon conjecture and not evidence. Cabral's exploit suggests that since he hit upon the South American continent before Columbus discovered it, the continent would have been found, in that age of daring mariners and high adventure, even if Columbus had never lived.

During the governorship of the fourth governor of Española, Diego Columbus, son of Christopher, the Spanish energetically pushed the exploration and colonization of the Caribbean islands. Juan Ponce de León was made governor of Puerto Rico in 1508, and he started a settlement on that island at San Juan three years later. At the same time both Jamaica and Cuba were being explored and a settlement was begun at Santiago de Cuba in 1514. Colonization was confined to these four larger islands, and the smaller islands of the Caribbean were used only as objects of slave-raiding expeditions. From Puerto Rico, Ponce de León set out in 1513 in search of the mythical fountain of youth and made the first recorded discovery of the peninsula of Florida, but his attempt to colonize it near the present Tampa in 1521 ended in failure and in his own death. Other explorers soon penetrated the Floridas, as all the land to the north and west of the Caribbean island settlements was called. An expedition commanded by Alonso de Pineda explored the coast of the Gulf of Mexico from the peninsula of Florida around to Tampico in 1519 and discovered the mouth of the Mississippi River. In this territory, called Amichel, a large colonizing expedition organized by Francisco de Garay attempted to found a settlement in 1523. Three years later Lucas Vásquez de Ayllón, a former member of the judicial tribunal which had been set up to act as an advisory council to Diego Columbus in Española, sailed to found a colony on the shores of the present South Carolina, probably near Cape Fear River, but his attempt ended in failure. Interest in the colonization of the Floridas was low because no gold could be found there and no promise of a strait through the mainland to the South Sea.

Expansion in other directions held greater attractions for the Spaniards. From the time when they began to realize that Columbus's Indians were not true Indians they commenced to search for a water passage through America to the Orient. Two years after Columbus's death, Pinzón and Juan Díaz de Solís retraced the route of his fourth voyage along the Caribbean coast of Central America in an endeavor to find such a waterway. Though they failed to find it, one result of their exploration was the establishment of the first

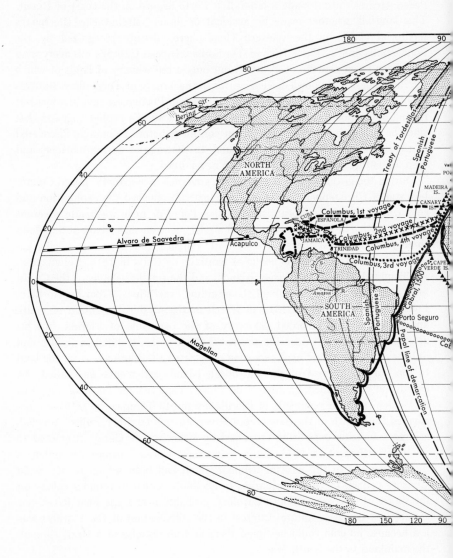

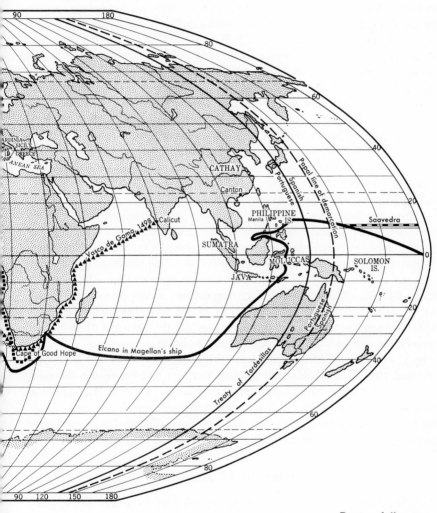

Routes of discovery.

settlement on the American mainland in 1510 at a place called Santa María la Antigua del Darién, east of the present Cristóbal in Panama. The first white man to cross the intervening land mass between Europe and Asia was the governor of this settlement, Vasco Núñez de Balboa, who with a party of sixty-seven men hacked his way through the tropical jungle at, fortunately, almost the narrowest part of the isthmus, in Panama or Darién, as it was then called. On this hazardous trip, Núñez de Balboa later reported to his sovereign, "Many times we have had to go a league, and two and three leagues, through swamps and water, stripped naked, with our clothes fastened on a shield upon our heads, and when we had come to the end of one swamp we have had to enter another, and to walk in this way from two or three to ten days." Arriving on the other side of the isthmus he discovered that a vast ocean, which he called the Mar del Sur or South Sea because he first viewed it facing southward at the Gulf of San Miguel, still separated the new American lands from Asia. Of this new ocean and all its bordering lands Balboa took possession for the crown of Castile to be owned by it "now and as long as the earth revolves, and until the universal judgment day of all mankind."

Balboa had found not a waterway but water, and his discovery stimulated new searches for a strait through America. Such a strait was found in 1520 by the chivalrous Fernão de Magalhaes or Magellan, who, after coasting along the South American continent from the bulge of Brazil southward, discovered near the southern tip of the continent the passageway that still bears his name. But Magellan's strait with its tempestuous waters proved an impracticable route for the fragile sailing craft of the sixteenth and seventeenth centuries, and the isthmus at Darién remained the principal thoroughfare between the east and the west coasts of the Americas.

By the time of Ferdinand's death in 1516 Spanish colonists had settled the principal Caribbean islands, and Spanish mariners had traced out the coast line of the American continents from Florida on the north to the estuary of the Río de la Plata on the south where Buenos Aires now stands, had crossed the Central American isthmus and discovered the Pacific Ocean, and were poised for the conquest of rich native empires on the mainland.

Conquest of Mexico

In the quarter century after Columbus stumbled upon the New World many of its mysteries were unraveled by geographical exploration and discovery. But the wealth of America seemed insignificant in comparison with that of the cultured Orient, which the Portuguese, thanks to the seafaring exploits of Vasco da Gama in 1497–1498 and the empire-building genius of the Marquis of Albuquerque after 1506, were now developing to their great advantage. Colonization in America was confined principally to a few towns and plantations established among the barbaric natives of Cuba and Española and to a miserable settlement on the isthmus at Santa María la Antigua del Darién,

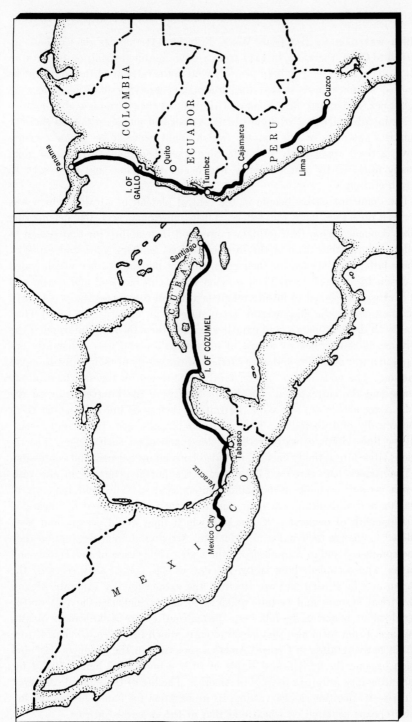

Conquests of Mexico and Peru.

which was soon to disappear. When Francisco Hernández de Córdova returned to Cuba, therefore, in 1517 from a slave-hunting expedition to Yucatan with a report of a semicivilized people living in the interior of the continent he aroused so much interest that the enterprising governor of Cuba, Diego de Velásquez, designated, first, Juan de Grijalva and then a young Cuban planter in his middle thirties, Fernando Cortés, as head of an expedition to the new country. The news of this country, which might prove to be a new treasure trove, arrived opportunely just at a time when Española's supplies of gold, mostly obtained by placer mining, had begun to decline and were soon to vanish entirely.

The dominant native people in the central plateau of Mexico, which was Cortés's objective, were the Aztecs. Their supremacy over the neighboring tribes depended upon their military power and their ability for that reason to collect tribute from them in the form of colored feathers, gold, and captives. These latter they needed for their ceremonies of human sacrifice which ended in ceremonial cannibalism. Their religion was a cult of blood and death, and its rites were designed to inspire religious awe and to impress the people with the greatness of the all-powerful Aztec state as an exemplar of force. They lived with death, violence, and catastrophe, and their theology interpreted the universe as being ruled by a host of fearful deities who were constantly engaged in a war of worlds and were careless of the effects of their struggles upon mankind. The gods had to be constantly propitiated by the sacrifices of the people and the entreaties of the priests, who were the intercessors with the gods. Aztec artists did not make portraits of their gods but represented them symbolically and abstractly. They pictured the rain god, for example, with billowy lines, drops of water, balls of cloud, and other such images. The religious rites, interestingly enough, included both infant baptism and confession.

The Aztecs had entered Mexico from the north, probably in the thirteenth century, coming as nomadic hunters clad in skins and ignorant of weaving and agriculture. On their migration they were assured by their god Nitzilopochtli of ownership of the land which they would occupy and were ordered to change their name to "Mexica." Arriving at their destination they soon conquered and in turn absorbed the higher civilization of the Toltecs and Mayas, who occupied those lands. By way of the Toltecs they received the Mayan arts of writing and architecture, the extraordinarily accurate Mayan calendrical system, and certain religious ideas, particularly the cult of the sacred snake, honoring the folk hero Quetzalcoatl—from Kukulcán in Mayan language. From them also they received corn, which had been developed from certain native grasses in Central America sometime in the shadowy past and which became the agricultural staple of their economy, as indeed it did for other sedentary primitive peoples of America. The life of these people centered on corn—its planting, its harvesting, its preparation for food—just as the life of Europeans centered on wheat and that of the Orientals on rice.

When the Aztecs first came to the notice of the Spaniards they were controlling a confederation of tribes extending from Tampico on the north to the south and southwest as far as the Isthmus of Tehuantepec and were carrying on trade on a local basis with tribes as far south as Panama. The headquarters of their domain, established around 1325, was a group of islands lying in the western corner of Lake Tezcoco and connected with the mainland by three long stone-faced causeways running north, west, and south from the central market place of the city. The gates in the city's great stone walls opening on these causeways provided the only means of entrance into the city. This city, called Tenochtitlán, the site of the modern Mexico City, received its supply of water from the hills of Chapultepec on the mainland by means of a long aqueduct. It was well supplied with markets, official buildings, and temples, and its streets were paved and regularly swept. Here in an area occupying about 1 per cent of the area of the present Federal District of Mexico lived a population estimated at from 30,000 to 1,500,000. "In conducting their affairs," Cortés reported to his emperor, "they live almost as we do in Spain and with as much harmony and order as there, and considering that these people are barbarians, far removed from the knowledge of God and from communication with other rational nations, it is a wonder to see how rational they are in everything."

Among the Aztecs were expert workers in clay, gold, copper, silver, precious stones, feathers, and woven cloth. Great stress was placed upon personal adornment, and in their clothing, made from the woven fiber of the native cotton and maguey plants, they used embroidered borders, tasseled fringes, and bright colors—scarlet from the cochineal insect, blue from the indigo plant, and purple from sea shells. Although no Aztecan textiles have survived the climate and the destruction of the Spaniards it is clear from the reports of the early chroniclers that they were masterpieces of design and color. The Aztecs had not discovered the uses of iron, and they lacked draft animals, having domesticated only guinea pigs, a species of mute and hairless dogs, and the so-called "Muscovy ducks," or musk ducks (*anas moschata*) which are native to South America and, unlike other ducks, are mute. To them, therefore, the sixteen horses on which Cortés and his men were mounted presented an awesome spectacle. Their writing system, taken over from the Maya, was almost entirely pictorial but contained a few phonetic elements. Their architecture was massive, and their houses, though plain on the outside, were often painted on the inside with brilliant colors. They were well built, an early Spanish chronicler reported, "of beautiful stone work and cedar wood and the wood of other sweet-scented trees, with great rooms and courts, wonderful to behold, covered with awnings of cotton cloth." The medical knowledge of the Aztecs compared favorably with that of Europeans of their day.

Under the Aztec system the common people were divided into twenty sub-tribes or clans, each of which was governed by an elected council. They held their land in common, cultivating the portions which were assigned to them and being required at harvesttime to deliver up to royal taxgatherers all the crops which they and their families would not need for sustenance until the next harvest. In addition they sowed, cultivated, and harvested the crops on the lands assigned in each town to the support of the temple and its priests and the lands belonging to Montezuma and his court. The common people lived monogamously in families, and their homes were built of sun-dried brick, wood, or reeds and were roofed with thatch. Only the nobles and members of the royal family were allowed to take concubines. The principal duty of women was to give soldiers to the state, and those who died in childbirth went directly to paradise. Children were deliberately trained in endurance to harden them for war. At the bottom of Aztec society was a numerous body of slaves, consisting of prisoners taken in battle or natives who had otherwise been reduced to bondage. Aztec civilization rested upon the institution of slavery.

The Aztec aristocracy consisted of the priests, the military, and the merchants. The ruler of the Aztecs was, strictly speaking, not a hereditary monarch but was chosen from a few families by a board of electors. His palace was luxuriously furnished with floor mats, wall draperies, incense burners, and more than one hundred baths. So fastidious were the Aztec nobles that they held bouquets of flowers to their noses whenever they had to approach a Spaniard! Adjoining the baths in the ruler's palace were zoological and botanical gardens. Under the Aztec class system the nobles and priests ranked just below the ruler's family. They paid no taxes but owed military service to the ruler. Only the members of this class were permitted to own personal property in land. At the time of Cortés's expedition the Aztec ruler was Montezuma II. According to the honest Spanish chronicler of the expedition, Bernal Díaz del Castillo,

The Great Montezuma was about forty years old, of good height and well proportioned, slender and spare of flesh, not very swarthy, but of the natural color and shade of an Indian. He did not wear his hair long, but so as just to cover his ears; his scanty black beard was well shaped and thin. His face was somewhat long, but cheerful, and he had good eyes and showed in his appearance and manner both tenderness and, when necessary, gravity. He was very neat and clean and bathed once every day in the afternoon. He had many women as mistresses, daughters of Chieftains, and he had two great Cacicas as his legitimate wives. . . . He had over two hundred chieftains in his guard, in other rooms close to his own, not that all were meant to converse with him, but only one or another, and when they went to speak to him they were obliged to take off their rich mantles and put on others of little worth, but they had to be clean, and they had to enter barefoot with their eyes lowered to the ground, and not to look up in his face. And they made him three obeisances, and said: "Lord, my Lord, My Great Lord!" before they came up to him, and then they made their report and with a few words he dismissed them, and on taking leave they did not turn their backs, but kept their faces towards him with their eyes to the ground, and they did not turn their backs until they left the room.

To conquer this great lord and his populous kingdom Cortés made elaborate preparations. Wrote Bernal Díaz:

He was very determined and headstrong in all business of war, not attending to any remonstrances on account of danger.... Where he had to erect a fortress, Cortés was the hardest laborer in the trenches; when we were going into battle, he was as forward as any.... In military service he practiced the most strict attention to discipline, constantly going the rounds in person during the night, visiting the quarters of the soldiers, and severely reprehending those whom he found without their armor and appointments.[2]

With a meager 400 white followers Cortés set out to subvert an empire, the most powerful in North America. If numbers could not accomplish this purpose, strategy, diplomacy, and a revolutionary religion would do so.

To reach the center of the Aztec confederation Cortés and his men were obliged to cross first the *tierra caliente* or hot, humid coastal strip which rings the Gulf of Mexico. At Zempoala, near the coast north of the modern Veracruz, Cortés concluded an alliance with the chief of the Totonacs, one of the confederated tribes. Zempoala was estimated by the Spaniards to have thirty thousand inhabitants. It was described by Bernal Díaz as a great city "full of white towers that glistened in the sun." Its wide streets were paved with polished cement that made the horses of the Spaniards slip and fall. From there the Spaniards ascended into the highlands of central Mexico. The success of their expedition was favored by several auspicious factors—the traditional expectation by the Aztecs of the return of their white god Quetzalcoatl from the East, predicted for the very year of Cortés's arrival; their apprehensiveness over several recent portents, including famines, earthquakes, floods, and fires, which they interpreted as warnings of evil to come; the blundering indecision of Montezuma; Cortés's good fortune in securing the services of loyal aides who knew the languages spoken by the Aztecs; his skill in playing upon the grievances of some of the tributary tribes, particularly the Tlascalans and Tezcocans, to win the support of several thousand of their warriors against the Aztecs; and his masterly finesse in securing possession of the person of Montezuma. The techniques of conquest which Cortés had used, employing local dupes—fifth columnists in modern parlance—spreading confusion and disunity among allies, infiltrating the centers of power, cajoling the weak-willed Aztec leaders, and invoking the sanctions of an alien ideology—these techniques familiar to successful conquerors in every age accomplished the downfall of the Aztec empire.

But Cortés's initial success in subjugating Montezuma's country by peaceful means was destroyed when, during his temporary absence at Veracruz, the indiscreet Pedro de Alvarado, whom he left in charge at Mexico City, took bloody action against the leaders of the Aztec religion. When Cortés and his men returned from the coast they were driven out of the city on *La Noche Triste*. Immediately they laid plans to regain possession of it by force. After a

<hr>

[2] Bernal Díaz del Castillo, *Historia verdadera de la conquista de la Nueva España* (3 vols.), trans. by the author, P. Robredo, Mexico, 1939.

prolonged military and naval siege ending in August, 1521, the audacious Cortés who, with his many thousands of Indian allies, outnumbered the city's defenders, occupied Tenochtitlán in what was the greatest military exploit of that age of intrepid *conquistadores*.

Fig. 2-1. Pedro de Alvarado, conqueror of Guatemala, an old painting in the Municipal Building in Guatemala City. (*Courtesy of Pan American Union.*)

Cortés, in conquering this highest civilization thus far found in the Americas, had acted without official authorization, for his orders had been revoked by Velásquez before his arrival at Veracruz and he had proceeded from there to the conquest of Mexico City only under authority conferred upon him by the town of Veracruz which he himself had established. His authority was now confirmed to him by the crown, and he was named governor, captain general, and chief justice of the new colony and was authorized to report directly to the king and no longer through the governor of Española. With the help of the zealous first bishop of Mexico, Juan de Zumárraga, Cortés undertook to destroy the political and religious structure of the conquered Aztecs. He demolished the main part of their capital city and proceeded to rebuild it along Spanish lines. He divided up the constituent village communities into *encomiendas*, which he assigned to his companions. Pagan temples, where hundreds of human victims had been sacrificed, were pulled down, a Catholic

Fig. 2-2. Cortés and the Cross, fresco by José Clemente Orozco, Dartmouth College, Hanover, N.H. (*Courtesy of Pan American Union.*)

cathedral was built, and mass baptisms of the natives were arranged. Mexico City now supplanted Española as the center of Spain's empire in America, and after the death of Diego Columbus in 1526 no new viceroy of Santo Domingo was ever appointed.

The victory of Cortés over the Aztec confederation was only the first of many conquests in Middle America. His exploit inspired new expeditions of exploration and conquest in all directions.

The Cordillera in Mexico assumes the rough configuration of a V with its point located at the Isthmus of Tehuantepec. Between the eastern range called the Sierra Madre Oriental and the western range called the Sierra Madre Occidental lies the wide, dusty, central plateau of Anáhuac, in which Cortés and

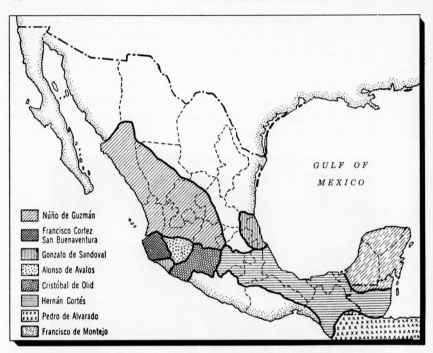

Early Mexican conquerors and the regions conquered.

his followers were now established. As the two lines of sierras converge to the south the mountains level out into hills and then disappear in the Isthmus of Tehuantepec, which has an elevation of only about 500 feet above sea level and which has therefore often served as a convenient route of transit from Atlantic waters across the continent to the Pacific. The mountains continue south of Tehuantepec but dwindle again to a narrow, comparatively low chain of hills in Panama.

In this region Andrés Niño coasted along the entire western shore of Nicaragua and Gil González Dávila explored that country and Costa Rica in 1522, discovering Lake Nicaragua, finding large quantities of gold, and baptizing thousands of natives. Meanwhile Pedrarias Dávila, who had succeeded to Balboa's power in the isthmus, had founded Panama and sent out an expedition which made the first settlements in Nicaragua—at León and Granada. One of Cortés's lieutenants, the impetuous Pedro de Alvarado, overran Guatemala, treating its Mayan natives with extreme brutality. "If you do not bring me the precious metal in all your towns," he threatened the Quiché chiefs, "I shall burn you alive and hang you." Then he cut from three of them the gold ornaments they wore in their ears. When the chiefs responded to these indignities by making war against him he conquered them and established himself there as proprietary governor. Cristóbal de Olid was also sent out by Cortés to explore Honduras, and there a settlement was made at

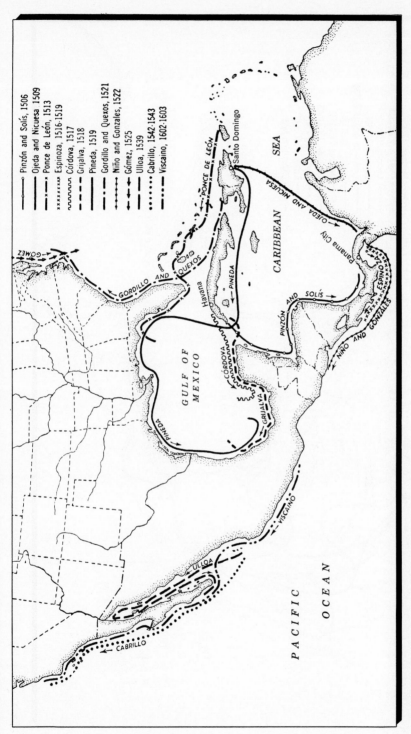

Early Spanish maritime explorations in Middle America.

Pinzón and Solís, 1506
Ojeda and Nicuesa 1509
Ponce de León, 1513
Espinoza, 1516-1519
Córdova, 1517
Grijalva, 1518
Pineda, 1519
Gordillo and Quexos, 1521
Niño and Gonzales, 1522
Gómez, 1525
Ulloa, 1539
Cabrillo, 1542-1543
Viscaino, 1602-1603

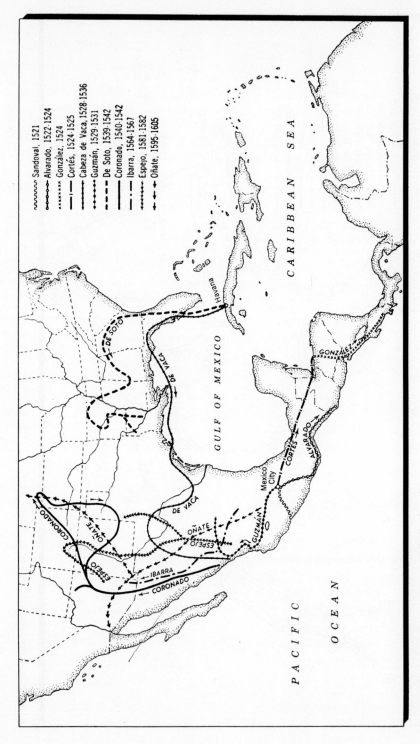

Early Spanish land explorations in Middle America.

Trujillo in 1525. At the same time Cortés himself was marching through this part of Central America, or Castilla del Oro (Golden Castile) as it was called. At the end of the following year Francisco de Montejo was commissioned as *adelantado* by the Emperor Charles V for the conquest and colonization of Yucatan. While he was engaged in this operation, lasting more than twenty years, the new bishop of Yucatan undertook the systematic destruction of the ancient Mayan temples, smashing their friezes, burning the records of their priesthood, and extirpating other evidences of pagan culture. But not until 1697 did the ruthless Spanish governor of Yucatan, Martín de Ursúa, conquer the last remnant of Mayan warriors defending themselves on an island in Lake Petén.

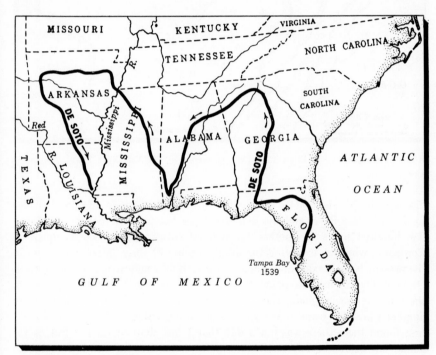

Route of De Soto's expedition, 1539–1542.

Meanwhile from the Caribbean islands Spaniards were making northward thrusts of exploration and conquest. Alvar Núñez Cabeza de Vaca started out as treasurer of an expedition headed by Pánfilo de Narváez, became separated from the main party, and with three companions crossed northern Mexico to the Gulf of California, where he finally found some of his compatriots. When he returned to Mexico City in 1536 his gilded account of his marvelous adventures among Indian cities in the country to the north helped to inspire Hernando de Soto, who was governor of Cuba and *adelantado* of Florida, to explore the piedmont region of Georgia in 1539, whence he went on west to

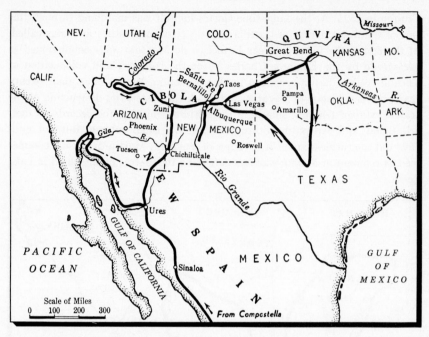

Route of Coronado's expedition, 1540–1542. (*Courtesy of The New York Times, January 7, 1940.*)

discover the Mississippi River near the present Memphis in 1541 and thence to the Arkansas River and the Red River. De Soto's route took him within a few hundred miles of another Spanish adventurer, Francisco Vázquez de Coronado, who was exploring the upper reaches of these latter two rivers in the present New Mexico and Kansas in search of a nonexistent golden city of Quivira. There, "in these plains as level as the sea," as Coronado reported to the king, he encountered "such a multitude of cows that it is impossible to number them, for while I was journeying through these plains until where I first found them there was not a day that I lost sight of them." But as for human life he found only uncivilized plains Indians "who travel around with these cows, who do not grow or harvest maize, and who eat the raw flesh and drink the blood of the cows they kill, and they tan the skins of the cows, with which all the people of this country dress themselves here."

But the territories in the present southeastern United States opened up by Narváez and De Soto were slow in being colonized by the Spaniards, partly because they furnished no gold and partly because the Indians there were hostile. Under orders from the viceroy of New Spain, Tristán de Luna y Arrellano tried to start colonies at Pensacola and in Alabama and Tennessee in 1559–1561 but had to abandon the attempt, as also did his successor, Angel de Villafañe. A few years later when French Huguenots began to encroach on the Atlantic coast of the Florida peninsula, threatening the route of the Spanish treasure galleons through the Florida-Bahamas channel, the new *adelantado* of Florida, Pedro Menéndez de Avilés, a distinguished naval officer and naval architect, countered their advance by founding the town of San Agustín (St. Augustine) in 1565. From there he proceeded first to wipe out the Huguenot settlement on the St. John's River and to replace it with a Spanish fort which he named San Mateo (St. Matthew). There the Jesuits began their ministrations, extending their missionary activity as far north as Chesapeake Bay. When these intrepid explorers and soul savers retired to Mexico in 1572, the Franciscans continued their work at St. Augustine, whence they extended their posts and missions northward to the sea islands of Georgia and South Carolina, only to be massacred in 1597. By the end of the sixteenth century all that remained of a century of Spanish colonizing efforts to the northward in Florida were the posts at St. Augustine and St. Matthew guarding the route of the precious treasure galleons.

One of the purposes of all these expeditions was to find a strait connecting the eastern and the western waters. After the return of Magellan's surviving vessel from its circumnavigation of the earth Cortés was instructed by the emperor to intensify his searches for such a strait. Cortés himself accordingly led an expedition to Lower California and later financed the voyage of Francisco de Ulloa, who first outlined the Gulf of California. But though all these efforts failed to find the strait through Middle America which the emperor and the Spanish traders desired, Alvaro de Saavedra opened up a Spanish trade route to the Philippine Islands in a pioneering voyage that took him from Acapulco, lying south of Mexico City, due west across the Pacific Ocean almost to the island of Guam in 1527–1528. His voyage was followed up by López de Villalobos in 1542–1543 and by Miguel López de Legaspi in 1564, who founded Manila in 1571 and became *adelantado* of the Philippine Islands. Another Spanish adventurer, Sarmiento de Gamboa, sailed into the South Pacific and discovered the Solomon Islands in 1567. These voyages gave a strong impetus to trade between New Spain and the Orient and resulted not only in increased attention to the western ports of New Spain, particularly Acapulco, but also in the eventual extension of the authority of the viceroy of New Spain over the *audiencia* at Manila.

Meanwhile explorations to the west and northwest of Mexico City had begun. The cruel Nuño de Guzmán, who had been president of the first *audiencia* set up in New Spain, organized an expedition and, lured on by tales of an island of Amazons and Seven Cities of Cíbola, commenced the conquest of the region known as New Galicia, now the state of Jalisco. There he founded the town of Culiacán in 1531. The discovery of the silver mines at Zacatecas, the richest in the world, by Juan de Tolosa in 1546, led to the occupation of this region and the intensive search for other mines in the Zacatecas lode farther north in New Biscay, comprising the present states of Chihuahua and Durango. The coasts of Upper California were explored in 1542–1543 by Juan Rodríguez Cabrillo, a Portuguese by birth. His journal of his expedition first used the word "California," in supposed allusion to a rumored black Amazon queen in that area. He passed by the Golden Gate without discovering the spacious harbor which lies behind it and later lost his life in the Santa Barbara Channel.

A further extension of conquest took the Spaniards into the northern borderlands beyond the silver mines into an area that was dominated by the hostile Chichimecas, Navajos, Apaches, Comanches, Yaquis, and other fierce nomadic tribes. Here they carried on silver-hunting and livestock operations under difficulties, maintaining their position precariously in this *tierra de guerra* by means of a chain of *presidios* or military posts. They founded Santa Fe in 1609 and a few other settlements in New Mexico but abandoned Texas only to reclaim it after a struggle with France in 1721. And they did not make any successful colonizing efforts in Upper California until the last third of the eighteenth century when, threatened by the advancing Russians, English, and French, Governor Gaspar de Portolá and Father Junípero Serra began settlements at San Diego (1769) and Monterey (1770).

The touch of Columbus's genius had caused new continents to emerge, as it were, from the ocean. Out of the western waters, through his discovery, rose

> ...two continents and countless isles,
> Taking slow shape through tales of strange adventurings.[3]

The crown that had sponsored the "Enterprise of the Indies," taking advantage of the service of hundreds of loyal adventurers in the new lands, had established a prior claim to them. But the Spaniards did not subdue their American empire by military force alone. Seldom did the Spanish forces, with or without their Indian allies, outnumber their enemies. Relatively speaking, only a handful of civilized Spaniards and Portuguese subdued the millions of aborigines who inhabited the American continents. At least equally potent with military force in accomplishing this result were diplomatic skill, a sense of religious mission, and patriotic zeal. The *conquistadores* carried out their exploits for God and country—and, of course, for themselves, for in America they could enjoy the fruits of their daring labors and the honors bestowed by their sovereign. Let no one argue that the Spanish people of Columbus's day were indolent and averse to manual labor. To that puritanical libel the arduous labors of the *conquistadores* are a sufficient refutation. The conquest of America was a stupendous national, religious, and individual achievement.

Additional Reading

Arciniegas, Germán: *Amerigo and the New World: The Life and Times of Amerigo Vespucci,* Alfred A. Knopf, Inc., New York, 1955.
Bolton, Herbert E.: *Coronado, Knight of Pueblos and Plains,* Whittlesey House (McGraw-Hill Book Company, Inc.), New York, 1949.

[3] Irene A. Wright, "Patronato, descubrimientos, descripciones," *Hispanic American Historical Review,* vol. 6, no. 5, February–August, 1926.

Castro, Américo: *The Structure of Spanish History,* Princeton University Press, Princeton, N.J., 1954. A profound and stimulating interpretation.
Chamberlain, Robert S.: *The Conquest and Colonization of Honduras, 1502–1550,* Carnegie Institution, Washington, D.C., 1953.
———: *The Conquest and Colonization of Yucatan, 1517–1550,* Carnegie Institution, Washington, D.C., 1948.
Covarrubias, Miguel: *Indian Art of Mexico and Central America,* Alfred A. Knopf, Inc., New York, 1957.
Díaz del Castillo, Bernal, *The Discovery and Conquest of Mexico, 1517–1521,* Farrar, Straus and Cudahy, Inc., New York, 1956.
Diffie, Bailey: *Prelude to Empire: Portugal Overseas before Henry the Navigator,* University of Nebraska Press, Lincoln, Neb., 1960.
Feuchtwanger, Franz (ed.): *The Art of Ancient Mexico,* Thames and Hudson, London and New York, 1954.
Hammond, George P., and Agapito Rey (eds.): *Narratives of the Coronado Expedition, 1540–1542,* University of New Mexico Press, Albuquerque, N.M., 1940. Documents relating to this expedition into southwestern United States.
Hodge, Frederick W., and Theodore H. Lewis (eds.): *Spanish Explorers in the Southern United States, 1528–1543 (Original Narratives of Early American History,* J. Franklin Jameson (ed.)), Charles Scribner's Sons, New York, 1907. Includes translations of the narratives of Alvar Nuñez Cabeza de Vaca, Hernando de Soto, and Francisco Vázquez de Coronado.
Idell, Albert (ed.): *The Bernal Díaz Chronicles,* Doubleday Dolphin Paperback, New York, 1956.
Keen, Benjamin: *Readings in Latin American Civilization: 1492 to the Present.* Houghton Mifflin Company, Boston, 1955, chaps. I, II, IV, V, VI.
León Portilla, Miguel: *The Broken Spears: the Aztec Account of the Conquest of Mexico,* translated by Lysander Kemp, Beacon Press, Boston, 1962.
MacNutt, Francis Augustus (ed.): *Fernando Cortes: His Five Letters of Relation to the Emperor Charles V* (2 vols.), Arthur H. Clark Company, Glendale, Calif., 1908. An indispensable source book on the conquest of Mexico.
Morison, Samuel Eliot: *Admiral of the Ocean Sea: A Life of Christopher Columbus,* Little, Brown and Company, Boston, 1942.
———: *Christopher Columbus, Mariner,* Mentor Books, New York, 1956.
———: *Portuguese Voyages to America in the Fifteenth Century,* Harvard University Press, Cambridge, Mass., 1940.
Morley, Sylvanus Griswold: *The Ancient Maya,* 3d ed., rev. by George W. Brainerd, Stanford University Press, Stanford, Calif., 1956.
Nowell, Charles E.: *A History of Portugal,* D. Van Nostrand Company, Inc., New York, 1952.
O'Gorman, Edmundo: *La Idea del descubrimiento de América: Historia de esa interpretación y critica de sus fundamentos,* Centro de Estudios Filosóficos, Mexico, 1951. A thorough analysis of the Columbian problem, favorable to Vespucius as the discoverer of America.
———: *The Invention of America,* Indiana University Press, Bloomington, Ind., 1961. A closely reasoned historical essay, modifying the conclusions of the above work.
Powell, Philip W.: *Soldiers, Indians, and Silver,* University of California Press, Berkeley, Calif., 1952. Describes the northward expansion of Mexico's mining frontier and the subjugation of the Chichimecas in the period 1550–1600.
Prescott, William H.: *History of the Conquest of Mexico,* Heritage Press, New York [1949?]. Required reading.
Romoli, Kathleen: *Balboa of Darién, Discoverer of the Pacific,* Doubleday & Company, Inc., New York, 1953.
Simpson, Lesley Byrd: *Many Mexicos,* 3d ed., rev., University of California Press, Berkeley, Calif., 1952.
Thompson, John Eric S.: *The Rise and Fall of Maya Civilization,* University of Oklahoma Press, Norman, Okla., 1954.

III

Southward the Course of Empire

In Spain's conquest of its new American empire the island frontier of the Caribbean was soon supplanted by a new mainland frontier in Middle America. The *conquistadores*, stimulated by Cortés's conquest of the rich Aztec confederation, made plans to advance from Panama down the west coast of South America to the wealthiest native peoples in the Western Hemisphere, the Incas of Peru.

Along that coast the western ranges of the Andes rise sharply from the narrow coastal shelf to elevations in gnarled ridges everywhere exceeding 10,000 feet, and they contain several volcanic peaks of more than 20,000 feet elevation. This towering Cordillera, which forms the dorsal column of the hemisphere, comprises the highest chain of mountains on the earth after the Himalayas, and has few passes under 12,000 feet. Starting close to the Pacific Ocean this formidable mountain barrier extends inland from 100 to 400 miles. The narrow coastal plains of Colombia and Ecuador, lying in the heart of the tropics, are covered with heavy jungle. The coast of Peru is a desert, habitable only where the rivers which originate in the Andes cut their way to the Pacific.

To the east the Andean ranges descend by heavily crevassed highlands, called *montañas*, into the Amazon lowlands. Continuing south they enclose the high piedmont plain or *altiplano* of Bolivia, which extends southward for several hundred miles between two mountain ranges. Here in the heart of the Andes on the border between Peru and Bolivia is located the highest fresh-water lake in the world, Lake Titicaca, at an elevation of 12,508 feet. It contains some unique fish which are commonly used as a source of food by the Indian population of the lake-shore area. In many parts of Latin America the elevation takes the curse off the tropics and renders the land habitable. Six per cent of the entire South American continent is elevated more than 10,000 feet above sea level and therefore enjoys temperate climates under a tropical sun. Each ascent of 330 feet reduces the temperature by 1° F. It was no mere coincidence that the aboriginal civilizations of Latin America reached their climax in the uplands of Guatemala; in the high central plateau of Mexico, called Anáhuac by the natives, which, though it lies within the tropics, enjoys a temperate climate by reason of its elevation of from 6,000 to 8,000 feet above sea level; and in the mountain valleys of the Andes in

Colombia, Ecuador, Peru, and Bolivia. This last-named area possessed, in addition to its temperate climate, other advantages conducive to the development of a high civilization, including rich soils in the large highland basins, an ample supply of water, and an abundance of building stone and clays suitable for making sun-dried adobe bricks. Everywhere the Andes are rich in minerals, in some places gold and platinum, in others copper, tin, silver, lead, and zinc.

Conquest of Peru

The wealth and civilization of the Incas became known to the Spaniards within twenty years after Columbus's discovery of the Western world. They were a conquering tribe of the Quechua linguistic group, whose ancestors built the structures in the Lake Titicaca region which, though in ruins, still give impressive evidence of the most highly developed culture of pre-Columbian America. At the time when the Spanish arrived, the empire of the Incas extended longitudinally some 2,000 miles from the northern part of Ecuador to central Chile and inland to the mountain regions of Bolivia and western Argentina, covering an area approximately equal to that of the Atlantic seaboard states of the United States. By means of their imperial policies these "Children of the Sun," as they called themselves, had been able to achieve an extraordinarily effective political and cultural integration among their subject peoples. Theirs was a mountain empire centering at Cuzco in southern Peru and interconnected by an elaborate system of roads, some of which were wide thoroughfares, others only footpaths for native couriers or *chasquis*. A main road ran the entire length of the empire from Quito on the north into central Chile, and a branch road went from Cuzco into the modern Bolivia. Another ran along the coast from the Gulf of Guayaquil southward to the desert of Atacama. Over these roads runners traveling in short relays could carry official messages as far as 1,200 miles in eight days.

The unit of government in this vast Inca empire was the *ayllu* or village community, which consisted not only of the people but also of the land which they tilled, for the people were almost mystically wedded to the land. The workers in each village were organized under the decimal system, each ten working under a boss and each group of ten bosses under a foreman up to the village chief who in turn was subject to the authority of the chief of the tribe, supposedly composed of 10,000 workers. The hierarchy continued up to the governor of the province, through him to the ruler of one of the four quarters of the Inca empire, and through him to the Inca himself, who was the final authority.

The economy of the empire rested upon an intensive cultivation of the soil and a diligent conservation of its resources. Over forty domesticated plants were cultivated, including corn, beans, squash, potatoes, cotton, and tobacco. Agriculturists terraced the steep mountain slopes for their crops, constructed elaborate works of irrigation, and systematically replenished the fertility of their fields with natural fertilizers, including human excrement and the bird droppings or *guano*, found on the rocky islets off the Peruvian coast and exploited as a government monopoly. Along the coast agriculture was supplemented by fishing.

The Inca empire in the early sixteenth century, it has been estimated, contained a population of from 4 million to 7 million and Cuzco, the capital, with its outlying villages probably numbered 200,000 people. Except for the royal family and a few noble families the great mass of the population consisted of commoners, who were given no opportunity to rise into the class of the aristocracy. For these latter were reserved not only all the high positions of state but also all the refinements of civilization, including fine clothing, more solidly constructed houses, and higher learning. They were the architects, the military leaders, the priests, and the teachers. Members of this aristocratic class directed the construction work which was carried on under the auspices of the government, and as priests they performed the elaborate religious ceremonies of the state religion. The office of the ruler, called the Inca, was hereditary, and he was venerated as a descendant of the Sun. He was, therefore, both the temporal and the religious leader of the people. Wherever he went he was carried in an ornate litter of gold and silver decorated with many-colored feathers. None of his subjects, not even the mightiest lord, dared to appear before him except with a burden upon his back and with bare feet. To preserve dynastic purity the reigning monarch had to marry his own sister, for the Inca had to be the son of both a son and a daughter of the preceding monarch.

The Incas had advanced beyond the Aztecs into the Bronze Age, and their craftsmen were expert in fashioning ornaments of not only bronze but also tin, copper, silver, and gold. When they did not find these metals in pure form they smelted them in furnaces, sometimes using a forced draft. In the manufacture of ceramics and textiles they were distinctly superior to the aborigines of Mexico. Their craftsmen were as skilled at making paper-thin ceramics as in fitting enormous stones together in their temple architecture, which they did with such precision that even today a knife blade cannot be inserted into the crevices between the stones. They accomplished these results without leaving behind any evidences of mechanical inventiveness. Indeed their technology in everything except the fabrication of bronze objects was a heritage from past civilizations of the Andean region. In textile manufacture they employed the animal fibers of the llamas and alpacas and occasionally human hair, either in their natural hues or colored with vegetable and mineral dyes. In this craft they displayed fabulous workmanship. Much of the Inca weaving was done for clothing, but some was done exclusively for the interment of the dead. Their clothing was similar to that worn today by the inhabitants of this region and consisted of wrap-around skirts, shawls, slit-neck ponchos, belts, and headbands.

The buildings of the Incas, constructed of stone, were massive and unornamented but did not use the principle of the arch. Along the coast their architecture was limited to the sun-baked adobe brick used by their predecessors. These Andean peoples had developed no system of writing, pictorial, ideographic, or phonetic. Apparently they conveyed numbers and possibly ideas by means of the *quipu,* an instrument of colored and knotted strings which could be arranged in various ways. This device was based on the decimal system. Each knot near the end of the string counted 1, each at an intermediate position on the *quipu* counted 10, and a knot farthest up counted 100. The Incas did not use wheeled vehicles but had domesticated the native llamas both as draft animals and as producers of animal fiber. These were maintained in vast herds as the property of the government and of the Cult of the Sun.

The entire economy of the Inca empire was strictly regulated in the interest of the government and the established religion. It was a system of state socialism in which property was collective and labor obligatory. According to the great Inca Tupac Yupanqui, "It is not meet that the sons of plebians should be taught the sciences reserved for the great; for they are low people ... ; it is enough for them to learn the craft of their parents, for governing and commanding is not a thing for the common man." All land was held by the government and all able-bodied individuals who were assigned to agricultural labor were required to perform that work under the supervision of government officials, tending first the fields set aside for the Cult of the Sun, next those to be cultivated for the benefit of widows and orphans and persons absent on government service, next the lands of the *curaca* or chief, and finally the lands of the Inca himself. The idle were severely punished. This paternalistic system of the Incas was extended to subject rival tribes. The Incas were not satisfied merely to collect tribute from conquered peoples but instead sought, with considerable success, to incorporate them in the empire. In the subjugated regions they built forts, stationed army garrisons, and settled colonists (*mitimaes*) to consolidate their control. They linked the new region to the empire by means of roads and carried off important hostages to Cuzco. In fact they sometimes transported whole villages in order to bring them under control and replaced them with already pacified colonists. But they often left the local chieftains in command when they found them cooperative and willing to accept Inca overlordship.

Newly conquered tribes, like those already pacified, were required to set aside certain lands for common ownership and tillage by the villagers and to assign the rest, first, to the Cult of the Sun and, second, as the property of the noble family of the Inca. The forced labor of the villagers on the collective farms constituted their tribute to both church and state. The products of their labor went into common storehouses, some for the use of the priests, some for the Inca and his family, and some for storage as a surplus against famine. No opportunity was allowed for the exercise of individual initiative or the accumulation of wealth. For that reason neither private trade nor currency was necessary. Children were required to follow the occupation of their fathers, and travel by private individuals from one village to another was forbidden.

Who had been the theoretician of Inca Communism? Who was its Rousseau, its Babeuf, its Karl Marx? The ruins of its civilization do not disclose answers to these questions. This Andean civilization seems in retrospect to have reached the limits of its potentials under irrigation farming at the time when Europeans arrived in the New World. Without iron, a system of money, and commercial interchange it probably could not have progressed much further. Already the ceramic and textile art of the Incas was becoming stereotyped and monotonous, perhaps because the overorganization of the empire was inhibiting artistic spontaneity. Even their art was being reduced to formulas by their passion for organization. It was being required to justify itself only by its utilitarian value. This very concentration of power in centralized political organization rendered the empire vulnerable to foreign attack. The mass of the people under the Inca were accustomed to regimentation and would not be reluctant to accept a new dictatorship.

The conquest of this fabulous empire by the Spaniards was entrusted to a shrewd, illiterate adventurer, Francisco Pizarro, and was seven years in preparation. Finally in 1531 Pizarro started south from Panama at the head of a large expedition carrying a contract from the Emperor Charles V which authorized him to subjugate this native empire and to make himself governor over it. Fortunately for him the divine hierarchy of the Incas included a bearded white god, Viracocha, who according to tradition had departed across the sea, and when the Spaniards first arrived the Incas thought that Viracocha had returned. Fortunately, too, the Inca empire was racked by internal strife between the dominant ruler Atahualpa, who, as only an illegitimate scion of the Inca family, was a usurper, and his deposed half brother Huascar.

The first encounter between Pizarro and Atahualpa was held in the great square at Catamarca, which was the Inca's northern headquarters. Pizarro first sent the Fray Vicente de Valverde, already optimistically denominated first bishop of Cuzco, to explain the mysteries of the Catholic faith to the Inca recumbent in his befeathered litter. The Inca asked to see the breviary from which the padre had read his preachments, but when he could not open its hasp he threw it to the ground saying, "The God who is my God still lives in His heaven and looks down on His children." At this seemingly sacrilegious act the Spanish troops, who had been secreted in a large building opening on the plaza, dashed out on horseback, the bells on the trappings of their horses ringing confusedly, drove the panic-stricken Indians into bloody retreat, and captured Atahualpa himself.

The Spanish takeover of Peru was facilitated by the centralization of this native empire. All that was required was a palace revolution. It did not implicate or concern the mass of the Inca's subjects, for they had been rendered inert by his methodical absolutism. Pizarro allowed Atahualpa to gather together a large ransom for his release but after appropriating the ransom, which has been generously estimated at the equivalent of $17,500,000, had the Inca ruler executed by strangulation. He then proceeded to occupy and plunder Cuzco, the capital, and to convert it into a Spanish city. To a common soldier fell by lot the principal idol in the temple, which was an image of the sun, all worked in finest gold with a wealth of precious stones, in the likeness of a human face surrounded by rays. He lost it in one night at gambling! In 1535 Pizarro, needing a city nearer the coast for communication with Panama, founded Ciudad de los Reyes, the City of the Kings, later named Lima. While

Fig. 3-1. Pizarro takes the Inca king Atahualpa prisoner, 1533. (*Courtesy of The Bettmann Archive.*)

he was thus absent from Cuzco a rebellion against his rule was organized by Huascar's brother and was suppressed by the Spaniards only after great effort. In the ensuing quarrel among Pizarro's associates over the division of authority in the Inca realms, Pizarro was attacked in his own house by a group of his enemies and was assassinated. The conquest of Peru degenerated into a bloody civil war among the conquerors.

This conquest later found its classic chronicler in the eminent Garcilaso de la Vega, the son of one of the conquerors and an Inca Princess of the Sun. He spent his early life in Cuzco and after the death of his father passed the rest of his life in Spain where he completed his famous *Royal Commentaries of the Incas* (*Comentarios reales de los Incas*) published in 1609 and 1617. Himself a mixture of both conqueror and conquered he described with vivid realism and objectivity the epic of Peru.

Occupation of Southern South America

The occupation of Peru, or New Castile as the Spaniards called it, established a new frontier of conquest. From this base, exploratory expeditions were sent out in many directions. Southward into Chile the Andean ranges continue as a coastal Cordillera rising abruptly from the sea. They strain the moisture out of the trade winds to create the great interior desert plains of Atacama. This is one of the most desolate areas on the earth's surface, redeemed only by its rich deposits of the natural fertilizer sodium nitrate. The geographical continuation of this valley to the south is the fertile alluvial central valley of Chile, which varies from ten to twenty miles in breadth. Over this section of Chile the majestic Mount Aconcagua towers 22,812 feet in the air, the highest peak in the Western Hemisphere. South of the central valley the Cordillera splits up into an archipelago of picturesque islands, pine-darkened precipices, and glacier-lined fiords.

From Peru the first reconnaissance of Bolivia, western Argentina, and Chile was made by Diego Almagro in 1535–1537. Soon afterward the colonization of Chile was begun when one of Pizarro's principal captains, Pedro de Valdivia, with Pizarro's permission followed the coast southward from Peru into central Chile, which he nostalgically named Nueva Estremadura from his home province in Old Spain. There in 1541 he founded a town which he named Santiago de Nueva Estremadura, the capital of modern Chile, and from there he sent back reports of his conquest to the king, which are among the most highly prized literary documents of early Chile. One of his men, Alonso de Góngora Marmolejo, later wrote a realistic narrative of these events in his *Historia de Chile* (*History of Chile*) published in 1575.

Valdivia's settlement of wooden houses at Santiago was almost snuffed out by the savage Araucanian Indians, the tall, muscular, warrior tribe of aborigines who jealously guarded their homeland in central and southern Chile against the Spanish invaders. But the little Spanish outpost perched on the fringe of a vast empire survived, and from it other settlements were made—at La Serena to the north and at Concepción to the south, which Valdivia envisaged as a commercial port for trade between Spain and Peru. The area of the new colony of Chile as defined in the concession made to Valdivia and his successor was to extend from the seacoast 100 leagues inland and southward to Magellan's strait. If this claim could be sustained it would include most of the region that now lies in western and southern Argentina. In pursuance of this claim one of Valdivia's men, Francisco de Aguirre, laid claim in 1553 to the settlement of Santiago del Estero, already founded by

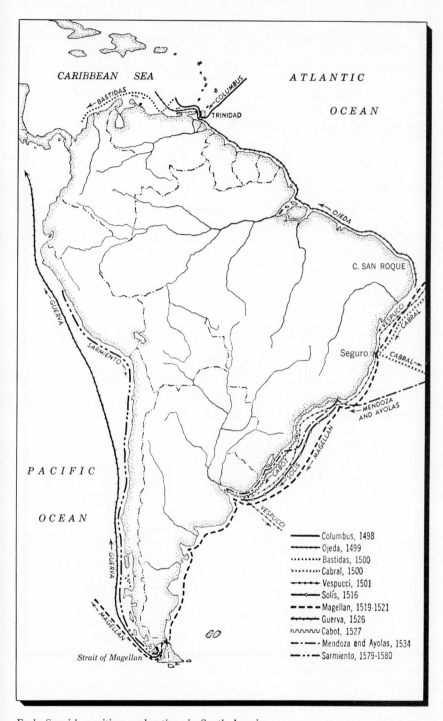

Early Spanish maritime explorations in South America.

67

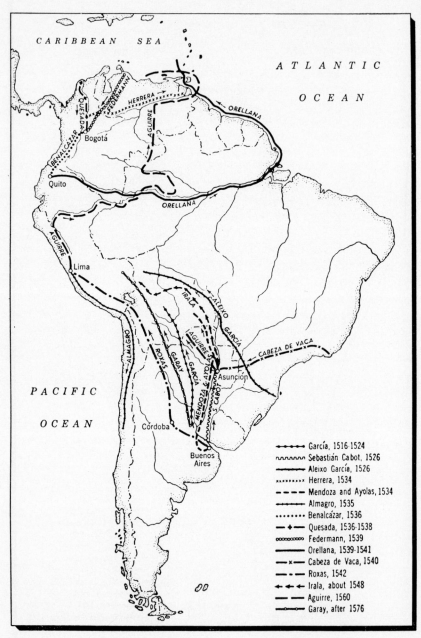

Early Spanish land explorations in South America.

García, 1516-1524
Sebastián Cabot, 1526
Aleixo García, 1526
Herrera, 1534
Mendoza and Ayolas, 1534
Almagro, 1535
Benalcázar, 1536
Quesada, 1536-1538
Federmann, 1539
Orellana, 1539-1541
Cabeza de Vaca, 1540
Roxas, 1542
Irala, about 1548
Aguirre, 1560
Garay, after 1576

men from Potosí in Upper Peru. This move marked the first step by the Chileans toward occupation of the region east of the Andes, but ten years later Chile was obliged to see the province of Tucumán in which it was situated transferred to Peru.

Valdivia, wrote one of his contemporaries, "was a man of good stature, and had a smiling countenance. His head was large, in just proportion with his body. He had become stout and bulky and broad-chested. A man of good understanding, though not cultured in his speech; liberal and gracious when he did a favor.... Two things he had that smirched his virtues. One that he hated men of noble birth. The other, that he was fond of women, and usually kept a common Spanish girl." This latter, Inés Suárez, deserves to be considered one of the founders of Chile.

The impetuous and imprudent Valdivia was killed in 1553 by the Indians. After a hard day of fighting against them he and his bedraggled followers, while retreating in orderly fashion, were set upon and defeated by the Indians, led by an Indian who from a boy had been brought up by Valdivia, his Indian name being Lautaro. His allegiance to his own people proved stronger than his gratitude to the Spaniards. After Valdivia's capture and murder at the age of fifty-six, his successor as governor, the young and snobbish García Hurtado de Mendoza, founded a settlement on the eastern side of the Andes which was named Mendoza. Other settlements were made by the Chileans in this area at San Juan and San Luis before the end of the century. This ultramontane province of which Mendoza became the principal town, called Cujo (Cuyo) or the saddlebag province, remained a part of Chile for more than two hundred years.

The Araucanian Indians in Chile, being formidable fighters and possessing little coveted gold and silver wealth, remained independent of Spanish authority and barred Spanish advance in the south just as effectively as the fighting Apaches and Comanches resisted Spanish expansion on the northern borders of New Spain. The exploits and vicissitudes that accompanied the founding of Chile were chronicled in a long heroic poem *La Araucana,* which was written by a young Spanish nobleman, Alonso de Ercilla y Zúñiga, who came out with Governor Hurtado. In it he sang:

> the valor in affray
> Of the undaunted warriors of Spain
> Who by the sword imposed a cruel yoke
> Upon the untamed Araucanian folk.

And yet, admiring the unconquerable spirit and native pride of the Araucanians he dedicated his poem to them! This most important epic poem of Spanish America went through edition after edition and became the most popular literary work of its day. Because it seemed to the governor not sufficiently adulatory of himself—in fact did not even mention his name—he commissioned Pedro de Oña to write another one, the strained and artificial *Arauco domado*

(*Arauco Subdued*), praising the governor as the conqueror of the Araucanians. The Indians, however, were not conquered. They rapidly adapted their strategy and tactics to the Spanish methods of warfare and acquired as spoils of war and by thievery a large supply of horses, thus increasing their mobility. The menace from the Indians in Chile continued until their final subjugation almost three and one-half centuries later. This Araucanian resistance, combined with Chile's lack of tangible wealth and its physical remoteness, kept it a poor, lawless, struggling, military frontier settlement until the beginning of the nineteenth century. It remained subordinate to Peru, for it was half a world away from Europe by way of the Pacific and its only alternative route to Europe was the difficult passage through Magellan's strait. By 1600 the population of Chile is estimated to have numbered only 10,000 Spaniards, 28,000 *mestizos,* and 600,000 Indians, making a total of 638,000. During the next two centuries its Indian population steadily diminished, numbering probably fewer than 100,000 by 1800. North of the Bío-Bío River, which was fixed as the boundary line between the Indians and the whites in 1612, the central valley of Chile was converted into a cattle-raising and agricultural country. Except for copper, mining was of inconsiderable economic importance.

While the first settlements were being made in Chile the Spaniards were reconnoitering the highlands southeast of Peru. There they soon discovered rich deposits of silver and lead. Coming down from Cuzco the first expedition established in 1538 a settlement which they called La Plata, or Silver, on the site of an Indian village Chuquisaca. But this first settlement in what is now Bolivia was soon eclipsed by Potosí, where the richest silver mines in the world were found and a Spanish settlement was established in 1545. As hordes of Spanish adventurers and prospectors flocked there, they turned it into a typical frontier mining town, with gambling halls, inflation of prices, and lawlessness. There gold leaf became so abundant and cheap that it was used to gild candles in the churches and the leaves of the cut flowers in the drawing rooms of the rich. By the end of the sixteenth century the population of Potosí reached 114,000. This colony, which was called Upper Peru or Charcas for almost three centuries, and Peru, to which it was administratively joined, became the world's richest source of silver and remained so for two centuries until surpassed by Mexico in the eighteenth century. By reason of its mineral wealth the combined Peru-Upper Peru became Spain's most prized possession and the center of its American empire. Other Spanish lands in South America were considered only subsidiary to it.

Exploring parties from Peru went into northern Argentina and Paraguay, starting in 1543. Seven years later the first permanent settlement was made in this region, later developing into the town of Santiago del Estero. But it was resented by the Chileans as an encroachment upon the territory which had been assigned to Valdivia. Finally after a decade of controversy Santiago del Estero was judged by the crown to be dependent upon Peru rather than Chile, but the Chilean claim to western and southern Argentina arising out of the concession to Valdivia persisted until the end of the nineteenth century. Meanwhile Spanish settlers pushed on into western Argentina, founding Tucumán in 1565. It became the metropolis of this area and a principal supplier of mules and cattle to the mines at Potosí. People from Tucumán then founded Córdoba in the center of the Argentine piedmont region in 1573, and established a university there in 1613. Meanwhile other settlements had been made at Salta, La Rioja, and Jujuy.

Along the Atlantic seaboard of South America Spanish adventurers had already begun to encroach on territory claimed by the Portuguese, who liked to believe that the territory assigned to them in the Treaty of Tordesillas extended as far south as the estuary of the Río de la Plata. The first whites who came to Brazil found no wealthy kingdoms comparable to those of New Spain and Peru. When they demanded gold from the cannibal natives their demands were not only resisted but they themselves were usually killed and eaten. Juan Díaz de Solís explored the coast as far south as the Río de la Plata in 1516, where he was enticed on shore by savages and killed. Ten years later Sebastian Cabot, sailing for the king of Spain, skirted the same coast, stopped at what is now Florianopolis on the island of Santa Catarina, built a fort which he named Sancti Spíritu on the lower Paraná River, and spent three years exploring the rivers as far south as the Río de la Plata. Since this river appeared to lead into the silver country to the west, of which he heard alluring tales, he named it the River of Silver (Río de la Plata).

The first settlement at the estuary of this river was attempted in 1536 by Pedro de Mendoza under a grant of territory made to him by the Emperor Charles V extending 200 leagues along the Atlantic coast south of the limits of the Portuguese claim. To settle the area granted to him Mendoza got up a lavish expedition of fourteen ships; 1,500 men thronged to his standard crying, "We are going to the Silver River." As they entered the Río de la Plata they breathed in the fresh clean air blowing from the wide river and built a town on its banks which they called Puerto de Santa María de los Buenos Aires or in German, as the Bavarian chronicler of the expedition wrote, *Guter Wind*.

There the Spaniards encountered a nomadic Indian tribe, named Querandíe, who wore only small loin cloths, ate the rhea and guanaco of the pampas, and supplemented this diet with fish, roots, wild fruits, and berries. For hunting and warfare these Indians used *bolas*, lassos, handbows and flint-pointed arrows, lances, and slings. The white settlers soon encountered their hostility and in a pitched battle against them suffered severe losses. The horses on which the Spanish noblemen rode to the fray proved a liability, for they were upset by the ingenious *bola* of the Indians, a long cord with weights on the end which was thrown around the horses' legs. The whites were now besieged in their stockade by several thousand Indians. As they sat there and watched their supplies of food dwindle, the fervor for adventure and wealth which had inspired them to come to the Silver River drained away. To each man was allotted only 6 ounces of wheat flour a day and a fish every third day.

So desperate was their plight that three of their number stole a horse and ate it secretly; the culprits after being tortured finally admitted their guilt and were hanged. From these hanging bodies three other Spaniards secretly by night hacked off pieces of flesh and took them home to still their hunger. The white settlement at Buenos Aires was then attacked in force by the Indians, was set on fire by flaming arrows, and was burned down. Only 560 men of the original expedition survived. Mendoza accordingly evacuated the fort. Racked with syphilis, disillusioned with the expedition in which he had sunk all his hopes and fortune, and convinced that La Plata was not a land of silver but instead a land of hunger and death, he abandoned his American venture and set out for Spain. On the return trip he died and was buried at sea. The first settlement at Buenos Aires thus guttered out.

But several of Mendoza's captains went up the Paraná River to look for the silver country around Potosí. One of them, Juan de Ayolas, was killed by the Indians while exploring the Chaco region; another, Domingo Martínez de Irala, succeeded to Mendoza's command at the latter's departure; and a third, Juan de Salazar de Espinosa, founded Asunción in 1537, the first settlement in Paraguay. Into this area five years later came the chronicler of the ill-fated Narváez expedition in North America, Alvar Núñez Cabeza de Vaca, who had been designated *adelantado* and governor of the province of Río de la Plata. He led an exploring expedition overland from the island of Santa Catarina. "All the people living in this country," he reported to the king of Spain, "are of the race of the Guarames, working at farming and hen and duck growing, as the country people of our own Spain; a domestic people it is indeed, and friendly to the Christians, and fit to win over with little trouble to the knowledge of our sacred Christian faith." These aboriginal Guaraní were rapidly Hispanicized in virtually every way except their native language, which their descendants speak to this day.

Less than a year after the arrival of the well-intentioned Alvar Núñez, his capital, Asunción, composed of more than two hundred houses of wood and thatch, was destroyed by fire. He and his companions, newcomers to Paraguay, were resented by Irala and other survivors of the Mendoza expedition, who now found themselves subordinated to him by orders of the king. When the unfortunate governor returned, sick with fever, from an unsuccessful journey up the Paraguay River in search of the kingdom of gold and silver and the land of the Amazons of whom the Indians had spoken, he was deprived of his power by Irala, thrown into prison, and sent back to Spain. Paraguay was then governed by Irala until his death in 1556.

Since the natural outlet for this country was downstream rather than overland, Juan de Garay founded a settlement at Santa Fe in 1573 to serve as a down-river port. Finally, seven years later, he made a new settlement, this time permanent, at Buenos Aires. The capital of modern Argentina, then, was founded originally as an offshoot of the capital of modern Paraguay. The

Europeans, finding here only sparse nomadic tribes, displaced the Indians and worked the lands themselves. For more than two hundred years this area remained in the backwash of Spanish colonization; it occupied only a secondary and peripheral place in Spain's imperial system. Having "no temples of beaten gold, or mythical races of men, or fountains of everlasting youth," it remained, like Chile, a conglomerate of raw frontier settlements subordinate and tributary to Peru.[1]

The Spaniards in Northern South America

Explorations to the north of Peru were inspired partly by reports of another wealthy Indian kingdom—the country of El Dorado or the golden prince—situated in the Andean highlands there. According to the story, the prince of that kingdom had himself periodically anointed with gum and sprinkled with gold dust. He then embarked on the waters of a lake in a boat which contained gold objects and which he emptied into the lake to propitiate the gods of the waterfalls. At the same time he plunged into the lake in order to give it the precious metal with which he was adorned. The locale of this story was originally vague and moved constantly eastward but was eventually fixed at Lake Guatavita in Colombia, a sacred lake of the Chibcha Indians.

These Indians belonged to an extremely heterogeneous and numerous cultural group that inhabited the northern Andes, Central America, parts of Venezuela, the Caribbean islands, and portions of eastern Bolivia. Both the cultural diversity in this area and all the evidence thus far discovered indicate that they were never politically united. The Chibcha or Muisca chiefdom occupied the high plateau east of the Magdalena River, and the principal towns were at Bacatá (Bogotá) and Tunja, which they palisaded for defense. There the Indians lived a primarily agricultural life, cultivating beans, squash, tomatoes, tobacco, cotton, corn, and potatoes. They manufactured coarse cloth and dressed in the conventional costume of the Andean Indians, consisting of breechclouts and slit-neck shirts for the men, and skirts and shawls for the women. Their conical houses were made of wood and thatch. They mined emeralds and were skilled craftsmen in casting gold and copper ornaments.

The Chibcha social structure consisted of two basic classes—the noble or ruling class and the commoners, from which latter class were chosen the warriors. The warrior group formed an elite fighting corps, and to them were assigned special privileges. The religion of the Chibcha showed many resemblances to that of the Maya and Aztec of Middle America. It included among its deities a white-bearded hero similar to the Aztec Quetzalcoatl. The priests inherited their offices through the female line, and they lived in

[1] William H. Hudson, *The Purple Land*, Modern Library, Inc., New York, 1904, p. 387.

temples where they performed religious ceremonials and acted as intermediaries between the people and the gods. The religious rites of the Chibchas included human sacrifice.

The Chibcha had domesticated no animals and had developed no handwriting. They were excellent craftsmen in pottery and metalwork, though they did not know the uses of iron or have much stone architecture. With a population estimated at 300,000 they formed the most populous state between Mexico and Peru. They were ruled by an absolute monarch called the Zipa, who was carried about on a litter and seated on a throne of gold. He inherited his office through his mother. When the Chibcha first encountered the Spaniards they had attained a level of culture midway between that of the nomadic plains Indians of the north and that of the Incas to the south. As a result of their frequent wars they had established hegemony over the neighboring tribes to the west in the valley of the Cauca River, and they carried on an active trade with related tribes in the humid lowlands of Colombia and Central America. But in fact they were not a people of wealth conceived in terms of the precious metals which the Spanish *conquistadores* were seeking. Nevertheless their legend of El Dorado lured many of these Spaniards onward through extraordinary hardships to the conquest of their kingdom.

The area north of Peru is dominated by the South American Cordillera. Its western chain, the Cordillera Occidental, which is the lowest of the three mountain ranges and rises to some 8,000 or 9,000 feet, lies between the Atrato and the Cauca Rivers. The central range, or the Cordillera Central, separates the Cauca Valley from the Magdalena and flattens out toward the north into one of the most fertile coastal-plain areas of Latin America. The eastern range, or Cordillera Oriental, rises east of the Magdalena and forms the high plateau on which Bogotá is situated. Proceeding northeast it broadens out into several mountain ranges that either dip into the sea in eastern Venezuela or sink into the Venezuelan coastal plain farther east.

Starting in the south one of Pizarro's captains, Sebastián de Benalcázar, who was left behind to guard Pizarro's rear in the expedition to Peru, took it on himself to conquer Quito, assisted by the civil war that was raging among native tribes there. He occupied the almost deserted town of Quito in 1533 and remained governor for over two years. But intrigued by the rumors of a fabulously rich kingdom to the north, he then abandoned Quito and entered the southern part of the territory of modern Colombia where he founded the town of Popayán and was eventually commissioned by the crown to be *adelantado* of the region of which it was the principal town. From Guayaquil somewhat later Francisco de Orellana went eastward to find a great river reported by the Indians. Moving down the Napo River he and some sixty companions entered the headwaters of the Amazon, which he named from the native women warriors whom he encountered there. "These women are very white and tall, and have hair very long and braided and wound about their heads," the chronicler of the expedition, Fray Gaspar de Carvajal, reported. "They are very robust and go about naked, [but] with their privy parts covered. With their bows and arrows in the hands, they do as much fighting as ten Indian men." The good father wrote this account with feeling because he lost an eye in the encounter with them! [2]

Continuing downstream Orellana proposed to return as soon as he could replenish his supplies of food, but finding none and having proceeded too far to turn back he and his party of Spanish adventurers had no alternative but to float onward down the sluggish, broadening stream. So great was their suffering that, as Father Carvajal reported, "We reached a state of privation so great that we were eating nothing but leather, belts, and soles of shoes, cooked with certain herbs, with the result that so great was our weakness that we could not remain standing." Some of the men, crawling on all fours or leaning on sticks, ventured into the jungle and gnawed at certain unfamiliar herbs which caused them to go insane. Orellana and his men finally reached the mouth of the mighty Amazon in the following year, 1541. A few years later this exploit was duplicated by a rebellious Spanish adventurer Lope de Aguirre.

Meanwhile expeditions launched from the Spanish settlements in the Caribbean were exploring the northern coast of South America, the so-called "Spanish Main." In 1508 Ojeda received a grant of territory extending from Cape Vela to the Gulf of Darién in what soon came to be called New Andalusía. But the first settlement that endured was not established until 1525 when Rodrigo de Bastidas established a town at Santa Marta, east of the mouth of the Magdalena River. His treatment of the Indians was exemplary, conforming to the high standards which his contemporary Bartolomé de Las Casas was advocating, but for that reason he was driven out by his Spanish colleagues. The importance of the settlement at Santa Marta diminished as the settlers soon afterward drifted away to join Pizarro in the dismantling of the Inca empire, and it was superseded in importance by a new coastal settlement, Cartagena, which was established to the west of the Magdalena River by Pedro de Heredia in 1533. The new port had an excellent harbor and became one of the chief centers of Spanish commerce and civilization in the New World. From these two settlements on the southern rim of the Caribbean, expeditions were launched into the interior. One of these, organized by a sturdy straightforward lawyer-turned-soldier, Gonzalo Jiménez de Quesada, went some 600 miles up the Magdalena River by boat and on foot and then turning off to the left climbed into the highland country of the Chibchas. After defeating them in battle the Spaniards occupied the entire plateau area of Cundinamarca and established a town there in 1538 at the site of one of the Chibcha villages, which they called Sante Fé de Bogotá.

[2] Jorge Hernández Millares (ed.), Fray Gaspar de Carvajal, O.P., *Relación del nuevo descubrimiento del famoso río grande de las Amazonas,* Fondo de Cultura Económica, Mexico, Buenos Aires, 1955.

To the country the homesick Quesada gave the name of New Granada, a name which survived to the middle of the nineteenth century. He was finally made captain general over it and perpetual magistrate in Bogotá in 1550, and from there he sent out an expedition in 1569 east of the Cordillera to find El Dorado—an expedition which ended disastrously.

Already an El Dorado of slave hunting and pearl fisheries had been opened up by the Spaniards along the Caribbean coast east of the settlements in New Andalusía or Colombia. This region offered special attractions to the Spaniards because the natives there could be more easily captured than the better-organized and more warlike tribes of the Caribbean islands and the North American mainland and because pearls were found in abundance in the waters around the island of Cubagua, just off the Venezuelan coast. There was established the first slave market in the New World, where native divers were used in the shark-infested pearl fisheries. The hazards of this forced labor so antagonized the free mainland Indians that when Bartolomé de Las Casas acquired an *encomienda* and undertook in 1521 to set up an enlightened free labor colony on the coast of eastern Venezuela he was driven out by the Indians. The importance of eastern Venezuela to the Spanish diminished with the destruction of their principal settlement in 1530 and the gradual depletion of the oyster beds after 1535. But with the development of other resources a new settlement, Santa Inés de Cumaná, which they established grew to become the metropolis of the area.

Along the Caribbean coast between New Andalusía and the pearl fisheries lay the territory that was named Venezuela by Ojeda because the Indian villages built out over Lake Maracaibo reminded him of Venice. There the first permanent settlement was made at Santa Ana de Coro in 1527 by Juan de Ampués, who had made such an enviable reputation for his kindness toward the Indians in the islands that he was sent by the *audiencia* of Española, in a burst of righteousness, to put a stop to slave hunting on the Spanish Main. But this area, having neither wealth nor strategic importance, was made a stepchild of the Spanish crown in the following year when it was granted by the Emperor Charles V as a concession to the great German banking house of the Welsers on condition that they colonize and develop the territory in order to liquidate the emperor's debt to the company.

Under the terms of a series of *capitulaciones y asientos* which Charles issued, the house of Welser was made responsible for transporting 300 Spanish colonists and 50 German miners to Venezuela within two years and for establishing two towns and three ports there. They were given permission to import 4,000 Negroes within four years. One of the members of this banking house, Ambrosius Ehinger, who was then in Española, was made *adelantado* and from there proceeded with about three hundred settlers to Coro where he drove Ampués from power. At the outset his primary objectives were to attract settlers and to develop trade, but these were thwarted by the shortage of labor. As a result Ehinger resorted to subjugation and enslavement of the natives, spending most of his time in quarrels with the *audiencia* at Santo Domingo over the limits of his authority and in expeditions of plunder and exploration in the interior until he was killed in ambush. His successor Georg Hohermut, who came out to Coro in 1535 with some five-hundred settlers, mostly Spaniards, was unable to prevent the colony from sliding into anarchy, misery, and bankruptcy. One of his associates, Nicolás Federmann, made an arduous journey overland to Bogotá in the highlands of New Granada but found it already occupied by Quesada. In 1546 the concession to the Welsers was voided by Charles V, though their claims to Venezuela were not definitely abrogated until after ten years of complicated litigation. Several years after Spanish authority was reestablished there Caracas was founded, and in 1576 it became the seat of administration of the combined provinces of Venezuela and New Granada.

Founding of Brazil

By the middle of the sixteenth century the Spaniards had effectively staked out their claims in the American continents north and south. Meanwhile the Portuguese had been somewhat nonchalantly following up the claims in America conceded to them in the Treaty of Tordesillas. Under the impetus given to overseas adventures by Prince Henry the Navigator, the Portuguese had ventured south along the coast of Africa and had reached the Sierra Leone on the Guinea coast by the time of Prince Henry's death in 1460. The rounding of the southern tip of Africa by Bartolomeu Días in 1487 focused the interest of the Portuguese upon the route to the Orient around Africa rather than by way of the west. This preoccupation with explorations in African waters explains in part the refusal of the Portuguese court to back Columbus's project. After the king of Portugal, John II, heard of Columbus's return from his first voyage he became sufficiently interested in western exploration to send out a secret expedition to trace his course, but when it returned unsuccessful from its timid western venture the Portuguese resumed their African explorations. The completion of Vasco da Gama's voyage to India in 1499—a voyage more sensational and more immediately rewarding than the voyages of Columbus—further dampened Portugal's interest in western exploration. After Cabral's discovery of the coast of Brazil in 1500, which added the claims of discovery to the claims based upon the Treaty of Tordesillas, a few voyages apparently were made to this coast unofficially by Portuguese navigators, of whom little trace survives. The first concession to cut the red brazilwood, highly prized in Europe as a dyewood, was given in 1503 to a Portuguese Jew, Fernão de Noronha, whose name is still perpetuated in the islands off the easternmost bulge of Brazil. But not until Sebastian Cabot, venturing for the king of Spain, established his settlement at Sancti Spíritu in 1527 did the Portuguese conclude that they would have to back up their treaty claims by actual settlement.

Disappointed at not finding El Dorado in Brazil, the Portuguese established a coast-guard service to exercise surveillance over the long Brazilian coast, where brazilwood was becoming a principal item of export and poaching by the French was common. They soon discovered the suitability of the territory to sugar production. To Portugal goes the credit for being the first nation in the history of European expansion to develop an agricultural society south of the equator. On the wide coastal plain on the eastern bulge of Brazil where pleasant prairies roll down to the sea from the Brazilian coastal mountains—the Serra do Mar—the Portuguese created an agricultural colony. They did not find sugar cane growing indigenously there but took it from Madeira and the Cape Verde Islands to Brazil around 1521 and made their first serious and successful effort to cultivate it near Pernambuco. After Sebastian Cabot returned to Spain from exploring the coast of Brazil, the Portuguese bestirred themselves to counteract his activities and strengthen their own territorial claims in South America under the Treaty of Tordesillas. They therefore sent out their first colonizing expedition under the young Capt. Martim Affonso de Sousa. Sousa's party explored the coast of Brazil from Pernambuco south to the present Uruguay and then turning back founded the first permanent European settlement in Brazil in 1532 at São Vicente. In this enterprise they received invaluable assistance from one of their compatriots, João Ramalho, who had been shipwrecked on the Brazilian coast twenty years earlier and who now conducted Martim Affonso to an Indian village in the highlands to the west of São Vicente where later was established the city of São Paulo.

The Portuguese interests in Brazil were threatened not only by the Spaniards but also by the French who were developing a project for a colony there. In an effort to counter them the Portuguese crown, following a pattern already set in its government of the Azores, divided the Brazilian coast from Maranhão on the north to the island of Santa Catarina below São Vicente on the south into fifteen "captaincies" (*capitanias*). Each captaincy extended from 50 to 100 leagues along the coast, with undefined limits in the interior. These were assigned to twelve captains donatory (*capitães donatários*) or governors on a semifeudal basis, each proprietor undertaking the obligation to carry out and finance colonization in his captaincy and in return receiving virtually sovereign powers there. They remained subject, however, to the ultimate sovereignty of the crown. In addition the crown reserved the right to the public revenue, to the royal fifth of all the minerals and precious stones discovered there, and to a monopoly of the trade in spices, brazilwood, and slaves. These trade monopolies would be handled on a concession basis, for the Portuguese crown itself did not engage in trade.

This attempt at government-sponsored colonization in Brazil met with limited success. Only five of the proprietors succeeded in establishing permanent colonies—Pernambuco, Bahía, São Vicente, Espírito Santo, and Ilhéos —and of these only Pernambuco and São Vicente became really prosperous. Their prosperity rested upon sugar. In other captaincies the new captains donatory either made no attempt at colonization or were so lacking in the qualities required for colony building that they failed to attract colonists or were defeated by the difficulties encountered and soon abandoned the attempt. Their captaincies degenerated into resorts for pirates and contraband traders in brazilwood. The large authority assigned to the captains donatory in this plan of colonization tended to discourage colonists who were ambitious for an independent life in the New World.

But though in general the captaincies, except those mentioned, were unsuccessful they roughly established the territorial outlines of the present coastal states of Brazil. Some of the proprietary claims in these captaincies survived into the eighteenth century, but in 1549 the Portuguese crown deprived the proprietors of much of their political authority by sending out the first governor general, the young and able Thomé de Sousa, to establish a centralized control and to defend the country from invaders. Taking with him some 320 soldiers, 400 convicts, and 6 Jesuits, who were the first to go to America, he established his residence in Bahía, or to give its full name, São Salvador de Bahía de Todos os Santos, located on the shores of a spacious bay, nearly 100 miles in circumference. There the Jesuits established a college, and from there they extended their missionary activities in all directions. Their most famous mission, the mission of St. Paul, to the south soon became a vigorous settlement, the forerunner of the modern São Paulo.

Europeans in the New World

Columbus's ironhearted venture westward into the "Ocean Sea" with his three tiny vessels had been followed by an extraordinary burst of colonizing energy. Europeans spilled over into the new hemisphere, led on by myth, romance, and hope of chivalric adventure and financial profit. *Conquistadores* set out with intrepid zeal to explore new deserts and jungles. They were harassed by pestilential "little flies" or *mosquitoes*, fought deadly serpents and jaguars, battled the even deadlier natives, performed prodigies of valor, and reduced aboriginal civilizations to subjection. Their sufferings were recompensed by the prospect of high adventure in strange lands among strange people every new day, by exciting glimpses of mountains, lakes, and oceans never before seen by white men, and sometimes by the acquisition of plunder beyond the dreams of avarice. They had faith in the impossible, and they often brought the impossible to pass.

> Capitanes de ensueño y de quimera,
> rompiendo para siempre el horizonte,
> persiguieron al sol en su carrera.

> (Captains of the dream and the chimera,
> always pushing forward to the horizon
> they pursued the sun in its course.) [3]

[3] Manuel Machado y Ruiz, "Los Conquistadores," *Horas de Oro: Devocionario Poético,* Imprenta Castellana, Valladolid, 1938, p. 21, used by permission.

Many of the conquerors were soldiers of fortune, adventurers incapable of leading a settled life and not interested in doing so. They were careless of life and limb and accustomed to hardship, always seeking out "the unpeopled world behind the sun." Such, for instance, was Alvar Núñez Cabeza de Vaca who traversed the North American continent on foot across Texas and northern Mexico and then, moving to South America as *adelantado* of the province of the Río de la Plata, led an expedition on foot for several hundred miles from Santa Catarina to Asunción in the Guaraní country. The conqueror of Guatemala, Pedro de Alvarado, left his governorship of Chiapas to fit out seven ships for an expedition against Quito in the Andean empire of the Incas. Juan Valenciano, who accompanied Jiménez de Quesada in the conquest of the Chibchas on the high plateau of Bogotá, soon afterward left on a pilgrimage to Jerusalem. The restless Hernando de Soto fought with Francisco Pizarro against the Incas in Peru and then moved on to the Floridas where he tramped into the back country as far as the Mississippi River and beyond, and there his restless soul found peace under the quiet waters of the river. These men were the shock troops of empire who prepared the way for settled living by those who came later.

Within two generations after Columbus, Spaniards and Portuguese explored most of the Western Hemisphere from northern Mexico to Patagonia, charted its main river systems, and founded most of the cities of modern Latin America. While beset by death on every side they were inspired by dreams of personal independence, glory, and wealth. For them America was above all a land of opportunity, a rainbow of hope. It would supply them with social security. It would enable them to acquire a fuller sense of belonging to their generation and age. A man who in the homeland would have had to resign himself to field labor under the orders of an avaricious landowner and who could only hope to eke out an unhappy existence became important in the New World. Here he could have Indians to wait upon him; he could maintain a harem of Indian women, which he could not do in any other part of the Christian world; he could own lands, could serve as captain in military campaigns, and might even be called upon to give advice to his *adelantado*. In America his dreams became real.

From the Indians the Europeans learned ways of accommodating themselves to the strange environment of the New World. The newcomers in Brazil built their houses of wood and straw after the Indian fashion, they protected themselves with palisaded forts, as did the native Tupi, and they learned to eat manioc as a substitute for wheat. The frontiersmen even walked in file, Indian fashion, one behind the other. They used the Indian canoe for river transportation, and they learned from the Indians how to use native herbs for the treatment of wounds and diseases. Their religion also was affected by pagan rites and beliefs. The Europeans in America, instead of Europeanizing the Indians, often were themselves Indianized in the process.

Some of the white newcomers went completely native. When Cortés, skirting the coast of Yucatan with eleven ships and 500 soldiers, learned that two Spaniards were being held prisoner by a *cacique* some four leagues inland he sent beads for their ransom. But one of the Spaniards was married to an Indian woman, had three sons by her, had his ears pierced and his face tattooed. He refused to leave. The other when he came into the presence of Cortés could not, so the ancient chronicler Bernal Díaz reported, "be distinguished from a native, and he had hardly the pronunciation of his own language.... His color was as dark as a native, and he was marked like them. He had a few rags about his shoulders and waist, an oar in his hand, and the remnant of an old book of prayers tied in a bundle on his shoulder." A more notorious example was that of the Portuguese castaway, Diogo Alvares, who was wrecked on the Brazilian coast in 1510 and who was spared the fate which befell his companions at the hands of their cannibalistic captors by displaying his prowess with a gun salvaged from his wrecked vessel. For this he was named Caramurú or man-of-lightning by his captors and was accepted by them as a chief. Through his influence he was able to keep some of the Indians along the Brazilian coast friendly to the whites. His career was later commemorated in *Caramurú*, an epic poem on the discovery of Brazil, which was published in 1781 by Friar José da Santa Rita Durão.

The surge of the Iberian peoples into the Western Hemisphere was a middle-class movement, imbued with the traditions of individual enterprise and local autonomy which prevailed in the mother countries. It was neither a crown enterprise, on the one hand, nor a rabble adventure, on the other. The lead was taken by members of the lesser nobility and by entrepreneurs who either were "on the make" or hoped to use American wealth to achieve rank in their mother country. In the overseas lands of Spain the original enterprisers were not the grandees, few of whom came to America, but *hidalgos* and energetic middle-class leaders. The discoverers and conquerors and the other newcomers who came from Europe were motivated by the same urges that impelled later immigrants from Europe, even into the twentieth century. They sought new opportunities in a new environment. They wanted to improve their lot in life and to find security and possibly wealth for themselves and their families. Many of the Portuguese who settled in Brazil were impoverished gentry who became large landholders in the New World. Other immigrants included peasants from the mother country and from the Azores and Cape Verde Islands and fugitives from justice. These were the people who opened up the American continents and determined the course and manner of their colonization. Not until later did the crown intervene to impose a layer of upper-class officials and to assert the royal prerogative. But the *conquistadores* had already determined their own leadership. Their newly won interests predisposed them to look with jaundiced eye upon imposed leadership and royal claims.

In relation to all the hardships involved in the conquest and occupation of America, the magnitude of the undertaking, and the customs of the day, the achievement should be judged not by how badly but by how well the conquerors behaved. Isolated individual acts of cruelty do not establish a national characteristic. In the Europe of that day human life was cheap and barbaric practices not uncommon. The Spaniards and Portuguese, in their dealings with the American aborigines, rejected the policy of total war, so common in our own day. Is it fair to blame the Iberian conquerors of the sixteenth century for not setting a higher standard of imperialism than the British and the Belgians set in the nineteenth century? Their theology may have been too refined for American savages and their religious zeal excessive, but they were usually motivated by the high purpose, which they avowed on many occasions, to ennoble (*enoblecer*) the lands of the New World. They aspired to develop its economic resources, to civilize its barbaric inhabitants, and to save them in Christ's name.

These high aims were often defeated, for often the more civilized the conqueror the more impatient he will be in dealing with barbarism. And the Iberian peoples of the conquest period were among the most civilized, cosmopolitan, and urbane in Europe. They were the heirs of the Roman Empire, convinced believers in the unity of Christendom, and carriers of the Renaissance. Some of the conquerors, coming of humble origin or belonging to the impoverished lesser nobility or having no hope of inheritance because of illegitimate birth, came to the New World primarily for the purpose of finding islands of gold. But in general the passion for gold among Spaniards was not so dominating a motive as it is with our twentieth-century contemporaries in a capitalist world. In the Europe of the conquest period capitalism had not yet become the prevailing economic system.

By 1550 Spaniards and Portuguese had completed their major conquests in the New World and had begun the process of consolidating their empires. Their settlements, starting with Columbus's modest colony in Española, spread over the hemisphere from Florida on the north to Chile and La Plata on the south, sparsely sprinkled over an area more than 6,000 miles from north to south and an equal distance from east to west. Most of their settlements were located on the littoral, but New Spain was centered in the high plateau of central Mexico. They were also exploiting the mines in the high interior plateau or *altiplano* of Upper Peru. In the next century as they sought to extend their settlements farther into the interior and to develop their seaports for an expanded trade with the mother countries they would encounter increased competition from jealous European rivals.

Additional Reading

Baudin, Louis: *A Socialist Empire: the Incas of Peru,* translated by Katherine Woods, D. Van Nostrand Company, Inc., Princeton, New Jersey, 1961.
Bennett, Wendell C.: *Ancient Arts of the Andes,* Museum of Modern Art, New York, 1954.
Calógeras, João Pandiá: *A History of Brazil,* trans. and ed. by Percy Alvin Martin, University of North Carolina Press, Chapel Hill, N.C., 1939, chap. I.

Encina, Francisco A.: *Historia de Chile desde la prehistoria hasta 1891,* Editorial Nascimento, Santiago, 1940–1946.

Flornoy, Bertrand: *The World of the Inca,* Vanguard Press, Inc., New York, 1957.

Galdames, Luis: *A History of Chile,* trans. and ed. by Isaac Joslin Cox, University of North Carolina Press, Chapel Hill, N.C., 1941, chaps. I–III.

Gandía, Enrique de: *Historia de la conquista del Río de la Plata y del Paraguay, 1535–1556,* A. García Santos, Buenos Aires, 1932. A detailed chronicle.

Greenlee, W. B.: "The First Half Century of Brazilian History," *Mid-America,* vol. 25, 1943, pp. 91–120.

Heaton, H. C. (ed.): *The Discovery of the Amazon,* trans. by Bertram T. Lee, The American Geographical Society, New York, 1934.

Henao, Jesús María, and Gerardo Arrubla: *History of Colombia,* trans. and ed. by J. Fred Rippy, University of North Carolina Press, Chapel Hill, N.C., 1938.

Keen, Benjamin: *Readings in Latin American Civilization: 1492 to the Present,* Houghton Mifflin Company, Boston, 1955, chaps. III, VII, VIII.

Lancaster, C. M., and P. T. Manchester: *The Araucaniad,* Vanderbilt University Press, Nashville, Tenn., 1945.

Levene, Ricardo: *A History of Argentina,* trans. and ed. by William Spence Robertson, University of North Carolina Press, Chapel Hill, N.C., 1937, chaps. I–VIII.

Mason, John A.: *The Ancient Civilizations of Peru,* Penguin Books, Inc., Baltimore, 1957.

Murphy, R. C.: "The Earliest Spanish Advances Southward from Panama along the West Coast of South America," *Hispanic American Historical Review,* vol. 21, pp. 3–28, 1941.

Osborne, Harold: *Indians of the Andes: Aymaras and Quechuas,* Harvard University Press, Cambridge, 1952.

Parr, C. M.: *So Noble a Captain: The Life and Times of Ferdinand Magellan,* Thomas Y. Crowell Company, New York, 1953.

Prescott, William H.: *History of the Conquest of Peru,* Heritage Press, New York, [1957]. Required reading.

Rowe, J. H.: "The Incas under Spanish Colonial Institutions," *Hispanic American Historical Review,* vol. 37, pp. [155]–199, 1957.

Steward, Julian H., and Louis C. Faron: *Native Peoples of South America,* McGraw-Hill Book Company, Inc., New York, 1959.

Vernon, I. S. W.: *Pedro de Valdivia, Conquistador of Chile,* University of Texas Press, Austin, Tex., 1946.

von Hagen, Victor W.: *Realm of the Incas,* New American Library, New York, 1957.

Wilson, W. J: "The Spanish Discovery of the South American Mainland," *Geographical Review,* vol. 31, pp. 283–299, 1941.

IV

The Foreign Challenge

Charles I, King of Spain and grandson of Ferdinand and Isabella, became the ruler of two worlds when he was crowned Charles V, Emperor of the Holy Roman Empire, in 1519. The empire which he governed, the most extensive in history, included not only Spain and Spain's overseas territories but also the Low Countries, Austria, the Germanies, Carinthia, Carniola, Tirol, Sicily, Sardinia, Naples, and other territories in Europe. Under Charles the royal standard flew in Brussels and Vienna, in St. Augustine and Valdivia. In this imperial congeries each unit largely retained its own individuality. Aragon and Castile remained autonomous under the emperor and preserved their own political institutions and traditions. Spain's vast imperial extent and the mineral treasures in its overseas domains—as famous as the storied riches of Ophir and the Queen of Sheba—made the empire of Charles V the first world power of the modern age. Pride in her imperial glory under Charles V animated the *conquistadores* in America. In Brazil, Portugal possessed a territory that supplemented her more extensive holdings in Africa and the Far East. The wealth of these American areas, which the Iberian nations staked out for themselves in the fifteenth century, gave them a prosperity which made them the envy of Europe and stimulated international rivalries to wrest their colonies from them. Whenever Spain and Portugal faltered in empire building or tolerated weakness in their far-flung lands, their European competitors moved in to seize control from them.

The Motives of International Rivalry

Rivalry in the New World was strongly affected by the religious struggle in Europe. It became a part of the contest between Catholics and non-Catholics which began with the Reformation in 1517 and continued through the Counter-Reformation and the religious wars of the seventeenth century. In that contest the overseas dominions became the spoils of religious imperialism. The policies that were put into effect in the New World by Spain and Portugal were often devised either to implement the religious beliefs of the most Catholic of royal houses or to counteract Protestant heresies. The history of these policies as written by later historians has often been influenced, even to the point of serious distortion, by the national and religious biases of their writers.

The exploit of Columbus made America a frontier of Europe. As soon as the newly discovered lands in the West were acknowledged to be a "fourth part" of the earth, that is, a continent of America and not a part of Asia, efforts were begun to incorporate them in western civilization. The achievements of the *conquistadores*, dramatic and glamorous as they were in opening up the western continents to European civilization, formed only a short prelude to colonization. The cultural complexes of Spain, France, Portugal, the Netherlands, and eventually England were transferred to the New World. The new lands had to be settled and governed by Europeans and the claims of each nation there had to be defended against the claims of other nations. The conquest of each area was only the introductory aspect of its history. The original discoverers and conquerors, Spain and Portugal, would have to resist pressure from the latecomers. They would have to fight off the challenge of the have-not nations.

The coastal rim and temperate highlands of Middle America and the coastal rim of South America were largely brought under the subjection of Spain and Portugal before any permanent colonies were established by other European nations in the Western Hemisphere. The claims of these pioneers of empire did not go undisputed by France, England, and the Netherlands, each of which left both its political and its cultural stamp upon this area and contributed to the area's heterogeneous nature and distinctive styles of living. The resulting contests for dominion in the New World were incidental accompaniments of the great dynastic and imperial wars in Europe. And yet through all the challenges presented, Spain and Portugal succeeded in maintaining their dominant position in the Western Hemisphere for more than three centuries. The duration of their empires for so long a period was tribute in itself to their success as imperial powers. In history mere survival is often the highest achievement.

The claims of Spain and Portugal were not only territorial but also maritime. The tradition of the closed sea had been established in the Middle Ages when the Hanseatic towns claimed the Baltic Sea as their own and Venice the Adriatic. To the arguments of the great Dutch pioneer in international maritime law, Hugo Grotius, against the closed sea in his tract *Mare liberum*, which was published in 1608 and which was well calculated to serve the national interests of his native Netherlands, Spain and Portugal did not succumb. Instead, Spain, following on her new Mediterranean, the "Ocean Sea," the precedents long maintained on the old Mediterranean, claimed sovereignty over the western Atlantic until 1670 and over the Pacific Ocean until the end of the eighteenth century. The Portuguese also adhered to this doctrine of the *mare clausum,* or closed sea, claiming as their own the Atlantic Ocean south of Morocco and the high seas eastward of the Cape of Good Hope. These claims of Spain and Portugal to closed preserves on the high seas were contested by the new rising maritime nations of France, England, and the Netherlands, who were determined to establish exclusive maritime rights for themselves. The eventual result of their flouting of the Hispanic maritime monopoly was to open the seas to themselves and their commerce on their own terms and as it suited them.

As the Spanish were the first to arrive on the American scene they claimed the rights and advantages of first discoverers. But in South America they were obliged to share these with the Portuguese who, though laggard in discovery and colonization in the Western Hemisphere because of their larger interests in the Far East, nevertheless eventually confirmed by successful colonization the rights granted to them by the Treaty of Tordesillas. The position of hegemony in the world which Spain and Portugal acquired in the sixteenth century aroused the bitter envy of their European neighbors. The power position of the Iberian nations and the counteracting challenge to it underlay much of the international rivalry of the sixteenth and seventeenth centuries —a rivalry which continued almost uninterruptedly "beyond the line" in the Americas despite a long series of dynastic "peace" settlements in Europe. The imperial privileges of Spain and Portugal were disturbing to a Europe whose international policy was dominated by the balance of power.

The power of Spain both in America and in Europe was increased by the union of the Spanish and Portuguese crowns in 1580. The lines of battle were already forming when in that year the Portuguese dynasty, the house of Aviz, died out in the person of Cardinal Henry, who left no direct heir. The shrewd Philip II of Spain saw in the death of the Portuguese king an opportunity to gratify the old ambition of his people to possess the whole peninsula and to strengthen his nation for the onrushing struggle with England. By asserting his own dynastic claims through his Portuguese mother, by making a display of his large army, and by generous bribes he was able to gain control of the Portuguese crown. With the union of the Spanish and Portuguese crowns their overseas interests were merged. But since the relationship thus established was merely a personal union, the king of Spain governed the Portuguese colonies through his Portuguese ministers. At the same time he used Portuguese resources to build up the navy which he would send against England and secured the assistance of Portugal in his war against the Dutch. During the period of sixty years, between 1580 and 1640, when the crowns of Spain and Portugal were thus united, Latin America formed part of a tremendously aggrandized empire. To Spain's possessions in the Western Hemisphere and the Philippine Islands in the Pacific were added the entire African and Asiatic empires of Portugal, including coastal settlements and trading posts from Lisbon to Canton. The Pacific Ocean itself became a Spanish-Portuguese lake.

Encroachments by the French, English, and Dutch

Almost immediately after Columbus's discovery of the western continents the European competitors of the Iberian nations began a long struggle to destroy the new ascendancy of Spain and Portugal which they deemed prejudicial to themselves. Energetic slave traders, smugglers, and emigrants of France, England, and the Netherlands became, in effect, agents of state policy to batter down Spain's commercial monopoly and her territorial empire. These nations would not be deterred in fulfilling their national ambitions by the prior, and, as they regarded them, exorbitant claims of the firstcomers in the New World. Lying like Spain and Portugal on the western rim of Europe, they possessed the same advantageous location for colonial enterprise in America as their Hispanic rivals. Like them also they had a numerous corps of expert seamen, national unity, and the adventurous spirit of the Renaissance. Neither France, which was torn by religious schism, nor anti-Catholic England, nor Protestant Netherlands would feel any strong religious inhibitions against tangling with the Catholic sovereigns.

As the sixteenth century advanced, the challenge of the French, English, and Dutch to the Hispanic colonies became stronger and more threatening, but it was slow to take the form of successful colonial settlement. These nations found that the wealth resources of the Americas had already been appropriated by the firstcomers. Moreover, they lacked the colonial experience which the Spanish and Portuguese had acquired in occupying, first, the Moorish-held lands in their own home peninsula and, later, their lands in America. Successful colonization in America would not become possible to them until they should first either exorcise the Hispanic threat or at least reach a practicable delimitation of territory there. All the English ventures into the Hispanic hemisphere in the sixteenth century established only a lawyer's claim and no permanent settlement there. The French engaged in fishing and exploring expeditions in Newfoundland and the St. Lawrence Valley and thrust themselves into lands in the south claimed by Spain and Portugal. When they challenged the Hispanic peoples in Florida and Brazil, they were soon driven out. The Dutch, preoccupied as were the Portuguese with trading operations and the establishment of colonies in the Far East, did not seriously invade the American hemisphere until near the end of the sixteenth century.

France, whose population was double that of Spain and whose Brittany sailors were probably as experienced as any in Europe, was the first nation to dispute the claims of Spain and Portugal to the New World. French vessels began to arrive on the Grand Banks of Newfoundland as early as 1500. French pirates seized a large part of the jewels and gold which Cortés dispatched to the king after his final conquest of Mexico. French raiders harassed the Portuguese traders in brazilwood along the coast of Brazil and in 1530 destroyed a Portuguese colony which had been established at Pernambuco some ten years earlier. More energetic than Henry VIII as a challenger of the dominant colonial powers were Francis I and his Valois successors who, partly because of the defiance which they hurled against the Hapsburgs in Italy, found it expedient, if not indeed necessary, to challenge the Hapsburg claims also in America. Francis I referred contemptuously to the claims of Spain and Portugal to world empires under the papal grants and declared that he "had never seen a clause in the last will of Adam conceding such exclusive control to Kings Manoel and Charles."

England under the Tudors lagged behind Spain, Portugal, and even France in colonial expansion. She made no successful colonizing effort in the Americas until after the death of the last Tudor, Elizabeth I, but limited herself rather to a negative policy of harassing the imperial powers. A few English explorers, starting with John Cabot in 1497 and continuing through Martin Frobisher, Sir Francis Drake, Sir Humphrey Gilbert, Sir Walter Raleigh, and Thomas Cavendish, in the 1570s and 1580s, carried the British flag into the hemisphere of Columbus. The redoubtable William Hawkins made a landing on the coast of Brazil around 1530, took back a "King of Brazil," and presented him to King Henry VIII. Somewhat later an English fort was apparently built along that coast, probably at Bahía. William Hawkins's son John invaded the closed reserve of the Spanish Indies in 1563 and began to trade with the colonists of Española, avid for English goods and Negro slaves. Wherever he found compliant officials he paid the royal license and customs dues required of Spanish traders, but when he encountered perverse officials he either forced trade at the cannon mouth or plundered and burned their towns. Five years later he came to grief at Veracruz in an encounter with a Spanish fleet bringing the new viceroy of Mexico, Martín Enríquez de Almanza.

Of the English freebooters the most famous, Francis Drake, a cousin of John Hawkins, was knighted by Queen Elizabeth herself on board his flagship, the *Golden Hind*. On his piratical voyages the fastidious "Francisco Drak," as the Spaniards called him, carried all possible dainties and perfumed waters, many of them presents from the queen, and dined to the music of viols. He had the calculated audacity to take with him artists who painted for him pictures of the Spanish coasts along which he sailed, thus marking out spots for future depredations. To the English backers of one of his plundering voyages Drake distributed dividends of 4,700 per cent! The exploits of Drake and his fellow freebooters who went out to "singe the King of Spain's beard" finally culminated in the outbreak of war between England and Spain which had been smoldering since the death of England's Queen Mary in 1558. England's defeat of Spain's mighty Armada in 1588 caused the first crack in the Spanish imperial system.

With the conquest of Mexico by Cortés, the Caribbean, which had been the earliest region of Spanish discovery, colonization, and commercial monopoly in America, yielded its primacy to Spain's continental possessions in America. It became a "focus of envy" of several European nations. As Spain's interest and strength in the islands dwindled, interlopers and buccaneers from these nations moved in to contest Spain's control. When their freebooting and filibustering exploits were encouraged by their sovereigns they became the instruments of high policy. The reduction of Spain's territorial monopoly in the Caribbean began in 1623 when the British started a settlement on St. Christopher's (St. Kitts), an island in the Leeward group, and followed it two years later with an occupation of Barbados. So commenced the process of whittling away chunks of Spain's American empire which ended finally with Spain's loss of Cuba and Puerto Rico in 1898. English animosity against Spain was stimulated by the publication in 1648 of *The English-American his Travail by Sea and Land: or, a New Survey of the West-India's* by Thomas Gage, who had resided and traveled for twelve years in Central America as a Spanish Dominican friar and who, after he returned to England and turned Protestant, assisted in the formulation of Cromwell's "Western Design" against Spain's lands in America. Cromwell's armies conquered Jamaica in 1655, and soon afterward Cromwell's successor, Charles II, appointed as lieutenant governor of the island the pirate scourge of the Spanish Main, the cruel, lascivious, hard-drinking Sir Henry Morgan.

Meanwhile, the French were picking up random islands in the Windward and Leeward groups, including Guadeloupe and Martinique, and were gaining a foothold on the large island of Española, which had been the cradle of Spanish colonization in the New World. France's claims there were established by a colony of enterprising retired pirates, *boucaniers* or buccaneers, who settled down on the little island of Tortuga off the northwest coast of Española. They rustled cattle from the Spanish, hunted wild oxen and boars, roasted the meat on spits or *boucans,* and then sold it to English and Dutch freebooters. These undisciplined renegades had sought refuge there to avoid punishment for the crimes they had committed. As described by a French priest who observed them,

They were without any habitation or fixed abode, but only rendezvoused where the cattle were to be found, and some sheds covered with leaves to keep off the rain and to store the hides of the beasts they had killed until some vessels should pass to barter for them with wine, brandy, lime, arms, powder, bullets and cooking vessels which they needed and which are the only movables of the buccaneers.... They were dressed in a pair of drawers and a shirt at the most, shod with the skin of a hog's leg fastened on the top and behind the foot with strips of the same skin, girded around the middle of their body with a sack which served them to sleep in as a defence against the innumerable insects which bit and sucked the blood from all parts of their bodies that were left uncovered.... When they returned from the chase to the *boucan,* you would say that these are the butcher's vilest servants who have been eight days in the slaughter-house without washing themselves.[1]

The claims unwittingly laid by these brutalized wretches were recognized in 1697 when by the Treaty of Ryswick Haiti was acknowledged to be a possession of France.

In the general disintegration of Spain's control in the Caribbean, the

[1] Abbe du Tertre, quoted in Arthur Percival Newton, *The European Nations in the West Indies, 1493–1688,* A. and C. Black, Ltd., London, 1933, p. 170, used by permission.

Dutch acquired a few small islands in the Antilles—Curaçao, Bonaire, Aruba, St. Eustatius, Saba, and St. Martin—which were confirmed to them in the Treaty of Westphalia in 1648, and they began a colonizing effort in Guiana. Even the Danes planted a colony on the almost uninhabited island of St. Thomas, one of the so-called "Virgin Islands," and shrewdly made it a free port and hence a center of illicit trade with the Spanish colonies. At the same time they occupied the neighboring island of St. John, and in 1733 they bought from the French West India Company the island of Santa Cruz, thus completing their claims to the Virgin group. On the Caribbean islands, therefore, English, French, Dutch, and Danish populations of non-descript character squatted in uneasy juxtaposition, jockeying with one another for island territory, uniting for defense against Spain's spasmodic attempts to conquer them, and serving as pawns of empire in the dynastic squabbles of their sovereigns. In the Treaties of Breda in 1667 between Great Britain, the Netherlands, and France and in the Treaty of Madrid of 1670 between Great Britain and Spain a definitive settlement of colonial possessions in the Caribbean was arrived at and a pattern of island ownership established which in general has continued to the present.

French and Dutch in Brazil

Many years before the union of the Portuguese and Spanish crowns, Portuguese activities in Brazil were defied by the French. In 1555, two years after Thomé de Sousa had resigned as governor general because he was tired of the New World, the French established a settlement on the beautiful bay which the Portuguese had already named Rio de Janeiro and which the French now ambitiously renamed France Antarctique. This project of colonization headed by a vice admiral of Brittany, Nicolas Durand de Villegaignon, was sponsored by French Adm. Gaspar de Coligny as a refuge for his Huguenot coreligionists. But the colony of Villegaignon, himself a Catholic who abjured Catholicism while he was governor of the colony at Rio de Janeiro, became so torn by religious factionalism that it fell an easy prey to a Portuguese flotilla which destroyed the French fort on Villegaignon's island in the harbor in 1560. When this flotilla retired to Bahía the French reoccupied the island at Rio de Janeiro and began to stir up the Indians against the Portuguese all the way from São Paulo in the south to Espirito Santo in the north. They had considerable success among these warlike, primitive Indians, members of the Tupi culture group, who represented almost the lowest stage in cultural development among the American aborigines and who moved about completely naked through the coastal areas and highlands of central Brazil, living by hunting and fishing. Here, as later in North America, the French found it convenient and natural to ally themselves with the native inhabitants against their fellow Europeans.

The new Portuguese governor of Brazil, Mem de Sá, having failed to drive the French out, formed an alliance with Indian tribes hostile to the French and sent a second expedition to Rio de Janeiro in 1565. This expedition established a rival fort behind the famous Sugar Loaf or Pão de Assucar and from that strategic location engaged the French, established on Villegaignon's island in the harbor, in intermittent fighting for a year and a half. It finally compelled them to abandon the island and return to France. The victorious Portuguese then moved their settlement around the Sugar Loaf to a promontory of land opposite the island which they named São Sebastião, the beginning of settlement on the actual site of Rio de Janeiro. They continued to have trouble with the Indians, however, who were stirred up by the French and harassed their settlements. As the Portuguese resisted them and drove them farther and farther inland they acquired a new knowledge of the interior of the country of which their settlements occupied the mere coastal fringe. By the end of the sixteenth century they had colonized and established their claim to the coast of Brazil from the eastern tip of the continent at Natal, which they settled in 1597, to below São Paulo on the south. Over this long coast the Portuguese governor general presided protectively with the support of his strong military and naval forces at Bahía, the capital of colonial Brazil. But their hold on this long stretch of coast was precarious.

Along the coast of Brazil to the north of the bulge the Portuguese encountered a new threat from the indefatigable French. There a group of both Protestant and Catholic traders from western France established a trading post at Maranhão in 1594, which they operated without molestation for some twenty years. Their colonial project was much encouraged by the French King Henry IV, whose assassination at the hands of the crazed Ravaillac in 1610 was a heavy blow to the colony. Two years later another French expedition, under the French Huguenot nobleman Daniel de la Ravardière, founded a larger settlement on the island of Maranhão. Against these French interlopers, heedless of the line of Tordesillas, the Portuguese, under the leadership of the greatest of Brazilian colonial generals, Jerônimo de Albuquerque, organized an expedition. Employing the very tactics which Mem de Sá had earlier used successfully to dislodge the French from Rio de Janeiro, the Portuguese built a fort on the mainland and used it as a base of operations against the French. After driving out the French they remained in possession of St. Louis, which they rechristened São Luis. Some members of the Portuguese expedition then proceeded farther north along the coast, founded a settlement called Santa María de Belém, the modern Pará, in 1616, and drove out other interlopers.

But the Portuguese had reached the northern limit of their expansive power and were not interested in going beyond the line of Tordesillas in the north. When the French returned in 1624 to begin the settlement of French Guiana, west of the Tordesillas line and beyond a protective range of mountains, the Portuguese left them alone. To protect their northern frontier, however, the Portuguese had already created along this coast the state of Maranhão, extending from the bulge northward to the Amazon River. It was made independent of the governor general in Bahía and directly responsible to the government in Lisbon and continued in this virtually autonomous position until 1774.

The defeat of Spain's Armada in 1588 exposed the Portuguese possessions to attack by the English and the Dutch. In the previous year Bahía was raided by an English corsair, and three years later São Vicente was captured by another of the Elizabethan "sea dogs," Thomas Cavendish, who then proceeded by way of Cape Horn to make the third circumnavigation of the earth. In 1595 Pernambuco was captured and sacked by another English sea captain, James Lancaster. To the Portuguese these raids were annoying and destructive, but they resulted in no permanent loss of territory to England in America. Much more formidable were the incursions of England's ally the Netherlands, which as it waged its valiant war of independence against Philip II, joint ruler of Spain and Portugal, was determined to undermine his empire in America and to establish Dutch colonies there. In this effort the Dutch followed the example and received the support of England.

The Netherlands became a part of the empire of Charles V in the early sixteenth century, and Dutch ships became the principal maritime carriers for Spain and the Indies. But when the Dutch rose in revolt against Spain in 1568 they proceeded to prey upon Spanish shipping on all the seas and on Portuguese commerce after the union of the Spanish and Portuguese crowns. Consequently they were denied by Philip II further access to Portuguese ports in 1595 and accordingly decided to go themselves to the sources of Portuguese wealth in the Spice Islands of the Orient and America. By the operations of the Dutch East India Company, organized in 1602, they almost completely excluded the Portuguese from the trade of Sumatra, Java, and the Moluccas during the seventeenth century and laid the basis for the Dutch commercial empire in the East Indies.

Expanding their world-wide commerce, the Dutch sent vessels up the Amazon and Orinoco Rivers in search of sugar, tobacco, and dyewood. More than a hundred of their vessels annually loaded salt in Venezuela, and others made a series of raids on the coastal towns of Chile, Peru, and Brazil, starting in 1598. These raids continued even after the Netherlands concluded a political truce with Spain in 1609, for this truce was not made applicable to South America. In Brazil, Dutch adventurers established two plantations on the Xingú River, a south tributary of the Amazon, and cooperated with the English in setting up a trading post nearby and another on the northern bank of the Amazon. By 1625 some ten or twelve Anglo-Dutch settlements had been made in this area and an Amazon Company had been organized to exploit its resources. These trading nations, realizing that Brazil's mother country had been itself reduced to a virtual colony of Spain and that Brazil was poorly defended, were well on the way to establishing a permanent colony in Brazil.

It was their activities in the Amazon region that led the Portuguese to found Belém.

After the truce between the Netherlands and Spain was ended and hostilities were resumed, the Dutch continued on their expansive course in America. In 1621 the Dutch West India Company was organized and was given exclusive privileges to trade and found colonies in America. It was also entrusted with the waging of war against Spain and Portugal in that part of the world. As an agent of the Netherlands government it became a gigantic privateering company with colonization as a secondary activity. One of the expeditions of this company was sent to the west coast of South America, where it blockaded Callao, the port of Lima, for five months. The expedition then proceeded to Guayaquil, the port of modern Ecuador, which it captured and plundered. These Dutch raids continued until Dutch independence was recognized by Spain in the Treaty of Westphalia ending the Thirty Years' War in 1648. While the Dutch were thus throwing the Spaniards on the defensive in both the Old World and the New, the English succeeded, under safeguards thus provided by the Dutch, in establishing their first colonies on the mainland of North America.

Meanwhile, the Dutch West India Company was founding colonies on the coast of Brazil, as well as in New Netherland at the mouth of the Hudson River in North America. The Dutch captured Bahía in 1624 and held it for almost a year until they were driven out by a combined Spanish and Portuguese fleet. Four years later a Dutch admiral, Piet Heyn, seized the entire Spanish treasure fleet—an event which was unique in the annals of the fleet— and the Dutch were emboldened to embark upon their grand Brazilian venture. They seized Olinda, the capital of the colony of Pernambuco and the principal commercial city of northern Brazil, together with its port Recife in 1631. With Olinda as their capital, the Dutch extended their control both to the north and to the south, and here along a coast some 1,200 miles long they maintained a strong, efficiently organized colony for nearly twenty-five years. They were never able to capture Bahía and had to accept it as their southern limit, but they extended their colony northward as far as Maranhão.

The patron of Dutch Brazil, the Dutch West India Company, was more interested in profits than in colonization, and it badgered the young Johan Maurits, Count of Nassau Siegen, a grandson of the martyred hero of Dutch independence, William the Silent, into becoming governor general of Dutch Brazil in 1636. Maurits or Maurice, to give his name its English spelling, sought to conciliate his Portuguese neighbors in every way, appointing Portuguese to his grand council and opening up his ports to free trade with the ports of Portuguese Brazil. He employed several artists, including the talented Frans Post, to paint pictures of the native inhabitants, the animals, fruits, towns, and forts. Under his governorship Brazil was widely advertised in Europe as a source of sugar; the commerce of the colony prospered; the colonial government was perhaps never better administered; the town of

Pernambuco, called Mauritsstad, was founded; a natural history museum was established; and the first scientific natural history of Brazil was written. But Maurice failed to satisfy the company, which was leading the mercantile oligarchy in the Netherlands in resistance to the nationalist policies of the reigning house of Nassau-Orange. He also antagonized the Calvinists in the Netherlands who disapproved of his toleration of Catholics. His leadership of a Protestant colony in Catholic Brazil was in turn resented by the Brazilian *crioulos* and the members of the religious orders. In discouragement, therefore, the efficient governor resigned in 1644. Almost immediately Dutch fortunes in Brazil began to decline.

Meanwhile, the union of the Portuguese and Spanish crowns came to an end with the accession of the Duke of Braganza to the Portuguese throne as King John IV. The Portuguese, now freed from their alliance with Spain, immediately concluded an alliance with the Netherlands, recognizing the Dutch colony in Brazil. But this cavalier treatment of Brazil as a mere pawn in the politics of the mother country aroused the nascent nationalist sentiment of the Brazilians. They rose up against the Dutch, threw them out of Maranhão, and then confined them to their capital, Olinda-Pernambuco. Finally in 1654 they compelled the Dutch to surrender and to sign in the following year a capitulation evacuating all places which they held in Brazil. By the end of the century all that remained of the Dutch Empire in America were the Caribbean islands of Curaçao, Aruba, Bonaire, St. Eustatius, St. Martin, and Saba, and Surinam or Dutch Guiana, which the Netherlands took in exchange for New Amsterdam or New York in 1657.

This uprising of the Brazilians against the Dutch is interpreted in Brazilian history as an early manifestation of nationalist feeling. For it the Brazilians themselves were responsible. It was indicative also of the racial cooperation upon which the Brazilians pride themselves, for the leaders in this uprising were a white planter, João Fernandes Vieira, an Indian, Felipe Camarão, and a Negro, Henrique Días. By treaty in 1661 Portugal obtained from the Dutch a renunciation of all their territorial claims in Brazil but agreed in return to recompense the Dutch in the amount of some 4 million crowns to be paid by Brazil and to continue the commercial privileges which the Dutch enjoyed in Brazil. Thereafter the Portuguese found it difficult to enforce their policy of commercial exclusivism. They were obliged to permit their colonists in Brazil to trade not only with the Dutch but also with the English and to continue their trade with the Spanish.

Spanish-Portuguese Rivalries

In occupying the Philippine Islands in the 1570s, Spain disregarded the Treaty of Tordesillas which had placed those islands within the Portuguese hemisphere. During the period of Portuguese-Spanish union from 1580 to 1640 the line of Tordesillas ceased to have any meaning and was disregarded.

Brazilians accordingly began to expand into areas beyond the line. In 1639 the governor of Pará sent out an expedition under Pedro Teixeira, the first since the expeditions of Orellana and Ursúa a century before, to explore the upper tributaries of the Amazon River. This expedition, after eight months of travel, finally reached a Spanish settlement in what is now eastern Ecuador. When Portugal regained its independence from Spain in the following year it thus remained in control of the most practicable route into the Amazon Basin. Its claim to this route, all of which lay west of the line of Tordesillas, was never effectively contraverted by Spain.

The Dutch occupation of the Brazilian littoral during the quarter of a century from 1630 to 1654 inspired the Brazilians to make efforts at expansion in other directions, which eventually, after the separation of the Portuguese and Spanish crowns, brought them into conflict with Spain. Among the new frontiersmen the so-called *bandeirantes* of São Paulo, bearers of flags or banners, explored and settled the Brazilian hinterland, establishing cattle ranches in the valley of the São Francisco River, grazing their cattle over the interior provinces as far north as Maranhão and Pará, and building settlements southward into Paraná, Santa Catarina, and Rio Grande do Sul. Generally *mamelucos* or mixtures of white and Indian, they carried on by land in the second century of colonization in America the adventurous exploits of the Portuguese maritime discoverers of the previous century. They were actuated by the same commercial urges, the same spirit of enterprise, the same mania to be always on the move, the same challenges of enormous distances to be traversed, dangers to be overcome, and legends to be vindicated. Bearers of the Portuguese standard, many of them carried with them copies of Camões's epic, *Os Lusíadas*.

Into the *llanos* and savannahs of the central part of the South American continent went these *bandeirantes*, capturing Indians and escaped Negro slaves, and opening up the mining regions of Minas Gerais. From the Indian villages in the interior which they conquered they brought back to the sugar plantations of the coast large numbers of slaves—according to the probably exaggerated reports of the Jesuits, 300,000 between the years 1614 and 1639. On this Brazilian frontier, life was raw and violent and social inequalities based upon wealth and status ceased to exist. In the grazing lands of the south these *gaúcho* cattlemen and horsemen found herds of wild cattle, descended from animals left by the first Spanish settlers. They herded these and also developed a trade in mules with the mining country to the north. Traveling often as communities with their families they traversed the hill and plains country which is now southern Brazil, Paraguay, even eastern Argentina and Uruguay, settling in one spot for a season, raising their crops, and then moving on. Unwittingly they thus expanded the boundary claims of Brazil. Wherever they came in contact with Spaniards they either traded with them or fought with them.

The severance of the Portuguese-Spanish union brought a resumption of the territorial rivalries between the two nations in the south and southwest. Both countries claimed the coast between São Vicente and the La Plata estuary, the Spanish arguing rightly that the Tordesillas line crossed the coast line near São Vicente and the Portuguese claiming that it extended as far west as the head of the La Plata estuary where Buenos Aires was located. Directly opposite Buenos Aires the Portuguese built a fort and a settlement in 1680 which they called Nova Colônia do Sacramento and which was immediately captured by the Spanish governor and then restored to the Brazilians on orders from the Spanish crown. Claims and counterclaims, settlements and countersettlements followed in this disputed area. After the Spanish founded Montevideo in 1726 the aggressive *Paulistas* tried unsuccessfully to seize it. Failing in this exploit they fell back to the lagoon area along the coast, where they founded the town of Rio Grande do Sul. This and Nova Colônia remained the southernmost outposts of the Portuguese empire in Brazil.

As title to this intervening area continued to be disputed, Portugal and Spain attempted to settle their claims by a treaty concluded at Madrid in 1750. In it they undertook to pursue a policy of "perpetual peace and good neighborliness" not only in South America, among their respective subjects, but also on the high seas. But if they should become engaged in hostilities in Europe their subjects in South America should "go on living in peace with one another as if there were no war between their Sovereigns, and without engaging in the slightest hostilities, either alone or in conjunction with their allies." In the territorial clauses of the treaty, Portugal agreed to give Nova Colônia to Spain, Spain agreed to give to Portugal the seven Jesuit missions in the interior with their thousands of Indians, and they agreed upon a boundary line between the Spanish settlements in Uruguay and the Portuguese settlements in Rio Grande do Sul in accordance generally with the rule of *uti possidetis* which allowed each territorial claimant to keep what it already in fact possessed. Thus diplomacy sought to legitimize the conquests of the *bandeirantes*. But the Indians in the seven missions resisted transfer to Brazil, allegedly under the leadership of the Jesuit fathers, and Portugal consequently postponed the surrender of Colônia. The treaty therefore was allowed to lapse and was annulled in 1761.

During the Seven Years' War (1756–1763) when Spain and Portugal found themselves in opposite camps, the Spanish established a settlement in the territory of Rio Grande do Sul and were later driven out by the Portuguese. In reprisal the first viceroy of La Plata, Pedro de Ceballos, gathered together a large army and a fleet of vessels and seized both Colônia and the island of Santa Catarina adjoining Rio Grande do Sul on the north. He was preparing also to recapture this latter province when news arrived that the Spanish crown, which was preparing to enter the Anglo-French war for the independence of the United States and felt it necessary to reestablish friendly relations with Portugal, had agreed to a new treaty in 1777—the Treaty of San Ildefonso—in which the Spanish relinquished their claims to Rio Grande do Sul and the conquered island of Santa Catarina. The Spanish retained the seven Jesuit missions east of the Uruguay River and finally received Colônia from the Portuguese. Thus early these border areas north of the La Plata estuary acquired the character of a buffer zone which they have ever since possessed.

The Hispanic Triumph

Despite repeated assaults the Spaniards and Portuguese kept their empires in America virtually intact for over three hundred years. During the century after Columbus they established themselves in almost impregnable positions. They adopted and put into effect the measures necessary to defend their large stakes there. They could not allow the rich kingdoms of New Spain and Peru or the prosperous sugar colony of Brazil to be snatched from them. Their defense was successful. None of their rivals acquired or kept for long any but fringe areas. The centers of Spanish and Portuguese power in America were never successfully assaulted. The Spanish system of commercial exclusivism was frequently violated. Foreign pirates carried on forced trade with ports in the Caribbean and elsewhere in defiance of the Laws of the Indies. But these seldom resulted in the alienation of Spanish territory. In the more than a century and a half of voyages by the Spanish treasure fleet only one annual fleet was captured in its entirety—in 1627 by the Dutch admiral, Piet Heyn. This almost perfect record of defense of the treasure fleet seems all the more remarkable when one considers the many enemies who lay in wait to pounce upon it.

The English, often lauded as successful empire builders in America, were more often defeated than victorious in their encounters with the Spaniards. When Drake captured Cartagena he took an unfortified port. At the close of the colonial epoch England possessed in America, in general, only such areas as had come to her by default of Spain, not by her own strength of arms. The later myth of an invincible England was not borne out in her relations with the Spanish Empire. Even England's victory over the Spanish Armada did not give her any considerable imperial advantage in America. Fifty years later the Spanish fleet was larger than ever before and still controlled American waters. The Elizabethan sea dogs never succeeded in capturing the Spanish treasure fleet. England's star of empire did not begin to rise until after she began to win victories over the Dutch in the middle of the seventeenth century. But the English still presented no serious challenge to the Spanish position in America.

The ultimate ineffectiveness of the foreign challenge to the Spanish and Portuguese Empires in America can be judged by the results. At the end of the eighteenth century Portugal's position in Brazil was secure; the threats from the French, the Dutch, and the English had been long since exorcised. Spanish America attained its greatest extent as late as 1790 when Spain laid claim to Nootka Sound north of California. Though defeated in this claim her empire nevertheless extended at that time from California and the northern limits of the Louisiana territory south to Cape Horn. In comparison with this vast extent of territory, British America to the north and the young United States seemed insignificant. Spain, supported by her overseas empire, was still territorially one of the great powers of the world.

Additional Reading

Aydelotte, Frank: "Elizabethan Seamen in Mexico and Ports of the Spanish Main," *American Historical Review*, vol. 48, pp. 1–19, 1942.

Boxer, Charles R.: *The Dutch in Brazil, 1624–1654*, Oxford University Press, New York, 1957.

———: *Salvador de Sá and the Struggle for Brazil and Angola, 1602–1686*, University of London, London, 1952.

Crouse, N. M.: *The French Struggle for the West Indies, 1665–1713*, Columbia University Press, New York, 1943.

Keen, Benjamin: *Readings in Latin American Civilization: 1492 to the Present*, Houghton Mifflin Company, Boston, 1955, chaps. XI, XVIII.

Levene, Ricardo: *A History of Argentina*, trans. and ed. by William Spence Robertson, University of North Carolina Press, Chapel Hill, N.C., 1937, chap. X.

Newton, Arthur Percival: *The European Nations in the West Indies, 1493–1688*, A. &. C. Black, Ltd., London, 1933. An excellent, detailed account of two centuries of international rivalry in the Caribbean.

Nowell, Charles E.: "The French in Sixteenth-Century Brazil," *Americas*, vol. 5, pp. 381–393, April, 1949.

Parry, John Horace, and P. M. Sherlock: *A Short History of the West Indies*, The Macmillan Company, London and New York, 1956.

Sluiter, Engel: "Dutch Maritime Power and the Colonial Status Quo, 1585–1641," *Pacific Historical Review*, vol. II, pp. [29]–41, March, 1942.

———: "Dutch-Spanish Rivalry in the Caribbean Area, 1594–1609," *Hispanic American Historical Review*, vol. 28, pp. [165]–196, 1948.

Williamson, James A.: *Hawkins of Plymouth*, A. & C. Black, Ltd., London, 1949.

———: *English Colonies in Guiana and on the Amazon*, Oxford University Press, New York, 1923.

Wright, Irene A. (ed.): *Spanish Documents Concerning English Voyages to the Caribbean, 1527–1568*, Hakluyt Society, London, 1929.

V

The Structure
of Imperial Government

Upon Spain, among all the nations of Europe, fell the initial responsibility for undertaking the task of assimilating distant lands nationally, linguistically, and religiously. As the first to assume the "white man's burden" she pioneered in devising an imperial system and in drawing the blueprints for the expansion of Europe. In both conquest and imperial administration the outstanding characters of the sixteenth and seventeenth centuries were Spaniards.

The Spanish Theory of Empire

The Spanish theory of empire, as applied in America, rested upon the following principles: (1) that the right of eminent domain over all the newly discovered lands belonged to the crown of Castile, (2) that private ownership of the land by both Spaniards and Indians could be enjoyed only by royal grant and royal favor, and (3) that all the white and Indian residents of the New World must be dealt with as subjects of the crown. The crown insisted that the claims of the Indians to the lands which they possessed and cultivated should be respected, and it thus sought to protect them from the rapacity of some of the *conquistadores*.

In opening up the new lands in America, Spain did not use the technique of the trading and colonizing company, which was later developed by England and the Netherlands. Her one experience with such a company—the Welsers in Venezuela—was thoroughly unsatisfactory. Most of the early Spanish expeditions to America, though encouraged or at least approved by the crown, were private ventures, financed and carried through by the adventurers themselves. Spain and Portugal did not plant colonies in the New World; they merely undertook to regulate and govern those established by Spanish and Portuguese conquerors. The discoverers and colonizers received from their sovereigns little but paper authorizations and high-sounding titles. They were recompensed for their expenses and hardships by the prospect of finding riches in the lands which they expected to discover and by the enlarged opportunities likely to open up to them in the New World. Many of the *conquistadores* gained their only reward in *repartimientos* and *encomiendas* of Indians.

99

But in a broad sense, the discovery, exploration, and colonization of America by Spanish adventurers was a national enterprise. These adventurers carried out their exploits as agents of the crown and for the glorification of the sovereigns whom they served. Even the Italian-born Columbus was only a barely acceptable interloper. Quite naturally Spain's imperial policy was nationalist and exclusivist. The crown early adopted a plan of selective emigration to its overseas domains, partly to prevent the depopulation of Spain and partly to maintain the racial and national homogeneity, the *limpieza de sangre* (purity of blood) of the new lands. For this reason, as early as 1501 Isabella denied passage to America to Moors, Jews, and all non-Catholics and soon afterward excluded all who had been condemned by the courts of the Inquisition. The crown also closed the American lands by law to all foreigners. It was the crown's intention that they should be settled only by loyal Christian Spaniards who would extend Hispanic culture, spread the religion of their homeland, and in general, enhance the prestige of the mother country. The colonization of America was inspired not only by commercial and religious motives but also by a type of imperialist fervor, which reflected both the new nationhood Spain had recently achieved and the Renaissance emphasis upon cultural nationalism. By 1574, or only a little over three-quarters of a century after Columbus's discovery of the New World, it was peopled by an estimated 160,000 Spaniards, distributed in 200 cities which they had founded and controlling uncounted millions of Indians.

From the beginning, Isabella, the first European ruler of America, held explicitly that only her Castilian subjects would be legally permitted to go to the Indies. But this restriction was later modified to allow Spaniards from other parts of the Hispanic peninsula the privilege of helping to conquer and exploit the new lands in America. Indeed many of the sixteenth-century *conquistadores* came from parts of Spain other than Castile and were assisted in their conquests by non-Spaniards. As early as 1540 the expedition of Francisco Vázquez de Coronado north of New Galicia certainly included five Portuguese, two Italians, a Frenchman, a Scot, and a German, and perhaps other foreigners. Although the theory of a Castilian monopoly of the Americas was thus early breached, the theory of legal ownership by Castile did mean that the institutions created by Ferdinand and Isabella for the government of Castile and found workable there would be transferred to their American domains. Philip II later officially ruled that in the absence of pertinent legislation for the colonies Castilian precedents would be followed.

"Through donation of the Holy Apostolic See and other just and legitimate titles," declared the crown in the Code of the Indies, "we are Lord of the West Indies, the Islands, and mainlands of the Ocean Sea already discovered or to be discovered, and they are incorporated in our Royal Crown of Castile." [1]

---

[1] Law I, Title I, Book III, of the *Recopilación de Leyes de los Reynos de las Indias* (3 vols.), Consejo de la Hispanidad, Madrid, 1943, vol. I, p. 523.

All parts of Spain's overseas empire in the New World therefore belonged to the crown of Castile. They were crown colonies in the fullest sense of the phrase and could not be alienated from the crown "totally or in part, under any condition, or in favor of any person." And yet, strictly speaking, they were not colonies at all but rather kingdoms, each separately subject to the king, as was Castile itself. They were integral parts of the Spanish monarchy. Theoretically the Spanish Empire was a federation of kingdoms (*reinos*), held, as were the Spanish dominions in Europe, as fiefs of the crown. Each component part in America was governed by a king—and all of them by the same king enthroned in Madrid. The crown to which they belonged as personal property governed a federalized empire, that is, a bevy of kingdoms for whose government he was equally responsible. Theoretically every kingdom in the New World was the equal of every kingdom under the crown of Castile in the Old World. The incorporation of the Indies in the crown of Castile implied also a juridical equality between the residents of the overseas domains and those of Spain itself. This concept of empire was gradually abandoned or at least was not vigorously asserted by the Bourbon rulers who succeeded the Hapsburgs on the Spanish throne in 1700, but it was later revived by the Americans to justify their claims to independence when the legitimate Spanish monarchy disappeared.

In the Spain of the sixteenth century the medieval theory of the divine right of kings had been tempered by the injunctions of churchmen and the free advice of the people. Public expression of views was remarkably free in the Spain that was approaching its Golden Age of literature and art. Even subversive socialist doctrines were unrestrainedly disseminated, and churchmen did not hesitate to warn the sovereigns to follow right policies toward their subjects. The monarchy was constantly affected by pressures for popular self-government. Although the powers of the sovereign were being aggrandized and the monarchy was becoming a more highly centralized institution, the theory of royal absolutism under God had been modified by the customary practice of local autonomy and by the more modern notion that kings are only the servants of the people. Absolutist theory was circumscribed by man-made laws and customs. These limitations upon divine-right monarchy imposed restraints upon the arbitrary exercise of royal authority not only in Spain itself but also in Spain's overseas empire.

As a matter of policy the Spanish crown did not entrust the government of its new lands to their discoverers or conquerors. After the period of conquest ended, as generally happened around 1550, the Spanish makers of imperial policy quickly replaced the original adventurers with administrators, lawyers, and judges—*letrados* who were familiar with Castilian institutions and who introduced the bureaucratic system of the homeland into the New World. They did not deem it either necessary or desirable to maintain control over the empire by military force. Their system lasted as long as it did because the crown recognized limitations upon imperial authority and permitted considerable flexibility in operation. Even corruption and subornation were tolerated as an alternative to a rigid enforcement of the Laws of the Indies because they contributed to the harmonious working of the imperial machinery. The crown realistically concluded that the arm of the state was simply not long enough to do everything that the crown wanted done. In particular the imperial authorities had to acknowledge that their system was often tenuous and inapplicable in the peripheral parts of the empire.

This was so, partly because of the vast distances separating the mother country from its colonies in the Indies. The vessels that they sent across the Ocean Sea, though they were perhaps the largest of the time, were subject to attack by both men and storms. When royal officials in the Americas asked the court for instructions they expected to receive them within four to six months, but they might wait a year or a year and a half for them. Meanwhile they had to use their own discretion. The king's viceroy was not at the end of a telephone wire; he was at the end of a long, slow, and cumbersome line of communication.

The history of Spain's imperial administration cannot be written from a mere study of the laws promulgated by the Council of the Indies, for wide disparities existed between the letter of the laws and their actual application. The Laws of the Indies themselves and outstanding Spanish jurists, such as Bobadilla and Solórzano, held that laws which were contrary to good practice, although issued by the king, should be respected by governors but not executed. The habit of "obeying" but not complying with the laws was expressed in the formula *obedezco pero no cumplo* (I obey but I do not comply). This formula was not a means of defying authority but rather "an institutional device for decentralizing decision making." [2] It was an intentional loophole provided by the imperial authorities in the interest of flexibility for the purpose of allowing local officials discretion in applying general legislation which they deemed unsuitable to their jurisdictions. After refusing to execute a law, these officials could explain to a distant council local requirements from their own surer knowledge, and they would receive in due time instructions more appropriate to their needs. The imperial authorities of Spain did not attach as much importance to uniformity of legislation as we do today, but made more allowance for local variations. They were willing to modulate doctrinaire legalism with reason.

Imperial Institutions of Government

Spain's imperial system was conciliar in character. As the Spanish crown under Ferdinand and Isabella, Charles V (1516–1556), and Philip II (1556–1598) consolidated the realm these monarchs eliminated the restraints imposed

[2] John Leddy Phelan, "Authority and Flexibility in the Spanish Imperial Bureaucracy," *Administrative Science Quarterly,* vol. 5, pp. 59–60, June, 1960. The rulers of Spain and Portugal are listed chronologically in Appendix III, p. 584.

upon their royal authority by the *cortes* and replaced it by councils which administered the component parts of the realm in the name of the king. For determining imperial policy and administering the overseas kingdoms the Spanish crown set up in 1524 a Supreme Council of the Indies (*Consejo Supremo de Indias*), under the presidency of Friar García de Loaysa. It exercised the same jurisdiction over the Indies that the Royal Council (*Consejo Real* or *Consejo de Castilla*) exercised in Spain. Its jurisdiction was complete, covering all financial, civil, military, judicial, ecclesiastical, and commercial matters. Nothing in the Indies was exempt from its control. It was the supreme legislative body, the supreme executive, and the supreme court of all Spain's overseas lands, and in its handling of American matters it was exempt from interference by all other councils in Spain. With the king's consent it adopted and promulgated ordinances for the overseas domains, approved or disallowed all American legislation, defined the boundaries between jurisdictions, filled all important offices in the American kingdoms, determined all matters of church government, and heard appeals from civil suits in America and from suits in Spain involving the Indies. To it and through it nominally to the king all colonial officials were responsible. Its five members were appointed by the crown and were collectively accountable only to the crown.

During the reigns of Charles V and Philip II the Council of the Indies was subject to their control, but during the seventeenth century as the Spanish kings became weaker the Council acquired an almost independent position as formulator and executor of imperial policy for an autocratic crown. Not until the eighteenth century, under the more vigorous Bourbon sovereigns, were some of the Council's powers taken away from it and vested in a minister of state. In 1714 a minister of marine and Indies was given charge of all matters relating to trade, war, finance, and navigation in the overseas kingdoms, but the Council retained its control over political and judicial functions there. Finally in 1790 all the powers of the Council were transferred to the Royal Council and the legal theory that the American territories belonged to the crown rather than to the nation thus lost its significance. The Council of the Indies survived, however, as a purely advisory body and though abolished in the famous liberal constitution of 1812 was reestablished by Ferdinand VII in 1814 and continued until 1834 when, Spain's empire having almost entirely disappeared, it ceased to have any further reason for existing.

The ordinances and other decisions of the Council of the Indies became so voluminous and contradictory that their codification was ordered by the meticulous Philip II in 1570. They were finally published in what is probably the most famous of all colonial codes, under the title *Recopilación de Leyes de los Reynos de las Indias,* in 1680. And yet, strictly speaking, the Laws of the Indies were not totally comprehended in this code, for the Indies were governed by regulations emanating not only from the Council of the Indies but also from the king, the ministry of the Indies, viceroys, *audiencias, cabildos, consulados,* intendants, and international concordats and treaties. The imperial system of Spain under the Hapsburgs cannot be reduced to a neat table of organization showing a clear line of authority from one part to another. It was a finely meshed interlocking mechanism, legalistic where legalism was required and flexible where flexibility was called for. But under the Bourbons after 1700 it gradually broke down through sheer bureaucratic top-heaviness, legalistic red tape, administrative paralysis, and an excess of paternalism. It suffered from all the shortcomings of the old colonial system, shortcomings that were common to all imperial powers before the rise of the idea of popular self-government. In 1784, for example, the bishop of Oaxaca in New Spain submitted to the Council of the Indies certain recommendations for the improvement of relations with the Indians; fourteen years later he

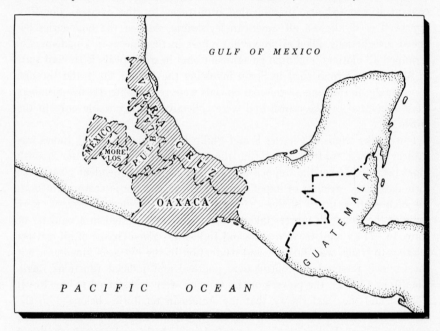

Territory in which towns were granted to Cortés.

was informed that the Council had not yet found time to examine his proposals!

In the hierarchy of officials required to administer the overseas domains, the Spanish crown naturally utilized many offices already established and familiar in the homeland. To many of the early leaders of the conquest of America, starting with Columbus, the crown gave the title of *adelantado,* a title which had been assigned to governors of frontier provinces during the reconquest of the Spanish peninsula from the Moslems and which conferred large military and judicial powers. As the name suggests, the *adelantados* were the promoters of colonization on the frontiers of an expanding empire. The *adelantado* operated as a governor, under the authority of the crown, of a private military and colonizing enterprise. He enjoyed proprietary authority over his lands, sometimes made hereditary. He was obligated to establish a certain number of settlers there, to found a specified number of towns within a specified time, to appoint officials in his jurisdiction, and to assign the Indians to *encomiendas*—all this at his own expense. After Columbus, most of the *adelantados* were men of substance, possessing titles and property, not mere adventurers. Some of them were notable town planners and founders of colonies. One of their first acts, after subjugating their new lands, was to establish a municipality in accordance with Spanish tradition. The *adelantado* selected the site, laid out the streets and the market place, and appointed a town council or *cabildo*. In all his military and colonizing activities he operated as a private concessionaire of the crown. He was engaged in a hazardous business and was likely to suffer death if he took his obligations seriously and removal from office if he did not.

As life in the overseas settlements became stabilized and both men and nature were brought under control, many of the *adelantados* were replaced by royal governors. For the private enterprise and almost complete discretionary authority of the original entrepreneur was substituted the direct authority of the crown. The crown's highest agent in the colonies was the viceroy, who, as the name suggests, was the personal representative of the king, a living image of the crown. He alone, among all other officials in the colony, was entitled to receive royal honors. The first viceroy in the Indies was Antonio de Mendoza, a member of a powerful family at the court of Charles V, knight of the military order of Santiago, and Spanish ambassador to Hungary. He was appointed in 1529 at a time when the crown had been prejudiced against the valiant conqueror of New Spain by his jealous political rivals. Cortés himself made a trip to Spain in an attempt to regain his authority, but nevertheless in 1530 his power was transferred to the *audiencia*, which under the able leadership of the good bishop of Santo Domingo, Sebastián Ramírez de Fuenleal, governed the colony for the next four years until Mendoza arrived. When Mendoza finally reached Mexico City in 1535 he took over the executive authority of the *audiencia*.

The new viceroyalty controlled both New Spain and the whole Caribbean region. After the conquest of Peru a second viceroyalty was created, centering in Lima and embracing the entire South American continent except Portuguese Brazil and Venezuela, which was considered appurtenant to the Caribbean jurisdiction and subject to the *audiencia* of Santo Domingo. In all, New Spain was governed by a succession of sixty-two viceroys, ten of whom were ecclesiastics, and Peru by forty-one. In the sixteenth century Peru was considered more important than New Spain by reason of its greater wealth and population, and the usual salary of 41,000 ducats paid to its viceroy was correspondingly higher than the salary of 24,000 ducats paid to the viceroy of New Spain. But these roles—and relative salaries—were reversed in the eighteenth century when Mexico edged out Peru as a source of wealth and continued thereafter as Spain's most profitable colony.

The powers of the viceroy were, in theory, absolute under the crown, but in fact they were distinctly limited. He was only a royal commissioner and had to refer all decisions of policy to the king and his Council of the Indies. He supervised the financial affairs of his viceroyalty but could not exert final authority over the exchequer. His nominations of subordinate officials, both lay and ecclesiastical, were subject to final approval in Spain. At his elbow sat the members of the high judicial and administrative tribunal of the vice-royalty, the *audiencia*, who were independently appointed by the crown, were not responsible to the viceroy, acted as administrators of the colony in his absence, and would assuredly report any of his derelictions to the Council of the Indies. By the orders of this Council his hands were tied even in dealing with matters of minor administrative detail, such as the purchase of brass rather than iron cannon for colonial defense. Under these conditions the vice-roy's lot was sometimes not a happy one.

The term of the viceroy was fixed originally at six years and was later reduced to three, but in fact he usually served at the pleasure of the king. As a class the viceroys were perhaps no better and no worse than the Roman pro-consuls of ancient times or the viceroys and governors general of the modern colonial empires of England, France, and the United States. Some of them were grandees of Spain, chosen because of their high standing at court. Some were men of wisdom and statesmanship; they were not only distinguished and honorable representatives of the crown but they made outstanding contributions to the development of the dominions placed under their jurisdiction. Such, for example, was the first viceroy of New Spain, the above-mentioned Antonio de Mendoza, who served in Mexico City from 1535 to 1550. During his administration the first mint for the coinage of money was established, merino sheep and silkworms were introduced to constitute the basis of a textile industry, and the enormously rich silver mines of Zacatecas were opened up. In this raw colony, conquered for Spain only fifteen years before his arrival, Mendoza quickly established a reputation as an excellent administrator. After serving for fifteen years in New Spain he was transferred to Lima as viceroy of Peru, where, though he was already an ill man, he came to be known as "the good viceroy" before his death in 1552.

Less humane and broad-minded was the third viceroy of Peru, Francisco de Toledo (1569–1582). A skillful and honest administrator he sought to adapt the crown's so-called "New Laws" of 1542 to the requirements of the Spanish colonists in Peru by introducing the *mita* system of forced labor, which will be discussed in the next chapter. He also prepared a book of assizes or *Libro de tasas* which undertook, among other things, to regulate the relations between the Spaniards and the Indians and which established his reputation in history. In this he recognized the local Indian organization with its own village council or *cabildo abierto* chosen by popular election. But he also undertook to establish Spanish supremacy in Peru by executing the claimant to the Inca crown, Tupac Amarú, and wiping out the surviving Inca empire that he ruled in the mountains of eastern Peru and Bolivia. Using the murder of a friar in the Inca stronghold as a pretext, in 1571 he sent out an expedition which captured the Inca and brought him back to his ancestral capital, Cuzco. There, despite the Inca's appeals to the *cabildo* and to the bishop, Toledo had him beheaded in the main square and confiscated the property of the royal family. This purely political execution and the subsequent resettlement of some 1.5 million of his followers in Spanish *reducciones*—conclusive proof of Toledo's organizing ability—kept the native followers of the Inca quiescent for more than two hundred years. But when Toledo reported to his sovereign what he had done he was, according to tradition, rebuked. "You were sent to Peru to serve kings, not to kill them," Philip II was reported to have said to him.

The second most important and powerful political institution in the Spanish kingdoms in America was the *audiencia,* an institution that was transferred from Spain to America and was there given enlarged powers. It was in fact a corporation which enjoyed a continuous life, regardless of the coming and going of viceroys. When a viceroy was in office he presided over the *audiencia,* but its authority often exceeded his. It could, for example, even hear appeals against the viceroy's own executive decisions. The *audiencia* was originally only a judicial tribunal or a law court, but during Diego Columbus's long absences from Española to press his numerous suits for the restoration of the powers granted to his father the *audiencia* of Española assumed executive powers. The same thing occurred when the first inquisitor of Peru, the shrewd, ascetic Pedro de la Gasca, returned to Spain. It became the regular practice, therefore, for the *audiencia* to administer a colony in the absence of the viceroy. It came thus to exemplify the double concept of justice in Spanish theory and practice, combining the executive and judicial powers in the same person or institution. For this reason, and because of the distances separating the American lands from the mother country, the *audiencia* assumed large administrative, advisory, and ecclesiastical powers which its counterparts in Spain did not exercise. Composed of magistrates of high rank, talent, education, and experience it served as a royal court of appeals, like the *audiencias* in Spain, but in America it became in addition a *junta* or committee of government.

The institution of the *audiencia* was soon extended to other Spanish provinces in America—to New Spain in 1528, to Panama in 1537, and eventually to all the viceroyalties and other territorial jurisdictions. The boundaries of the jurisdictions assigned to the *audiencias* in America became, in general, the boundaries of the nations of Latin America after they gained their independence. All the *audiencias* had coordinate jurisdiction. Theoretically no one of them was subordinate to another, though in fact the *audiencia* which was located in a capital that was the seat of a viceroy was the most powerful and dominated the *audiencias* in the subordinate jurisdictions.

From the decisions of the *audiencias* appeals could be taken only to the crown and these only in certain defined categories. The *audiencia*, besides discharging judicial responsibilities, sat in executive session as a political advisory body, called an *acuerdo*, and also as a supervisory body or *junta de hacienda* in matters of finance. It had competence in all matters involving the powers and responsibilities of the viceroy or the president of a colony. In its deliberations the viceroy could not participate and vote unless he was a lawyer. By law the *audiencia* was required to make a general inspection or *visitación* of the colony every three years, and on such an inspection it could bring charges against any or all officials, including the viceroy, could make recommendations for change and improvement in administration, and in general could inquire into all the affairs of the colony. Since the terms of the members of the *audiencia*, called *oidores*, often overlapped, the tribunal as a whole when once set up never went out of existence. The members were almost always peninsular Spaniards, that is, they were appointed by reason of position or distinction acquired in Spain. They were forbidden to marry in America without the king's approval, to have any business dealings there, to purchase or own any real estate, to accept hospitalities and gifts in the colonies, or to serve as godfathers in colonial families. Creoles or American whites were, therefore, usually considered ineligible for membership because of their local involvements, and when in the later colonial period they were occasionally appointed as judges they were sent to distant kingdoms.

All these officials, as well as lesser officials such as *presidentes, gobernadores,* and *corregidores* were subject to a *residencia*, which was a judicial review or royal postaudit of all the acts of an official during his tenure of office. When a *juez de residencia* or judge of *residencia* arrived to conduct an inquest he would exhibit his royal instructions at a meeting of all the local officials, including the dean and chapter of the cathedral. Each member would then take the paper of instructions, kiss it, place it on his head, and promise to obey and execute the orders therein contained as coming from their legitimate master and natural lord. All of them would then put down their wands and resign their offices. The royal instructions would be publicly announced through the city and read in the market square by the public crier. The judge would then begin his investigation into the acts of the previous administration. Sometimes an official's successor held the powers of *residencia* and was thus enabled to review all the acts of his predecessor. Before him any person might come, make complaint, and offer evidence against the offending official, who in turn would be given opportunity to defend himself. An official who was thus undergoing *residencia* was suspended from the exercise of his office, and if found guilty he was punished and required to pay the expenses of the *residencia*. From the decision of the judge of the *residencia* there was no appeal except to the Council of the Indies.

The effect of the *residencia* upon Spanish colonial administration has been variously estimated. In some cases, it seems certain, the apprehensiveness of royal officials over a regular impending *residencia* had a paralyzing effect, crushing out their initiative and driving them to a too scrupulous compliance with instructions. The *residencia* has been interpreted as a symptom of a bureaucratic disease which eventually overwhelmed the Spanish Empire and caused its destruction. It undoubtedly had the effect of requiring officials to hew strictly to the line of their official duties. At the same time it served as a means by which the *encomenderos* and other pressure groups might have their grievances heard. In some cases, when the viceroys were weak men, it undoubtedly had a corrupting influence, for, as was said, a royal official had to accumulate from his office enough money, first, to recoup the original cost of the office, second, to sustain himself and his family in Spain for the rest of their lives, and third, to buy off the judges of the *residencia*. But the ill effects of the *residencia* can easily be overemphasized. Like most of Spain's governing institutions in the New World this institution varied so considerably with regions and personalities as to defy generalization about its usefulness. It must have been considered useful by the crown, for it was not finally abolished for lower colonial officials until 1799 and was continued for viceroys to the end of the colonial period.

As a further check upon the actions of royal officials the crown could and often did send out an inspector general or *visitador general* at any time to scrutinize all colonial affairs down to the most minute details. One of the earliest of these was Francisco Tello de Sandoval, who was sent to Mexico City in 1544 to supervise the enforcement of the so-called "New Laws" and who remained for three years while those laws were being adapted to American conditions. The greatest of these *visitadores* was José de Gálvez, who more than two centuries later helped to improve the administration of New Spain, established there a lucrative tobacco monopoly for the crown, and worked out a statesmanlike plan of imperial defense.

In the lesser kingdoms in America the crown's principal administrative official was either a *presidente* or a captain general. These officials governed territories which were theoretically subordinate to the viceroys but were in fact virtually independent of them. Each served as chairman of his local *audiencia*. In provinces that were plagued with frontier problems or that were strategically situated from a military point of view, the chief executive official was often called a captain general, and he usually enjoyed more political independence of the viceroy than did the *presidente*. As noted above, the *audiencias* in these subordinate jurisdictions were nominally independent of the *audiencias* in the viceregal capitals. As the colonial period advanced, some of the lesser colonies themselves qualified for viceregal status. A brief review of the political evolution of the colonies will suggest the complicated nature of Spain's imperial system.

All the subordinate jurisdictions of New Spain were denominated captaincies general except one. After the death of Diego Columbus in 1526, the Caribbean islands and Venezuela were made a captaincy general subordinate to the viceroy of New Spain. In 1543 Central America as far south as Panama was made the captaincy general of Guatemala, subordinate to the viceroy of New Spain. Toward the close of the sixteenth century the Philippine Islands also became a captaincy general and were made directly responsible to the Council of the Indies. The fourth territorial division of New Spain included the mining and frontier regions north and west of Mexico City. It was erected in 1548 into the presidency of New Galicia.

No fundamental changes were made in these territorial arrangements until the end of the Seven Years' War (1756–1763) which added to the Spanish Empire all of Louisiana west of the Mississippi River and thus confronted Spain with new problems of imperial defense. In 1764 this newly acquired area was attached to a new captaincy general of Havana for better defense of the northern lands of New Spain against the murderous Yaqui, Apache, and Comanche tribes as well as against the English and the Russians. The crown, in pursuance of the recommendations of its great *visitador general,* José de Gálvez, detached from the viceroyalty of New Spain the northern provinces, the so-called *"Provincias Internas,"* of the two Californias, Sonora, Sinaloa, New Biscay, Coahuila, New Mexico, and Texas and in 1776 united them as a buffer territory under a military government (*Comandancia General*) which was made directly responsible to the crown. Spanish occupation of these lands had been impeded not only by the barrier of the formidable Indian tribes but by the difficulties of developing desert agriculture. In 1773 Spain's administrative control of this area of Middle America was further fragmented when Venezuela was detached from the independent captaincy general of Havana and was made a captaincy general under the viceroy of New Granada, which had been created for a second time in 1739. Another reduction of territory in this area occurred in 1795 when Spain ceded to the French Directory the highly prosperous eastern part of the island of Española, thus allowing this island-cradle of the Spanish Empire to go completely under French control.

From the beginning all the subordinate jurisdictions of Peru were called presidencies except one. Panama was a presidency with its own *audiencia* after 1535, and until a viceroy was appointed for Lima in 1544, Panama really administered Peru. Subordinate to the viceroy of Peru were also the presidencies of Upper Peru or Charcas, created in 1559, and Quito (Ecuador) created in 1563. Chile remained under a military government as a remote frontier region until it was made a presidency and given an *audiencia* in 1609. In the eighteenth century two new viceroyalties were created within the former area of the viceroyalty of Peru. In 1739, as mentioned above, the captaincy general of New Granada was made a viceroyalty and to it were attached the presidencies of Quito and Panama and later the captaincy general of Venezuela. A viceroyalty of Buenos Aires was created in 1776 with jurisdiction over the entire La Plata River area, including the modern Argentina, Paraguay, Uruguay, the presidency of Upper Peru or Charcas, and the so-called "saddlebag

Viceroyalties in Latin America around 1800.

111

area" of Cuyo, which had long been claimed by Chile. This new viceroyalty therefore included everything east of the Andes and south of Brazil. As the seat of a viceroyalty, it was hoped, Buenos Aires would be better able to force Portugal out of Nova Colônia do Sacramento across the estuary and to stamp out the smuggling trade of the Portuguese and the British carried on from there. Chile itself was made a captaincy general in 1778 and became practically independent of the viceroy of Peru, whose effective authority was thereafter confined only to Peru.

The Church in America

The Spanish Empire was a religious institution, and the authority of the crown over its American kingdoms was staunchly supported by the church, which served as the religious arm of the royal government. Spanish imperial administration was a unique blend of nationalism and religion. The sovereign of Castile, by virtue of the papal grant of the *patronato* in the New World, became the secular head of the church in America early in the sixteenth century. He exercised temporal jurisdiction over it, collecting the tithes and disbursing them on behalf of the church establishment. Since the crown used the tithes for the support of the church the royal revenues were not directly benefited, but the crown thus acquired virtually complete financial control over the church. Similarly through the right of patronage the king nominated all important ecclesiastical officials in America, and his nominees were invariably appointed by the Pope. The consent of the king and of his Council of the Indies was therefore essential before any ecclesiastical official could go to Spain's colonies or any church decrees could be issued or any cathedrals, churches, or other religious establishments could be erected. By the end of the eighteenth century eight archbishoprics were functioning in Spanish America located in Santiago de Cuba, Mexico, Guatemala, Lima, Quito, La Plata (Chuquisaca) in Charcas, Caracas, and Bogotá.

Because the crown considered non-Catholics enemies of Spain it imposed restrictions upon the religious liberty of its subjects both in Europe and in America. Crown and church agreed on the necessity of protecting the purity of Catholic doctrine and preventing the Indies from being racked by the religious dissensions of contemporary Europe. These might indeed produce dangerously explosive effects among the native peoples of the New World, who were being slowly tamed to Christian civilization. Through the religious agency of the Holy Office or the Inquisition the crown therefore sought both to eliminate religious heresy and to prevent the infiltration into the empire of British, Dutch, German, and other non-Catholic foreigners who might subvert the Spanish government and its religion. The Holy Office was introduced into Castile and Aragon by Ferdinand and Isabella in 1481 as a means of purging the newly formed Spanish body politic of the poisons of unorthodoxy. The purpose of the crown was to use it as a means of maintaining "the purity of the Holy Faith and good morals" and thus to prevent the divisive political effects of religious heterodoxy.

When this church tribunal was transferred to the Americas, courts were set up at Mexico City and Lima in 1569 and at Cartagena in 1610. Already in 1560 the Spanish crown had forbidden the publication of anything concerning

Fig. 5-1. Central America's oldest cathedral, built in 1534, Antigua, Guatemala. (*Courtesy of Foto-Arte, Guatemala.*)

America without previous authorization of the Council of the Indies. One of the functions now assigned to the Inquisition was to examine the books that were imported into or published in America. Under the law, until agents of the Inquisition judged a book to be acceptable they could not allow it to be shipped to the colonies or circulated in them. A bookseller who was found guilty of buying or selling a prohibited book was required to cease his business for two years. If he purchased a private library he was required to furnish a complete inventory of its contents to the judges of the Inquisition, and every person who entered the colonies with books was obliged to do the same. Catalogues of books also had to be sent to the Holy Office and could be retained and destroyed by it. The penalty for violation of these regulations was the payment of heavy fines, which were required by law to be paid into the royal treasury. Even the judges of the *audiencia* were subject to the authority of the Inquisition. Its authority extended also to the censorship of theatrical productions and the enforcement of edicts against sorcery, necromancy, magic, the practice of astrology, and the casting of horoscopes, for, declared the Holy Office, "there is no human art or science capable of manifesting the things which are to come." [3]

The Holy Office did not undertake a general policing of the reading material of the colonials; it concerned itself mainly with books of religious heresy. But by 1790 the courts of the Inquisition, according to their own catalogue, had condemned 5,420 authors, not to mention many anonymous works. The works condemned included those of Voltaire, Rousseau, and Montesquieu and Daniel Defoe's *Robinson Crusoe!* The authority of the Holy Office was only sporadically enforced. The bookdealers of Sevilla found ways of evading the law, and they transferred to avid American readers great quantities of books, including many that were proscribed by the Holy Office. Despite the orders of the Inquisition, an interchange of books and ideas between America and Europe was carried on throughout the colonial centuries, as will appear in a subsequent chapter. As a result, the crown's attempts to regulate the reading habits and cultural interests of the Americans proved largely ineffective.

The Inquisition, in fulfilling its mission of stamping out heretical ideas, was authorized to take action against persons who had apostatized, that is, fallen away from, the Catholic faith. These included Jews, Moslems, and Protestants, though few of them were found in Spanish America. If found, however, and convicted of apostasy, they were condemned in a pronouncement read out in an *auto de fé* or public "act of faith." Sentences might be relatively light, but in cases of heinous offense the pronouncement was death. The execution of these sentences devolved upon the civil authorities; they were not carried out by the church. In all, it is believed that not more than one hundred and possibly as few as sixty apostates were burned at the stake in New Spain and Peru during the entire colonial period. Most of the proceedings of the courts of the Inquisition were concerned with cases of immorality, blasphemy, sacrilege, polygamy, Judaism, and religious heterodoxy. One of the purposes was to discipline the clergy, to enforce higher standards of morality among them, and to discourage solicitation of the confessional. The Indians did not come under the jurisdiction of the Inquisition.

The Inquisition, which has been luridly described by writers hostile to Spain, cannot be fairly appraised unless it is studied as a national security

[3] Quoted in Irving A. Leonard, *Baroque Times in Old Mexico*, University of Michigan Press, Ann Arbor, Mich., 1959, p. 88.

system and in relation to the spirit of the age. Because it was kept under strict regulation and its judges were of high caliber, it was a more responsible institution than, for example, the Star Chamber in England, which served a similar purpose. Spain's record in dealing with religious dissidents compares not unfavorably with the contemporary efforts of other European nations to handle the problem. In this respect the Spaniards were no worse than other peoples of their day and in some respects they were better than most. On the Boston common in 1659 four Quakers were hanged for their religious views, and many of the English colonies in North America imposed severe penalties upon Baptists and Catholics. In some matters, such as witchcraft, the Spanish record was comparatively quite enlightened, and Spanish America furnished no parallel to the Salem witchcraft episode of 1692. France, as a result of the revocation of the Edict of Nantes in 1685, forced hundreds of thousands of French Huguenots to flee to foreign lands. The objectives and methods of punishment followed in all these cases seemed appropriate in a period which had not yet evolved a conception of religious toleration. Spain, in attempting to carry out her objectives in the national interest as she conceived it, simply followed the practices of the day. The inquisitors were men who, like those they judged, were imprisoned within the illusions of their time, of their country, and of their kind—all of which adds up to the conclusion that in assessing the deeds of nations in the past it is well not to place all the blame on one nation or to ascribe all merit to another.

After 1700, with the loosening of traditional restraints on individual morality and social cohesion under the influence of the Enlightenment, the Inquisition declined in importance. Prosecutions became less frequent and the vigor of the Holy Office deteriorated. The impact of the Enlightenment and the general spirit of the times created laxness among the churchmen. The friars and secular clergy in America, as elsewhere, succumbed more and more to luxurious living. Religious practices were often only slackly observed, and violations of the vows of chastity and celibacy by the clergy, particularly in Peru, became notorious. Though the Holy Office ceased to be effective in accomplishing its purposes it survived in Spain as an institution until 1833.

Economic Relations

The basic elements of the administrative system that Spain formulated for her American kingdoms in the early sixteenth century continued virtually unmodified until the late eighteenth century. For her the successful administration and preservation of a well-ordered empire possessed high prestige value. The overseas domains gave the Spanish crown importance in international politics and stature as a great power. To maintain the empire undiminished was, from the time of Columbus, a cardinal objective of Spanish policy. The administrative machinery and the diplomatic strategy followed by the court were devised to bolster and defend the imperial system on which Spain's position and prosperity depended.

Admitting that prestige considerations alone were sufficient to justify Spain in defending her empire, what material benefits did she, in addition, derive from it? The economic advantages of empire were definitely not paramount in Spanish policy in the early fifteenth century when she found herself involved, almost by accident, in empire building. The missionary endeavor in America to bring souls to Christianity was not motivated by material considerations; it did not bring money directly into the royal treasury but instead proved to be a costly effort for the crown. Spain did not consciously evolve a theory of mercantilism to establish the economic advantages of overseas lands to the mother country. The Spanish policy of exclusivism was designed to counter the exclusivism of the Protestant countries of Europe—to match the exclusivism of the Protestant Reformation with the exclusivism of the Spanish Inquisition. Exclusivism was not synonymous with the later theory of mercantilism, as developed by the British, with its peculiarly economic implications but was more broadly national, religious, and political. When the economic benefits of empire later became more important to Spain she swung over to the theory of mercantilism, but really never succeeded in practicing it successfully, as her experience with the Caracas Company and the economic innovations under Charles III (1759–1788) demonstrated.

Spain's overseas lands were clearly not necessary to her as outlets for a discontented, rebellious population expendable from the homeland, as was true of some of England's colonies in North America. Indeed the Spanish kingdoms in America were officially closed to elements deemed undesirable in the mother country, including Jews and Moslems, criminals, and immoral people. The Spanish imperial system placed heavy emphasis upon law and Christian morality and insisted upon a strict observance of both in the overseas kingdoms. These kingdoms offered enlarged opportunities to loyal subjects of the crown and gave new scope to their individual economic enterprises in creating wealth both for themselves and for Spain.

In a direct economic sense the colonies were valuable to Spain as sources of raw materials and of revenue. The products of the Indies, particularly the tropical colonies, had high commercial value to a Europe which was beginning to industrialize, but of this value Spain was not to be the ultimate beneficiary, since she remained backward in manufacturing. Any estimate of the income which Spain derived from America must take into account the considerable foreign exchange which she obtained from the sale of the products of her colonial monopoly in the Germanies, the Netherlands, Italy, France, and England. The access of unprecedentedly large quantities of gold and silver into Europe by way of Spain helped to strengthen the capitalistic system by expanding the basic circulating currency medium. To the countries of northern Europe, thoroughly committed to private capitalistic enterprise, the large benefits of the wealth of the Indies eventually flowed, either through the normal channels of trade or through their plundering expeditions. Upon them, however, as well as upon Spain and Portugal, descended all the evils of inflation which accompanied the importation of so much wealth from the Indies and which produced a crisis in their delicately balanced price structure. Even before the abdication of Charles V in the middle of the first century of American colonization, his European dominions had experienced a spectacular rise in prices which, though it raised the standard of living, also widened the gap between the rich and the poor and produced social consequences which have continued into our own time.

The crown's principal American income was derived from the various taxes which were collected by royal officials (*oficiales reales*) in each kingdom. These officials included a treasurer, a comptroller, and sometimes in addition a factor, who converted produce into cash for the royal treasury, and an accounts inspector (*veedor*) who extracted the king's share from the profits of the mines. This share, the royal *quinto*, was fixed originally at one-fifth, later one-tenth, and then one-twentieth. It was simply an income tax, which was collected in accordance with the Spanish law and tradition that held that all the subsoil resources of the empire belonged to the crown. Since the crown did not itself engage in mining it collected a royalty from those who did. The amount of the royalty depended upon three factors: (1) the crown's current policy of either encouraging or discouraging mining operations, (2) the accessibility of the mines and the difficulties of extracting and transporting the ore, and (3) the nature of the mineral—gold, silver, and the precious stones being rarer in Europe and therefore more highly esteemed than copper and iron. By the middle of the eighteenth century when mining operations had become fairly well stabilized the royal share of the profits was generally reduced from one-fifth to one-twentieth.

Since the king was the great *encomendero,* royal officials collected a *tributo* from the Indians who were not assigned to a private *encomendero* and who were thus fully free subjects of the king. They thus adopted the tribute system which was common among the Indians, and indeed in some cases they took over and used the Indian tribute rolls for this purpose. They collected from goods imported into the colonies a tax which was called by its Arab name *almojarifazgo,* and which ranged from $7\frac{1}{2}$ to 10 per cent. After 1566 Spain also levied a tax of $2\frac{1}{2}$ per cent upon exports from the colonies. Another principal source of income was the sales tax or *alcabala* which was levied on every transfer of a product from its raw to its manufactured stage. When originally introduced in the 1570s it was fixed at 2 per cent, but it was raised to 4 and then 6 per cent in the following century and to 10 per cent in the eighteenth. From a tax on stamped paper which was required in all official transactions and from the income from royal monopolies on salt, gunpowder, snow, liquor, quicksilver, playing cards, and, in the latter part of the eighteenth century, tobacco, the crown derived additional revenues. One of the special taxes was the tax levied after 1591 to pay for the Invincible Armada, and this was still being collected a century later! Another source of revenue was the *cruzada* or sale of indulgences of which the crown was given a monopoly by the church and which it collected from 1535 to the end of the colonial period. This revenue had been assigned to the Spanish monarchs by the Roman pontiffs to finance their politico-religious wars of the Reconquest in the Iberian peninsula, and its continuance was now justified in America as a means of promoting the conversion of the pagans to the Catholic religion. As the government of Philip II fell more and more deeply into debt the king resorted to the sale of colonial offices and made it possible for purchasers to hold such offices for life or turn them in as part payment on other more lucrative offices. Major offices such as those of the viceroy, judges of the *audiencia,* and fiscal officers were usually not disposed of in this way, but lesser offices were auctioned off at public sale, usually at astonishingly high prices, and sometimes new offices were created for no other purpose than to be sold. The same practice was followed in Brazil by the Portuguese crown. But the sale of offices was normal throughout Europe at the time. The innovation of the Spanish and Portuguese sovereigns was to treat certain offices not as the perquisites of court favorites but as open to others.

The Spanish administrative system in the Indies included an elaborate system of checks and balances. It has been called a "network of mistrust," but it should rather be viewed as a means of ensuring efficient administration and preventing abuse of power. Viceroys kept the *audiencias* under surveillance, *audiencias* kept vigilant watch over the viceregal establishment, and frequently *visitadores* or royal inspectors arrived to review the record of both viceroy and *audiencia.* A new royal check was introduced in the 1760s when the office of *intendente* was first created in an effort to improve local administration and the collection of royal revenues. The office was taken over from the administrative experience of France. It was set up in America by the Spanish Bourbons in order to increase royal authority in the hinterlands of their empire, to brace the interior provinces against the Indians, and to achieve for the colonies an increased measure of internal security. The *intendente* system, moreover, carried royal authority directly into the more remote parts of the empire and superimposed it upon the exploiting and almost irresponsible *corregidores.* It was intended to provide both internal order and external defense for those growing nuclei of settlement which were remote from the seats of viceregal power in the American capitals.

Despite, or perhaps because of, all this royal vigilance the crown was often deprived of its lawful income by conniving, bribe-taking officials. When a foreign vessel loaded with contraband goods anchored off a colonial port, local planters and merchants would cover an itching official palm with gold in order to smuggle ashore the forbidden merchandise, which very often the local dealers had been unable to obtain from the Spanish galleon fleet. Sometimes even the viceroys violated the royal trust in this way; in Lima trains of mules carrying smuggled goods passed along the street directly under the balconies of the viceroys. But this was an exception. Corruption was generally confined to lesser officials, who worked in cooperation with local ruling groups in subordinate provinces and municipalities to defraud the royal treasury. Peculation and fraud—the antecedents of the modern *mordida,* or bite, of Mexico— were rife in the Spanish and Portuguese provinces in America. Royal inquisitors and investigators seemed powerless to prevent this expression of local willfulness or independence, this defiance of central authority. And yet the lax enforcement of imperial regulations revealed an essential tolerance of the court toward colonial practices and may help to explain why Spain's imperial relationship with her American subjects survived into the nineteenth century.

By the end of the sixteenth century Spain's income from the Indies was accounting for approximately one-quarter of the total revenues of the crown. This proportion declined in the seventeenth century but vastly increased in the eighteenth century primarily because of the enlarged output of the Mexican silver mines. At that time Mexico was Spain's richest colony and was furnishing the major part of the income which the mother country derived from America. It seems certain that without the income from the Indies Spain would not have been able to sustain her European position and her world empire as long as she did.

As befitted a commonwealth of kingdoms the advantages of the imperial relationship were reciprocally shared. The bulk of the American revenues were spent in America. The crown paid the churchmen, built the churches, supplied the pensions of the conquerors and their children, furnished Indian supplies, bore the expenses of military defense, and supported the entire civil establishment from the viceroys down to the humblest clerk. All this it did in order to maintain its imperial prestige, to keep the empire economically productive, and to "ennoble" the American kingdoms. Spain considered the preservation of the empire so important that she herself made many sacrifices to maintain it. Several of the component parts of the empire in the New World, notably Española and Chile, were financial liabilities to the crown throughout the colonial period and had to be supported by it from revenues obtained elsewhere.

The Administration of Brazil

The Spanish system was extended to Portuguese Brazil in 1580 when the Spanish and Portuguese crowns were united under Philip II. Portugal had become increasingly impoverished by her involvement in Africa and the Far East. Toward her colonial settlements in America she followed a policy of *laissez faire* or salutary neglect. The Portuguese crown was less committed to executive absolutism and centralized authority than were Ferdinand and Isabella and their successors. The Portuguese system of colonial administration was less rigid, less regimented, less elaborate, almost less rational, and perhaps for that reason less resented in the colonies than the Spanish. It was a mixture of local autonomy and royal control, with the former generally predominating. The authority of the governor general, who was assigned nominal control over all the Brazilian lands of Portugal in 1549, was limited in fact by the powers already assigned to the captains donatory, who continued to govern their princely domains as private proprietors and petty rulers. The power given to the governor general in Bahía was large, but he was generally unable to exercise any of it outside the capital. The commander of the Brazilian coast guard himself advised his government that colonization could not go forward unless the colonists disregarded royal ordinances which had been issued without reference to actual conditions in the New World. The attempt by the Portuguese crown to bring an increased measure of centralized control into Brazil's political life therefore remained largely ineffective.

Brazil was governed in fact not by the king in Lisbon or by the governor general in Bahía but by the municipal councils, the captains major (*capitães mores*), who preserved order in certain local areas, and the heads of pioneer families in the largely unpeopled frontier regions. In the government of the towns the municipal councils were often assisted, as in the Spanish colonies, by a popular assembly (*junta do povo*). Local autonomy was the prevailing political system in colonial Brazil.

This was strengthened by Portugal's policy, the reverse of Spain's, of allowing all foreigners, provided they were Catholic, to enter its American colony and of sending religious dissenters and the inmates of its prisons there. These latter added to the lawless element, always common in a frontier community, and made life difficult for colonial administrators. Many of these men were "unbridled stallions," to quote the Brazilian sociologist-historian Gilberto Freyre. Responding to the sexual enthusiasm of the native Brazilian women they began immediately to produce that fusion of races of which modern Brazil boasts. Family men of steady habits did not leave Portugal to settle in Brazil, for they could easily find occupation in the underpopulated homeland and were not provoked by religious or political oppression to migrate. Near the close of the eighteenth century Brazil was secretly described by the good viceroy, the Marquês of Lavradio, Dom Luiz d'Almeida Portugal, to his successor, Dom Luís de Vasconcelos e Sousa, as "inhabited for the most part by people devoid of education, licentious in character, heterogeneous in cast, and unaccustomed to any subjection except to the Government and Magistrates." Portugal's American colony attracted vagabonds and scoundrels and also caused fairly respectable settlers to degenerate into "a human scum." They were roughened and toughened by their contact with frontier conditions in America.

The relaxed character of Portugal's imperial system was well exemplified in the relations of the Portuguese crown with the religious orders in Brazil. It generally found itself at loggerheads with the dedicated Jesuits in the colony who pled for royal intervention to improve the moral tone of the colony and to end the slave trade in Indians. In these matters the home government usually chose not to interfere with the prevailing practices of local landowners, wealthy families, merchants, and rich traders. John III established the Inquisition in 1536 but did not apply it rigorously. The Portuguese crown did not engage in business activities in Brazil. It merely encouraged certain economic enterprises by granting tax exemptions, conferring titles of nobility upon their operators, and protecting them from foreign competition. In general it allowed the colonists to create the type of economy and society that they wanted. Almost the only area of Brazilian life into which the Portuguese crown consistently entered was mining. Here, particularly as the mining of gold and diamonds became increasingly profitable in the eighteenth century, royal officials collected the royal fifth.

After the union of the Portuguese and Spanish crowns the viceroys had no greater success in centralizing Brazilian affairs than had their predecessors, the governors general. The title of viceroy for the Portuguese crown's chief agent in Brazil was continued by the Braganzas after they ascended the throne in 1640 and was used, except for brief intervals, until the Portuguese royal family itself arrived in Brazil in 1808. The agency responsible for the government of the colonies under the crown was an Overseas Council (*Conselho Ultramarino*) which was created for the eastern Indies in 1604 and was given jurisdiction over Brazilian affairs in 1642. It exercised the same powers as Spain's Council of the Indies, including supervision over the sale of public offices in Brazil and the sailings of the royal fleets or *frotas*.

General Characteristics

The structure of imperial government which Spain developed and Portugal to a limited extent emulated was an overseas extension of the administrative system of the homeland modified, sometimes significantly, by the new conditions in America. In so far as it was built upon any other system it followed the Roman pattern of closely knit imperial units directed from the center. It was humanitarian and national in purpose, was elaborate and logical in construction, and was the most carefully planned imperial system of the age. It was a complete system of governmental organization. As a paper mechanism for accomplishing results it was admirable. All the channels of decision making and action taking were constructed and every contingency provided for. It was devised to cope with new problems arising in an area where precedents were lacking and most of the subject peoples were uncivilized. If anything, it was too legalistic and overelaborated and required too many lawyers to interpret it and too many bureaucrats to carry it into effect.

In general the imperial system of the Hispanic nations, though it originated in the centralism of the Castilian crown and the Hapsburg monarchy, was flexible enough to be adapted to local conditions in America. As originally worked out, it was the best imperial system in the world, and judged by its results, it was the most successful, for it implanted a new culture upon the inhabitants of almost an entire hemisphere and produced among them a unity of customs and language which continues to be one of the outstanding phenomena of our modern world. This imperial system was created to govern a territory more extensive than the Roman Empire at its greatest magnitude. If it did not make the Spanish, like the Roman, a thousand-year empire, it nevertheless preserved the empire for three hundred years and vestiges of that empire for over four hundred. Even the fiscal system which furnished the sinews of empire served as a model for the later tax system of the independent nations of Latin America. The sources of revenue which the crown had tapped proved indispensable to them.

Additional Reading

Aiton, Arthur Scott: *Antonio de Mendoza, First Viceroy of New Spain,* Duke University Press, Durham, N.C., 1927.

Bernstein, Harry: *Modern and Contemporary Latin America,* J. B. Lippincott Company, Philadelphia, 1952, chaps. 1, 10, 17, 24, 32.

Butler, Ruth L.: "Mem de Sá, Third Governor-General of Brazil, 1557–1572," *Mid-America,* vol. 26, pp. 111–137, 1944.

————: "Duarte da Costa, Second Governor-General of Brazil," *Mid-America,* vol. 25, pp. 163–179, 1943.

————: "Thomé de Sousa, First Governor-General of Brazil, 1549–1553," *Mid-America,* vol. 24, pp. 229–251, 1942.

Calmon, Pedro: *Historia da civilização brasileira,* 4th ed., rev., Companhia Editora Nacional, São Paulo, 1940.

Calógeras, João Pandiá: *A History of Brazil,* trans. and ed. by Percy Alvin Martin, University of North Carolina Press, Chapel Hill, N.C., 1939, chap. II.

Cardozo, Manuel S.: "The Brazilian Gold Rush," *Americas,* vol. 3, pp. 137–160, October, 1946.

Castañeda, C. E.: "The Corregidor in Spanish Colonial Administration," *Hispanic American Historical Review,* vol. 9, pp. 446–470, November, 1929.

Desdevises du Dezert, G.: "L'Eglise Espagnole des Indes à la Fin de XVIIIᵉ Siecle," *Revue Hispanique,* New York and Paris, vol. 39, no. 95, pp. [112]–293, February, 1917.

Galdames, Luis: *A History of Chile,* trans. and ed. by Isaac Joslin Cox, University of North Carolina Press, Chapel Hill, N.C., 1941, chaps. IV–VI.

Gibson, Charles: *The Inca Concept of Sovereignty and the Spanish Administration in Peru,* University of Texas Press, Austin, Tex., 1948.

Greenlee, William B.: "The First Half Century of Brazilian History," *Mid-America,* vol. 25, new series, vol. 14, pp. 91–120, April, 1943.

Hamilton, Earl J.: "Imports of American Gold and Silver into Spain, 1503–1660," *Quarterly Journal of Economics,* vol. 43, pp. 436–472, May, 1929.

Hanke, Lewis: "Free Speech in Sixteenth-Century Spanish America," *Hispanic American Historical Review,* vol. 26, pp. 135–194, May, 1946.

Haring, Clarence H.: *The Spanish Empire in America,* rev. ed., Oxford University Press, New York, 1952. Scholarly treatise, by a distinguished Harvard professor.

Hill, Roscoe R.: "The Office of Adelantado," *Political Science Quarterly,* vol. 28, pp. 646–668, December, 1913.

Keen, Benjamin: *Readings in Latin American Civilization: 1492 to the Present,* Houghton Mifflin Company, Boston, 1955, chaps. X, XIII, XIV, XIX.

Levene, Ricardo: *A History of Argentina,* trans. and ed. by William Spence Robertson, University of North Carolina Press, Chapel Hill, N.C., 1937, chaps. XI–XVIII.

Madariaga, Salvador de: *The Rise of the Spanish American Empire,* The Macmillan Company, New York, 1947. A thorough analysis by a distinguished Hispanophile.

Marchant, Alexander: "Feudal and Capitalistic Elements in the Portuguese Settlement of Brazil," *Hispanic American Historical Review*, vol. 22, pp. 493–512, August, 1942.

Moore, J. P.: *The Cabildo in Peru under the Hapsburgs*, Duke University Press, Durham, N.C., 1954.

Parry, J. H.: *The Sale of Public Office in the Spanish Indies under the Hapsburgs*, University of California Press, Berkeley, Calif., 1953.

———: *The Spanish Theory of Empire in the Sixteenth Century*, Cambridge University Press, New York, 1940.

Phelan, John Leddy: "Authority and Flexibility in the Spanish Imperial Bureaucracy," *Administrative Science Quarterly*, vol. 5, pp. [47]–65, June, 1960.

Priestley, Herbert Ingram: *José de Gálvez, Visitor-General of New Spain, 1765–1771*, University of California Press, Berkeley, Calif., 1916.

Schurz, William L.: *The Manila Galleon*, E. P. Dutton & Company, Inc., New York, 1939.

Shiels, W. Eugene, S. J.: *King and Church: the Rise and Fall of the Patronato Real*, Loyola University Press, Chicago, 1961.

Simonsen, Roberto C.: *História econômica do Brasil, 1500–1820*, 2 vols., Companhia Editora Nacional, São Paulo, 1937.

Smith, R. S.: "Sales Taxes in New Spain, 1575–1770," *Hispanic American Historical Review*, vol. 28, pp. [2]–37, 1948.

Van der Kroel, J. M.: "Francisco de Vitoria and the Nature of Colonial Policy," *Catholic Historical Review*, vol. 35, pp. 129–162, 1949.

Zavala, Silvio: *The Political Philosophy of the Conquest of America*, Editorial Cultura, Mexico, 1953.

———: *New Viewpoints on the Spanish Colonization of America*, University of Pennsylvania Press, Philadelphia, 1943. A stimulating interpretation of certain aspects of Spain's motives and methods in the New World.

Zimmerman, A. F.: *Francisco de Toledo, the Fifth Viceroy of Peru, 1569–1581*, Caxton Printers, Ltd., Caldwell, Idaho, 1938.

VI

Indian and African

The success of the American enterprise would depend in part upon the ability of the imperial powers to exploit the riches of their new lands. This in turn would require an adequate and reliable labor force. Possession of the land alone was not enough. The land had to be first subjugated and then cultivated and developed. Could not the New World itself, already inhabited by a sturdy muscular people, supply its own labor force? The attempt by the white Europeans to use the Indians in this way produced complications that have continued into modern times.

Indians as a Labor Force

The magnitude of the task of opening up the newly discovered western lands suggested the utilization of native labor to Columbus at the very beginning of European colonization in America. As laborers the Indians who surrounded each settlement appeared to offer the help that the newcomers needed. The Spaniards, quite naturally as conquerors of the country, expected the natives to support them, particularly after their own small supplies of imported foodstuffs were exhausted. But they soon discovered to their dismay that the populations of the Caribbean islands had no reserves of food and indeed lived nearly always on the verge of starvation. In lieu of the tribute, either in gold or cotton, which Columbus began to exact from them in 1495 he allowed them to furnish a certain amount of labor and thus began their exploitation. Four years later when he came to terms with the rebellious colonists under Roldán he granted them the right to the labor of the Indians. But the problem of finding an adequate and suitable labor force to develop the enormous newly discovered resources continued to be acute.

When the two races first came into contact they were entirely unknown to each other and were widely separated in time. The Caribbean Indians, in particular, unaccustomed to labor discipline, could not be made to work even for wages, and they resisted assimilation by the white newcomers. These Indians, complained the colonists, preferred living in the woods, eating spiders and roots "and other filthy things," to living with the Spaniards. They persisted in going about naked, despite the explicit injunctions of the crown that they should clothe themselves. They would not dig gold unless they were forced to do so. They did not even seem to understand the punishments meted out to them by their new overlords. They could not appreciate the advantages of trade and commerce and were so unenlightened that they did not even understand taxes. Their adherence to their old ways of living both baffled and antagonized the Spaniards and raised the question whether or not they could be considered capable of governing themselves and leading Christian lives.

Hostilities with the native races, who had no previous experience with European culture and were therefore considered inferior, began immediately. The conquest of America became a gigantic collision of races and of modes of living unparalleled since the meeting of the Romans and the barbarians. The psychological reaction of the aborigines to this collision we have no way of estimating, for they left no record of it. The Indians at the time of the conquest had not developed a feeling of racial solidarity, a sense of Indianism. They were conquered not by the Spaniards but by their own people who betrayed rival tribes to the white invaders. Their own separatist rivalries and not Spanish military force brought about their undoing. They defeated themselves with the guidance and aid of the whites. If it had not been so, the conquest of America by a handful of *conquistadores* would have been impossible. The Indians had no bond of racial unity, and thus were fair prey for a divide-and-conquer policy by the Spaniards.

The Spanish imperial authorities, having no experience to guide them, experimented, on a trial-and-error basis, with various Indian policies. They might have adopted a policy of extermination. Such a policy, if it could have been successfully carried out, might have prevented the growth of a serf system, might have produced less class stratification, and might have created more democratic political and social conditions than actually developed in America. But the crown rejected this policy even before the discovery of the populous Aztec confederation and the Inca empire demonstrated its impracticability. From the beginning the crown assumed that the native inhabitants were capable of understanding, that they were a *gente de razón,* that is, rational human beings, even before the Pope proclaimed them to be such.

Ferdinand and Isabella based their claim to sovereignty over the aboriginal inhabitants of the Indies upon Columbus's discovery and their claim to spiritual responsibility for the Indians upon the papal bulls of 1493. The policies that they worked out were accordingly directed toward incorporating the Indians in the empire. They assumed a paternal and humanitarian attitude toward them and undertook the obligation of Christianizing and civilizing them. This would prove to be a much more formidable task than the United States assumed after World War II in reeducating the populations of Germany and Japan. If the native Americans would submit to their new Spanish overlords the crown would give them all the privileges enjoyed by residents of Castile, treating Indian and white alike.

Spain worked out its Indian policy on a high intellectual plane with much conscientiousness and dialectic. To the credit of the Spanish sovereigns they decided at the outset to explain and interpret this policy to the Indians. They therefore required their commanders in the Americas to read to the Indians a formal document or *requerimiento* prepared by an eminent member of the Council of Castile, Dr. Juan López de Palacios Rubios, calling upon the Indians to acknowledge the Pope and the king in his place as their lord. The natives were informed in this document:

> If you do so, His Majesty will greet you with all love and affection and leave your wives and children free so that you may do with them as you wish, and will give you many privileges and exemptions.... But if you do not, or if you maliciously delay in doing so, by the help of God, I will enter into your lands and will subdue you to the yoke of obedience to the Church and to their Majesties and I will take your wives and children and make slaves of them, and will sell them as such, and will take all your goods and do you all the mischief I can, as to vassals who will not obey and will not receive their lord. And I protest that all the death and destruction which may come from this is your own fault, and not His Majesty's or mine or that of my men.[1]

The effect of the policy thus proclaimed to the Indians was to give them no alternative to submission to a monarch whom they had never seen and a religion of which they had never heard. Their only choice was between voluntary and forced submission. They must accept not only the religion but also the civilization of the newcomers. They responded, some with bafflement thinking the *Ave Maria* was something to eat, some with sullen resentment, many with passive resistance, and some with open rebellion. After the Indians of the Sinu region had listened to an interpreter translate this *requerimiento* to them they replied that "there could be nothing without God" and that, referring to the part which said that the Pope was lord of the universe and that he had made a gift of their land to the king of Castile, "the pope must have been drunk when he did it because he gave what was not his to give and the king who requested and took the gift must have been a little crazy because he asked for something that belonged to others."

As mentioned above, Queen Isabella insisted upon regarding the Indians as rational human beings. In her instructions to the third governor of Española, Nicolás de Ovando, in 1501, she declared that the Indians were to be treated as free subjects of the crown and were to be converted to Christianity. They were first exposed to organized missionary effort when twelve Franciscan friars who came out with Ovando began to work among them. But the impingement of the Spanish culture and religion upon the simple natives complicated their lives and aroused their resentment, with the result that Ovando soon complained to the crown that the colony's native labor supply was dwindling and that the natives were resisting conversion. Many of them hanged themselves rather than submit.

The policy of the Spanish crown toward the natives in its new American

---

[1] Silvio Zavala, *New Viewpoints on the Spanish Colonization of America,* University of Pennsylvania Press, Philadelphia, Pa., 1943, p. 8.

colony was set forth in detail in new instructions to Ovando in 1503, which struck a compromise between Queen Isabella's desire to protect the Indians and the colonists' desire to make them work. The natives would no longer be kept in slavery as chattels but would be elevated to the status of freemen. They would be required to work, but to work as wage earners, not as slaves. In return they would be provided with missionary schools and with storehouses of food. Their land was declared inalienable, and they were to be organized in villages, each with a church, a native *cabildo*, its own corps of officials, hospitals, and other municipal institutions. Each Indian village was to be placed under a Spanish *patrón* who would see that the natives under his charge worked and who would at the same time look after their physical welfare and their spiritual needs. The grant to their Spanish *patrón* was made by the governor or the viceroy under a formula transferring the Indians "whom I commend to your care in order that you may make use of them on your *haciendas* [estates] and in your mines and transactions in the manner directed by their Highnesses [Ferdinand and Isabella] in their ordinances."

The *encomienda* system, which was accordingly introduced into the New World by Ovando, was obviously intended at the outset to combine the objectives of Indian employment with Indian protection. The Indians were now turned over, under a system of *repartimiento* or distribution, in groups of 50 or 100 to work for a Spanish *patrón* in his mines or on his farms. Sometimes the labor of a certain number of natives was guaranteed to a Spanish official as a part of his salary. In addition, as the instructions to Ovando authorized the actual enslavement of rebellious Indians and of Indians who were taken prisoner, slave-hunting expeditions to neighboring islands were organized and large numbers of Indians were reduced to the condition of chattel servitude. Such Indians were marked with a branding iron to denote their ownership and slave status. In extenuation of the conquerors, it must be pointed out that the Indians themselves practiced slavery and that the European type of slavery was in many cases preferable to the Indian type. The slaves of Indian captors were often used for sacrifice to native gods, but the Indians who fell into the hands of the Spaniards escaped this fate. Although the conditions of Indian labor varied considerably from place to place and depended to a large extent upon the individual master, the Indians probably fared better under European masters than under Indian masters. *Encomienda* service, it should be noted, was not required of *mestizos*. They enjoyed free status.

As usually happens when a primitive civilization meets an advanced civilization, the pristine culture of the native population in the islands suffered a severe setback. After the arrival of the Europeans the native Carib stock began immediately to be diluted through interracial mixture and a new breed of *mestizos* appeared. Slave-hunting expeditions from Española to other islands multiplied after the death of Isabella in 1504 and were carried out in some cases under the auspices or at least with the approval of the crown, which derived revenue from them. The pacific Arawaks of Española were not accustomed to regimented work, and natives who resisted enforced labor were often killed while trying to escape. Many more succumbed to the white man's diseases, especially tuberculosis, cholera, rickets, smallpox, measles, and yellow fever, and to their excessive addiction to alcohol. The native population of Española, which is optimistically estimated to have numbered 200,000 at the time of Columbus's first arrival, dwindled to 60,000 by 1508, to 46,000 by 1510, to 20,000 by 1512, and to only 14,000 by 1514. Fewer than 200 natives of pure stock were found in 1542. Within a half century after Columbus first introduced his lithe, headdressed "Indians" to the astonished court of Isabella, pure-blooded natives had almost completely disappeared from the Caribbean islands. But these figures, so often cited to demonstrate Spanish brutality, ignore the *mestizo* element in the islands, which must have been numerous by 1542. Even today Indian characteristics are marked in the biological heritage of the Caribbean peoples.

A similar decline in the Indian population of Mexico occurred. Upon the arrival of the Spaniards, the Indian population was estimated to be 9 million to 11 million, but within half a century, it had dropped to only 4.4 million. Meanwhile, however, the process of mestization had been going on and the total number of inhabitants in Mexico had probably increased. The reduction in the native population of the Caribbean islands and Mexico was not attributable solely to inhumane treatment by the Spanish conquerors. But certain members of the regular clergy in America chose to regard it as such.

Champions of the Indians

Against the cruel maltreatment of the natives the Dominican friar, Antonio de Montesinos, first raised his voice in a sermon in Santo Domingo in 1511. Another critic of this system was Bartolomé de las Casas, who had been trained as a lawyer and who had come to Española in 1502. He accompanied a Spanish expedition to Cuba, and there he was awarded an estate with its native laborers under an *encomienda* arrangement. From his actual experience with this system Las Casas concluded that it was vicious, and he dedicated his great talents thereafter to destroying it, making himself the "indomitable Quixote of the brotherhood of men" and carrying his case directly to the crown on many occasions.[2]

The question of the treatment of the Indians embraced the larger question of the rightfulness of the conquest, which was heatedly debated now, perhaps for the first time, by an imperial nation. The Spanish conscience was deeply troubled by the moral implications of the "white man's burden." As a result Ferdinand prohibited further abuse of the *encomienda* system in the famous Laws of Burgos which he issued in 1512. These laid down specific

---

[2] Pedro Henríquez-Ureña, *Literary Currents in Hispanic America,* Harvard University Press, Cambridge, Mass., 1946, p. 18.

requirements for the better protection of the natives, the payment of wages, and improved diets. But they were unacceptable to settlers in America, who insisted that unless they were given the labor of Indians in perpetuity they could not cultivate the land or earn any profits or even contribute to the support of religious work among the Indians. They were not depriving the Indians of their lands, they explained, because ordinary Indians never were lords of the land or landholders in the preconquest days. The requirement of personal service was therefore actually beneficial to the Indians because it redeemed them from idleness and gave them contact with a civilized people. Of this *encomienda* system, by which whole Indian villages or *pueblos* were entrusted to Spanish overlords, Cortés, after his conquest of Mexico, became an outstanding champion.

The needs of the American settlers, therefore, in the treatment of the natives, as in many other matters, repeatedly nullified court policy and compelled the court to change the laws in order to make them enforceable. The Americans, having a typically Hispanic resentment against authority, would not be controlled effectively by the crown and found ways of squirming out of the reach of its long arm. On the matter of the treatment of the natives, a rift very early appeared between the Spaniards in the New World and the Spaniards who formulated and carried out the policy of the court. It betokened the cleavage that would later develop between the *criollos* or native Americans on the one hand and the *gachupines* or peninsular Spaniards loyal to the crown on the other.

In the controversy over the *encomienda* system as a method of compulsory labor the views of the colonists sometimes prevailed. All that the crown could do was to attempt to mitigate the system. In theory the Indians remained vassals of the monarch of Castile. They were considered immediate wards of the sovereign but were entrusted or "commended" to an *encomendero* for his use. The indefatigable Las Casas, in luridly exposing the evils of this system, did not hesitate to employ exaggeration in order to persuade the crown to take action favorable to the Indians. When he personally observed conditions in the shark-infested pearl fisheries, he wrote that "the tyranny which the Spaniards exercise over the Indians in fishing for pearls is one of the cruelest in the world. There is no hell in this life nor any desperate state in this world that may be compared to it." He idealized the primitive innocence of the aborigines and gave currency to the charge that Spanish imperialism was basically cruel, bigoted, and exploitative.

But Las Casas was so blunt and intolerant that he built up opposition to himself and to the Indian cause which he championed. His action, giving aid and comfort to the enemies of Spain, was treasonable in the technical sense, though dictated by a higher law, and in this way it exemplified the individualistic tradition of Spain. He laid the basis for that Black Legend of Spain's inhumane treatment of its subject peoples in the New World which was repeated by Spain's enemies and rivals and which has colored their interpretation of Spanish imperialism ever since. At the same time his humanitarian zeal in the cause of the American Indian helped to establish the cult of the noble savage which was later to form an important element in the Enlightenment of the eighteenth century.

After Ferdinand's death in 1516 Las Casas found a sympathetic response in the regent, the Cardinal Archbishop of Toledo, Francisco Jiménez de Cisneros, acting for the insane Queen Juana. Las Casas was sent out to Española by the Cardinal in the anomalous capacity of Protector of the Indians, but his efforts in that direction were so thwarted by the Americans that in 1517 he and other religious leaders in the colonies made a suggestion to the new sovereign Charles V which Las Casas ever afterward regretted. He suggested that Negro slaves be imported to work on the Caribbean plantations. Negroes had already been introduced into America as slave laborers, but now Charles V, following Las Casas' recommendation, granted an *asiento* or contract in 1518 to a Flemish trader to carry 4,000 Negroes to the New World. This was the forerunner of many similar *asientos* granted to Flemish, Italian, Spanish, Portuguese, and other slave merchants. The Spanish crown itself did not directly engage in the trade.

Negroes in Spain's overseas lands would be used as slaves, but Indians were to be treated as wards of the crown. They must be brought around to an acceptance of the institutions, culture, religion, and language of their new mother country and would enjoy equal rights with all other free subjects of the crown. If the Indians were abused, their persecutors would be punished. To this policy Charles V was guided not only by the persuasiveness of Las Casas, who became a Dominican friar in 1522, but also by the logic of the great Spanish jurist Francisco de Vitoria, whose lectures delivered at the University of Salamanca in 1532 proclaimed the natural right of the natives of America to freedom and the obligation of the crown to protect them from exploitation. Spain thus deliberately undertook to exercise a civilizing trusteeship over the red natives of America. It thus anticipated by three centuries the concern for the Indians which was proclaimed by some of the *criollo* leaders of the independence movement and even the twentieth-century campaigns to incorporate the Indians more thoroughly in the economy and political life of the independent Latin American nations.

The Spanish crown embodied this new moral ethic for the treatment of subject peoples in the "New Laws of the Indies for the Good Treatment and Preservation of the Indians" in 1542. These abolished future enslavement of Indians throughout Spanish America, freed all chattel slaves for whom no good title of ownership could be shown, and declared all others freed at the death of their owners. If the risk of death of Indians in the pearl fisheries could not be avoided, the emperor decreed in a burst of humanitarian zeal, "then let the pearl fishery cease; for, as is reasonable, we value much more highly the preservation of lives than the profit which may come to us from the pearls." No more *encomiendas* were to be granted, and many already created were to be abolished for the future. The Indians assigned in an *encomienda* were placed under the protection of the crown and were henceforth required to pay tribute in goods rather than personal services. Under the edict of the crown the *encomienda* system could not be used legally as an excuse for chattel slavery because the tribute which the Indians were required to deliver under it to the *encomendero* was explicitly prescribed and written down and could not take the form of personal service. The Indians under *encomienda* were now permitted to resume the communal village life to which they had been accustomed for centuries, subject only to the requirement of payment of a certain fixed annual tribute in money, corn, or poultry, for example, to their *encomendero* and through the *encomendero* to the crown.

After the New Laws, therefore, the *encomienda* relationship could not be construed as implying any property ownership in Indians. It entitled the *encomendero* only to their tribute and established a kind of pension system for the benefit of the *encomendero*. Perhaps half the Indians in Spanish America were thus brought under the private *encomienda* system. The remainder continued to be subject directly to the king, and their labor was regulated by the royal *corregidor*.

As an institution the *encomienda* persisted into the eighteenth century. It was not abolished but was only reformed and regularized by the New Laws. *Encomenderos* continued to transmit their *encomiendas* to their heirs from generation to generation and to require their Indian vassals to furnish them with tribute. They could also hire them out for work with other employers for wages set by law. Under the operation of the New Laws most of the *encomenderos* were reduced to pensioners by the 1570s. As a class they declined both in numbers and in influence as the crown became the great *encomendero*. It became such by virtue of the humanitarian policy formulated in the New Laws of 1542.

Crown Policy versus American Needs

The New Laws laid down a policy of protection and benevolence toward the Indians which compared favorably with the contemporary laws of other European countries in the treatment of their laboring class. But this enlightened policy was unacceptable to the Americans, including many of the clergy, because of their dependence upon Indian labor. So strong was the protest in New Spain that the *visitador* who was sent out to put the New Laws into execution, Tello de Sandoval, was dissuaded from carrying out his royal orders. In Peru the Spanish landowners rose in revolt under the leadership of Gonzálo Pizarro, brother of the murdered Francisco, and they defeated and killed the viceroy, Blasco Núñez Vela, in a battle near Quito.

As a result of American resistance, the labor system that was subsequently followed was not exactly the voluntary labor system that the crown desired but rather a compromise system called the *cuatequil* or forced wage system.

Under this system, the Indians who were under the *encomienda* of the king were subject to periodical *repartimientos* or work assignments. They were dispatched in rotation to laboring tasks by public officials called *jueces repartidores,* who herded them in gangs to the town square where they could be hired for wages by those to whom their labor was assigned. The Indians were required by law to come to the market place and make themselves available for hire. But they must be paid wages for their work, and their employer was required to show that their work for him was necessary and in the public interest.

This was a system by which the Indians were conscripted by crown officials to perform certain types of labor for a wage, such as work in the mines, in the churches, and in the universities, and personal services for clergymen and public officials. It became widely prevalent in most of the Indies and developed in Peru on a large scale under the name of *mita,* a short form of the Indian word *mitachanacuy,* which meant to take turns according to families. For the coercion implicit in the *encomienda* system the crown sought to substitute the coercion of public officials, who would prescribe for the Indian workers reasonable hours and conditions of work. Indian labor was made subject to state regulation in the interest of the Indians. This regulation, for obvious reasons, was most consistently and effectively applied in and around the viceregal capitals and tended to become lax in the peripheral areas beyond the reach of the Spanish authorities.

The *mita* system continued throughout the colonial period and was not legally abolished until 1821. Under it the Indians who were subject to work assignments constituted varying proportions of the male Indian population. In Peru under Viceroy Toledo, it amounted to one-seventh at any one time but later rose to one-sixth and eventually to one-fifth. In Chile one Indian in every six was required to work in the mines and one in every five to work in the fields. Under the *mita* system the responsibility for procuring Indian labor was usually left to the local chieftain or *curaca* because it was found that the Indians responded better to their local leaders than to white overseers. Many "noble" Indians therefore continued to hold land under the Spaniards and performed this and other government tasks for them. Meanwhile, alongside these two systems and operating for the benefit of the *mestizos* and of the great majority of the Indians who were not subject to assignment under the *cuatequil* or the *mita,* a system of voluntary wage labor grew up.

As the economy of the colonies developed, the Spanish settlers were increasingly obliged to depend upon the available local labor force and to overcome the impediments placed in their way by the crown. The *mita* system responded to their labor needs in only niggardly fashion and was hedged about with irksome regulations. They therefore contrived ways of persuading Indian families to settle on their agricultural holdings and to keep them there by a system of debt peonage. Thus evolved the *hacienda,* or the paternalistic, agrarian estate, with its complement of a fixed agricultural labor force. In areas where the *hacienda* developed, the Indians living in communities of nominally free landowners were reduced to the status of corporate peasants, remaining illiterate and following the political dictates of their *hacendado*. The same system of debt peonage came to prevail in many mines and in the sugar and textile mills. An employer would advance an Indian a small sum of money and then on the pretext of having him work off his debt would shut him up in his workshop. Instead of paying him in cash for his work he would supply him with meat, alcoholic liquor, and clothes at a profit to himself of sometimes 50 or 60 per cent. He thus kept the workman forever in debt and exercised almost as much control over him as if he had purchased him as a slave. This became the characteristic labor system in Spanish America after the middle of the seventeenth century.

The distribution of Indians under the *repartimiento,* the *encomienda* establishing the obligation of personal service by the Indians, and the *mita* were institutions which sought to reconcile the private needs of the Americans with crown policy, almost always to the disadvantage of the aborigines. The *encomienda* with its feudal attributes and its American equivalents of kings and vassals was transformed into a manorial system with lords and serfs. Thus was repeated in America, as in a microcosm, the social and political transformation that had occurred in Europe during the Middle Ages. The Indians, once lords of the land and owners of America, were dispossessed. They lost control of their continents. Their native aristocracy was relegated to a position of intermediary between the communities of serfs and their white overlords. But though they lost their distinctive aboriginal patterns of living they did not acquire upper-class Hispanic patterns. It is probable that many Indians did not realize they were being subjugated to new white masters. They simply went on working as before and many of them continued to live a life apart from their conquerors, either in the Indian sections of towns or in their own rural communities, where they practiced both private and communal ownership of property. In their communities they were subject first to their local *cacique* and through him to their Spanish overlord. But in most matters of village administration they enjoyed rights of self-government, choosing their own municipal officials and assigning to them the same names and duties as those of officials in the Spanish towns. They lived much as they had lived before the conquest, occupying floorless thatched cottages and subsisting on *frijoles* (beans), *tortillas* (maize cakes), chili, and occasional strips of dried beef. To the Indian communal village the modern Mexican *ejido*, to be discussed later, bears a recognizable resemblance.

After the initial shock of the impact of the white invasion, the Indians seldom developed enough sense of racial grievance to rebel as Indians against the Europeans. When they did rebel against their new Spanish overlords, as, for example, the Indians of New Galicia did in 1541 in the Mixtón War, they were crushed and the survivors were reduced to slavery. But after the promulgation of the New Laws it was difficult to justify the enslavement of even those Indians who were captured in war. A justification had to be presented in each case and required the express approval of the king. In Peru no uprising of Indians as Indians occurred until 1780. In other rebellions in which Indians participated they joined with *mestizos* to resist abuse, not mistreatment of the Indians as such.

Missionary Activities

Both church policy and imperial policy were concerned with the welfare of the Indians. The annals of unselfish humanitarian service can show few chapters that equal the efforts of the Catholic missionaries and the Spanish authorities on behalf of the aboriginal inhabitants and their descendants. Counteracting the Black Legend, they wrote a Golden Legend of Spain in America. They tirelessly sought to stay the hand of the *conquistadores* and to prevent the physical annihilation of the natives. In the forefront of this crusade for humane treatment of the Indians stood the passionate and eloquent Las Casas and his Dominican brothers. One of the latter, Bernardino de Minaya, did not hesitate to advise Pizarro to "explain to the Indians the reason for our coming: to make God known to them and not to rob them or despoil them of their lands," only to receive the harsh rejoinder from Pizarro that he had not come for any such reasons but had come to take their gold away from them. Father Minaya then made a pilgrimage to Rome to plead the cause of the Indians. Almost equally solicitous of the welfare of the natives were Vasco de Quiroga, the bishop of Michoacán; Juan de Zumárraga, the first bishop of Mexico and an *oidor* of the *audiencia;* and the Jesuits and other churchmen. Even the Araucanians had their defender in the Dominican priest Gil González, who contended in the 1560s that they should not be warred against because they "defended a just cause, that is their liberty, homes, and property." One of the friars, the dedicated Toribio de Benavente, best known by his Indian name Motolinía, was not above putting the protection of the Indians on a utilitarian base. To the *encomenderos* he explained, "If we did not defend the Indians, you would have no one to serve you. If we favor them it is to conserve them, so that you may have servants." When the Indians in the Spanish islands of the Caribbean disappeared, the *encomiendas* likewise disappeared, having no Indians to operate them.

Columbus's discovery gave Spain and later Portugal greater opportunities for the conversion of a pagan world than had come to Europe since Pope Urban II launched the first crusade in 1095. The task of converting the American Indians to Christianity was carried out under the auspices of the Spanish crown, not the Pope. Ecclesiastics in the colonies performed their functions always within the limits imposed by Spanish authority. The mission early became the principal means by which the religious orders brought salvation to the aborigines of America and in the process extended their own influence over them. In these missionary areas the Indians lived in villages which were organized on a communal basis under the paternal direction of one or several priests. There the Indians residing under religious tutelage were protected against exploiting white settlers. The missions embodied the conception of the missionaries of the ideal Christian community. They were conceived as "frontiers against paganism." In the missions, primary schools were maintained for instruction in the languages of the Europeans, in religion, in agriculture, in music and other arts, and in crafts. The missions were operated as self-sufficient units and all contacts with the outside world were either banned or closely regulated. The purpose was to enable the Indians to earn their livelihood from their own work while living in close association with their religious leaders.

In the Portuguese settlements the missionaries were the first *bandeirantes*, so to speak, pioneering in the exploration of the country under the sign of the cross. They moved peaceably and unmolested even among the savage Tapajosos, who killed their enemies with poisoned arrows, and they vainly sought to deter their countrymen from reducing these and other Indians to slavery. They preached vigorous sermons against slavery—sermons filled with hell-fire and damnation and appealing to papal encyclicals, imperial *cedulas,* and human conscience. Their efforts finally received the support of the Portuguese crown, which in 1570 declared that all Indians "except those captured in a just war" were exempt from slavery. In 1609 the crown decreed the emancipation of all Indian slaves.

But these laws against the enslavement of Indians could not be effectively enforced, because, as in the Spanish colonies, humanitarian and ameliorative measures on behalf of the natives were opposed by the colonists themselves who did not want their use of the only available local labor force restrained. In the north the priests could make little headway against the stout opposition of the old proprietor of Pernambuco, Duarte Coelho Pereira, but in Bahía and the southern captaincies the Jesuits were more successful. There around 1610 on the banks of the Uruguay River they established the Seven Missions, the famous Jesuit *reducciones,* which have been beautifully described by a modern Brazilian writer Erico Verissimo in his novel translated into English under the title *Time and the Wind.* In them they maintained a virtual theocracy in which the priest ruled often as not only a religious but also the highest secular authority, protecting the Indians from exploitation by the whites and from the bad example often set by them.

The Jesuits were notable colony builders. In various parts of Brazil they helped to build up the economy of the country by producing hides and skins, tobacco, cacao, sugar, cotton, and *yerba maté.* Their *fazendas* were the most prosperous, their sugar mills were models of efficiency, and they maintained Christian communities for the purpose of converting the Indians from paganism to Christianity and from a primitive nomadic existence to a settled agricultural life. But these settlements were the target of continued attack by the coastal planters, who complained that the Jesuit fathers were interfering with their own slave-raiding expeditions and were in fact exploiting the Indians for their own profit.

As a result of this mission activity, civil administration was almost completely suspended in favor of administration by religious orders in certain peripheral or frontier areas of the Spanish and Portuguese empires in America. In Paraguay, for example, the Jesuit "reductions" among the Guaraní and other tribes eventually became so firmly established as to constitute a state within a state. By 1702 their Indian population, dwelling in some thirty villages, numbered 114,000. There the Indians were initiated into a settled and civilized life and were given opportunities to work at agriculture and various arts and crafts under the direction of the Jesuit fathers. They were required to work two days a week in rotation on the common lands and thus to defray the expense of maintaining and decorating the church, supporting the missionaries, helping the sick, and laying up stores for hard times. In the rest of their time they were free to work the parcels of land assigned to each family for its sustenance, but their daily lives were closely regulated by the priests through drumbeats and shouted announcements. Equality for all in housing, food distribution, and clothing was assured. These theocratic communities were intermediate states—neither native settlements nor European provinces. They were "in but not of the empire." They operated in accordance with principles of Christian socialism and largely independently of the civil authorities. But since they served as a part of the imperial system by which savage Indians on the frontier who could not be easily brought under the temporal *encomienda* system were subdued, they were encouraged and even subsidized by the crown. Through them civilization advanced into the interior.

The missionaries, men of the cross in hooded robes of black or brown or white, continued to walk through the American wilderness in their bare or sandaled feet, visiting remote Indian villages, preaching in the native languages, healing, teaching, opening up new pathways for civilization, and seeking by peace and piety to redress the violence of the conquest. According to Motolinía, in Mexico alone they baptized nearly five million Indians between 1524 and 1536. They were *conquistadores* of the spirit, making their "apostolic conquests." Sometimes they suffered martyrdom at the hands of savage Indians in reprisal for the Indian blood spilled by Spaniards who had conquered by the sword. Among the colonists themselves, who in the barbaric environment of the New World had greater need than in the Old World for the ministrations of the church, the friars also found ample fields for missionary labor.

The influence of the church in New Spain was greatly strengthened by the report in 1531 that the Virgin Mary had miraculously appeared to a poor Indian named Juan Diego and had requested him to build a temple in her honor. This Virgin of Guadalupe, whose coming tremendously impressed the credulous Indians, was made the patron saint of the country. Similarly in other parts of Hispanic America, allegedly miraculous events were used to win converts to the church, reinforcing the genuinely pious acts and exemplary lives of local friars and saints. One of the Portuguese Jesuits, Manoel da Nóbrega, early began to work among the irreligious Portuguese settlers in Brazil, and both he and a missionary colleague, José de Anchieta, founder of a Jesuit *colegio* or school at São Paulo, acquired great influence in the administration of the colony. In the college at São Paulo the devoted Father Anchieta carried on a school for the Indians and taught them not only the European languages but also agriculture and handicrafts. He and his colleagues effectively used the converted Indians in the defense of the colony against the French.

The church in Latin America influenced every phase of colonial life. It claimed extensive temporal authority, acquired large landed estates which it held in *mortmain,* and, through its money-lending activities, often played a decisive role in the economy of the colonies. Almost from the beginning of colonization it was a strong agent in preserving loyalty to the crown. The religious zeal of the early Spanish conquerors and the control exercised over the church in America by the imperial authorities through the *patronato real* and the Inquisition combined to entrench Catholicism firmly and to protect it from financial want, physical attack, and heretical competition. No other religion had a chance in colonial Latin America. So inseparably were the interests of the church merged with the interests of the crown that in the colonial history of Hispanic America it was often impossible to differentiate between ecclesiastical and political functions. To the crown the church was a useful instrument of polity and control; to the church the monarchy was a mainstay of physical support.

Negroes in America

Alongside the Indian serfdom in America grew up the practice of Negro slavery. In the Spanish colonies this was unaffected by the New Laws. In Portuguese Brazil the Jesuits, for the better safeguarding of their cherished Indian protégés, encouraged the importation of Negro slaves, as Las Casas had already done in the Spanish colonies, in order to provide the planters with a supply of substitute labor. After the middle of the sixteenth century, therefore, Negroes were brought in by Portuguese slave traders with the encouragement of the Portuguese government to replace the Indians as laborers on the plantations of the north. They were culturally much more advanced, worked harder, and adapted themselves better to tropical conditions than did the natives, possessing a relatively greater number of sweat glands than the lighter-skinned races. During the late sixteenth and seventeenth centuries most of them were imported from Angola, and during the eighteenth and early nineteenth centuries from Guinea. They were redeemed from paganism by being baptized, sometimes in wholesale lots, into the church. By 1585

Pernambuco alone contained almost ten thousand Negroes. Bahía soon became the greatest Brazilian distributing point for Negro slaves from Africa and remained such for the following three centuries. During that time, it is estimated, between six and eight million African Negroes were brought into Brazil—strong ebony-colored men and women to cultivate the soil, conquer the forests, plant the cane fields, dig the mines, and build up the wealth of the country. In the black belt of northern Brazil, with its large plantations and its fields of sugar cane, an agrarian aristocracy and a racial situation developed which were similar in many ways to those in the "cotton South" of the United States before the Civil War.

Both in Brazil and in the Spanish colonies Negroes occupied the lowest position in society. But for Negro slaves emancipation was legally possible, and many of them either bought their freedom or escaped to freedom. Some freed and rebellious Negroes drew together in settlements of their own. In 1545 it was estimated by a resident of Española that there were as many as seven thousand ex-slaves or escaped slaves living in Negro colonies in the island. Similar colonies were reported by Francis Drake when he anchored his freebooting ships along the isthmus in the 1570s. These colonies of *cimarrones,* as they were called by the Spanish, or maroons in English, were often hunted down and, despite their constant vigilance against attack, were recaptured or exterminated. In Brazil such a colony, calling itself the Palmares Republic, was established in Alagôas during the struggles of the Portuguese with the Dutch. Numbering as many as twenty thousand inhabitants, it was finally destroyed in 1695 by an army of mixed-blood planters after twenty years of fighting.

Meanwhile the traffic in Negro slaves from Africa was pressed to meet exigent American demands for labor. As early as 1560 it was reported by the *adelantado* of Florida that Puerto Rico contained a Negro population of 15,000 and Haiti, 30,000. Negro workers were much more highly prized than Indian workers. At Cartagena on the tropical coast of the Spanish Main vessels loaded with Negroes constantly arrived, bringing in an estimated ten or twelve thousand a year. On their sea voyage the Negroes were, as the solicitous Father Bertrand Fleurian reported, "thrown one on another in the hold of the ship, without beds, clothing, and almost without food, loaded with chains, and plunged in their own filth. . . . Even cattle on board ship are not so ill used as are these miserable creatures." On the coffee plantations or *habitations* of French Haiti, Guinea Negroes were preferred as slaves by the *grands blancs* or French great whites—great by virtue of their large landholdings. These Negroes, as one of the great whites declared, could be "formed and disciplined according to the master's own ideas." On the sugar plantations of Cuba and northeastern Brazil Negro slaves performed the field labor, while some of their number acted as servants in the *casa grande* or big house of the proprietor. In the towns they were the beasts of burden, supplementing the labors of horses and mules.

Interracial Adjustments

Racial fusion began almost as soon as the white discoverers landed on the shores of the New World. They came without race prejudice, without any consciousness of being a white elite, and on some of them the family ties of the Old World hung loosely. The Spanish sovereigns, ignorant of the differences in culture between Europeans and the American aborigines, recommended intermarriage, their purpose being to bring the Indians into the political and social structure of the empire and to introduce the family system into the New World. From the beginning they encouraged racial mixture or *mestizaje*. In the Laws of the Indies they prohibited the Indian custom of selling daughters in marriage, banned polygamy, and required the marriage of couples living in concubinage. This policy, as it worked out, seemed to be directed not at building up exclusively Spanish communities in the overseas empire but rather at the adulteration of Spanish blood there. The Spanish and Portuguese conquest of the populous lands in the west marked the beginning of a process of racial fusion which eventually worked to the disadvantage of the mother countries by producing a new race of Hispanic Americans, or Latin Americans, as they came to be called. In early Chile, for example, some of the Spanish conquerors had as many as 30 concubines each and in one frontier post in 1580 in Chile 60 children were born to 160 Spanish soldiers within a single week! Where such sexual promiscuity was practiced and the requirement of a Christian marriage was ignored, society tended to become matriarchal in character and continues so to the present.

The crown's policy of Europeanizing or Hispanicizing rather than exterminating the American natives coincided with the best interests of the colonists themselves. It was generally applied in the overseas kingdoms of Spain after 1502 and saved the natives, except those who inhabited the Caribbean islands, from extermination. But it could not have its intended effect of Europeanizing them because the natives were too numerous, and at least in New Spain and Peru, their native cultures were too highly developed and too deeply ingrained. Captains general and viceroys assumed authority over Indian *caciques*, and *audiencias* were substituted for native councils. A layer of Spanish political administration was imposed upon native rule, without, however, interfering overmuch with local practices. The customary law of the indigenous American peoples did not disappear with the conquest but on the contrary persisted, continuing even into the twentieth century in some places and influencing the legal system of Latin America. The *cabildo abierto* itself can be traced to customary Indian councils.

Similarly the religion of the conquerors was, at least at first, superimposed upon native religious practices, but became itself considerably paganized in the process. Pagan priests were replaced by Christian priests, and on the sites of heathen temples razed to the ground new Christian churches were erected. In many Indian villages the residents remained faithful to their pre-Christian cults and, though nominally converted to Christianity, even continued their cannibalistic practices. In the Laws of the Indies the Spanish sovereigns commanded that "the good laws and customs which the Indians formerly had for their good government and order, and the usages and customs which they have retained since they became Christians that are not opposed to our holy religion nor to the laws of this book . . . may be retained and enforced." Despite the theories of political absolutism and Christian evangelism which actuated the Spanish monarchs they allowed a considerable latitude to local, even native, administration. In general their policy was to interfere with aboriginal customs only to the extent deemed essential to the interests of the crown. In race, customs, and religion it is difficult to say which people were the conquerors, which the conquered. The introduction of Negroes into America also resulted in racial fusion and helped to diversify and enrich the culture of the Americas. Like the Indians the Negroes were drawn into the European tradition but at the same time were able to retain many of their own customs and modes of life.

Additional Reading

Aguirre Beltrán, Gonzalo: "The Slave Trade in Mexico," *Hispanic American Historical Review,* vol. 24, pp. 412–431, 1944.

Basadre, Jorge: "El Régimen de las Mitas," *Letras,* Lima, tercer Cuatrimestre, 1937, pp. 325–364.

Hanke, Lewis: *Bartolomé de las Casas: Bookman, Scholar and Propagandist,* University of Pennsylvania Press, Philadelphia, 1952.

————: *Bartolomé de las Casas: An Interpretation of His Life and Writings,* Martinus Nijhoff, The Hague, 1951.

————: *The Spanish Struggle for Justice in the Conquest of America,* University of Pennsylvania Press, Philadelphia, and Oxford University Press, New York, 1949. Policies and practices of Spain in relation to the Indians.

Keen, Benjamin: *Readings in Latin American Civilization: 1492 to the Present,* Houghton Mifflin Company, Boston, 1955, chaps. IX, XX.

Kirkpatrick, F. A.: "The Landless Encomienda," *Hispanic American Historical Review,* vol. 22, pp. 765–774, November, 1942.

Kubler, George: "Population Movements in Mexico, 1520–1600," *Hispanic American Historical Review,* vol. 22, pp. [606]–643, November, 1942.

Marchant, Alexander: *From Barter to Slavery: The Economic Relations of Portuguese and Indians in the Settlement of Brazil, 1500–1580.* Johns Hopkins Press, Baltimore, 1942. A thorough monographic treatment of a limited subject.

Padden, Robert Charles: "Cultural Change and Military Resistance in Araucanian Chile, 1550–1730," *Southwestern Journal of Anthropology,* University of New Mexico, Albuquerque, N.M., vol. 13, pp. 103–121, Spring, 1937.

Romero, Fernando: "The Slave Trade and the Negro in South America," *Hispanic American Historical Review,* vol. 24, pp. 368–386, 1944.

Simpson, Lesley Byrd: *The Encomienda in New Spain: The Beginning of Spanish Mexico,* University of California Press, Berkeley, 1950, superseding the author's earlier *The Encomienda in New Spain: Forced Native Labor in the Spanish Colonies, 1492–1550,* University of California Press, Berkeley, 1929. A monographic study.

VII

Ways of Life

From the beginning the culture of Hispanic America, exemplified in its art, architecture, and literature, was both a transplantation and a fusion. In it the mind of the Spanish Renaissance flowered; in it also the spirit of America's aboriginal peoples found new expression. As the age of the *conquistadores* faded into history and life became more settled the peoples of Hispanic America developed a rich artistic creativity. They became sharers in Spain's *Siglo de Oro* (Golden Age), when, as has been aptly said, the mind of Spain was the mind of Europe. It became also the mind of America.

Learning and Culture

The outstanding centers of colonial culture were the two viceregal capitals, Mexico City and Lima. In learning, New Spain early took the lead. The first printing press in the New World was set up in Mexico City in the 1530s and the first book published in the Western Hemisphere was printed there in 1539, of which unfortunately no copy survives. There Bishop Diego de Landa wrote his straightforward *Relation of the Things of Yucatan (Relación de las cosas de Yucatán)*, which remains a principal source of information about the Mayan civilization. The life and customs of the Aztecs were similarly chronicled by the Spanish friar Bernardino de Sahagún, a pioneer in American anthropology, in his *General History of the Things of New Spain (Historia general de las cosas de la Nueva España)*. This lifework of the tireless Franciscan scholar was confiscated in manuscript in 1577 by the conscientious viceroy, Martín Enríquez de Almanza, on orders of Philip II, was sent to Spain, and was lost there for two centuries.[1] An earlier work, *Of the General and Natural History of the Indies, Islands and Continent of the Ocean Sea (De la historia general y natural de las Indias, islas y tierra-firme del Mar Océano)*, written by one of the *conquistadores* in Castilla del Oro and Española, Gonzalo Fernández de Oviedo, between 1535 and 1557 is a monumental history. These and the *True History of the Conquest of New Spain*

---

[1] Diego de Landa, *Relación de las cosas de Yucatán,* ed. and trans. by A. M. Tozzer, Papers of the Peabody Museum, Harvard University, Cambridge, Mass., vol. XVIII, 1941; and Bernardino de Sahagún, *General History of the Things of New Spain.* Florentine Codex, trans. by Arthur J. O. Anderson and Charles E. Dibble, University of Utah Press, Salt Lake City, Utah, and School of American Research, Santa Fe, N.M., 1950.

(*Verdadera historia de la conquista de la Nueva España*), by the forthright
Bernal Díaz del Castillo, already mentioned, and Motolinía's *History of the
Indians of New Spain* are important literary records of Middle America in
the conquest era.[2] The latter has been pronounced "the greatest piece of
popular history in the Spanish language." For South America, works of comparable scholarship were produced by the Jesuit father Bernabé Cobo in his
History of the New World (*Historia del Nuevo Mundo*) and by the Inca
Garcilaso de la Vega in his *Comentarios reales de los Incas*. Peru's first printing press was set up in 1579 by an Italian printer, Antonio Ricardo.

Spaniards in America early turned their attention to the founding of
schools and other institutions of learning. A college was established in 1536
in Tlaltelolco near Mexico City by the first bishop of New Spain, Father
Zumárraga, to train an Indian clergy. The first university in America was
organized in Santo Domingo two years later. A university was authorized for
the capital of New Spain in 1551 and began to function in 1553 during the
administration of the second viceroy, Luis de Velasco. Another institution of
higher learning, which was decreed by the Emperor Charles V for the capital
of the viceroyalty of Peru in the same year, eventually evolved into the University of San Marcos. It was originally attached to a Dominican monastery,
but in the 1570s under the encouragement of the viceroy, Francisco de Toledo,
it broadened its program by establishing chairs of law, Latin, and the Quechua
language. The graduates of these American universities, according to the
Laws of the Indies, were entitled to the same privileges as those of the
distinguished University of Salamanca. In the seventeenth century five more
universities were established in America and in the eighteenth another ten,
in addition to many colleges, seminaries, and other centers of learning. In
them professional training in law, theology, the ancient languages, mathematics, and medicine was given.

But many of these so-called universities were only poorly equipped colleges attached to convents. Higher education was shaped largely by the
church and rested upon the authority of the Bible, Aristotle, and the church
fathers. But it was not exclusively theological and dogmatic. Scientific investigation which sometimes defied accepted theology was tolerated. A conspicuous example of the fearless rationalist was Carlos de Sigüenza y Góngora,
professor of mathematics at the University of Mexico, an understanding
friend of the gifted poetess Sor Juana Inés de la Cruz, and one of the first
scientific minds of the American hemisphere. When a complete eclipse of the
sun occurred in Mexico City in 1692 Sigüenza calmly studied it through his
telescope while the cathedral bells rang for prayer and the Indian women and
children, abandoning their stalls in the market, went shrieking and flying at
full speed into the cathedral. With his keen mind and universal interests
Sigüenza anticipated the searching scientific minds of the Enlightenment.

[2] Motolinía's *History of the Indians of New Spain*, trans. and ed. by F. B. Steck, Academy of American Franciscan History, Washington, D.C., 1951.

The Spanish Americans created a notable colonial culture, superior to that of the English colonies in North America and comparing favorably with European culture. The viceregal capitals displayed refinements comparable to those of the courts of Europe. The tone of their cultural life was set by the viceroy's court, and learning, scholarship, and the fine arts were cultivated by the educated leisure class who were scornful of business. It could not reasonably be expected that the total cultural achievement of Latin America would equal that of Europe as a whole, considering the ocean distances to be spanned and the rawness of much of the American environment. But if Spanish America lacked a Paris and a Madrid it had a Mexico City and a Lima which achieved cultural eminence in their respective kingdoms. Approximating Hamburg and Marseilles in population, they far outshone those European cities in creative activity of the mind and spirit.

The American residents of the great empire of Spain showed a surprisingly close rapport with the cultural life of the homeland. In intellectual and literary matters they were preoccupied with European models until well into the eighteenth century and remained as subordinate to the mother country in these matters as in their political and economic life. In the cultural capitals of America the interchange of books and ideas with Europe was constant, allowing only for the hazards of ocean transit. Latin American culture suffered, as did that of Spain, from the blight of that curious literary movement *gongorismo,* a cult of preciousness and literary decline associated with the Spanish writer Luis de Góngora y Argote in the early seventeenth century. Americans afterward became full partners in the Golden Age of Spain, extending over almost the first three-quarters of the seventeenth century, and shared the shining distinction of Cervantes, Lope de Vega, El Greco, Velázquez, and Murillo.

As was to be expected, the development of the Spanish American peoples measured in terms of European cultural achievements was uneven. Some of them were remote from foreign sources of stimulation and could provide only a small audience to creative artists and thinkers. Situated on the outer edges of the empire they were not distinguished for intellectual activity because they were preoccupied with more practical matters. For this reason Chile, for example, remained the most backward Spanish province in scholarship and science. It did not receive a printing press until 1812. In remote Bolivia, on the other hand, copies of Cervantes' *Don Quixote* were received immediately after it was published, allowing only the time required for shipment from Spain. The acceptance by Spanish Americans of the European baroque style in the seventeenth century was shown in the design and ornamentation of their cathedrals and in the writings, for example, of the expatriate Mexican dramatist Juan Ruiz de Alarcón, the poet Bernardo de Valbuena, and many lesser figures.

Cultural development in Spanish America was not seriously inhibited by cramping official restrictions. In general only those creative writers who advanced dissident views on religion were subjected to censorship. But what constituted dissident views on religion was sometimes broadly construed. Latin America's greatest colonial poetess, the Carmelite nun Sor Juana Inés de la Cruz, was reprimanded by her bishop for her preoccupation with secular writings. Nevertheless through her charm and intellectual power the convent of San Jerónimo in Mexico City where she lived became a literary and social center, and there she received the most distinguished people of Mexico. But torn between the intellectual life and the religious life she finally gave up her intellectual pursuits, sold her library of more than four thousand volumes, and disposed of her astronomical instruments, and with her own blood wrote a prayer to Christ. While nursing victims of the plague in Mexico City in 1695, she contracted the disease and died at the early age of forty-four. Her creative genius was not seriously stifled by authority, and the three volumes of plays and poems which she wrote are a priceless legacy from colonial times. If the official requirements of religious orthodoxy seemed to hamper free intellectual inquiry, even these were relaxed in practice in the eighteenth century. As late as 1773 a Colombian botanist, José Celestino Mutis, was charged with heresy by the Inquisition for teaching the doctrines of Copernicus, but was acquitted.

In its intellectual life, Brazil was less active than the Spanish kingdoms. Its aboriginal culture was primitive, lacking not only monumental buildings such as those of the Mayas, Toltecs, Aztecs, and Incas but also sculpture and fabrics like those of the native peoples of Mexico and Peru. Here there were no Indian palaces and temples to excite the admiration of the conquerors and no trained native craftsmen to turn out works of art and artisanship. The patriarchal organization of society and the wide distribution of population in Portuguese Brazil did not encourage the establishment of schools. As a result schooling was limited to the children of the master class and was confined to reading, writing, arithmetic, Latin, and French for the purpose of preparing them for higher study abroad and for professional careers.

Colonial Brazil established no universities or other schools of higher learning comparable to those in Mexico and Peru. A printing press which was set up in Rio de Janeiro in the middle of the eighteenth century was ordered destroyed by the Marquês Sebastião José de Carvalho e Mello, and another was not set up until 1808. The first and only novel written in Brazil during the colonial period, *The Adventures of Diophanes* (*Aventuras de Diófanes*) by Teresa Margarida da Silva, had to be printed in Lisbon. Illiteracy was almost universal among the women and was quite general among the men except those who were active in cultural life, business, and the church. The Jesuit Father José de Anchieta, who wrote in Portuguese, Spanish, Latin, and the Indian languages, became the first important Brazilian literary figure, enthusiastically describing the country's colorful landscape and aboriginal peoples. The first scientific treatise on the natural history of Brazil was prepared by Jorge Marcgrave during the Dutch period and was published in 1648. Though the Inquisition was not formally established in Brazil, its methods were sometimes applied there to check heretical writings. But in general the Brazilians enjoyed complete freedom to import books from abroad. These circulated widely in the colony and kept literate Brazilians informed of cultural and scientific developments in Europe. Brazil's culture and art in the seventeenth century were much influenced by the ornate baroque school associated with the Spanish literary obscurantist, Luis de Góngora y Argote.

Class Alignments

The Iberian society that was transplanted to the New World was not rigidly stratified. The Hispanic way of life permitted considerable social mobility among the classes below the rank of grandee and was noteworthy for its horizontal equality within classes. Heirs of an ancient Mediterranean culture, Spaniards and Portuguese appreciated the social utility of allowing leaders to emerge from the middle class and sometimes even the lower class.

In America this system was affected by the concepts of social stratification that characterized the leading aboriginal civilizations. It was also modified by the racial fusion which introduced the new factors of race and color. As the class structure ranged from the very high to the very low, one's place in it was determined not only by birth and wealth but also by race and color. This was the heritage of Latin America. And yet boys of humble Indian parentage who showed talent were sometimes provided with the means of education. Such was Espinosa y Medrano, an unknown youth in the little Andean town of Calcanso who was so precocious that he was sent to school and later to the university by the bishop of Cuzco and became a professor, an orator, and the most famous literary critic in Peru.

In general the top social class was formed by the European-born whites, an elite and often segregated group who were the highest imperial officials and churchmen. They were called *peninsulares* in the Spanish kingdoms and *reinões* or inhabitants of the kingdom (Portugal or *reino*) in Brazil. In addition a distinctive American society began to form when the first *conquistadores* completed their conquests and settled down in the New World. The members of this society, called *criollos* in the Spanish lands and *crioulos* in Brazil, lived on the income from their *encomiendas*, their *haciendas* or *fazendas*, or their mineral properties, all of which were worked by Indians and Negroes. The line between *peninsulares* and *criollos* was thin, but it would become sharper with the passage of time. Beneath these upper strata of power lived literally millions of Indians, Negroes, and mixed peoples. After Hispanic culture had exerted its civilizing and stabilizing effects upon them, many attained a standard of living which was higher than that of the European peasant class.

At the apex of society stood the viceroy, who was the personal representative of the king. By the end of the administration of the fourth viceroy of New Spain, Martín Enríquez de Almanza (1568–1580), the viceregal office had crystallized into a pattern that it followed for another two centuries. In the court of the viceroy the pomp and magnificence of the court in Spain were imitated. He was sometimes a patron of art and letters, and in the viceregal palace he entertained musicians, poets, dramatists, and scholars. In the courts of the successive viceroys, Mancera and Paredes, in Mexico City, the sensitive Sor Juana was often honored. The viceroy was expected to grace with his august presence the pageantry of religious festivals and the poetical tournaments at which the Americans displayed their literary talents.

The arrival of a new viceroy was the American equivalent of a coronation. All the splendor and wealth that the capitals of the viceroyalties— Mexico, Lima, Bogotá, and Buenos Aires—could muster were displayed on the occasion of the viceroy's formal entry into his new seat of power, and all members of capital society vied with one another to do him honor. As he proudly rode into the city, mounted on horseback and preceded by the militia, the members of the *audiencia,* and other local officials, members of the city corporation walked alongside his horse on foot supporting a canopy over the viceroy's head, and two ordinary members of the council or *alcaldes* acted as equerries holding the bridle of his horse. As befitted his rank he was received by the troops with a royal salute. As soon as he arrived in the capital he would go to the chambers (*sala*) of the *audiencia* where he would take the oath of office, swearing "by God and the holy Mary to perform well and faithfully the duty of viceroy and president, attend to the service of his Majesty, obey the laws and ordinances of the kingdom, administer justice to litigants, and preserve the secrecy of the *audiencia."* The climax of his triumphal entry came when he was received at the cathedral by the archbishop and cathedral chapter and attended a mass and *Te Deum.* In Lima this formal ceremony was followed by five days of bullfights and feasts, at the end of which representatives of the university, colleges, convents, and nunneries presented themselves to him and acknowledged him as their protector. When the pleasure-loving Archbishop García Guerra was installed as viceroy of Mexico in 1611 he decreed that bullfights should be held every Friday for an entire year. Associated with the viceroy in the highest stratum of colonial society were the judges of the powerful *audiencias,* the captains general, the *presidentes,* and the high churchmen.

Processions, spectacles, bullfights, and fiestas were popular in colonial Latin America. In the secular processions, gaily decorated horses pranced, and mummers dressed as Moors or Indians performed their antics. In the religious processions, marchers carried statues of saints, and musicians played religious songs. Often these processions culminated in the performance of an outdoor religious play. Among those who enjoyed social status, luxurious levees and dances were common, and these were interspersed with musical concerts and poetical contests, in which the participants vied with one another in devising florid metaphors.

The *criollos* because of their European backgrounds and more or less white complexions enjoyed a privileged position above all other strictly colonial social groups. Offspring of a *quarterón* or *quinterón* and a mulatto or *tercerón* were called *saltos atrás* (throwbacks) because, reported two young Spanish visitors to Spanish America in the 1740s, "instead of advancing towards being Whites, they have gone backwards towards the Negro race." [3] "The greater or less degrees of whiteness of skin decides the rank which a man occupies in society," concluded the observant German visitor to America, the Baron Alexander von Humboldt in 1811. "When a common man disputes with one of the titled lords of the country," the Baron added, "he is frequently heard to say: 'Do you think me not so white as yourself?' " Under decrees of Philip II free Negroes and mulattoes were required to pay tribute and perform labor in the mines and fields. They could not hold public office or be admitted to the priesthood unless they first acknowledged their color limitation and received a special dispensation for it. Both in Spanish lands and in Brazil the color line could be obliterated by money, wealthy *mestizos* and mulattoes being allowed to purchase a certificate of whiteness from royal officials. But in Brazil the military regiments and the *irmandades* or brotherhoods, which were patterned after those in the mother country and which performed a social service function for their members, preserved the color line. Some of them reserved their treasured membership only to whites, and membership in them was equivalent to a certificate of whiteness. Others were reserved for mulattoes and were closed to the blacks. Still others were organized only by and for the free blacks.

But though many of the creoles aped the manners of the viceregal court, others shaped their manner of living more independently. This was particularly true of those who could not claim, either in fact or by law, the advantage of a completely white skin. Many of the members of these classes inferior to the royal aristocracy eschewed ostentation and betrayed without apology the simple traits of the cattleman, the frontiersman, and the jungle pioneer. To them the French customs followed by the elite class in both Spain and America under the Bourbon kings were repugnant. In their America, perfumed wigs and alabaster statuettes seemed out of place. They were contemptuous of the extravagance and sophistication of the gilded society of the viceregal courts and unwilling to bow obsequiously before the representatives of the crown. Indicative of their underlying resentment were their snide satires of the peninsular officials displayed in their colorful *máscaras*

[3] Jorge Juan and Antonio de Ulloa, *A Voyage to South America,* trans. from the Spanish by John Adams, in John Pinkerton (ed.), *A General Collection of the Best and Most Interesting Voyages and Travels,* Longman, Hurst, Rees, and Orme, London, 1808–1814, vol. 14 [1813], p. 30.

and fiesta parades, in which they burlesqued, usually with impunity, the foibles of the imperial dignitaries. They found ingenious ways of not complying with unrealistic royal orders, particularly orders which adversely affected their hard-won economic status or limited their opportunities for making money.

As the motive of many of the Spanish *conquistadores* and Portuguese *bandeirantes* was to carve out domains in America for themselves and their descendants, their aspirations clashed with the centralizing policies of the crown. Their pretensions in the New World often challenged the claims of their sovereigns. To curb these pretensions was one of the main purposes of the crown in restricting the *encomienda* system in the middle of the sixteenth century. The Laws of the Indies consistently pursued a nationalizing objective. As royal authority was extended, the *encomiendas,* usually granted originally only for two or three lifetimes, gradually reverted to the crown. Though the crown granted titles of nobility to some creoles and Indians in its overseas dominions it did not grant enough to create a preponderating American nobility. The only noble class consisted of the peninsular officials composing the viceregal courts, and these were constantly being transferred either to other seats of government in America or back to Spain. In the colonial period many instances of tug of war occurred between these official representatives of the crown and the local landowning class. Therein is found a basic cause for the schism which later opened the way to independence.

Urban and Rural Life

Spaniards by interest and long tradition preferred urban to rural life. They congregated in municipalities. The town in Spanish America therefore was usually a transplantation from the homeland rather than an indigenous growth. One of the first acts of most of the early *conquistadores,* acting as *adelantados* or royal grantees, was to found a town. Such towns, particularly those established in the areas where the aboriginal peoples had developed a settled agricultural life, became nuclei of Spanish culture, while the countryside around them largely retained the cultural complexion that it had had before the conquest. Town life became the prevailing mode of life in Spanish America. But many Spaniards who came to America, although they did not come from the farmer class, became interested in agriculture and ranching. As they settled down in the vast expanses of the New World, the land took on a new interest for them, and though they resided on their *estancias* and *fazendas* they gravitated to the town for their intellectual and social life. They considered community living the ideal life and preferred to dwell in the cities and to leave the cultivation of their land to the Indian and black slaves.

The town in colonial Spanish America was not the row of straggling log huts in a forest clearing that the English settlers in North America later built on the Ohio and Indiana frontier. Instead it was a highly defensive urban community built on the model of the fortresslike towns of Castile and Andalusía and created consciously in accordance with a definite plan. The streets followed the familiar gridiron pattern of a Roman camp, and in the center of the town was laid out a large central square or plaza where the cathedral and the principal government offices were located. Towns that were built on the sites of Indian settlements that were based upon communal living, as in Mexico, Peru, and Central America, were often planned with certain common lands or lands held by all the townsmen and open to the use of all. To each resident were assigned both a town lot and a suburban lot, together with the use of the common pasture lands and woodland. The town was governed by a local council or board of aldermen called a *cabildo,* or *ayuntamiento,* whose members (*regidores*) in the beginning were appointed by the *adelantado.* The early *cabildos* enjoyed considerable local autonomy and were about the only governments in which the creoles had any opportunity to influence official policy and to acquire administrative experience. They chose the local judges or magistrates, who were called *alcaldes.* To the *cabildo* fell the duties of providing for local police, levying local taxes, building roads, hospitals, and bridges, issuing building permits, regulating processions, and controlling the town markets. The members were not allowed to engage in business and could not hold any other salaried position under the government.

The viceregal capitals were centers of lively cultural and social activity. The first public theater was built in Mexico City in 1597, and a few years later another was constructed in Lima. These cities were visited by noted scholars, artists, dramatists, poets, and scientists from the mother country, and from them native writers departed for frequent visits to the capitals of Europe. An interesting glimpse of Lima, as it appeared in 1629, is furnished by a contemporary observer. In this city of approximately 60,000 inhabitants, including 30,000 Negro slaves and 5,000 Indians, Father Bernabé Cobo recorded, most of the dwellings were constructed of adobe and brick with balconies and porches of richly carved wood and gardens adorned with images and statues. The private homes were surpassed in grandeur and luster by the public buildings, most of which bordered the principal plaza, which, Father Cobo declared, "is larger and better planned than any other I have seen, even in Spain." In the center of the big plaza was the market, "where all kinds of fruit and other foods are sold by Negresses and Indian women in such numbers that the square looks like an ant hill; and on fiesta days, in order that this crowd of people should not remain without hearing mass, a mass is said for them on a balcony or corridor which runs along the facade of the main church commanding the whole square." [4]

[4] Padre Bernabé Cobo, *Historia de la fundación de Lima,* Raúl Porras Barrenechea, compiler, *Pequeña antología de Lima, 1535-1935,* G. Sáez, Madrid, 1935, pp. 122-130.

At approximately the same time Mexico City, the wealthiest and most cultured of all the towns of New Spain, was described by another observer as follows:

Their buildings are with stone and brick very strong, but not high, by reason of the many earthquakes, which would endanger their houses if they were above three storeys high. The streets are very broad; in the narrowest of them three coaches may go, and in the broader six may go in the breadth of them, which makes the city seem a great deal bigger than it is. In my time it was thought to be of between thirty and forty thousand Spaniards, who are so proud and rich that half the city was judged to keep coaches, for it was a most credible report that in Mexico in my time there were above fifteen thousand coaches. It is a by-word that at Mexico four things are fair; that is to say, the women, the apparel, the horses, and the streets. But to this I may add the beauty of some of the coaches of the gentry, which do exceed in cost the best of the Court of Madrid and other parts of Christendom, for they spare no silver, nor gold, nor precious stones, nor cloth of gold, nor the best silks from China to enrich them. And to the gallantry of their horses the pride of some doth add the cost of bridles and shoes of silver.[5]

Towns in Spanish America made a precocious growth. As population increased towns grew into cities, and frontier settlements grew into towns and were brought more completely into the Spanish imperial system. Under a law of 1630 the ordinances of cities, towns, and other local administrative bodies, including universities, communes, hospitals, and colleges in America, were made subject to the previous approval of the viceroy and *audiencia* and finally the Council of the Indies. The planning of towns was carried out in accordance with detailed and usually enlightened regulations laid down by the monarch and the Council of the Indies. These prescribed the number of streets that should radiate from the plaza, the location of the parish church and the town hall, the use of narrow crooked streets for protection against the sun, and the setting aside of recreational areas. But the regulations when incompatible with local requirements could usually be altered by the town authorities.[6]

As Spain's system of hierarchical administration was extended, local initiative was inhibited by the crown's policy of municipal consolidation. Town authority weakened toward the end of the sixteenth century. Municipalities were merged into larger provincial units upon which was imposed the authority of the crown in the person of a royal governor, called *gobernador* in the older settlements and *corregidor* in the newer. In the larger districts this official was appointed by the crown, in the smaller by the viceroy. He exercised control over the military, police, and judicial affairs of the towns,

[5] Thomas Gage, *The English-American his Travail by Sea and Land: or, A New Survey of the West-India's,* ed. with an intro. by John Eric S. Thompson under the title *Thomas Gage's Travels in the New World,* University of Oklahoma Press, Norman, Okla., 1958, p. 67, used by permission.

[6] Zelia Nuttall, "Royal Ordinances Concerning the Laying Out of Towns," *Hispanic American Historical Review,* vol. 5, pp. 249–254, May, 1922.

heard appeals from the *cabildo,* and in general supervised local government. He made and unmade *regidores* and became the real governor of the towns. Upon him devolved responsibility for maintaining order among the Indians and collecting the *tributo* (tribute) from them. Since his only recompense was usually a specified percentage of the revenues of the town he often employed unpopular methods of getting it and connived with the local *alcaldes* or bosses under his jurisdiction to collect high prices for the merchandise he sold to the Indians and to pay low prices for their products. Since this office usually went at public auction to the highest bidder, it often fell into the hands of unscrupulous persons. The *corregidores* were regarded generally by the local inhabitants as money grabbers and exploiters. By them much of the local autonomy which the towns enjoyed in the beginning was undermined.

Throughout the process of municipal decay the *cabildo* usually retained its local prestige. Its function was to look after the needs of the townspeople, to solve their neighborhood problems, to fix the prices of foodstuffs and other salable goods, to plan public fiestas, to protect the poor from injuries by the rich, and to serve as an intermediary between the ecclesiastical authority and the townsfolk. However limited its authority in fact, it represented an interest different from that of the hierarchy of royal officials and provided the principal field of governmental activity and authority for the creoles. In the town councils, with their *alcaldes* and *regidores,* the creoles, representing local interests, gained experience and exercised influence in government. Even after the *cabildos* lost much of their local power the tradition of their past vitality survived to be recalled in coming days of struggle. In most communities the *cabildos* were oligarchic and included only local aristocrats who were wealthy enough to buy membership in them and who used their positions to protect their own interests. But they constituted a semipopular organization in which the germ of independence was later nurtured.

Outside the towns the prevailing system of land tenure was the large estate or *latifundio.* The concentration of land in large holdings has been one of the persistent problems of Latin America ever since the early colonial period. It was sometimes encouraged and at other times discouraged by the crown as the social system of the Old World was transferred to the New. In the vast expanse of America the *conquistadores* carved out for themselves princely estates; Cortés, for example, was granted the entire valley of Oaxaca. Large landholdings became characteristic of the church, and when land found its way into the hands of religious establishments it was seldom transferred again to private hands. The church, serving as the principal welfare agency and banker in America, often acquired land as incidental to its educational, charitable, and money-lending activities and by pious donation. On its lands the missionaries pioneered in agricultural development and made Latin America the richer for their interest in progressive farming methods and the introduction of new crops. By the end of the eighteenth century the church controlled probably one-half of the habitable land of New Spain either through outright ownership or by mortgage. The church was the largest land-lord in America; church interests were therefore closely tied up with the maintenance of the prevailing system of Indian labor and the caste system implicit in it.

Brazilian Ways

In Brazil agriculture was stressed even more than in the Spanish colonies, and the few towns were only places from which to ship crops. Both produc-tion and settlement were concentrated in the north in the area centering around Pernambuco and Bahía. This area became the world's main source of sugar. Probably no other part of the world-wide dominions of Portugal contained such a large concentration of rich agriculturists as did northern Brazil. By 1580 Pernambuco reported some fifty sugar mills and an annual export of 4,000 hogsheads of sugar and molasses. Bahía had a more diversified agriculture, exporting some 2,400 hogsheads of sugar and molasses but pro-ducing also cotton, bananas, rice, tobacco, and coffee. The economy of this region was organized around a plantation, each plantation being a small in-dependent village in which the great house was surrounded by the slave quarters, shops, stables, and mills. The great house was the center of a vast estate, with fields stretching out into the distance far beyond the limits of actual settlement. The center of the industrial life of the estate was the sugar mill or the *engenho* where the cane was crushed and the juice extracted from it. But the estate also produced liqueurs and wines from tropical fruits, and cloth, soap, and candles, generally, however, only for local use. It was a self-sustaining unit, needing to import usually only wine and olive oil.

Many of the plantation owners (*fazendeiros*) in northern Brazil accumulated large fortunes and became notorious for their extravagant living, particularly at their town homes in Olinda, later a suburb of Pernambuco. Their status in society was determined by the number of slaves that they possessed, for slaves signified capital, labor force, and prestige. Because of the scarcity of money in colonial Brazil, slaves constituted the most desirable form of capital. As their families increased so grew the capital investment of the master. The masters themselves scorned manual labor, used slave-borne litters and sedan chairs instead of carriages, and spent great sums on parties and fine clothes. In Europe the Pernambuco planter became a byword for wealth, and Brazil meant only the wealthy sugar-exporting colonies of the north. When the fine lady of a rich plantation owner went to church she decked herself out in all the brocades and precious stones that she could comfortably wear, and if she possessed more than she could wear she was followed to church, as Gilberto Freyre has noted, by her most beautiful slave girls wearing the silks and jewels that she herself could not wear. But except for the regular sallies of these ladies to church, they remained in the background of the social life of Brazil. In not a few cases, however, the *senhora* of an improvident plantation owner managed the estate herself, supervising its economy, its industry, and its household chores, and assuming responsibility for the illegitimate children of her husband. By the end of the sixteenth century Brazil's population, resulting from both immigration and natural increase, was reliably estimated to number almost 750,000, but it included only about 40,000 Portuguese, many of whom had been emptied out of Portuguese prisons or were fugitives from justice in the mother country.

The southern captaincies of Brazil had little importance and remained a frontier region of small, struggling, scattered settlements extending along a 1,000-mile coast and showing little promise of their future dominating position in Brazilian life. The only exception in the south was São Paulo, which was already an active, self-sufficing colony, containing a considerable admixture of Indian blood. And yet in 1620 there was only one bed in São Paulo, and it was requisitioned from the owner, much against his will, for the use of the *corregedor* when he visited the town. Rio de Janeiro, which became the seat of the viceroy in 1763, was, despite its beautiful location, a filthy, ill-smelling, and disease-infested town. From the large, unpaved *praça* or square, which was the main approach to the town from the bay, narrow streets and byways branched off. They were bordered by snuff and tobacco shops, hairdressers' shops, bakeries and butcher shops, shops of craftsmen in gold and other metals, grain shops, clothing and hat shops, and taphouses. Many of the town houses had latticed balconies extending completely around the house. From their narrow slits of windows the women, remaining in Moorish seclusion, could peer out to see what was going on in the street without themselves being seen. Toward the end of the eighteenth century they sometimes were carried in their sedan chairs to the *praça* for conversation with their neighbors, but in general they only left their homes to attend mass in the early morning hours wrapped in voluminous cloaks and shawls which concealed everything but their eyes.

On the Brazilian frontier west of São Paulo, Rio de Janeiro, and the other seaboard settlements life was rough and hard. Here the *gaúchos* or cowboys of the south and the north grazed their herds on the prairie backlands of Pernambuco, Minas Gerais, Piauhy, and Maranhão and had their cow branding and steer throwing. The herdsmen, driving their cattle before them, brought population to the most inaccessible regions of the back country, from the basin of the São Francisco south as far as the hills and savannas of Rio Grande do Sul. Cattle and cattle raising prepared the way for the later agricultural development of interior Brazil. The women on the cattle frontier spun and wove the clothing for all the members of the household, and the young women learned the use of firearms alongside their brothers both for killing game and for defense against the wild Indians. The frontier developed a nomadic, predatory civilization quite distinct from the agricultural patriarchal life of the littoral. In both cultures the spirit of individualism was strong. The frontiersman was self-reliant and contemptuous of all authority. Similarly the planter of the littoral, living in feudal independence as lord of his plantation, of his slaves, and of his family, was disinclined to accept the restraints of both the government and the church.

Over the rolling lands in southern Brazil, Uruguay, and Paraguay, called the Continente and disputed between Spain and Portugal, roamed gangs of cattle thieves, who sacked and plundered the huts of the ranchers and despoiled their women. From their depredations the ranchers lived in terror, eking out a precarious subsistence from their fields and cattle. Their poor homes were built of giant bamboo and clay, were straw-thatched, and had only hard-trodden earth for a floor. Beside their huts stood the wooden crosses of their dead killed in the interminable border fighting or by Indian raiders from the hills. The lives of the women on this Brazilian frontier were strenuous and lonely, spent in bearing and rearing children, cooking, washing, and sewing. Illiterate and remote from the coastal towns, they knew none of the refinements of civilization. The men were crude and violent, and their lives were occupied with the primary passions, fighting duels, and engaging in indiscriminate amours. They knew how to subdue the wild ponies, to rope and tie cattle, to bleed and butcher them, and to fight the wars that came with every new generation, seldom knowing why they fought.

The partial removal of the limitations upon the foreign trade and commerce of Brazil, which occurred after the separation of Portugal from Spain in 1640, and the discovery of new and unexpected mineral wealth toward the close of that century brought new prosperity and an extraordinary population increase to the country. At Sabará, located near the headwaters of the São Francisco River and some 300 miles north of Rio de Janeiro, occurred in 1698 the greatest gold strike in the history of the world up to that time. A gold rush ensued which almost depopulated some of the seacoast towns. Many of the sugar factories and tobacco plantations ceased to work because their managers left for the gold fields, driving their slaves with them. Vila Rica soon attained a population of 100,000 and became the center of a new cultural renaissance. With the increase in wealth, social life acquired a corresponding importance and inspired a new interest in the arts. Even pianos were brought up from Rio de Janeiro on muleback. The churches in the mining towns gleamed with wealth; beaten gold was used to decorate the altars; and the luxury of the baroque art was indulged in. There worked the crippled sculptor-architect Francisco Antônio Lisboa, called "Aleijadinho," perhaps Brazil's outstanding colonial genius. In 1720 the gold region was erected into a large new captaincy called Minas Gerais (General Mines). In the northern part of the new captaincy diamonds were found a few years later. The diamond deposits were immediately declared to be crown property subject to exploitation only by crown officials. From them came the world's principal supply of diamonds for the next 150 years. The discovery of gold and diamonds enormously augmented the wealth of Rio de Janeiro, the principal port for the mines, and its population increased from 25,000 to 100,000 between 1750 and 1800. The center of Brazilian economy now began to move from the northeast to the south central part of the country. The opening up of the General Mines also hastened the peopling of the interior and stimulated the importation of Negro slaves from Africa.

Spanish America with an estimated 20 million people in 1780 and Portuguese America with an estimated 3 million had larger populations than their mother countries. In size their capitals surpassed many of the important cities of the homelands. The population of Mexico City was estimated at 90,000 in 1790, that of Havana at 76,000, and that of Lima at 50,000. The gloss and glitter of their capital society reflected the customs and habits of Europe, but it was confined to the relatively small groups that surrounded the viceregal "courts." Outside the capitals, life was often raw, wild, and coarse; and in every juris-diction, actual frontiers of settlement existed. Already the redoubtable friars were beginning to penetrate the Spanish borderlands to the north where a first mission was set up at San Diego in California in 1769 by the Franciscan, Junípero Serra. In Brazil groups of *bandeirantes* or *crioulo* pioneers were push-ing their way farther and farther into the backlands or *sertões*. The feeling was growing that Latin America belonged to the people who had settled there and who were slowly conquering it. They boasted the largest cities in the Western Hemisphere—cities which compared favorably with those of the homelands and far surpassed those of the United States of North America, which achieved its independence between 1776 and 1782. The intellectual and artistic achievements of Latin America, attested by its masterpieces of art and architecture, placed it at the head of civilization in the New World. At the end of the eighteenth century the Spanish Renaissance joined with the Latin American baroque to create a true *mestizo* art, nativist and original. At the same time the products of Latin America's soil and mines were assuming new importance to foreign merchants and manufacturers in the burgeoning era of the Industrial Revolution. Colonial Latin America had long since come of age in every respect except politically. It clearly would not remain indefinitely content with a politically subordinate status in relation to Europe.

Additional Reading

Calmon, Pedro: *História social do Brasil,* 3d ed., Companhia Editora Nacional, São Paulo, 1941.

Costa, Luiz Edmundo da: *Rio in the Time of the Viceroys,* trans. from the Portuguese by Dorothea H. Momsen, J. R. de Oliveira & Cia., Rio de Janeiro, 1936. Interesting description of social life and customs in Brazil's capital in the eighteenth century.

Freyre, Gilberto: *Casa-Grande y Senzala,* 2d ed., Schmidt, Rio de Janeiro, 1936, trans. into English by Samuel Putnam as *The Masters and the Slaves,* New York, Alfred A. Knopf, Inc., 1956. Classic sociological description of the plantation economy of northern Brazil.

Gage, Thomas: *Travels in the New World,* ed. and with an intro. by John Eric S. Thompson, University of Oklahoma Press, Norman, Okla., 1958. A contemporary de-scription of Mexico and Central America by a Dominican friar turned Protestant.

González Peña, Carlos: *History of Mexican Literature,* rev. ed., trans. by G. B. Nance and F. J. Dunstan, Southern Methodist University Press, Dallas, Tex., 1943.

Henríquez-Ureña, Pedro: *Literary Currents in Hispanic America,* Harvard University Press, Cambridge, Mass., 1946. A brilliantly interpretive literary history.

Instituto Internacional de Literatura Iberoamericana, E. Herman Hespelt (ed.): *An Anthology of Spanish American Literature,* Appleton-Century-Crofts, Inc., New York, 1946. An excellent compilation of Spanish American literature for readers of Spanish.

Jacobsen, J. V.: "Nóbrega of Brazil," *Mid-America,* vol. 24, pp. 151–187, July, 1942.

Keen, Benjamin: *Readings in Latin American Civilization: 1492 to the Present,* Houghton Mifflin Company, Boston, 1955, chaps. XII, XVI.

Konetzke, Richard: *Colección de Documentos para la Historia de la Formación Socia! de Hispanoamérica, 1493–1810,* 2 vols., Consejo Superior de Investigaciones Científicas, Madrid, 1953–1958. Vol. I, 1493–1592; vol. II, 1593–1690.

Kubler, George A.: *Mexican Architecture of the Sixteenth Century,* 2 vols., Yale University Press, New Haven, Conn., 1948.

Lanning, John Tate: *Academic Culture in the Spanish Colonies,* Oxford University Press, New York, 1940. A series of lectures both erudite and readable.

Leonard, Irving A.: *Baroque Times in Old Mexico: Seventeenth-century Persons, Places, and Practices,* University of Michigan Press, Ann Arbor, Mich., 1959. Life in New Spain in the seventeenth century.

————: *Books of the Brave,* Harvard University Press, Cambridge, Mass., 1949. A monograph on the book trade and literary interests of Spain's colonists in America in the sixteenth century.

————: *Don Carlos de Sigüenza y Góngora, a Mexican Savant of the Seventeenth Century,* University of California Press, Berkeley, Calif., 1929.

Levene, Ricardo: *A History of Argentina,* trans. and ed. by William Spence Robertson, University of North Carolina Press, Chapel Hill, N.C., 1937, chaps. XIX–XXI.

Moore, John P.: *The Cabildo in Peru under the Hapsburgs: A Study in the Origins and Powers of the Town Council in the Viceroyalty of Peru, 1530–1700,* Duke University Press, Durham, N.C., 1954.

O'Sullivan-Beare, Nancy: *Las Mujeres de los conquistadores: La mujer española en los comienzos de la colonización americana,* Companía Bibliográfica Española, Madrid, 1956(?). The role of women in the conquest and settlement of America.

Ots Capdequí, José María: *Instituciones sociales de la América española en el período colonial,* Imprenta López, Buenos Aires, 1934.

Poppino, R. E.: "Cattle Industry in Colonial Brazil," *Mid-America,* vol. 31, pp. 219–247, October, 1949.

Porras Barrenechea, Raúl (compiler): *Pequeña antología de Lima, 1535–1935,* Imp. de G. Sáez, Madrid, 1935. A useful anthology.

Putnam, Samuel: *Marvelous Journey: A Survey of Four Centuries of Brazilian Writing,* Alfred A. Knopf, Inc., New York, 1948.

Royer, Franchón: *The Tenth Muse, Sor Juana Inés de la Cruz,* St. Anthony Guild Press, Paterson, N.J., 1952.

Ruiz, Hipólito: *Travels of Ruiz, Pavón and Dombey in Peru and Chile (1777–1788). With an Epilogue and Official Documents Added by Agustín Jesús Barreiro,* trans. by B. E. Dahlgren, Field Museum of Natural History, Botanical Series, vol. 21, Chicago, 1940.

Stanislawski, Dan: "Early Spanish Town Planning in the New World," *Geographical Review,* vol. 37, pp. 94–107, 1947.

Torres-Ríoseco, Arturo: *The Epic of Latin American Literature,* University of California Press, Berkeley, Calif., 1959, chap. 1.

VIII

Apogee of Centralism

Under the Hapsburgs, Spain and her kingdoms in America formed a commonwealth of nations. The occupation and settlement of the overseas areas were encouraged by the crown for reasons of wealth, patriotism, imperial prestige, and piety, and those areas became incorporated parts of the empire, contributing to its strength and receiving benefits in return. As the Spanish makers of imperial policy incorporated the new American lands in the empire they utilized many of the institutions of centralized political control which had been used successfully in the homeland, but they tempered them to American requirements and allowed a considerable latitude in applying them. The taxes that Spain collected in her American kingdoms were lower than those in Spain, and the Indian policy which she followed there was definitely not formulated or carried out only to benefit the crown. In commercial exchange the entrepôt depleted her own resources in order to meet the commodity needs of the Spanish Americans. The old imperial system of the Hapsburgs implied a two-way operation, a reciprocally beneficial exchange between the European homeland and the American kingdoms. A different system based upon exploitation would be self-defeating, as the Hapsburgs had learned to their cost in the Netherlands.

Mercantilism

Spain did not originate nor, until many years after the accession of the Bourbons in 1700, did she exemplify the economic theory of mercantilism. But as that theory came to dominate the statecraft of Europe in the eighteenth century Spain was thrust into mercantilistic competition with her European rivals and her imperial policy was altered. The political and some of the economic institutions of the Hapsburg regime survived, but they were now increasingly used to benefit the European metropolis at the expense of the peripheral areas of the empire. Under the impact of mercantilist theory as applied by the Bourbons, the Hapsburg commonwealth of nations was transformed into a mother-country–colony relationship and the political system of the Spanish monarchy became correspondingly more rigid.

Mercantilism, particularly as developed and practiced by Colbert in France, narrowed imperial policy exclusively to commercial policy and emphasized its

157

utility in protecting the mother country. It thus became a means of building up a nation's economic power for political purposes and of making it stronger than its neighbors. It emphasized national greatness, prestige, and wealth. The wealth that was most highly valued was bullion, that is, gold and silver, and happy was the nation that could get and retain large quantities of it! The function of colonies was to supply the mother country with the means of wealth either in the form of bullion and precious stones or in the form of raw materials—marketable wealth—which could be converted into bullion. The overseas territories of a nation came to be viewed simply as estates to be worked for the advantage of the mother country. These territories must therefore be prohibited from trading with foreign nations, and they were expected to maintain a tributary relationship to the mother country.

Mercantilism as a system of statecraft was not thought out until the seventeenth century, but in Spain some of the policies of Charles V and Philip II pointed in this direction. Spain rigorously, and Portugal somewhat less rigorously, insisted that the American territories should feed their raw materials only to the mother country and must not produce or manufacture any articles that would compete with those of the mother country. In turn the products needed by the Americans, whether produced in the mother country or not, must be delivered to them only in the ships of the mother country manned by her sailors. The mother country thus undertook to absorb all the external trade and commerce of her overseas possessions and to meet all their requirements for materials needed from outside. She would thus become a great entrepôt of trade, monopolizing the wealth derived from the American kingdoms and supplying them with all their needs. Her economy was complemented by that of the kingdoms, and so long as this complementarity or partnership could be maintained in a total shared imperial relationship it would presumably be advantageous to the Americans. These were the old and generally accepted principles which eventually shaped the imperial system of both Spain and Portugal, as well as the old colonial system of England in America. To it Spain and Portugal added little that was original or new. Their imperial system was no worse—but also no better—than that of other contemporary empires.

The agent of the Spanish crown in supervising commercial relations with the Indies was the *Casa de Contratación* or House of Trade, which was set up at Sevilla in early 1503. At first it was only a kind of private commercial house for the crown, but as the trade with America burgeoned it became a government bureau, appointed by the Council of the Indies and having complete official responsibility for the administration of trade. Nothing could legally be sent to America or brought back from America except by permission of the *Casa*. It received all gold and silver bullion, pearls, and precious stones from the overseas dominions, kept ledgers of all trade transactions with them, and exercised complete control over navigation. Under its control the annual fleet system was set up in the middle of the sixteenth century and was operated thereafter for two centuries. Under the *Casa* the crown limited Spain's commerce with America to a *consulado* or group of merchants in Sevilla, which was organized as a crown monopoly in 1543.

But Spain and Portugal were poor nations, sparsely populated, and backward in manufacturing as compared with the countries of northern Europe. Since they were unable to supply even their own domestic requirements, obviously they could not meet all the requirements of the Americans. Their people lacked the mechanical inventiveness and technical skills required by an industrial age. Besides, the merchants of Sevilla and Cádiz, who were the principal beneficiaries of Spain's imperial system, did not encourage an abundant flow of manufactures to America because they preferred a regime of scarcity and high prices. In a broad sense, therefore, the Spanish Empire fell because Spain did not accept the Industrial Revolution, as did her neighbors in Europe. Without industry of her own, she could not fulfill her part in the imperial compact.

Into Sevilla through its port of Cádiz came ships from the Netherlands, England, France, and other parts of Europe, and there their cargoes were transferred to Spanish vessels for shipment to Spain's colonies. As the trade of the empire increased, Spanish merchants were very often obliged to become simply factors of foreign commercial firms to which they lent their names. Since they could not discharge their obligations to these foreign firms solely in the wine, olives, wool, fresh and dried fruits, hides and leather, silk cloth, iron, and other products of Spain, they had to pay in coin. Spain therefore became a distributing center for gold and silver to the manufacturing and commercial nations of Europe, and much of her precious bullion escaped her. By the end of the seventeenth century she was able to supply only about one-sixth of her own requirements and the requirements of her overseas dominions from her own resources. All the rest she was obliged to import from other countries. Under the criteria of the mercantilist system she was already failing as an imperial power. She did not establish the industrial structure which a metropolis must have in order to discharge its duties in an imperial organization. As a result she simply served as a channel through which the wealth of the Indies passed into the rest of Europe. "Spain kept the cow and the rest of Europe drank the milk," ran the popular saying. Others said that Spain was "a sieve, which, whatever it receives, is never the fuller."

The crown vacillated in its policy toward manufacturing in its American kingdoms. Despite the mercantilist theory to which it was committed it did not consistently require them to take Spanish goods in preference to their own manufactures, and even in a few cases it encouraged production in America of things which Spain itself could furnish. By an early sixteenth-century decree Spain stipulated that every ship going to the Indies must carry grapevines in order to stimulate a wine industry there. A later monarch, Philip II, attempted to reverse this policy by banning wine production and the olive industry altogether in America, but his order was not carried out. Philip II also sought to restrict the growth of textile manufactures, which, building on the sure foundations of cloth production established by the aborigines, had already had a phenomenal development in New Spain and which competed with an industry that was one of the most important in Old Spain. But his viceroy found it impracticable to carry out this order. As a result, this and other industries flourished in the Indies. Both New Spain and Peru developed strong textile industries, using native cotton and wool and silks imported from China. In factories or workshops called *obrajes,* soap, chinaware, hats, glass, and leather were manufactured for local consumption and for sale in the mining areas of America. Ironworks were constructed, and tanning and milling operations were carried on. Gold, silver, and wood were fashioned into exportable objects in several of the kingdoms, and ocean-going vessels of fine mahogany were built in the shipyards of Guayaquil. As for Portuguese America, Brazil remained largely dependent upon Portugal and, through Portugal, England for its requirements of manufactures, including cheese, flour, medicines, acids, ironware, tin, furniture, mirrors, glassware, paper, and leather goods.

The products of all Europe were carried to the ports of Spain's empire in America in the galleon fleet (*galeones*), which rendezvoused at Portobelo on the Caribbean side of the narrow isthmus, and in the *flota,* which made Veracruz on the Gulf coast of New Spain its principal port of call. This trade was entirely controlled by the crown and was operated in the interest of the wealthy merchants of Sevilla and Cádiz. The galleons were large men-of-war, built high with three or four decks and capacious storing space, and were difficult to maneuver in battle, especially when heavily loaded with merchandise. As they proceeded westward across the Atlantic from Spain—some six or eight convoying from twelve to sixteen merchant vessels—they and the vessels which they convoyed carried cargoes of clothes and textiles, hardware and iron utensils, glassware, wine, books, paper, and the numberless other artisan-made products of Europe—not so much of Spain as of France, England, and the Low Countries. The galleons also carried plenty of balls and shot, not only for their own defense but also for delivery to the Spaniards in America for defense against the foreign pirates, French, English, and Dutch.

Not long after the silver and gold mines of Peru were acquired through Pizarro's conquest, the Spaniards made an attempt to establish an ocean route to the west coast of South America by way of Magellan's strait. In 1539 an expedition, financed by the bishop of Plasencia in Castile, undertook this hazardous trip, but only one of the five vessels reached Peru. Magellan's strait, therefore, demonstrably lacked commercial value as a transit route, and the cold, wind-swept route around Cape Horn, discovered by a Dutch navigator in 1616, proved even more impracticable. Spain, therefore, very early established a direct route to America. To operate as the entrepôts in this trade she licensed three American ports: Veracruz in New Spain; Cartagena in New Granada, and Nombre de Díos (later Portobelo to the west of Nombre de Díos) on the Isthmus of Panama. The last-named town, though squalid and disease-infested, was built on the only practicable harbor on the Atlantic side of the isthmus. It served as the legal port of entry for all of Spain's commerce with South America after 1584.

Spain's transatlantic commerce was carried on in the following manner. With full sails flying the galleon fleet leaves Sevilla for its annual voyage to America at a time determined by the Council of the Indies. When it reaches the Antilles the galleons proceed to the hot, steaming coast of the Spanish Main where at the well-guarded port of Cartagena they unload their cargoes destined for that port. Meanwhile word goes out through all the Spanish lands that the fleet is in and can be expected to arrive at Portobelo within a month. Hastily the armed ships that have been waiting at Callao load on chests of gold and silver from Potosí, quinine or Jesuit bark and sugar from Peru, bales of vicuña wool and casks of cacao, and after picking up additional cargoes at Guayaquil and Buenaventura they arrive at old Panama on the Pacific coast of the isthmus. The galleon fleet at Cartagena now weighs anchor and sails to Portobelo. Here in this fetid coastal port the commerce of Peru and Spain are joined. From Panama to Portobelo come trains of mules loaded with wedges of silver which are unloaded in the public market place and lie there like heaps of stone in the street. A large tent is erected in the plaza, and there the treasures of Peru are exchanged for the luxuries and utensils of Europe under price contracts signed and sealed by the commodore of the galleons, representing the Spanish merchants and the crown, and the governor or *presidente* of Panama. At this annual Portobelo fair, lasting only a few weeks, one of the largest commercial exchanges anywhere in the world is carried on. After the fair the bustling crowds of merchants, tavern keepers, and roustabouts drift away and Portobelo sinks back into its torrid sleep.

Meanwhile the merchant fleet or *flota* which had detached itself from the galleons in the Antilles has proceeded under naval escort to Veracruz by way of Puerto Rico, the island called Española, and Cuba. At Veracruz the Spanish vessels unload their European cargoes, most of which will be sold in the fair at Jalapa, a town in the *tierra templada* above Veracruz. Some of these crates and boxes will be laboriously transported overland by muleback to the Pacific port of Acapulco, lying 200 miles south of Mexico City, and will then be loaded on the "Manila galleon" for the long voyage to the Spanish Philippines. The cargo which the *flota* vessels stow away in their holds at Veracruz, the products of New Spain and the Philippines, are not so rich as the cargo which the galleons have picked up at Portobelo. At Havana both squadrons of vessels—the *flota* and the galleons—now rendezvous. From that spacious port, well protected by its forbidding castle-fort, a little fleet or flotilla of light, fast vessels is dispatched to Spain with full accounts of the commercial exchanges accomplished, the latest intelligence from America, and occasionally an urgent plea for reinforcements of convoy to protect the treasures of the Indies from pirates reported to be lurking in the Florida coves. Finally venturing out on this most hazardous part of the trip, the treasure fleet moves warily northward through the Florida channel to Cape Hatteras and then, taking advantage of the trade winds, sails eastward to Terceira in the Azores and thence to Sevilla, having been absent from the homeland more than two years.

A harrowing incident of this return voyage in the year 1637 was dramatically recounted by the Dominican friar Thomas Gage. In that year the galleon convoy on which he traveled left Havana at the appointed time but before the *flota* from Veracruz arrived. As reported later by the friar:

Don Carlos de Ybarra [the admiral of the fleet], seeing it stayed longer than the time appointed and fearing the weather, and the new moon of that month, which commonly proveth dangerous in the Gulf of Bahama, resolved to stay no longer, but to set out to Spain. On a Sabbath day, therefore, in the morning we hoisted sails, being in all seven and twenty ships..., and one by one we sailed out of Havana to the main sea, where we that day wafted about for a good wind, and also waiting for our guide, which was not yet come out of Havana to guide us through the Gulf of Bahama. That night we wished ourselves again in Havana, thinking that we were compassed about with a strong fleet of Hollanders, for many ships came amongst us, which made us provide for a fight in the morning. A council of war was called, and all that night watch was kept, the guns prepared, red cloths hung round the ships, orders sent about both to the galleons and to the merchants' ships what posture and place to be in. That which I was in was to attend the Admiral, which I hoped would be a strong defense unto us. Our men were courageous and ready to fight, though I liked not such martial business and discourse, but a place was prepared where I might lie hid, and be safe among some barrels of biscuit. All the night I had enough to do to hear the confessions of those in the ship, who thought they could not die happily with the shot of a Holland bullet until they had confessed all their sins unto me, who towards morning had more need of rest than of fighting, after wearying my ears with hearing so many wicked, grievous, and abominable sins. But the dawning of the day discovered our causeless fear, which was from friends, and not from any enemies or Hollanders. The ships which were joined unto us in the night were as fearful of us, as we of them, and prepared themselves likewise to fight in the morning, which showed unto us their colors, whereby we knew that they were the fleet which we expected from Vera Cruz to go along with us to Spain. They were two and twenty sail, which little thought to find us out of Havana, but within the haven lying at anchor, waiting for their coming, and therefore in the night feared us much more than we them. When the day cleared our doubts, fears, and jealousies, then the martial colors began to be taken down, the joyful sound of trumpets with the help of Neptune's kingdoms echoed from ship to ship, and the boats carried welcoming messages from one to another. The Spanish *"brindis"* with *"Buen viaje," "Buen pasaje,"* was generally cried out, and the whole morning was spent in friendly acclamations and salutations from ship to ship.[1]

[1] Thomas Gage, *The English-American his Travail by Sea and Land: or, A New Survey of the West-India's,* ed. with an intro. by John Eric S. Thompson under the title *Thomas Gage's Travels in the New World,* University of Oklahoma Press, Norman, Okla., 1958, pp. 334–335, used by permission.

By means of such heavily convoyed voyages Spain maintained her commercial ties with the Americans and sought to supply them with their European requirements. All the lawful trade with them she sought to keep in her own hands, and from it she rigidly excluded all foreign vessels, forbidding them even to navigate American waters. But as her overseas empire increasingly became an economic liability her own failure to industrialize only aggravated her economic plight. She lagged behind the rest of Europe in manufacturing and consequently could not fulfill her imperial obligations. In a broad sense Spain's decline was due precisely to her discovery of America. She eventually ceased to be a world power because her overseas commitments strained her economic capacity.

The Americans therefore carried on a great deal of unlawful trade, much of it in connivance with Spanish officials. They were eager to buy cheap foreign goods and to dispose of their own surplus products, and at times when crown officials were scrupulously enforcing the law they found ingenious ways of circumventing it. Determined to trade, they were not inclined to look closely into the credentials and nationality of the traders. At the welcome signal of a cannon shot fired from a foreign vessel anchored in an out-of-the-way harbor the residents of nearby towns would flock to the vessel by night. Only a few of them would be permitted to come on board for trading at one time, and these were carefully scrutinized by the smuggler's crew. But sometimes, obviously with the knowledge and permission of local officials, smuggling vessels anchored in the open roadsteads. Buenos Aires, after its final founding in 1580, and the entire La Plata region became centers of smuggling activity through which non-Spanish foreign goods found their way overland to Chile and Peru. A foreign trader reported that he saw as many as twenty-two Dutch ships lying in the harbor of Buenos Aires at one time in 1657. To suppress this clandestine trade was one of Spain's reasons for creating the viceroyalty of the Río de la Plata in 1776.

During the seventeenth century smuggling activity in Spanish America steadily increased. Under cover of the slave trade, which was authorized by successive *asientos* of the crown, the Americans received quantities of contraband, particularly after the English took over the contract for supplying slaves to the Spanish Main by the Treaty of Utrecht in 1713. The Americans also welcomed the foreign goods which they obtained clandestinely from the Caribbean bases of France, the Netherlands, and England. By these means they effectually undercut the Spanish crown monopoly and its restrictive commercial practices and bypassed the annual fleet to obtain the foreign goods which they needed, including flour, pitch, tar, beef, pork, brass, ironware, woolens, cottons, canvas, shoes, and nails. It has been estimated that their illicit trade eventually exceeded their legal trade in both volume and value and was carried on so extensively as to cause a decline in the prices of goods brought in by the Spanish galleons and offered for sale at the fairs at Cartagena and Portobelo.

Imperial Innovations of the Bourbons

Spain's imperial system in America was obviously becoming too rigid and formalistic. As the machinery of centralized government increased, honesty among the imperial bureaucrats declined. The Laws of the Indies, though intelligently conceived, seemed to be almost impossible of precise application in America, for they did not adequately take into account the diversity of customs and requirements there. Though the defects in the laws were the defects common to the age they were freely disobeyed by the Americans as suited their convenience. Prohibited books were brought into the New World and were distributed in great numbers. Foreigners to whom the American continents were closed came in with relative freedom, and throughout the continents smuggling was engaged in on a great scale.

As Spain's imperial system was coming to be regarded as anachronistic in America, disrespect for law increased and official corruption became prevalent. Like the English colonists in North America, Spanish Americans were becoming restive under European monopolies and contemptuous of the crown's laws, which were not of their making and not always to their liking. They were discontented with control from abroad which kept them a dependent area suspended from Europe, subject, as the Venezuelan declaration of independence later stated, to only "a peninsular corner of the European continent." The natural flow of their trade was prohibited by innumerable royal *cédulas*. Even their trade with the Philippines and other places in the Far East was strictly forbidden by a series of royal orders from 1582 on except for one galleon a year shuttling between Manila and Acapulco. Except for this one annual cargo the Spanish Americans were made dependent upon Spain even for their Oriental goods. Like the English in North America, they felt that their development was being sacrificed to that of the mother country. They complained of an excess of interference by a host of crown officials, including inspectors, controllers, tax collectors, and legal agents, in short, of a statism which was controlled from abroad. Their widespread violation of the laws of the crown could easily shade into open revolution.

The resentment of the Americans against Spain's paternalism was aggravated by the centralizing policies of the Bourbons. After Spain's *Siglo de Oro*, which ended soon after the middle of the seventeenth century, her international position markedly deteriorated. By the end of the seventeenth century she was sunk in poverty and decadence and her population had declined to only 5.5 million. Her commerce was feeling the pinch of the British navigation system, begun in 1651, which was the counterpart of her own system of commercial exclusivism. With the accession of the Bourbon dynasty to the throne of Madrid in 1700, Spain began to lay plans for a closer political and commercial unification of the empire. The pro-French orientation which the Bourbon kings gave to Spain in the eighteenth century and which was signalized in foreign policy by the Family Compacts of 1733 and 1762 made it a virtual satellite of France. When Spain's armies lost Cuba to Britain in 1762, Spain in order to redeem the island had to yield the Floridas to England and in addition accepted from the French king the cession of his unprofitable and sparsely populated trans-Mississippi colony, Louisiana, thus considerably complicating her administrative problems in North America. Spain's territorial holdings in North America were further enlarged and her problems of administration complicated by her acquisition of both East and West Florida from Britain in 1783.

But as Spain thus extended her empire she increased her contacts with foreign powers and stimulated their jealousy. To discharge her enlarged imperial responsibilities Spain began a drastic modification in her imperial system. Scandalous abuses in the administration of the overseas dominions were called to the attention of the king in the secret report of Adm. Jorge Juan and Adm. Antonio de Ulloa in 1736, but they went unredressed by Philip V. When his Bourbon successors, in a well-intentioned effort to eliminate misgovernment in the colonies, began to pull more of the strings of empire into the hands of the crown, as shown, for example, by their deliberate policy of absorbing all outstanding *encomiendas* and by instituting the system of *intendentes* (intendancies) on the French model, they antagonized local American interests and stirred up a resentment which later merged into patriotic resistance. The irreconcilability of the crown's centralizing policy with American requirements made Spain's control increasingly ineffective. The *intendente* system, for example, though set up by the Spanish crown in the 1780s as a means of strengthening royal authority and making it more efficient, was utilized by the Americans to reinforce localism. The *intendente* was made the spokesman for local interests and local aspirations and became the official around whom the members of the *cabildo* could rally after the beginning of the liberation movement. The intendancy system was thus converted by the Americans into an instrumentality of regional and imperial disintegration.

In the latter third of the eighteenth century Spain virtually abandoned her policy of keeping the Americans in economic leading strings. In practice her policy of commercial exclusivism had, of necessity, been considerably relaxed during the period of the union of the Spanish and Portuguese crowns (1580–1640), which in effect merged the colonial trade of both. During the latter part of that period it was further tempered by the opening up of trade between Dutch Brazil and large parts of Portuguese Brazil. When Spain accepted alliance with France in 1700 and became involved in the War of the Spanish Succession, her American subjects opened up new, though still contraband, trade with French ship captains. At the close of the war her commercial policy yielded to the force of arms when in the Treaty of Utrecht Spain was obliged to concede to England a thirty-year contract to supply 4,800 Negro slaves annually to her American colonies and the right to send a British ship, the *navío de permiso,* of not more than 500 tons burden and loaded with British goods to call at Spanish ports during the season of the fairs. Soon afterward the ports of northern Spain, long jealous of the commercial monopoly that Cádiz and Sevilla enjoyed in the American trade and long accustomed to considerable freedom of trade in Europe, began to organize trading companies similar to those of the English and the Dutch. These were given trading monopolies in certain parts of America on condition that they drive out foreign interlopers. Through the efforts of one of these companies, the Caracas Company, or, to give it its full name, the *Real Companía, Guipuzcoana de Caracas,* Venezuela took on a new commercial importance.

But as the eighteenth century advanced, the system of Spanish trade monopolies in America was increasingly called in question by both theorists and administrators in Spain. Would not the unity of the empire be promoted if Spanish and American ports were opened to free trade with each other and commercial privileges were granted which would tend to equalize all parts of the monarchy? Accordingly the annual fleet system, which required all American trade to move under convoy between the Isthmus of Panama or Veracruz and the Spanish ports of Cádiz and Sevilla and which was only irregularly followed in the eighteenth century, was finally abandoned for the isthmus in 1740 and for Veracruz in 1779. With this beginning of the decline of the Cádiz-Sevilla monopoly the trade of the West Indies was thrown open to seven new ports of Spain in 1765. Three years later the same was done for Louisiana, in 1770 for Yucatan, in 1776 for Buenos Aires, in 1778 for all of Spanish America except New Spain and Venezuela, and in 1789 for these two remaining colonies. Finally twenty-three American ports were specifically opened to free trade with Spanish ports. With the complete disappearance of the Cádiz-Sevilla monopoly the *Casa de Contratación* was abolished.

The effects of the removal of these restraints to free trade were startling. Between 1778 and 1788 the value of trade between the American kingdoms and the mother country increased by about 700 per cent. The number of hides exported from Buenos Aires rose from 150,000 to 800,000 a year. But the free trade that was thus established was not free trade in our twentieth-century sense of the term. It was free trade only within the empire and still preserved the trade monopoly of the mother country. It was therefore calculated to advance the interests of Spain quite as much as those of the Americans. As such it did not completely satisfy the latter, many of whom were beginning to agitate for free trade with all commercial nations. Spain's subjects in Louisiana and West Florida, upon the recommendation of Governor Bernardo de Gálvez, were finally authorized in 1781, in an unprecedented action by the Spanish crown, to carry on trade with Spain's ally—France—and a limited trade with the French West Indies for a term of ten years. After war broke out between Spain and England in 1796, Spain's subjects in America were obliged to develop trade with the non-Spanish world. As their commercial ties with Spain were cut and the mother country's vessels were swept from the sea, they found it both possible and necessary to open up trade with England.

Their grievances against Spain's still restrictive commercial system were therefore intensified. Their newly whetted desire for cheap imported manufactures from the foreign world and enlarged markets abroad for their raw materials could not be satisfied by the resumption of exclusive trade with Spain. The initiation of even limited free trade with the foreign world, however, was disadvantageous to Latin America's nascent manufacturing industry, as, for example, textiles in New Spain and Peru and wines in Argentina and Chile, because they could not compete successfully with European textiles and wines in an unrestricted market.

Centralism for Brazil

In Brazil the Portuguese crown's policy of commercial monopoly was early breached, for the Dutch, while settled in their coastal colony centering at Olinda, established free trade with most of Portuguese Brazil. But after the fall of the Dutch colony Portugal undertook to reestablish her monopoly through the medium of a commercial company, the *Companhia do Brasil,* or Brazil Company, which was alone authorized to carry foreign products into Brazil and to carry specified products of Brazil out of the colony. The company operated two fleets annually in the Brazil trade. Against the crown's policy of commercial monopoly the Brazilians rose in rebellion at least twice, in 1684 and in 1710–1711, but each time their rebellions were suppressed. A violent resistance movement in Minas Gerais in 1737 against the attempt of royal officials to augment the crown's income from the mines was similarly defeated. Brazilians, like the Spanish Americans, carried on an extensive illicit trade with the British.

Brazil felt the full force of imperial restraints during the reign of the spendthrift John V of Portugal (1706–1750). The colony was exploited, its trade and wealth were monopolized by the mother country, all commerce that could compete with that of Portugal was rigidly prohibited, and Portuguese officials in Brazil practiced flagrant corruption and bribery. Brazilian resentment against these abuses was mounting when at the king's death in 1750 the Marquis of Pombal became prime minister. He immediately began efforts to rehabilitate not only his impoverished homeland but also Brazil and to improve the relationship between mother country and colony.

For this purpose the autocratic Pombal imposed a new administrative centralization upon Brazil. He put the province of Maranhão back under the colonial government, suppressed the eleven surviving donatory or proprietary grants, revived the title of viceroy for the king's chief agent in the colony, and transferred the capital from Bahía, which was dominated by the aristocratic planters of the north, to the bustling commercial center of Rio de Janeiro in the south. He abandoned the annual fleet system in 1765 and initiated an enlightened economic policy which brought renewed prosperity to Brazil's sugar and cotton industry. But at the same time he sought to strengthen the commercial ties between Portugal and Brazil by assigning certain trade monopolies in the colony to Portuguese companies—an action which benefited the colony in some respects but drew criticism from the Brazilians.

Pombal's centralizing or nationalizing policy impelled him also, first, to deprive the Jesuits in Brazil of their control over the Indian communities and then in 1759 to order the expulsion of the Jesuits from Brazil, as well as from Portugal, and the confiscation of their property. His pretext for this drastic action was the Jesuit resistance to those parts of the Treaty of Madrid of 1750 which dealt with the mission Indians. But the expulsion of the Jesuits benefited the coastal planters of Brazil by removing the benefactors and protectors of the Indians. To prevent this result Pombal issued a royal decree in 1758 abolishing all forms of Indian slavery, a decree which was more honored in the breach than in the observance in Brazil. Perhaps Pombal most aided Brazil by allowing some Brazilians to replace Portuguese officeholders in the colony and thus to acquire experience in office and insights into problems of administration. But this policy was abandoned after his fall from power in 1777.

Pombal's efforts at the consolidation of royal control over Brazil proved immediately beneficial to the colony and perhaps in the long run postponed the independence movement there. After his downfall the Portuguese crown attempted to prohibit manufacturing in Brazil. A decree of 1785 forbade all industrial activity in the colony, since a contrary policy, it declared, would render "the inhabitants totally independent of the metropolis." This and other efforts by the crown to control Brazil from overseas and to exalt the homeland at the expense of the colony were distasteful to some of Portugal's American subjects. The caliber of the Portuguese officials charged with enforcing this control was often far from satisfactory. These officials, complained one of Brazil's best viceroys, the Marquês de Lavradio, "think of nothing further than fulfilling the time for which they have been sent here, in order that they may afterwards claim promotion; and during the time of their residence, their only study is to accumulate all that they can, in order that on their return they may benefit their families." Against such incompetent time servers, who naturally became symbols of royal authority, colonial resentment mounted.

Criollos and Peninsulares

In America the advantages of Spain's imperial controls were almost entirely monopolized by the *peninsulares,* or *godos* (Goths), that is, by the Spaniards from the mother country, called *chapetones* in South America and *gachupines* in New Spain. As the movement of protest against Spain gained momentum one of the principal grievances of the creoles or native white and *mestizo* leaders was their exclusion from high office in the colonies. These white subjects of Spain, born in the New World and already calling themselves American rather than Spanish, felt that their fortunes and potentialities were limited by the more favored European whites. Their own America was being exploited to feed the fortunes of court favorites from abroad. As one of these creoles, Francisco de Terrazas, wrote of "la triste Mejico" (sad Mexico), in a metrical complaint early in the sixteenth century:

> Madrastra nos has sido rigurosa
> y dulce Madre pía a los extraños.
> (To us she has been a harsh and severe stepmother,
> To the *peninsulares* a mild and gentle mother.) [2]

Of the 166 viceroys and 558 captains general, governors, and presidents who held office in Spain's American kingdoms—in all 724—only 18 were creoles. The same exclusion of creoles from the high church offices occurred. According to the Mexican historian, Lucas Alamán, of 706 archbishops and bishops appointed by the crown under the *patronato*, only 105 were creoles. On the eve of the revolutionary outbreak in New Spain all the bishoprics except one were held by Europeans. The Laws of the Indies themselves made no distinction between *peninsulares* and creoles, but in fact officials close to the crown tended to reserve the royal patronage for their friends and for their younger sons. They constituted an official aristocracy from which the creoles were largely excluded. Though they numbered probably not more than one-tenth of the total population of European descent found in America, they were the viceroys and presidents, the members of the *audiencia*, the royal treasurers, chiefs of the army, and ecclesiastical dignitaries.

And yet the creoles were surely not justified in expecting the Spanish crown to appoint them to high administrative position in church and state, any more than George Washington could have expected George III of England to appoint him governor of the royal colony of Virginia. In such a position a creole as an agent of the crown in his own homeland would have labored under many disadvantages from the outset. He could not, for example, observe the aloofness and respect for royal prerogative which were inseparable from his office so long as his domain remained a subordinate part of the realm and subject to the crown. If the crown chose to appoint him to such an office was it not admitting a degree of local self-government which was inconsistent with the maintenance of imperial authority? From the viewpoint of the interests of the crown, the creole's love of the land and his pride in his American birth disqualified him for royal favor under an imperial system. But even the appointment of a few creoles to high offices was not enough to abate the grievance of the creoles, who came to feel that they were entitled to staff all the administrative posts in their own countries. If their ambitions for viceregal posts had been

[2] Francisco de Terrazas, *Poesías,* Edición Antonio Castro Leal, Librería de Porrúa Hnos. y Cía., Mexico, 1941, p. 87.

gratified, however, would not Spain have lost control over her American territories? Would she not have been virtually obliged to acknowledge their independence?

To the political barrier against the creoles was added a social barrier. The jealousy and contempt of the creoles for the *peninsulares* were heightened by the tendency of the latter to form liaisons with creole women which, though they sometimes led to marriage, usually produced a mass of illegitimate offspring who were assigned an inferior position in society. Class cleavages were thus accentuated and class feelings embittered. Especially galling to the creoles was the calm assumption of superiority, the "old-country" pride and superciliousness of the Spaniards of European birth. As early as 1557 the creoles in Chile writhed under the discrimination and contempt of the new governor, Valdivia's successor, García Hurtado de Mendoza, who handed out *encomiendas* lavishly to his peninsular retainers and who insultingly declared that not more than a handful of Chileans knew the identity of their fathers. As the creoles themselves developed a local aristocracy they looked down upon the newcomers from Spain as a *nouveau riche* who deprived them of the social and political influence in their own native lands to which they felt entitled by reason of their intrinsic merit and accumulated wealth. The Americans became convinced that they were being edged out of the benefits of the imperial system.

In addition the creoles were almost entirely excluded from big business in their own countries, for the Spanish commercial houses found it to their interest to be represented by the more intelligent, ambitious, and hard-working peninsular factors. The latter entrenched themselves in the *consulados* or guilds of merchant importers in New Spain and Peru, which in turn served as agents of the organized mercantile communities or *consulados* of Sevilla and Cádiz. Through their virtual monopoly control over the import and export trade of the colonies, they deliberately maintained, in their own interest, an economy of scarcity and high prices for imported goods. These associations, which were at the same time chambers of commerce, admiralty courts, banks, and business corporations, wielded great influence—an influence which was uniformly exerted in behalf of the economic interests of the mother country. In the last decade of the eighteenth century the number of *consulados* in Spanish America was increased from the original two in Mexico City and Lima to ten, new ones being created in Caracas, Guatemala, Buenos Aires, Havana, Cartagena, Santiago, Guadalajara, and Veracruz. Meanwhile the number of peninsular merchants in America had considerably increased, and the source of migration shifted from Estremadura and Andalusía to the northern parts of Spain. These Basque, Catalonian, and Galician newcomers proved to be more vigorous and frugal than their predecessors. Against them and their more enterprising business methods creole resentment mounted. This resentment also appeared in the relations between peninsular and creole clerics.

In 1767 Charles III, one of the "enlightened despots," under pressure from the powerful Duke of Alba, forfeited one of the mainstays of the crown's power in America by ordering the expulsion of the Jesuits and the confiscation of all their accumulated wealth. This he did, as the decree of banishment by the viceroy of Mexico explained, for the purpose "of preserving intact his sovereign prerogatives, and of keeping his loyal and beloved people in subordination, peace, and justice, and for other very grave reasons which he conceals in his royal heart." The mission activity of the Jesuits had weakened in the later seventeenth century but had revived again after the middle of the eighteenth. The Jesuits had acquired enormous landed wealth through donations by the faithful and through the favors of governing officials, and on their estates or "temporalities" they carried on extensive and highly profitable agricultural and industrial operations. By the act of expulsion, which was consonant with the spirit of the Enlightenment, Charles III removed from the colonies, as well as from Spain itself, the chief exponents of scholasticism in education and helped to encourage humane learning. But by this act, also, as Salvador de Madariaga has explained, the king "with his own hands cut the most solid link between his Crown and his subjects overseas." [3]

The members of the Jesuit order, through their missionary labors among the Indians and their work in education, had acquired large influence in the Americas, and the royal order of expulsion, as well as the abrupt methods used in carrying it out, produced great excitement and some resistance, particularly among the Indians and *mestizos* who had been befriended and protected by the Jesuits. As the Jesuits, numbering over 2,200, quietly retired from America under the edict of expulsion their *reducciones* or Indian communities in Paraguay were thrown open to slave raids. Some of the Jesuits, thus driven from Spain and her American kingdoms and full of hate for the Spanish crown, now began to cooperate with England in plans for the destruction of the Spanish Empire, and even after the suppression of the order by the Vatican in 1773 they continued to work against Spain's interests. Their departure from America opened up new opportunities for the remaining religious orders, particularly the Franciscans, who in a burst of missionary activity inspired by Father Junípero Serra founded eighteen missions in Upper California between 1769 and 1804.

The Spanish and the Portuguese who were born in the lands of America had many devious ways of circumventing royal authority. Their great physical distance from the mother country and the very momentum of the natural economy of their lands worked in their favor. Time worked in their favor, too. As their power grew, so grew their numbers. They became contemptuous of the agents of the king and the royal courtiers who surrounded them. Moreover, the intellectual climate both in Europe and in America was becoming hostile to empire. Colonialism or the subjection of one people to another was coming to be considered immoral and contrary to nature. Under these in-

[3] Salvador de Madariaga, *The Fall of the Spanish American Empire,* The Macmillan Company, New York, 1948, p. 282.

fluences the control of Spain and Portugal over their American lands gradually eroded away. The national fervor of the mother countries weakened as they fell increasingly under the cultural influence of France and the Enlightenment.

Suggestive of the reaction of the creoles to the numberless acts of restrictive and punitive legislation by the mother country was their nonchalant attitude toward imprisonment. It carried no stigma. When thrown into prison the creole seldom showed any emotion. He spent his time writing letters, framing appeals, and receiving visitors from morning till evening; when released he accepted his freedom with equanimity, returned the visits which he had received in prison, and resumed without prejudice his customary position in society. This attitude toward judicial punishment has carried over into modern Latin America as a heritage of the passive resistance which the creoles practiced.

Spain's policy toward the Americans under the later Bourbons was a contradictory mixture of enlightenment and repression. Though the Bourbons liberalized the economic system of the Hapsburgs, they enforced it more rigidly than the Hapsburgs had done. By closing the loopholes in the system they antagonized their subjects overseas. As the Bourbons were less nationalistic and less concerned to impose their own standards of morality upon the Americans, they largely abandoned the attempt to exclude foreign, secular, and divisive ideas from the New World. The old Hapsburg conception of Spain's holy mission to carry Christianity to the heathen and to legislate morality was scrapped. Indeed, it may be argued that Spain lost her American empire because under the Bourbons the monarchy ceased to be a religious institution. When Spain altered the character of her imperial system and relaxed the bonds of empire under the influence of the Enlightenment her power in the world collapsed.

In relation to the creoles Spain did not maintain her position in America by military force. Prior to the middle of the eighteenth century Spain's armed forces in America consisted of only a few companies of militia and even fewer regulars. The standing army that was established there after 1768, like the army which the British were maintaining at the same time in their colonies in the north, was established in response to the international situation, namely, the danger of foreign war and aggressions and not for the purpose of keeping down the local populations. In order to enable the towns in America themselves to repel foreign invaders, Charles III even authorized them to organize citizen militias, thus giving the creoles and *mestizos* their first opportunity to serve in the royal armies. Later, when the independence struggle began, the major part of this new army sided with the rebels against Spain, and the military training which they had received proved an invaluable asset to the American cause. Meanwhile, under the operation of the intendant system the *cabildos*, particularly those in the capital cities, were becoming increasingly active in the political and financial affairs of their municipalities.

The political and fiscal changes which the Bourbon court made in the government of the colonies in the late eighteenth century, though they brought tangible benefits to the Americans, were resented because they represented the philosophy of reform from above, did not provide for representation by the creoles in the formulation of imperial policies, and were devised to serve first the interests of the crown and Spain. Similar objections, stemming from the ferment of the Enlightenment, were shaking the contemporary English and French Empires in America. Spain's political system in America eventually failed for the same reasons that those other empires failed. It was worked out primarily in terms of the crown's interests and those interests, as interpreted by the later Bourbons, were allowed to override the new ideas and new demands of their subjects in America in the latter eighteenth and early nineteenth centuries. The Spanish system reflected, as was natural, the environmental limitations of the homeland. Its major defect was that however ideal in conception and however flexible in practice it may have been it was still an imperial system predicated upon a metropolis-colony relationship. This was the heart of the system and it could not be excised while life remained in the body.

Additional Reading

Bernstein, Harry: *Modern and Contemporary Latin America,* J. B. Lippincott, Philadelphia, 1952, chap. 2.

Hamilton, Earl J.: "Monetary Problems in Spain and Spanish America, 1751–1800," *Journal of Economic History,* vol. 4, pp. 21–48, May, 1944.

Juan, Jorge, and Antonio de Ulloa: *Noticias secretas de América,* published originally as two volumes in one, London, 1826; republished by Editorial-América, Madrid, 1918.

————: *A Voyage to South America,* trans. from the Spanish by John Adams, in John Pinkerton (ed.), *A General Collection of the Best and Most Interesting Voyages and Travels,* Longman, Hurst, Rees, and Orme, London, 1808–1814, vol. 14 (1813).

Keen, Benjamin: *Readings in Latin American Civilization: 1492 to the Present,* Houghton Mifflin Company, Boston, 1955, chap. XV.

Loosley, Allyn C.: "The Puerto Bello Fairs," *Hispanic American Historical Review,* vol. 13, pp. 314–335, August, 1933.

McAlister, Lyle N.: *The "Fuero Militar" in New Spain, 1764–1800,* University of Florida Press, Gainesville, Fla., 1957.

Nettels, Curtis, "England and the Spanish American Trade, 1680–1715," *Journal of Modern History,* vol. 3, pp. 1–32, March, 1931.

Ots Capdequí, José María: *Nuevos aspectos del siglo XVIII español en América,* Editorial Centro-Ins. Gráf., Bogotá, 1946.

Smith, R. S.: "The Institution of the Consulado in New Spain," *Hispanic American Historical Review,* vol. 24, pp. 61–83, 1944.

IX

Twilight of Empire

Political liberty was the heritage of Latin America. Popular rights and institutions of municipal and parliamentary government had been established in Spain in the Middle Ages. At a time when these rights and institutions existed nowhere else in Europe, except perhaps in the Italian city-states, they were recognized by the sovereigns of Spain. This tradition of personal liberty and self-government was transplanted to America with the immigrants from the homeland. As embodied in the writings of the great Spanish jurists, Francisco Suárez, Francisco de Vitoria, Juan de Mariana, and other Spanish Catholics it was taught in all the universities of Spanish America. Spain's subjects were deeply imbued with the doctrine that political power could be wrested by the people from a tyrannical ruler. They acted upon this doctrine in the wars of independence in the early nineteenth century. Their purpose was to vindicate liberalism as conceived by the philosophers of the Enlightenment against the authoritarianism of the Bourbons.

Beginnings of Schism

The winning of independence by the American subjects of France, Spain, and Portugal in the Americas between 1791 and 1825 came as the culmination of a slow, long-developing separation between them and their mother countries. It was the product of an estrangement, an incompatibility, that had begun three centuries earlier. In fact the discovery of America by Columbus only accelerated the fragmentation of empire. It encouraged the breakdown of the universalism associated with the medieval Christian church and the Holy Roman Empire. Ironically Columbus's exploit, which was an enterprise of empire, brought about the eventual collapse of empire.

The Hispanic peoples who came to America brought with them a tradition of localism and particularism, which were indigenous in the mother countries. These qualities were intensified in the Americas by geography, race, and international conflict. Consequently a wide disparity between the law of the crown and American practice appeared. As early as 1554 Charles V was informed by one of his advisers that his commanders in the Indies "think only of themselves and their families, and, as they are so far away, they are within a hair's breadth of rebellion." They were already developing an American psychology. From the first founding, the American settlements began to be differentiated from the homelands. The settlers acquired individual personalities and a sense of cleavage from Europe. Their birth into independence was stimulated by their own peculiar environmental conditions, their increasing irritation with certain consequences of the imperial and monarchical tie, and their sharpened questioning of established institutions under the influence of the Enlightenment. Their essential uniqueness was also gradually revealed by their racial difference from the mother country. The Liberator, Simón Bolívar, was able to bring all these factors of separation into focus with extraordinary perception when he wrote of his Spanish American compatriots in his famous Jamaica letter in 1815: "We are neither Indian nor European, but a species midway between the legitimate proprietors of this country and the Spanish usurpers." The American was a new man.

The evolution of imperial government in America paralleled the growth of absolutism in Europe, particularly as it developed under the French and Spanish Bourbons, swallowing up the historic liberties of the settlers in the New World and subjecting them to arbitrary and often avaricious authority. The more royal intervention, the less the Americans prospered and the more resentful they became. The settlers remained on good terms with the mother country as long as they did not have to think about her. Their independence came as the climax of a centuries-long struggle between the centralizing drift of royal policy, based on the assumed needs of the European mother country, and the decentralized requirements of the Americans. It was the result of a spiritual tug of war that began with the first contacts between Europeans and Americans and that was finally won by the Americans. The persistent dualism between Spain as a crown-dominated nation-state and the Spaniards overseas in an evolving American society was finally resolved in favor of the latter. The centripetal forces of union were opposed by the centrifugal influences generated in America. Or expressed differently, the impulses which kept the Americans attached to their European mother countries were overwhelmed finally by the impulses radiating from their New World environment. The centralization against which they rebelled was European imperialism. They determined to find meaning now in their own experience, in the realities of their own lands.

What the creoles opposed was not so much Spain's abusive exercise of power over them as the possibility of its exercise. They probably lived better than the bulk of the Spanish people, excepting of course the grandees and others of the highest class. In the disintegration of the Spanish monarchy, which was brought about by Napoleon Bonaparte, the Americans found both pretext and justification for rebellion. The wars of independence were the work of active minorities—of men who had imbibed the revolutionary ideas of the Enlightenment, or who had envisaged enlarged possibilities for Latin American trade with independence, or who ambitiously hoped to carve out conspicuous careers for themselves in the liberated nations of America. The leaders of the revolutionary movements were men who had an interest, a stake in independence.

The masses who followed their leadership only gradually drifted into independence. From time to time they were galvanized into spasmodic activity by a revolutionary group or by a few dynamic leaders, including notably Simón Bolívar, José de San Martín, Antonio José Sucre, José Antonio Páez, Miguel Hidalgo y Costilla, and José María Morelos, who at certain moments were capable of unifying the forces opposed to Spain and giving them a common patriotic impulse. By the tireless efforts of these *caudillos* the will to independence in Spanish America was cultivated and nurtured into an irresistible separatist force. The Masonic connections of many of these leaders of the wars of secession may have helped to give some of the movements an anticlerical bias. By reason of the substantial identification of church and state, the anti-Hispanism that culminated in the revolutionary movements almost necessarily included a strong element of anticlericalism.

In these movements the creoles were the moving forces, recruiting their battalions largely from the *mestizos*. The wars of independence in Spanish America were fought by troops such as the following cavalry unit in Bolívar's northern army, as described by a contemporary observer:

> As for the troops themselves, they were from 13 to 36 or 40 years of age—black, brown, sallow complexion, according to the cast of their parents. The adults wore large mustachios, and short hair, either wooly or black, according to the climate or descent. They had a ferocious savage look.... Mounted on miserable, half-starved, jaded beasts, whether horse or mule, some without trousers, small clothes, or any covering except a bandage of blue cloth or cotton around their loins...; others with trousers, but without stockings, boots or shoes...; and some wearing a kind of sandal made of hide, with the hairy side outward.... A blanket of about a yard square, with a hole, or rather a slit, cut in the center, through which the wearer thrusts his head, falls on each side of his shoulders, thus covering his body, and leaving his bare arms at perfect liberty to manage his horse or mule, and lance.[1]

The revolutionary leaders also sought to win the support of the great mass of the Indian population and now for the first time began to recognize them as sharers in the American tradition, glorifying their ancient empires and berating the Spaniards for their past cruelties to them. Mariano Moreno, for example, passionately championed the Indian victims of the *mita* against the mineowners in Upper Peru. Several other leaders of the revolutionary movement were influenced by the intense concern of the philosophers of the Enlightenment to improve the condition of the indigenous American population. One of the earliest products of the romantic movement in Brazil was the long poem "O Uruguai," published by José Basílio da Gama in 1769 and idealizing the Indian. But in general the struggle for power between the creoles and the *peninsulares* did not concern the Indians. They, for the most part,

---

[1] G[ustavus] Hippisley, *A Narrative of the Expedition to the Rivers Orinoco and Apuré, in South America; which Sailed from England in November 1817, and Joined the Patriotic Forces in Venezuela and Caraccas,* John Murray, London, 1819, pp. 414–415. Spelling modernized.

except in Mexico, remained inert and indifferent, waiting to see on whose banners victory would finally rest and to which conqueror they should yield their allegiance.

The empires of France, Spain, and Portugal in America were, in a broad sense, casualties of the Enlightenment and the revolutionary spirit that it engendered and that culminated in the American War for Independence, the French Revolution, and finally the revolutionary upheavals in Latin America. In the eighteenth century the Americans swung into the current of the Enlightenment and by the end of the century were fully caught up in the revolutionary ideology of their day. Under the new learning of the Enlightenment, they challenged the dogmatism, the scholasticism, and finally even the imperialism of the past. Their wits were sharpened for political and even military encounter by the philosophic and theological dialectic which was encouraged by the universities from Mexico City in the north to Córdoba in the south. The prevalent rationalism of the age led to attacks upon authority and stimulated the deep-seated individualism of the Americans. The wars for independence came as the culmination of the cleavage between Europe and America that began in the sixteenth century. Intellectual rejection preceded political revolt, until finally almost all Latin America was suddenly swept into the current of the modern revolutionary movement. The revolution against European paternalism began long before a single army was raised or a single musket fired. Thereafter it had only to receive political recognition. The intellectual protest was only a tool utilized to accomplish an end considered desirable. The end that was initially sought by many of the revolutionary leaders was only separation from Spain under the monarchy and fuller recognition of local autonomy within the empire. This led eventually to a demand for complete independence to be won only by hard fighting.

The Enlightenment in Hispanic America

Revolutionary discontent, which stirred the American colonies of Britain to independence in 1775–1783 and which split France into civil war after 1789, had a contagious effect in Latin America. The liberal ideas generated by the United States in its Declaration of Independence, its Articles of Confederation, and its Constitution of 1789 called up sentiments and traditions which were deeply rooted in the minds of Latin Americans. These documents and the French Declaration of the Rights of Man circulated widely in St. Domingue and in certain sections of New Granada, Venezuela, and La Plata and inspired the ambitious creoles with dreams of independence. The native American upper classes, long resentful of the domination of peninsular officials, were ready and in some cases eager to take advantage of the deterioration of the power position of their mother countries to raise the standard of revolt against them.

In the movement which the creoles launched against Spain they were strongly influenced by the writings of the French Encyclopedists and rationalists, in particular, Montesquieu's *Spirit of the Laws,* Voltaire's essays, Diderot's *Encyclopedia,* and Rousseau's *Social Contract.* They were also impressed by Adam Smith's *Wealth of Nations,* which was first published in 1776 and which advocated the removal of official restraints upon international trade. Smith's work was translated into Spanish in 1794. Not only was it given wide currency in the colonies, particularly by the Peruvian scholar and scientist, José Hipólito Unánue, but it also circulated in Spain, where it stimulated liberal thought. As the Spanish Americans read and discussed the revolutionary ideas of their day they were encouraged by the intellectual renaissance which was occurring in Spain itself. Besides, they were emboldened by the apparent sanction which England, France, the Netherlands, and even Spain gave to revolution by recognizing the independence of the revolted North American colonies of Britain between 1778 and 1785. While they were themselves resisting the centralizing policies of the crown they saw their mother country encourage the decentralization of the British Empire—a decentralization which was achieved by force.

From the sixteenth century onward the Americans received large numbers of books from abroad and closely followed the changing currents of European ideas. During the latter part of the eighteenth century the gap between intellectual movements in Europe and in America dwindled to the time required for an ocean passage. As the Inquisition became moribund, the educational institutions in Spanish America became increasingly secularized. The ideas and writings of the revolutionaries in the British colonies and in France were brought to America by creoles who traveled abroad. One of these was José Antonio Rojas, who traveled through Europe as far as Russia gathering up books which he sent back to his homeland Chile. Thus the epoch-making books of Locke, Raynal, Voltaire, Montesquieu, and Rousseau found their way into many private libraries—especially those of ecclesiastics. Indeed Rousseau's works were principally circulated in both Spain and America in the Spanish edition of the *Journal de Trévoux,* a periodical published by the French Jesuits. In the literature of the Enlightenment, Spain's treatment of the American natives was represented as scandalously abusive, as evidenced, for example, in the Abbe Guillaume Raynal's phenomenally popular *Philosophical and Political History of the Indies,* which went through fifty-four editions in thirty years, and the continued popularity of Las Casas' *Brief Relation of the Destruction of the Indies,* which Raynal sometimes simply parroted. Works such as these, though they quite unfairly condemned Spain, crystallized creole resistance to colonialism.

The ideas of individual freedom and political independence to which the Enlightenment gave winged expression stimulated an intellectual awakening which centered in New Spain, Peru, and New Granada. In their capitals literary societies were formed, largely composed of creoles, and literary journals were founded to disseminate new and often republican ideas. Talk of natural rights and of the imprescriptible duty of a colony to throw off the yoke of an unfeeling mother country filled the air. Freemasons cooperated with Jacobin societies in secretly encouraging revolutionary action against His Catholic Majesty.

Preliminary Rebellions

The wars of independence in Spanish America were foreshadowed by several smaller insurrectionary movements, some of which were fomented by creoles and inspired by economic grievances. Discontent with Spanish rule appeared in many places during the eighteenth century. An uprising in isolated Paraguay resulted in the assertion of local independence for four years against the authority of the viceroy in Lima. The creoles in that remote settlement were habitually critical of the protective role which the Jesuits assumed over the Indians whom they wanted to use as laborers on their plantations. In 1721 a governor, Diego de los Reyes, who was sympathetic with the Jesuits was deposed, and the Paraguayans demanded some voice in the choice of the officials who would rule over them. Their leader, José de Antequera y Castro, even spoke in favor of the "sovereignty of the people." They had to yield to the authority of the viceroy in 1725, but their resentment flamed up again in 1730 in another four-year uprising, led by Fernando de Mompó. He asserted the right of the people to resist the authority of the king; and his followers, who called themselves *comuneros* or the popular party, adopted republican forms and set up a *junta* which governed the capital, Asunción, until it was finally crushed in 1735. This seems to have been a popular resistance movement directed against both the crown and the Jesuits but perhaps not having independence as its explicit object.

At about the same time, 1730, several thousand *mestizos* at Cochabamba in Upper Peru (Bolivia) launched a protest movement against excessive local taxation as a result of which they gained the right to elect as *alcaldes* and *corregidores* some of their own number to the exclusion of *peninsulares*. Whether the imperial collections were, in fact, excessive or not, the Americans became convinced that they were so and became increasingly restive under them. To them the taxes imposed on raw materials and manufactured articles in particular seemed burdensome and unjustified. A creole revolt broke out in Venezuela in 1749, led by Juan Francisco de León, against the most important and successful of the commercial companies, the Caracas Company, which was dominated by unpopular Basques and was closely allied with the crown. The *alcabala* or sales tax was the principal grievance both of a creole uprising in Quito in 1765, which resulted in some 400 casualties, and of an uprising in Santiago de Chile in 1776, which forced the captain general of Chile to call a *cabildo abierto* or town meeting of prominent citizens and to grant concessions to the rebels.

An uprising more akin to a native Indianist movement against Spanish rule broke out in November, 1780, when one of Tupac Amarú's descendants, José Gabriel Condorcanqui, the Marquis of Oropesa, calling himself Tupac Amarú II, organized a rebellion in Peru against the Spanish authorities. His people, including children only eight and ten years old, were being required to work as long as sixteen hours daily in the textile mills. They worked in locked rooms in the *obrajes* or cloth factories (sweatshops), were paid pitifully low wages, and if they failed to complete their tasks were brutally beaten. Tupac Amarú protested against the treatment of the Indians in the mines, in the *obrajes,* and on the farms; he asked that they be put under the jurisdiction of their own *alcaldes* rather than the hated *corregidores;* and he insisted that the king's order, as he understood it, abolishing the *corregidor* system be put into effect. But he and his Indian followers were defeated by the viceroy's forces, and he was captured in the following year. As punishment, his tongue was cut out, and he was tied to four horses and torn into four parts in a public execution in the plaza at Cuzco. The justification for his execution was found in the fact that he headed a revolutionary movement dangerous to Spanish power and so was guilty of treason. But after his execution many of the reforms which he had demanded were granted.

In the same year an even more serious outbreak took place in certain towns of the viceroyalty of New Granada, provoked by the new taxes which Spain levied upon all her American subjects to support her war alliance of 1779 with France. Every American was required to contribute from one to two *pesos* for the support of the war, and the tobacco and alcohol excises were increased. A motley army of protest numbering between 30,000 and 40,000 gathered in Socorro, elected a central directing committee or *común,* and marched against Bogotá under the cry "Long live the King and down with bad government!" They demanded that the new taxes be abandoned, that the annual tribute collected from the Indians and the *alcabala* or sales tax be reduced, that the tobacco monopoly be abolished, and that the creoles be recognized as entitled to governmental positions, for, they declared, the peninsular officials "believe that they are the masters and that all Americans of any kind are their inferiors and servants." The rebels proved strong enough to defeat the royal troops, and they set up a provisional government which dispatched commissioners to England to obtain a loan. The archbishop of Bogotá then came forward with an offer of mediation which resulted in the abolition of the tobacco tax, the reduction of other taxes, and the recognition of the right of creoles to be appointed to certain offices. The viceroy, however, subsequently repudiated this settlement, known as the Pact of Zipaquirá, on the ground that it had been made under duress. The *mestizo* peasant leader of the uprising, José Antonio Galán, was then executed and the others were dispersed.

The Spanish authorities perhaps experienced the greatest difficulty in stamping out unwanted ideas in New Granada, which, facing the ocean highways to Europe, maintained close contacts with the outside world. In New Granada the developments in the new republic of the United States and the revolutionary uprisings in Europe were enthusiastically approved by the radical intellectuals. Antonio Nariño, a wealthy creole who had been a member of the *cabildo,* published and circulated in 1794 a Spanish translation of the French Declaration of the Rights of Man which had been adopted by the French National Assembly in 1789. For this publishing effort he was found guilty of treason by the *audiencia* and was banished to Africa. The *audiencia,* to show their disapproval of the document and being unable to find a Spanish translation, then burned the French original.

Probably none of the uprisings mentioned above had independence from Spain as an objective. They were simply protest movements against certain officials or royal orders. Their object was to secure the removal of hated officials or the redress of grievances, particularly economic grievances. Their principal result was to keep alive a mood of rebelliousness among the Americans which would burst forth in full force in the early part of the nineteenth century.

This mood was accentuated by the change in Spain's imperial policy which followed the execution of Louis XVI in 1793. This execution brought the Enlightenment to an end. In the lurid light of the horrifying French Terror, Spain's policy hardened into opposition to the consequences of the Enlightenment in America. The fear induced by the excesses of the French Revolution severely constricted Spain's previous liberalism. After the downfall of the Bourbons in France the crown in Spain imposed a more rigid censorship upon its subjects in an attempt to keep out ideas which challenged the rights of the crown and the laws of the empire and which, if not suppressed, might even threaten the continuance of the Bourbon throne in Spain.

Independence of Haiti

The influence in Latin America of the revolutionary ideas which filled the very air in the last quarter of the eighteenth century was nowhere better or earlier displayed than in the French colony of St. Domingue. This colony, occupying the old Spanish island of Española, fell to France in the Treaty of Ryswick in 1697 and the Treaty of Basle in 1795 and became France's richest overseas possession. It was overwhelmingly populated by Negro slaves, most of them of recent African origin, kept in rigid subjection by the small minority of free mulattoes and wealthy whites who formed the elite. Of its total population of about 536,000, some 480,000 were slaves. The colony was governed by a governor general, who enjoyed virtually absolute powers, and by an intendant, who had complete control over finance. The colonial assembly represented only the white elite; even freed Negroes were denied the privilege of holding public office and of practicing the professions. This white elite welcomed the outbreak of the French Revolution as offering them an opportunity to shake off control from Paris. But they could not manage their own revolution and soon saw it pass into the hands, first, of the mulattoes, and then of the blacks.

The revolutionary impulse was brought from France to St. Domingue by a freedman, Vincent Ogé. For his armed rebellion there against the whites he was sentenced to be broken on the wheel. His execution in 1791 only encouraged new outbreaks. The black masses found a champion in a gifted exslave François Dominique Toussaint, later called L'Ouverture, who was steeped in French revolutionary ideas. Under his leadership they gained their freedom both from their white masters and from France in an orgy of destruction. In their drive for independence from France they received support from some of the most influential persons in the colony who, despite the prospect of black supremacy, expected independence to revive for them the great commercial advantages which they had derived during the War of the American Revolution from their lucrative trade with neutral nations. Wrote one of his white associates in government in 1799:

> Toussaint is the real leader of the Negroes, and the white inhabitants who have become reconciled regard him as a friend. . . . No personal vanity ever separates Toussaint from anyone else on the island. His whole mode of living is republican simplicity. . . . He is an excellent diplomat in all that concerns the island, but he is naive and trusting in all that concerns himself personally. The usual form of address the Negroes use is "Father."

By 1801 Toussaint had extended his control over the entire island. Assisted by epidemics of yellow fever, his armies were able to beat off the attempts of Napoleon Bonaparte's brother-in-law, Gen. Victor-Emmanuel Leclerc, to restore them both to bondage and to France in 1802–1803. The independence of this first of the free Latin American nations was then proclaimed by the leader of the army on January 1, 1804, under the name of Haiti with the illiterate commander in chief of the army, Jean Jacques Dessalines, as governor general for life. "I have saved my country," Dessalines vaingloriously proclaimed to his people. "I have avenged America. . . . Never again shall a colonist, or a European, set his foot upon this territory with the title of master or proprietor." Toussaint had been captured by Leclerc through a ruse in 1802 and had died a prisoner in France in the following year. Haiti's struggle for freedom, thus finally succeeding, had been persistently pressed successively against the French monarchy of Louis XVI, the French Republic, the government of the Directory, the Consulate, and finally the armies of the Emperor Napoleon. Haiti became the first independent Negro nation in the world and when it declared itself a republic in 1806 it became the first republic to be founded in the Western Hemisphere after the United States. The new nation included only the western portion of the island, the eastern portion remaining under the control of French and Spanish armies.

Precursors of Spanish American Independence

Except in Haiti the example of the French Revolution had little direct revolutionary effect upon America. The creoles in Spanish America, Catholic and monarchical in outlook, generally were repelled by the antireligious and antimonarchical character of the popular upheaval in France. They were finally impelled to revolution not in resistance to the old Catholic monarchical order but in defense of it. Attesting the continuing widespread loyalty to the crown, the early resistance movements were organized under the slogan "Long live the King and death to bad government." The local self-made, white or nearly white creole aristocracy, proudly calling themselves Americans and resentful of Spain's restrictions upon their political activity, opposed the peninsular aristocracy, which derived its power from the court in Madrid. From an economic standpoint they were jealous of the peninsular business interests, which profited over them only by reason of Spain's imperial system.

From the beginning a few creole leaders audaciously conceived of outright independence from Spain as the ultimate objective. The true precursor of the independence movement in Spanish America was Francisco de Miranda. A native of Caracas, this impetuous would-be liberator was born in 1756. While fighting with the Spanish in the War of the American Revolution he resolved to launch a similar revolutionary movement in his own country. The independence of England's colonies in North America, he later wrote, "was bound to be in the future the infallible preliminary of ours." After the end of the war for North American independence he spent much time in European capitals and in the United States agitating and seeking aid for the cause of Latin American independence. In England he failed to secure Pitt's backing for a filibustering expedition under his leadership in 1798 only because of a change in European conditions. "That man," declared Napoleon to a friend after talking with Miranda, "has a sacred fire in his soul." Finally selecting the United States as his base of operations this ambitious revolutionary sailed from New York in 1806 on board the *Leander* at the head of an expedition against Venezuela.

Miranda, convinced of the blessing of destiny on his expedition, was thus described by one of approximately two hundred enthusiasts from the United States who sailed with him on the *Leander:*

His imagination and feelings were an overmatch for his judgment. He is more rash and presumptuous in projects, than dexterous in extracting himself from difficulties.... In the contour of his visage you plainly perceive an expression of pertinaciousness and suspicion. Upon the whole, without saying he is an elegant, we may pronounce him a handsome man....

He used his mental resources and colloquial powers with great address to recommend himself to his followers. He assumed the manners of a father and instructor to the young men. He spoke of the prospect of success, and of the preparations made for him with great confidence. The glory and advantages of the enterprise were described in glowing colours. At another time he detailed his travels, his sufferings and escapes in a manner to interest both their admiration and sympathy. He appeared the master of languages, of science and literature. In his conversations he carried his hearers to the scenes of great actions and introduced them to the distinguished characters of every age. He took excursions to Troy, Babylon, Jerusalem, Rome, Athens and Syracuse.... After all, this man of renown, I fear, must be considered as having more learning than wisdom; more theoretical knowledge than practical talent; too sanguine and too opinionated to distinguish between the vigour of enterprise and the hardiness of infatuation.[2]

When this dramatist of revolution landed on the Spanish Main with his party of filibusters he was soon driven off by a Spanish force. His expedition was then convoyed by Adm. Lord Thomas Alexander Cochrane to the neighborhood of Coro where Miranda spent his time in vigorous revolutionary propaganda, but to no avail. The Venezuelans were not yet sufficiently aroused to take revolutionary action against Spain. Furthermore, they were suspicious of Miranda's reliance upon foreign support in his campaign for independence, fearing that the result would be only a change of masters. Independence when it came would have to be locally inspired. The further development of events in Europe and the inspiriting efforts of Bolívar would be required to stimulate them to action.

After the British navy under Lord Nelson gained command of the sea at Trafalgar in 1805 England could more effectively work toward her objective of liquidating Spain's empire in America and conquering new markets and sources of supply there for her expanding factory system. In the following year a British filibustering expedition made a landing in the viceroyalty of Buenos Aires, which, if successful, might have resulted in the establishment of a Latin American Canada. It was a by-product of the Dutch-British struggle for the Cape of Good Hope, which the British captured in 1806 under the leadership of Sir Home Popham and Gen. William Carr Beresford. Popham had been in close relations with Miranda and had become intrigued by the possibilities of South American independence. Whether he received orders or not from his government to attack Buenos Aires is uncertain. But in 1806 he and Beresford sailed from the Cape of Good Hope with a fleet of about twelve vessels and 1,200 men bound for the estuary of the La Plata. As they entered Buenos Aires on June 27 they encountered only token resistance and the cowardly viceroy, the Marqués de Sobremonte, fled into the interior. The British remained in possession of the city for over six weeks, endeavoring in every possible way to conciliate its more than 55,000 residents. One of General Beresford's first acts was to issue a proclamation guaranteeing freedom of property and religion and reducing the tariff. For the first time the merchants of the port were able to enjoy legal trade with the British. But these acts failed to win the allegiance of the *Platenses*, whose resentment against foreign

---

[2] [James Biggs], *The History of Don Francisco de Miranda's Attempt to Effect a Revolution in South America*, 2d ed., Edward Oliver, Boston, Mass., 1810, pp. 288–291.

intervention mounted. The resistance was organized by a Frenchman who was serving in the Spanish army, Jacques or Santiago Liniers. Aided by a force of fighting men who sailed from Colonia across the estuary to Buenos Aires he descended upon the British and with the support of angry creoles fighting from their housetops and in the streets forced the British to surrender. In an incident probably unique in the annals of the British navy one of the British warships, stranded in the estuary by a sudden drop in the water level, was obliged to surrender to a force of cavalrymen who splashed out from shore to capture it!

The triumphant *porteños,* or residents of the port of Buenos Aires, now met in *cabildo abierto* and chose Liniers as deputy to the absent viceroy and as commander in chief of the troops. These troops, organized into five battalions, were to play a major role in the later revolution against Spanish authority. A later *cabildo abierto,* meeting in February, 1807, transformed itself into a war council or *junta de guerra* and ordered the suspension and imprisonment of the viceroy. When the British occupied Montevideo and from that port attempted a second descent on Buenos Aires in June, 1807, under Lieut.- Gen. John Whitelocke, they were again driven out, with heavy losses. A new national spirit now appeared among the creoles in Buenos Aires, for they had twice delivered themselves from a foreign enemy by their own efforts. They had flexed their muscles for future revolutionary combat. After the first attack they had appealed to Spain for help but had been told to rely upon their own resources. Their contempt for their royal masters was increased by this refusal of cooperation. If the local forces could drive off the British why could they not also drive out the Spanish? Why could they not then open up their port to trade with all nations?

Napoleon Bonaparte was the unwitting *deus ex machina* of Latin American independence. In carrying out his continental system, which required the economic self-sufficiency of the continent under his sway, he found it necessary to come to terms with the Bourbon king of Spain, the dull-witted Charles IV. But the real ruler of Spain was Manuel de Godoy, the so-called Prince of the Peace and the lover of the queen. With him Napoleon concluded an agreement at Fontainebleau on October 27, 1807, designed to bring Portugal into the continental system. By this treaty Portugal was to be divided into three parts, one small part going to the King of Etruria, another to Godoy himself, with the title of King of the Algarves, and the third to be sequestrated by France until the end of the war. But when news of this arrangement reached Spain it proved so unpopular that riots against Godoy broke out at Aranjuez in March, 1808, and Godoy himself was captured. The weak Charles IV, lacking patriotic sentiments and fearing that in the outbursts against Godoy even his own son Ferdinand might have him assassinated, finally abdicated in favor of Ferdinand. He and Ferdinand were then inveigled to Bayonne by Napoleon where both of them renounced their claims to the throne in favor of Napoleon's brother Joseph Bonaparte.

In Spain a new national spirit began to emerge, giving the signal for the rise of an independence movement in America. Preparations were immediately made to repel the French interloper. Patriotic *juntas* or committees sprang up even before Joseph arrived. When he finally entered Spain in July, 1808, he was driven out. By December the national Spanish resistance movement was organized by the establishment of a central governing *junta* (*Suprema Junta Central Gubernativa*) in Sevilla which represented the local patriotic *juntas* and was loyal to Ferdinand. As the imperialistic ambitions and the continental system of the Emperor of the French thus met their first serious challenge he countered by pouring his armies into Spain. The Spanish governing *junta* thereupon retired to Cádiz, leaving Madrid and Sevilla in the possession of the French forces of occupation. Two governments, one acting in the name of Ferdinand, the other in the name of Joseph Bonaparte, thus competed for the allegiance of the Spanish people.

News of these turbulent events in Spain produced confusion in Spain's colonies. With the overthrow of Charles IV the American kingdoms of Spain became kingdoms without a king. The empire was decapitated and its power in America devolved upon the four viceroyalties. Agents from Napoleon's government immediately arrived demanding recognition. Soon afterward envoys of the Spanish revolutionary *juntas* came demanding not only recognition but also aid in throwing out the French invaders. When Napoleon's emissary arrived in Caracas announcing the accession of Joseph Bonaparte to the Spanish throne and bringing orders from the French Emperor to the captain general, thousands of Venezuelans gathered up their arms, surrounded the residence of the captain general, and demanded the proclamation of Ferdinand VII as their king. The French representative had to be spirited out of the town by an armed guard for his own safety.

In general throughout the colonies the *peninsulares* and the creoles united in their resistance to the French envoys, but they could not agree on the course to be followed in the future. The *peninsulares* desired to restore the *status quo* as it had existed under Charles IV from which they had profited so much. But the creoles sought to take advantage of the altered state of affairs to advance their own interests and to strike for more local self-government. Many of them had become wealthy from the new trade opportunities opened up by the European wars and had thus acquired the means of resisting Spain's imperial claims upon them. To bolster their position they argued that with the deposition of the sovereign, Ferdinand VII, the imperial tie, which under the Hapsburgs had been a personal union between the American jurisdictions and the crown, had been broken and sovereignty had therefore reverted to the people. This argument, very similar to the natural rights doctrine of England's former colonists in North America, was advanced by the Buenos Aires pamphleteer Mariano Moreno anonymously in his famous *Representación de los hacendados* in September, 1809, prepared at the request of the *consulado* or trade association of the port. When the sovereign disappeared, Moreno argued, the people had a right to legislate for themselves. So effective was this argument, combined with the pressure of the *consulado,* representing the diverse agricultural exporting interests of the viceroyalty, that the viceroy, Baltasar Hidalgo de Cisneros, was constrained to open the port to English trade.

Amidst the confusion that ensued in the colonies after the collapse of the Bourbon monarchy two early and abortive outbreaks occurred—one in Quito, the other in Upper Peru or Charcas, which was a part of the viceroyalty of the Río de la Plata. In Quito on August 10, 1809, was proclaimed the first *grito* of independence in Spanish America. The revolutionists there, led by Selva Alegre, deposed the president, Ruiz de Castilla, set up an independent *junta,* raised troops, and issued proclamations, couched in the terms of the French Declaration of the Rights of Man, to the other colonies asking for their recognition and support. But this revolutionary movement was soon overthrown in August and September, 1809, by the viceroys of adjoining Peru and New Granada.

Jealousies between the *audiencia* and the president formed the background of the outbreak in Upper Peru centering in Chuquisaca and eventually spreading to La Paz. They were stimulated by the intrigues which were set in motion there by Ferdinand's sister Carlota Joaquina, who claimed his royal rights while he was in exile. Amidst these jealousies and intrigues the *audiencia* of Upper Peru deposed the president, who was favorable to Carlota's intrigues and then was itself overthrown by creoles in May, 1809. In an uprising in La Paz two months later, the victorious creoles set up an independent government and began to raise an army to oppose the Spanish authorities. But Upper Peru, like Quito, lay between two viceroyalties, those of Buenos Aires and Peru, and the leaders of the rebellion in La Paz were marked for destruction. An armed force was dispatched against them by Viceroy Cisneros of Buenos Aires which was to join a force sent by the viceroy at Lima, José de Abascal. The latter under Gen. José Manuel de Goyeneche, a ferociously loyal creole, arriving before the force from Buenos Aires, encountered stout resistance at La Paz but finally took the city by storm and subjected it to savage punishment, pursuing the leaders into the country round about. The revolution was thus stamped out. It failed largely because of the isolation of Upper Peru and because public opinion had not yet been sufficiently stimulated to revolutionary effort. Indeed Upper Peru was to be the last of the Spanish American colonies in South America to gain its independence.

Meanwhile Napoleon's armies were overrunning Spain, the Spanish nationalist movement was temporarily crushed, and only the *junta,* now located at Cádiz, remained of the authority of Ferdinand. Practically every vestige of a national Spanish government disappeared. In this dire situation the *junta* placed such powers as it had in the hands of a regency, which now revived the Cortes, or parliament, that had fallen into abeyance under the Bourbons. Included for the first time in the new Cortes, which met at Cádiz in 1811, were a few representatives from Spanish America, but too few to satisfy the creoles there, too few indeed to prevent their grievances from being disregarded. The Cortes, for instance, rejected their demand for representation of the American dominions in the Cortes on a basis of population and hedged on their demands that most of the restraints upon American trade should be abolished, that monopolies should be suppressed, and that at least half the royal offices in America should be assigned to creoles.

What was more serious, both the *Junta Central* in Cádiz and the Cortes denied the right of the Americans, in the absence of the king, to set up governments of their own, thus rejecting the doctrine of the residual sovereignty of the people. But to counter the revolutionary impulses in America and to strengthen the unity of the empire before Napoleon's onrushing armies, the *junta* did abandon the Bourbon philosophy that the American territories were merely the private property of the crown and agreed to treat them as incorporated parts of the empire. They insisted, however, that the absence of the king made no difference in the status of the overseas possessions, which still remained "an essential and integral part of the Spanish monarchy," as the Cádiz *junta* declared in 1809. Even the Spanish liberals failed to comprehend Spain's problem in America. They seemed bent upon smothering the creoles in the imperial embrace and snuffing out their aspirations for a larger measure of freedom within the empire. They sought to reimpose the repressive regime of the Bourbons before the Americans made the first overt moves for secession from the empire. They treated them like orphans of empire and drove some of Spain's most loyal defenders in America to accept the cause of independence. Even as late as 1810 probably most of the creoles in Spanish America were disinclined toward a complete rupture with the mother country. They were opposed to what they regarded as Spain's unenlightened government and its commercial system, which had once more become restrictive, but if they had been granted the liberties within these areas to which they considered themselves entitled they might have been content to remain within the empire. They did not make the decision for independence until the Spanish Empire itself ceased to exist. With its disappearance, a struggle for power began between the viceroys who were the legitimate successors to imperial authority in America and the creoles. As the viceroys demonstrated their inability to maintain and exercise the power of Spain a process of fission began which opened the way for the rise of local leaders of independence.

Additional Reading

Fisher, Lillian Estelle: *Champion of Reform: Manuel Abad y Queipo,* Library Publishers, New York, 1955.

Keen, Benjamin: *Readings in Latin American Civilization: 1492 to the Present,* Houghton Mifflin Company, Boston, 1955, chaps. XVII, XXI.

Korngold, Ralph: *Citizen Toussaint,* Little, Brown & Company, Boston, 1944.

Lanning, John Tate: *The Eighteenth-century Enlightenment in the University of San*

Carlos de Guatemala, Cornell University Press, Ithaca, N.Y., 1956. Interaction between the European Enlightenment and a colonial university in America.

Lynch, John: *Spanish Colonial Administration, 1782–1810: The Intendant System in the Viceroyalty of the Río de la Plata,* University of London, Athlone Press, London, 1958.

Madariaga, Salvador de: *The Fall of the Spanish American Empire,* The Macmillan Company, New York, 1948. A provocative treatment rich in generalization and strongly Hispanic in point of view.

Marchant, Alexander: "Tiradentes in the Conspiracy of Minas," *Hispanic American Historical Review,* vol. 21, pp. 239–257, 1941.

Robertson, William S.: *Iturbide of Mexico,* Duke University Press, Durham, N.C., 1952.

————: *The Life of Miranda* (2 vols.), University of North Carolina Press, Chapel Hill, N.C., 1924.

Rodman, Selden: *Haiti: the Black Republic,* Devin-Adair Co., New York, 1954.

Whitaker, Arthur P. (ed.): *The Western Hemisphere Idea: Its Rise and Decline,* Cornell University Press, Ithaca, N.Y., 1954.

————: *Latin America and the Enlightenment,* Appleton-Century-Crofts, Inc., New York, 1942. A series of stimulating essays.

X

The Winning of Independence

The wars for the independence of Spanish America, the Liberator, Simón Bolívar, later explained, were due to "the Laws of the Indies, the rule of the old executives, the influence of religion and of foreign domination, . . . the ferocity of our enemies and our national temperament." As in the case of Haiti, these wars, extending from 1808 through 1825, were civil wars. At the beginning the common objective of the resistance leaders was a larger measure of autonomy within the Spanish Empire. Not until the long-developing divergencies between the mother country and the Americans were exposed in the fall of the Spanish monarchy and not until the smoldering disaffection had been given an emotional character by skilled propagandists, such as Antonio Nariño, Mariano Moreno, and Bolívar, did the open break come. These leaders had to overcome not only the apathy of their compatriots toward revolutionary change but also their genuine attachment to the rule of Spain, whose traditions had fixed themselves deeply upon the American spirit and ways of living.

The revolutionary *juntas* were originally formed for a defensive purpose —to resist the pretensions of Napoleon's puppet government in Spain. But though they professed to desire the restoration of Ferdinand's authority, many of their actions pointed toward independence. They became convinced that Spain's imperial policy, whether carried out by king or Cortes, was invariably formulated in such a way as to make the crown, the crown's agents, and the mother country the principal beneficiaries. Bolívar even complained, with the perfervid exaggeration of a revolutionary, that Spain's American subjects were "forbidden to grow European crops, or to store products which are royal monopolies, or to establish factories of a type the Peninsula itself does not possess." Spain's imperial system seemed to them to be incorrigibly doctrinaire and anachronistic. Into the movement for secession from Spain were poured all the memories of previous independent action—of former uprisings against the king and his viceroys, of acts of resistance to foreign influences, of every conspiracy and movement which tended to give the Americans a common and a unique experience. The separatist tendencies of three centuries of history were now summoned to create and justify a mood of rebellion.

All the Spanish dominions in America except Guatemala and Peru revolted almost simultaneously. Sometimes the revolts started in the provinces, but usually they began as urban movements fanning out into the countryside, and their success usually depended upon the character of the creole leadership in the cities and the support which they received from the rural districts. As the reins of authority over America fell from the hands of the Spanish monarch, the *cabildos* in the cities of Spanish America picked them up. They assumed and exercised the sovereignty that the king abandoned. It was in the towns that the creoles were made most aware of the political, economic, and social pressures of Spain's imperial system and saw most vividly the flaunting corruption of crown officials. When popular opinion in the towns crystallized in favor of resistance it usually was expressed in the *cabildo,* which provided a forum for the expression of popular views and reached decisions by vote of the whole body. In the mounting protest against imperial restraints the *cabildo* of the principal city often took the lead, now resuming the role which it had played in earlier times as a spokesman for an entire province. These *cabildos* stood forth as the representatives of the local urban oligarchies, mostly creole, against the crown and its officials. From them emerged the revolutionary *juntas.*

Beginnings of Resistance in South America

At Buenos Aires the opponents of Spanish rule resisted the viceroy Cisneros, who took over authority from Liniers in June, 1809, from the moment of his arrival. They secretly plotted against him and shrewdly contrived to gain the support of several of the best regiments in Buenos Aires, who, when the crisis of independence came, threw in their lot with the revolutionists. This crisis occurred when news of the dissolution of the central *junta* in Spain before the invading French armies reached Buenos Aires. The revolutionaries then compelled the *cabildo* to call a *cabildo abierto,* which the viceroy, perceiving that his power was undermined, unwillingly consented to. This meeting declared the authority of the viceroy at an end and set up a *junta gubernativa* of nine persons headed by the revolutionary agitator, Mariano Moreno, who has been called the Tom Paine of the revolutionary movement in the south. The date, May 25, 1810, when Cisneros, the last Spanish viceroy of Buenos Aires, was deposed, is still celebrated as Argentina's first independence day. After his expulsion, the Río de la Plata was placed by the Cádiz *junta* under a new viceroy, Gen. Francisco Javier de Elío, but he was prevented by the revolutionaries in Buenos Aires from assuming his post.

Following the example of Buenos Aires, Santiago in the Chilean captaincy general deposed its royal representative, the governor García Carrasco, in July, 1810, and converted its municipal *cabildo* into a nationalist *junta.* In the following year Chile threw off the reins tying her to the viceroyalty of Peru and held her first free congress. Caracas joined in the movement in early 1810, deposing the captain general, setting up a *junta* independent of

Cádiz, and forming a federal type of government. In Bogotá the *cabildo* prevailed upon the reluctant viceroy, Antonio Amar y Borbón, to call an assembly of leading citizens, and, encouraged by the establishment of the liberal regency in Spain in 1810, the creoles of New Granada began to advocate independence and set up *juntas* throughout the country. Under the leadership of the *junta* in Bogotá a congress convened in late 1810 and established the "Republic of Cundinamarca" to be ruled by a president and vice-president, but it acted in the name of the king of Spain.

These actions were ostensibly taken in loyalty to Ferdinand, who was being held a prisoner by Napoleon. Thus far independence was advocated by only a few creole intellectuals and agitators. The Cuban representative who presented the grievances of the Americans to the Cortes in Cádiz in 1810 explained, "Those who demand reforms do not desire to establish a state which will be juridically independent but they insist only that Spain recognize the personality of the colony." The mother country and the colonies could live together harmoniously and prosperously, he argued, if the metropolis would only decentralize its governmental system. But the Americans already in fact enjoyed economic independence. Although they did not deliberately employ the pressure tactics of the economic boycott which had proved so effective for England's colonists in North America in the 1770s at the time of their break with the mother country, the Spanish Americans, by championing and practicing a policy of free trade with the non-Hispanic world, in effect limited the economic position of the mother country in America. As their commercial interests ran counter to those of Spain they increasingly traded with foreign nations in defiance of imperial regulations. This course of action was made possible for them by Napoleon's invasion of Spain, which wiped out the principle of commercial restriction upon which Spain's economic policy was based and thus enabled the creoles to carry into practice for the first time the principles of Adam Smith. Economic independence was practically forced upon them, and their ports were thrown open to foreign commerce. Their previous clandestine trade became legal, and smuggling was no longer punished by the long arm of the royal government. The immediate result was a considerable increase in their trade with England and with the United States, particularly after the repeal of Jefferson's Embargo Act in 1809 enabled Yankee ships to carry on trade with the ports of Spanish America. In those ports foreign commercial houses established branch agencies which added their weight to the growing movement for independence. As Americans tasted the benefits of their new economic freedom their sentiment for political independence was strengthened. "We have already seen the light," exclaimed Bolívar, "and it is not our desire to be thrust back into darkness."

The first successful declaration of independence in South America was made by citizens of Asunción whose remoteness in their interior province could be considered a guaranty of immunity from punishment for their daring act. This region, located up the Paraná River from Buenos Aires, had long nursed a strong feeling of local independence and jealousy of Buenos Aires. The commerce of Paraguay was hampered by the duties collected at the port on the Plata, and the Paraguayans complained of the military service which they were required to render. After the expulsion of the last Spanish viceroy from Buenos Aires in May, 1810, the *cabildo* in Asunción showed a disinclination to recognize the supremacy of the *junta* in Buenos Aires, and the Paraguayans defeated an army sent against them by Buenos Aires. In May, 1811, while prominent citizens of Asunción convened in the government house were debating with representatives of the Spanish court whether the government of the country should be carried on in the name of Ferdinand VII, Dr. José Gaspar Rodríguez Francia, who had made up his mind that it should not, walked up to the table, calmly laid a pair of loaded pistols before him, and said: "These are the arguments which I bring against the supremacy of Ferdinand VII." Almost literally at the point of pistols, Dr. Francia thus forced the first declaration of independence from Spain. After this bold action the ambitious Dr. Francia was unanimously chosen by Congress to serve as first consul of an independent Paraguay.

In the Spanish dominions in the northern part of South America the forces of independence were welded into unity by Simón Bolívar, who, like Miranda, was a native of Caracas. Bolívar, born in 1783, was orphaned of his father at the age of three and of his mother at the age of fifteen. He was, nevertheless, able by means of his inherited wealth to live and travel extensively in Europe. He was early tutored by Andrés Bello, who would later become one of South America's leading literary figures and first rector of the National University of Chile. In Rome in 1805 in the presence of another tutor, the dynamic Simón Rodríguez, Bolívar vowed that he would liberate his native land. "I swear before you," he cried in ecstatic words that his tutor later wrote down, "I swear before the God of my fathers, by my fathers themselves, by my honor and by my country that my arm shall not rest nor my mind be at peace until I have broken the chains which bind me by the will and power of Spain."

Bolívar returned to Caracas in early 1807 and joined in secret meetings of his townsmen working for revolution and independence. In all this he was strongly influenced by the writings of Voltaire and Rousseau. The deep sorrow which he felt over the death of his young wife, María Teresa Rodríguez del Toro, was transmuted into a deep passion for the independence of his country. As soon as a revolutionary *junta* was formed he joined it. On July 5, 1811, the Congress of Venezuela adopted a resolution of independence from Spain, the second adopted in Spanish America. This Congress, meeting at Valencia, then put Gen. Francisco de Miranda in charge of its army and promulgated a constitution of the Venezuelan Republic. But the new government was soon wrecked by a devastating earthquake which occurred on Holy Thursday in 1812 and which almost completely destroyed Caracas, killing nearly 10,000 persons in that capital and 20,000 in the country as a whole. It was promptly interpreted as showing God's disapproval of the insurrection. The survivors, diverted from the revolutionary movement and thrown into a panic, hastened to appease the anger of heaven by forming funeral processions, chanting hymns, and publicly confessing themselves in the streets. Couples who had lived together out of wedlock now submitted to a marriage ceremony, and children who had been disowned by their parents were reclaimed. With society thus disorganized, the cause of independence seemed lost as the Spanish forces moved to take advantage of their opportunity. Miranda was betrayed into their hands by Bolívar and some of his companions and was sent to Spain where he died in prison four years later.

Discouragement and Defeat

The removal of Miranda enlarged Bolívar's power in the northern colonies. The nervous, lithe, resolute young leader now infused a new spirit into the motley band of creoles, volunteers from foreign countries, *mestizos,* mulattoes, Indians, and freed Negroes who comprised the patriot armies. But they were no match for the disciplined royalist forces. As the latter gained the ascendancy in Venezuela, Bolívar, the indomitable revolutionary, crossed into New Granada. Like George Washington, he was inspired by an intrepid zeal for freedom, and though he might lose battles he would win the war. His defeats seemed only to give him new strength. He was gifted with a formidable tenacity of purpose, his conceptions of strategy were bold and original, and his quick intelligence could always find ways of overcoming obstacles. Meanwhile Cundinamarca issued a declaration of independence on July 16, 1813, and in the following year Antioquia and other states of New Granada did the same. Bolívar, given a military commission by the revolutionary *junta* at Cartagena, drove the Spaniards from the mouth of the Magdalena. He then defeated them at Cúcuta, and proclaiming "War to the Death" against the Spaniards, crossed the Andes eastward and reentered Caracas in August, 1813. There he assumed dictatorial powers and selected an assembly of notables into whose hands he resigned his powers. He was then in turn vested with dictatorial authority to last until Venezuela and New Granada should drive out the Spanish forces and become united.

But the royalist forces soon gained the upper hand again in Venezuela and forced Bolívar to flee back to New Granada. All that the governing *juntas* and Bolívar's armies could now do was to carry on defensive holding operations. Events in Spain worked against them, for there an outburst of nationalist fervor drove Joseph Bonaparte from Madrid and restored Ferdinand VII to his throne. The new liberal constitution which the Spanish Cortes promulgated in 1812 was hailed by some of the American revolutionaries as a harbinger of increased self-rule within the empire, and it

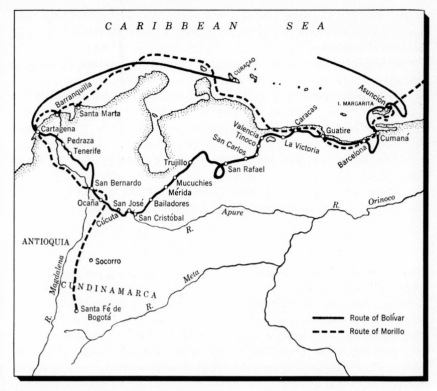

Campaigns of Bolívar and Morillo, 1810–1815.

abated their zeal for independence. But Ferdinand, like his Bourbon cousins in France, never learned anything or forgot anything. After his restoration to the Spanish throne in 1814 he dissolved the Cortes of Cádiz by the *golpe de Valencia* and determined to crush out the independence movements in America. Ferdinand, his subjects whispered among themselves, had "the heart of a tiger and the head of a mule." The fatuousness of the crown's policy, particularly the failure to perceive not only the fact but also the implications of the virtual economic independence of Spain's American subjects, made reconciliation impossible.

As the independence movement in America waned, the Spanish forces redoubled their attempts at reconquest. General Pablo Morillo arrived in New Granada in 1815 with more than ten thousand Spanish troops, invested Cartagena, and finally compelled its surrender. At the end of that year he boasted that he had not "left alive, in the Kingdom of New Granada, a single individual of sufficient influence or talents to conduct the revolution." In June, 1816, his army marched up the Magdalena River and entered the capital, Bogotá. "Every person, of either sex, who was capable of reading and writing, was put to death," he reported after entering the city. "By thus cutting off all who were in any way educated, I hoped to arrest effectually the spirit of revolution."

This brutal counterrevolutionary action, though it appeared to succeed, actually gave new stimulus to the independence movement. Bolívar, who had fled to Jamaica and thence to Haiti, prepared to lead an expedition to Venezuela. "There is nothing," he passionately declared, "that we have not suffered at the hands of that unnatural stepmother—Spain." But though his forces captured the island of La Margarita and the mainland town of Barcelona, he was defeated by Morillo and forced to retreat into the lower valley of the Orinoco, leaving the Spaniards in control of the valley of the Magdalena, all the cities of New Granada, and the northern coast of Venezuela. The light of independence had almost flickered out.

Revolutionary Movement in La Plata

In the south the independence movement was hampered not so much by Spain's military opposition as by divided councils and lack of firm leadership in Buenos Aires and by the preoccupation of the revolutionary leaders there with finding a Bourbon prince to govern the former viceroyalty of La Plata. That viceroyalty, having been created as late as 1776, had not achieved the same high degree of centralism as had other parts of Spain's empire in America. In the component parts of this viceroyalty allegiance was local, the tradition of virtual autonomy for each *cabildo* was strong, and government was largely a regional matter. After the beginning of the movement against Spain jealousies among the revolutionary chieftains and bitter historic antagonisms between the rural pampas and the city of Buenos Aires produced a condition of domestic instability which prevented united action for independence. Moreover, the *consulado* by conducting its affairs in such a way as to favor the merchants of Buenos Aires over those in Montevideo, Asunción, and Córdoba stirred up resentments that encouraged the spirit of nationality in Paraguay and the Banda Oriental and federalist tendencies in the interior provinces of Argentina. Starting with Mariano Moreno in 1810, one patriot or rather one ambitious leader after another first gained and then lost power over the Buenos Aires *junta* in rapid succession. Moreno was driven out by the moderate Cornelio de Saavedra, who in turn was forced to leave in 1811 to be succeeded after two years of leaderless chaos by the appointment of Gervasio Antonio Posadas as supreme director. After his fall from power he was succeeded by his nephew, Gen. Carlos María de Alvear, and he in turn by Col. Ignacio Alvarez Thomas. In March, 1816, Juan Martín de Pueyrredón was chosen supreme director by the Congress of Tucumán.

In the viceroyalty as a whole outside the port city of Buenos Aires there were three centers of disaffection, and war was almost constant on several fronts. Across the estuary in the Banda Oriental (Uruguay) the vigorous *gaucho* Gen. José Gervasio Artigas challenged the Spanish party which was headed by the commandant of the Montevideo garrison, General Elío, and was aided by the Spanish Princess Regent Carlota Joaquina in Rio de Janeiro. In two successive sieges of Montevideo, Artigas, supported by the newly organized Argentine navy under a Scotch-Irishman Adm. William (Guillermo) Brown, was able to gain control of the country. But his plans for a republican form of government and a large measure of state's rights for the Banda ran counter to the ideas of the Buenos Aires *junta,* which itself then appealed to Carlota for aid against Artigas. In the ensuing war Artigas was forced to seek refuge with Dr. Francia in Paraguay, and Brazil annexed the Banda as the Cisplatine Province in 1821.

Against the independence movement in the second area of disaffection, Paraguay, the members of the Buenos Aires *junta,* as we have noted, took action as early as 1810 when they sent out an expedition under Manuel Belgrano to conquer that country's allegiance. Belgrano was a creole educated in Spain who had become secretary of the *consulado* in Buenos Aires. In his official capacity he had been tirelessly presenting the advantages of free trade to the Spanish colonies. He had also designed the Argentine flag. One of the finest characters of the revolution, this public-spirited citizen was not trained as a military man. He and his army were forced to withdraw from Paraguay, which then went its independent way. The Paraguayans, after repulsing Belgrano and thus assuring themselves of political independence from the Río de la Plata province, then declared their independence of Spain and deposed their Spanish governor in May, 1811.

The *junta* in Buenos Aires, representing cattlemen and merchants of the port area, was also opposed by a third sector of the old viceroyalty, the outlying rural districts. In the interior provinces, including San Juan, Mendoza, Tucumán, Salta, and Córdoba, the loyalists remained in control and refused cooperation with the revolutionary *junta* in Buenos Aires. Their resistance was directed not primarily against Spain but against Buenos Aires and Lima, which were centers of commercial monopoly hateful to them. On their northern frontier along the old overland route between Buenos Aires and Lima they were constantly assailed by Spanish forces from Upper Peru. Into all these areas the *junta* sent military forces to compel allegiance to Buenos Aires. They were successful in the interior provinces where after their victory they took bloody reprisals against the loyalists, probably at the instigation of Mariano Moreno. Among those executed on orders of Moreno was Liniers, who had been working with the Spanish party. But when the Buenos Aires forces entered Upper Peru they were defeated by the royalist army at Huaquí in June, 1811. On a second attempt Belgrano's troops were also defeated and driven back in October, 1813. Upper Peru remained solidly royalist, keeping the northern Argentine provinces in continual turmoil and forcing them to rely upon local *caudillos* for protection.

The revolutionary movement, then, had a divisive effect upon the old viceroyalty of La Plata, breaking it up into four areas with competing interests and objectives. When the creoles gained control of the areas outside the port city they wanted independence not only from Spain but also from Buenos Aires. The failure of Buenos Aires to preserve the extensive territorial limits of the old viceroyalty and to maintain its control over the entire area seriously disrupted the economic life of the city by stopping shipment of silver from the mines of Potosí, of tobacco and *maté* from Paraguay, and of hides and skins from the interior provinces.

Until this time the leaders of the revolutionary *junta* at Buenos Aires had not issued any declaration of independence. They were discouraged by the British from doing so on the ground that Britain, which was assisting them, could not continue, as an ally of Spain, to aid an overtly anti-Spanish movement there. In 1811 the Buenos Aires *junta* purged the *cabildo* of its pro-Spanish members, refused to recognize the authority of the Cádiz *junta,* and took over the *patronato* or control of ecclesiastical affairs, which had formerly been the prerogative of the crown. Secret societies, of which the most important was the Lautaro Lodge and Patriotic Society, were also working for independence. When a new national assembly met in Buenos Aires in January, 1813, representing all the provinces except the Banda and Paraguay, the members significantly refrained from taking an oath of allegiance to Ferdinand VII, now restored to the throne of Spain. Still acting without a declaration of independence or a constitution, the assembly went on to choose the name United Provinces of the Río de la Plata as the name of their country. They also adopted an official seal, selected a national anthem, terminated the colonial labor systems of the *mita* and the *encomienda* as well as Negro slavery, forbade the symbols of the old regime, including family crests, the entailing of estates, and titles of nobility, abolished the Inquisition, provided for the coinage of money, and took other legislative action appropriate to an independent national government. In fact they were governing a new nation, for they admitted no authority in the United Provinces superior to their own, but they could not officially declare their independence because if they did so they not only would alienate patriots who still recognized Ferdinand VII but would find themselves at war with Spain's ally, England, upon whom the country depended for its economic well-being.

Upon the next assembly, which was summoned to meet in Tucumán, devolved the obligation of finally declaring the independence of the United Provinces. A declaration of independence was issued there on July 9, 1816, as a clarion call to united action at a time when the prospects of independence seemed dark throughout Spanish America. The revolutionary governments in Venezuela and New Granada had completely collapsed, Bolívar was in exile in Jamaica, the revolutionary movements in Quito and Chile had been conquered, and the royalists were preparing an army in Upper Peru to invade Argentina. Even in Mexico the original leaders of the revolution had been shot.

One of the active members of the Lautaro Lodge in Buenos Aires was a professional army officer who returned in 1812 from twenty years of honorable service in the armies of Spain to aid his desperate countrymen. On a visit to England José de San Martín had become acquainted with Miranda and had imbibed his enthusiasm for Spanish American independence. He now was assigned command of the southern armies. Abandoning the old plan of the *junta* of assailing Spain in Upper Peru more than 1,200 miles from his base of supplies, he venturesomely proposed to cross the high Andes into Chile, capture the principal port, Valparaíso, and launch a combined military and naval assault against the Spanish forces in Peru. If he could gain possession of the oldest and strongest citadel of Spanish power in South America, the independence not only of his own Platine confederation but of other American dominions of Spain would be assured.

With this bold purpose before him San Martín assumed the governorship of the province of Cuyo, whose capital, Mendoza, nestled at the eastern end of the Uspallata Pass over the Andes. There San Martín, drawing on his

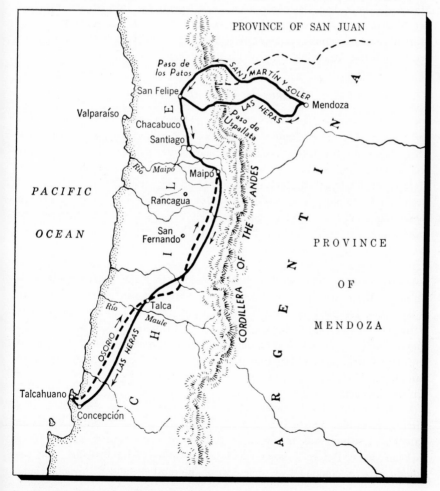

San Martín's Chilean campaign, 1817–1818.

expert knowledge and experience of the skills of warfare, began to collect and organize an army. For over two years he made toilsome preparations until January, 1817 when with an army of about five thousand men he commenced the terrible journey over the frozen Andean passes nearly 13,000 feet above the sea. He had already seen to it by means of a clever strategem and the cooperation of a friendly Indian tribe, the Pehuenche, that the captain general of Chile, Gen. Marcó del Pont, expected him to cross by the lower southern passes to Talca and San Fernando, whereas San Martín now took his men over the northern passes of Uspallata and Los Patos. For the journey through these passes he had an experienced guide. He had already shrewdly dispatched an engineer, Alvarez Condarco, to present a copy of the Chilean declaration of independence to the Spanish general, sending him under a flag of truce by way of the Los Patos Pass and instructing him to study the pass thoroughly as he went through it. But, as San Martín had expected, Gen. Marcó del Pont had the declaration of independence burned and expelled San Martín's emissary by the shortest route, namely the Uspallata Pass. San Martín's engineer emissary therefore had an opportunity to study both passes over which the Argentine army of liberation soon afterward traveled.

Victory in Chile and Peru

Chile was ripe for San Martín's assault. There a group of wealthy creoles had long chafed under Spain's restrictions and looked forward to the time when they could break the Spanish commercial and political monopoly. Their propagandist and spokesman was Juan Martínez de Rozas, the Mariano Moreno of Chile. With him collaborated closely a wealthy Irish liberal Bernardo O'Higgins, who was a friend of Miranda. The conflict between these creoles and the royalist supporters took form in the rivalry between the *cabildo* and the *audiencia*, which also contained a majority of *criollos*. The overthrow of the Spanish viceroy in Buenos Aires on May 25, 1810, gave a signal for a popular revolt in Chile. The creole leaders of the revolt were promptly arrested. The *cabildo* then demanded that the governor, the contemptible Brig. Francisco García Carrasco, appear before them and give an explanation. He not only refused to do so but proceeded to exile the leaders of the revolt and angrily forbade the *cabildo* to hold any further meetings. But his tactless conduct so antagonized even the *audiencia* that they replaced him with a wealthy, conservative, eighty-five-year-old creole, Mateo de Toro Zambrano. This deposition of the Spanish governor was a first step toward Chilean independence.

A further stimulus to independence was given by the circulation of a stirring pamphlet entitled *Catecismo político-cristiano* (Politico-Christian Catechism), which was the work of Antonio José de Irisarri, calling for a national *junta*. Before a *junta* could be appointed Toro resigned, and the *cabildo abierto*, composed of some 350 of the most prominent men of Chile, resolved that a new government should be formed. Their resolution, adopted on September 18, 1810, marks the independence day of Chile. When the new governing *junta* assembled it first created a military force and then declared Chilean ports open to free trade and all monopolies, sale of offices, and farming of taxes abolished. In all this Rozas was the moving spirit, and close contact was maintained with the revolutionary *junta* in Buenos Aires. During this period of revolutionary ferment Chile's first newspaper, *La Aurora*, was founded by a priest, Camilo Henríquez Gracias. It was printed on a press which was imported from the United States and which was the first in Chile's history.

Meanwhile arrangements were made for the election of a first all-Chilean Congress. But when the Congress assembled on July 4, 1811, it showed such a conservative complexion, even taking an oath of allegiance to Ferdinand VII, that it was purged of many of its conservative members by a young creole cavalry officer, José Miguel Carrera, who had recently returned from Spain. He then staged a *golpe de estado* which resulted in the setting up of a *junta* of five, and later three, members with himself as first consul and dominant member. Then imagining himself another Napoleon he contrived by devious methods to abolish Congress and to make himself military dictator. He had to reckon now with the opposition of Rozas who gathered together an army and prepared to resist him. But instead of fighting against Rozas, Carrera persuaded him to commit the fatal blunder of negotiating with him, as a result of which he was able to exile Rozas across the Andes to Mendoza where Rozas soon died.

But Chile was easy of access by sea from Peru, thus far unaffected by the revolutionary movement, and could be punished for her rebellion. There the viceroy, Fernando Abascal, put in operation in 1813 plans for a joint invasion of Chile and Argentina. The expedition against Chile was to be launched from the island of Chiloé, the northernmost island of southern Chile, for this island had been administered as a military district directly subject to Lima since 1787. Operating from its base on that island, the Spanish expedition pushed north and overran the provinces of Valdivia and Concepción. When Carrera rushed to the field to defend the country from the invaders at the line of the Maule River, a *junta* headed temporarily by Bernardo O'Higgins and later by Col. Francisco de la Lastra carried on the government in Santiago. But the Chilean cause was weakened by the defeat of the French forces in Spain and the restoration of Ferdinand VII. Through the mediation of an English naval officer, Commander Hillyar, the Santiago *junta* consented to a truce with the Spanish forces in May, 1814, under which the revolutionary authorities agreed to recognize the sovereignty of the Spanish king on condition that the Spanish forces would be withdrawn and the country would be left in the hands of the creoles. But this Treaty of Lircay, which meant home rule for Chile within the Spanish Empire, proved as unacceptable to the viceroy in Lima as to the Chilean patriots and was repudiated by both. In a decisive three-day battle at Rancagua in October, 1814, the Chileans were defeated. O'Higgins, who commanded the Chilean troops in the battle, made a brilliant defense but was overwhelmed by the superior Spanish forces, largely because Carrera in Santiago failed to furnish him with necessary support.

Even before the Spanish reconquest many of the Chilean creoles, wealthy and conservative, had become disgusted by the factional quarreling of the revolutionary leaders and had begun once more to favor the old regime. Without resistance from them, the viceroy's troops now entered Santiago and restored Spanish authority throughout the country. The cause of Chilean independence seemed hopelessly lost, and some three thousand Chilean patriots including O'Higgins, Carrera, and other officers crossed the Andes and placed themselves under the command of San Martín. But the royalists in Chile, following the example of the vengeful royalists of Spain, took severe reprisals against the defeated creoles, transporting some of them to Juan Fernández Island, confiscating their property, and eventually launching a veritable reign of terror against them. In particular they aroused creole resentment by restoring all the old institutions, including the *audiencia* and the Inquisition, and challenged the new prosperity of the creole merchants by making heavy financial levies on them and terminating free trade. These actions ended all hope of cooperation between the Chilean creoles and the government of Ferdinand VII and turned the patriots toward San Martín as their deliverer.

San Martín conducted his army of more than five thousand through the Andean passes without losing a single soldier, a piece of baggage, or a cannon and fell upon the unwary Spanish at Chacabuco in early 1817, administering a sharp defeat to them. By gaining another victory in the battle of Maipó a year later he brought royalist authority in Chile almost completely to an end. The grateful Chileans had already offered to make him supreme dictator of their country, but when he refused they offered the post to O'Higgins, who had returned to Chile with San Martín's army. This illegitimate son of a liaison between an Irish-born viceroy of Peru, Ambrosio O'Higgins, and a woman of distinguished Chilean family was the leader who issued Chile's proclamation of independence on February 12, 1818.

Immediately after San Martín established himself in Chile he began to recruit, organize, and drill his forces for the liberation of Peru. "He is a tall, erect, well-proportioned, handsome man," he was described by an English naval officer, "with a large aquiline nose, thick black hair, and immense bushy dark whiskers, extending from ear to ear under the chin; his complexion is deep olive, and his eye, which is large, prominent, and piercing, is jet black; his whole appearance being highly military." [1] His single-minded devotion to independence and the simplicity and earnestness of his manner infused new

[1] Captain Basil Hall, *Extracts from a Journal, Written on the Coasts of Chili, Peru, and Mexico, in the Years 1820, 1821, 1822* (2 vols.), A. Constable and Company, Edinburgh, 1825, vol. I, pp. 213–214.

energy into the revolutionary cause. In this cause he received the aid of Thomas Lord Cochrane, who had been removed from the British navy in a gross miscarriage of justice and had thereupon been engaged in 1817 by the Chilean agent in London to organize a navy for Chile. In mid-1820 Cochrane anchored off Callao, the port of Lima, and established a blockade of the whole Peruvian coast.

Fig. 10-1. José de San Martín, portrait by José Gil, 1818. (*Courtesy of Pan American Union.*)

Peru had not yet experienced any revolutionary violence. It had long been the center of Spain's military and political power in America, the redoubt of the crown's authority. In this conservative, aristocratic viceroyalty even the wealthy creoles were royalists. But San Martín hoped to fan the undercurrent of revolutionary sentiment there into an explosion that would aid his cause. For this purpose he introduced a new "engine," as he called it, public opinion. "The Spaniards," he explained, were "incapable of directing it, have

prohibited its use; but they shall now experience its strength and importance."
He accordingly began to make propaganda appeals to the people of Peru
and undertook to convert them to independence. In this effort he was convinced that time worked in his favor. He was also opportunely helped by the
insurrection against Ferdinand's regime in Spain, launched by Col. Rafael
Riego, which prevented the crown from reinforcing its armed forces in America.

In fulfillment of San Martín's program one of his colonels conducted 1,000
troops from Pisco through the heart of the country, disseminating revolutionary propaganda as he marched and thus recruiting hundreds of Spanish
deserters before he rejoined San Martín's forces at Huacho. All this was
criticized as a dilatory maneuver by the blunt-spoken Lord Cochrane, who
was accustomed to the more direct methods of the British navy. While his
squadron was anchored in the roadstead at Callao, he and 240 volunteer
seamen from his squadron carried out an audacious exploit. They embarked
in fourteen small boats under cover of darkness, rowed into the harbor,
boarded one of the Spanish frigates, the *Esmeralda,* lying under the guns of
the castle, overpowered her crew, and steered her triumphantly out under fire
of the castle guns with a loss of only eleven killed. Cochrane then cooperated
with San Martín in investing Lima and forcing the Spanish viceroy, Gen.
José de la Serna, to evacuate the city in July, 1821.

To the further disgust of Lord Cochrane, San Martín showed great deliberation in occupying the captured city. San Martín explained:

I do not want military renown. I have no ambition to be the conqueror of
Peru—I want solely to liberate the country from oppression. Of what use would
Lima be to me if the inhabitants were hostile in political sentiment? How could
the cause of independence be advanced by my holding Lima or even the whole
country in military possession?—Far different are my views. I wish to have all
men thinking with me and do not choose to advance a step beyond the gradual
march of public opinion. . . . I have been gaining, indeed, day by day, fresh allies
in the hearts of the people.[2]

When San Martín finally entered Lima, a city of 70,000, he did so only
after being invited by the local *cabildo.* He came unattended except by a
single aide-de-camp, wisely keeping his army out of the city for several
weeks in order to spare the residents the humiliation of a triumph and to
avoid pillage and destruction. At his suggestion an assembly then met and
proclaimed the independence of Peru on July 28, 1821. The troops were drawn
up in the great square of Lima and from a platform erected in the center
of the square San Martín, accompanied by leading dignitaries of the city and
displaying for the first time the flag of independent Peru, called out in a loud
voice, "From this moment Peru is free and independent, by the general wish
of the people and by the justice of her cause, which God defend!" The cries
"Viva la Patria! Viva la Libertad! Viva la Independencia!" were taken up

[2] Quoted in *ibid.,* pp. 215–216.

by the crowd of people in the plaza, the church bells of the city joined in
the chorus, and cannons were discharged to herald a new era in Peru's history.
San Martín himself assumed the supreme executive power as protector,
promising to surrender the government to the people as soon as Peru should
be actually free. In one of his first proclamations he granted freedom to
every person born after the day of independence, and he extended immediate
freedom to all slaves who enlisted in his army. He then proceeded to organize
a government which promulgated a provisional constitution and summoned
a Congress. Soon afterward his hand-picked executive for Peru, Bernardo de
Monteagudo, forcibly expelled from the country hundreds of so-called "Old
Spaniards" who refused to accept the new revolutionary regime.

Triumph of Bolívar

While the revolutionizing armies of San Martín were overrunning Chile
and Peru, Bolívar was reinvigorating the independence movement in the
north. From his headquarters at Angostura (later renamed Ciudad Bolívar)
on the lower Orinoco he was confirmed in his dictatorial military powers by
the Venezuelan Congress. He gained the support of the tough, hard-riding
horsemen of the plains (*llaneros*) who shifted their allegiance from Morillo
to José Antonio Páez and joined his growing army of liberation. After receiv-

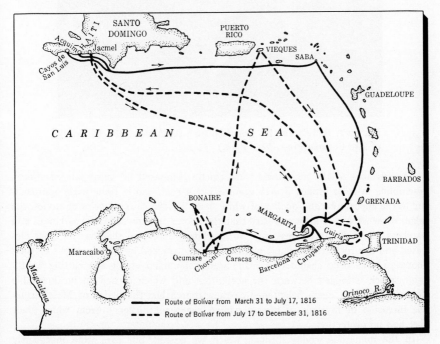

Expeditions of Bolívar in 1816.

ing additional military reinforcements of English and Irish veterans of the Napoleonic Wars he moved against the Spanish forces and drove them before him toward Lake Maracaibo. The anguished crossing of the Andes by an English legion supporting Bolívar was described by one of the veterans of the campaign as follows:

Fig. 10-2. Bolívar and his troops crossing the Andes, 1819. (*Courtesy of The Colonial Press, New York.*)

The surfaces of the mountains were chiefly composed of sharp-pointed stones, resembling in color broken Scotch granite, but harder, and in some parts approaching to the appearance and quality of white flints. By this latter species of stones, the edges of which are so keen and hard that the poorer Indians use them as knives and hatchets, the feet of the men were so shockingly lacerated that on the more elevated and dry rocks their course might have been tracked by bloody marks of their footsteps. The deep gashes thus made were soon filled up by the cutting brittly sand, which is lodged between the acclivities, and which caused an inconceivable degree of torture, again heightened as they approached the plains of Maturín, by the intrusion of myriads of insects named *chegoes* [chiggers], from which their feet had no protection. . . .

In the numerous woods through which we passed, our ears were incessantly assailed by the screams of the flying monkeys, who united to express their indignation at our trespass on their peaceful seclusion.... At night, the different sounds of these and other animals, united with the howlings of the storm, the creepings of the numbers of lizards over the troops as they reposed, and the consciousness of being surrounded not only by snakes in abundance, but by the small kinds of lions and tigers with which these woods are plentifully stocked, all conspired to banish sleep, and to keep the mind completely alive to the horrors of the situation.... The precaution and comfort of having fires round the camp could not be taken, as the descent of the rain, which resembled the burst of a water-spout, extinguished them as soon as kindled. At the same time the ground on which we lay was covered with water to the depth of from six to nine inches, so that we were obliged to prop up our heads with anything we could procure, to avoid suffocation.

During our progress we necessarily passed many standing pools of water.... When it happened that one of these pools, which were sometimes of vast extent, lay directly across our path, so as to render it necessary to march a long way round, many of the most fatigued and reckless of existence among the troops preferred wading through them. In several of such instances, a species of fish, called the raya, oftentimes seized their thighs and the calves of their legs, and tore large pieces from them leaving those who survived altogether incapable of further service. Some of the men so bitten were obliged to be left behind, as they could not walk.... These unhappy persons would earnestly implore their comrades to shoot them, instead of abandoning them to starvation.... Many of the troops had ulcers which deprived them of their toes—one of the many disagreeable consequences of low living and unwholesome food; and others were lamed by the thorns of the sensitive plant, which penetrated the soles of their feet....

We continued our irksome journey until we came near the branch of the Cordillera of the Andes, which stretches across the route from Cumaná to Maturín.... We had previously deemed our progress sufficiently calamitous, and had never contemplated this new and stupendous difficulty, to surmount which the little strength we had left seemed wholly inadequate.... A spirit of despondency spread over the whole party. And many but for the laudable efforts of their officers, would have laid themselves down to perish without another exertion.[3]

But Bolívar did not allow himself to show any despondency, and he led his troops into battle against the Spaniards, defeating them at Tunja and winning a decisive victory over them at Boyacá in August, 1819. "The whole Spanish army, in complete rout and surrounded on all sides, after having suffered heavy casualties, surrendered its arms and gave itself up as our prisoner," read Bolívar's official communiqué of the battle. "The advantages won by the Republic as a result of the glorious victory of yesterday are incalculable," continued his report. "Never before had our troops obtained a more decisive triumph." Their losses numbered only thirteen dead and fifty-three wounded.

The central plateau of New Granada and the Magdalena River valley were now cleared of the Spanish. A decisive victory at Carabobo in Venezuela

[3] Anonymous, *Recollections of a Service of Three Years during the War-of-Extermination in the Republics of Venezuela and Colombia* (2 vols.), Hunt and Clarke, London, 1828, vol. I, pp. 135–140.

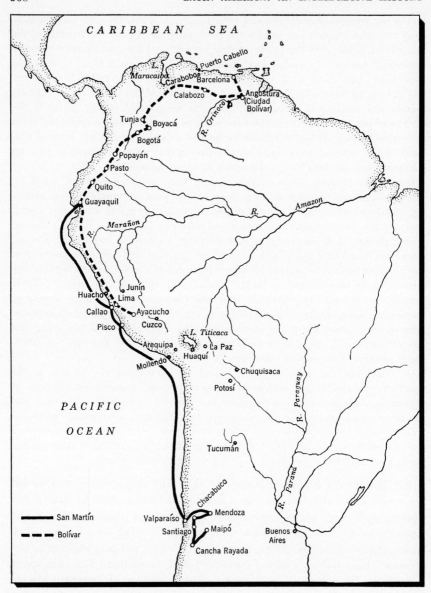

Routes of San Martín and Bolívar.

in June, 1821, virtually ended the war in the north, leaving the Spanish in possession only of Panama and of Puerto Cabello on the Venezuelan coast. The victorious armies of Bolívar in the north and those of San Martín in the south were now separated only by the former presidency of Quito.

When Guayaquil, a town of about twenty thousand people and the chief port of the presidency of Quito, declared its independence in 1820 San

Martín sent a division of his army to support the resistance movement there. Bolívar also sent troops under Antonio José de Sucre, the youngest of his principal aides, and the combined armies defeated the Spanish troops at Pichincha in May, 1822. Bolívar then proceeded to annex both Quito and Guayaquil to New Granada. On July 26 and 27, 1822, the two liberators met in a historic conference at Guayaquil. The details of their meeting can be deduced only from the partial record kept by Bolívar's secretary and from its results. Bolívar was apparently more optimistic than San Martín about the future possibilities of the Spanish Americans for self-government and united action. He hoped that they would set up republican governments and then would form a federal union under a single ruler, probably himself, whereas San Martín envisaged a South America composed of independent nations ruled over by European princes. These and other disagreements between the high-strung, ambitious, and idealistic Bolívar, then thirty-nine years old, and the more mature and moderate San Martín made it apparent that South America was too small for the two of them. In the future military operations which would be necessary, San Martín offered to serve under Bolívar, but the latter rejected his offer.

Since San Martín had no further personal ambition he resolved to retire. He had the great heart to abandon the project to which he had dedicated himself rather than precipitate war over his differences with Bolívar. Only by withdrawing from the struggle could he advance the great object of his life. Though a career military officer he seemed paradoxically unwilling to use force to make his views prevail. A leader of fine character and a God-given power of command, he lacked the stern quality and the iron will of Bolívar. His interview with the latter at Guayaquil must have been for him a severe psychological trauma. He now accordingly returned to Lima where at the age of forty-three he resigned the supreme authority to the Peruvian Congress and refused the command of the armies of Peru which was offered him. As a citizen of another state he was willing that Peru, if it felt competent to its own defense, should work out its own destiny uninfluenced and unrestrained by him. "The presence of a fortunate soldier, however disinterested he may be," San Martín told the Peruvian Congress in his farewell address, "is dangerous to newly established states." He then passed out of history, dying in France twenty-eight years later.

As a strategist San Martín, an experienced military officer, operated according to the textbook, carefully safeguarding his lines of supply, skillfully making use of counterintelligence and propaganda to confuse his adversaries, and taking only calculated risks. Bolívar, though he was not trained for military service, showed an inborn instinct for it, but he remained essentially a guerrilla fighter, gifted at improvisation, resourceful in emergencies, brilliant in conception and execution. He never developed the technique of combined land-sea operations, as did San Martín, though he could undoubtedly have used it to advantage against the Spanish forces along the Caribbean coast and later in his attack on Quito. San Martín was a military captain, not a revolutionary leader. Bolívar was both.

From this time onward Bolívar was the chief leader of the revolutionary movement. After the strong hand of San Martín was removed in Peru, the independence leaders saw the capital again occupied by Spanish forces in June, 1823. Bolívar named Sucre supreme military chief to recapture it. He himself then entered Lima and was proclaimed the deliverer of the country. The royalists remained entrenched, however, in the almost impregnable mountains of Upper Peru centering around Potosí and La Paz, where efforts of Andrés Santa Cruz, another of Bolívar's generals, to dislodge them ended in his precipitate and shameless flight. Bolívar was regarded as the only leader who could mop up these strong royalist remnants. After accepting the position of dictator from the Peruvian Congress he marched his armies across the snow-clad Andes and defeated the Spanish on the plain of Junín

Fig. 10-3. Antonio José de Sucre. (*Courtesy of Pan American Union.*)

in August, 1824. Four months later Sucre, outnumbered some 6,000 to 9,000, defeated the viceroy's entire remaining army on the plain of Ayacucho in eighty minutes of fighting and captured the viceroy, La Serna, himself. The revolutionary armies then occupied the old Inca stronghold of Cuzco and moved into La Paz, Potosí, and Chuquisaca. Under Sucre's direction a new Congress in Upper Peru declared the independence of their country on August 6, 1825, and gave it the name of Bolivia in honor of the Liberator.

End of Spain's Rule in Mexico

Freedom had now been won for all of Spain's dominions in South America. Two great revolutionary armies operating in a gigantic pincers movement over a vast continent had closed in on the last of the royalist forces. The sweep and heroism of their exploits through steaming jungles and snow-covered mountain slopes matched those of the *conquistadores* who had won most of the continent for Spain three centuries before. Quite different, however, was the struggle for independence in Spain's dominions in North America, for there it assumed from the beginning the character of a social upheaval threatening the entire fabric of life and pitting class against class, Indian and *mestizo* against Spaniard, have-nots against haves. Whereas the revolutionary movements in South America were primarily municipal movements directed by creoles who held positions in the *cabildos* and who used the *cabildos* in promoting independence, the revolutionary armies in New Spain down to 1821 were composed principally of rural or semirural Indians and *mestizos,* not creoles. The resistance movement there, as earlier in Haiti, was directed against the creoles as much as against the *peninsulares* and so was soon suppressed. Not until it was brought under creole control with Agustín Iturbide as its leader did it succeed.

When Napoleon invaded Spain the royal *audiencia* in New Spain was determined that the rich territory over which it exercised jurisdiction should remain loyal to the *junta* at Sevilla acting in the interests of Ferdinand VII and should not either become a satellite of Napoleon or yield to the allurements of independence. But the viceroy, José de Iturrigaray, was constrained by pressure from creole members of the *cabildo* and from other prominent creoles to call a *junta.* The summoning of this *junta* in 1808 marked a first step toward independence, and as such was opposed by the peninsular members of the *audiencia* who were loyal to Ferdinand. When the *junta* nevertheless met, it sought to put itself at the head of the new movement for all of New Spain, even usurping the authority of the *audiencia.* This was too much for the upholders of the authority of the crown who with their peninsular retainers invaded the palace and took the viceroy prisoner. The *audiencia* then installed the senile Pedro de Garibay as viceroy in his place. The failure of this Mexican attempt at the establishment of self-rule in 1808 discredited the creole leadership of the independence movement. When the movement was revitalized two years later it was therefore led by new leaders who were not connected with the *cabildo* in Mexico City.

The father of the revolution in Mexico was Miguel Hidalgo y Costilla, who was born in 1753 of old creole stock. He was educated for the priesthood and served successively as rector of the College of San Nicolás Obispo at Valladolid, later renamed Morelia, and as curate in the village of Dolores in the province of Guanajuato. He encouraged the members of his curacy to cultivate vineyards, to plant mulberry trees for silkworms, to raise bees, and to develop brickmaking, tanning, and other industries. Being fond of music, he organized members of his church in an orchestra. He was described by a contemporary who knew him as follows: "He was of medium height, stoop-shouldered, of dark complexion and quick green eyes, his head bent a little over his chest, and his hair rather gray and bald.... He was vigorous, though neither active nor swift in his movements; taciturn in ordinary conversation but animated in argumentation of the academic style when he became interested in the heat of a dispute. A little careless as to his clothing, he wore only such garb as small-town curates customarily wore in those days." [4]

In 1800 Father Hidalgo was denounced by the Inquisition on the grounds that "he spoke disdainfully of the Popes; that he showed little respect for the apostles and for Saint Teresa; that he doubted the virginity of the Mother of Christ; that he declared fornication to be no sin; and that he lived an immoral life, forgetting the obligations of priesthood and indulging in music, dances, and games. Several persons averred that the home of the curate ... was known as 'Little France!' " He was alleged to have praised certain books that were banned in the *Index Expurgatorius* and to have steeped himself in French revolutionary literature. He was spreading revolutionary sentiments, declaring that kings were tyrants and that Mexico would one day gain her independence. His curacy of Dolores was located in the so-called "Provincias Internas"—the name given officially to the area northwest of Mexico City, which was made partially independent of the viceroyalty in 1776. It was an area where popular resentment and separatist feeling against Spanish officialdom in Mexico City were strong.

As Spanish authority declined under Iturrigaray and his weak successors, Francisco Javier de Lizana y Beaumont and Francisco Javier Venegas, Father Hidalgo joined with other malcontents in plotting rebellion. He and his fellow conspirators, Ignacio Allende and Juan Aldama, planned their uprising for December 8, 1810, but their plans were discovered by the authorities of Querétaro and they were warned by the wife of the *corregidor,* Doña Josefa María Ortiz, who sympathized with their purposes. On Hidalgo's advice they decided to launch their uprising immediately and did so with the ringing of the church bell in Dolores a little before midnight on September 15. They

[4] Lucas Alamán, *Historia de Méjico* (5 vols.), Impr. de J. M. Lara, Mexico, 1849–1852, vol. I, p. 354.

freed the prisoners from the village jail, gathered together a band of about six hundred villagers, and began to march toward Mexico City, 200 miles away, raising the *grito* of Dolores "Long Live the Virgin of Guadalupe and death to the *Gachupines*." This battle cry, shouted by the motley army with the fervor of pilgrims as they marched onward through the desert, was echoed by thousands of Indian *peones* who rushed to join the ranks with their sickles, stones, and slings. In this crusading cry they appealed to the guardian divinity of Mexico, the traditional Virgin of Guadalupe, and at the same time defied the Spaniards, contemptuously called "the spurred ones who were pricking the sides of Mexico with their heels." It marked the beginning of Mexican national feeling.

The Indians were swept into the revolutionary movement in part by the lure of loot but in part also by the urge to regain the independence of which they had been deprived both by the *gachupines* and by the creoles. A horde of them, exalted by their new-found patriotism and filled with centuries-old resentments, attacked the public granary—the Alhóndiga—in Guanajuato which was defended by the intendant himself and a small armed force of about five hundred men. Against its stone walls the mob of Indians advanced like the waves of the sea, forcing one another onward until they dashed against the stones. At Hidalgo's request a miner known to his comrades as Pipila moved toward the great door of the Alhóndiga carrying lighted pitch and combustibles and, unmindful of the shower of bullets around him, set fire to it. As it crashed in a heap of embers the Indians swarmed into the building. Almost incredible acts of heroism were performed on both sides. The mob finally took the granary and either killed its defenders or made them prisoners. An orgy of plunder and drunkenness ensued.

Hidalgo, proclaiming himself "Generalissimo of America," soon afterward announced his revolutionary program. He ordered all owners of slaves to liberate them within ten days under pain of death for failure to do so, decreed the restoration of lands to the Indians and the abolition of all tribute and other exactions from the Indians, and forbade the further use of stamped paper in judicial proceedings. But he was completely lacking in military training and skill and could not keep together his undisciplined hordes, numbering now between 60,000 and 80,000. As they approached Mexico City they were defeated in engagements near Querétaro and Guadalajara and began to disperse. When Hidalgo was asked to accept a pardon (*indulto*) offered by the Spanish Cortes in order to avoid further bloodshed he defiantly replied: "In the discharge of our duty we will not lay aside our arms until we have wrested the jewel of liberty from the hands of the oppressor. We are resolved to enter into no arrangement which does not have for its basis the liberty of the nation and the enjoyment of those rights which the God of nature has given to all men—rights which are inalienable and which will be sustained if necessary by the shedding of rivers of blood."

Meanwhile the viceroy, Venegas, accompanied by his generals, had gone to the cathedral in Mexico City and besought the image of *Nuestra Señora de los Remedios* to protect the capital from insurgent attack. Before the entire congregation he made her a general in the royalist army. Hidalgo and his officers were soon captured through the treachery of one of their own number, Lieut. Col. Ignacio Elizondo. They were executed, and their heads were cut

Fig. 10-4. Miguel Hidalgo y Costilla, by José Clemente Orozco, from a fresco in the Government Palace in Guadalajara. (*Courtesy of Pan American Union.*)

off and exhibited in iron cages at the four corners of the public granary of Guanajuato for ten years as a grim warning to other rebels. Obviously, emotionalism and resentment alone would not be sufficient to drive out the *gachupines*. Nor were the methods of mob action and terrorism which Hidalgo used acceptable to the Mexican creoles. Because of the methods used by Hidalgo, the creoles would not support the independence movement until they could gain control of it and direct it into respectable channels.

One of Hidalgo's associates was a fellow priest, José María Morelos y Pavón. Like Hidalgo he had fathered several children. Less than 5 feet in height, black-bearded, and stout of figure, he was placed in charge of the revolutionary movement in the regions south of Mexico City. There he organized an effective fighting force, tolerating no banditry by his troops and promptly demoting all incompetent subordinates. One of his advisers was the young Quintana Roo, who later became the chronicler of the Mexican revolutionary movement. Morelos possessed military and political capacity which Hidalgo lacked, and he soon gained control over all Mexico from the Isthmus of Tehuantepec northward to the vicinity of Tampico on the Gulf of Mexico and to Colima on the Pacific coast, excepting only the cities of Guanajuato, Valladolid, Guadalajara, and Mexico City. At Chilpancingo a Congress summoned by him issued the first declaration of Mexican independence on November 6, 1813. Morelos became both the chief executive and the military head of the new government, but the title which he preferred was "The Servant of the Nation."

Under his leadership the Mexican movement became definitely committed to a socially revolutionary and equalitarian program of action. Appreciating more clearly than Hidalgo the importance of incorporating the Indian in the national life, he abolished by fiat all caste distinctions in the areas which he controlled, prohibited slavery, and ordered the confiscation of all the property of the rich. Of this confiscated wealth he distributed half among the poor and used the remainder for the support of his revolutionary army. He also broke up the large *haciendas* and distributed the land among the *peones*. This program was approved by the first Mexican constitutional convention which Morelos convened in 1814 at Apatzingán in Michoacán. The constitution which this assembly drew up recognized the sovereignty of the people, provided for a representative system of government, abolished special privileges, and proclaimed an end of slavery. So strong was the aversion to one-man rule of the viceregal type that the constitution established a three-man executive, each member of which would exercise the powers of chief executive for a period of four months.

But the Mexican revolutionary movement had already begun to decline. The guerrilla type of warfare which Morelos and his followers were obliged to wage did not provide the dramatic successes needed to sustain the interest of the *mestizos* and Indians. A mere campaign of harassment would not assure independence. Moreover, the objectives of social revolution which had been promulgated by Hidalgo and Morelos in the interest of the *mestizo* and Indian masses repelled the creoles, who were the only source of trained military personnel and whose support was essential to victory. Even independence itself seemed less attractive to the creoles after the promulgation of the Spanish constitution of 1812, for that constitution, adopted by the Cortes in Sevilla and accepted by the viceroy of Mexico, offered amnesty to political prisoners and granted the liberal freedoms of speech and the press. What was more important this constitution established political equality between Spaniards and creoles and provided for representation of the American dominions in the government of the empire under a limited monarchy. Would not the business interests of creole merchants profit from continued membership in the Spanish Empire on these terms? This prospect appealed particularly to the merchants of Veracruz and Mexico City, who, by reason of their geographical situation and under the encouragement of the crown, had established a virtual monopoly of the commerce of New Spain. They failed to perceive or at least to press the advantages which free trade with the non-Spanish world would bring to Mexico generally, for they feared that it would bring their privileged status to an end.

This reaction of powerful creole business groups against independence strengthened the hands of Spain. In 1814 Ferdinand was restored to the Spanish throne, the constitution of 1812 was nullified, and the Inquisition, which had been abolished, was once more established. Morelos was captured by the Spaniards in the following year, stripped of his priestly robes, and shot in the back. During the following five years the revolution continued only as guerrilla warfare under the leadership of Guadalupe Victoria, Vicente Guerrero, and other rebels. By 1820 Spain appeared to have successfully pacified the country. The Jesuits, who had been expelled in 1767, were restored, and the administrative authority of Spain was once more imposed. Reaction had triumphed.

Under the surface, however, revolutionary ferment was actually increasing. It was stimulated by the pamphleteering of José Joaquín Fernández de Lizardi, a passionate fighter for freedom and justice and author of a picaresque tale, *El Periquillo sarniento* (*The Itching Parrot*), which has been called the first Spanish American novel. The Mexican creoles, who had disapproved of the rabble movement of Hidalgo and Morelos, were finally aroused to demand independence when the Spaniards themselves rose against the perverse Ferdinand in 1820 under Colonel Riego and forced him to restore the liberal, anticlerical constitution of 1812. To Mexican conservatives the prospect of being governed by a liberalized Spanish government was more unpalatable than independence.

But in their new zeal for separation from Spain the Mexican creoles determined to prevent a recurrence of the Hidalgo-Morelos fiasco. They looked for leadership to Agustín Iturbide, a creole with some Indian blood, who was devoutly Catholic and conservative in his outlook. At the time of Hidalgo's march on Mexico City he had taken up arms on the Spanish side, and he later distinguished himself in campaigns against Morelos. Trusted by the viceroy he was given the task of crushing the guerrilla warfare in the south led by Guerrero. But instead of giving battle to the insurgent leader he concluded an agreement with him on February 24, 1821, called the Plan of Iguala because it was first made public in that town. This plan contained three principal clauses and was skillfully devised to win the support of all groups in Mexico. It proclaimed independence from Spain but offered Ferdinand the crown under a constitutional form of government, declared that the Roman Catholic religion was the only faith that would be tolerated in the country, and asserted equal rights for Spaniards and Mexicans regardless of color or blood. With this plan as a rallying point the turncoat opportunist, Iturbide, gathered around him a large army called the Army of the Three Guaranties (Trigarantes), and virtually compelled Gen. Juan O'Donojú, the captain general in Mexico, acting as viceroy, to recognize his authority. In the treaty which he as the representative of the Mexican Empire concluded with O'Donojú at Córdoba on August 24, 1821, he secured O'Donojú's consent to serve as a member of a regency and to dispatch commissioners to Spain to offer the crown to Ferdinand or, in the event of his refusal, to other members of the Spanish royal family in a specified order. The independence movement which Hidalgo and Morelos had launched eleven years earlier was coming to fruition through the leadership of a royalist officer and the compliance of a weak-willed viceroy. The latter now conveniently died of yellow fever.

To the proclerical, conservative elements in Mexico the independence movement seemed to have fallen into the right hands. When the Mexico City *cabildo* again took the oath of loyalty to the Spanish constitution of 1812, conservative groups rallied around Iturbide to resist the continued rule of a now seemingly liberal Spain and the local *cabildo* representing it. With their support Iturbide's army entered Mexico City in triumph, bringing Spanish rule virtually to an end. Iturbide then summoned a *junta,* placed himself at the head of it, and called a constitutional convention, appealing to all factions—Freemasons, creoles, republicans, clericals, liberals, and the army—to support the government of the new nation. But he soon received word that his Treaty of Córdoba with O'Donojú had been declared "illegal, null, and void, as respects the Spanish government and its subjects" by the Cortes in Madrid. He therefore staged a *golpe de estado* in May, 1822, which made him emperor of Mexico under the title of Agustín I.

We have a prejudiced but interesting description of this native Mexican emperor, the fortuitous heir of the revolutionary movement started by Father Hidalgo, from the pen of the United States minister, Joel R. Poinsett:

I was presented to His Majesty this morning. . . .

The emperor . . . received us with great politeness. Two of his favorites were with him. We were all seated, and he conversed with us for half an hour in an easy unembarrassed manner, taking occasion to compliment the United States, and our institutions, and to lament that they were not suited to the circumstances of his country. He modestly insinuated that he had yielded very reluctantly to the wishes of the people, but had been compelled to suffer them to place the crown upon his head to prevent misrule and anarchy.

He is about five feet ten or eleven inches high, stoutly made and well proportioned. His face is oval, and his features are very good except his eyes, which

Fig. 10-5. Agustín de Iturbide acclaimed as emperor of Mexico at Moncada Palace on May 19, 1822. (*Courtesy of Duke University Press and the Museo Nacional de Antropología, Mexico.*)

were constantly bent on the ground or averted. His hair is brown with red whiskers, and his complexion fair and ruddy, more like that of a German, than of a Spaniard. As you will hear his name pronounced differently, let me tell you that you must accent equally every syllable, I-tur-bi-de. I will not repeat the tales I hear daily of the character and conduct of this man. Prior to the late successful revolution, he commanded a small force in the service of the Royalists, and is accused of having been the most cruel and bloodthirsty persecutor of the Patriots, and never to have spared a prisoner. His official letters to the viceroy substantiate this fact.... With a pleasing address and prepossessing exterior, and by lavish profusion, he has attached the officers and soldiers to his person, and so long as he possesses the means of paying and rewarding them, so long he will maintain himself on the throne; when these fail he will be precipitated from it....[5]

The empire over which Iturbide ruled was one of the largest in the world, being surpassed only by those of Britain, China, and Russia. To the north it extended to the limits of Texas and California; to the south it included Central America. Throughout the colonial period these isthmian countries had maintained close political connections with the viceroyalty of New Spain. But they had enjoyed a separate administrative status under the *audiencia* and captains general of Guatemala, whose jurisdiction extended throughout

[5] [Joel R. Poinsett], *Notes on Mexico,* H. C. Carey and I. Lea, Philadelphia, 1824, pp. 67–68.

Central America down to Panama. In this area no real warfare was carried on against Spain. Although disaffection was rife and revolutionary attempts were made, the authorities, assisted by the clergy, who were mostly pro-Spanish, succeeded in maintaining order and keeping the people under their control. But after Mexican independence was established, Chiapas, then a part of Guatemala, separated from Spain and joined Mexico. Soon afterward, on September 15, 1821, a popular assembly in Guatemala City declared the independence of all of Central America. Two months later, on November 28, 1821, a *cabildo abierto* in Panama, which geographically belonged to Central America but maintained closer ties with New Granada, declared the independence of that country from Spain and its annexation to New Granada. So unimpassioned were the Panamanians, however, over the change from colonial status to independence that they allowed their Spanish governor to continue in office.

After Guatemala's action the more conservative districts of Central America, distrusting Guatemala's leadership and attracted by Iturbide's program, decided to join Mexico. In the following year the towns of Central America acting through a creole "consultative committee" in Guatemala annexed all of Central America except Panama to Mexico. But when Costa Rica, Salvador, and parts of Honduras refused to approve this decision Iturbide sent in an army which forced them into union with Mexico. When the vain, incompetent, and unscrupulous Iturbide himself was deposed as emperor of Mexico in March, 1823, his general in Central America, Vicente Filísola, was unable to prevent the representatives of these countries from declaring, on July 1, 1823, the independence of Central America "from Spain, Mexico, or any other power." The leadership of this independence movement was furnished by Dr. José Cecilio del Valle, a distinguished legal authority and friend of the English utilitarian reformer and libertarian, Jeremy Bentham.

Independence of Brazil

As in Spanish America, the impetus to independence in Portugal's enormous American colony was given by the Napoleonic Wars. But independence came to Brazil not through violent social upheaval, as in France's colony Haiti, or by fifteen years of intermittent war, as in Spanish America, but in less than a year as a result of an almost bloodless coup. The peaceful separation of Brazil from Portugal stands out in marked contrast to the sanguinary struggle by which the independence of Spanish America was achieved.

Nationalism had appeared in Brazil in early colonial days, originating sometimes in economic grievances, sometimes in resistance to unreasonable acts of despotic governors, sometimes in the developing pride of the colonists as Brazilians. Their claims to local autonomy were often championed by the town councils, as in Spanish viceroyalties, and often by officials of the church, for the church in Brazil repeatedly quarreled with the Portuguese authorities over jurisdictional and other matters. Rivalry between the local sugar magnates, proprietors of vast estates, and the Portuguese who carried on the business operations of the country and monopolized the public offices was chronic.

The Brazilians, like other Americans, were profoundly moved by the intellectual ferment of the eighteenth century. In the gold and diamond country, centering at Ouro Prêto (Black Gold), in the latter part of that century occurred an unusual literary renaissance. There lived and worked a group of poets and other literary figures who represented the finest expression of Brazil's colonial spirit in literature and who were strongly influenced by the French Enlightenment. Many of them were educated in the University of Coimbra in Portugal, a center of liberal ideas, and when they returned to their native country they were distressed by its backwardness and thralldom. They therefore stimulated a vigorous nativistic spirit which gave rise to the most brilliant intellectual movement in colonial Brazil. In literary and scientific societies, which they organized on the pattern of the French salon, they conspired for the independence of Brazil. In these plans they were supported by local ecclesiastics and by certain leaders of the mining industry who opposed the collection of what they regarded as extortionate taxes by the crown. Some of these freethinkers were social revolutionaries interested in everything new and determined to make over the life of the New World. They dreamed dreams and saw visions of a new America. One of them, José Joaquim de Maia, while a student in France, conferred with Thomas Jefferson, who was then serving as minister in Paris, and by him was inspired by the example of the war for independence of the United States. In their writings and other propaganda for independence many of the members of the so-called *"Escola Mineira"* (Mines School), for example, Santa Rita Durão, José Basílio da Gama, Ignácio José Alvarenga Peixoto, Thomaz Antônio Gonzaga, Claúdio Manoel da Costa, and Manoel Ignácio da Silva Alvarenga, revealed wide reading, resourcefulness and fertility of ideas, and profound insights. But their conspiratorial actions were repugnant to the authorities, who moved against them in 1789. The Ouro Prêto conspiracy was ferreted out, and its leader, a young army officer and ex-dentist, Joaquim José da Silva Xavier, nicknamed Tiradentes or the tooth puller, was hanged in Rio de Janeiro "for the hideous crime of rebellion and high treason." One of his associates committed suicide and others were exiled to Africa.

Portugal had been almost uninterruptedly allied with England since the fourteenth century and had been united with her in a defensive alliance since the Treaty of Methuen in 1703. When after the outbreak of the Napoleonic Wars she refused to support the continental system of the emperor of the French she defiantly kept open in the Hispanic peninsula a door of access to Europe for the commerce of the outside world. Portugal was therefore occupied by French troops. As the invading armies of France under General

Junot came up over the mountain rim surrounding Lisbon on November 29, 1807, a fleet of some forty-eight vessels dropped down the Tagus River and put out of the harbor carrying almost the entire Portuguese court, including thousands of noble families and Prince John, who was regent for his insane mother María I. Under convoy of a British squadron they reached Bahía, the old capital of Brazil, in January and proceeded on to Rio de Janeiro, which became the royal capital. Prince John now took over the authority of the last viceroy of Brazil, Count Arcos, and the mother country and chief colony exchanged places. For the first time a European royal court was established in America. Brazil gained prestige as the new seat of the Portuguese Empire, and Rio de Janeiro took on the appearance of the capital of a sovereign state. The arrival of the royal court in Rio de Janeiro choked off liberal agitation and probably prevented the establishment of a Brazilian *junta* which might easily have led the country toward independence.

From now on Brazil, as the headquarters of the Portuguese government in exile, enjoyed great advantages. Even before the royal fleet arrived, the regent issued a decree opening Brazil's ports to the commerce of all friendly nations and reducing the tariff on imported goods. This act, particularly gratifying to the British, virtually gave Brazil its economic independence. Thereafter its subordination to Portugal was merely political. After the arrival of the court in Rio de Janeiro a military establishment was created, the first printing press was set up, an imperial library and a national bank were founded, new port works were constructed, and all the royal ceremonials and trappings of a European court were introduced. The regent also encouraged a group of French artists headed by Joaquim Lebreton to found an academy of fine arts in Rio de Janeiro. Brazil was more Europeanized than ever before. The regent, showing more wisdom than the Spanish government, granted his American colony the rights for which the subjects of Spain in America had been vainly clamoring. In 1815 he elevated Brazil to equal status with the mother country in the United Kingdom of Portugal, Brazil, and the Algarve. But in reality Brazil as the seat of the court became the mother country, and Portugal was virtually reduced to a dependency. On the death of the insane Queen María in the following year, Prince John became king of the united kingdom as John VI.

But all this was not pure gain for Brazil, for John's wife, Carlota Joaquina, who was the sister of the deposed Ferdinand VII of Spain, was involving the colony in profitless intrigues with its neighbors in South America. Besides, since the Portuguese court could not collect taxes in the mother country to maintain its extravagances during the French occupation it undertook to raise new revenues in Brazil through increased taxes. This action heightened the tension between the Portuguese and the *crioulos* or *mazombos* which had already occasionally reached a stage of active hostility during the eighteenth century. The Portuguese were resented as foreign exploiters. They held the principal offices and monopolized the trade in goods which the *mazombos* produced. Portuguese culture dominated Brazilian life, and since Portugal was subservient to Britain, Brazil became virtually a British colony, an integral part of the British commercial system. Brazilian nativist feelings were offended by these foreign intrusions.

The antagonism between the Portuguese and the *mazombos* was stimulated by the example of the insurrection of the Spanish Americans against their mother country after 1810. The contagious spirit of the insurrection was at work among the creoles in Brazil. As discontent grew, a republican outbreak occurred in Pernambuco in 1817 caused by resentment of the creoles in the garrison there against their peninsular officers. This nationalist uprising was directed against the Portuguese as foreigners, as aristocrats, and as exploiters, and it was stimulated by the Masons and by a group of liberal churchmen who were imbued with French revolutionary ideas and English economic theory. It soon spread to four other regions, Itamaraca, Paraíba, Alagoas, and Rio Grande do Norte. The severe measures taken by the authorities to suppress this revolution further embittered popular feelings against the Portuguese.

Meanwhile popular sentiment in Portugal, now relieved of the French incubus, was increasingly clamoring for the return of the king from Rio de Janeiro. In 1820 Portugal, influenced by the example of the Spanish revolution of that year and restive under the "bondage" of Lord Beresford, who had been designated as regent by King John, drove out the English regency and adopted a liberal constitution, which required the return of the king to Lisbon. The king preferred to remain in Rio de Janeiro, but, urged by his Portuguese advisers and by his son Pedro, who if the king left would become regent of Brazil, he gave his approval to the constitution and reluctantly left Brazil for Portugal in April, 1821, taking with him the entire court as well as the treasury. The Brazilians were loath to see him go, for he had been a good sovereign and had not only given them legal equality in the Portuguese Empire but had increased their international position. As it turned out, his liberal policy of encouraging each part of the United Kingdom of Portugal to assume increasing responsibility for its own affairs worked, perhaps in unintended ways, to stimulate separatist feelings in the minds of the Brazilians. This policy was to have a divisive effect upon the kingdom. John VI must have sensed this effect, for before he departed from Rio de Janeiro he instructed his son Pedro, acting as regent and "Perpetual Defender" of Brazil, to preserve Brazil to the House of Braganza but "in case of any unforeseen circumstances which should make the union of Portugal and Brazil impracticable . . . to place the crown upon his own head."

Pedro helped to influence these "unforeseen circumstances" by encouraging the independence sentiments of the Brazilians as they gradually crystallized under the leadership of José Bonifácio de Andrada e Silva, a lawyer of São Paulo. He was swept along into the independence movement also by the agitation of the lodges of the Masonic order of which he was made grand master.

"Why should Brazil continue subservient to such a poor and insignificant country as Portugal?" the Brazilians asked themselves. Their country was more than fifteen times as large as the mother country. They developed feelings of grievance against Portugal and complained of its tyranny, particularly after the new Portuguese constituent assembly abolished the freedom of trade which Brazil had enjoyed since 1808. Especially distasteful to them was the treatment which their representatives to the Côrtes in Lisbon received. They were not admitted to the debates until the end of the sessions, and when they attempted to speak they were often rudely interrupted. Brazilians remembered that during King John's residence in Rio de Janeiro they had been encouraged to play and had actually played a more important role in the world than they were now playing. Was it now the purpose of Portugal to reduce them once more to colonial subjection?

The actual achievement of Brazilian independence came rapidly and without the disruption of civil war in 1822. It responded to the economic requirements of the agricultural population of the littoral and resulted largely from their agitation. It was a Brazilianist movement, an expression of *Brasildade* against a superimposed Portuguese authority. When the Portuguese garrison in Rio de Janeiro tried to cause trouble in January, 1822, Pedro shipped it back to Lisbon. He refused to comply with the orders from Lisbon that he return to "complete his political education." Soon afterward he accepted the title of Perpetual Defender of Brazil. In June he agreed to summon a constituent assembly, and in August he informed the diplomatic corps that Brazil was on the point of declaring its independence. Finally in September while he was returning from the south he received couriers with the latest dispatches from Europe informing him that all his Brazilian decrees had been annulled and he himself had been declared a traitor.

There on September 7, 1822, on the banks of the Ypiranga near São Paulo, Pedro tore the Portuguese colors from his uniform and proclaimed the famous *Grito do Ypiranga,* "Independence or Death. We are separated from Portugal." His personal act declaring Brazil independent was hailed with great enthusiasm, and he was proclaimed Constitutional Emperor Pedro I by the municipal council in Rio de Janeiro and crowned on December 1, 1822, at the age of twenty-four. The fortuitous presence of a prince at the time the new nation was born made it easy for Brazil, unlike her Spanish American neighbors, to begin her separate national existence as a monarchy. The persistence of Portuguese loyalists in some of the northern cities and the continuance of Portuguese garrisons in Montevideo, then a part of Brazil, made some mopping-up operations necessary. In these the Brazilians were brilliantly assisted by the ubiquitous Lord Cochrane, now employed in the service of Brazil as "first admiral of the national and imperial navy."

Within a span of a third of a century the political complexion of all Latin America had been transformed. A continent had been lost to Europe. To

Fig. 10-6. The Cry of Ypiranga. Dom Pedro is seen in the center of this historic painting on the field of Ypiranga as he voiced the cry "Independence or death," September 7, 1822. (*Courtesy of Pan American Union.*)

France after the loss of St. Domingue remained only a few small Caribbean islands and a mainland colony of Guiana. Spain had been ejected from all her continental New World empire; she retained only the islands of Cuba and Puerto Rico. Brazil's independence removed Portugal entirely from the Western Hemisphere. Gone were the imperial officials with their peninsular retainers and their instructions from Madrid and Lisbon. Viceroyal courts, *audiencias,* captains general, and *intendentes* had been swept into discard from California in the north to Tierra del Fuego in the south. The new nations were now free to create their own systems of government, to make their own economic arrangements, and to trade with whoever would trade with them. New leaders churned up by the maelstrom of revolutions were already offering new solutions to all the problems created by independence. But however revolutionary the break with the mother countries had been, varying from district to district, and however radical the effects of the removal of imperial controls, also varying from district to district, the legacy of the colonial past—social, cultural, religious, even economic and political—still persisted. That legacy was now subject to change by the method of direct revolutionary action under personal leadership, made respectable by the success of the wars of independence. In Brazil after independence the Braganzas succeeded themselves, as it were; but after the collapse of the power of the Bourbon rulers of Spain in America, new aspirants to the power of the Bourbons would arise.

Additional Reading

Arnade, Charles W., *The Emergence of the Republic of Bolivia,* University of Florida Press, Gainesville, 1957.

Belaúnde, Víctor Andrés: *Bolívar and the Political Thought of the Spanish American Revolution,* Johns Hopkins Press, Baltimore, 1938.

Bernstein, Harry: *Modern and Contemporary Latin America,* J. B. Lippincott Company, Philadelphia, 1952, chaps. 3, 11, 18, 25, 33.

Calogeras, João Pandiá: *A History of Brazil,* trans. and ed. by Percy Alvin Martin, University of North Carolina Press, Chapel Hill, N.C., 1939, chaps. III, IV.

Davis, Thomas B., Jr.: *Carlos de Alvear, Man of Revolution: The Diplomatic Career of Argentina's First Minister to the United States,* Duke University Press, Durham, N.C., 1955.

Edwards Vives, Alberto: *La Fronda Aristocrática,* 4th ed., Editorial del Pacífico, Santiago de Chile, 1952. A short history of Chile after 1810.

Galdames, Luis: *A History of Chile,* trans. and ed. by Isaac Joslin Cox, University of North Carolina Press, Chapel Hill, N.C., 1941, chaps. VII–IX.

Goebel, D. B.: "British Trade to the Spanish Colonies, 1796–1823," *American Historical Review,* vol. 43, pp. 288–320, 1938.

Griffin, Charles C.: "Economic and Social Aspects of the Era of Spanish-American Independence," *Hispanic American Historical Review,* vol. 29, pp. [170]–187, 1949.

Keen, Benjamin: *Readings in Latin American Civilization: 1492 to the Present,* Houghton Mifflin Company, Boston, 1955, chaps. XXII, XXIII.

Lecuna, Vicente (comp.), and Harold A. Bierck, Jr. (ed.): *Selected Writings of Bolívar* (2 vols.), Colonial Press, New York, 1951.

Levene, Ricardo: *A History of Argentina,* trans. and ed. by William Spence Robertson, University of North Carolina Press, Chapel Hill, N.C., 1937, chaps. XXII–XXXV.

Madariaga, Salvador de: *Bolívar,* Hollis and Carter, London, 1952. The Spanish view of the wars of Spanish American independence.

Manchester, Alan K.: "The Recognition of Brazilian Independence," *Hispanic American Historical Review,* vol. 31, pp. [80]–96, 1951.

Manning, William R. (ed.): *Diplomatic Correspondence of the United States Concerning the Independence of the Latin American Nations* (3 vols.), Oxford University Press, New York, 1925. An indispensable documentary collection.

Martin, Percy A.: "Artigas, the Founder of Uruguayan Nationality," *Hispanic American Historical Review,* vol. 19, pp. 2–15, 1939.

Masur, Gerhard: "The Conference of Guayaquil," *Hispanic American Historical Review,* vol. 31, pp. [189]–229, 1951.

————: *Simón Bolívar,* University of New Mexico Press, Albuquerque, N.M., 1948.

Peterson, H. F.: "Mariano Moreno: the Making of an Insurgent," *Hispanic American Historical Review,* vol. 14, pp. 450–476, 1934.

Robertson, William Spence: *France and Latin-American Independence,* Johns Hopkins Press, Baltimore, 1939.

Rojas, Ricardo: *San Martín: Knight of the Andes,* trans. by Herschel Brickell and Carlos Videla, Doubleday & Company, Inc., New York, 1945.

Schoellkopf, Anna: *Don José de San Martín, 1778–1850,* Liveright Publishing Corporation, New York, 1924.

Sherwell, Guillermo A.: *Antonio José de Sucre,* Byron S. Adams, Washington, 1924.

Street, John: *Artigas and the Emancipation of Uruguay,* Cambridge University Press, London and New York, 1959.

Trend, J. B.: *Bolívar and the Independence of Spanish America,* The Macmillan Company, London, 1946, and New York, 1948. A neat, concise account of the struggle for Spanish American independence and Bolívar's role in it.

Whitaker, Arthur P.: *The United States and the Independence of Latin America, 1800–1830,* Johns Hopkins Press, Baltimore, 1941.

XI

Organizing New Nations

The liberation movement in Latin America demonstrated that the process of forming nations there had been long at work. But of itself it did not produce new nations. It merely freed the American territories of France, Spain, and Portugal from their imperial connections. "As for the King," explained a Mexican *peón* to a visiting Englishman in early 1822, "his only fault, at least that I know about, was his living too far off; if a king really be good for a country, it appears to me that he ought to live in that country, not two thousand leagues away from it." [1] Political revolution alone does not necesarily transform society. The revolutionary struggle had removed the king from Spanish America and with him all political authority from abroad. But nationhood or nationality had yet to be achieved. This would require first of all the development of national feeling. The tie of monarchy, of a common allegiance to a European crown, which had been a unifying force in colonial America, was now dissolved. Though the former colonials had ceased to be imperially minded, they had emerged from the revolution regionally minded but scarcely nationally minded. Could they now find a moral equivalent for monarchy which would be adequate to sustain their economies, to reconcile personal rivalries, and to override geographical localisms? The answer would depend upon how they organized their new nations.

Conditioning Factors

The population of Middle and South America in 1815, when the territories were struggling to gain their independence from Spain, was estimated by Bolívar to be about 16 million. Of these some 6 million lived in Mexico, 2.5 million in New Granada, 1.5 million in Peru, 1 million in Argentina, 0.8 million in Chile, and 0.75 million in Venezuela. [2] In addition Brazil's population was shown by the census of 1817–1818 to number 3.8 million, of whom 1.9 million were Negro and mulatto slaves. Latin America as a whole was

---

[1] Quoted in Captain Basil Hall, *Extracts from a Journal, Written on the Coasts of Chili, Peru, and Mexico, in the Years 1820, 1821, 1822* (2 vols.), A. Constable and Company, Edinburgh, 1825, vol. II, p. 193.

[2] The figure for Argentina is considered excessive and was probably closer to 0.5 million. See Alejandro Bunge, *Una Nueva Argentina*, Editorial Guillermo Kraft, Ltda., Buenos Aires, 1940, pp. [95]–98.

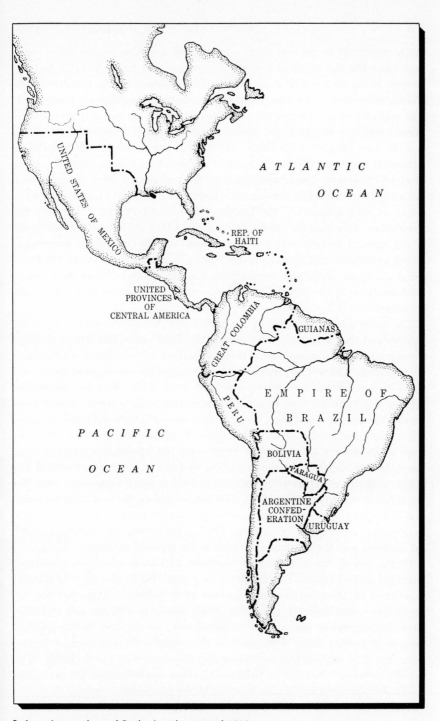

Independent nations of Latin America around 1825.

227

thinly populated in relation to its vast area of 8 million square miles, more than twice the size of all of Europe. But to say that Latin America had 2.5 persons to the square mile is misleading, for in almost all the countries large areas contained no population at all. Many areas were even largely unexplored. The majority of the inhabitants were located in the central plateau areas of Mexico and New Granada, the coastal fringes of Brazil, Venezuela, and Peru, and the level pampas of La Plata. There they were concentrated in nuclei of settlement, such as Mexico City, Rio de Janeiro, Bogotá, Buenos Aires, Córdoba, Santiago, Lima, and Caracas, with dispersed lines of settlement radiating from the urban centers and thinning out or even disappearing altogether as they approached the frontiers. The boundary lines separating the new nations were vaguely drawn. In most cases they could be discovered only in old colonial *cédulas* and had never been actually traced up waterways, across mountains, and through green jungles. Indeed, except where the territorial claims of Spain and Portugal in America impinged upon each other, the boundaries of the jurisdictions of viceroys and *audiencias* had not seemed important.

The geographical isolation of the new Latin American nations one from another and their long experience of individualized suspension from European mother countries imposed upon them a pattern of separatism or national particularism. The settled areas of each were generally remote from the settled areas of a neighboring country, separated from them often by impassable jungles, mountain barriers, or simply vast distances. As a result, national authority became more and more tenuous as it extended outward from the capitals toward the border areas. Each Latin American country had the character of an enclave set down in a larger area but having few relations with the adjoining enclaves. At the beginning of Latin American nationhood the intervening spaces between the enclaves covered a much vaster area than did the zones of settlement themselves. For the centralists, the geographical isolation of the local settlements seemed to emphasize the need for strong authority to overcome the obstacle of localism. For the federalists, this very geographical isolation was the supreme justification for regional autonomy.

In the case of the new Spanish American nations geographical conditions militated against political organization as a unit and so also did the colonial experience of those nations as separate viceroyalties, captaincies general, presidencies, and *audiencias* of Spain. Their disparate interests and character were accentuated in the wars of independence. As the lead in the political movement against Spain was taken by the *cabildos* these municipal bodies, being equal in relation to one another, became centers of particularism. The *cabildo* contained the germ of federalism, which would become the prevailing political characteristic of Latin America in the nineteenth century.

The very rationale of the wars was the desire of Spain's subjects in America for separation from authority. This desire gained momentum as the wars proceeded and became so powerful at the end of the wars that the hope of erecting a single independent union of the former American lands of Spain, originally cherished by some of the early revolutionary leaders, could only be considered a chimera. Certainly Miranda, San Martín, and Bolívar did not originally envision a Spanish America of some ten or fifteen separate republics replacing the Spanish Empire in America. "The whole vast extension of both Americas is what we conceive of as our fatherland. . . . All of us who inhabit the New World are brothers . . . worthy of constituting a nation," exclaimed a Peruvian newspaper in 1812. But when the Americans turned against the Spanish imperial system, unitarism and centralism became discredited. A secessionist spiral began which rendered increasingly impractical the maintenance of any kind of beneficent confederation of the Spanish American peoples and which ended in the fragmentation of the empire. Even Bolívar's hope of binding a few of the newly liberated nations in regional pacts or federations ultimately failed of realization. As a heritage of the revolution, Latin America was to remain a congeries of local units, and the number of local units was in fact much greater than the actual number of political units that were created during and after the war. The strong tendency toward local autonomy constituted a formidable obstacle to the establishment of any central authority, whether national, regional, or generically Spanish American.

But if this tendency, the product of the inaccessibleness of one nation to another, of their conflicting boundary claims, and of their predisposition to separatism, worked against an effective composition of the Latin American world, at the same time it rendered outright warfare between the members difficult. The history of the greater part of the Latin American area for a century and a quarter after independence was, as compared with that of other areas of the world, relatively unscarred by international conflict. Wars among the Latin American nations have been few, though when they have occurred they have been marked by extraordinary ferocity and bloodshed. Much more common have been local violence, banditry, and internecine strife. These have been the heritage of Latin America since the removal of the moderating hands of Spain and Portugal.

The physiographic separateness of the Latin American nations was a product of the colonial pattern of settlement. Their separateness was further explained by racial and linguistic dissimilarities among the peoples of the area. The rivalry and jealousy between Portuguese America and Spanish America had, if anything, been aggravated during the so-called "Portuguese captivity" by the Spanish crown between 1580 and 1640, and continued after independence to color their relations. The edges of Brazil abutted all the Spanish American nations of South America except Chile. At least portions of her boundaries with all of them were undetermined and hence bristled with boundary disputes. Toward the south Brazil's path of expansion was blocked by Argentina. Since both states were expansionist, the buffer areas lying between them would suffer from this Brazilian-Argentine rivalry. The conflict between them would go on steadily and with intermittent bursts of violence for decades to come.

These new nations, having long served, at least legally, only as suppliers of raw materials to the mother countries of Spain and Portugal, remained predominantly agricultural. Their commercial centers and port cities derived their livelihood from the exchange of the agricultural and mineral products of their supporting hinterlands for foreign manufactures. The local processing of raw materials had scarcely begun. Meat from slaughtered range cattle was converted into *charqui* or the jerked beef of commerce by the following process. It was removed dexterously from the carcass, was cut into strips, and was allowed to hang under cover until it acquired a black color and lost much of its moisture. It was then exposed to the sun until thoroughly dried and was made up into great bales, tied with a network of thongs to await shipment overseas. Mineral products were processed sometimes to the bar or pig stage. The copper ore that was mined in Chile, for example, was broken into pieces the size of a walnut. These were placed in a dome-shaped smelting furnace in alternate layers with firewood, and the wood was ignited. A blast of air was played upon the flames from two pairs of bellows from below, worked by cranks attached to the axis of a water wheel. When the ore was melted it was allowed to run out of a hole in the lower part of the furnace, was thrown into water while still hot, and was afterward scraped by iron instruments to remove the slag and dross. It was then melted again in the refining furnace and was drawn off into molds about 20 inches long, 12 wide, and 3 or 4 thick. When these bars cooled they were ready to be exported. The mines from which the ore was taken contained little machinery of any sort. All the ore was carried out of the narrow, almost perpendicular tunnels on the backs of laborers.

In the world's economy as it operated at the end of the first quarter of the nineteenth century these nations were distinctly peripheral, entering into world life only as they could help to sustain the already industrializing nations of Western Europe. Taking advantage of the free-trade practices of those nations and of the United States they expected to enjoy enlarging benefits from the trade which was opened up to them by the elimination of the Spanish and Portuguese commercial monopolies. As soon as they became in fact free from the mother countries their trade with the outside world burgeoned. The experience of Buenos Aires in 1806 when the port was thrown open to all foreign nations was repeated subsequently in each of the new nations. The harbor of Callao, for example, which before independence contained merely half a dozen empty merchant vessels, was reported by a foreign observer in 1821 immediately after independence to be "crowded with ships unloading rich cargoes, while the bay, to the distance of a mile from the harbor, was covered with others waiting for room to land their merchandise." [3] But the methods by which these nations might improve their economic position and at the same

---

[3] Hall, *op. cit.*, vol. II, pp. 64–65 (punctuation and spelling modernized).

time consolidate their newly won nationality remained to be worked out. At the time of the break with Spain and Portugal the Americans felt that they had been kept, as Bolívar complained, "in a sort of permanent infancy with regard to public affairs." They had been "cut off," he declared, "and, as it were removed from the world in relation to the science of government and administration of the state." Their own American strengths had been neglected and their growth hampered by controls from abroad. They had not been given opportunities to become familiar with the requirements of public life. But in their struggle for independence they had discovered new strengths and had unleashed new forces which might be difficult to control. Bolívar himself was disturbed by the restive spirit of his own troops—"obstinate, ignorant *llaneros*," as he characterized them. "We are over an abyss," he warned in 1821, "or rather, over a volcano that is about to erupt. I fear peace more than war." The revolutionary movement had created a new volcanism ominous for the future. Social discontents and demands had been aggravated by the disruption of the old imperial system and would inevitably color the actions of the governments of the new states, created to provide means for new autochthonous expression. In the new nations the romantic idea of the separateness, the uniqueness, the promise, and the superiority of the Western Hemisphere over old Europe was omnipresent. It found one of its finest poetic expressions in the *Silvas Americanas* of Andrés Bello, published in 1823, and his poem "La Agricultura de la zona tórrida" ("The Agriculture of the Torrid Zone"), published three years later, gave rise to a new Americanist impulse in Latin American literature.

Competing Concepts of National Organization

The history of Latin America since the wars of independence has been the history of attempts to reconcile individualism with authority. Unlike the North American colonists of England—Washington and his contemporaries—the Latin Americans had struggled not so much for their rights and liberties as individuals as for the political independence of their countries. And yet the impulse toward an assertion of their individual rights was strong almost everywhere in Latin America. As the new nations assumed responsibility for their own affairs they were naturally influenced strongly by the romanticism of the early nineteenth century and by the liberal ideas of the age. These ideas stressed national sovereignty, political equality of citizens, and division of power. They called for written constitutions which would provide for representative government through national congresses, a system of checks and balances among executive, legislative, and judicial branches, and the establishment of civil liberties, including freedom of speech, freedom of the press, and freedom of assembly. With the need and uses of written constitutions the Latin Americans were quite familiar from their centuries-long experience with the old Hispanic charters, the *fueros* of the towns. They had rallied around the Spanish constitution of 1812. In the drafting of their new constitutions for independent states they were influenced by that document and also to a lesser extent by the constitutions of the United States and of France.

But many of these provisions seemed doctrinaire in their new American setting. The Americans had had, strictly speaking, no experience in law making, except in the very limited ambit of the municipal *cabildo*. All the laws under which they lived were issued in the name of the king by the Council of the Indies. Bolívar himself, whose position of authority gave him an opportunity to influence the formulation of constitutional arrangements for Venezuela, New Granada, Ecuador, Peru, and Bolivia, believed that "the democratic and federal system" was unsuited to the character and customs of the people. The primary question seemed rather to be whether or not the new nations would set up effective central governments or would disintegrate into anarchy. Their Spanish and Portuguese traditions and their experience in colonial development and in the struggle for independence convinced them that less government meant more liberty. How could they, in their new national organizations, strike the optimum balance between authority and freedom, between the venerated traditions of their Hispanic culture and the realities of their American situation? The need for strong, stable government would have to be balanced against the liberal, democratic pressures of the period.

This was the issue which divided the centralists and the federalists in all the new nations. In organizing their new governments, would the independent nations of Latin America retain the French-Spanish tradition of centralism against which they had rebelled or would they adopt instead the Anglo-American system of decentralized authority? The centralists, of whom Bolívar was the leader in the five countries which his armies had liberated, advocated a strong, unified, national government. For them a centralized national government was the most desirable substitute for the centralized imperial system of Spain. The federalists, on the other hand, favored a decentralized system which would devolve authority upon the local areas. Thus was repeated in Spanish America the struggle that had racked the new United States of America during the period of the Articles of Confederation, that later divided Hamilton and Jefferson, and that lies at the heart of the perennial national government-states' rights conflict. The question as to what is a satisfactory relationship between the nucleus and the peripheral sections of a political area had been the core issue in the Spanish American wars of independence, and it loomed up now as the most important political issue confronting the new nations. On this issue the centralists took their stand in favor of strong executive authority, even monarchy in Mexico, the Río de la Plata, and Brazil, while the believers in the liberal democratic tradition favored federalism—a system which had been resurrected by the United States and whose practicability for the modern world had been demonstrated in its experience. The reasons for their respective positions were deeply rooted in their economic and social interests.

Their struggle for independence had given the people of the revolted colonies of France, Spain, and Portugal an opportunity to develop native leadership. As their faith in a faithless king, Ferdinand VII, waned, they placed their trust in new leaders, *caudillos,* who responded to their deep latent yearning for chieftains who would embody the attributes of their new nations. *Caciquismo,* as the Spaniards called rule by native chiefs which they encountered among the Indian tribes when they first arrived in America, had been dormant since Montezuma and Atahualpa, except as an occasional aggressive leader or *caudillo* emerged to espouse a local grievance or head a rebellious movement. The *caudillo* appeared with Roldán's rebellion in 1498, but the bloody swashbuckler Lope de Aguirre, who after killing Pedro de Ursúa led an expedition down the Amazon in 1561, appears to have been the first to give currency to the title in America and also the first to give it the bad reputation which it does not intrinsically deserve.

Throughout the colonial experience of the Latin American peoples, leadership had been furnished from abroad, by the kings in Paris, Sevilla, and Lisbon and by the agents of this foreign royalty in America. But in the independence movement the Americans found an opportunity to provide their own leadership. They provided it successfully and well. But their leadership lacked the sanction of legitimacy. It rested not upon the kind of authority that had been provided by the Spanish king but upon violence. Upon the new leaders therefore devolved more than the mere responsibility of leading a successful war. They were now expected to provide the leadership which had previously been expected of and sometimes furnished by the king as the fountainhead of justice. But they lacked the authority, both human and divine, which the sovereigns had enjoyed.

Into this vacuum of political authority moved the *caudillos.* After the downfall of the king and the disintegration of viceregal authority the *caudillos* redeemed Spanish America from anarchy. *Caudillismo* or the system of personal leadership was revived. Quite naturally the first exemplars of it in Haiti and in several of the countries newly emancipated from Spain were the military heroes of the wars of independence, who in many of the new nations contrived to gain personal power backed by their armies and by the local creole whites or, in the case of Haiti, by the lighter-skinned mulattoes. As the people were accustomed to look to a master—whether king, captain general, viceroy, supreme director, or military chieftain—despotism, often of the military type, became the characteristic of the government of the new states. *Caudillismo* or the principle of subjective personal leadership was the legacy of the wars of independence. But it would be tempered by the democratic remedy of revolution, which was also the legacy of the wars of independence.

The *caudillo* has nature's gift of being able to enslave the wills of other men and of leading them with him—into rebellion, into battle, even over the abyss. He wins the affection of great masses of men and makes them his people. He commands their confidence; he becomes the symbol of their prestige; he embodies the personality of the nation. He dominates even his rivals by his personal power and physical strength. The *caudillo* is heir to the Indian ruler who was also a sun god. He is the modern counterpart of the Negro chief in the African jungle, the homeland of many "Latin" Americans. He is likewise the exponent of a military feudalism similar to that of medieval Europe or ancient Egypt. He stands athwart the modern dogmas of republicanism, democracy, equality, and liberty. Acting in the name of the people and professing to serve their interests, he justifies his dictatorship.

The independence movement brought political autonomy to the nations of Latin America. But the cultural and economic bonds of these nations with Europe continued virtually as strong as before independence. Those bonds everywhere throughout Latin America replaced the political bonds of the colonial era. Just as Latin America had been culturally governed by France in the eighteenth century, it continued after independence to be dominated by French liberalism and French romanticism. But the political independence gained by the Latin American nations did not assure independence to individuals in the new nations. In the first of the Latin American revolutions, the uprisings which started in Haiti in 1793 and culminated in the independence of that country in 1805, elements of social revolution on the model of the French Revolution were present from the start. Here hordes of Negro slaves hoped to improve their lot and to gain individual freedom through mass revolt. The struggle for Mexican independence also started as a social uprising, and Morelos, its most effective early leader, was condemned by the Inquisition for espousing "the manifest heresy of the sovereignty of the people." But in all the other Spanish colonies and in the later stages of the revolutionary movement in Mexico the creoles who directed the campaign for independence from the mother country did not fight for an idealistic objective of individual liberty. Nor did the *crioulos* in Portuguese Brazil show any enthusiasm for a social revolution. Indeed the independence of Brazil was accomplished by the heir of the Braganzas representing the *crioulo* elite. The leaders of the revolutionary movements in Spanish and Portuguese America wanted freedom from imperial restraints but not the *liberté, égalité, fraternité* of the French Revolution. They scarcely comprehended to what extent they themselves subscribed to the very doctrines of government by a centralized elite against which they rebelled.

The wars of independence were liberal in the sense that they resisted centralized authority in favor of freedom. But the creole leaders of the Latin American secession movement sought freedom for themselves and for their class. The "patria" for which they fought extended only to their own class in the new states which they led; it did not include the *castas* or mixed breeds or the Indians. Their objectives were primarily political, not social. Most of them were not motivated by concern for the local Indian, Negro, and *mestizo* populations. They were inflexibly committed not to the ideals of equality and fraternity but to the preservation of their own lives, property, and position in society, unhampered by absolutist power exercised from abroad. The members of this albocracy, as Bolívar later called it, had an aristocratic outlook, as befitted the generation which, profiting from the equalitarian ideals of the French Revolution, nevertheless drew back with abhorrence from its equalitarian results. Moreover, their outlook had a racial basis; such equality as they acknowledged was an equality only for whites and therefore was predicated upon the necessity of maintaining a wider inequality.

For this reason the Latin American wars of independence were not, like the French or more recently the Mexican and the Russian revolutions, internal revolutions. They were political in character, not social. They did little to change the prevailing social system, to alter relationships between classes, or to modify patterns of living. In the ferment of the revolutionary movement, a few lower-class *mestizos* rose to high position in the military, political, and social scale, but the institutions which involved property, family, labor, and law were little affected.

Those who toiled in *hacienda* and *fazenda* under the old colonial system continued to do so after independence. The owners of the large estates were now exempt from the cramping restrictions of the mother country. While freed, as it were, from the restraints of an imperialism that had come to be regarded as foreign to their manner of living and their interests, they continued to maintain after independence the patriarchal manorial system which had constituted the basis of their colonial economy. They now easily resumed the amiable, convivial life to which they were accustomed and which had been scarcely interrupted even by the wars of independence. They had known all along that the cult of the noble savage which Rousseau and his Encyclopedist friends had so eloquently preached in the prerevolutionary period was only a ridiculous fiction. By means of either a *peón* class attached to the land by a system of virtually inescapable indebtedness or Negro and mulatto slave labor the large landowners on their often self-sufficient plantations continued to produce and sell, as in colonial times, the sugar and tobacco, coffee and cacao, cotton and bananas, maize and manioc, cattle and sheep that formed the staples of the Latin American economy. For them the winning of independence represented merely a recognition of the position which they had claimed and in fact enjoyed during the last century of Spanish control. The creole aristocrats would continue to be the dominant group in society. As they had established the patterns of colonial living they would also dominate the new national states. They had not championed the independence movement in order to promote the liquidation of their own class. They aspired to establish a social order similar to that of Spain but without Spain. Freed now from the legislation of the mother countries designed to protect the Indian communities they considerably extended their landholdings and consequently their power position as a class.

Haiti and Northern South America

French models were decisive in determining the character of the new government of Haiti. Here the example of autocratic government by the ruling elite under the *ancien régime* combined with the traditional master-slave relationship which had prevailed during the prerevolutionary period to impose continued absolutist practices upon this new nation of freemen. The excesses of the revolutionary struggle had destroyed its marvelous prosperity, not a single school could be found in the entire country, and the gospel that to be free is not to work dominated the thinking of the Haitian people. Though they owed their freedom from slavery as well as their national independence to the liberating ideas of the French Revolution they swung with the tide in France toward strong centralized rule. The most daring of all their revolutionary leaders, Jean Jacques Dessalines, imitating Napoleon, had himself proclaimed emperor in 1804, and established a military dictatorship using forced labor as a means of increasing the economic production of the country, which had been badly shattered by the revolutionary turmoil. To promote the unity of the country he endeavored, with genuine patriotic zeal but largely in vain, to reconcile the interests of blacks and yellows, Negroes and mulattoes. His empire was short-lived, and he was slain in ambush while suppressing a rebellion in 1806.

But the death of Dessalines did not end the rebellion. The forces of decentralization triumphed, and the west and south withdrew to set up a separate government in 1807 under the control of a mulatto Alexandre Petión, who had been one of Dessalines's aides in the independence movement. His liberal convictions had been strengthened by a visit to Paris and by his contacts there with revolutionary leaders. As president he contrived to concentrate most of the governing power in his own hands and was made president for life in 1816. It was he who persuaded Bolívar to make the abolition of slavery one of the objectives of the independence movement in South America. As president he initiated the policy of dividing the expropriated lands of the *grands planteurs* into small farms and establishing the system of peasant ownership which became a guaranty of social equilibrium.

The Negro government in the north of Haiti was headed by another lieutenant of Dessalines, Henri Christophe, who was likewise given the title of president for life but was crowned king in 1811. His rule was an outright military dictatorship, and he kept his Negro subjects under control by fear and by forced labor. In 1820 he committed suicide rather than surrender power to his subordinates. His death made it possible for the energetic Jean-Pierre Boyer, who had succeeded to power in the south, to reunite the country, and in 1821 Boyer took advantage of a revolt of the inhabitants of Santo

Domingo in the eastern part of the island against Spain to bring them also under his rule. The order and stability which the island enjoyed under his leadership for nearly a quarter of a century redounded to the advantage of the mulatto elite and seemed to indicate that unity, nationalism, and prosperity could best be achieved through a strong executive supported by military power. One evidence of the new strength of the nation achieved under Boyer was the conclusion of a treaty in 1825 by which Haiti secured recognition of its independence by France.

The same course of early fervor for the new gospel of liberty, equality, and fraternity and then disillusionment with its results was traced in the former American colonies of Spain and was reflected in their political organization. The revolutionary liberals in Spanish America rejected their colonial experience and all the forms of political and social organization associated with it. They repudiated also the religion of their fathers, for with the spread of the "enlightenment" many of them lost their religious faith or substituted for it a vague theism. They were strongly influenced in the beginning by the French Declaration of the Rights of Man and the French constitution of 1791. To those who wanted freedom in America the French Revolution offered hope and guidance. But as it advanced into the Terror, social chaos, political anarchy, the suppression of political parties, and finally the enthroning of an emperor—all in the name of liberty, equality, and fraternity—its American imitators turned against it. Their struggle for independence was waged against an aborted liberal movement; they could no longer look to French models. As they faced the enormous task of constructing new political edifices in their own liberated countries they therefore turned increasingly to examples furnished by the United States and England. These countries were actually sustaining a truly liberal system of government based on law and reason, with a free press, free assembly, free commerce, and a strong congress or parliament controlling the executive. But the appeal of this system was limited to liberals in Latin America. It was not attractive to the traditional conservative classes, because it limited privilege whenever privilege conflicted with human rights.

The republicanism of the constitutional arrangements which the new nations now made was largely spurious and existed in form only, having no roots in the political experience of the people. The imitativeness of the Spanish Americans in this respect was revealed in the first constitution of Venezuela, adopted in 1811, which was modeled after that of the United States and which showed the influence of the French Declaration of the Rights of Man. Embodying the federal principle it proved so weak that, under the exigencies of the Spanish *reconquista,* it was virtually set aside by the selection of Bolívar as dictator. The first constitution of New Granada, or the "Act of Federation of the United Provinces of New Granada," as it was called, also adopted in 1811, was based on the federal principle. It gave "the General Government the special and proper powers necessary to govern the nation" but reserved to the provinces "their liberty, sovereignty, and independence in whatever is not of common interest." All that was not of common interest or expressly delegated was reserved to the provinces. But this arrangement was not accepted as final and led to civil war between the centralists and federalists in 1813. Meanwhile a plural executive or triumvirate was established, consisting of one representative each from Cartagena, Socorro, and Antioquia. The centralists under Bolívar then succeeded in conquering Bogotá and bringing it into the federation. But like the federal government of Venezuela it collapsed before General Morillo's advancing armies.

The formation of Gran Colombia, as distinguished from the earlier United Provinces of New Granada, began in 1819. This larger Republic of Great Colombia, which was to include not only New Granada, but also the modern Panama, Venezuela, and Ecuador, came about in the following way. In December, 1819, the Congress of Angostura (the modern Ciudad Bolívar) in Venezuela outlined the basis for a constitution, which two years later was elaborated at Cúcuta in Colombia into a constitution for the larger republic. In this work Bolívar, who was the guiding spirit and military hero of the new nation, was assisted by Francisco Antonio Zea. Bolívar aspired to be the architect of regional confederation for the new nations of South America but was cynical about the ability of his countrymen to handle the institutions of popular self-government. "Generally speaking," he had cogently written in a "Memorial to the Citizens of New Granada" in December, 1812, "our fellow-citizens are not yet able to exercise their rights themselves in the fullest measure, because they lack the political virtues that characterize true republicans—virtues that are not acquired under absolute governments, where the rights and duties of the citizen are not recognized."

To the Congress at Angostura Bolívar now explained his constitutional ideas, calling attention to the necessity of strengthening democracy "since it is weak in itself." Though he admired the example of freedom set by the young United States of North America he felt that its constitutional system should not be taken as a model by the new and inexperienced nations of Spanish America. It would be impossible, he felt, to "assimilate the conditions and character of two nations as different as the Anglo-American and the Spanish American." The political system of the new nations must respond to their own conditions and requirements. He concluded therefore that federalism would mean the ruin of Venezuela, and he pled for the abolition of federalism and the strengthening of the executive. "Let us concentrate the powers in a president," he urged. "Let us give him sufficient authority to establish and maintain internal peace and external defense."

In the later Congress at Cúcuta in 1821 Bolívar was elected president of Gran Colombia, but his vice president, Francisco de Paula Santander, who was to act almost continuously as the real executive while Bolívar was absent fighting the last battles of independence, leaned toward federalism and the prevailing liberal doctrines of his day, to which he was strongly influenced by the English philosopher Jeremy Bentham. His insistence upon establishing a legal requirement in 1825 that "teachers of public law will henceforth teach the principles of Bentham's legislation" antagonized the church and was one reason for Bolívar's loss of confidence in him. Bolívar and Santander embodied for New Granada the conflicting systems, respectively, of centralism and federalism. Bolívar had a predilection for the British political system with its stabilizing institution of monarchy and was hopeful not only of imitating that system but of concluding an alliance with England. Santander on the other hand was dedicated to the principles of republican government exemplified in the United States.

To the south of Gran Colombia San Martín tried to establish monarchical government for Peru in 1821 while he was protector of that country. He considered monarchy the best form of government for all the new nations, particularly for Peru, where respect for royalty seemed deeply rooted in tradition. Accordingly, he sent two envoys abroad to secure a prince for the Peruvian throne, but the Peruvians soon expressed their disapproval of this scheme. When Bolívar reached Lima on his liberating expedition in 1823 he found that a Peruvian Congress had already laid the constitutional basis for a republic. Soon afterward it promulgated a constitution which established a centralized government with a president elected for four years and a unicameral legislature. Bolívar was chosen dictator, but he had ideas for a different type of constitution with more numerous and stronger checks upon popular action. These he incorporated in a new constitution for Bolivia, which provided for a highly centralized government with a president elected for life and a tricameral congress made up of censors, senators, and a house of tribunes. This oligarchic constitution with its complicated machinery of government was modeled upon some of those of ancient Greece and Rome as well as upon one of Napoleon's, but it proved entirely impractical for the politically unsophisticated Bolivians. Though it was adopted by the Bolivian Congress no serious attempt was made to put it into operation. In Lima, nevertheless, Bolívar's council of government, headed by Andrés Santa Cruz, adopted the same constitutional system for Peru and sought to have Bolívar elected president for life under it. Was Bolívar perhaps seeking to annex Peru to Gran Colombia and to make himself perpetual dictator over all the northern countries of South America? This apprehension of the Peruvians over Bolívar's designs was an early manifestation of popular opposition to *continuismo,* the continuation of a president in office beyond his elected term. Within less than six months the Peruvians turned against Bolívar's regime, set aside his constitution, and established a government of their own which was predominantly national.

Meanwhile New Granada was sliding into bankruptcy. Its emissary, Francisco Antonio Zea, who was sent to Europe for the purpose of securing desperately needed financial assistance, found the credit standing of his country so low that he was only able to negotiate a series of highly disadvantageous loans with British and French capitalists. When he returned home with his loan agreements the Congress at Cúcuta declared them null and void. Thereafter New Granada's pleas to European capitalists for monetary aid fell on deaf ears. Its failure to secure financial support abroad was rendered particularly serious by the heavy demands that Bolívar made upon Santander's government for military equipment and supplies for his conquest of Peru and Bolivia. As the government faced a deteriorating financial situation at home Santander and his associates, true to their liberal principles, refused to establish new local sources of revenue that would provide the government with its basic money requirements, preferring to give a restrictive interpretation to the responsibilities of the central government in this as in other fields.

Meanwhile Gran Colombia began to fall apart. The liberal program of the leaders in Bogotá, most of whom were Freemasons, had a decidedly anticlerical complexion which alienated the church though it did not provoke open rebellion. The establishment of the capital at Bogotá had displeased the Venezuelans, as did also Santander's propensity to fill the majority of official posts with his fellow *Granadinos*. His patronage practices seemed to represent blatant political favoritism which was inequitable and unjust to Venezuela. Finally Santander's removal of Bolívar's loyal revolutionary aide, Gen. José Antonio Páez, as commander general of Venezuela in 1826 created a serious breach which Bolívar undertook to repair. He was able to prevent Venezuela's secession at this time, but his leniency toward Páez, his friend of many battles, further widened the gulf between him and Santander. This personal disagreement, against the background of the conflicting economic interests of the central government and the provinces, sharpened the issue between the centralists and the federalists. Bolívar's reinstatement of the rebellious Venezuelan in his old position and his confirmation of Páez in his civil and military authority undermined the constitutional foundations of the central administration of the confederation and gave rise to charges that he was full bent on establishing dictatorial rule.

At this juncture Bolívar tried to impose his pet conservative constitution upon Gran Colombia. When a new constitutional convention assembled at Ocaña in 1828, therefore, it split into two principal parties—the Centralists or Bolivarians and the Federalists or Anti-Bolivarians. The Centralists desired to grant increased powers to the executive and to extend the presidential term from four to eight years. The Federalists, on the other hand, resisted these changes, which they regarded as tending toward monarchy, and proposed instead increased state autonomy, the extension of the suffrage, increase of civil liberties, and a short presidential term. To Bolívar these proposals were unacceptable. He felt that they aped the provisions of the Constitution of the United States of North America, which he regarded as unsuited to Spanish America by reason of the latter's lack of experience in self-government. In this controversy lay the genesis of the two historic parties of Colombia—the Conservative and the Liberal—which, however, were not organized as parties until 1848.

At Ocaña Centralists and Federalists failed to reach agreement, and the

Congress was dissolved. Bolívar, unable to obtain the adoption of his constitution and seeing the country plunge into anarchy, established himself as dictator by the authority of the legislature at Bogotá. By this act, a precedent for many later dictatorships in Latin America, he alienated his friends, including Santander, and confirmed the worst apprehensions of his enemies. "Glory is his ambition," wrote a sympathetic member of Bolívar's staff at this time, and he "is not always tolerant enough with those who contradict him." An attempt was made upon his life, but he was saved by his mistress, Manuela Sáenz de Thorne, wife of an English physician, who by reason of her devotion to Bolívar was sometimes called *La Libertadora*. Santander, for his supposed part in the plot against Bolívar, was exiled.

But Gran Colombia had nothing to hold its component parts together except Bolívar's strong-arm methods, his now waning prestige, and the weak tie of a tradition of common past membership in the viceroyalty of New Granada. When Bolívar resigned from the presidency in March, 1830, to die soon afterward of tuberculosis at the age of forty-seven, Gran Colombia was falling apart. Ironically, another Congress was then meeting in Bogotá seeking to settle the controversy between Centralists and Federalists. Venezuela had already determined upon separation, which it carried out in April. Quito went its independent way in August under a Venezuelan leader, Gen. Juan José Flores, now taking the name of Ecuador for the first time. "He who dedicates his services to a revolution," wrote the disillusioned Bolívar to General Flores, "plows the sea." Meanwhile, New Granada, sliding into the condition of instability which characterized it during most of the nineteenth century, lacked both the resources and the will to recover its lost partners in the confederation. In 1831 it was obliged to recognize the dissolution as a *fait accompli*. But the tradition of regional cooperation among them persisted to be revived again as recently as in the period following World War II.

The Confederation of Greater Peru

In the high Andean countries to the south also, Bolívar had dreamed of establishing a confederated government which would embrace the territory of the old viceroyalty of Peru. But this dream was partially destroyed by Sucre who invaded Upper Peru in 1825 with his Colombian army and destroyed the occupying Spanish forces. He then proclaimed the independence of Bolivia, adopted a national flag, arranged for a separate coinage of money, and after the adoption of Bolívar's constitution was elected president of the country. But both he, a Venezuelan, and his Colombian troops were resented by the Bolivians as foreigners. Moreover the establishment of Bolivia as an independent country was opposed by the Peruvians, who now actively circulated propaganda in Bolivia against Sucre. After Bolívar's departure from Lima they feared the continuing presence of Colombian troops on their southern flank. They finally invaded Bolivia and forced a humiliating treaty upon Sucre which required his Colombian troops to leave the country. Sucre without his troops would be helpless, and in August, 1828, he resigned as president, designating another of Bolívar's aides, Andrés Santa Cruz, as his successor.

Santa Cruz, being half Indian (Aymará), was more acceptable to the Bolivians than Sucre had been, and after establishing himself in power in May, 1829, he demonstrated his high administrative abilities by proceeding to organize and build up the country. He promulgated a new civil code, abolished slavery, improved the system of public finance, and sought to attract European immigrants to the forbidding Bolivian *altiplano*. Influenced undoubtedly by Bolívar's dream of regional federation he conceived the idea of setting up a Confederation of Greater Peru, somewhat along the lines of Bolívar's earlier dream. His opportunity came in 1835 when he was invited to assist two of the contestants, first, Gamarra, and later, Orbegosa, in a three-cornered civil war in Peru. Crafty and cruel he then crushed both Gamarra and the actual president, Felipe Santiago de Salaverry, and set up his Peru-Bolivian Confederation, composed of three states—North Peru, South Peru, and Bolivia—each with its own president and Congress. But over the combined state Santa Cruz was to act as a kind of superregent—or Inca—exercising whatever power was needed to maintain peace and order throughout the Confederation and having final authority in all foreign and military matters.

This Confederation rested upon unstable foundations. As it depended upon the personal leadership of the Bolivian dictator, Santa Cruz, it was resented by the Peruvians. The new capital of the Confederation, Lima, was disliked by the Bolivians. But the undoing of the Confederation was brought about by foreign complications, for it was regarded apprehensively by both Buenos Aires and Chile as upsetting the balance of power in South America. In particular the newly established conservative regime in Chile considered itself threatened by filibustering expeditions and conspiracies of exiled Chilean liberals hatched in Bolivian territory. But when the Chileans landed at Mollendo and captured Arequipa, Santa Cruz descended upon them and captured their entire force. A second Chilean expedition, launched against Lima, was more successful. Santa Cruz was defeated, his regional confederation collapsed in 1839, and he went into exile first in Guayaquil and later in Paris, where he died in 1865. After the dissolution of the Confederation each of the components—Bolivia and Peru—went its own anarchic way.

Central America and Mexico

Longer lived than either Gran Colombia or the Confederation of Greater Peru was the federation of the five Central American states—Guatemala, El Salvador, Honduras, Nicaragua, and Costa Rica—which was formed after they gained their independence from Mexico in 1823. In the debates between the Conservatives, who wanted a centralized government, and the Liberals, who favored a federal system, the latter were victorious, partly because of the resentment of the Central Americans against the imperial system of Mexico from which they had just freed themselves. The Central American patriots had no intention of resubjecting themselves to another autocratic centralism. They accordingly now set up a government, called the United Provinces of the Center of America, which allowed each state to send two senators to the federal Congress and based representation in the lower house upon population. The headquarters of the federation were located in Guatemala City, which had been the headquarters of the old captaincy general and which was now the capital of the largest and most populous state in the federation. But this arrangement favored the Conservatives, who were strongest in Guatemala and who soon secured the backing of the first president of the federation, Manuel José Arce, elected as a Liberal. His defection, under the blandishments of the Conservatives, left his former Liberal party leaderless and precipitated three years of civil war. From that war Central America was delivered by a Liberal creole from Honduras, Francisco de Morazán, who led his army victoriously into Guatemala City in 1829 and made himself dictator of Central America.

Morazán was an ardent and impatient Liberal. The program of the Central American Liberals, which was carried out under his leadership, included not only reprisals against the Conservatives, many of whom were still proroyalist, but also diminution of the powers of the Roman Catholic Church. Religious orders were banned, and the church itself was disestablished in 1832. Morazán encouraged immigration into Central America and sought to introduce the Anglo-Saxon jury system. For these acts the Liberals were accused of selling out the country to foreigners and of adopting foreign practices in preference to established Hispanic practices. Opposing Morazán's program, the proclerical Conservatives found a champion in a young, illiterate, native-born Guatemalan Indian leader, Rafael Carrera, who put himself at the head of a revolutionary Indian rabble and advanced upon Guatemala City. Although his motley army was defeated by Morazán, his movement caused such widespread demoralization that the federation of Central America fell apart in 1839. It had been steadily opposed by the official agents of Great Britain who followed a policy of "divide and conquer" in Central America. To the British it seemed that their economic interests would be best advanced by close cooperation with the conservative landowning class of whom Carrera was the spokesman. Only that class—the so-called Serviles— could assume the responsibility of providing the raw materials that Great Britain's omniverous industrial system required. After the collapse of the federation of Central America Morazán escaped to South America; when he returned to Costa Rica in 1842 he was condemned to death and shot.

In Mexico independence had been consummated not, as Hidalgo and his associates had originally planned, as a triumph of the provinces over the capital, but as a national movement emanating from the capital. But the unity which Mexico appeared to have attained with the accession of the flamboyant Iturbide to an imperial throne there in 1822 was illusory. Opposition to his regime was actively promoted both by the republicans and by the Masons. When he dissolved Congress in October, 1822, and prepared to promulgate a new constitution, his authority was challenged by the Scottish-rite Masons and by Antonio López de Santa Anna, commander of the port of Veracruz. Against him Santa Anna issued a *pronunciamiento* of revolution and compelled Iturbide to abdicate in March, 1823. Santa Anna was thus responsible for a *cuartelazo* or barracks revolt, the first in a long series which became characteristic of the political life of Mexico. The deposed emperor, only thirty-nine years of age, was granted a pension on condition that he would leave the country. When he nevertheless returned in the following year he was apprehended and executed. Santa Anna now became the dominant figure in Mexico. Behind the procession of presidents who exercised the nominal executive power he was the real ruler.

As the Iturbide government had been set up by Mexican conservatives who abhorred the swing toward liberalism in Spain, its downfall encouraged the Mexican liberals. Favoring an almost completely decentralized government, they now determined to organize the Mexican republic as a federation of semiautonomous states. Their views were embodied in the constitution adopted in 1824. This constitution established a federal type of government which was modeled after that of the United States and which divided the country up into nineteen artificial states, four territories, and a federal district, Mexico City. Congress was composed of two houses—a house of deputies and a senate. The president and the vice president, who might belong to different political parties, were to be chosen by the state legislatures for terms of four years. The Roman Catholic Church was established as the state church and toleration was not granted to other sects, though the Inquisition was finally abolished.

Centralism in Mexico, however, had strong defenders, one of whom Gen. Mier y Terán argued in the constitutional convention that governmental centralization best harmonized with the spirit and traditions of the Latin American peoples. The first president of the Mexican Republic, chosen under the constitution of 1824, was a federalist, Guadalupe Victoria, who established an almost unique record by completing his four-year term. But his vice president was a centralist, and his ablest minister, Lucas Alamán, who was carried over as minister of state from the Iturbide cabinet, admired the stability and aristocratic order of the old viceroyalty. He was basically unsympathetic with the liberal constitution and the liberal program. An admirer of the kind of government provided by the English upper classes, he desired the Mexican government to be centralized and strong enough to protect property and maintain order. He believed that foreign capital, foreign industry, and foreign technicians should be invited to come into Mexico, but that they should come under strict government supervision. A conservative and centralist at heart Alamán was distrusted by the liberals, who now found an ally in the first United States minister to Mexico, Joel R. Poinsett.

Poinsett conceived of his diplomatic mission as an opportunity, first, to advertise the virtues of the democratic political system of the United States in the neighboring republic to the south, second, to promote the penetration of Mexico by Yankee enterprise, and third, to counter British interests in that country. Inhibited by no qualms over meddlesome intervention, the aggressive envoy sought to instruct high officers of the Mexican government in the advantages and methods of republicanism and identified himself with the York-rite Masons (*Yorquinos*) in their feud with the Scottish-rite Masons (*Escoceses*). The pressure which he thus applied, reinforced by that of the disgruntled liberals who were unhappy over Alamán's emphasis upon central-ism, proved too great for Alamán, who fell from power in September, 1825. His fall, Poinsett exaggeratedly wrote to Secretary of State Henry Clay in Washington, was a victory for the United States over England. But Poinsett had made himself so unacceptable to the Mexican government that at its re-quest he had to be recalled.

The struggle between liberals and conservatives now degenerated into a crass contest for power, largely devoid of ideological content and manipulated by Santa Anna in his own interest. In the election of 1828 Vicente Guerrero, the "York-rite" candidate, was defeated by the "Scottish-rite" candidate, Gen. Gómez Pedraza, but despite his defeat in the election Guerrero secured the aid of Santa Anna, who was still commanding the garrison at Veracruz and who launched a revolt which resulted in the selection of Guerrero as president by Congress. Santa Anna, always the shrewd opportunist, then allied himself with the vice president, Anastasio Bustamente, ousted Guerrero, and put Bustamente in the presidency. By 1832 Santa Anna had ousted Bustamente and got himself elected president by the state legislatures. But he allowed his liberal running mate, Valentín Gómez Farías, to carry on the business of government as acting president. He would use Gómez Farías as a stalking horse and would watch from the sidelines to see whether Gómez Farías and his liberal colleagues could carry through successfully the changes in the liberal program which they wished to make. He would give the liberals their head, but if they went too far or too fast he would step out as the savior of the country.

As acting president Gómez Farías first took vigorous reprisals against the members of the former Bustamente government and forced Alamán into hiding. But his main objective was to bring the landed aristocracy, the army, and the Roman Catholic Church under the control of the national government. To do so would involve a substantial modification of traditional liberal theory, for it would require the strengthening of the powers of the central govern-ment and an assertion of its authority over sometimes almost autonomous subordinate units. *Laissez faire* as a principle of liberal action would be abandoned in favor of governmental intervention for the supposed benefit of the nation. Liberals would scrap one of their principles, namely the principle of decentralized authority, in order to accomplish their other objectives. In the policy of these liberals toward the Catholic Church, however, they were simply carrying out the traditional Spanish policy of the supremacy of the civil over the ecclesiastical power. Though Catholic in religion they were anticlerical in secular affairs.

The program of the liberals was now embodied in the so-called "laws of '33." These laws undertook first to deal with the problems of land monopoly by depriving the landed aristocracy of their almost feudal privileges. They also asserted the power of the national government over the Catholic Church, though still maintaining it as the official church. The liberals also nationalized the University of Mexico. In addition, Gómez Farías launched a program of national economic development. In all these acts he pointed the way toward many later "liberal" programs which would advocate the use of the national authority to attain liberal objectives that seemed to be otherwise unattainable. Henceforth Mexican liberalism would not be synonomous with federalism. Liberalism in many countries was undergoing this transformation in the 1830s, notably in the United States under President Andrew Jackson, where liberals were using Hamiltonian means to achieve Jeffersonian objectives.

As the clerical, conservative resistance to this imposed liberal program in Mexico mounted, Santa Anna saw his opportunity. He had been willing to flirt with such a transformed liberalism, but he now determined to arrest the trend in that direction and to espouse the new centralism on behalf of his conservative backers to protect their own interests. The army still remained largely unreconstructed by Gómez Farías's program. With its support Santa Anna dissolved Congress in 1834 and made himself president with dictatorial powers. Two years later his powers were confirmed by a special Congress, which was dominated by the conservative and clerico-military groups. A new constitution was then drawn up and adopted. Devised to serve the interests of the groups which drafted it, this constitution set up an aristocratic political system limiting the suffrage to citizens who could meet prescribed property qualifications and extending the term of the president from four to eight years with the possibility of reelection. It also undertook to convert Mexico into a thoroughly centralized government by reducing the states to departments completely dependent upon Mexico City. In this constitution of 1836, then, centralism, which had been backhandedly endorsed by the liberals, was imposed by the conservatives, who found their spokesman and protector in Santa Anna. But this constitution aroused so much opposition that several of the states in the northwest threatened secession. Texas in the northeast actually withdrew from the Mexican nation in the same year, never to be reunited with it, and the easternmost state, Yucatan, formally seceded in 1841 during the ensuing Caste or Social War, remaining outside the nation until 1848. The forces of localism were beaten down, but they were not defeated.

The process of organizing new nations in Middle America and northern South America during the first three decades of the nineteenth century brought into sharp relief the new problems of independence. These revolved around personal struggles for power, the conflict of economic interests, and rival political theories. In the former Spanish viceroyalties of New Granada, Peru, and New Spain eleven independent nations—Venezuela, New Granada, Ecuador, Peru, Bolivia, Mexico, Guatemala, El Salvador, Honduras, Nicaragua, and Costa Rica—came into being by 1830. The particularistic interests which had been encouraged by the break with Spain and by the geographical separateness and inaccessibility of one area from another were dominant. In New Granada and Lima a decade of political maneuvering and constitutional experimentation demonstrated that national feelings and local economic interests were already too strong to permit the unification of the area into the great federation which Bolívar envisaged. In Central America united action was longer sustained, but the same disruptive influences were operating there. The forces working for local autonomy were greater than those working for centralization. They were to be greater also in the new national states that were formed from the disintegrating federations. Rivalries between centralists and federalists continued, and these were accentuated by regional jealousies and struggles for power among ambitious *caudillos*. All these factors taken together explain much of the apparent disorganization which characterized the later history of these countries.

Additional Reading

Baur, J. E.: "Mulatto Machiavelli, Jean Pierre Boyer, and the Haiti of His Day," *Journal of Negro History,* vol. 32, 307–353, July, 1947.

Bernstein, Harry: *Modern and Contemporary Latin America,* J. B. Lippincott Company, Philadelphia, 1952, chaps. 4, 12, 34.

Bushnell, David: *The Santander Regime in Gran Colombia,* University of Delaware Press, Newark, Del., 1954.

Callcott, Wilfrid H.: *Santa Anna: The Story of an Enigma Who Once Was Mexico,* University of Oklahoma Press, Norman, Okla., 1936.

Chamberlain, R. S.: *Francisco Morazán, Champion of Central American Federation,* University of Miami Press, Coral Gables, Fla., 1950.

Chamorro, Pedro J.: *Historia de la Federación de la América Central, 1823–1840,* Ediciones Cultura Hispánica, Madrid, 1951.

Karnes, Thomas L.: *The Failure of Union: Central America, 1824–1960,* University of North Carolina Press, Chapel Hill, N.C., 1961.

Keen, Benjamin: *Readings in Latin American Civilization: 1492 to the Present,* Houghton Mifflin Company, Boston, 1955, chap. XXIV.

Kendall, L. C.: "Andrés Santa Cruz and the Peru-Bolivian Confederation," *Hispanic American Historical Review,* vol. 16, pp. 29–48, 1936.

Parker, F. D.: "José Cecilio del Valle: Scholar and Patriot," *Hispanic American Historical Review,* vol. 32, pp. 516–539, 1952.

Robertson, William Spence: *Iturbide of Mexico,* Duke University Press, Durham, N.C., 1952.

Trueba, Alfonso: *Iturbide: un destino trágico (Figuras y Episodios de la Historia de México),* Editorial Jus, S.A., Mexico, 1954. Presents Iturbide as the great misunderstood founder of the Mexican nation.

XII

Emerging Governments in Southern South America

Stresses and strains of a personal, economic, and ideological nature, similar to those which accompanied the formation of new governments in the countries of Middle America and northern South America, occurred in the countries of southern South America. The process of consolidating nationality in the new jurisdictions formed from the viceroyalty of the Río de la Plata and Chile displayed, though with interesting local variations, the same struggle between the forces of unity and the forces of disunity which racked the newly evolving states of the north. In Brazil a less traumatic transition occurred from colonial status to independence.

Triumph of Federalism in La Plata

In the provinces that had formerly been ruled by the viceroy of the Río de la Plata the conflict between centralists and federalists developed early in the struggle against Spain. There the objective, first, of home rule under Ferdinand VII and, later, complete independence had a disruptive effect, accentuating old jealousies, leading almost immediately to the secession of both the Banda Oriental (Uruguay) and Paraguay, and stimulating centrifugal tendencies in the interior provinces of Argentina. Upper Peru or Charcas, which had been a part of the viceroyalty of the Río de la Plata and which remained a royalist stronghold, also defied Buenos Aires and was finally lost to it when Bolivia began its separate national career in 1825. With these fragmenting tendencies the strongly centralistic *porteños* seemed powerless to cope, partly because in their leadership of the independence movement they were suspected of having ulterior motives and partly also because of their own disorganization. The expulsion of the viceroy had been entirely their work. To the provincials it seemed to have been unduly brusque, sudden, and perhaps unnecessary. Moreover, the misconduct of the revolutionary troops as they moved through the provinces against the royalist armies in Upper Peru antagonized the proud and conservative provincials.

The acute differences of opinion that developed between the unitaries or centralists of Buenos Aires and the federalists of the Argentine provinces provide the key to much of the later history of the region. While this bitter struggle raged, Argentina fortunately remained virtually free, alone among all of Spain's colonial areas, from attempts at reconquest. The result was a ten-year period of anarchy, which might conceivably have been shortened if the Spanish menace had been greater. This period of administrative chaos, which has scarcely been duplicated in the history of the most turbulent of the other Latin American countries, paved the way for the emergence of *caudillos* or local chieftains, who gave the region whatever stability it possessed. This stability, however, was developed outside the framework of the nation.

The conflict between Moreno and Saavedra in the first *junta* in Buenos Aires in 1810 disclosed the issues between the port and the provinces. These issues were implicit in the course of the revolution thus far as a radical urban movement and in the underlying social differences between the powerful metropolis of the country and the backward, even semibarbaric hinterland areas. Buenos Aires, which was the sole port of entry and export for the hides, wool, and other products of the provinces, wished to maintain its commercial preponderance and saw in the movement against Spain an opportunity to do so. As it made the initial moves for independence and undertook to direct the revolution it clearly seemed to be attempting to assert its own sovereignty over the entire area of the old viceroyalty on the pretext of combining all the forces of the country against Spain. Quite aside from any considerations of commercial supremacy, moreover, the intellectual leaders of the revolutionary movement in Buenos Aires were inclined to consider unitary action a good thing on theoretical grounds. Whether Moreno, for example, actually espoused unitary views or rather envisaged an ultimately federated structure, his revolutionary program was predicated upon unitary action by all parts of the old viceroyalty. The unitaries in planning the national organization of an independent Argentina proposed to apply the very doctrines of viceregal and imperial centralism which the Americans had successfully rejected in their struggle for independence.

The provinces, on the other hand, where the centers of population were separated by wide distances of open country and were far removed from the intellectual currents of the age, had rendered loyalty to the person of the viceroy in Buenos Aires as Spain's representative but not as the embodiment of the authority of the *porteños*. Such unity as existed in the colonial period had derived from subordination to Madrid, not to Buenos Aires. As the provinces were alienated from Madrid they also were alienated from Buenos Aires. To them it appeared that Buenos Aires was only supplanting Madrid as the center of power and was assuming all the responsibilities for guiding the revolutionary movement. When the bonds that united the viceroyalty to the Spanish court were broken each province felt free to act for itself.

As the La Plata province had been notorious for its resistance to Spanish mercantilism, so now the hinterland provinces, as the old viceroyalty fell apart, stubbornly resisted the new mercantilism of Buenos Aires. With the rough and ready responses which frontiersmen everywhere exhibit, the cattlemen of the pampas, living in physical and mental isolation and steeped in provincialism, now sought independence from all authority. If these hard-riding, hard-fighting *gauchos* of the pampas could not share the social advantages and living standards of the port they would not contribute to them. Their faces were turned not toward Buenos Aires or a far-distant, old-world society of which they knew nothing but toward their own lush grasslands and their own provincial towns of Tucumán, Santiago del Estero, Córdoba, San Luis, and Sante Fe. They were jealous of all centralized authority and in particular did not want Buenos Aires either to speak for them or to control them. They saw no reason for obeying the dictates of the port city. Thus early appeared the dualism—and the dueling—between the city and the interior provinces which explains much of Argentina's subsequent history.

With the admission to the Buenos Aires *junta* in December, 1810, of deputies from the provinces with whom Saavedra was in close alliance, Moreno, who depended upon the more radical *porteños* to promote the revolution, resigned and soon afterward died en route to England. But when this *junta* resigned its executive powers to a triumvirate in the following year, Moreno's followers got the upper hand, for all three members of the triumvirate were *porteños*. The influential position of secretary, which Moreno had formerly held, was now taken over by the active and intelligent *porteño* Bernardino Rivadavia. It was Saavedra's turn, now, to be expelled, and his followers soon afterward failed in an attempt to engineer a revolution against the triumvirate. The influence of Rivadavia, representing the *porteños*, was thrown toward the establishment of a strong central authority until he fell from power and a second triumvirate was set up in October, 1812.[1]

The first real Argentine national assembly was called by the triumvirate and met in January, 1813. It did not draw up a constitution or declare independence; neither did its members take an oath of allegiance to Ferdinand. But it adopted the name United Provinces of the Río de la Plata for the new union and laid the foundations of a national organization. Executive authority was lodged in a single supreme director instead of a triumvirate. The leaders felt that both national unity and the favor of European governments could best be achieved under monarchy. But unlike the Brazilians they were not so fortunate as to have a prince already at hand. They may have been persuaded to make this move by a plan which a few years earlier the Spanish prime minister, Godoy, had advanced for conciliating Spain's subjects in America. He had proposed that the Spanish crown send out a prince or princess with the title of prince regent to govern each of its kingdoms in America. This suggestion, which would have elevated the American dominions of Spain almost to coordinate status with the mother country in the empire, came too late to save the empire. But the idea of setting up a constitutional monarch to rule

[1] See the data on Argentina in Appendix IV, Latin American Chiefs of State.

the La Plata kingdom within the empire persisted. It could be accepted by the less enthusiastic revolutionaries who looked beyond the military situation of the moment and appreciated the future need for order and stability. Moreover, the system of constitutional monarchy gained favor even among liberals after the restoration of Louis XVIII to the throne of France and of Ferdinand VII to the throne of Spain. If they could set a Spanish or even a French prince on the throne of the Río de la Plata they would avert the danger of reconquest by Spanish armies and assure the independence of their country.

Accordingly, between 1814 and 1819 the revolutionary leaders in Buenos Aires made persistent efforts to secure a European prince who would unite and rule over the old viceroyalty of the Río de La Plata as a constitutional monarch. In 1814 Posadas dispatched two envoys to England and Spain for this purpose. Negotiations had already been begun to persuade the former Charles IV of Spain, then living in Italy, to name one of his younger sons for this American crown. In the following year Alvear conveyed to the British minister in Rio de Janeiro a suggestion of a British protectorate. An ingenious plan was presented to the Congress in Tucumán that an Inca married to a Braganza who was half Spanish would make an ideal sovereign! The new supreme director, Juan Martín de Pueyrredón, sought to find and place upon a prospective throne of the United Provinces a French prince who would reestablish order and maintain the stability of the provinces. In this effort he received support from the French government and the name of a candidate, Charles Louis of Bourbon, grandson of Charles IV of Spain. The Congress at Buenos Aires voted to accept him in 1819 under the conditions that France would arrange a marriage between him and a Brazilian princess, would secure the consent of the great powers of Europe, particularly England and Spain, and would furnish troops to support the new Buenos Aires monarchy if Spain opposed it. If England, however, offered armed opposition the whole project would be abandoned. England soon made known her unequivocal disapproval, the monarchical party in Buenos Aires was driven from office, and no further official efforts were made to establish a monarchical government in this region. But these efforts had already had the effect of heightening the political schism by creating new parties of republicans and monarchists. Some of the opposition to the leadership of Buenos Aires that appeared in the provinces during these years and later was animated by antimonarchism.

Several of the leaders of the new nation were, at heart, believers in constitutional monarchy, but failing to find a monarch they decided on a strong centralized republic. As unitaries they advocated the establishment of a national government invested with broad political and economic powers. They desired to reduce the provinces to mere administrative districts which would be controlled by the central government and which would be restrained by it from fomenting internal friction. Not all the unitaries were found in Buenos Aires, for centers of unitary sentiment existed in some of the provinces, particularly in the remote Andean provinces of the northwest, Catamarca, Salta, and Tucumán. The believers in a federal system, on the other hand, favored the widest possible economic, fiscal, and political autonomy for the provinces. They emphasized local self-determination, for which the provinces, they said, were already prepared by their practical experience in self-government. In economic matters they insisted that Buenos Aires should not monopolize the profits from foreign trade which were, they argued, derived from the production of the whole country. That part of the national income which Buenos Aires received from customs revenues, therefore, should be equitably distributed among all parts of the federation.

The unitaries attempted to set up their system in the first constitution, adopted in April, 1819. Representing the metropolitan, aristocratic element steeped in doctrinaire centralism, they were convinced that their creed offered the only solution to the problems of the country. If they had been willing to agree to a federal type of regime they might have been able, through this constitution, to reestablish the unity of the nation including all the areas of the old viceroyalty, except possibly Paraguay, and to avoid three decades of dissension. But the Congress which drafted this constitution in Buenos Aires was dominated by men who were doctrinaire and who were strongly influenced by the Napoleonic tradition of strong government. This group came mostly from Buenos Aires but included also some of the provincial delegates who represented conservative opinion in the provinces and who were in some cases commercially allied with the leaders of the port. The constitution which they drew up provided for an executive to be designated supreme director and to be chosen for a five-year term by the national assembly. The assembly was to be a bicameral body, membership in the lower house being proportional to population and membership in the upper house including one senator from each province. These provisions were enough to stir the jealousy of the provinces, but the further provision that the provincial governors should be appointed by the central government was quite unacceptable to them, undercutting as it did the control of the local *caudillos* or *gaucho* leaders of the provinces. They were determined not to submit to dictation from Buenos Aires.

The soul of the provincial opposition to the attempt to impose a unitary government and, as was suspected, to confirm Buenos Aires in its claims to a foreign-trade monopoly, was José Artigas. This leader of the revolutionary forces in the Banda Oriental was the real father of Argentine federalism. He espoused federalist doctrines not only because he resented the assumed primacy of Buenos Aires in the revolutionary movement but because he had strong doctrinal convictions in favor of a federal type of government patterned after that of the United States. He was willing that the capital of the federal union which he envisaged should be located in any provincial city except Buenos Aires. He gained the support of the *caudillos* of several of the other provinces who, though they did not all share his theoretical predilection for federalism, hoped to maintain their own provincial autonomy and their own semifeudal governmental and social system. In 1815 Artigas inspired the organization of a Federal League, including not only his own Banda but also Corrientes, Entre Ríos, Santa Fe, and Córdoba, in all of which disaffection with Buenos Aires was rife. To organize their resistance to Buenos Aires, Artigas even called a constitutional convention rivaling the Congress of Tucumán, but it came to nothing.

The antagonism between these provinces and the revolutionary unitaries resulted in civil war. So ominous was the provincial resistance to the leaders of the Congress of Tucumán that the supreme director, Pueyrredón, appealed to the Portuguese court in Rio de Janeiro for assistance in overcoming it, preferring a Portuguese army in the disaffected provinces to the turbulent Artigas and his fellow *caudillos*. His weak successor as supreme director, José Rondeau, continued this alliance with the Portuguese and tried to force the country to accept the domination of *porteños*. To this end he ordered San Martín, who was organizing his army at Mendoza for a descent upon the Spaniards in Chile, to move eastward against the federalist opposition led by Artigas, the governor of Santa Fe, Estanislao López, and the governor of Entre Ríos, Francisco Ramírez.

But San Martín, as noted above, refused to become involved in the civil war and instead, in a famous act of disobedience which was justified by the event, pursued his campaign against the royalists in Peru. The army in the north which was operating against the Spanish in Upper Peru and which was ordered to aid in suppressing the revolt in Entre Ríos mutinied at the instigation of the *caudillo* of Córdoba and refused to fight the provincial forces. In the battle that was fought at Cepeda on February 1, 1820, the armies of López and Ramírez were able to win a crushing victory over Rondeau's forces and to overthrow the centralist constitution of 1819. Buenos Aires, it was thus determined, was not to dominate a unitary government of a united Argentine nation. And yet the victorious *caudillos* were neither vindictive nor even antinationalist. They did not, for example, attempt to set up independent national republics. All that the provinces had been asking for was a proper voice in the central government, respect for their local rights, and assurance that a monarchical regime would not be set up. In the Treaty of Pilar which López and Ramírez now signed with a representative of the *cabildo* of Buenos Aires they agreed to the summoning of a new constitutional convention by the three riverway provinces of Corrientes, Entre Ríos, and Buenos Aires to draw up a federal form of government. They could not include the Banda because that province, thanks to the reckless folly of Buenos Aires, had been already overrun by Portuguese armies and annexed to Brazil. The principle of federalism, not unitarism, thus triumphed, but it was to be applied not to the whole original area of the United Provinces of the Río de la Plata but only to these three provinces. Starting from this limited beginning further national development would be possible, but it must be based upon the federal principle.

The Gauchos

Meanwhile, the central government ceased to exist and most of the provinces lapsed into anarchy, from which they were eventually redeemed only by the despotism of local *caudillos*. Each province desired to govern itself under laws of its own choosing. Many of them accordingly held conventions and drew up new constitutions between 1819 and 1825. Santiago del Estero separated from Tucumán early in 1820, and Catamarca followed suit in August, 1821. At the same time Salta and Jujuy declared their independence of the central government. San Juan separated from Mendoza in March, 1820, but did not set up its own constitutional administration until 1821. Córdoba and Corrientes adopted their first constitutions in 1821 and Entre Ríos in the following year. But generally these constitutions were lightly regarded by the *caudillos*, who made it their chief business to maintain order without constitutional scruples. These vigorous *gaucho* chieftains exercised a natural leadership over men. "Look you," one of them, the notorious Facundo Quiroga, *caudillo* of the province of La Rioja, was reported to have said to a companion, "if I should go into the street, and say to the first man I met, 'Follow me,' he would follow me!" But these uncouth leaders over uncouth followers were maligned by *porteño* commentators, who allowed their predilection for the culture of Buenos Aires and Europe to blind them to the often beneficent contributions which the *caudillos* made to the life of their own provinces. Writing later critically of these provincial leaders, particularly of this same Facundo, Domingo Faustino Sarmiento, himself a product of the provinces, represented their resistance to the domination of Buenos Aires as a conflict between barbarism and civilization.

In this disunited nation, euphemistically called the United Provinces of the Río de la Plata, the cultural contrasts between city and country were perhaps more picturesquely revealed than in any other Latin American country. The city of Buenos Aires, facing toward Europe and emulating its cosmopolitan culture, conceived of itself as an embattled fortress surrounded by barbarian foes. From its suburbs westward, northward, and southward stretched the far-flung pampas, treeless except for an occasional *ombú* tree and flat as a sea at rest. Over these seemingly interminable and lonely plains roamed the *gauchos*—the cowboys who looked after the immense herds of cattle, horses, and sheep which grazed on these fertile grasslands.

These plainsmen, a mixture of Indian nomad and white European, whose faces were blackened by exposure to the sun and wind, dressed themselves in long white cotton drawers held up by a woven belt into which was thrust a long knife. They wore huge iron spurs and carried a coiled lasso lying over the rump of the horse. Their food consisted generally only of roasted beef (*asado*) and *maté* or Paraguay tea sucked from a gourd through a tube. They rode their horses like centaurs, as if attached to them. Their only law was the law of the strong. The pampa that they knew was raw and brutal, but its vastness reflected the eternal, and at night it seemed to match the infinitude of the myriad-starred heavens. Reported an observant United States diplomat in 1832:

Fig. 12-1. An Argentine *gaucho*.

Untaught either in letters, manners, religion or morals, always mounted, they never quit the back of the horse except to throw themselves on a hide to sleep. They hear mass and hold their convivial meetings on horseback. In some respects they are the most efficient cavalry in the world. Dismount them, they are nothing—for they are scarcely able to walk. Constantly engaged in hamstringing and slaughtering cattle, they have engrafted the ferocity of the butcher on the simple habits of the shepherd, and are both ignorant and cruel.[2]

[2] Francis Baylies, Dispatch, July 24, 1832, in *Diplomatic Correspondence of the U.S.,* Carnegie Endowment for International Peace, New York, 1932.

With their earthy humor, their plaintive folk songs, and their fatalistic contempt of death, the *gauchos* formed a buffer between the white settlements and the savage Indians, serving unwittingly as a vanguard of civilization and waging continual war against the plains Indians who were always lying in wait just beyond the horizon. Each *gaucho* depended only on himself and acknowledged no superior.

The later discovery of the *gaucho* as an authentic native character, described by Sarmiento in his *Facundo* in 1845 and by José Hernández in his long epic poem *Martín Fierro* published in 1872, marked an important stage in the emancipation of Latin American literature from foreign servitudes. The latter became the most popular work ever written in Argentina and went through edition after edition. The *gaucho* theme has also been brilliantly developed by Ricardo Güiraldes in his unforgettable classic *Don Segundo Sombra,* which moves with the rhythmic gallop of the plainsman's horse and pulses with the excitement of the rodeo and the fiesta.

The split personality of the Argentine nation, divided between city sophistication and pampa rudeness, predisposed it to feuds and dissensions. The *gauchos* held the balance of power, and in their political inexperience they could easily be united behind a favorite leader or chief. Among these picturesque cattlemen wealth and social position were measured by the head of livestock and the square leagues of grazing land that the *gaucho* owned. A typical *gaucho* was Francisco Candioti, who was lord of 300 square leagues of territory in Entre Ríos across the Paraná River from Santa Fe. There he owned 250,000 cattle and 300,000 horses and mules. As a youth he had made a trip to Peru with a few mules for sale and with an enterprising business eye perceived the need for these useful animals in the commerce of the interior towns and the mines of Upper Peru. His annual trip to Peru thereafter became the Argentine equivalent of the North American "long drive" from Texas north. These trips were described as follows by two English visitors:

Candioti's mode of journeying to Peru with his annual caravan, and with five or six thousand mules, was this: having brought them from his estates on the east side of the Paraná by making them swim, under the direction of many herdsmen, over that stream, he collected them into *potreros,* or large paddocks, in the vicinity of Santa Fé, till he had got together the number he required. He then loaded thirty or forty huge wagons with the merchandise most wanted in Peru; and taking with him, under the guidance of his own vigilant eye, five hundred tame oxen to serve as relays in the drawing of these wagons, and his six thousand mules driven, *en masse,* by forty or fifty *gaucho* peons, he set his face to the plains, and commenced his journey towards Santiago, Tucumán, and Salta, leaving Córdoba to the left.

The country covered with grass, and copiously irrigated by streams, afforded sustenance for his cattle wherever he chose to make halt; and he had to encounter on his journey the obstruction of neither ditches nor fences, any more than he had to incur the expense of a single farthing for the maintenance of his numerous cavalcade. Beside his draught bullocks, he had with him a sufficient number of others for daily slaughter as he proceeded; and neither himself nor his men thought farther provision necessary, than beef, *maté* (Paraguayan tea), salt, water, and watermelons. None of these, except the salt and *maté*, could be said to cost Candioti anything; and these were very cheap. . . .

Whenever the caravan came to a halt, the bullocks, being loosed from their yokes, were let out to pasture on the plain. The herd of mules, too. And while half the cortege of peons were riding round and round them to keep them together, the other half were busied in lighting fires upon the sward, roasting beef, boiling water, eating melons, or stretching themselves out under the shade of the wagons for repose.

At a given hour the refreshed party was sent off to relieve the working one. And when man and beast were sufficiently rested and fed, off again marched the cattle and caravans. In fine moonlight they travelled from evening till morning, and rested during all the hours of solar heat. But when the nights were dark, they necessarily stopped, kindled their fires, and kept . . . watch over their herds of cattle —as wandering at large, under the inspection of the peons, they grazed within sight of the numerous fires kindled to prevent their straying from the spot of encampment.

Candioti was of course the presiding genius of the journey. Sleeping less than any of his peons, he was ever the last to lie down and the first to rise. He invariably got up at midnight, and at some other hour of the night or morning, to see that the watches were properly relieved, and the cattle kept compactly together. The whole discipline of this moving camp was not only in accordance with his own precise regulations, but was seldom infringed, because so vigilantly superintended. He would pardon drunkenness in a peon, impertinence (upon an apology made for it), absence, gambling, and even theft. But never was he known to forgive a man whom he once caught asleep when he ought to have been awake.[3]

In such men the desire for independence was strong, the life of the pampas exhilarating, and the love of the land and its animal wealth a controlling motive. They possessed a native resourcefulness and ingenuity which was contemptuous of book learning. They were self-made men who did not owe either their property or their mode of life to royal favor or inheritance. In the broad pampa each town developed its own special character, its own government, its own regional interests; and these militated against the formation of a unified nation. Federalist sentiment was profoundly rooted in the blood and the habits of the Argentine plainsmen. In contrast, the unitary philosophy was conjured up by certain theorizing *porteños* who did not understand the force of the federalist tradition.

Unitary Reaction

An Argentine nation did not exist. In Buenos Aires the *porteños* who supported the policies of Moreno and Rivadavia were outright nationalists; the littoral provinces, including Entre Ríos, Corrientes, Santa Fe, and Buenos Aires, insisted upon keeping their own autonomy within a federal union limited both geographically and administratively; and the provinces of the

[3] J. P. Robertson and W. P. Robertson, *Letters on Paraguay,* John Murray, London, 1839.

interior, though each contained a small unitary-nationalist party, defended the autonomy of their local *caudillos* hoping, however, that the provincial governments might be financed by the customs revenues of Buenos Aires.

In the province of Buenos Aires, with its capital the port city of the same name, anarchy reigned after Cepeda. There in the eight months after the defeat of the *porteños* in battle eight successive governments were set up and overthrown. Stability was not achieved until Gen. Martín Rodríguez was chosen governor in 1820 with the energetic and enthusiastically patriotic Bernardino Rivadavia as his chief minister or minister of government. During the three years of Rodríguez's term, Rivadavia, who had unitary convictions, carried through a program which not only gave the province of Buenos Aires an outstanding position among the Argentine provinces but served as an example for similar action by some of them. Rivadavia, the real chief of the unitary party in Buenos Aires, had a bold and original mind. He had lived in France after the restoration of the Bourbons and had there fallen under the influence of French socialist ideas. Later becoming a disciple, friend, and correspondent of the leader of English utilitarianism, Jeremy Bentham, Rivadavia conceived programs of action on a grand scale and was impatient to make over Buenos Aires province in accordance with his own centralistic conceptions. But in his determined campaign to abolish what he called "ancient abuses" he antagonized both the large landowning class and the priesthood.

One of Rivadavia's early innovations was a new electoral law which provided for universal manhood suffrage. During his ministry the University of Buenos Aires was established in accordance with plans drawn up several years before, and a course in Bentham's utilitarianism was introduced there. In addition, an agricultural school and a national archives were organized, and a system of widespread primary education was put into operation, organized in accordance with the Lancaster system. For the financial rehabilitation of the province Rivadavia introduced an annual budget system, established the first money market or bourse and the first bank of issue, and started a foreign debt by negotiating in London a loan of 1 million pounds primarily for the construction of a port and waterworks at Buenos Aires and the establishment of new settlements along the Indian frontier. He also introduced the first general tariff, which levied 15 per cent duty *ad valorem* on imports from overseas but only a nominal 4 per cent on imports from other Argentine provinces. This was not the only method by which exchange among the now disparate provinces was encouraged, for free scholarships at the university were provided for students from the provinces.

More controversial than any of these measures was Rivadavia's land-reform system or emphyteusis, which had already been suggested by Belgrano. This was based upon the old civil-law concept of a heritable leasehold and has been compared to the later single-tax system of Henry George. Under this system government lands were no longer to be sold outright but were to be rented, at rates determined by commissions of landowners, to citizens who would bring and keep them under cultivation or otherwise improve them. The rental would be based upon the value increment added to them by the lessee. Equally unenforceable and even more unpopular were his measures against the church, which included requirements that no one under twenty-five years of age should take a vow to join a religious order and that abolished ecclesiastical tithes, independent church courts, and certain monastic establishments. As Rivadavia underestimated the power of the landowning class when he pushed his emphyteusis reform he also showed by his open attack on the sacerdotal power that he underestimated the influence of the clergy with the Argentine people. Indeed, the resistance of the clergy to his reform proposals inspired an abortive revolt.

Rivadavia judged the time inopportune for the governor of Buenos Aires province to call the constitutional convention of all the Argentine provinces to which the governors of the riparian provinces had agreed in the Treaty of Pilar. But meanwhile Buenos Aires joined with Entre Ríos, Corrientes, and Santa Fe in concluding a treaty of peace and alliance in 1822. In this so-called "Treaty of the Quadrilateral" these four provinces agreed to aid one another in the event of invasion by a foreign power and not to declare war against their neighbors without first consulting one another. They also established free trade among themselves and free navigation of the rivers, and they reaffirmed their desire for a new all-Argentine constitutional convention, to be called by the governor of Buenos Aires.

The call for such a convention was issued by Rodríguez's successor, Gen. Juan Gregorio de las Heras. Of the fourteen provinces represented in this convention when it met in Buenos Aires at the end of 1824, six favored federalism, four unitarism, and four were complacently willing to leave the matter to the Congress. The unitaries by working upon these undecided delegates were able to gain the ascendancy, but by only a bare margin. By the trick of doubling the representation of each province in the convention the unitaries then further improved their position, for since the convention was meeting in Buenos Aires a greater number of *porteño* delegates would be able to attend while provincial delegates were absent.

At this time also, auspiciously for the unitaries, Brazil declared war against Buenos Aires, alleging that that province was trying to dismember the empire by supporting rebels in the Banda Oriental or Cisplatine Province. After Brazil's annexation of this province a dissident group—"the immortal 33"—who refused to accept Brazilian dominance had crossed the river to Buenos Aires under the leadership of Juan Antonio Lavalleja, and, reversing the former policy of Artigas, asked for annexation to Buenos Aires. When the Buenos Aires Congress accepted this offer Dom Pedro declared war in December, 1825. The outbreak of war seemed to necessitate the strengthening of central authority among the Argentine provinces and particularly encouraged unitary sentiment in the littoral provinces which were bound to be most affected by military operations.

The new constitution of 1826, speeded up by these developments favorable to the unitaries, was no more successful in imposing unitary control upon the provinces of the Río de la Plata than had been its short-lived predecessor, the constitution of 1819. More than the adoption of the new name—the Argentine Republic—would be required to make it a unitary nation. The constitutional convention designated Rivadavia as the president of the new Argentine Republic for a term of five years and provided in the constitution that the president should thereafter be chosen by an electoral college composed of representatives from each province. A bicameral legislature was to be set up, with a lower house elected directly by the people of the provinces on the basis of population and with a senate composed of two senators from each province chosen by indirect election to serve for terms of nine years. But the governors of the provinces were to be appointed for terms of three years by the president of the republic from lists of nominees submitted to him by the provinces. This latter feature was, of course, certain to be repugnant to the provinces, which were wedded to federalism. Moreover, the province of Buenos Aires was denied the hegemony which it hoped to enjoy by reason of its numerous population and commercial preeminence. What was worse, it lost both its identity and its capital, for the convention put the province directly under the national government and nationalized the city of Buenos Aires as the new federal capital, thus giving rise to a new highly disgruntled federalist faction in the province of Buenos Aires itself.

From the beginning the provinces had regarded the Congress with suspicion as only a tool of the unitary party. The opposition of six of them, led by Juan Bautista Bustos of Córdoba, was sufficient to destroy the constitution which was the handiwork of the Congress. When they were asked in early 1827 to pass upon the new constitution, province after province refused to approve it. But the common danger from the war against Brazil counseled against an open break between federalists and unitaries, at least until after the war was over. The provinces allowed Buenos Aires to fight the war almost alone. Although both its navy and army were victorious in early encounters with the Brazilians, Rivadavia was forced by the domestic situation to make overtures for peace. When these backfired against him he became so discredited that he retired to Europe in 1827, where he died eighteen years later. Rivadavia was a child of the French Revolution pitted against the *gauchos*, and he lost. His policies served the needs of the *porteños* in their relations with Europe rather than the needs of provincial businesses, *estancieros*, and the mass of the Argentine people.

The Rosas Era

Rivadavia's resignation brought an end to unitary control, and his successor, a federalist Dr. Vicente López, who was chosen by Congress as a provisional president, dissolved the Congress and convoked an assembly of Buenos Aires province, which chose the leader of the federalist party there, Manuel Dorrego, as governor. The Argentine Republic which had been envisaged in this second attempt at constitution making for a united nation thus collapsed. Indeed it was never formed, and the provinces simply continued in their previous independent status, dominated by their own local *caudillos*, quarreling with one another, and jealous always of the *porteños* who controlled their contacts with the outside world. "The provinces will be torn to pieces, perhaps," declaimed Facundo, "but never dominated."

As the war against Brazil continued, Buenos Aires received some assistance from her neighboring riparian states. When Great Britain offered mediation to end the conflict it was accepted, with the result that the area in dispute ceased to be either the Banda Oriental of Argentina or the Cisplatine Province of Brazil and became instead the independent Oriental (Eastern) Republic of Uruguay, set up under the joint protection of Buenos Aires and Brazil. Uruguay is a historical accident. Its nascent nationalism, though assiduously nurtured by Artigas and his associates, was not strong enough of itself to produce a nation. Nationhood emerged here as an artificial creation made necessary by Argentine-Brazilian rivalry. With a total population in 1828 of around 70,000 and only 5,000 in its capital, Uruguay owed its national existence to its situation as a buffer area between Buenos Aires and Brazil.

The treaty of peace ending the war was ratified by a new Congress which Dorrego summoned to draw up a federal type of constitution and which met at Santa Fe. Civil war had only been postponed by the war against Brazil, and upon the ratification of the treaty with Brazil, it broke into the open, taking the form now of factional struggles which were motivated by either personal ambition or desire for vengeance and were almost entirely devoid of ideological significance. It was Dorrego's misfortune that the two generals, Juan Lavalle and José María Paz, who won fame in the war against Brazil, belonged to the unitary party. Lavalle immediately launched an attack against him, and by a military *golpe de estado* overthrew his government. Capturing Dorrego he had him summarily shot. For this action Lavalle was pronounced guilty of high treason by the Congress at Santa Fe. But this was a futile gesture, for while the Congress was winding up its ineffectual career, General Paz moved into the interior, and there, after defeating both Bustos of Córdoba and Facundo of La Rioja, proceeded to gain military ascendancy over nine provinces with himself at the head. To meet this threat López of Santa Fe came to terms with a new *gaucho* federalist chieftain of Buenos Aires, Juan Manuel de Rosas. With their cowboy militia from the pampas they won a decisive victory over Lavalle, as a result of which Rosas was elected governor of Buenos Aires province in 1829.

The cooperation of the federalist provinces was broadened in 1831 by the conclusion of a Littoral Pact, among the four littoral provinces—Corrientes,

Buenos Aires, Santa Fe, and Entre Ríos. In this pact they agreed to a defensive and offensive alliance, gave a mutual guaranty of one another's independence, and formed a provisional union. The four provinces established freedom of trade among themselves, but each continued to collect its own taxes, to operate its own schools, and to handle its own boundary problems. The headquarters for the league was located at Santa Fe and equal representation was allowed to all the constituent provinces. The pact provided for the admission of other provinces and, what was more important, specifically recognized the right of Buenos Aires to exercise control over both foreign and military relations, as it had long been doing in fact. A kind of embryonic constitution, this pact marked a step toward unification, a step taken in accordance with federalist principles. With the capture of Paz soon afterward, the whole interior movement collapsed.

Rosas was a vigorous and picturesque leader, who was to dominate Buenos Aires, indeed the whole of Argentina, for almost a quarter of a century and whose influence persists even into the twentieth century. While he was in complete rapport with his *gaucho* comrades of his native pampas and shared their love of the open field and their blunt directness, he had also acquired standing among the business interests of the port as a wealthy businessman and owner of a *saladero* or meat-salting monopoly. Closely connected with the Anchorena family, the wealthiest family in Buenos Aires province, he had served them as steward or overseer, managing their extensive *estancias* and other possessions until he himself became one of the richest men in the province. His honest and effective administration of the province from 1829 to 1832 and his forceful methods gave him an influence over the *caudillos* of other provinces which no previous leader of Buenos Aires had been able to establish. Though a federalist he gave the country a unity which it had previously lacked, but it was a personal unity. He was the *caudillo* of *caudillos*. His own preeminent position led him to discourage the Littoral League as a possible rival to Buenos Aires. When in 1832 this league, then including six provinces in its representative committee at Santa Fe, issued a call for a federal congress, Rosas opposed it, fearing, as he explained, that it would divide the federal party and would enable the unitaries to take advantage of this division to attack them. Above all, he deplored a resumption of civil war. The provinces capitulated before his opposition rather than risk civil war. He preferred to show what could be done in the way of consolidating Argentine nationality without a national structure of government.

Rosas was described at this time by the diplomatic representative of the United States in Buenos Aires, as follows:

His education had been very slight, but he had certain qualities which gave him a commanding influence with the *gauchos*. He possessed much personal beauty, having a large commanding figure and a fine face. And he was a *rubio* [blond]—you must understand that term is applied to those with florid complexions and light eyes, indicating a descent from the pure Gothic race (the ancient lords of Spain), without any intermixture of Moorish or Jewish blood.... In addition, he was inimitable in all athletic exercises: he could manage a horse and throw the lasso with as much dexterity as the most thoroughbred *gaucho*....

Rosas is now the Chief of this "Republic" of Buenos Aires, and by a decree of the Legislature is invested with dictatorial powers. He has no knowledge either of international or even municipal law, and no acquaintance even with the common forms of public business. Reared amongst the cattle and the *gauchos*, it is his influence over the latter—and the patronage of the Anchorenas—which has elevated him to his high station.

His disposition, in my opinion, is not bad, and his intentions are honest (but in this opinion I differ from many intelligent Americans here). . . .

The two brothers Anchorenas have a commanding influence over the Governor. They are facsimiles of the old Spaniards: proud, bigoted, narrow-minded, and oppressive, hating all foreigners—especially Protestants.[4]

When Rosas's term as governor of Buenos Aires province expired in 1832 he refused reelection three times. In his place one leader after another either proved incompetent to handle the problems of provincial government or refused to undertake them. Meanwhile his wife, Encarnación, and his daughter, Manuelita, carried on an active political campaign to get him back into the governorship, representing their cause as "apostolic." Finally after more than two years Rosas acceded to the pressures, which were undoubtedly encouraged by him, and agreed to accept the governorship again on the condition that he be given dictatorial powers. The representative *junta* accepted this arrangement with the provisos, however, that he should not disestablish the Catholic Church and that he must keep the government federalist in nature. These imposed no hardship on him, for he was a conservative in religious matters and actually favored, and later carried out, a vigorous proscription of unitaries. But Rosas insisted that his election should be decided in a popular plebiscite. When it returned 9,315 votes in his favor to only 5 against him, he was inaugurated governor in March, 1835, to serve originally for a five-year term.

During the period of Rosas's domination of the life of the La Plata region from 1835 to 1852 the issue of centralism versus federalism was dealt with not as an academic problem but by methods of practical politics. During those years Rosas was in fact Argentina. He kept the provinces united by means of bilateral pacts, his influence with the provincial governors, and his position of strength as governor of the most populous and richest province. The idol of his party, he was supported by the wealthy because he alone seemed able to maintain order and ensure prosperity, and he exerted a glamorous appeal to the lower classes as a typical *gaucho*. His pictures were carried in processions, and his person was almost deified. Secret patriotic societies, using the symbol

[4] Francis Baylies, *op. cit.*

of the Argentine maize and calling themselves *Mazorca* after it, were organized by his supporters to advance his program and to eliminate his unitary enemies who were denounced as anti-Argentine and proforeign. The opposition was discouraged and was forced either underground or into exile, the universities were purged of unitary propagandists, and many of Argentina's intellectuals, who, like intellectuals elsewhere, had a theoretical predilection for centralized institutions, expatriated themselves to Uruguay, Chile, and other foreign countries. These included Domingo Faustino Sarmiento, Bartolomé Mitre, Juan Bautista Alberdi, and others who later distinguished themselves as exponents of Argentine centralism.

In many ways Rosas resembled his contemporary in the United States, Andrew Jackson. During the Rosas era Argentina underwent a social evolution from the aristocratic and unitary control which had prevailed during the later viceregal and early independence periods to a new type of democratic and federal society. His accession to power came as the culmination of a long struggle between the urban and the rural classes, between the landholding patrician minority and the plebian majority. He appealed to the "disinherited" and was supported by the great mass of the Argentines as well as by the conservatives who had been disillusioned by the preceding anarchy, particularly by the chaos of the year 1820. After these excesses the need for a strong government filled the air. Under Rosas the colonial mode of life was broken and a new Argentine nation finally emerged.

Like Jackson, Rosas, in carrying out his domestic program, particularly of assistance to the agricultural areas, made war on the national bank. The bank, which had contrived to gain a virtual commercial monopoly and had identified itself with the government in fact as well as in name, was closely affiliated with the unitary party. When its charter expired in 1836 Rosas announced its dissolution. This act was a staggering blow to the party but a boon to the cattle-raising provinces, which were thus relieved in some measure of subjection to the Buenos Aires money interests. Another act by which Rosas won increased popularity in all the interior agricultural provinces was the promulgation of a tariff law in 1835, which provided a definite stimulus to agriculture, particularly grain growing. Since the expansion of foreign trade was not desirable if attained only at the expense of local interests, the act sought to encourage domestic manufactures on a scale sufficient to meet the domestic demand. It also liberalized the port regulations in Buenos Aires for the purpose of stimulating commercial relations between that port and the upriver ports and in turn improving their position in overseas markets. As a consequence, Buenos Aires now received increasingly large cargoes of upriver produce, which were floated down the river in small craft and *chalapas* (flat-bottomed boats). Although Rosas was only the federalist governor of Buenos Aires province he seemed to be putting the interests of the nation—of all parts of the nation—above the narrow interests of the port city. He thus established himself as the *de facto* leader of the nation and laid the basis for a durable federation of provinces which would finally be given a constitutional structure in 1853.

In the national interest also Rosas initiated the policy of making peace with the hostile Indians of the pampas. When in the later colonial period the Indians made incursions even into the outskirts of Buenos Aires, the viceroys and the *cabildo* had thrown across the pampa a chain of small frontier forts. These became the nuclei of towns, but these towns and the frontier *estancias* were constantly threatened by Indian attack. Rosas was familiar with frontier life because as the steward of the Anchorenas he had managed an estate in southern Buenos Aires province. He had first risen to prominence there in 1820 when he had organized a band of several hundred armed *peones* for defense against the Indians. In his campaign against them he had recovered thousands of cattle and acquired vast prestige among the cattlemen. In his expedition of 1833 when he was commissioned by the legislature of Buenos Aires to move against the Indians he began instead to negotiate treaties with them, fixing the southern limits of white settlement in the provinces of Buenos Aires, Santa Fe, Córdoba, San Luis, and Mendoza. The Indians agreed not to cross these boundary limits without military passes. Their *caciques* were kept mollified by regular gifts of horses, *yerba maté*, tobacco, and salt. This policy of Rosas seemed to him preferable to a long series of Indian wars. It preserved peace on the frontier for more than twenty years.

The Argentine provinces lacked a national government in name, though in fact they had a national champion in Rosas at Buenos Aires. In his dealings with foreign nations even more than in his domestic program, as will be shown later, Rosas was able to establish the primacy both of Buenos Aires and of the as yet unorganized nation. The problems of the period were being given national solutions but within the limits of federalism and without any doctrinaire preconceptions. Though the fashion of making constitutions prevailed elsewhere in Latin America during this period, Argentina abandoned the attempt after the two unsuccessful tries of 1819 and 1826 and was satisfied with the personal leadership provided by Rosas. From the system of one masterful *caudillo*, ruling the strategically situated and wealthy province of Buenos Aires and dominating in varying degrees the *caudillos* of some thirteen other provinces, would emerge in 1853 the Argentine Confederation. Significantly, during the Rosas period none of the provinces declared its independence of Buenos Aires to become a separate nation. Before the accession of Rosas to power Paraguay and Uruguay had been lost to Argentina, but no such losses occurred under him. His sincere federalist convictions responded to the predominating federalist convictions of the Argentines. Instructed by the two earlier abortive attempts by the unitaries to impose their centralism upon the country, Rosas refused to make a third attempt. Clearly any such attempt if made in accordance with federalist principles would ensure the supremacy of the provinces over the port and would only confirm the Rosas system.

Achievement of Constitutional Order in Chile

In Chile the struggle between the capital and the provinces, between centralists and federalists, did not assume the same proportions as in the La Plata region. The capital, Santiago, a city of some forty thousand inhabitants, was not the port, and during the revolutionary struggle it was less inclined to independence than were the provinces. The first Congress, after it was purged of its conservative elements by Carrera, laid the basis for a constitutional system in 1811 by providing for the gradual abolition of Negro slavery, setting up new courts of justice, and putting the church on a constitutional basis as a state church which would be subject to control by the government. The first attempt at constitution making came in the following year when Carrera, then at the height of his dictatorship, issued a provisional constitution, which though republican in form sought mainly to justify his own short-lived usurpation of power. When O'Higgins was chosen supreme director in 1817 after the second expulsion of the Spanish he at first cooperated with Buenos Aires in negotiating for a European prince to become monarch of the country. He offered to accept a prince from any neutral power that would extend protection to Chile. But he soon drew back from these negotiations and established a dictatorship himself, buttressed by a constitution.

By reason of the perils of the time this constitution, though sanctioned by unanimous popular vote, placed virtually all power in the hands of the supreme director. The legislative body of five men was to be appointed by him, and the courts were made dependent upon him. The tradition of military rule in Chile was strong, going back to the days of the captaincy general, and was justified in part by the need for resistance to the savage Araucanian Indians in the south. This tradition was strengthened by the wars of independence and by the later preoccupation of the wealthy landowners with the rebuilding of their estates which had been devastated by the war. In particular, the area around Concepción in the south had been reduced almost to a desert by the incessant warfare between the Chileans and the Spaniards and more recently between the Chileans and the Araucanians, who were now led by a ruthless Chilean renegade, Vicente Benavides. To the creole aristocracy which replaced the Spanish aristocracy in Chile, strong military rule seemed to offer the best assurance of continued peace and order.

O'Higgins was an enlightened dictator who was strongly influenced by the liberal ideas of his time and regarded his dictatorial rule only as a transition to a republican type of government. His strong methods were evidenced mainly in his repression of freedom of speech and the press and in his treatment of the remnant of the Carrera faction. Aided by Ramón Freire, the creole *intendente* of Concepción, O'Higgins moved against the lingering royalist strongholds in the south, particularly those on the island of Chiloé. In order to help prepare San Martín for his northern expedition he established the first Chilean navy, starting with a converted English merchant ship. To this he added other vessels until he built up a considerable fleet under Adm. Manuel Blanco Encalada. This was the fleet with which Admiral Cochrane later blockaded Callao and raided Guayaquil, thus preparing the way for the revolutionizing of Peru and Quito. O'Higgins also founded a national library and a national institute, the nucleus of the later University of Chile, both of which had been originally conceived by Carrera. These and other improvements in the capital, Santiago, including new boulevards, paved streets, and a new public theater, began to give it the appearance of a modern town. But many of these improvements were made possible by a loan of 1 million pounds which O'Higgins secured from British bankers and the British government at an enormous discount.

The elimination of the Carrera faction, with the execution of the three brothers in Mendoza, and the defeat of the royalist elements in the south of Chile made O'Higgins's dictatorship, however benevolent and constitutionally correct, seem increasingly anachronistic. Besides, O'Higgins's sponsorship of the theater and his favors to Protestant foreigners, particularly the English, alienated the clergy. At the same time his attempts to eliminate cock- and bull-fighting, dice games, and gambling were resisted by other elements as high-handed suppression of legitimate pleasures. When he suppressed titles of nobility and tried to abolish coats of arms and the entailing of estates, he incurred criticism from the wealthy upper classes. So strong did the opposition become by 1822 that he felt obliged to call for the election of a new constitutional assembly. In the elections O'Higgins applied considerable pressure to secure the kind of assembly he wished, and when it met it was so favorable to him that it drew up a constitution extending his power for ten years. This arrangement only increased the dissatisfaction with his system of government, though apparently not with him personally, and revolts broke out in Concepción, in La Serena, and even in Santiago, with the result that he offered his resignation to the assembly in January, 1823, and retired to Lima.

The overthrow of O'Higgins opened up a decade of bitter conflict between the Conservatives, called *pelucones* or "bigwigs," and the Liberals called *pipiolos* or upstarts. At first the Conservatives gained the upper hand, and the new Conservative Congress drew up a constitution, largely the work of Juan Egaña. But they scrapped it a few months later when they chose Ramón Freire, the thirty-six-year-old *intendente* of Concepción, as perpetual supreme director. He was confronted with the difficult task of redeeming Chile's financial position, which was going from bad to worse. By reason of the postwar depression the government was unable to meet even the interest payments on the British loan which O'Higgins had concluded. In this dire situation Freire proposed to grant a monopoly of the revenues from the sales of tobacco, alcohol, playing cards, and other items to the business house of Portales, Cea, and Company on condition that the company assume responsibility for paying the interest on the debt. But this proposal aroused strong opposition from the Liberal outlying provinces, which protested that the government was careless of their interests and was willing to sacrifice them to this Santiago-Valparaíso business monopoly. Here then was a revelation of a basic cleavage between town and country. In order to placate Liberal sentiment Freire was obliged to abandon the arrangement with Portales after two years. He also began to move against the church by fixing twenty-five years as the minimum age when persons could take final vows, reducing the number of monasteries, and secularizing their lands, but in doing so he only sharpened the conflict between Conservatives and Liberals. Finally he resigned in disgust in 1826, and turned over the government to his Liberal vice president, Francisco Pinto, and a Liberal Congress.

The Liberals now tried the experiment of federalism and drew up a constitution which provided a large measure of autonomy for the eight provinces. But federalism for Chile was obviously artificial, and even the Liberals only lukewarmly supported it while they controlled the central government. The country was bankrupt and could hardly support one national government, not to mention eight strong provincial governments. Besides, federalism had a much weaker basis in Chile than in Argentina, for the settled parts of Chile occupied a less-extended area and were therefore more compact, it had a stronger tradition of centralized and military government, and it was still faced with the problem of subjugating hostile Indians south of the Bío-Bío River. For these reasons a strong central government seemed necessary and was steadily advocated by the Conservatives, led by Diego Portales, head of Portales, Cea, and Company, and by Juan Egaña. The federal scheme in Chile proved so impractical that it lasted only two years and was abandoned by President Pinto himself in 1828. To take its place a new constitution, largely the work of José Joachín Mora, was drawn up. But Pinto's Liberal party had shown itself largely bankrupt of programs, and when Pinto resigned in 1829 the Conservatives, led by Joachín Prieto, started a revolution. After six months of conflict between Liberals and Conservatives, almost contemporaneous with civil war in Argentina, a decisive battle was fought at Lircay in which the Conservatives completely routed the Liberals and assumed control of the government. At the very time when Bolívar was vainly struggling to hold his Gran Colombia together and Rosas was moving into executive control in Argentina the Conservative Diego Portales became virtual dictator of Chile.

Portales, then only thirty-seven years of age, had had a business career and had not been involved in politics until his company received the monopoly from Freire in 1824. From that time on he took a prominent part in Conservative party activities and in the revolution of 1829–1830 risked everything that he owned. After the Conservatives occupied Santiago he was made chief minister for foreign affairs, war, and marine in the new provisional government and became the first civilian dictator of Chile after the Conservative victory at Lircay. A gifted leader of high character, Portales was never president in fact, but he was the real power in the Chilean government, able to make and unmake presidents.

At the outset of his regime Portales moved vigorously against the opposition, depriving Liberal army officers of their rank, exiling both Freire and Mora, proscribing other Liberal leaders, and even rejecting an appeal from the exiled O'Higgins to be allowed to return to Chile. In order to keep the belligerent Liberals under control Portales established a national guard manned by Conservative officers and founded a military academy limited almost entirely to members of his own aristocratic class. By these means and by a rigid press censorship he established his Conservative party firmly in power. A new constitution, the seventh in Chile's short national history, was drawn up and adopted in 1833.

In the constitutional convention Mariano Egaña, who prepared the original outline of the constitution, argued for a strong executive, while Manuel José Gandarillas argued in favor of a strong Congress. The resulting constitution represented a compromise between these conflicting viewpoints. The president, who was given considerable powers, was to be chosen by indirect elections for a term of five years and could be reelected for another term of five years. His cabinet members were given the privilege of sitting in Congress, but they could not vote. When Congress was not in session the president, with the consent of his council of state, could declare a state of siege; but when Congress was in session, only it could authorize him to do so. The Congress was a bicameral body, elected by popular vote; when it was not in session a commission composed of members of both houses acted in its place as a continuing committee. The suffrage was limited to male citizens twenty-five years of age and over who could read and write and who owned a specified amount of property. Under this constitution the government of Chile was completely centralized and the provinces were reduced to departments headed by governors appointed by and responsible to the government in Santiago. As in previous Chilean constitutions, no provision was made for religious toleration, and church and state remained united. The Chilean government, however, claimed and in fact exercised the right of the *patronato*, inherited from colonial times, of nominating candidates for the higher ecclesiastical offices.

Before the constitution was promulgated General Prieto was elected president and Portales temporarily retired to private life. By the end of this, the first dictatorship of Portales, Chile was successfully launched upon its national career under a constitution which would keep a Conservative aristocracy in control of the government for almost thirty years—until 1861 —and would give the country an extraordinary degree of political stability. Under the guidance of a small group of conscientious and serious-minded landowners, who have been compared with the contemporary Whig landed aristocracy of England, Chile was to enjoy several decades of quiet and orderly growth, in sharp contrast to that of some of her neighbors. The constitution adopted in 1833 would serve, with amendments, as the basic frame of government for Chile until 1925.

Constitutional Monarchy in Brazil

Under a constitutional monarchy Brazil attained the same high degree of stability after declaring its independence from Portugal. This vast country, unlike the Spanish American areas, embarked upon its national career as a unit. This was all the more remarkable since it was even more geographically and economically diversified than Chile, not to mention the La Plata provinces. Heterogeneity and localism were the heritage of Brazil. This enormous country was really a group of "island" areas separated from one another by physical barriers of rivers, mountains, and jungles, and each imbued with its own local patriotism. Here the states of the sugar-producing northern bulge had little in common with the royal capital, Rio de Janeiro, or with the southern cattle-raising states. And all of them were separated from the hinterland areas by geographical obstacles—in the north by jungles and swamps, and in the middle and south by steep coastal escarpments. That these diverse areas, preoccupied with their various local interests and possessing little idea of national solidarity, did not either fly apart or, more probably, fly at one another's throats when independence was achieved seems to set Brazil apart from the Spanish viceroyalties.

Brazil was predisposed to greater unity and stability than the new Spanish countries by the fact that its population was dispersed through the countryside and was predominantly agrarian and pastoral. Here a pattern of a homogeneous rural class prevailed as contrasted with the town system of the Spanish countries. The centers of population along the seaboard and on the inland plateau calling themselves cities were really only sprawling villages spreading out into ranches, small estates, and country houses. The quiet of their urban life was broken only by the squeaking of the oxcarts, the bustle of caravans of loaded horses and mules, and the songs of Negroes and cowboys who had come to town from neighboring ranches. Negro laundresses washed clothes in the town fountains, and carriages rolled through the streets bumping over the stones and holes. Townsfolk who had to go abroad at night were preceded by a slave with lantern in hand. Some of the inland cities, as, for example, those in the gold and diamond country that had enjoyed a precocious growth in the eighteenth century, had dwindled to ghost towns. Vila Rica in the mining region looked like "a stage where a show has just been finished."

As a result rural aristocracy of the colonial period continued its dominant role in the life of the country after independence and entrenched itself in power even more firmly after the abdication of Dom Pedro I. Brazil's Indians were widely dispersed and were not tied to established town units as were the Indians in the Andean highlands and in the Mexican plateau of Spanish

America. They therefore did not provide the base for that *caciquismo* or competing nuclei of regional feeling which was a divisive force in Spanish America. In addition, the transition to independence in Brazil, unlike that in the Spanish colonies, was gradual, not sudden. Slow if unintended preparations for it were made during the fourteen years when the Portuguese court was situated in Rio de Janeiro; and the change when it occurred was not accompanied by civil war or violent social dislocations. Brazil did not suffer the losses which Spanish America suffered during the struggle for independence in property destruction, setbacks to economic progress, political anarchy, and disrupted leadership. Moreover, the leaders who brought about the independence of Brazil, representing largely the creole landed aristocracy, looked with disfavor upon political experimentation. But the basic continuing element of stability, which all the other new nations of the Americas lacked, was monarchy. The Braganzas provided a unifying center of Brazilian nationalism and gave it a conservative centralized complexion which kept the nation together and enabled it to survive as a single unit the overthrow of two monarchs.

Pedro I like his mother was ambitious and intemperate. When he became emperor his formal education and political experience were deficient, but he relied upon his quick intelligence to enable him to fulfill his new role. At the age of nineteen he had been married to Leopoldina Cristina, daughter of Emperor Francis I of Austria, without having seen her beforehand. His queen had many intellectual interests, was well educated, and became very popular with her Brazilian subjects, partly because of her generosity and kindness and partly because she espoused the interests of Brazil against those of Portugal. But Pedro was emotionally unstable and undisciplined, dissolute and addicted to coarse jokes and fits of passion. His private life was scandalous, particularly with the flamboyant Marchioness of Santos, for whom he built a house next to the palace.

Pedro tended to favor the Portuguese element in Brazil, for not all the Portuguese had left the country with his father, John VI, in 1821. When a constitutional assembly met in 1823 to draft a basic charter for the monarchy the nature of the new government was thoroughly debated. The republican and anti-Portuguese elements, led by the three Andrada brothers, wished to impose constitutional limitations upon the monarchy, to emphasize the federal nature of the government, and to ensure a large measure of autonomy to the provinces. Pedro, influenced by his Portuguese advisers who wished a centralized government, thereupon dismissed the assembly, exiled the leaders, including the Andrada brothers, and appointed a committee of ten to draw up a constitution.

The constitution which they presented in the following year declared Brazil to be a constitutional monarchy governed by the House of Braganza. Since it largely preserved the prerogatives which the emperor had claimed for himself it was accepted by him and was imposed upon the country. It recognized the right of the emperor to appoint and dismiss the members of his cabinet, to approve or veto legislation, to prorogue the parliament, and even to dissolve it when the safety of the empire required. It made Brazil a unitary nation, reducing the provinces to little more than administrative subdivisions of the central government and entrusting the emperor with the power to appoint and dismiss the provincial governors. It also gave him unlimited power to select the members of the council of state, which was a body of ten members separate from the cabinet and holding office for life. The parliament was to consist of two houses, a lower house chosen on the basis of limited suffrage for terms of four years, and a senate named by the emperor for life terms from triple lists of nominees chosen indirectly by the electorate. Most important of all, the constitution conferred the *poder moderado* or regulating power upon the emperor, authorizing him to "watch incessantly over the maintenance of the independence, equilibrium, and harmony of the rest of the political powers."

Largely because this constitution was presented by Pedro as a gift to the people and because it was almost immediately violated by him, opposition soon appeared. In particular, he set aside the article guaranteeing personal liberty, established censorship of the press, and by these and other arbitrary actions showed that he interpreted his government not to be responsible to parliament. Moreover, he consistently favored the Portuguese elements in the country putting them over Brazilians in the government. When he readmitted the Jesuits to Brazil he antagonized the liberals who formed the nucleus of the nascent republican movement. Organized republican resistance to Pedro's regime appeared in Pernambuco in the north in 1824 where a short-lived "Confederation of the Equator" was set up under the leadership of Manoel de Carvalho Paes de Andrade. The revolution spread to the neighboring provinces of Paraíba, Rio Grande do Norte, and Ceará, but was soon suppressed by Lord Cochrane acting as Pedro's defender.

The emperor's partiality for the Portuguese was shown by his acceptance of a treaty concluded with Portugal in 1825 in which his father, under pressure from Britain, recognized the independence of Brazil but at the same time required Brazil to pay an indemnity of 2 million pounds sterling of which three-fourths was a debt which Portugal owed to Britain. This treaty was bitterly opposed by the Brazilians. In the following year Pedro became technically the heir to the throne of Portugal when his father died, but he wisely declined to assert his claims to it, advancing instead the claims of his seven-year-old daughter María da Gloria. But Pedro's younger brother, Miguel, also claimed the vacant throne, insisting that under the Salic law a woman could not ascend the throne in preference to a male claimant. An attempt was made to end this rivalry by a marriage between María da Gloria and Miguel, and the little girl was actually married to her uncle by proxy. But when the marriage was later canceled, civil war broke out in Portugal between the Liberals supporting Gloria and the Conservatives supporting Miguel. Pedro backed the claims of his daughter, but his Brazilian subjects looked with a dubious eye upon his involvement in the Portuguese controversy.

Even more dubious and less successful in its outcome was Pedro's involvement in the war with Buenos Aires over the Cisplatine Province, which ended in the loss of this province and its establishment in 1828 as the independent republic of Uruguay. During this unpopular and costly war Pedro's German mercenary troops mutinied and had to be disbanded. Many of them took up land and became the progenitors of the large German colonies in the southern provinces of Paraná, Santa Catarina, and Rio Grande do Sul.

Pedro's unpopularity was increased by the suspicious death of his popular queen after a violent quarrel between them over his mistress. As his regime weakened from internal causes, his republican opponents were stimulated to action against him by the example of the successful French revolution of 1830 overthrowing Charles X. At this point Pedro committed the indiscretion of dismissing his liberal cabinet and appointing in its place a cabinet composed of conservatives of the Portuguese party, as he had a constitutional right to do. Defying public opinion he refused to reinstate the liberal ministry declaring, "I will do everything for the people, but nothing by the people." Monarchical absolutism could not phrase a better *credo*, but it was contrary to the wishes and spirit of the Brazilian people. His policy was not only anathema to republican sentiment but it antagonized also the landowning, slaveholding class and, most important of all, the army. The hero of Brazilian independence had become a tyrant. When his army deserted him he dramatically and unexpectedly abdicated his throne in April, 1831, in favor of his five-year-old son Pedro, whose name was thus conveniently shortened from Pedro de Alcantara João Carlos Leopoldo Salvador Bibiano Francisco Xavier de Paula Leocadio Miguel Gabriel Rafael Gonzaga! The former monarch then sailed on a British ship to England and thence to Portugal, where he spent the few remaining years of his life in a finally successful effort to place his daughter on the throne of the Braganzas. He never again saw the young Pedro whom he left behind in Rio de Janeiro.

The abdication of Pedro I marked the end of the political influence of the Portuguese element in Brazil, but Portuguese culture, notably in art forms and architecture, continued to be dominant, for the native Brazilian landholding aristocracy, who now supplanted the local Portuguese aristocracy, had been schooled in the Portuguese tradition. The manner in which the Brazilians achieved their independence in 1822 and disposed of their first emperor in 1831 illustrated the moderation and restraint which have characterized much of their subsequent history. Less mercurial and less addicted to violent overturns of government than the Spanish Americans they have written a more placid history than the latter. With them violence was usually localized in the frontier areas and was confined to struggles against nature and wild Indians. But violence was not approved by the conservative seaboard classes who controlled the government.

During the ten years while the young Pedro was in his minority and a regency tried to govern Brazil the country almost fell apart. The national economy had already been seriously weakened by the forced liquidation of the Bank of Brazil in 1829. Brazil now repeated belatedly the decade of anarchy which had characterized the history of several of the Spanish American countries immediately after they gained their independence. The conflicts of liberals versus conservatives, federalists versus centralists, northern provinces versus southern provinces, and Brazilians versus Portuguese, though they did not take form in general revolution, produced widespread confusion and revealed the essential artificiality of Brazilian nationalism.

The first government of three regents was reduced to that of one regent, the Liberal priest Antônio Diogo Feijó of São Paulo, by constitutional amendment in 1834. Other provisions of this *Acto Adicional* gave the provinces the right to elect their own legislatures and control their own finances but still required that the provincial governors should be appointed by the national government. But this *Acto,* establishing, in effect, a republican government in Brazil and restoring the federal system, did not curb disaffection in the provinces. In Pará the soldiers took over their garrison and set up a republic which lasted for five years. Brazil's southernmost province, Rio Grande do Sul, had never been so closely linked with the empire as the coffee and sugar provinces had been. There the so-called "War of the *Farrapos*" or "War of the Ragamuffins" began in 1835 when the *gaúcho* republicans of Rio Grande do Sul entered the chief city and port of Porto Alegre, expelled the governor appointed from Rio de Janeiro by Feijó, and established the Rio Grandense Republic. Under that name it went its independent way for a decade—from 1835 to 1845. Even in the most stable provinces—Rio de Janeiro, São Paulo, Minas Gerais, and Bahía—factional struggles were rampant.

When the Conservatives wrested power from Father Feijó in 1837 and established a wealthy senator, Pedro de Araujo Lima, as regent they attempted to undo the *Acto Adicional* by reestablishing a centralized government and destroying provincial autonomy. The provincial assemblies were made little more than advisory bodies under the supervision of governors appointed from Rio de Janeiro. But by these methods the Conservatives proved to be no better able to pacify the country than the Liberals had been. New revolutions broke out in Bahía and the revolution in Rio Grande do Sul spread to Santa Catarina. As a result the demand arose on all sides that Pedro be declared legally of age, although the constitution declared explicitly that he would become of age only on his eighteenth birthday. The national assembly accordingly staged what was virtually a parliamentary revolution and, after securing the consent of the fifteen-year-old Pedro, proclaimed him Dom Pedro II Emperor of Brazil in July, 1840. The fateful *"já quero"* of the adolescent boy ended the regency and with it a decade of virtual republicanism. The reestablishment of the monarchy revitalized the empire, checked the trend toward decentralization and republicanism, and brought a new element of stability to Brazil.

With the accession of this indubitably Brazilian monarch, quite different from his father, the centrifugal trend in Brazil was checked and a strong basis for national solidarity and stability was laid, to last for almost fifty years. The centralism which Gran Colombia, the federation of Greater Peru, and the Central American federation had established but failed to maintain, which the La Plata provinces were achieving in practice after much travail almost without knowing it, and with a conservative landed aristocracy was imposing in Chile seemed now to be assured in Brazil. But the centralism that was established there through the power of the ruling class of the great landowners and under the leadership of the wise and tactful Dom Pedro II was nevertheless a constitutional centralism. As it rested upon a constitutional base and parliamentary institutions it could not become uncontrollably arbitrary. The monarch though enjoying virtually unlimited powers must remain a constitutional *caudilho*.

Common Problems of the New Nations

The issue of centralism versus federalism which seemed to be the main source of discord in all the seventeen new nations as they struggled to work out their unaccustomed problems of self-government after 1810 can be viewed as also a struggle between conservatives and liberals as those terms were understood in the early nineteenth century. The centralists or conservatives represented generally the propertied classes with vested interests in society as it existed under the old regime. They were closely affiliated with the Roman Catholic Church, which had been the established church of colonial days, and they wished to maintain the authoritarian, even the royalist, traditions of those days. They therefore advocated strong government. The federalists or liberals, on the other hand, heirs of the Enlightenment and the early French Revolution, were most numerous in the professional and mercantile classes. They owned little property, particularly in land. They were restive under authority, whether of the crown, the church, or local aristocratic propertied classes. The chief instigators of the independence movement, they wished to preserve both to themselves and to their new national societies the advantages of local self-rule and not to allow government to be monopolized by conservative and authoritarian ruling groups. Very often the strength of these two movements ebbed and flowed with the ebb and flow of the liberal-conservative struggle in Europe.

In the larger aspect the issue that divided the Latin Americans in their attempts to organize the new nations was not political but rather social and economic. The political systems that were evolved, ranging from Morazán's liberal system in Central America to Brazil's monarchical system, embodied the social and economic views of the groups or coalition of groups that were able to make their interests prevail at the time. Often, it seemed, the system that was finally adopted and embodied in a constitution represented a successful effort by traditional oligarchies to put their political desires into operation. But some deference had to be paid both to public opinion, which was now better able to express itself than under colonial restraints, and to regional conflicts, which had been intensified by the removal of the crown's authority. Not only had the number of administrative units been increased as a result of the overthrow of the viceroyalties of New Spain, New Granada, Lima, and Buenos Aires, with their various administrative subdivisions, but within the nations that were formed from them ports vied with hinterland, lowland with highland, town with country, and exporting interests with agricultural interests. Even in those countries where the forces of centralism seemed to be in the ascendancy the forces of localism would continue to offer a strong challenge to the exercise of national authority. In other areas where national feelings had little basis in tradition, as in the Central American countries, Ecuador, Bolivia, and Uruguay, the centrifugal forces continued to be dominant.

Additional Reading

Amunátegui y Solar, Domingo: *Historia de Chile* (2 vols.), Nascimento, Santiago de Chile, 1933.

Bealer, L. W.: "Juan Manuel de Rosas" in A. C. Wilgus (ed.), *South American Dictators during the First Century of Independence,* George Washington University Press, Washington, D.C., 1937.

Bernstein, Harry: *Modern and Contemporary Latin America,* J. B. Lippincott Company, Philadelphia, 1952, chaps. 13, 26.

Burgin, Miron: *The Economic Aspects of Argentine Federalism, 1820–1852,* Harvard University Press, Cambridge, Mass., 1946.

Calogeras, João Pandiá: *A History of Brazil,* trans. and ed. by Percy Alvin Martin, University of North Carolina Press, Chapel Hill, N.C., 1939, chap. V.

Carcovich, Luis: *Portales y la política internacional hispano-americana,* Imprenta Universitaria, Santiago de Chile, 1937.

Galdames, Luis: *A History of Chile,* trans. and ed. by Isaac Joslin Cox, University of North Carolina Press, Chapel Hill, N.C., 1941, chaps. X, XI.

Gandía, Enrique de: *Historia de la república argentina en el siglo XIX,* A. Estrada y Cía, S.A., Buenos Aires, 1940. An excessively detailed history written from the unitary viewpoint.

Gil, Federico G.: *Genesis and Modernization of Political Parties in Chile,* University of Florida Press, Gainesville, 1962.

Levene, Ricardo: *A History of Argentina,* trans. and ed. by William Spence Robertson, University of North Carolina Press, Chapel Hill, N.C., 1937, chaps. XXXVI–L.

Marín, Raúl: *Conceptos políticos y administrativos de Portales,* Imp. el Imparcial, Santiago de Chile, 1937.

Nichols, M. W.: *The Gaucho: Cattle Hunter, Cavalryman, Ideal of Romance,* Duke University Press, Durham, N.C., 1942.

Quesada, Ernesto: *La Epoca de Rosas, su Verdadero Carácter Histórico,* Moen, Buenos Aires, 1898, republished by the Faculdad de Filosofía y Letras, University of Buenos Aires, Talleres S. A Casa Jacobo Penser, Ltda., Buenos Aires, 1923. A sympathetic treatment.

Romero, José Luis: *Las Ideas Políticas en Argentina,* Fondo de Cultura Económica, Mexico, 1946. A brilliant and provocative analysis.

Sarmiento, Domingo Faustino: *Life in the Argentine Republic in the Days of the Tyrants; or, Civilization and Barbarism,* trans. by Mrs. Horace Mann, Hurd and Houghton, New York, 1868, and Hafner Publishing Company, New York, 1960.

Street, John: *Artigas and the Emancipation of Uruguay,* Cambridge University Press, 1959.

Tinker, Edward Larocque: *Life and Literature of the Pampas,* University of Florida Press, Gainesville, 1961.

Torres-Ríoseco, Arturo: *The Epic of Latin American Literature,* University of California Press, Berkeley, Calif., 1959, chaps. 2, 4.

XIII

Defending Their Nationality

After Spain lost her American kingdoms she refused to move toward a commercial rapprochement with them, as England had more wisely done in relation to her revolted colonies in North America after 1782. Indeed Spain's commercial stake in America had declined markedly in the latter eighteenth century as she failed under the free-trade system to compete successfully in the commerce of the Americas with her European trade rivals—Holland, England, and France—which based their trade upon individual enterprise and cooperative organization. Spain lost commercial preeminence in America before she lost political control, and by persisting in her refusal to recognize the independence of the New Spanish American nations after they had unmistakably established it *de facto* she postponed reconciliation with them. Not until after the death of Ferdinand VII in 1833 and the accession of a more liberal regime did Spain give serious consideration to political recognition and the reopening of trade relations with the new nations of Spanish America. Meanwhile those nations were being drawn more closely into the commercial orbit of Spain's rivals.

Latin America's Relations with England and the United States

As the leaders of independence looked chiefly to France for their ideological inspiration they staked their economic future on the favor of Britain. The final breakdown of Spain's imperial system under the hammer blows of Napoleon gave the English merchants the commercial opportunities which they had long sought and enabled them to legalize a trade which they had been carrying on clandestinely—and profitably—since the seventeenth century. While England was fighting Spain she was able to cut off the mother country's communications with her overseas dominions and thus to build up a lucrative commerce with them. When she later allied herself with the Spanish *junta* in resistance to Joseph Bonaparte she concluded an agreement with the *junta* permitting her to trade with the Spanish territories overseas on condition that she assist in bringing them back under the control of Spain. Though her good offices to this end were later rejected she was able to maintain her commerce with them.

To England as well as to other foreign trading nations Brazil's ports were opened up by the Portuguese crown in 1808. The new, close relationship between Britain and Brazil was signalized by the negotiation of a commercial treaty by the British minister, Lord Strangford, and the Prince Regent, John, in 1810, which made Brazil almost an economic protectorate of England. The treaty gave England's merchants in Brazil immunity from visit and search in their homes and warehouses, allowed them extraterritorial rights in legal disputes, and lowered the import duties on their merchandise to 15 per cent, while the Portuguese were paying 16 per cent and merchants of other countries 24 per cent. England thus took advantage of her position of political command in Portugal to gain commercial preeminence in Brazil. In the next year sixty-five British businessmen were settled in Rio de Janeiro, and by 1816 more than a hundred. England's merchants specialized in trade in bulk goods, machinery, iron products, wines and other liquors, groceries, books, paper, and textiles.

The virtual elimination of England's trade with the United States during the second war between them from 1812 to 1814 made the developing commerce with Latin America increasingly attractive, if not essential, to England. After the war the new protective tariff of the United States enacted in 1816 imposed almost the same limitations on British trade with the United States as had the war itself and further stimulated the expansion of England's commerce with Spanish America. By 1822 that commerce was valued at almost 6 million pounds. The assistance which English volunteers, such as the English and Irish foreign legion in Bolívar's army and Lord Cochrane in San Martín's expedition against Peru, rendered to the cause of independence in Spanish America had a beneficent effect upon England's commerce with the new nations. Both British merchants and the British government were quick to follow up their advantages there, though the British government itself remained officially neutral, as attested by its Foreign Enlistment Act of 1819. To the ruling classes in England the revolutionary movements there were abhorrent. England and other nations as well, Bolívar complained bitterly on several occasions, had remained only "apathetic bystanders" in the Spanish American wars for independence. Not until the commercial interests became dominant in the London government, as they did under George Canning in 1822, did England's policy toward the revolted states of Spanish America become more realistic. That development, combined with France's victory over the Spanish liberals in the following year, made acceptance of the independence of the Spanish American nations palatable to the British, particularly after independence clearly became established in fact.

In the United States, on the other hand, where resistance to an oppressive European mother country was respectable, public opinion was sympathetic to the Spanish American revolutionists from the beginning. Besides, the prospects of an expanding commerce with them were just as attractive to the Americans of the North as to the British. During the Napoleonic Wars several of the east coast ports of the United States profitably pressed their trade advantages with the countries on the east coast of South America, thus introducing many exotic products into the United States and opening up new outlets for its manufactures. In 1810 the United States began to send commercial agents to the revolted colonies—Robert K. Lowry to Caracas, Joel R. Poinsett to Buenos Aires and Santiago, and William Shaler to Havana. The favorable public opinion was reflected in the adoption of a resolution by Congress in 1811 expressing sympathy with the revolutionists. On the eve of the War of 1812 Congress appropriated $50,000 for the relief of the earthquake victims in Venezuela, and the agent who delivered it, Alexander Scott, was instructed to inform the Venezuelan authorities that the United States took a sincere interest in their struggle for independence from Spain, hoped they would establish a republican government, and was informing the governments of Europe of its interest in the independence of the Spanish provinces.

After the peace of Ghent many naval veterans of the second war of the United States against Great Britain took service on corsairs of the revolutionary governments in South America. The leading champion of Latin American independence in Washington was Henry Clay, Speaker of the House of Representatives from 1815 to 1820, who eloquently urged recognition of the revolted colonies as new governments, particularly after Argentina's declaration of independence in 1816. With public opinion so well disposed to the revolutionists the United States government could not effectively enforce its neutral duties, with the result that many privateersmen were fitted out by the South American revolutionists in United States ports, particularly in Baltimore and New Orleans, whence they carried on operations against the Spanish forces bent upon reconquest.

The official policy of the Madison and Monroe administrations was, like that of Britain, to exploit the newly opened trade with the revolted Spanish Americans and to maintain neutrality until they had demonstrably established their independence. Official intervention on their behalf or even premature recognition might bring the wrath of Europe upon the United States. As early as 1808, however, the Jefferson administration had expressed its "strongest repugnance" to the transfer of either Cuba or Mexico from the weak hands of Spain to those of either France or England, and Congress in 1811 reaffirmed this "no-transfer" principle with special reference to the Floridas. The United States itself derived territorial advantage from the breakup of the Spanish Empire by occupying West Florida at the request of the inhabitants there. Its subsequent efforts to secure Spain's recognition of this annexation were not finally consummated until 1821, when its treaty of February 1819 with Spain was ratified. The long delay counseled a policy of scrupulous official neutrality for the United States in the struggle between Spain and her American dominions.

Soon after that treaty was ratified by Spain, the United States felt itself free to extend recognition to the new nations. This it did by formally receiving a *chargé d'affaires* from Gran Colombia and a minister plenipotentiary from the empire of Mexico, and by sending ministers plenipotentiary to the governments of the United Provinces of the Río de la Plata and to Chile. After the promulgation of the Monroe Doctrine it received a *chargé d'affaires* from the new empire of Brazil and a minister plenipotentiary from the United Provinces of the Center of America, and in 1826 it sent a *chargé d'affaires* to Peru. Except for Portugal's earlier recognition of the United Provinces of the Río de la Plata in July, 1821, the United States was the first foreign nation to recognize any of the new Hispanic-American states. In all these actions it imposed no conditions and asked for no concessions in return for recognition.

Meanwhile both England and the United States had become disturbed over the plans of the Holy Alliance powers to assist Spain in reconquering her American colonies. When it seemed that France might intervene in Latin America as an ally of Spain, Secretary of State John Quincy Adams bluntly warned her in May, 1818, that the United States "can neither accede to nor approve of any interference to restore any part of the Spanish supremacy in any of the South-American Provinces." But this warning was not enough. The United States learned that plans for joint intervention by the European allies of Spain were to be concerted at the meeting of the powers to be held in 1823. If carried out they would jeopardize the free trade which both England and the United States enjoyed in Spanish America, and they appeared to be particularly threatening to the United States which had already recognized the independence of those nations. A victorious coalition of Spain, France, and possibly Russia, overrunning the territories which Spain claimed in Middle and South America, would surely take reprisals against the United States and might threaten its security if not, indeed, its independence.

To forestall this threat of coalition action in the Americas the British foreign minister, Canning, proposed to the United States minister in London, Richard Rush, that their two governments issue a joint declaration against European intervention to restore the colonies to Spain. While the Monroe administration was deliberating upon Canning's proposal, Canning himself let France know that his government was unalterably opposed to the intervention of the Holy Alliance powers in the Americas. "The British Government were of opinion," he informed the French ambassador in London, the Prince de Polignac, on October 4, 1823, "that any attempt to bring Spanish America again under its ancient submission to Spain would be utterly hopeless; that all negotiation for the purpose would be unsuccessful; and that the prolongation or renewal of war for the same object would be only a waste of human life, and an infliction of calamity on both parties, to no end." To this declaration Polignac, on instructions of his government, responded unequivocally, "that his Government believed it to be utterly hopeless to reduce Spanish America to the State of its former relation to Spain, that France disclaimed, on her part, any intention or desire to avail herself of the present state of the Colonies, or of the present situation of France toward Spain, to appropriate to herself any part of the Spanish possessions in America," and "that she abjured, in any case, any design of acting against the Colonies by force of arms." This pledge of nonaction by France, coupled with England's explicitly stated aversion to intervention, doomed any Holy Alliance plan that might have been conceived for the reconquest of the Americas. At the same time, Austria, whose Emperor Francis I was the father-in-law of Dom Pedro I, was supporting the independence of Brazil and throwing its weight against European intervention, possibly for the purpose of undermining England's dominant position in Portugal.

In Washington the Monroe administration was troubled not only by Canning's avowal to Rush of the plans of the Holy Alliance but also by Russia's encroachments southward into the Pacific Northwest toward territory claimed by the United States. But even under these serious threats Secretary of State Adams counseled against a joint declaration with Britain in favor of a unilateral warning. A joint declaration, he feared, might prevent the future acquisition by the United States of territory in the Western Hemisphere, perhaps Cuba. Besides, he believed in the doctrine of the two spheres, namely, that the American system was different from the European system and should be kept separate from it. The famous Monroe Doctrine was therefore not issued as a joint declaration by the United States and Britain but was embodied in President Monroe's message to Congress on December 2, 1823. In it Monroe declared first that "the American continents, by the free and independent condition which they have assumed and maintain, are henceforth not to be considered as subjects for future colonization by any European powers"—this despite the fact that large areas in both the American continents had not yet been effectively occupied or colonized by any nation. Monroe, in the second place, warned against any attempt by the powers of the European alliance "to extend their system to any portion of this hemisphere." With the new American governments, he asserted, which had "declared their independence and maintained it, and whose independence we have, on great consideration and on just principles, acknowledged, we could not view any interposition for the purpose of oppressing them, or controlling in any other manner their destiny, by any European power, in any other light than as the manifestation of an unfriendly disposition toward the United States."

Here were explicitly set forth both the noncolonization and the nonintervention principles as policies of the United States determining its relation with the new states of Latin America. To the new states, these principles of the Monroe Doctrine were interesting and might be important if carried out by the United States. But when Clay, following up the doctrine in January, 1824, introduced a resolution in Congress proposing to commit Congress explicitly to the support of the doctrine it was not approved.

Colombia, whose vice president enthusiastically hailed Monroe's message, asked the United States in the following July to enter into an alliance with her on the basis of the principles stated in the message, but the Monroe administration in reply simply expressed the hope that France and the other members of the Quadruple Alliance would not resort to force against it and explained that, "if they should, the power to determine our resistance is in Congress." Brazil and Mexico also asked the United States bluntly what it would do to prevent European aggression and received similarly disappointing answers. One of the motives which prompted Gran Colombia, Mexico, and Central America to invite the United States to attend the Congress of Panama in 1826 was the hope that there the principles of the Monroe Doctrine might be translated into definite engagements, but the United States Congress hesitated so long before appropriating money for a mission to the congress that when the two United States delegates could finally be appointed one of them died on his way to Panama and the other had not set out when news arrived of the adjournment of the congress to meet later at Tacubaya in Mexico. Whatever illusions of closer cooperation among the nations of the Western Hemisphere may have been conjured up in the minds of the Latin Americans by Monroe's message, therefore, were effectually dispelled. The actions of the United States did not match its brave words. From those words alone Latin America could derive little comfort.

The unilateral nature of Monroe's declaration, issued to prevent action deemed threatening to the "peace and safety" of the United States and to preserve its commercial stake in Latin America as against England, stimulated both a political and commercial contest between the United States and England for the favor of the new American states. Canning, who had previously feared France's designs upon those states, now began to fear the United States, and he instructed his agent to the Congress of Panama in 1826 to prevent the ascendancy of the United States over them, even to encouraging the Spanish American states to form a league among themselves and to reach an accommodation with Spain. Under the fear of commercial competition from the United States and also possible commercial retaliation from the Spanish American states if England did not recognize them, Canning proceeded to extend recognition to them after 1824, even though the mother country, Spain, had not yet done so. Indeed, except for Mexico, which was recognized by Spain in 1836, none of the former Spanish colonies was formally recognized by Spain until after 1840; recognition of Honduras came as late as 1894. Recognition by powerful Britain, therefore, meant much to these new states and signalized, far more than did the earlier recognition by the parvenu United States, their admission into the family of nations. Besides, England, unlike the United States, was a capital-exporting nation and as such could, if favorably disposed, bolster up their bankrupt economies. As Canning himself said, Britain's steadily increasing investments there represented more than mere commercial speculations. As a result, throughout the nineteenth century England's position in Latin America was both economically and politically stronger than that of the United States.

Early Attempts at Pan-Hispanic Union

The idea of a Pan-Hispanic union of the American states which Canning's representative at the Congress of Panama was instructed to encourage had been foreshadowed by Bolívar in his Jamaica letter in 1815. Their common three-centuries-old colonial tradition under the same sovereigns, their common political inheritance, legal system, and language, their cooperation in the joint movement of independence from Spain, the resulting absence of strong national states, and the widespread feeling among the revolted colonials that the whole of America, not just New Granada, Venezuela, or Chile, was their country, made such a union seem natural, if not indeed inevitable. Besides, a federal union had been successfully established by the former English colonies in North America. The initiative was taken by Gran Colombia when in 1821 it invited several of its neighbors to negotiate with it treaties of union or perpetual federation. Such treaties were concluded by Gran Colombia with Chile and Peru in 1822, and with Mexico and the United Provinces of the Río de la Plata in 1823, though the treaty with the latter amounted to little more than a declaration of good will. In the following year Gran Colombia concluded a treaty with Central America which provided for mutual assistance in maintaining their independence from Spain. After the final defeat of Spanish arms at Ayacucho, Bolívar as president of Gran Colombia and Peru believed that the time had come for the realization of his dream of a grand federation of American states—a federation that would include Great Britain and that would come to the aid of any one member which, as he explained, "might suffer at the hands of a foreign enemy or from internal anarchic factions." Spain's continued refusal to terminate the technical state of war was a cause of concern to all of them. Besides, the formation of a union might be a prelude, Bolívar believed, to their joint liberation of Spain's two remaining American colonies, Cuba and Puerto Rico, and to a general abolition of slavery. He accordingly suggested that the Spanish American states—not including either Brazil or the United States—should meet at the centrally located Isthmus of Panama, which he envisioned as serving the same purpose for the American states as the Isthmus of Corinth for the ancient Greeks. At Panama he hoped there might be formed "a league more extensive, more remarkable, and more powerful than any that has ever existed on the face of the earth." In all this Bolívar looked to Britain, rather than to the United States, for assistance.

Only four of the Spanish American governments—Gran Colombia, Mexico, Central America, and Peru—were represented in the congress at Panama. In the matter of practical results it was a failure, partly because of the growing suspicion of Bolívar's ambitions, partly because it presupposed a degree of responsible national action which was still lacking, and partly because the foreign threat had now abated. Though the congress drew up a "Treaty of Perpetual Union, League, and Confederation," none of the states except Gran Colombia ever ratified it. The headquarters of the federation were to be established at Tacubaya, and some of the delegates proceeded there for a continuation congress, which, however, never met. This plan for a Hispanic-American federation was prematurely conceived and doctrinaire, but it remained nevertheless an attractive objective to be steadily striven for. Since Tacubaya was designated as the capital of the visionary federation, Mexico considered that it had a mandate to carry forward the idea. It accordingly sent out invitations to other Spanish American nations to attend conferences in 1831, 1838, 1839, and 1840, but no such conferences were held. The next conference did not assemble until after the outbreak of the war between Mexico and the United States.

Embattled Mexico

The causes of that war were rooted in the conflict of interests between the United States and Mexico in both Texas and California. Texas, virtually unsettled at the time Mexico gained its independence, began soon afterward to be occupied by settlers from the United States, led by Stephen Austin. They settled on lands in the Brazos River valley which had been granted to Austin by the Iturbide government with the proviso that they should not be taxed for seven years. Between 1825 and 1830 about 15,000 settlers from the United States thronged into Texas, and by 1836 their population east of the Nueces River totaled almost 30,000, not including some 3,000 Negro slaves. They soon made it apparent that they would not remain satisfied with alien rule. As early as 1825 one of the *empresarios,* Haden Edwards, set up at Nacogdoches an independent republic which he called Fredonia, but it was soon suppressed.

These actions of the Texans aroused the apprehensions of the Mexican government. In 1830 the Mexican secretary of states, Lucas Alamán, explained to the Mexican Congress the dangers of further immigration from the United States and in return secured from his congress a law which forbade the further entrance into Mexico of foreigners who were not provided with Mexican passports, prohibited citizens of adjoining nations from settling in the frontier states and territories of Mexico, and suspended all unexecuted colonization contracts. At the same time Mexico began to encourage Mexicans to settle in its border areas, tightened the restrictions on squatters, forbade the further introduction of slaves, and united Texas with the more populous Coahuila to form a new state in which Mexicans were politically dominant.

The Texans immediately and strenuously protested, demanding, at first, restoration of their privileges under Mexican law and, after 1835, complete separation from Mexico. They were undoubtedly encouraged in their resistance by the knowledge that both the Adams and the Jackson administrations in the United States, regretting the boundary treaty with Spain in 1819, repeatedly sought to buy Texas from Mexico. Adams's efforts through Poinsett to secure a rectification of the boundary which would push it west to the Brazos River, the Colorado River of Texas, or even the Río Grande failed. But Jackson renewed the effort through his minister, Anthony J. Butler, who offered Mexico an unspecified sum for a boundary which would extend along the Río Grande to 37 degrees north latitude and thence run due west to the Pacific Ocean or for any other line which would bring San Francisco Bay into the United States. But Mexico steadfastly refused to sell any of her territory.

The Texans were not so easily put off. When their seven years of tax exemption expired in 1831 they tried, often successfully, to evade payment of the customs duties and other taxes which Mexico now sought to collect. The developing friction between them reached a climax with the promulgation of the centralist or unitary constitution of 1836, for the Texans favored the federal constitution of 1824, which was now superseded. Anglo-American in outlook, they did not want to be absorbed into a strong, dominating Mexican nation centered in Mexico City, and on March 2, 1836, they declared their independence. Santa Anna then took immediate and bloody reprisal by exterminating every Texan within the Alamo. Soon afterward he was captured and his army was almost completely destroyed by Sam Houston at San Jacinto. Texas thus gained its independence, encountering almost no further resistance from Mexico. In the following year, 1837, its independence was recognized by the United States, in 1839 by France, and in 1840 by England.

For nine years Texas remained independent while Mexico, the United States, England, and France jockeyed for position there, the latter two trying to keep Texas an independent, low-tariff, cotton-producing nation which would rival the United States. Both England and France offered to mediate between Mexico and Texas for the recognition of Texan independence on condition that Texas would not join the United States. But Texas wanted to join the United States, and in 1844 President Sam Houston asked for annexation, using the threat that if his offer were spurned Texas would form closer relations with England or establish a transcontinental confederation extending to the Pacific.

Meanwhile in Mexico the unfortunate reputation which Joel Poinsett had given to the United States was aggravated by the similar interventionist activities of his successor, Anthony J. Butler. Both Poinsett and Butler were too active as missionaries of the United States system of popular republican government and seemed to feel that they could impose this unquestionably desirable system upon Mexico by persuasion or possibly even by coercion.

Numerous border incidents which had occurred in the undefined boundary areas had given rise to recriminations and claims of one nation against the other. Relations became so strained that in 1842 a United States naval officer commanding the Pacific Squadron, Commodore Thomas A. Jones, concluding that war must inevitably come or perhaps had already broken out between the United States and Mexico, seized Monterey in Mexican California. He was immediately ordered to restore it to the Mexican authorities, but in the following year Mexico in retaliation ordered all citizens of the United States to leave its northern provinces and imposed new restrictions upon trade across the border.

Meanwhile the claims of the United States against Mexico had been fixed at $2,026,139.68 by an arbitral commission in 1841, but Mexico paid only three of the five installments. Mexico's major grievance against the United States was the Texas question, and in 1844 she warned the United States that the annexation of Texas, whose independence she had not acknowledged, would be regarded as an act of war. When Texas was nevertheless annexed to the United States by joint resolution of Congress in March, 1845, Mexico at once broke off diplomatic relations. The union of Texas with the United States was soon afterward unanimously approved by the Texas constitutional convention and was ratified by a popular vote.

Under the ordinance of annexation the boundaries of Texas were to be fixed by the United States, and the boundary dispute which followed led directly to war. Texas claimed a southern boundary extending to the Río Bravo (Río Grande). The Mexican government, on the other hand, insisted that Texas had not extended south of the Nueces River since 1775 when the boundary line between Texas and Nuevo Santander had been officially fixed at that river. This dispute seemed ripe for settlement by negotiation, and overtures to this effect were made by President James K. Polk to the Mexican government, now headed by José Joachim Herrera. After preliminary negotiations Polk sent John C. Slidell of Louisiana to Mexico with instructions to secure a recognition of the Río Grande boundary in exchange for a relinquishment of Mexico's unpaid debts to the United States and to offer Mexico up to 25 million dollars for California and all the other territory north of the latitude of El Paso. If Slidell could not buy all this territory he might offer 5 million dollars for New Mexico. But Slidell could not even secure an audience with Herrera, who was soon driven from office by the still more belligerent Paredes.

The war spirit was rising in both countries. Even before the failure of Slidell's mission, the Polk administration had instructed its consul at Monterey, California, to assure the Californians that they would be gladly received into the United States if they won their independence from Mexico. Soon afterward Gen. John C. Frémont participated in an armed revolt, the so-called "Bear Flag revolt," against Mexican authority near San Francisco Bay. At this juncture Polk, anxious to forestall British and French designs upon California and to save it for the United States, resurrected the Monroe Doctrine in his annual message to Congress on December 2, 1845, declaring, "as our settled policy, that no future European colony or dominion shall, with our consent, be planted or established on any part of the North American continent." Thus Polk sought to use the doctrine as a justification for the territorial expansion of the United States at the expense of Mexico, in this process limiting it, however, to "the North American continent."

Already on instructions from President Polk, United States troops, commanded by Gen. Zachary Taylor, had entered the disputed territory between the Nueces River and the Río Grande, and on April 26, 1846, they were attacked by Mexican forces there. When news of this encounter reached Washington, opportunely at a time when Polk was already drafting a war message, he promptly informed Congress that United States blood had been shed upon United States soil by Mexico. "War exists," he concluded, "and, notwithstanding all our efforts to avoid it, exists by the act of Mexico herself." Congress responded with a declaration of war which was approved by a vote of 173 to 14 in the House and 42 to 2 in the Senate.

Mexico was soon invaded by troops from the north. General Taylor crossed the Río Grande and advanced toward Monterrey. By the end of 1846 both New Mexico and California had been taken over by United States forces. In this time of national crisis the one-legged Santa Anna came to power again. In 1845 he had been captured by the armies commanded by Paredes, had been brought to trial, and had been condemned to permanent exile from the country. But from his place of exile in Havana his return to Mexico was now facilitated by the Polk administration which cherished the naïve illusion that Santa Anna in Mexico City might be friendly to the United States. Upon returning to his country he overthrew Paredes and made himself president again, with Gómez Farías as his vice president.

Meanwhile Gen. Winfield Scott was advancing from Veracruz toward Mexico City, and when he entered the city Santa Anna turned the presidency over to Manuel de la Peña y Peña and exiled himself to Venezuela. The new president concluded a treaty of peace with the diplomatic representative of the United States, Nicholas P. Trist, at Guadalupe-Hidalgo on February 2, 1848, granting the Río Grande boundary of Texas, ceding New Mexico and Upper California to the United States, and requiring the United States in return to cancel her claims against Mexico in the amount of $3,250,000 and to pay an additional $15,000,000. This treaty was accepted by the United States Senate on March 10, 1848, although a strong sentiment had developed in the United States for the annexation of all of Mexico, now prostrate before it. Some Mexicans also urged that their whole country be turned over to the United States, and they asked General Scott to declare himself dictator of Mexico, to keep his troops in occupation of the country, and to declare it annexed to the United States. But Scott declined their proposals and in July, 1848, withdrew all his troops from the country.

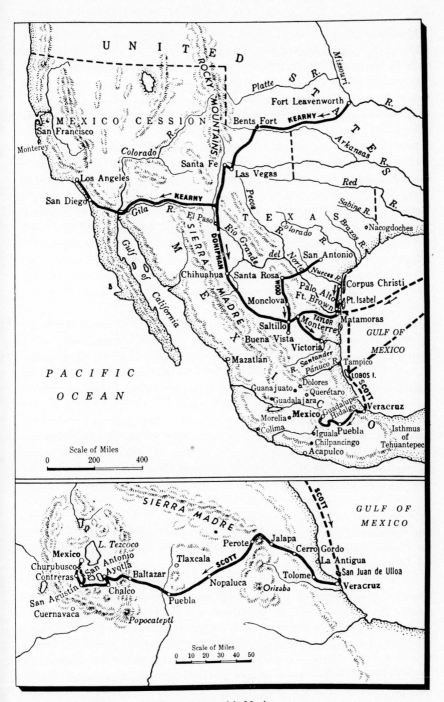

Routes of United States forces in the war with Mexico.

Mutilated Mexico now passed through five chaotic years marked by frequent changes of administration, economic demoralization, and bloody Indian wars. In the midst of this bitter internecine struggle, which pitted class against class and family against family and sometimes took the form of blind destruction of property, the ubiquitous Santa Anna returned from his exile in New Granada and, backed by the conservative classes led by Lucas Alamán, once more gained control of the government. He now proclaimed himself "Perpetual Dictator" with the title "Most Serene Highness," dissolved congress, abolished the state legislatures, and built up a large army. He also agreed to enter into negotiations with the United States for the sale of the Gila River valley in the northwest. The Treaty of Guadalupe-Hidalgo had fixed the boundary between Mexico and the United States west of the Río Grande to run "along the whole southern boundary of New Mexico (which runs north of the town called Paso) to its western termination" according to Disturnell's map of 1847. But this map was found to be inaccurate, and a compromise settlement was accordingly worked out between the United States commissioner, John Russell Bartlett, and the Mexican commissioner, Pedro García Condé.

This compromise proved unacceptable to the United States. A new envoy therefore arrived in Mexico, James Gadsden of South Carolina, sent by the Pierce administration to settle the dispute, to secure payment of additional United States claims against Mexico, and to buy more territory for the United States. Gadsden was instructed to secure Lower California and the entire southern watershed of the Río Grande, for which he could offer as much as 50 million dollars, or in any case to secure at least a route for a southern railroad to the Pacific. The treaty which was concluded in 1853 accomplished the latter purpose, placing El Paso in the United States and transferring to it some 19 million acres south of the Gila River for 10 million dollars. The treaty allowed citizens of the United States free use of the Colorado River and the Gulf of California and gave the United States and its citizens the right of transit across the Isthmus of Tehuantepec. In addition it abrogated the article of the Treaty of Guadalupe-Hidalgo which bound the United States to prevent southwestern Indians from making raids across the boundary.

Santa Anna's high-handed methods in this affair and other acts of his administration stimulated the forces of local autonomy, which had not been quieted by his assumption of dictatorial powers. They inspired a federalist revolt which began in the state of Guerrero in 1854 and was headed by a full-blooded Indian, Juan Alvarez. So successful was this so-called "revolution of Ayutla" that Santa Anna, after making a desperate and unsuccessful effort to find a royal ruler for Mexico, resigned in 1855. His power in Mexico thus collapsed for the last time, the homes of his ministers were sacked, his own property was burned, and he went into exile in New Granada, finally dying in 1876. He left Mexico poorer than he found it, for he had been able neither to stimulate national feeling nor to prevent foreign action detrimental to it. Indeed he appeared to have actually connived with Mexico's enemies to advance his own political fortunes. During the thirty years of his domination Mexico fared badly in her domestic life but worse in her international relations.

Defense of La Plata

Much more successful in opposing foreign intervention was the Rosas government in Buenos Aires. There a law enacted in 1821 requiring military service for foreigners who had been resident in Buenos Aires for more than two years caused trouble with France. When it was applied to French citizens in 1829 the French consul in Buenos Aires summoned to his aid a vessel of the French squadron off the coast of Brazil. Buenos Aires warships were seized, and the Buenos Aires government was forced to come to terms with the French. The French consul even went so far as to advise his government to send the entire French fleet against Buenos Aires and to seize Patagonia as indemnity for the mistreatment of French citizens. What use he expected his government to make of that desolate region was not explained.

Another international incident, harmful to Argentina, was created by the British occupation of the Falkland or Malvinas Islands lying off Patagonia in South Atlantic waters and commanding the eastern approach to the Strait of Magellan. These islands, presumably discovered by the English explorer John Davis, had been claimed for France by Louis Antoine Bougainville in 1764, but in 1767 they were ceded by France to Spain under the Family Compact between the two Bourbon thrones. When Spain accordingly sought to drive out the British who had built a fort, Fort Egmont, on the islands she nearly precipitated war with her rival. In 1771 when Spain's international position was low she agreed to allow the British to remain in the islands, leaving unsettled, however, the question of their ultimate sovereignty. But the islands were abandoned by the British in 1774 and then were reoccupied by them in 1833, over the ineffective protests of the Buenos Aires government, which claimed them as the heir of Spain.

This kind of humiliating treatment was not to be endured after Rosas came to power. When the inexperienced and quarrelsome French vice-consul, Aimé Roger, made demands upon the Rosas government arising out of the enrollment of several French citizens in the militia and the imprisonment of another, who was charged with corresponding with enemies of the state, Rosas handed him his passports in March, 1838. But the French consul was backed by his government, and the French admiral, Le Blanc, stationed off Montevideo presented Buenos Aires with an ultimatum, which the Argentine foreign minister rejected in a dignified manner. For two and one-half years— from March, 1838, to October, 1840—the French maintained a blockade of the entire Argentine seacoast, though without declaring war. Buenos Aires was not the only Latin American area which felt the lash of the truculent French monarchy at this time, for in Mexico the port of Veracruz was captured by a French fleet in 1838 in the so-called "Pastry Cook's War." The claims which France sought to collect from Mexico by this means included the claims of a French citizen who operated a pastry shop at Tacubaya and who thus gave his name to the "war." In the end Mexico was obliged to conclude a treaty with France recognizing the latter's claims. Mexico's capitulation may have encouraged France in its punitive action toward Buenos Aires.

In the midst of the French blockade of Buenos Aires, Argentina's plight was worsened by the outbreak of war with the Riverista faction in Uruguay, whose independence had been guaranteed by both Argentina and Brazil at the end of their war in 1828. As soon as Uruguay thus gained its independence its congress promulgated a new constitution and chose Fructuoso Rivera as president. After his term expired in 1834 he launched a revolution against his successor Manuel Oribe, and in the ensuing civil war the two historic Uruguayan parties were born—the *Colorados* (Reds) who adhered to Rivera and the *Blancos* (Whites) who followed Oribe. Both had been members of the patriotic "33" who had exiled themselves to Buenos Aires after 1821 in protest against Brazil's absorption of their country. Oribe received support, even troops, from Rosas but was nevertheless driven from power and sought asylum in Buenos Aires. The victorious Rivera, egged on by the numerous unitary *émigrés* in Montevideo and by the French, now turned on Rosas and declared war against him in 1839.

At this time when Buenos Aires was beset both by the French fleet and by Uruguay, the unitary and even the federalist enemies of Rosas turned against him. The French blockade caused great suffering in the upriver provinces, paralyzing their commerce and giving rise to a peace movement there. Since Rosas had failed to maintain friendly relations with foreign nations, the governor of Corrientes, Domingo Cullen, refused in 1838 any longer to recognize his right to conduct foreign relations for the entire country. When Rosas discovered that the governor was engaging in a conspiracy against him, his reprisal was swift and complete, for the punitive expedition which Rosas sent against him captured and shot him.

Equally thorough was Rosas's suppression of the so-called "Maza conspiracy" in the following year. This alleged conspiracy grew out of the activities of an association called *Joven Argentina* or *Asociación de Mayo,* a kind of political debating society which was inspired by the contemporary young Italy movement and which opposed despotism generally and Rosas in particular. Founded by the socialist leader, Esteban Echeverría, it included many young military officers among its members and was headed by young Col. Ramón Maza, a son of the federalist president of the Buenos Aires provincial legislature. When the Mazas were found to be conspiring with Lavalle, with the unitaries in Montevideo, and with the French squadron which was blockading Buenos Aires in 1839, the young Maza was arrested and shot, and his father was ordered to leave the city. When he refused he was assassinated. Rosas was blamed for the assassination, but no evidence was adduced to connect him with it. On the other hand, the haste with which the unitaries sought to take advantage of it suggested that some of them might have been responsible.

At the same time Rosas was obliged to contend with the continued revolutionary activities of the two generals who had won fame in the Brazilian war, Lavalle and Paz. The former, assisted by Rivera and protected by the French fleet, seized the island of Martín García, lying in the river opposite Buenos Aires, and threw the city into a panic. The northwestern provinces of Tucumán, Salta, Jujuy, Catamarca, and La Rioja also rose up at this time to support Lavalle and to deprive Rosas of the authority to conduct foreign relations for the Argentine provinces. They were joined by some of the principal *estancieros* in Buenos Aires province who were hostile to Rosas and who were cooperating with the Maza conspiracy. Under these critical circumstances Rosas was obliged to come to terms with the French in order to eliminate at least one enemy. In the convention which he concluded with Vice Adm. Baron de Mackau in October, 1840, he agreed to pay an indemnity, to give the French most-favored-nation privileges, and to respect the independence of Uruguay in return for a promise from France to dissuade the unitary *émigrés* there from intriguing against him.

The French blockade and the harassments of civil war caused serious economic dislocations in Buenos Aires and bankrupted the government. To remedy this situation Rosas abandoned some of the national objectives which he had striven for at the time of the tariff act of 1835 and, recognizing that the shortages imposed by the blockade had prevented the attainment of self-sufficiency in manufactures, opened the port to commodities which had previously been excluded. With this virtual return to free trade the provinces felt abandoned. They could see no difference between Rosas's type of federalism and unitarism. But their protests availed little, for with the French threat ended, at least temporarily, Rosas was free to move against the armies of Lavalle and of the dissident northwestern provinces. With an army of 10,000 men, his general, Oribe, decisively defeated Lavalle near Córdoba in November, 1840, and scattered the armies of the northwestern provinces. Lavalle was pursued and shot near the borders of Bolivia, and the leader of the anti-Rosas movement in the northwest, Marco Avellaneda, father of a later president of Argentina, was captured and beheaded.

Rosas now determined to strike directly at Montevideo in order to overthrow the *Colorados* there and to wipe out this center of resistance to his regime. In early 1843 therefore Oribe laid siege to the port, which was defended not only by its *Colorado* army and Argentine *émigrés* but also by foreign elements, including an Italian legion commanded by the young soldier of fortune, Giuseppe Garibaldi. To England and France, Rosas explained that he was punishing Uruguay because of Rivera's interference in Argentine affairs, but before long both the English and French governments intermittently joined in the defense of Montevideo at the solicitation of both the *Colorados* and the Argentine *émigrés*. The latter would go to any extreme—even the possible dismemberment of Argentina—to defeat Rosas. In addition Paraguay, which was now governed by Carlos Antonio López and was disgruntled at Rosas's interference with the river trade, came to Uruguay's aid with an alliance and 4,000 troops. The British refused to recognize Rosas's siege of Montevideo and sent two envoys to negotiate a peace with him, demanding that Rosas raise the siege, guarantee the independence of Uruguay, and restore the free navigation of the Paraná River by removing the chains which he had strung between two forts blocking its exit. Rosas refused these demands. An Anglo-French fleet then drove away the blockading Argentine squadron commanded by Adm. Guillermo Brown, broke the chains, captured the river forts, and established a blockade of Buenos Aires in September, 1845.

But this European intervention redounded to the advantage of Rosas, for he was seen now to be defending the independence of his country, perhaps also Uruguay and other South American nations, from European fleets and armies. Elsewhere in Latin America, even in Montevideo, public opinion turned in his favor. The British, too, realizing that they had blundered into a military impasse which would be prejudicial to their commercial interests, sought to make peace. Their *entente cordiale* with France which had been established in 1841 after the fall of Palmerston's government and which made possible the Anglo-French cooperation in the La Plata region ended with Palmerston's return to power in 1846. The early efforts of the British to patch up a truce with Rosas, first through envoy Thomas Samuel Hood and later through Lord Howden, failed partly because of the intransigence of Rosas's Argentine enemies in Montevideo and partly because of the uncooperativeness of the French. Whereas England wanted peace and disengagement from an embarrassing situation, France clearly wanted to secure commercial and even territorial concessions.

Finally the British concluded a separate peace in November, 1849, which was a complete victory for Rosas. The British promised to return all captured ships and cargoes, agreed to give the Buenos Aires government a twenty-one-gun salute, and formally recognized the sovereign rights of the Rosas government both to control the interior rivers of the country and to punish Uruguay for interfering in the affairs of Buenos Aires. The outbreak of the revolutions of 1848 in Europe had already impelled Garibaldi to leave Uruguay to fight for the freedom and unity of Italy and clearly made necessary the ending of the French blockade of Buenos Aires. But the French continued to aid in the defense of Montevideo until August, 1850, when they concluded a peace with Rosas on almost the same terms as the English treaty of the preceding year.

Little attention was paid by the United States to the Anglo-French armed intervention in the La Plata area despite the Monroe Doctrine. During the first French blockade of Buenos Aires in 1839 the United States offered its good offices to France, but they were politely declined. During the later intervention the United States was preoccupied with its own war with Mexico. Whereas it emerged from this war in 1848 victorious, with vast new territorial acquisitions, its position in Latin America was weakened by the war. England, on the other hand, emerged from its encounter with Rosas in the following year both politically and commercially strengthened. Against the joint Anglo-French intervention in the La Plata area, the United States had not at any time invoked the Monroe Doctrine. Indeed, its own seizure of Mexican territory made the doctrine seem to Latin Americans who remembered the doctrine at all to be of dubious advantage to them.

The wave of foreign interventions in the 1840s excited grave apprehensions throughout Latin America and led to the summoning of the first exclusively Spanish American conference. The early cooperative efforts of the American nations to safeguard their independence from possible reconquest by Spain were renewed in 1847 at a time when Spain was invading Ecuador and the United States was overrunning Mexico. Under pressure from these developments the foreign minister of Peru, convinced "that the people of South America need to unite and to form alliances to repel foreign and ominous pretensions against the American cause," invited them to send representatives to a conference in Lima. In the midst of the United States–Mexican War and the Anglo-French blockade of Buenos Aires, therefore, representatives of five South American governments—Bolivia, Chile, Ecuador, New Granada, and Peru—met and concluded a treaty of confederation in which they agreed to use their land and naval forces under certain circumstances for the maintenance of the sovereignty and independence of each signatory state. But neither this nor the other treaties signed at the conference were ever ratified. The need for some such measure of collective guaranty, nevertheless, continued to be demonstrated by the developments of the following decade.

International Intrigue in Central America

Foreign interference in the five Central American nations impelled them toward repeated attempts to revive their shattered federation. The collapse of the Central American Confederation in 1839 was followed by several years of civil war in almost every separate country. Each new government coming into power by force had to maintain itself by the same means or be overthrown. The ideal of reestablishing the federation continued to be an objective of the liberals, the followers of Morazán, in all those countries and was particularly strong in El Salvador, Nicaragua, and Honduras. Only Costa Rica, which was dominated by Great Britain, showed little interest in the revival of the union, and her isolated position enabled her to remain comparatively aloof from the political struggles which centered around it.

The idea of union was strongly opposed by the conservatives who controlled the governments of all these Central American nations until the early 1870s and in the case of Nicaragua until 1893. They took their cue from the government of Guatemala which was dominated by Rafael Carrera as an absolute despot until his death in 1865. Through his efforts liberals who occasionally came to power in neighboring countries were promptly driven from office. Carrera and the conservatives and church elements who supported him successfully resisted all attempts to reestablish the federal union and intervened by intrigue and force to frustrate all plans of the union-minded liberals in other countries of Central America. The conservatives had deplored the expense which had been incurred and which they had been obliged to pay during the period of the Confederation, and they had learned to dread the return of the liberals to power. They were the greatest single obstacle to the restoration of the union. Associated with them was the British government, which worked actively against the revival of the federation and fomented discord among its former members. Over the government of Guatemala, Great Britain acquired a commanding influence by means of a large loan guaranteed by the revenues of the state. When El Salvador, leader of the prounionist forces, protested against British meddling in Central America, her ports were blockaded by a British fleet.

The agitation and plotting of the Central American liberals in favor of union and of the Central American conservatives opposing union cut across national boundaries and in themselves served to promote the idea of union. In El Salvador, Nicaragua, and Honduras, the liberals, as well as many conservatives, resented the influence exerted upon them from Guatemala and continued to champion the union. In almost every year between 1840 and 1854 these three nations met to discuss plans for forming some sort of central government. Twice during those years they almost succeeded in establishing one. The first of the unions was formed in 1842 by delegates from these three countries meeting at Chinandega in Nicaragua. The treaty which they adopted provided for a council consisting of one delegate from each republic and presided over by a supreme delegate. It also provided for a supreme court to be chosen by the state legislatures. This federal government sent troops to aid El Salvador in a war against Guatemala two years later and finally brought the war to an end through the mediation of the supreme delegate. In that same year, however, the federation had to be terminated when El Salvador and Honduras attacked Nicaragua because the latter was harboring their political exiles.

British encroachments in Central America led to the second attempt at union among the weak nations of that area in 1849. English log-cutting settlements had been established on the Campeche coast south of Yucatan since the seventeenth century, but England in treaties with Spain in 1786 and 1815 relinquished all claims to sovereignty there. In the latter treaty England agreed to keep her log cutters north of the Sibun River in the Belize region.

But the English did not keep their promise, and they were still occupying the entire coastal area when Central America declared its independence from Spain. After the Central American Confederation was formed the English successfully resisted the efforts of Morazán to persuade them to withdraw north of the Sibun River and to evacuate the Mosquito Coast. They not only remained where they were in violation of their treaty commitments but established themselves in the strategic Bay Islands which belonged to Honduras. In 1841 they placed the islands under the control of Belize. South of Belize the British claimed the entire Mosquito Coast extending from Cabo Gracias a Dios on the north to Boca del Toro on the south. Near the end of the war between the United States and Mexico, the British officially took possession of the mouth of the San Juan River in the name of "His Mosquito Majesty."

Since Britain thus occupied the Atlantic terminus of perhaps the best transisthmian canal route, Nicaragua appealed to the United States for help, even asking for admission to the Union. Though this latter request was not favorably acted upon, Nicaragua was able to conclude a treaty with the United States recognizing its sovereignty over the canal route but containing no specific guaranty. At the same time, 1849, Honduras signed a treaty with the United States agreeing to cede to it Tigre Island in the Gulf of Fonseca at the western terminus of the Nicaraguan canal route and allowing it to construct a naval base there. The southward advance of the British toward Panama also alarmed New Granada, particularly after her overtures to both the British and the French for treaties guaranteeing the neutrality of the isthmus and her sovereignty there were spurned. New Granada accordingly turned to the United States and in 1846 concluded a treaty in which she guaranteed to citizens of the United States "the right of way or transit across the Isthmus of Panama" and received in return from the United States a guaranty of "the perfect neutrality" of the isthmus and of "the rights of sovereignty and of property which New Granada has and possesses over the said territory." By this treaty New Granada obtained the support of the United States in maintaining sovereignty over her province of Panama, which, after two years of rebellion and independence under the name State of the Isthmus, had just been recaptured by New Granada in 1844.

The British contested this extension of United States influence over the isthmus, and the British minister in Central America concluded a treaty with Costa Rica protecting her claims to the San Juan River canal route as a riparian nation having an interest in it. At his suggestion a British naval expedition even seized Tigre Island, but this act was later disavowed. The rivalry between England and the United States over the isthmus was to be settled in Washington in negotiations between the British minister, Sir Henry Bulwer, and Secretary of State John M. Clayton. In an effort to avoid a serious conflict they agreed in the treaty which they signed in April, 1850, that neither the United States nor Great Britain would "ever obtain or maintain for itself any exclusive control" over any ship canal through Central America or fortify it or "occupy, or fortify, or colonize, or assume or exercise any dominion over Nicaragua, Costa Rica, the Mosquito coast, or any part of Central America." They agreed further that neither would acquire "any rights or advantages in regard to commerce or navigation through the said canal which shall not be offered on the same terms to the citizens or subjects of the other." Any canal which should be constructed would be neutralized, and the tolls charged would be equal to the citizens and subjects of both nations. But by an exchange of notes preceding the ratification of the treaty Bulwer and Clayton agreed that its provisions did not apply to "the British settlement in Honduras commonly called British Honduras (as distinct from the State of Honduras), nor the small islands in the neighborhood which may be known as its dependencies."

Considerable bickering and recrimination between the United States and Britain grew out of this treaty, the United States insisting that the treaty required the British to withdraw entirely from Central America and the British denying that the words "assume or exercise" were intended to have a retroactive effect.

England erected the Bay Islands into a crown colony in 1852. This action, as well as Britain's continued exercise of a protectorate over the Mosquito Indians, caused much resentment in the United States and led to protracted negotiations between the two nations. As a result the British concluded a treaty with Honduras in 1859 in which they gained recognition of their control over the Mosquito territory but agreed in exchange to transfer the Bay Islands back to Honduras. In the same year they negotiated a treaty with Guatemala fixing the southern boundary of Belize at the Sarstoon River. In the following year they made a treaty with Nicaragua abandoning their protectorate over the Mosquito Indians and recognizing Nicaragua's title to the Mosquito Coast. By these actions the British allayed the apprehensions of the United States over their interference with its own interests in Central America, but they did not relieve the uneasiness of the Central American nations.

In the dispute between the United States and Britain which culminated in the Clayton-Bulwer Treaty the Central American nations played a fairly passive role. But they were stimulated to make another effort to unite for self-protection. In 1849 after Great Britain's occupation of Greytown or San Juan del Norte at the mouth of the San Juan River the three governments of Honduras, El Salvador, and Nicaragua again signed a treaty of confederation. As foreign complications became more serious they endeavored to strengthen their union still further by meeting in a congress at Tegucigalpa in 1852. At that congress they agreed to give their president power to represent all three of their governments in dealings with foreign powers and the right also to intervene by force in the internal affairs of the member states in order to maintain order. But El Salvador and Nicaragua refused to ratify this arrangement.

The apprehensions of the Latin American nations generally over the acquisitive urges of the United States were quickened by the filibustering activities of the adventurous William Walker of Tennessee, the "grey-eyed man of destiny." Upon the invitation of the liberals of León in Nicaragua, desperately determined to overthrow the conservatives, Walker made it his "destiny" to establish himself as dictator of Nicaragua in 1854. His object appeared to be not only to carve out for himself an empire in Central America but also possibly to create a Central American federation with himself at the head. When he attempted to reintroduce slavery and to reopen the African slave trade in Nicaragua, his efforts were commended by slaveholders in southern United States as pointing possibly toward the annexation of another slave state to the Union. His work was praised in the Democratic platform of 1856 as an attempt to "regenerate" Nicaragua. He was supported in a more practical manner by the money, arms, and recruits sent him by Morgan and Garrison, two New York businessmen, who were seeking to wrest control of the Accessory Transit Company from Cornelius Vanderbilt.

Vanderbilt's company had begun to operate there during the gold rush to California when he had secured a concession from Nicaragua to carry passengers across the isthmus using small steamers on the San Juan River and Lake Nicaragua and a coach line from the lake to San Juan del Sur. Friction which developed between his company and the British at San Juan del Norte (Greytown) was terminated by the British evacuation of that port. When Walker now voided Vanderbilt's concession and granted a new one to his two backers he sealed his doom. He also found himself faced with the united opposition of Central America, backed in its opposition by the British and the French. Armies came against him from Guatemala, El Salvador, Honduras, and even Nicaragua itself, and Costa Rica cut off his communications with the outside world by way of the San Juan River. By these united efforts Walker's army was dispersed and he himself was obliged to return to the United States. But he immediately organized another expedition and returned to Nicaragua. There he was arrested and brought back to the United States by a United States naval officer, who for this act was removed from his command by President Buchanan. A third expedition by Walker to Central America was broken up by the British navy, and he was executed by the Hondurans in 1860.

Fears of the "Yanqui Colossus"

While England was posing as the protector of Latin America at mid-century, meanwhile pushing her commercial interests there, the United States, despite its Monroe Doctrine, came to be feared as a nation that cherished imperialistic designs upon Latin American countries. One object of its desire was Cuba, which, along with Puerto Rico, remained a part of Spain's empire but which nevertheless was regarded by the independent peoples of Spanish America as spiritually and racially identified with them. To this island the United States had long applied the no-transfer principle, which indeed had been first foreshadowed in a resolution relating to Cuba adopted by Jefferson's cabinet as early as 1808. Several offers were made to Spain for the purchase of Cuba by succeeding presidents, and after the Mexican War when the acquisitive impulses of the United States were rising, President Polk offered Spain as much as 100 million dollars for the island. To this offer the Spanish minister replied that his government "sooner than see the island transferred to any power, . . . would prefer seeing it sunk in the ocean." If Cuba could not be added to the United States by purchase, expansionists would find another way to annex it. Filibusters, centering their activities in the Southern states of the United States, now made many attempts to revolutionize the island and add it to the Union as another slave state.

The leading filibuster of this period was Narciso López, who, influenced undoubtedly by patriotic motives, allowed himself to be used as a tool by the slavery expansionists in the United States. After consulting Jefferson Davis, Robert E. Lee, John C. Calhoun, and Senator Henry S. Foote of Mississippi, he gathered together an expedition in New York, but when it was ready to descend upon Cuba it was broken up by Federal authorities. López now secured the backing of Governor John A. Quitman of Mississippi and organized another expedition in New Orleans. But when his party of about 750 men reached Cuba it found no answering response among the Cubans. López returned to the United States and was brought to trial at New Orleans but was acquitted by jury action. Undaunted he led another expedition to Cuba in 1851 but this time was captured and garroted in Cuba. With him some 50 citizens of the United States, including a nephew of the attorney general, who was López's second in command, were captured and shot by the island authorities, and 135 others who were captured were freed only through the intercession of the United States minister to Spain.

Not only were Cuba's neighbors in Latin America disturbed by the filibustering enterprises launched from bases in the United States, but both England and France became apprehensive that these activities might lead to the annexation of Cuba to the United States. Upon the "anxious desire" of Spain, therefore, they asked the United States in 1852 to conclude with them a tripartite agreement disclaiming, "now and for hereafter, all intention to obtain possession of the island of Cuba" and binding themselves to prevent any powers or individuals or any one of themselves from obtaining any exclusive control or assuming or exercising any dominion over the island. But this overture was rejected by the United States as contrary to its traditional policy of avoiding international commitments and as likely to tie its hands against its own future acquisition of the island.

This seemed to be rendered imminent by President Pierce's announcement in his inaugural address in March, 1853, that his administration would "not be controlled by any timid forebodings of evil from expansion" and by his appointment of notorious expansionists to the most important diplomatic posts, James Buchanan to England, John Y. Mason to France, and Pierre Soulé to Spain. The new administration was soon given a pretext in the *Black Warrior* affair, in which the Cuban port authorities seized a United States packet ship that was unable to produce on sudden notice a complete manifest and fined it $6,000. Accordingly the Pierce administration instructed Soulé in Madrid to offer Spain as much as 130 million dollars for Cuba and, if Spain refused to sell, to direct his efforts toward detaching that island from "the Spanish domination and from all dependence on any European power." These vague instructions were interpreted by Soulé as justifying strong action to secure Cuba, and when the Spanish government again refused to sell he met with Buchanan and Mason in Belgium and signed with them the famous Ostend Manifesto. In this they declared that if Spain persisted in her refusal to sell Cuba, "then, by every law human and Divine, we shall be justified in wresting it from Spain, if we possess the power. . . . Under such circumstances, we ought neither to count the cost, nor regard the odds which Spain might enlist against us." This manifesto was immediately disavowed by the Pierce administration, but the Democratic platform of 1856 called for the annexation of Cuba, and the Democrats nominated and elected Buchanan, the real author of the manifesto, as President.

In the United States the new President, Buchanan, undertook to bring a part of northern Mexico into the United States, offering as excuses the continuing chaos in that country, the increasing claims of citizens of the United States against Mexico, and the possibility of European intervention there. In his annual message in 1858 he asked Congress to authorize him to assume a "temporary protectorate over northern Chihuahua and Sonora," and in the following year he asked Congress for authority to use military force to invade Mexico for the purpose of collecting claims and restoring order. But these threats against Mexico could not be carried out because of the disintegration of the Union in civil war. Both the Pierce and Buchanan administrations also sought to obtain territory in Santo Domingo, and a treaty was drafted for the cession of Samaná Bay to the United States. As late as 1860 both factions of the Democratic party were still advocating the acquisition of Cuba on terms "honorable to us and just to Spain." But all these annexationist projects were shelved by the Civil War.

The United States had meanwhile developed large commercial interests in Latin America. The trade between it and countries to the south was fairly stable because it was reciprocal. Trim clippers from Baltimore, New York, and Boston carried on a brisk commerce with South American ports, exchanging the cotton, flour, grain, tobacco, and other products of the United States for precious metals in Peru, unwrought copper in Chile, coffee in Brazil, the Guianas, and Venezuela, hides in Uruguay and Argentina, and cacao, coffee, and indigo in Venezuela. An occasional Boston or Baltimore vessel made the Peruvian harbor of Callao a port of call on its route to China. North American cottons were highly prized in the west coast countries of South America. From Peru the North American clippers brought back rich cargoes of *guano,* the bird droppings of centuries which had accumulated on the islands off the Peruvian coasts and which were needed to replenish the fertility of the tired soils of Maryland, Virginia, and the Carolinas. Between 1852 and 1861 Baltimore alone imported Peruvian *guano* valued at more than 14 million dollars. The economic interest of the United States in the South American *guano* became so great and the restrictions of the Peruvian *guano* monopoly so irksome that in 1856 the Congress in Washington passed an act authorizing United States citizens to take possession of hitherto undiscovered or unexploited *guano* islands in the name of the United States and assimilating such islands to the domestic coasting trade. Several such *guano* island specks in Latin American waters were accordingly acquired by the United States.

Supplementing the growing commercial interest of the United States in Latin America during the 1850s was a new scientific interest in the river systems, fauna, flora, and other natural resources of the lands to the south. The appeal of these countries to the United States resulted also in part from their attractive potentialities as new areas of development by slaveholding interests who were eager to expand the area of their "peculiar institution" and thus to counterbalance the growing influence of the Northern free states. The annexation of semitropical, Latin American areas to the United States would help to preserve the slavery system upon which, they were convinced, their prosperity depended, and the expansion of commerce with these areas would benefit the United States as a whole.

For these reasons the United States at mid-century showed considerable interest in opening up the river systems of South America to foreign trade and commerce. The Pierce administration sent out a naval vessel, the *Water Witch,* in 1853 to make a survey of the tributaries of the Río de la Plata and report on the commercial condition of the countries bordering it. But more interesting to the United States was the Amazon. This river and its tributaries have a total navigable length as great as the distance around the earth at the equator. The Amazon and other large river systems—the Orinoco, the Paraná-Paraguay, and the São Francisco—cut through the eastern mountain escarpment of South America and drain the central interior plains. These plains, seldom lying more than 1,000 feet above sea level, extend from Venezuela to Patagonia and constitute fully one-half of the area of the southern continent. The headwaters of all the rivers draining this interior basin are connected either by short portages or, as in the case of the Orinoco and the Amazon, by the curious Casiquiare river-canal, which flows in two directions. These rivers provide a network of interior communication for an area that seemed ripe for exploitation.

As a result an exploration of the Amazon Basin was made by two United States naval officers, William L. Herndon and Lardner Gibbon, in 1851 and 1852. The originator of this expedition, a Virginian, Matthew Fontaine Maury, hoped that it would corroborate his theory that the ocean currents and trade winds flowing north from Pará made the United States the natural outlet for the trade of the Amazon and all its tributaries. His lively imagination conjured up a fleet of United States steamboats plying the Amazon waters and carrying on a reciprocally profitable commerce between Brazil and the United States. He further hoped that the Amazon Valley might serve as an area of settlement both for the slaves and for their white masters in the southern part of the United States.

As Herndon's party with their Indian guides ran the dangerous rapids in the upper tributaries of the Amazon their nerves were quickened by the rapid gesture of the *puntero* indicating the channel, by the graceful position of the *popero* giving the boat a broad sheer with the sweep of his long paddle, by the "railroad rush" of the canoe, and by the wild, triumphant, screaming laugh of the Indians as the boat reached the bottom of the rapids. Sea cows abounded in the river and were highly prized by the Indians for their flesh, which tasted like pork, and for their fat. Enormous turtles swarmed out of the river at night, deposited their eggs in the sand, and retreated to the water before dawn. Porpoises also sported in the river, and alligators appeared after the party entered the main trunk of the Amazon. On one occasion the Indian guide shot a large bat of the vampire species, which measured about 2 feet across its extended wings and had a delicate fur of a glossy, rich maroon color. Parrots and lizards were plentiful, and a strange bird, called the *alma perdida* or lost soul, sometimes in the deepest night sounded its wailing melancholy cry from the depths of the jungle.

The Indians who lived in the tiny villages of fifteen or twenty houses along the river were a gentle, quiet race, submissive to the local priests and much addicted to drinking and dancing. They hated all forms of work and lived little above the level of the beasts. Filthy and mangy, some of them had the revolting habit of eating mosquitoes which they caught on their bodies in order to reclaim the blood taken by the insects. The Indian dandies made a resplendent sight in their savage decorations, including heavy ornaments which hung from holes in their lower lips. The tribes followed the practice of binding the heads of infants between boards, front and rear, in order to flatten them.

The members of the Herndon-Gibbon expedition and their official sponsors in the United States envisaged a flourishing future trade between the Amazon ports and southern ports of the United States and also hoped "to settle and to revolutionize and republicanize and Anglo-Saxonize that valley." The suspicions of the Brazilians that such motives underlay the expedition explain why they viewed it with misgivings and, instead of opening their interior waters freely to foreigners, granted to one of their own citizens, Irineo

Evangelista de Souza, by imperial decree in 1852 the exclusive privilege of navigating the Amazon for thirty years. Not until 1866 when the policy of the United States toward Latin America was no longer being formulated by slaveholders eager for territorial expansion and a Liberal ministry had come to power in Rio de Janeiro did Brazil open the King of Rivers to foreign vessels. But Brazil's great river valley was still attractive to the slaveholders from the United States and became a haven of refuge to hundreds of die-hard Confederates after Appomattox. Fugitives from the Southern carpetbag governments, they migrated to Brazil to begin life anew.

While foreign enterprisers were obliged to contend with obstacles in the physical environment of Latin America they sometimes also faced obstacles imposed by governments. Brazil, for example, by law in the 1840s required foreign firms to employ a certain proportion of native clerks in their establishments. But foreign companies were disinclined to allow meddling Latin American governments to complicate their business activities still further and deny them the profits to which their enterprise entitled them. The strong foreign nations were obviously not averse to punishing a Latin American country which interfered with their profits. This punishment took the form of naval blockades, military action, and seizure of territory. The mid-century interest in the isthmus connecting North and South America was inspired by concern over the construction and control of an interoceanic canal, and that concern was largely commercial in nature.

But all this foreign interest had political implications. Against foreign encroachments Latin America could count on very little protection from outside forces. If the British navy had earlier served as a guaranty of the independence of the Latin American countries, it could not be considered as such after Britain herself began to maintain naval blockades and annex territory there. Similarly whatever guaranties the Monroe Doctrine might have been deemed to offer to Latin America were nullified by the seizure of Mexican territory by the United States and by its acquisitive gestures toward other Latin American areas during the 1850s. Indeed the Monroe Doctrine itself had been resurrected by President Polk and used as a justification for territorial expansion by the United States at Latin America's expense. Though Polk in reviving the doctrine reiterated also the injunctions against European intervention in the Western Hemisphere, particularly in his special message to Congress in April, 1848, opposing the transfer of Yucatan to a European nation, the United States did nothing to enforce even this principle of the doctrine.

In the international arena the Latin American governments were obviously "on their own," and the treatment which they received at the hands of foreign nations would depend upon their own strengths and negotiating abilities. The Congress of Panama and the later attempts at confederation or union among some of the Spanish American nations showed the importance which was given to cooperative action, at least by the Spanish-speaking countries, to protect their own security and to promote their common interests against foreign threats. Their alarm at the victory of the United States over Mexico, at the activities of the filibusters in Central America and Cuba, and at the rampant spirit of "manifest destiny" in the United States inspired another attempt at regional action by several Spanish American governments. Representatives of the three Pacific nations of Chile, Ecuador, and Peru met at Santiago de Chile in 1856 and, stressing the union which existed among them "as members of the Great American Family," signed a Continental Treaty in which they agreed to use their land and naval forces under certain circumstances to maintain the sovereignty and independence of each signatory nation. Peru was authorized to communicate the treaty to other governments, including, significantly, Britain but not the United States, and to invite them to join this federation or league of American nations. But like the other cooperative arrangements of this sort the Continental Treaty was never carried into execution. Under these circumstances, it was perhaps remarkable that none of the Latin American governments was actually subverted by foreign powers.

Additional Reading

Albion, R. G.: "British Shipping and Latin America, 1806–1914," *Journal of Economic History*, vol. 11, pp. 361–374, 1951.

Bernstein, Harry: *Origins of Inter-American Interest, 1700–1812*, University of Pennsylvania Press, Philadelphia, 1945.

Davis, W. C.: *The Last Conquistadores: The Spanish Intervention in Peru and Chile, 1863–1866*, University of Georgia Press, Athens, Ga., 1950.

Dozer, Donald M.: "Pathfinder of the Amazon," *Virginia Quarterly Review*, vol. 23, pp. 554–567, Autumn, 1947.

Ferns, Henry Stanley: *Britain and Argentina in the Nineteenth Century*, Oxford University Press, New York, 1960.

————: "Beginnings of British Investment in Argentina," *Economic History Review*, 2d series, vol. 4, pp. 341–352, 1952.

Manchester, Alan K.: *British Preeminence in Brazil: Its Rise and Decline*, University of North Carolina Press, Chapel Hill, N.C., 1933.

Nichols, T. E.: "The Establishment of Political Relations between Chile and Great Britain," *Hispanic American Historical Review*, vol. 28, pp. 137–143, 1948.

Nuermberger, G. A.: "The Continental Treaties of 1856: an American Union 'exclusive of the United States,'" *Hispanic American Historical Review*, vol. 20, pp. 32–55, 1940.

Perkins, Dexter: *The Monroe Doctrine, 1823–1826*, Harvard University Press, Cambridge, Mass., 1927.

Ramírez, J. Fernando: *Mexico during the War with the United States*, trans. by W. V. Scholes, University of Missouri Press, Columbia, Mo., 1950.

Rippy, J. Fred: *Joel R. Poinsett, Versatile American*, Duke University Press, Durham, N.C., 1935.

Robertson, William S.: "French Intervention in Mexico in 1838," *Hispanic American Historical Review*, vol. 24, pp. 222–252, 1944.

Roeder, Ralph: *Juárez and His Mexico, a Biographical History* (2 vols.), The Viking Press, Inc., New York, 1947.

Salit, C. R.: "Anglo-American Rivalry in Mexico, 1823–1830," *Revista de Historia de América*, no. 16, pp. 65–84, 1943.

Stewart, Watt: *Henry Meiggs, Yankee Pizarro*, Duke University Press, Durham, N.C., 1946.

XIV

Constitutionalism versus Personalism

By the mid-1830s, the pattern of political and constitutional action was formed along national lines in most of the Latin American countries. The pattern varied in each country according to the strength of traditional action, economic class interests, and international pressures, and it continued to develop along the same lines during the next thirty years without unusual incident in most cases. The conservatives and the liberals offered different solutions to the perennial problems of establishing the proper balance between liberty and order. As a solution the former prescribed the strengthening of the central government, and the latter advocated the concentration of power in local units of government. Brazil, established as a constitutional monarchy, remained one under Dom Pedro II. Chile continued in the hands of a landed, Whiglike aristocracy. Varying degrees of dictatorship and disorder prevailed in most of the other countries. Argentina finally emerged, after many vicissitudes, as a national unit. And Mexico underwent a major constitutional struggle.

The Brazil of Dom Pedro II

Under the young Dom Pedro II, who was crowned amidst enthusiastic popular acclaim in 1841, Brazil began a period of peace and economic progress almost incomparable in South America. His general, Luiz Alves de Lima e Silva, renamed the Duke of Caxias, quickly suppressed the revolutions in Maranhão, Minas Gerais, and São Paulo. Under Dom Pedro's conciliatory policy Rio Grande do Sul returned to the Brazilian union in 1845 and was granted complete amnesty. A small revolution that broke out in Pernambuco in 1848 was quickly suppressed, and for the following forty years Brazil enjoyed internal peace. The accession of Pedro II to the throne represented a victory for the great landowners who formed a traditional ruling oligarchy and who, controlling the sugar-growing northeast, largely fixed the pattern of Brazil's economy and society. But at the time of Pedro's accession the power of the old sugar-growing patriarchal society was beginning to be challenged by a new coffee economy centering in São Paulo and Rio de Janeiro in the south. The sugar magnates were also meeting increased competition from the sugar industry of the Antilles, which showed more enterprise in taking advantage of the new, complicated, and expensive sugar machinery. Moreover, the social system of northern Brazil was disrupted by the abolition of primogeniture in 1835. As coffee plantations multiplied in the south, coffee began to supplant sugar as the mainstay of Brazil's economy. In fact as coffee increased in importance it became the primary source of both domestic prosperity and foreign exchange.

The emperor frankly accepted the idea that he governed under a constitutional and parliamentary system. He could hardly do otherwise, for the period of the regency and the method by which he himself had been summoned to the throne—by a parliamentary revolution—had firmly established the idea of parliamentary government. But he was a simple man with no delusions of grandeur. Indeed he seemed to value his position lightly and often said that he was the best republican in the empire and that his main function was to prepare Brazil for republicanism. He did, however, have the constitution amended to make the executive power stronger than it had been under the regency. By means of the *poder moderado* or superintending power thus conferred upon him he was able to rule as well as to reign. It gave him the right to approve legislation, to select his own council of state, to appoint and dismiss cabinet members, provincial presidents, and certain other officials without reference to Parliament, to dismiss Parliament, and to have a hand in the selection of senators. All this, of course, did not please the liberals who wanted increased local autonomy, combined with removal of restrictions on voting and an elected rather than an appointed upper house of Parliament, but the emperor's policy toward them was conciliatory.

At the age of eighteen Dom Pedro was married by proxy to Thereza Christina, the twenty-one-year-old daughter of the King of Naples. It is reported that he turned his back when he first saw his bride's face, but unlike his father, he became a model husband. His manner, again unlike that of the Braganzas, was dignified but unostentatious. Tutored by José Bonifácio de Andrada he was a diligent student all his life, but no pedant. He devoted all his time to his books and to imperial duties, but he was not self-important. As one of his biographers has written, "He drove about in rickety old carriages with absurd-looking horses; he kept no court properly so called; he would gobble through his state dinners in a hurry to get back to his books; he would call cabinet meetings at inconvenient hours of the night if an idea struck him. Though his subjects loved and trusted him, the general tendency was rather to laugh at his peculiarities." By these methods, whether calculated or not, he made himself the most powerful political force in the nation. An amiable, energetic, shrewd, and wise ruler he was characterized by Victor Hugo as a "grandson of Marcus Aurelius." His democratic manners and his wise policies concealed the fact that he was an absolutist ruler and that the final authority in Brazil centered in him.

Ruling the largest nation in the Western Hemisphere—a nation which was divided into eighteen states and contained a population of seven or eight million—Pedro II undertook to improve internal communications, to open western lands to settlement, to encourage immigration, and to attract foreign investment. As a result, large amounts of foreign capital entered the country, coming mostly from Britain. Foreign commerce doubled between 1849 and 1856. During those years the first railway systems were constructed, more than twenty thousand European immigrants arrived annually, and the treasury receipts increased by 50 per cent. But in 1856 Brazil suffered a financial crisis which brought on a seven-year depression. Foreign trade remained stationary, public revenues declined, and the public debt grew. Prosperity began to return, however, as the Civil War in the United States drew to a close and the market for coffee there improved. Brazil soon became the most prosperous and powerful nation in South America, enjoying internal stability, peace with her neighbors, and the benefits derived from improved methods of transportation, communication, industry, and agriculture which foreign capital provided. Public affairs were characterized by conformity and decorum, and practically every phase of social life revealed the important influence of religion.

And yet Brazilian life was marked by many disturbing antinomies. Ever since the days of the *bandeirantes* it had exhibited a polarity between the coast and the backlands, between European culture and American traits, between the centralism of the imperial government and the individualism and *caudilhismo* of the *sertão*, between the religious imperialism of the church and the physical conquest of the land by the rugged *aventureiros*. In this heyday of romanticism the clergy were corrupt, literature lacked robustness, and public opinion showed an almost total absence of critical thought. Brazil's constitutional system as it was administered was favorable to the formation of a ruling elite. Government was monopolized by the upper class, who, though they had undeniable capacities for governing and a commendable toleration for dissident viewpoints, were smug and complacent and did not truly reflect the views of the numerical majority of the nation, nor did they keep abreast of the intellectual currents of the times. Upon the government of Brazil the nascent middle class and the large working classes could not exert the slightest political influence. Under Dom Pedro II educational opportunities at the higher levels for the upper classes were considerably extended, but primary and secondary education was neglected. At the end of the imperial era, the total enrollment in primary schools was only 250,000 out of a total population of more than 13 million. Illiteracy was still widespread; chattel slavery, continued from the colonial period, was under the protection of the government; and the commerce, banking, railroads, and mining interests of the country were largely controlled by foreigners.

Conservative Control in Chile

No less stable but more varied was Chile's political development during the three decades after the adoption of its conservative constitution in 1833 under the leadership of Diego Portales. Portales's aims for Chile, like Dom Pedro's aims for Brazil, were first pacification of the country and then development through foreign capital investment. After 1831 Chile was governed successively for three decades by three Conservative presidents: Gen. Joachín *Joaquín* Prieto who was the hero of the civil war, Gen. Manuel Bulnes, and Manuel Montt. During these years a class of conservative *hacendados,* closely allied with the church, controlled Chilean political life under a constitution that was admirably adapted to their type of government. This conservative landed oligarchy provided Chile with a period of generally tranquil growth, honest administration, economic development, and intellectual stimulus, all of which, of course, served their own class interests but also promoted the interests of the nation.

President Prieto undertook first to establish internal security and to guarantee safe conditions of travel, for certain areas of Chile were still wild and infested with bandits and could be safely traversed only with an armed guard. The financial condition of the country also required attention, for the foreign debt of 1 million pounds which O'Higgins had borrowed had accumulated unpaid interest and was now almost 5 million pounds. In order to improve Chile's financial position Prieto's minister of finance, Manuel Rengifo, funded the internal debt, established strict economy in government, and carried through a new tariff law for the purpose partly of securing increased revenues and partly of providing protection for local Chilean interests against foreign competition. The moderate Conservative faction which Rengifo headed advocated a policy of conciliation of the Liberals in order to secure their support for these measures of national improvement. For this purpose they urged that the proscriptive decree of 1830 issued by Portales dismissing all Liberal military officers from the army be reversed. They also were critical of the extreme proclerical policies of President Prieto. This faction accordingly began to build up Rengifo for the presidency, but he, unwilling to split the Conservative party, pledged support to Prieto. Nevertheless the schism in the party became so serious that Portales was recalled to public life and began his second dictatorship as minister of interior and war in 1835. Rengifo was then forced to resign.

The return of Portales to power was so distasteful both to the Liberals and to the moderate Conservatives that they abstained from voting, and Prieto was installed in office for a second term by his own Conservative party dominated by Portales. Against him the former president, Ramón Freire, who had been living in exile in Peru, thereupon organized a revolution based on the island of Chiloé. He was soon captured, and although sentenced to death was instead exiled to Sydney, Australia. Since he had organized his revolution not only on Peruvian soil but seemingly also with the connivance of Peru, Chile's already bad relations with Peru became further strained. The causes of this unfriendliness went back to the wars of independence when Chile had financed San Martín's expedition against Lima with the expectation of being reimbursed for the costs of the expedition. But she had never been paid nor had she received from Peru any payments on the small part of the British loan of 1 million pounds which she had transferred to Peru in 1822 to enable Peruvian patriots to finance their war against the viceroy's forces. In the early 1830s, moreover, a tariff war opened up between the two countries when Chile levied duties on Peruvian sugar and Peru retaliated with duties on Chilean wheat.

Against this backdrop of Chilean-Peruvian hostility, the formation of the Peru-Bolivian Confederation under Gen. Andrés Santa Cruz in 1835 introduced a new element of discord. Since Chile could hardly be expected to acquiesce complacently in the creation of this strengthened coalition of nations on her frontiers, Freire's expedition from Peru may have been encouraged by Santa Cruz in order to weaken the Chilean government or to distract its attention from his Confederation. His action was deemed provocative by Portales, who now determined upon war against him. In this course he was encouraged by the Peruvian exiles in Chile who were eager to assist anyone who would overthrow Santa Cruz. As a first hostile action against Santa Cruz, who wished to avoid war, Portales sent the Chilean fleet to Callao where it seized the Peruvian navy. He followed up this action by an ultimatum, dispatched by Manuel Egaña, demanding the dissolution of the Peru-Bolivian Confederation, the limitation of naval armaments by Peru, and indemnity for Freire's expedition. When Santa Cruz quite naturally rejected these demands, Egaña, in accordance with his instructions, declared the two nations to be at war in November, 1836. This action was confirmed by President Prieto in the following month. In the war against Santa Cruz, Chile was soon joined by Rosas who resented the asylum which Santa Cruz was giving his unitary foes and who did not wish to see a strong nation established on Argentina's northern border.

This war, for which Portales was responsible, stimulated the opposition to his rule in Chile and in turn drove him to strengthen his dictatorship and to inaugurate a reign of terror. This caused his undoing, for in June, 1837, while he was reviewing troops north of Valparaíso, he was seized by a group of officers in a military coup. These mutineers then marched against Valparaíso with the intention of seizing the government, but they encountered resistance from the Valparaíso garrison. In the course of the fighting Portales, who was then forty-four, was assassinated. The army mutiny was soon suppressed and the leaders executed. Portales's death made him something of a martyr and had the effect of strengthening the government in its war against Peru, particularly when the rumor circulated that Santa Cruz had engineered the army mutiny and the capture of Portales.

Chile took the offensive in the fighting against Santa Cruz by first sending a naval expedition under Adm. Blanco Encalada against southern Peru. He had been assured by the Peruvian exiles in Chile that their countrymen would flock to his standard, but on the contrary he found little local support and was himself captured by Santa Cruz near Arequipa. Under duress he signed a treaty formally recognizing the Peru-Bolivian Confederation and promising to return the Peruvian navy, captured in the previous year, but the Chilean government repudiated the treaty and sent a second naval expedition under Gen. Manuel Bulnes. First he and then Santa Cruz occupied Lima, but both were driven out by the epidemic there. Finally a decisive battle was fought between them at Yungay on January 20, 1839, in which Santa Cruz was completely routed and forced to find refuge in Ecuador. The Peru-Bolivian Confederation collapsed, and the war, which had been a war against Santa Cruz and his Confederation, ended. As a result Chile's prestige was greatly enhanced, and the hero of the war, General Bulnes, returned to Santiago to become president of Chile.

The continuation of the Conservative party in power was to be expected not only because it had just won a war against a formidable foreign rival but because the administration controlled the election machinery. Under the centralized constitution of 1833 the president appointed the *intendentes,* judges of returns, and other election officials. The constitution had established educational and property qualifications for voting, but these were not enforced until after 1840 when Congress passed the necessary implementing legislation. The delay in enacting this legislation was deliberate on the part of the *hacendados,* for it enabled them meanwhile to register their agricultural laborers who, of course, would vote as told. Having thus assured themselves of the support of these regimented voters they now saw to it that the new legislation applied only to future registrations and did not interfere with the voting rights of those already registered. Another bloc of supporters whom the *hacendados* could depend upon was the national guard, which had been organized by Portales on a purely Conservative basis and whose members had been allowed to register for voting. Moreover, if the opposition became too vocal or too strong the president could always declare martial law and could then cause the arrest of opposition candidates for disturbing the peace. But after the assassination of Portales the bitter proscription of Liberals was softened and a reaction against the repressive features of this system appeared. Even O'Higgins was granted permission to return to Chile. By such means the landed oligarchy maintained complete control over the Chilean government. But they maintained good government and tolerated constructive criticism from members of their own class.

Under this kind of leadership Chile, during the administration of General

Bulnes, who came to power in 1841, experienced an unprecedented burst of internal development. This was made possible in part by the policy of political reconciliation and general amnesty which was now inaugurated and which liberated new, dynamic forces into the nation's life. The rapprochement with Peru which followed the overthrow of Santa Cruz in 1839 and Spain's final recognition of Chile in 1844 gave Chileans a feeling of well-being in their international relations and stimulated the regenerative elements in the nation. In 1840 the first steam navigation line was opened up, handling both the coastal trade and commerce with Europe. This company, capitalized in London, was organized by a citizen of the United States, William Wheelwright. In particular, Chile's commerce with the United States was stimulated by the gold rush to California, which created a new demand there for Chilean grain. Increased industrial development became possible with the beginning of coal mining at Talcahuano.

While these bases were being laid for an expanded commerce and industry, the effective frontiers of Chile were extended. No real effort had hitherto been made to settle Chilean Patagonia, the area adjoining the Strait of Magellan, but in 1843 the Chilean flag was hoisted there and in 1847 a settlement was made at Punta Arenas, now Magellanes, the southernmost city in the world. But in order to reach Punta Arenas, Chileans had to pass along a vast stretch of their seacoast which was still unsettled by Europeans. The limits of effective occupation ended at Concepción at the Bío-Bío River which was the frontier against the Araucanian Indians who occupied almost all of this southern area of the country. Valdivia in the isolated southern part of this Indian territory was used as a penal colony.

Efforts were now begun to colonize this area with Germans. Incentives in the form of free land and settlement rights were offered by the government in a colonization law passed in 1845, and in the following year nine German families arrived and settled in Valdivia, thus beginning the German migration to that area. In 1850 an additional 300 Germans settled there, and though they encountered the usual difficulties of pioneers in a new and rugged environment their numbers grew steadily. They completely transformed the area of Valdivia and Llanquihue, bringing their German language, educational system, Lutheran religion, and habits of industry, and they soon dominated the business and intellectual life of southern Chile. This enclave of Little Germany, eventually numbering some thirty thousand, constituted the largest single foreign population element in Chile and remained both culturally and politically unassimilated.

Chile, which had been one of the most backward parts of the Spanish Empire, began in the middle of the nineteenth century to swing into the intellectual currents of the time. The Chileans had shown little interest and no leadership in education. By 1846 there were only fifty primary schools with no more than three thousand pupils in the entire country, and higher education was confined to the Instituto Nacional and a medical school, staffed largely by non-Chileans. The only university in name was the moribund University of San Felipe, which had been founded under Philip V and which was wholly ecclesiastical. Educational leadership in Chile was furnished mainly by foreigners, of whom the Venezuelan, Andrés Bello, and the Argentine, Domingo Faustino Sarmiento, were the most conspicuous.

Fig. 14-1. Andrés Bello, leader in Chilean education. (*Courtesy of Fondo de Cultura Económica, Mexico.*)

During the presidency of General Bulnes, Chile experienced a real intellectual awakening. A Chilean literary society was founded in 1842, and in the same year the University of Chile was established, the old University of San Felipe having been formally suppressed by the government in 1839. For the new university with its five faculties, Bello, Chile's outstanding poet and scholar, was selected as rector. In the same year, 1842, the first normal school was established, with Sarmiento as principal. Sarmiento, one of the Argentine unitary exiles in Chile, had been connected with *El Mercurio,* the oldest newspaper in Chile, founded in 1827, and later became editor of the first daily newspaper in Santiago, the government-subsidized *El Progreso.* These educational innovations, including also a national conservatory of music and a school of fine arts, were carried out under the direction of the minister of justice and education, Manuel Montt.

Whether this intellectual ferment in Chile, encouraged by the Conservatives, was the cause or the result of new liberal thought is difficult to say, but it stimulated the liberal, anticlerical movement which in turn worked against continued Conservative domination of the nation. Questions were now asked about the relationship between the government and the Catholic Church, which for the first time made the status of the church an acute issue in Chilean politics. Under the constitution of 1833 church and state were united, but a rift, caused by the new liberal thought, now began to develop between them. Though the government remained under the control of the Conservative oligarchy, anticlerical tendencies appeared even there, and the government undertook to bring the church under its control. It did not do so, however, through a genuine anti-Catholic movement or Kulturkampf, as in some Latin American countries, but rather by means of a series of relatively mild legal enactments. These exempted non-Catholics from the Catholic marriage ceremony, forced priests, who had customarily kept the vital records, to register all marriages, established government supervision over priests, set the minimum age at twenty-five years for taking vows to the church, and forbade priests to continue the custom of laying the national flag on the ground and walking on it. Though this legislation was unpalatable to the church and though the archbishop resigned in protest, it was not modified. Through it all, church and state remained united.

As another outgrowth of the intellectual awakening of 1842 a new Liberal party was organized in 1849 and the era of political harmony, which had begun at the end of Prieto's administration, came to an end with the revival of bitter partisanship. The Liberals, opposing the ruling oligarchy, demanded a curtailment of executive power, the elimination of censorship of the press, and the establishment of more representative government. Their movement derived unexpected strength from the contagious spirit of the European revolutions of 1848. A Chilean radical leader Francisco Bilbao, who in 1844 had inveighed against the Chilean aristocracy and then moved to France, witnessed the February revolution there, returned to Chile, and in 1850 founded the *Sociedad de la Igualdad* (Society of Equality) which became the nucleus of a small intellectual and working-class party. A fighter for freedom, Bilbao attributed the lack of freedom in Latin America to the influence of the Catholic Church. Whereas Protestant North America, he said, was free to experiment, Latin America was free only to accept the dogmas of the church. He and his *Sociedad,* with their newly established *El Amigo del Pueblo* as

their newspaper organ, soon developed a political organization which supported the Liberals in the presidential campaign of 1850.

The Liberal candidate in that election was José María de la Cruz, who was
intendente of Concepción. The campaign was marked by violence which
culminated in an attack by an armed mob upon the offices of Bilbao's
Sociedad de la Igualdad and the suppression of his organization. Martial law
was declared by the government, opposition newspapers were closed, and
Liberal leaders were sent into exile. But these measures only drove the opposition into conspiratorial action against the official candidate, Manuel Montt.
Montt had been closely identified with the Chilean renaissance of 1842 as
minister of justice and education and had indeed been responsible for the
establishment of several of the new institutions of learning at that time. He
was serving as minister of the interior when Bulnes was reelected in 1846
and was hand-picked by Bulnes as his successor. He was declared elected, but
the Liberals refused to acknowledge his victory. Revolution broke out in both
Concepción and La Serena, which were Liberal strongholds and which the
Liberal candidate had apparently carried. Civil war continued for two months
and was finally suppressed only when Bulnes himself assumed command of
the army and defeated the rebels in a pitched battle with heavy casualties.

Montt, who thus in the midst of civil war became the first civilian president
of a nation of some 1.5 million people, was a leader of the Conservative party,
but he was neither hidebound in his conservatism nor politically vindictive.
One of his first acts was to grant amnesty to the insurgent Liberals. His conservatism was the moderate kind which many Liberals could accept. In his
attitude toward the church he pleased the Liberals by abolishing ecclesiastical
tithes. He also moved against the abuse of land monopoly by imposing an
income tax on land, abolishing entails (*mayorazgo*), and encouraging the
division of large estates. German migration into southern Chile for the further
development of that area was also promoted. But still more important were
the measures of cultural and economic development which this able, energetic
president inaugurated. More than five hundred public schools were established, normal school instruction was opened to women, and Chile's first
astronomical observatory was founded. Railroad construction was pushed, and
the first railway connecting Santiago and Valparaíso was built by the United
States entrepreneur, William Wheelwright, who obtained his capital in Europe.
English capital was particularly attracted to Chile, especially to Valparaíso,
which became more of a British than a Chilean port. Exports of copper,
nitrates, and *guano* achieved new importance, and between 1845 and 1857
Chile's foreign commerce tripled, making Valparaíso the busiest port on the
west coast south of San Francisco. The "Age of Montt," as it was called, was
a period of unexampled intellectual progress and prosperity for Chile.

The three decades of Conservative domination from 1831 to 1861 brought
great gains to Chile. Operating under the constitution of 1833 the successive

administrations of Prieto, Bulnes, and Montt were able to consolidate national sentiments and to promote the material advancement of the nation. Under their leadership Chile enjoyed an extraordinarily long period of constitutional stability and internal order. It moved forward in every way except in education for political life. The control of Chile by the aristocratic classes whom these leaders represented was being increasingly challenged by the new liberal elements who desired to extend the franchise and broaden the base of Chilean politics. The tug of war between them became more acute as Montt's second term approached its end, and in the administration of his successor, the young liberals definitely gained the ascendancy.

Rise of Liberalism in Colombia, Venezuela, and Ecuador

The struggle between the conservative classes who benefited from existing social and economic conditions and wished to keep them as they were and liberal groups who favored modification of those arrangements occurred in most of the other countries of Latin America during the second third of the nineteenth century. It was a continuation of the struggle that had divided the colonies in their wars for independence from Spain, and it was not stilled either by the winning of independence or by the formulation of new constitutional arrangements for the independent nations. Indeed it rather reflected the unsuitability and the tenuousness of those arrangements. These social and economic stresses, aggravated by rivalries between town and country, port and hinterland, exporters and farmers, fixed the general political pattern, which, however, was sometimes altered by political quixotism and opportunism. In contrast to the ordered development of Brazil and Chile, the former under a constitutional monarchy, the latter under a conservative oligarchy, the history of the remaining countries of Latin America was turbulent, characterized by violent oscillations in power of these rival groups. Politics was a precarious business, and fortunate was the *caudillo* who after losing the support of the ruling groups did not also lose both his property and his life.

An ideological struggle between competing conservatives and liberals characterized the politics of the nations into which Gran Colombia dissolved in 1830. During the ensuing three decades the conservatives who were in the ascendancy in New Granada, Venezuela, and Ecuador when these nations began their separate existence gradually lost ground as the forces of liberalism became stronger. In New Granada the controversy between centralists and federalists, the conservatives and liberals of that day, was settled in 1832 by the adoption of a centralized or unitary constitution. But under this conservative constitution Francisco de Paula Santander, who became president in 1832, pursued many liberal policies, particularly in relation to the church, advocating public education and religious toleration. By his enlightened leadership and his insistence upon law as the only basis for effective government he laid the foundations of Colombian nationality and stable government.

"If the sword gave us independence," he declared, "the law will give us liberty." A man of peace, he sought to govern always under the law and not in defiance of the law; he established the *civilista* tradition or the tradition of civilian leadership for his country. His methods, however, became increasingly arbitrary and his influence, therefore, waned. The decline of his authority in the late 1830s enabled the conservatives to reestablish their power. This they did with Tomás Cipriano de Mosquera as president and with a new conservative constitution adopted in 1843. Signalizing their close relationship with the church they readmitted the Jesuits who had not legally operated in New Granada since their expulsion in 1767.

But party differences remained indistinct until 1849 when both political groupments there achieved organization for the first time. In that year the Conservative party was founded by Mariano Ospina Rodríguez and José Eusebio Caro with a program favoring a centralized administration and strong support of the Catholic Church. In that same year the Liberal party was organized, also for the first time, by Gen. José Hilario López and Manuel Murillo Toro, who were influenced by the liberal ideas of the English utilitarians, Jeremy Bentham and John Stuart Mill, and by the contemporary liberal movement in Spain. This new Liberal party took the color red as its symbol and enlisted the support of workers, students, and intellectuals. Its program called for a federal system of government, separation of church and state, religious toleration, and extension of the suffrage.

In that same year and with this program the Liberals came to power under Gen. José Hilario López. They immediately expelled the Jesuits, abolished slavery, and embodied their principles in a constitution in 1853 which established manhood suffrage and complete religious freedom. López himself unsuccessfully urged the separation of church and state. The issue of a centralist or federalist type of government was a continuing source of political controversy, but it no longer divided New Granada along traditional party lines. Both parties were now seeking to harmonize the centralist and federalist tendencies. When Mariano Ospina Rodríguez, an out-and-out conservative, was chosen president in 1857 he frankly accepted the idea of federalism, and during his administration, a new federalist type of constitution was adopted in 1858 fixing the name Granadine Confederation for the new federal state. This was made possible by the conciliatory and indeed ambiguous policies of the president in this era of good feeling. President Ospina readmitted the Jesuits, but he yielded to the Liberal request that a new president should be elected in a free popular election after four years.

This was not to happen peacefully, however, for the opportunist Mosquera, veering with the climate of the times, had now espoused the Liberal party, and he launched a revolution against Ospina on the grounds that the president was not faithfully carrying out the provisions of the federalist constitution. He was successful in establishing himself in office two years later, this time as a Liberal president, and proceeded to expel the Jesuits and to arrange for the drafting of a new liberal constitution. This constitution, the so-called "Ríonegro Constitution," named for the place in Antioquia where it was drawn up, was completed in 1863. With its adoption Liberal power and ideology reached its climax. Not only did it confirm the federal form of government but it created a federal form in which the autonomy of the states was more extensive than in any of the preceding constitutions. The nation was now given the name of the United States of Colombia, and the national government agreed to return some of its powers to the states, which were designated in the constitution as "small republics." The constitution also provided for a strong legislative body and a weak, short-term central executive, for the purpose, it was believed, of curtailing the privileges of the wealthy landowners who had consolidated their power in the central governing oligarchy. The president, who was to be elected by popular vote every two years, was made responsible to the legislature. Capital punishment was abolished, and the maximum term of imprisonment was fixed at ten years. Freedom of the press and freedom of speech and religion were affirmed, and both the church and the armed forces were forbidden to interfere in government.

The liberal movement of the early nineteenth century, with its emphasis upon local autonomy and broadly based popular government, had had a slow evolution in New Granada, but it attained full stature in the Ríonegro constitution of the United States of Colombia in 1863. That constitution, made possible by the success in revolution of Tomás Cipriano de Mosquera, who had moved from conservatism to liberalism, was adopted and put in force only by the Liberal party, victors in the struggle. Conservative contributions to it were neither wanted nor given. As earlier in Central America during Morazán's time, liberalism in Colombia had become militant, aggressive, and doctrinaire. When Victor Hugo later read the Ríonegro constitution he pronounced it "a constitution not for men but for angels." But it became and remained a rallying point for Colombian Liberals, and under it they continued in power for more than two decades, becoming increasingly radical and anticlerical. With the adoption of this constitution romanticism reached its zenith in Colombia. In literature it found its highest expression in the romantic novel *María*, published by Jorge Isaacs in 1867, which is a tale of Isaacs's own pastoral homeland, the Cauca Valley.

During the period of three and one-half decades after the establishment of Venezuela as a separate nation it underwent the same transition as New Granada from conservatism to liberalism and from centralism to federalism, accompanied similarly by violence and bloodshed. The Venezuelan constitution of 1830, drawn up by the Conservative party which opposed the participation of the people in affairs of state, kept Roman Catholicism as the state religion and provided for a centralized, oligarchic government similar to that provided in the constitution of New Granada of the following year and in the Chilean constitution of 1833. Under these constitutions in all three cases the Conservatives enjoyed political ascendancy for more than three decades, gradually losing out to Liberals in the 1860s as the currents of nineteenth-century thought veered in a new direction and the economic interests of ruling groups were modified by changing world conditions.

The champion and leader of Venezuelan conservatism was Gen. José Antonio Páez, a rough and ready *mestizo* plainsman of meager education. He had joined the early revolutionary movement against Spain as a common soldier in the Venezuelan *llanos* and so distinguished himself among his comrades by his enormous physical strength and courage that he was accepted by them as their natural leader. Though he suffered from acute epileptic seizures he was selected by Bolívar as one of his aides in the wars of independence. The true father of Venezuelan nationality, General Páez was responsible for the separation of Venezuela from Gran Colombia and for establishing it as an independent nation. Under the constitution of the new nation he was elected first president for the four-year term from 1831 to 1835, a term which was marked by internal peace, economic progress, and political conciliation. During the troubled terms of his successors Páez continued to hold the reins of power as commander in chief of the army and was chosen president for a second time in 1839.

But the rising resentment against the continued Conservative domination of the country found a spokesman in Antonio Leocadio Guzmán who founded the journal *El Venezolano* to resist the Conservatives and to promote the interests of the newly formed Liberal party. So influential did the Liberals become that they received several cabinet posts in the administration of José Tadeo Monagas, who though elected president of Venezuela as a Conservative in 1847 almost immediately began, like his contemporary Mosquera in New Granada, to make overtures to the Liberals. This shift can be explained partly by the growing strength of liberalism, which was obvious to any political leader who found it necessary to respond to popular pressures in order to remain in power, and partly by the example of the revolutionary spirit in Europe, which in the events of 1848 revealed how disruptive a thwarted liberalism could be. But Monagas's willingness to cooperate with the Liberals and his attempts at the same time to establish executive supremacy at the expense of the Conservative legislature alienated Páez who led two revolutionary movements against Monagas but was defeated and driven into exile in the United States in 1850. Monagas became increasingly dictatorial and personal in his rule, and when during his second term he sought to impose a new constitution which would further centralize the powers of government in his hands and extend his term for six years with no prohibition against reelection he was forced to resign in 1858.

Venezuela now lapsed into anarchy and civil war from which the Conservatives sought to redeem it in 1861 by recalling Páez from exile. But Páez had been too long out of contact with changing currents of Venezuelan opinion and was too old to give the firm leadership which he sought to exercise. His overthrow two years later by a Liberal coalition led by Gen. Juan Cristóstomo

Falcón and Guzmán Blanco, son of the founder of *El Venezolano,* signalized the bankruptcy of conservatism and enabled Falcón to come to power with Guzmán as his vice president. Páez retired again to exile in New York where he died ten years later.

Venezuelan Liberals were now riding the high crest, and they embodied their principles in a new constitution in 1864 which, like the Colombian constitution of the previous year, broadened the suffrage, increased local autonomy, and made Venezuela a federal republic. So Venezuela joined the ranks of the Latin American nations which at least paid lip service to the principles of local self-government and increased popular participation in government. But if the Venezuelan Liberals were less doctrinaire than those of Chile and Colombia they were also, as events were to show, less firmly established in politics. It must not be supposed that theirs was a lower-class movement. They were not proposing to admit the masses of half-caste and outcast *peones* to political life. Mid-century liberalism in Latin America represented at best a stirring among the upper classes. It appealed particularly to the younger, freethinking, and intellectual members of ruling groups, who were restive under traditional restraints, who were attuned to new foreign trends toward enlargement of the area of personal liberty, and who equated liberalism with political and economic progress.

After the dissolution of Gran Colombia, Quito, like her two former partners in the Confederation, began her national career under a conservative constitution, adopted in 1830. This constitution, drawn up by a congress which met at Ríobamba, first adopted the name Ecuador for the new nation and provided for the establishment of a highly centralized government under a president elected by a unicameral legislature for a term of four years. Roman Catholicism was made the religion of the country to the exclusion of all other religions. Under this constitution Juan José Flores, a Venezuelan who had been one of Bolívar's lieutenants and who was responsible for Quito's withdrawal from Gran Colombia, became the first president. The conservative cast which he gave to the Ecuadoran government, favoring both the church and the military and repressing all dissidents, was tempered under his more liberal successor Vicente Rocafuerte, and the constitutional system was liberalized in a new constitution adopted in 1835. The new President proved to be a skillful politician. A nationalist, he sought to give his country the kind of constructive administration which his contemporary Diego Portales, whom he greatly admired, was giving to Chile. In particular he opposed and sought to reduce the power of the Negro troops whom Flores had brought into the country from Venezuela. He justified his rough treatment of revolutionaries by the necessity of maintaining order and ensuring economic progress. But he had to yield the presidency to Flores again in 1839. Flores now established an even more repressive rule. He promulgated a new constitution embodying his principles of government and extending his term to eight years, but in

March, 1845, he was driven into exile by a Liberal uprising and his property was confiscated.

Liberal government, thus inaugurated, was established earlier in Ecuador than in Chile, New Granada, or Venezuela and under it the country soon fell apart. This process of national dissolution was facilitated not only by the absence of national feeling but also by the physiographic separateness of various regions of the country, particularly the coastal and highlands regions. Guayaquil, the principal port, was connected with Quito, the capital, only by a 300-mile path traversing some of the most difficult terrain in Latin America. During the fifteen years from 1845 to 1860 when the Liberals nominally controlled the country, radical opposition to the Roman Catholic Church became widespread, the country lapsed into anarchy and civil war, and each area, particularly port and capital, went its own way under its own *caudillo*. Liberalism thus discredited itself or was discredited by Conservative resistance in Ecuador, therefore, before it reached its apogee in Chile, Colombia, and Venezuela and was ready by 1860 to be succeeded by the forces of a new conservative nationalism.

Caudillo Rule

In much of Latin America ideas were less potent than personalities. Theories of government dissolved in the presence of an energetic *caudillo*. Liberalism or conservatism was strong in proportion to the strength of its leader. In other words principles of government, more or less doctrinaire, were less important than the principle of leadership. This was particularly true, but not exclusively so, in the more backward, isolated regions of Latin America, which were out of touch with the outside world and were therefore more easily dominated by local *políticos*. There the struggle for personal power was nakedly revealed without the necessity of masquerading under principles. *Personalismo* was the only important political theory; but it was more than a theory—it was a hard fact of political life. In Haiti the contest of ideas was subordinated to the struggle for power between mulattoes and blacks. In Peru, Bolivia, and Paraguay, factors of geographical isolation and large, in some cases predominant, Indian populations either kept the doctrines of nineteenth-century liberalism unknown or made them seem unrealistic.

Under these circumstances constitutions were only pieces of paper neither reflecting nor responding to actual political conditions. They were often devised mainly to sustain a regime in power and so served, in effect, as an invitation to revolution. The pattern of government was usually defined, in Montesquieu's classic terms, as one of checks and balances between legislative, executive, and judicial branches, the legislature making the laws, the executive enforcing them, and the judiciary interpreting them, but in fact the pattern of government was usually one of executive supremacy, the president coming to power either by a farcical election or by a *golpe de estado,* then establishing himself in power with a new constitution which recognized him as constitutional president, then the gradual strengthening of his power into a dictatorship, and finally his overthrow by another ambitious *caudillo* in another *golpe de estado.* Under this pattern of government the only nationalism that appeared was a nationalism imposed by *caudillos* who established their personal authority over the national territory and who convinced themselves that aggressive policies of national action would benefit the vested interests that kept them in office and so would prolong their own tenure of power.

Liberal stirrings began to appear in Haiti in the early 1840s, provoked particularly by both the restrictive and the exclusive nature of the regime of Jean Pierre Boyer. There the president alone could initiate legislation before Congress. That body was only a rubber stamp for executive action, and the members were chosen under a highly limited system of selection and in elections in which the executive freely intervened. Under this system a group of young liberals, who desired some share in government for themselves, became restive and started a rebellion in 1843 which resulted in Boyer's exile. The liberal system which they now inaugurated was embodied in a new constitution providing for popular election not only of local officials but also of the members of Congress and of the president. But, as soon appeared, it was too doctrinaire to suit the political realities of this nation of illiterate and superstitious Negroes, many of whom had reached adulthood in savage Africa. It resulted in an almost complete paralysis of government and a disintegration of the nation. The Spanish-speaking residents of the eastern end of the island declared their independence in 1844 and successfully maintained it. In the south of Haiti a revolution among the black masses broke out. Although it was suppressed, the liberal regime in Port-au-Prince was thoroughly discredited and was soon overthrown.

The liberals by encouraging the hostility of the blacks toward the mulattoes had started something which they could not control and had to see power pass now into the hands of the blacks, who were to dominate the Haitian government for more than a quarter of a century. They were first established in power by a captain of the palace guard, Faustin Soulouque, who was chosen president in 1847 and who made himself a champion of the blacks, using ruthless military methods. In 1849 he proclaimed himself Emperor Faustin I. But his autocratic pretensions and his savage persecution of the elite eventually caused his undoing. His successor, Febre Geffrard, chief of his general staff who overthrew him, was able finally to gain recognition of the Haitian government from the United States in 1864 after the slaveholding element had lost its influence in the government in Washington. Both he and, after his overthrow in 1867, his successor, Sylvain Salnave, sought to advance the interests of the Haitian population, overwhelmingly black, by the methods of military dictatorship and so encountered continuing opposition from the liberal mulatto elite. Their opposition culminated in civil war in 1868–1870 which resulted in a liberal triumph. But political developments in Haiti in the middle third of the nineteenth century cannot be strictly described as contests between liberals and conservatives but were only contests between, on the one hand, self-styled liberals who represented the mulatto elite and, on the other, the black masses who sought their general advantage through the leadership of a black chief and the methods of dictatorship. The objective of both was to rule or ruin.

Peru's development to 1860 was even less influenced than Haiti's by ideological considerations. After a dozen changes of constitution and a period of anarchy following the collapse of the Peru-Bolivian Confederation a *mestizo* leader, Ramón Castilla from Tarapacá, began to establish some stability there, serving as president for twelve years, from 1845 to 1851 and from 1855 to 1861. But as in Ecuador, national unity was difficult of attainment in a country as geographically broken up as was Peru. Geographical regionalism was reflected in a political particularism which stressed local differences, local privileges, local personal leadership, and rivalries of neighboring regions, particularly of the mountain towns of the interior against Lima. Behind the narrow, flat land shelf skirting the sea towered the sharp escarpment of the Andes, and on the Andean plateaus, almost inaccessible from the coast, were located several of Peru's most populous cities. Here where the monarchical spirit, older even than the Spanish conquest, strongly survived, real constitutional government along the lines suggested by Montesquieu and the Constitution of the United States proved quite impracticable. Castilla's government, therefore, was largely arbitrary and uninhibited by constitutional considerations, but the constitution which he finally promulgated in 1860 and which was centralist in character survived until 1919.

The governments of both Bolivia and Paraguay represented outright personalism unmitigated by constitutional limitations, though both of them, of course, had constitutions on paper. Only a strong Santa Cruz was able to reduce the anarchy and to harmonize the rivalries of the six leading towns of the Bolivian *altiplano*, each one a nucleus of localism and isolated from the others by weeks of mule travel over bleak mountain trails. With his overthrow Bolivia relapsed into an anarchy which went a long way toward belying its justification for existence as a national entity. Only the accession of José Ballivián in 1841, proclaimed president by the army, brought a period of stability, peace, and economic development, but he resigned in disgust in 1847 and left the country. The emergence of another strong leader, José Mariano Melgarejo, in 1864 revived the almost moribund Bolivian nationality.

The political history of Paraguay to 1862 can be told in the careers of two men. The first was the shrewd, austere, and mysterious Dr. José Gaspar Rodríguez Francia, the father of his country. After the beginning of the independence movement he wrote the "By-laws of Government" for an independent Paraguay and in deference to the power of Fulgencio Yegros, a member of the revolutionary *junta,* provided for two executives, each of whom should control half the military forces of the country and serve as president for periods of four months. But in 1814 he persuaded the Congress to abolish this dual presidency and to make him dictator for five years. The Congress which met two years later gave him the position for life, and for the next twenty-four years he governed the country as *El Supremo,* largely isolating it into a self-sufficient, hermit nation in order to preserve its independence from Argentina and Brazil and maintaining both internal order and his own power through his control of the army. Upon his death in 1840 power passed into the hands of a wealthy *mestizo* lawyer and landed proprietor, Carlos Antonio López, who made himself a constitutional dictator, though a benevolent one. Operating under a constitution which allowed Congress to assemble once every five years, largely for the purpose of validating the acts of the president, he remained president until his death in 1862. Even then no significant political change occurred, for his son, Francisco Solano López, who was commander in chief of the army, stepped into the presidency with the backing of the army. In this backward, remote, and landlocked nation with a population largely composed of Guaraní aborigines speaking their own native tongue, power went to him who could claim it, that is, who could control the army. Neither the transfer nor the exercise of power was hampered by political theory. The principle of leadership was implicitly followed without reference to subtle considerations of popular representation or local autonomy. In the leader was embodied the nation.

The quality of leadership in all these nations usually responded to the existing political and economic environment. Among peoples who for centuries had lived under traditions of servile followership, government necessarily rested to a considerable extent upon force and was operated largely for the benefit of the propertied class. In the more sophisticated societies conservative and liberal ideologies competed for influence in government. Latin America, even in its most backward areas, felt the contagion of these ideas which were rampant in Europe and also in a more limited sense in the United States. Consequently the tradition of force, on the one hand, and of subservience to it, on the other, often proved unworkable in the maturing popular milieu of Latin America in the middle of the nineteenth century. Experimentation with more popular forms of government was making some headway and the forms of the old established order were increasingly called in question.

An Underdeveloped Continent and a Half

At mid-century Latin America was becoming an increasingly attractive area to foreign nations. It was an area which seemed ripe for commercial exploitation and financial investment by the industrialized capitalist nations. To foreign investors and visitors it seemed that Latin America's needs were great and living standards were far below nineteenth-century requirements.

The city of Rio de Janeiro, the capital of the empire of Brazil, for example, had no sewers or privies, even in the estates of the wealthy with their spacious yards and gardens; after ten o'clock in the evening the sewage was carried out of the houses in buckets on the heads of slaves and was emptied into the bay. The general width of streets in the old part of the city was from 12 to 18 feet, the pavement inclining from the houses on each side to the middle of the road, where the drainage gutter ran. In these narrow streets two carriages could barely pass without scraping each other, and for that reason no steps or other projections were permitted.

The typical home of the Mexican or Argentine *peón* was a straw-thatched one-story hut with a dirt floor and occasionally a lean-to where the cooking was done. The typical town dwelling was a tile-roofed square house abutting on the narrow street and enclosing an open patio. This patio was a courtyard of varying dimensions surrounded by an open-sided passage or colonnade on all sides. Off the patio all the rooms of the house opened, often by means of half doors. Windows were few or entirely lacking. Along the passageways surrounding the patio were storage cupboards, hooks for hanging meat, flour mills, clay urns, woven baskets, hammocks, and other household essentials. In drought areas the patio often contained huge clay vases sunk half or two-thirds into the ground for storing rain water collected from the roofs for drinking purposes. Clothes were washed in the town fountain or in nearby streams or lakes.

Such a town house provided both privacy and protection to its occupants. In the patio and its surrounding passageway both the workaday and the family life of the household centered. Here too religious relics were displayed. On appropriate brackets and small tables in Mexican parlors were placed images of the Divine Shepherdess, the Divine Child, and Our Lady of Sorrows in high glass cases before which an oil lamp constantly burned. On the walls hung pictures of the Blessed Trinity, St. John Nepomuceno, protector of honor, St. Joseph with the Child in his arms, and the devoted St. Sebastian of Aparicio with the oxen kneeling before him. Such a home provided a retreat from the noises of the street as well as from street riots. It gave both domestic comfort and protection. It could usually be entered only through the front door, which opened either directly from the street or from behind a high, iron-piked wall. When civil disturbances broke out, as they not infrequently did, the occupants could thus "hole" themselves up in the house for the duration of the rioting.

The typical farm or ranch house also followed this architectural pattern, but it was somewhat more open and easy of access. For a busy *ranchero* or *estanciero* his home was also his place of business. Candioti's home in the Entre Ríos pampa was thus described by a visitor: "There was not a carpet in the whole house. The chairs were common rush-bottom chairs; the tables were of deal, not even painted. The beds were stretchers, with wide bottoms; curtains to them, or sashes for the windows, there were neither. And in the very drawing-room, or *sala,* there were upon a horse-rack the whole of Candioti's horse-gear. The patio of his house was continually filled with *capataces*—overseers—calling for orders, or with peons bearing messages, and leaving or taking away horses." [1]

Wealth among the Latin American peoples consisted mainly of land, yielding grain, cotton, and cattle. For both upper-class society and the *mestizo* laboring class the frequent fiestas provided spectacles of carnivals and masquerades and opportunities for dancing, cockfighting, bullfighting, and gambling. The latter was the universal sport and was indulged in by all classes. On days of fiesta the towns swarmed with crippled beggars, thieves, pickpockets, and mangy dogs. The attire of the lower classes in all the west coast countries of South America and in the Argentine was the poncho, a cotton or woolen blanket, sometimes black and sometimes varicolored, with a slit in the center through which the wearer passed his head. Educational facilities were either nonexistent or rudimentary. A visitor to Ecuador reported in 1867 that the library of the University of Quito, which had 285 students, consisted of "eleven thousand volumes, nearly all old Latin, Spanish, and French works. The cabinet is a bushel of stones cast into one corner of a lumber-room, covered with dust." In the capital of Ecuador, a city of 40,000, not a single bookstore was to be found.[2]

Of industry there was little in Latin America. Metropolises like Rio de Janeiro could boast of artificers and artisans who worked iron and copper or made hats and guitars. In the capital of Brazil, lime for building purposes was manufactured from the sea shells that lined the beach. Some coal was mined for the use of foundries and forges, textiles were woven, and sugar was partially processed.

If Latin American industry was rudimentary, transportation was primitive. It was as slow, except where railroads had been built, as in the days of Aztecs and Incas. Mules, burros, and human backs transported most of the produce of Latin America. The streets of Rio de Janeiro were filled with hawkers crying their wares of vegetables, flowers, fruits, roots, fowls, eggs, pastries, skillets and stewpans, knives and tumblers, silverware, china, handkerchiefs, dresses, shoes, jewelry, and even books. In rural areas of Latin America human transportation was sometimes supplemented by oxcarts. Such a cart was described by a traveler in Chile in the early 1850s as follows:

A clumsy pair of solid wheels, hewn from transverse sections of a tree, and without tires, are working ungreased upon a rude axle—to which are fastened a couple of saplings projecting some distance behind and joined in front so as to form a tongue. This tongue is strapped to the yoke, which, resting on the back of the oxen's necks, is tied to their horns with leather thongs.

[1] J. P. Robertson and W. P. Robertson, *Letters on Paraguay,* John Murray, London, 1839.
[2] James Orton, *The Andes and the Amazon,* Harper & Brothers, New York, 1870, pp. 68–84.

The body of the cart is simply a hide laid upon the saplings, and rests about a foot from the ground. These dumpy little vehicles are common throughout the country... laden to their utmost capacity, with a driver on top stirring up the team with a long pole.[3]

Where streams were too deep to be forded, suspension bridges made of rawhide cables interlaced with cane were built to accommodate both human and animal traffic. Only with difficulty could pack animals be prevailed upon to cross them, and the swaying of these precarious *puentes de cimbra* often afflicted their human passengers with a debilitating dizziness. The crash of such a bridge in Peru, plunging its human passengers into the surging torrent below, provides the theme of Thornton Wilder's sensitive tale *The Bridge of San Luis Rey.* In the absence of such suspension bridges travelers could sometimes cross the larger streams by launches. But this type of ferry service could not be depended upon on remote routes of travel. Transportation up and down the larger navigable streams, such as the Amazon and Paraná, was provided by luxurious steamers. Steaming up the Amazon from Manaus toward Tabatinga in 1865 Prof. Louis Agassiz of Harvard University and his wife recorded in their journal: "Nothing can be more comfortable than the travelling on these Amazonian boats. They are clean and well-kept, with good-sized staterooms, which most persons use, however, only as dressing-rooms—since it is always more agreeable to sleep on the open deck in one's hammock.... The table is very well kept, the fare good, though not varied. Bread is the greatest deficiency, but hard biscuit makes a tolerable substitute."

Human life was almost entirely lacking along the banks of the upper Amazon in Brazil. The Agassiz journal continues: "One often travels for a day without meeting even so much as a hut. But if men are not to be seen, animals are certainly plenty. As our steamer puffs along, great flocks of birds rise up from the shore, turtles pop their black noses out of the water, alligators show themselves occasionally, and sometimes a troop of brown capivari [hog-sized rodents] scuttles up the bank, taking refuge in the trees at our approach."[4]

This Latin American expanse of an undeveloped continent and a half abounded with opportunities for foreign engineers, foreign shipping companies, foreign mining interests, foreign banking houses, and foreign capital. But the terrain, the climate, and the local governments often presented insuperable obstacles to their enterprise. In the Andes of Peru a "Yankee" engineer, Henry Meiggs, fleeing from his creditors in San Francisco, built the Central Railway of Peru which, rising without benefit of cograils, to a height of 15,665 feet by way of the canyon of the Rimac River, was one of the most daring feats of railway construction in the world. It passed through sixty-five tunnels, and for many miles of its course ran on a narrow shelf of rock cut

[3] Edmund Revel Smith, *The Araucanians,* Harper & Brothers, New York, 1855.
[4] Prof. and Mrs. Louis Agassiz, *A Journey in Brazil,* Ticknor and Fields, Boston, 1868.

out of the sheer sides of the canyon. In the construction of the railroad across the Isthmus of Panama the railroad builders also encountered almost intolerable difficulties—pestilential swamps alive with alligators and other reptiles, mosquitoes and sand flies so numerous that the laborers were compelled to cover their faces with gauze veils while they worked and to spend their nights on shipboard, and complete scarcity of local building materials. Fresh laborers of almost all nationalities were brought in by thousands to replace those who died or deserted, but the climate was fatal to all alike. All food supplies required by the builders and every piece of material needed for the construction of the railroad had to be brought in from outside Panama, being transported in some cases for thousands of miles. Even the local trees were unsuitable for ties and telegraph poles, and timber for these purposes had to be imported either from other Central American countries or from the United States.

The problems created by these conditions could not be solved by constitutional manipulation, by personal leadership, or by enterprising foreign capital alone. It required the cooperation of all three factors to bring Latin America into the current of the mid-nineteenth century. The economy of these countries was still largely local, directed toward production for home consumption or the export of a few raw materials. As yet the possibilities of the Industrial Revolution for Latin America were only dimly glimpsed and the masses of the people had not been even slightly affected by it.

Additional Reading

Amunátegui y Solar, Domingo: *Pipiolos y pelucones,* Imp. y Lito. Universo, Santiago de Chile, 1939.

Baur, J. E.: "The Presidency of Nicolas Geffrard of Haiti," *Americas,* vol. 10, pp. 425–461, April, 1954.

———: "Faustin Soulouque, Emperor of Haiti: His Character and His Reign," *Americas,* vol. 6, pp. 131–166, October, 1949.

Bernstein, Harry: *Modern and Contemporary Latin America,* J. B. Lippincott Company, Philadelphia, 1952, chap. 27.

Calogeras, João Pandiá: *A History of Brazil,* trans. and ed. by Percy Alvin Martin, University of North Carolina Press, Chapel Hill, N.C., 1939, chaps. VI–VII.

Corrêa da Costo, Sergio: *Every Inch a King: A Biography of Dom Pedro I, First Emperor of Brazil,* trans. by Samuel Putnam, The Macmillan Company, New York, 1950. Sympathetic to Dom Pedro.

Donoso, Ricardo: *Desarrollo político y social de Chile desde la constitución de 1833,* 2d ed., Imprenta Universitaria, Santiago de Chile, 1942.

Edwards, Alberto: *El Gobierno de don Manuel Montt, 1851–1861,* Nascimento, Santiago de Chile, 1932.

Galdames, Luis: *A History of Chile,* trans. and ed. by Isaac Joslin Cox, University of North Carolina Press, Chapel Hill, N.C., 1941, chaps. XII, XIII.

Gibson, William M., ed.: *The Constitutions of Colombia,* Duke University Press, Durham, N.C., 1948.

González, Natalicio J.: *Proceso y formación de la cultura paraguaya,* Editorial Guarania, Asunción and Buenos Aires, 1938.

Haring, Clarence H.: *Empire in Brazil: A New World Experiment with Monarchy,* Harvard University Press, Cambridge, Mass., 1958.

Jones, Tom B.: *South America Rediscovered,* University of Minnesota Press, Minneapolis, 1949. An ingenious weaving together of travel accounts "to reconstruct southern South America as foreigners saw it in the years from 1810 to 1870."

Keen, Benjamin: *Readings in Latin American Civilization: 1492 to the Present,* Houghton Mifflin Company, Boston, 1955, chaps. XXV, XXVI.

Palmer, T. W., Jr.: "A Momentous Decade in Brazilian Administrative History, 1831–1840," *Hispanic American Historical Review,* vol. 30, pp. 209–217, 1950.

Pierson, William W., and Federico G. Gil: *Governments of Latin America,* McGraw-Hill Book Company, Inc., New York, 1957.

Verissimo, Erico: *Brazilian Literature: An Outline,* The Macmillan Company, New York, 1945. A neat, authoritative summary.

Williams, Mary W.: *Dom Pedro the Magnanimous, Second Emperor of Brazil,* North Carolina University Press, Chapel Hill, N.C., 1937. A fascinating hero-worshipful biography.

XV

The Struggle for Liberalism

Liberalism appeared to have triumphed in Argentina with the victory of the federalists over the unitaries at Cepeda in 1820. Thereafter authority in the La Plata provinces was decentralized and *caudillo* rule became the prevailing form of government. But personalist government on a local level did not necessarily meet all the requirements of the liberal program. Within the limits of the federal system national leadership in certain matters was provided by Rosas, the governor of Buenos Aires province. In Mexico, liberalism, despite its auspicious start, was subverted by Santa Anna and only after his downfall could it emerge triumphant. In both Argentina and Mexico the struggle between the liberals and conservatives took dramatic forms in the decades of the 1850s and 1860s.

Argentine Federalism

In Argentina, whose riparian provinces were dominated by Rosas and whose interior provinces were controlled by local *caudillos* generally subservient to him, unsophisticated personalism was becoming discredited. There the conflict between *porteños* and provincials, city dwellers and *gauchos,* unitaries and federalists, which went back to the wars of independence, had been mitigated by the accession to power of the strong federalist leader Rosas, a Buenos Aires *gaucho.* But his was a personal regime; and dictatorship, dependent as it was upon the arbitrary decisions of a leader, became increasingly distasteful to the Argentines, not only to the unitaries, who felt an implacable hatred for Rosas, but even to federalists. They developed a certain common feeling in their united opposition to the continuation of the Rosas regime. Moreover, Rosas failed to provide a truly national government for the disparate Argentine provinces, and he governed without a constitution. The experiment of constitution making had been suspended after the failure of the unitary constitution of 1826 and was not resumed by Rosas, to the disappointment of the federalists who had steadily looked forward after their victory at Cepeda to the adoption of a federalist constitution for a united Argentine nation. But for Rosas the time never seemed ripe for drawing up a constitution, or, as was surmised, his own personal ambitions advised against it. Or, perhaps more accurately, he feared that a constitution once adopted either would become a dead letter or would be used to the disadvantage of certain provinces which under it might be required to solicit alms from the federal government and thus lose some of their autonomy. He remained irrevocably committed to a federal system consisting of autonomous provinces.

Rosas's reputation as a national leader was enhanced by his success in foreign relations. But his very success in defending not only Buenos Aires but other provinces against foreign assaults for which he was not responsible aroused jealousies and produced economic repercussions which increased his unpopularity. In a dictatorship the dictator must bear responsibility for everything that goes wrong. For these foreign attacks, which were inspired largely by Rosas's unitary enemies and perpetrated by truculent English and French admirals, Rosas was made the scapegoat. During the foreign blockade of Buenos Aires, he lost the support of the merchants, whose trade was cut off, and of the small artisans in the city and the small farmers in the province, who were forced to reduce their levels of living. This result occurred when he was obliged to depreciate the value of Argentine money by issuing fiat currency to finance his defense against foreign enemies. In the littoral provinces resentment was particularly strong because of the closing of the rivers made necessary by the military operations.

There the opposition to Rosas was led by Gen. Justo José de Urquiza, the *gaucho* governor of the province of Entre Ríos. Urquiza had cooperated with Rosas in the war against the Rivera faction in Uruguay, which had intrigued to detach the Mesopotamian provinces of Argentina from the littoral alliance with Buenos Aires. Resisting these intrigues Urquiza established a considerable military reputation by defeating Rivera in battle in 1845. His estrangement from Rosas began in the following year when he tried to arrange a reconciliation between Rosas and the governor of Corrientes, which Rosas rejected. He became convinced that Argentina must form a national union under a federal regime and that Rosas was blocking the desire of the provinces for such a union. Through his capable administration of Entre Ríos province, befriending education, maintaining freedom of the press, and assisting the farmers with loans at low rates of interest, Urquiza gained for himself a formidable political power. In 1851 he launched a revolt against Rosas, charging that Entre Ríos had never delegated to Rosas any power except control over foreign relations and calling for the organization of a true federal republic.

Urquiza appealed to the other Argentine provinces for support but received none except from Corrientes. He did, however, enlist the aid of the anti-Rosas faction in Uruguay, whose capital, Montevideo, was still being besieged by Rosas. He also received assistance from Brazil, which, upon the dubious argument that she was a guarantor of the treaty of 1828 establishing the independence of Uruguay, now agreed to intervene in the war. With the backing of the Brazilian fleet commanded by Admiral Grenfell and with an army of some 10,000 men of his own, Urquiza raised the eight-year siege of Montevideo in a daring campaign in October, 1851. He then took his army, now numbering 24,000 men, across the Paraná River and threatened Buenos Aires. At Monte Caseros he confronted Rosas in battle on February 3, 1852, and completely routed the Buenos Aires forces. Rosas returned to Buenos Aires with only a few followers, wrote out his resignation, sought asylum in the British legation, and then sailed to England where he spent the rest of his life, living quietly as an impoverished country gentleman until his death in 1877. He had not taken the precaution of establishing a bank account in Europe, and he boasted truthfully that he had never made a cent from public office. His property was now confiscated by the new provincial authorities.

The highly literate unitaries have set the tone of most subsequent appraisals of Rosas. Their hatred of the man and of his federalist system led them to depict him as an unscrupulous and bloodthirsty tyrant and his *Mazorca* supporters as the vigilante agents of a fiend. This is the portrait given in the novel *Amalia* published in 1851 by the Argentine writer, José Mármol, and it colors much of the writing in English about the era of Rosas in Argentina. "Rosas was a maniac," wrote Sarmiento summarily. And in another judgment he declared, "Rosas is a type of imbecile, and this appears to me to explain most of his actions." This allegation was later developed medically by an Argentine physician, José M. Ramos Mejía, in two works, *Las Neurosis de los Hombres Célebres en la Historia Argentina*, first issued in 1878–1882, and *Rosas y Su Tiempo*, published in 1907.[1] To the unitaries must be credited the picture of Rosas as an exemplar and defender of barbarism which has projected itself into modern times.

Rosas was a strong ruler without doubt, and the absolutist nature of the power which he exercised cannot be denied. But the so-called "Rosas Terror" was short-lived, occurring only in 1839 and 1840, and although other periods of his long regime were disfigured by much loss of life—an estimated twenty thousand people were killed during his regime—he cannot be held responsible for all the blood shed in the civil wars from which the country suffered during his tenure of power, for the unitary opposition to him was arrogant, stubborn, and irresponsible. When Buenos Aires was at peace, Rosas only rarely took bloody reprisal against his adversaries. On the other hand, he greatly improved the tone of public administration and maintained the dignity of the country in foreign affairs. He created a new sense of national responsibility and gave Argentina a unity which it had not possessed before. He assumed power over an anarchy and left it a nation. But his regime was an improvisation depending upon the judgment and prestige of the dictator. Under Rosas the provinces of the Río de la Plata continued to be only a ramshackle congeries of separate units, which, particularly in the light of what Argentina later became, appeared to be inadequate. Including now a

---

[1] In the former work Ramos Mejía also undertook to prove Dr. Francia of Paraguay insane.

population of some 800,000 they were ready for a stronger national cohesiveness. Rosas's persistent opposition to the formation of a constitutional union had split his own federal supporters, and his regime was finally overthrown by these dissident federalists who determined to create a nation organized along federal lines.

Urquiza and Constitutional Federalism

After the overthrow of Rosas, Urquiza was able to secure the withdrawal of Brazilian troops, and Vicente Fidel López was made governor of Buenos Aires province as Rosas's temporary successor. López had composed the Argentine national anthem in 1813 and had served as interim president after the overthrow of Rivadavia in 1827. Under their joint agencies a convention was summoned to meet at San Nicolás de los Arroyos in May, 1852. After Urquiza's victory at Caseros he sent out Bernardo de Irigoyen to line up the provinces behind the new project for creating a constitutional federal union. With the influential example of Caseros he succeeded in gaining the support of eleven of the thirteen Argentine provinces, including, as he thought, even Buenos Aires province. The *acuerdo* which was drawn up at San Nicolás reaffirmed the Littoral Pact of 1831 which, it was now agreed, should serve until a definite government could be set up. It made Urquiza the provisional director of the revived federal union and commander in chief of its armed forces. But this *acuerdo* was unacceptable to the members of the new provincial legislature of Buenos Aires and was rejected by them largely because they were unwilling to follow the leadership of the provinces, objected to the provision of equality of the provinces under the *acuerdo,* and feared that Urquiza, whose background was similar to that of Rosas and who resembled him in many ways, was going to establish a new dictatorship. When Urquiza thereupon dissolved the Buenos Aires legislature and exiled its leaders, the worst fears of the *porteños* seemed to be realized. Their response was to rebel against his authority, as they did in September, 1852, under the leadership of Valentín Alsina. The city was blockaded by the naval forces of the constitutionalists under a mercenary seaman from the United States, Adm. John Halsted Coe, from the following December till July, 1853, when the *porteños* bought off the besieging fleet with gold and Admiral Coe went over to the Buenos Aires government with all his ships.

Meanwhile a constitution for the Argentine Confederation—the first federalist constitution in Argentine history—had been drawn up at Sante Fe. It was promulgated on May 25, 1853, the anniversary of Argentine independence. As a guide to the formulation of this constitution one of Argentina's outstanding constitutional lawyers, Juan Bautista Alberdi, prepared and circulated among the delegates to the constitutional convention his own *Bases y puntos de partida para la organización política de la República Argentina,* which served as the basis of the new constitution, originally drafted by him.

This constitution of 1853 as finally adopted established Argentina as a federal republic with a president and vice president chosen for a six-year term by a purely formal electoral college, as in the United States. The president was to be assisted by a cabinet, whose members were appointed by him and could sit and participate in Congress but could not vote. Congress consisted of two houses—the lower chosen on a proportional basis by population, the upper of an equal number of senators from each state chosen by the state legislatures. The powers of the central government over the states included the right to grant generous subsidies to them, the right to impeach the governors and to intervene the states, that is, to replace the local governor and other officials with federal interventors, and the right to approve the state constitutions before they went into effect. The Roman Catholic religion was made the official religion of the nation and the president was required to be a Catholic. The church itself received subsidies from the government, which, however, reserved to itself the *patronato* or control of the secular affairs of the church and the right of nominating officials for appointment to ecclesiastical positions.

Buenos Aires, which soon afterward ceased its open rebellion against the constitution, nevertheless continued in sullen opposition and refused to accept it. For the next seven years the province with its capital, the principal port of the nation, remained outside the Argentine Confederation. It now drew up a constitution of its own somewhat similar to the repudiated unitary constitution of 1826 and conducted its affairs as an independent state uncooperative with the new federal government. This new federal government was headed by Urquiza, who served as president from 1854 to 1860 with his capital at Paraná, the seat of government of his own state of Entre Ríos. The new president immediately took steps to legitimize his children, reported to number 108, and to marry one of the mothers!

As recommended by Alberdi, the new government concluded a series of treaties with the United States, Great Britain, and France in 1853 opening up the Paraná and Uruguay Rivers to those foreign countries—a concession which these nations had sought in vain to obtain from Rosas. The government of the Confederation also concluded a treaty with Brazil confirming their mutual obligation to defend the independence of Uruguay against attempts by any other nation to alter its form of government or seize control over it. Urquiza encouraged the migration of foreigners to Argentina, and the modern tide of immigration set in with the establishment of new colonies in Entre Ríos, Corrientes, Santa Fe, and other littoral provinces. Railroad construction was also pushed as a means of opening up new regions and expanding commerce, both domestic and foreign.

Urquiza found it necessary to conclude treaties of commerce and other conventional arrangements with Buenos Aires, but these were generally unsatisfactory and led to a tariff war between them in 1856. An effort was made to counteract the geographical and commercial advantages which the province possessed in its principal port by building up Rosario as a rival to Buenos Aires, and the stimulus which eventually made Rosario the second commercial city in the nation began at this time. Though Rosario began to serve as an outlet for the growing grain-producing pampas of eastern Córdoba and Santa Fe it could not really outdistance Buenos Aires in foreign trade. This commercial inadequacy finally impelled the federal government to try to bring Buenos Aires into the union by force. At Cepeda in October, 1859, Urquiza met and defeated a Buenos Aires army under Bartolomé Mitre and forced the recalcitrant state to enter the federation. Urquiza showed great restraint, dealing with the conquered *porteños* through a mediator, Francisco Solano López, the young son of the president of Paraguay, and refusing to enter the city as a conqueror. He and his government also accepted the constitutional amendments which Buenos Aires insisted upon as a condition for its entry into the union. These required, among other things, that no city should be elevated into the national capital without the consent of the province in which it was located. This so-called "Agreement of San José de Flores" nationalized the customs-house of Buenos Aires but assured the province of Buenos Aires of its income for the next five years. Under the federalist constitution of 1853, therefore, as thus amended in 1860, Argentina finally achieved national unity.

Even after these concessions Buenos Aires continued, under Urquiza's successor, Santiago Derqui, to be uncooperative. Her union with the other Argentine provinces had been brought about under duress, she was not given the prominent role which she thought she deserved in the Confederation, and the capital of the Confederation remained at Paraná. In 1861 when the national Congress refused to accept the credentials of the Buenos Aires deputies, who had been defiantly elected in accordance with the provincial rather than the national constitution, Buenos Aires renewed its rebellion against the national government. Again Urquiza met Mitre in battle—at Pavón in the province of Santa Fe—but this time he abandoned the field to him. Urquiza now retired from public life, and his former protégé Derqui went into exile. Mitre, who was governor of the province of Buenos Aires, became provisional president of the Argentine federation and transferred the capital from Paraná to Buenos Aires. In the following year he was elected president.

Mitre, whose father was a teacher at the army post of Fort Carmen de Patagores on the Río Negro, spent much of his childhood on Argentina's Indian frontier. During the Rosas regime he became a unitary exile in Uruguay and Bolivia and founded the military school of the latter nation. As a young colonel of artillery he participated in the rebellion that overthrew Rosas in 1852. He considered himself a military man but showed no great capacity in that line. As minister of war and marine for the province of Buenos Aires he personally led expeditions against the Indians from 1855 to 1860 but was barely able to keep them confined behind the barrier forts. Later as the founder of the great Buenos Aires newspaper *La Nación*, he not only made himself influential in politics but helped to create an outstanding tradition of journalism in Argentina. His numerous historical works, written from the unitary viewpoint, established him in the front rank of Latin American historians. But unitarism as a program and movement for Argentina was effectually destroyed by Rosas before his overthrow, and when Mitre became president he loyally accepted the federalist constitution of 1853. On the question of the organization of the federal capital Mitre was willing to federalize either the capital or the province of Buenos Aires but was unable to carry the majority of the *porteños* with him on this proposal. A compromise arrangement was therefore worked out in 1862, to continue for five years, whereby Buenos Aires province remained autonomous, and the port city of Buenos Aires served as the capital of both the province and the nation. Under this arrangement the federal government collected the import duties.

Mitre sought, with only moderate success, to reconcile the provinces to his administration. Disorders occurred in Córdoba, San Juan, Catamarca, and Mendoza. The assassination of the aggressive *caudillo* of La Rioja by federalist army officers was deemed necessary in order to prevent his meddling in neighboring provinces. Revolts broke out in Corrientes, Mendoza, Santiago, and San Luis in 1866, which engaged the attention of federal troops for more than a year and hampered the military operations against Paraguay, to be discussed later. But the legal balance and cooperation between the province and the federal government were maintained under the constitution while Mitre, a *porteño*, served as president. A satisfactory accommodation seemed to have been worked out between the strategically placed, cosmopolitan port city and province of Buenos Aires and their country cousins. Only after long agitation and much bloodshed had the constitutional question of unitarism or federalism been finally settled in favor of the latter. This settlement guaranteed that Buenos Aires, though rich and powerful enough to dominate the country, would not be able to do so. It would be subject to checks by the provinces and could not maintain a power monopoly. The basis was thus laid for a balanced national development of federated provinces. In Argentina then, as in Chile, Colombia, Venezuela, and other countries of Latin America, the contest between conservatives and liberals in the middle third of the nineteenth century was resolved substantially in favor of the liberals with the decentralization of authority among the local units and a corresponding limitation of the powers of the national governments. Among the La Plata provinces this federal system was consecrated in the constitution of 1853, which remained in force for almost a century.

Militant Liberalism in Mexico

With the final downfall of Santa Anna in 1855 Mexico also was ripe for reform along liberal lines, corresponding to the trend of the times. The basis for such a movement had been laid in the laws of 1833 which had been carried through by the acting president, Valentín Gómez Farías, and later subverted by Santa Anna. As the romantic ideals of political freedom and equalitarianism again became popular, influenced by the literature and example of France and Spain, they found expression in the literary work of the members of the famous Academy of San Juan de Letrán in Mexico, including Guillermo Prieto, Romualdo Pacheco, Ignacio Rodríguez Galván, and Fernando Calderón. These ideals, thus emphasized in patriotic poems and novels which marked the beginnings of a Mexican national literature, inspired the liberals to work for a curtailment of the powers of the central government, which had been expanded and allowed to encroach upon individual liberties under Santa Anna, and a corresponding devolution of authority to the states and other local units of government.

The liberals became convinced that the Mexican independence movement had worked out only to the advantage of the military and the Roman Catholic Church. They did not deny that these two groups were necessary, but they assumed the duty of limiting the tyrannies of both in the interest of the nation. In particular they insisted that the church should restrict itself to saving souls and should not intervene in the civic and secular life of the nation. Government itself should have no control over the life of the individual citizen except to the extent required to maintain order. The state must not be used as an instrument for the achievement of certain ideals, the accomplishment of a social mission, the improvement of its citizens, or the imposition of ideas.

Their movement, appealing generally to the large class-conscious, illiterate, and inarticulate aboriginal population, aroused grave concern as disruptive of the social and religious order. As a political movement it was led by Benito Juárez, a full-blooded Zapotecan Indian born in the sheep-grazing state of Oaxaca in 1806. Juárez had practiced law in his native state, had won a political reputation for ability and honesty in several minor offices, was elected governor of Oaxaca, and was named minister of justice and ecclesiastical affairs in the cabinet of President Juan Alvarez.

In this position Juárez immediately aroused the bitter enmity of both the army and the church by issuing in November, 1855, the so-called *"Ley Juárez,"* which deprived both military and ecclesiastical courts of the jurisdiction that they had customarily exercised over certain civil matters. As a result the government was denounced by the clergy, Juárez was excommunicated by Pope Pius IX, and Alvarez was forced to surrender the presidency to his secretary of war, Ignacio Comonfort. But these changes did not moderate the reform movement, which on the contrary, intensified its campaign against the privileged classes. In the so-called *"Ley Lerdo,"* promulgated in June, 1856, and named for Miguel Lerdo de Tejada, a liberal leader from Veracruz, the government now suppressed the Jesuits, further curtailed the powers of the church, and forbade both civil and religious organizations to hold real estate which was not used specifically for purposes of worship. These provisions cut directly at the landed power of the church, which owned ap-

Fig. 15-1. Benito Juárez, detail from a mural painting by Diego Rivera in the Mexican National Museum of History. (*Courtesy of Pan American Union.*)

proximately one-half of the land of Mexico; they were intended to force the church to sell the land and thus make it available to the landless agricultural workers.

Some of these reforms were embodied in a new constitution which was drawn up by a constituent congress and issued in 1857. This constitution was largely the work of Melchor Ocampo. Though it followed the general governmental pattern of the constitution of 1824, it contained guaranties of personal liberty, which were intended to prevent its perversion into a justification of dictatorship at the hands of another Santa Anna. It emphasized the federal nature of the Mexican nation by stressing states' rights and the authority of Congress rather than the president. The principles of the liberal movement were further embodied in provisions which forbade clerical participation in affairs of state and abolished special courts, such as those of the army, the church, and the large *hacienda* owners. The purpose of these provisions was to enable the federal government to terminate special privilege and monopoly and to assert the national authority over them. Under this new constitution Comonfort was elected president and Juárez vice president.

Even greater was the fury of the clerico-conservative classes against this new constitution than against the previous *Ley Juárez* and *Ley Lerdo*, for it undercut the very ground on which they stood. In the predominantly agricultural Mexico of that day, land was the basis of wealth and prestige. But land monopoly was not the source of the power of the *hacendados* alone;

on it also rested the power of the church. They united in opposition to the constitution and demanded its repeal in the Plan of Tacubaya which they drew up. The archbishop of Mexico officially denounced the constitution and withheld the sacraments from those who supported it. When Comonfort responded to these pressures by timidly advocating changes in the constitution, Congress repudiated him and drove him into exile in 1858, replacing him with Juárez as president.

For the next ten years Mexico was racked by the so-called *"Guerra de la Reforma"* (War of the Reform) centering around the constitution of 1857. At first the clerico-conservatives gained control of Mexico City and installed Gen. Félix Zuloaga as president. Thereupon Juárez and his congressional allies recruited an army to oppose him under the banner of the constitution of 1857. He shrewdly established his headquarters in the populous port of Veracruz where he could finance the war by collecting customs duties. Throughout the war Juárez received his support principally in the east and in the northwest. His reform program for Mexico, evolved in the intervals between battles, went beyond the constitution of 1857, particularly in respect to the church. It included not only defense of the main provisions of the constitution but also the elimination of tithes, the suppression of monastic orders, the establishment of religious toleration, the separation of church and state, the legalization of civil marriage, and the nationalization of all church property that was not used for religious purposes. Under this conception the power of the Mexican government would be used against the ranking social classes for the benefit of the masses of the nation, largely Indian and *mestizo,* in order to create a hitherto nonexistent rural middle class. It contained the elements of a true social revolution.

After many bloody battles Juárez victoriously moved into Mexico City in December, 1860, and asserted his claims as president under the constitution of 1857. He immediately began to proscribe church officials, expelling the archbishop from the country and putting into force his anticlerical decrees. Under these he proceeded against the monastic orders and took over lands of the church. But his adversaries now, as a desperate expedient, resolved to call in foreigners to conquer him. The situation in Mexico, divided by a bitter war of classes and sliding into bankruptcy, seemed ready-made for foreign intervention. The Mexican conservatives could not, however, expect to receive aid from the United States, which indeed under President Buchanan had supported Juárez in the expectation of being rewarded with a cession of Mexican territory. They therefore turned to Europe for help and worked particularly for the establishment of a French protectorate over their country. The Mexican clerical, José de Hidalgo, approached the Emperor Louis Napoleon with proposals that France establish a Spanish Bourbon prince on the throne of Mexico.

These proposals were encouraged by French speculators who had invested heavily in Mexican bonds and who were dismayed when Juárez under the duress of the civil conflict in Mexico was forced to suspend interest payments on Mexico's foreign debt. This debt included a loan of 3,375,000 francs, which had been made by a Swiss banker, Jecker, to the Miramón government of Mexico preceding that of Juárez and which after the failure of Jecker in 1860 had been taken over by the Duc de Morny, illegitimate half brother of Louis Napoleon and president of the *Corps Législatif* of France. These claims were officially backed by the French government. The British also became interested in moving against Mexico after the British vice-consul at Taxco was murdered.

The Tragedy of Maximilian

Finally Mexico's three principal foreign creditors—France, England, and Spain—agreed in the Convention of London in October, 1861, to use their joint forces "on the coasts of Mexico" and "for other operations" to collect their claims against Mexico, but at the same time they agreed not to seek "any acquisition of territory or special advantage and not to exercise in the internal affairs of Mexico any influence of a nature to prejudice the right of the Mexican nation to choose and to constitute freely its form of government." With these assurances that their intervention would not take the form of occupation of Mexico's territory or violation of its political autonomy the intervening powers sought to justify their action to the United States, which was then opportunely preoccupied with the Civil War and was for that reason in no condition to object to a European debt-collecting intervention against Mexico. Even if the Lincoln government had been strong enough to protest against this intervention, did a mere debt-collecting action constitute a violation of the Monroe Doctrine? And was the Monroe Doctrine of any effect anyway? At the suggestion of Great Britain, provision was made for the accession of the United States to the London convention, but this invitation was not accepted by the United States.

Napoleon III was craftily plotting more than a mere debt-collecting expedition. He was intrigued by the possibility of setting up a puppet monarch in Mexico, who might be expected to serve the interests of France or at least to curb the further spread of republicanism. When England and Spain became convinced that Napoleon's ultimate object was the overthrow of the Mexican government they withdrew from the venture, leaving the French troops to press on alone. The British, though continuing to sympathize with the purposes of the expedition and hoping to reap some financial benefits from it, did not wish to invite a war with the United States. The Spanish chose to concentrate their attention upon their war with Peru, arising out of their seizure of the Chincha Islands, and upon their intervention in Santo Domingo. By the summer of 1863 a French army of 36,000 men, led by Gen. Elie Fréderic Forey, occupied Mexico City, where they were welcomed by the conservatives, clericals, and monarchists. Juárez was forced to abandon the city and withdraw to San Luis Potosí. At the time when liberal principles were triumphant in Chile, Colombia, Venezuela, and other Latin American countries they were banished from the seats of power in Mexico, but only through the forcible intervention of a reactionary European monarchy.

The members of the conservative-monarchist group who now governed Mexico, supported by French bayonets, convinced themselves that a foreign monarch was the answer to Mexico's problems and would be their own salvation. They resolved to undo nearly a half century of republicanism in Mexico. The commander of the occupying French army now chose a Council of Notables which in April, 1864, persuaded the Archduke Ferdinand Maximilian, brother of the Emperor Francis Joseph of Austria, to accept the proffered throne of Mexico. Before accepting the throne Maximilian extracted a promise from Napoleon, in the Convention of Miramar, that, "however events in Europe may turn out, the assistance of France shall never fail the new Empire." In return Maximilian agreed to repay France for the expenses of the intervention and to pay for the maintenance of the French army in Mexico after July 1, 1864. To reimburse the French and to finance his royal venture Maximilian issued a loan of 201 million francs before he reached Mexico, turning over 66 million to the French treasury and retaining only 8 million for Mexico. In addition he agreed to grant special privileges to French concessionaires, but he refused to give Napoleon the privilege of exploiting the mines of Sonora under the protection of French troops. As a Catholic he solicited and received the approval and blessing of the Pope, with the understanding that he would restore the church properties confiscated under the Reform.

Maximilian set out for Mexico with grandiose and naïve plans for the absorption of Central America, the isthmus, and the northern part of South America into his new Mexican empire and for the marriage of one of his brothers to the daughter of the emperor of Brazil. In late May, 1864, he arrived in Mexico with his wife Carlota, daughter of Leopold I of Belgium, ostensibly at the invitation of the people of Mexico. As his vessel sailed by the fort San Juan de Ulloa, built upon a small rocky island, he caught a first view of the principal port of his new empire, the miasmic Veracruz. To one side lay the French fleet, and in front, scattered along the coast of the mainland, were the graves of thousands of French soldiers who had landed here with high hopes of consummating their emperor's bold plan of conquest. His arrival had been announced. Yet all was silent as the grave. There was no motion in the harbor and none upon the coast. The new ruler of Mexico stood in sight of his kingdom and was on the point of landing. But his subjects remained in concealment. No one came to receive him.

"An uncomfortable feeling stole over us all," wrote one of the members of the emperor's party. "But the Emperor maintained a sarcastic tranquillity.

It seemed as if he endeavored to turn his tolerably cutting satire against himself." [2]

Maximilian was warned by the French rear admiral that he would be exposed to dangers on his journey to Mexico City and that plans had been laid to take him and Carlota captive along the way. Finally the Archduke was welcomed by General Almonte, who had held the reins of government until his arrival. He then proceeded without serious mishap to the capital and was crowned emperor by order of the Council of Notables, which was under the control of the French army. His government was immediately recognized by France, Austria, Spain, Great Britain, Portugal, Belgium, Prussia, Italy, and Sweden, but not by the United States.

Maximilian, who was a Mason, soon alienated the church by refusing to restore the property confiscated from it by Juárez. He failed to retain the support of the conservatives because of his liberal views, and he did not make sufficient reforms to win the support of the republicans. He had to look, nevertheless, both to the church and to conservative business groups for funds to support his regime. He sought therefore to raise money by exacting forced loans from the church and by making new government concessions to mining interests, construction concerns, and railroad companies. He concentrated in the central government the power to make such concessions for mining and commercial operations and railway development. Administratively he undertook to restore the centralist regime of Santa Anna by reorganizing Mexico into departments whose governors were responsible only to the national authorities in Mexico City.

Against Maximilian's government Juárez kept up a steady guerrilla warfare, receiving support from the United States and also from veterans of the Union army after Appomattox. As long as the Civil War in the United States continued, Secretary of State Seward could only warn France against any permanent occupation of Mexican territory, but after the victory of the Lincoln government, the tone of his protests became stronger. In November, 1865, he informed the United States minister at Paris that the continued presence of French troops in Mexico was "cause of serious concern to the United States," and President Johnson's annual message of December 4, 1865, hinted at the possibility of United States resistance in the defense of republicanism in Mexico against foreign interference. Soon afterward Seward warned France that her Mexican project would inevitably jeopardize her friendly relations with the United States, and in February, 1866, he bluntly demanded that Napoleon set a time limit for the evacuation of his troops from Mexico.

The presence of a Union army of over one million unemployed veterans in the United States eager to drive the vastly inferior French army out of Mexico furnished an impressive sanction backing up Seward's warning. In-

[2] Countess Paula Kollonitz, *The Court of Mexico*, M. A. Saunders, Otley, and Co., London, 1868.

deed Seward had to restrain high-ranking army officers, including Gen. Ulysses Grant and Gen. John Schofield, from immediately marching into Mexico. When Schofield was given leave of absence by General Grant to organize Juárez's armies, Seward diverted him from this undertaking by means of a skillful ruse. He sent him to France on a special mission with instructions to put his "feet under the Emperor's mahogany" and talk him out of his Mexican venture, but he deliberately neglected to furnish Schofield with the necessary credentials! Though Seward thus prevented overt intervention in the hostilities in Mexico he maintained 50,000 troops in Texas under Gen. Philip Sheridan ready at a signal to cross into Mexico and support Juárez.

These gradual pressures applied by Seward and Juárez's harassments of the French armies were reinforced by the turn of events in Europe. There Napoleon's subversion of the Mexican government was subjected to increasingly scathing criticism by Liberals in the French Chamber, particularly after the connection of the Duc de Morny with the scheme was revealed. In the diplomatic situation in Europe France was becoming isolated. In 1865 Napoleon had allowed himself to be persuaded by Bismarck to remain neutral while Prussia drove Austria out of the German Confederation. Bismarck's overwhelming victory over Austria at Sadowa was considered a defeat not only for Austria but also for France and a portent of the Franco-Prussian War of 1870. It behooved Napoleon, therefore, to prepare his defenses for the oncoming war by abandoning his costly overseas intervention in Mexico. He accordingly responded favorably to Seward's demand for a time limit on his intervention, but under the compulsion of the European diplomatic situation he actually withdrew his troops before the date agreed upon. This he did despite the anguished pleas of Carlota that he continue to support her husband on the Mexican throne. When Napoleon pulled his last army out of Mexico in early 1867, he left Maximilian at the mercy of Juárez. Maximilian's throne, unsupported by the French, immediately collapsed. In May, 1867, he surrendered to Juárez and was shot by a Mexican firing squad at Querétaro in the following month. His distraught widow Carlota lingered on in Europe, hopelessly insane until her death sixty years later.

France was not the only nation that took advantage of the breakup of the United States in the Civil War to push its political interests in the American hemisphere. Just two weeks after Lincoln became President of a truncated union, the Spanish government of Isabella II reasserted its claim to the Dominican Republic under secret arrangements made with its traitorous president, Pedro Santana, and began to govern it again as a Spanish colony. The Spanish minister in Washington, Tassara, was warned by Lincoln's Secretary of State Seward, that the United States would "meet the further prosecution of enterprises of that kind in regard to either the Dominican Republic or any part of the American continent or islands with a prompt, persistent, and, if possible, effective resistance," but this tough policy was not backed up by Lincoln. Spain, therefore, continued in occupation of the island republic for four years until, as her policies there became increasingly unpopular both in the island and in Spain, Isabella abrogated the act of annexation in mid-1865, just a few weeks after Lincoln's assassination.

The execution of Maximilian was necessary, Juárez explained, in order "that the existence of Mexico as an independent nation be not left to the goodwill of foreign potentates." If Maximilian had been allowed to live even in exile in Europe he would have been used, Juárez continued, by the enemies of Mexico "as a weapon for the restoration of a regime disastrous to the democratic institutions of the country." With the downfall of Maximilian's imperial house of cards Mexico's independence and nationality were again assured and European threats against the Western Hemisphere in violation of the Monroe Doctrine became discredited. In addition Mexico's liberal constitution of 1857 was vindicated, after a civil war which had been marked by unprecedented brutality and bloodshed extending over ten years, and Juárez was installed in the presidency for the third time.

Mexico thus joined the ranks of the Latin American nations which in the 1860s committed themselves to liberal principles of government. Of cardinal importance was the principle that nationality and progress were not dependent upon strong central authority or, as in the case of Mexico, upon a superimposed monarchical rule. On the contrary, their national development would be best furthered by limiting the authority of the central government and by making possible the corresponding expansion of agencies of local self-government. This system, imposing a minimum of governmental and social restraints, would liberate individual energies for productive national effort and the creation of national wealth. But did this system sufficiently recognize the need for directed national effort to achieve national goals, particularly in times of economic stress and war, and did it adequately take cognizance of the strong emphasis of the Latin Americans upon the principle of leadership and their susceptibility to *caudillismo?* Could not a governmental apparatus be developed that would put science and art at the service of the people, that would use its authority to improve their living conditions, that would give the disinherited, the so-called *"léperos,"* a new and more dignified place in society, that would in short enforce liberal principles and destroy reactionary prejudices? Toward such a positive program of governmental action that would use the power of centralized government to put liberal principles into effect the Mexico of Juárez was pointing the way. In the process liberalism would undergo a fundamental transformation.

Additional Reading

Bernstein, Harry: *Modern and Contemporary Latin America,* J. B. Lippincott Company, Philadelphia, 1952, chaps. 5, 14.
Calcott, Wilfrid H.: *Church and State in Mexico, 1822–1857,* Duke University Press, Durham, N.C., 1926.

————: *Liberalism in Mexico, 1857–1929,* Stanford University Press, Stanford, Calif., 1931.
Crawford, William Rex: *A Century of Latin-American Thought,* Harvard University Press, Cambridge, Mass., 1944. A brilliant digest of Latin American thinkers and their ideas.
Davis, William C.: *The Last Conquistadores: the Spanish Intervention in Peru and Chile, 1863–1866,* University of Georgia Press, Athens, 1950.
Hyde, Harford M.: *Mexican Empire: The History of Maximilian and Carlota of Mexico,* Macmillan, New York, 1946.
Jeffrey, William H.: *Mitre and Argentina,* Library Publishers, New York, 1952.
————: *Mitre and Urquiza: A Chapter in the Unification of the Argentine Republic,* Drew University Studies, no. 4, Madison, N.J., 1952.
Keen, Benjamin: *Readings in Latin American Civilization: 1492 to the Present,* Houghton Mifflin Company, Boston, 1955, chap. XXVII.
Knapp, Frank Averill: *The Life of Sebastián Lerdo de Tejada, 1823–1889: A Study of Influence and Obscurity,* University of Texas Press, Austin, 1951.
Levene, Ricardo: *A History of Argentina,* trans. and ed. by William Spence Robertson, University of North Carolina Press, Chapel Hill, N.C., 1937, chaps. LI–LIV.
Ruiz, Ramón Eduardo (ed.): *An American in Maximilian's Mexico, 1865–1866: Diaries of William Marshall Anderson,* Huntington Library, San Marino, California, 1959. Observations of a visitor from the United States.
Scholes, Walter V.: *Mexican Politics during the Juárez Regime, 1855–1872,* University of Missouri Press, Columbia, Mo., 1957.
Scobie, J. R.: "The Aftermath of Pavón," *Hispanic American Historical Review,* vol. 35, pp. [153]–174, 1955.
Walford, A. J.: "General Urquiza and the Battle of Pavón (1861)," *Hispanic American Historical Review,* vol. 19, pp. 464–493, 1939.
Zea, Leopoldo: *Dos etapas del pensamiento en Hispano-América: Del romanticismo al positivismo,* El Colegio de México, Mexico, 1949.

XVI

The Triumph of Republicanism in Brazil

Liberalism, as defined in its nineteenth-century sense, triumphed in many parts of Latin America in the last third of the century. Intellectual currents flowing from Europe and, to a lesser extent, from the United States contributed to the ferment in Latin America which called in question many of the traditional systems of belief and action inherited from colonial times. In literature it was marked by a new romantic freedom of expression, a wider use of the popular idiom, and the discovery of new themes in hitherto neglected local life and customs, including those of the Indian and the *gaucho*. The exemplars of this romantic movement in literature were Esteban Echeverría and Domingo Faustino Sarmiento in Argentina, Gonçalves de Magalhaes, Antonio Gonçalves Dias, and Joaquim Manoel de Macedo in Brazil, and José Caicedo Rojas, José Manuel Marroquín, and Jorge Isaacs in Colombia. Their sympathetic treatment of new themes was accompanied by a tendency to critical self-examination which was reinforced by the social and economic pressures of the new industrial age. The liberals accepted the nineteenth-century cult of progress with its emphasis upon material advance, mechanical skills, and technical efficiency, and in many countries they looked to foreign capital as a means of bringing these advantages to their countries. In those countries where this new liberalism came into vogue it profoundly disturbed customary conditions of feudal, oligarchic, and authoritarian rule.

The upsurge of liberalism, with its emphasis upon decentralization of government, criticism of the church on rational grounds, and resistance to privilege, became especially apparent at the middle of the century. With a long background of preparation, liberalism became an organized political movement at that time in several countries and moved toward positions of power in government. In Brazil its advance was handicapped by the presence of a popular monarchy, but it advanced nevertheless as a republican movement reinforced by the ideology and religion of Positivism until the monarchy fell in 1889. In Chile and Argentina liberalism gradually took over control of the government in the 1870s. Mexican liberalism, solidly based on the now vindicated constitution of 1857, was transmuted into a social science monopolized by the wealthy elite under the quasi dictatorship of Porfirio

Díaz. In other Latin American countries the progress of the liberal movement followed this same pattern, developing, as it came to power, its own bureaucracy, oligarchy, and defensive power mechanism.

War of the Triple Alliance

The liberal movement in Brazil was stimulated by the reaction against Brazil's involvement in the War of the Triple Alliance in which she joined with Argentina and Uruguay against Paraguay. At the beginning of the war in 1865 Brazil was probably the strongest and best-ordered nation in South America. By her successful cooperation with the *Colorado* faction in Uruguay and with Urquiza, governor of Entre Ríos, to overthrow the Argentine dictator Rosas in 1852, Brazil greatly enhanced her position in South America. In 1851 she extended her southern border at Uruguay's expense by annexing the region between the Ibicui and Cuareim (Quarai) Rivers and forcing Uruguay to accept the latter river as its northwestern boundary. At the same time Brazil also acquired exclusive rights of navigation on Lake Mirim and the Yaguaron River (Jaguarão) on Uruguay's northeastern boundary. In addition she emerged from her war against Argentina on good terms with the new Argentine government headed by Urquiza. Her position of preeminence did not seem to be threatened by the Argentine provinces, which despite the adoption of the new federal type of constitution in 1853 were still weakened by the uncooperativeness of the province of Buenos Aires. Brazil soon obtained from the new Urquiza government one of the objectives for which she had fought against Rosas, namely, the opening of the navigation of the Paraguay, Paraná, and Uruguay Rivers to commerce with the outside world, thus providing means of ingress and egress for a considerable part of her back country, opening it up to settlement and foreign trade, and enabling her further to press her territorial claims westward to the foot of the Andes. These claims she had cherished since colonial days, and the opening up of her western lands stimulated her desire for access to the upper reaches of the Paraná and Paraguay Rivers controlled by Paraguay.

The War of the Triple Alliance grew out of a tangled complex of international rivalries, personal ambitions, and geographical conditions in southern South America. Brazil's traditional westward thrust seemed to jeopardize Paraguay's nationhood, and the final consolidation of the Argentine provinces in 1860 placed a strong rival on Paraguay's southern border, threatening the continued access of the commerce of that landlocked nation to the sea.

Francisco Solano López, the president-dictator of Paraguay, realizing that either Argentina or Brazil could strangle his nation, stimulated his people to a passionate hatred of both nations. His country had been treated as an inferior by both, and its nationality might be extinguished at any time by either. The unsettled condition of Paraguay's boundaries caused constant complications with both of her powerful neighbors. Paraguay perhaps continued to exist as an independent nation only because of their jealousy of each other. A *mestizo* with little education, Solano López had been groomed by his father, Carlos Antonio López, for the rulership of Paraguay. At the age of eighteen he was made a brigadier general in the Paraguayan army and in 1854 was sent abroad as a diplomatic representative of his government to England and France. In France he acquired an excessive admiration for the emperor of France and developed a Napoleon complex. After succeeding his father as president of Paraguay with the backing of the army he contrived to acquire a powerful ascendancy over his country. He became ambitious to give it a place in the sun and perhaps hoped to create a greater Paraguay which would include the Argentine provinces of Entre Ríos and Corrientes, and possibly Uruguay and which would vie with Argentina and Brazil for preeminence in South America.

This uncouth Guaraní *caudillo* was thus described by the unsympathetic United States minister at Asunción:

He dressed grotesquely, but his costume was always expensive and elaborately finished. He wore enormous silver spurs, such as would have been the envy of a Gaucho, and the trappings of his horse were so completely covered with silver as almost to form a coat of mail. After his return from abroad, he adopted a more civilized costume, but always indulged in gorgeous display of gold lace and bright buttons. He conversed with fluency and had a good command of language, and when in good humor his manners were courteous and agreeable. . . . He had however a gross animal look that was repulsive when his face was in repose. . . . He was an inveterate smoker of the strongest Paraguayan cigars. His face was rather flat, and his nose and hair indicated more of the negro than of the Indian. His cheeks had a fulness that extended to the jowl, giving him a sort of bulldog expression. In his later years he grew enormously fat, so much so that few would believe that a photograph of his figure was not a caricature. He was very irregular in his hours of eating, but when he did eat, the quantity he consumed was enormous. His drinking was in keeping with his eating; he always kept a large stock of foreign wines, liquors and ale, but he had little discrimination in the use of them. Though he habitually drank largely, yet he often exceeded his own large limits, and on such occasions he was liable to break out in the most furious abuse of all who were about him. He would then indulge in the most revolting obscenity, and would sometimes give orders for the most barbarous acts. When he had recovered from these debauches he would stay the execution of his orders, if they had not already been enforced.[1]

For years this vain, autocratic, ferocious, and tragic ruler prepared his nation for war, and by 1865 he had built up an army of 60,000 excellently drilled and disciplined troops, which was militarily stronger than the combined armies of both his supposed rivals. He knew that they were not prepared to wage war and felt confident that Brazil, in particular, would not have either

---

[1] Charles A. Washburn, quoted in Julian Hawthorne, *Spanish America,* Peter Fenelon Collier, New York, 1899, pp. 439–440.

the means or the inclination to fight on foreign soil. The pretext for the war was Brazil's intervention in Uruguayan politics. Brazil felt a paternal interest in Uruguay, for whose independence she had become jointly responsible with Argentina in 1828. Besides, her financial stakes in Uruguay were considerable. In particular, the Visconde de Mauá, a large Brazilian financier who owned a bank in Montevideo, constantly pressed upon Dom Pedro the need for maintaining order and stability in Uruguay.

Ireneo Evangelista de Souza, Baron and later Viscount of Mauá, made himself one of the wealthiest men in Brazil largely through his connections with British mercantile and banking interests and his developmental enterprises in his own country. A native of Brazil's southernmost state of Rio Grande do Sul he established close business relations with Uruguay and secretly provided the Uruguayan government with assistance which contributed to the downfall of Rosas in 1852. At the same time he constructed the first Brazilian railroad, the *Estrada de Ferro de Petrópolis,* running from the port some forty miles inland to the mountains at Petrópolis, where the summer palace of the emperor was located. Branching out from this modest venture he became actively concerned with the construction of nearly all the Brazilian railroads that were built during the third quarter of the nineteenth century. An adventuring financier of boundless enthusiasm he pioneered in the construction of iron foundries, shipyards, and other industries in Brazil. He promoted port improvements in Pôrto Alegre, gasworks and other public utilities in Rio de Janeiro, the development of steam navigation on the Amazon River, and the laying of the first submarine cable connecting Brazil with Europe (1874). Altogether the Baron of Mauá was an enterpriser of ingenuity and perseverance in the tradition of the great industrial and financial promoters of the nineteenth century.

When Dom Pedro went to the aid of a revolutionary chief, Venancio Flores, leader of the *Colorado* faction in Uruguay, against the *Blanco* president, Atanasio Aguirre, Solano López undertook to discipline Brazil. He did so apparently at the solicitation of the *Blancos* in Uruguay, who sought Paraguayan help as a counterpoise to the openly expressed sympathies of both Argentina and Brazil for their *Colorado* rivals. In particular they were apprehensive that Brazil might annex their country again as a new Cisplatine Province, and they resented Brazil's financial penetration of their country as a possible step in that direction. When Brazil's property interests in Uruguay seemed threatened by the failure of the Aguirre government to maintain order, Dom Pedro sent an ultimatum to Aguirre in August, 1864, demanding that the Uruguayan government guarantee the security of foreign life and property and pay indemnities for any damages done to them. Uruguay ignored the ultimatum, but López of Paraguay made common cause with Aguirre and sent a stiff note of protest to Brazil, which Brazil in turn ignored. Brazil then invaded Uruguay to compel the Aguirre government to comply with its ultimatum and by doing so, of course, openly allied itself with and assisted the cause of the *Colorado* revolutionists there. With Brazil's assistance these revolutionists soon overthrew the Aguirre government.

López of Paraguay now moved in to assist the defeated Uruguayan *Blancos* and to advance his own imperial aspirations. As a signal for hostilities he seized a Brazilian steamer, *Marquês de Olinda*, which was plying up the Paraguay River toward Matto Grosso. He followed up the seizure of this vessel by invading Matto Grosso and capturing the fort at Coimbra and the town of Corumbá. He next struck at the southernmost Brazilian state of Rio Grande do Sul which, if annexed, would give him access to the sea. These belligerent actions of the Paraguayan ruler evoked a wave of jingoism in Brazil which was particularly strong among the *gaúchos* of Rio Grande do Sul. They felt a kinship with their *gaucho* neighbors in adjoining Uruguay and were eager to tackle the Paraguayan army, not realizing that as a rough-and-ready cavalry they were hopelessly outnumbered and outtrained by their adversaries.

But Uruguay and the southern provinces of Brazil were separated from Paraguay by the Argentine province of Corrientes, and President Mitre of Argentina refused to allow either belligerent to march its troops across Argentine territory. López, thus thwarted in his designs upon southern Brazil and Uruguay, was enraged by Mitre's insistence upon maintaining the neutrality of his country and declared war against Argentina. In March, 1865, he began offensive operations against not only Brazil but also Uruguay and Corrientes. By this act the Paraguayan dictator drew Urquiza, who since his retirement as president of the Argentine Confederation had continued as the virtually independent ruler of Entre Ríos, into the armed coalition against him. López's enemies could now move against him directly by way of both the Paraná and the Uruguay Rivers. In the following May his principal enemies, Brazil, Argentina, and Uruguay, the latter with Flores now in control, concluded a secret treaty of alliance promising not to lay down their arms until López was overthrown. They agreed further that none of the allies would make peace without the concurrence of the others and that the treaty of peace should fix the Paraná and Paraguay Rivers as the boundaries between Argentina and Paraguay as far as the territory of Brazil, thus assigning to Argentina the region of Misiones and the entire Chaco territory from the Bermejo up to Bahía Negra. At the same time they promised one another to respect Paraguay's independence as a nation. Mitre was made commander in chief of the combined armies, and Brazil was put in charge of naval operations.

The allies were not prepared for war. Brazil's regular army numbered fewer than fifteen thousand, but the emperor now gave all his time and his tireless energy to preparing the nation for participation in the hostilities. At his call fifty-seven battalions of volunteers were soon organized. The Brazilian navy was enlarged until it included eighty-five ships of war, of which thirteen were ironclads. In June, 1865, the Brazilian navy defeated López on the Paraná just below the southern boundary of Paraguay, and at about the same time Brazilian troops drove back a Paraguayan army invading Rio Grande do Sul. The allies succeeded in establishing a foothold on Paraguayan territory in early 1866 but were soon driven out by the embattled Paraguayans after a series of bloody engagements. They had to cope not only with the ferocious resistance of the fanatically patriotic Paraguayans but also with the cholera, which their hospital and medical services were inadequate to handle and which accordingly decimated their ranks. Besides, they were handicapped by lack of skillful leadership, by their poor supply facilities, and by their ignorance of the topography of the areas of Paraguay in which they were obliged to fight. The Brazilian fleet meanwhile laid siege to the strong fortress at Humaitá guarding the approach to Paraguayan territory on the Paraná River and forced the fortress to surrender in August, 1868. In the ground operations against Paraguay the Brazilian forces were led by the emperor's favorite general, Marshal Caxias, a Conservative who replaced Mitre as commander in chief of the allied armies. Caxias, who had successfully put down the separatist movement in Rio Grande do Sul between 1845 and 1855, now began to win victories over the Paraguayans and by 1869 occupied Asunción.

López showed a desperate ferocity as his enemies closed in on him. At the height of his military effort he commanded an army of 150,000 men. When his officers were defeated in battle he had them shot, and when they surrendered to the enemy he took reprisals against their families. In March, 1870, he was caught by the Brazilians while trying to escape through the woods and was speared by a common soldier. With his death, it has been said, "his country died with him." A provisional government was set up even before his death which denounced him as "an assassin of his country and an enemy of humankind," and after his death his property and the property of his Irish mistress, Eliza Lynch, were confiscated.

For Paraguay the war was virtually a successful experiment in self-immolation, for almost all the able-bodied men were killed and the women and girls had to carry on the essential services, even to fighting in the armed forces. The total population of the country was reduced by possibly 50 per cent—from an estimated 500,000–1,500,000 before the war to only 150,000–250,000 after the war. Under these circumstances polygamy was inevitably resorted to, but a half century later women still outnumbered the men four to one. After the war Paraguay transferred to Brazil the disputed territory between the Apa and the Branco Rivers, thus slightly expanding the area of the Brazilian state of Matto Grosso to the south. In 1876 she ceded to Argentina the much more valuable Misiones territory and the area between the Bermejo and Pilcomayo Rivers, the so-called "central Chaco," which became the Argentine territory of Formosa.

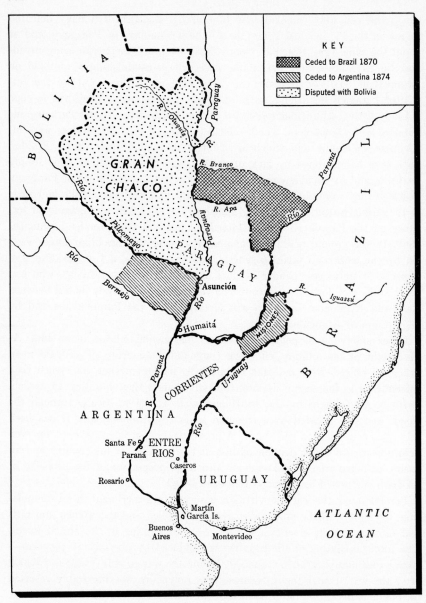

Territorial cessions to Argentina and Brazil following the Paraguayan War.

Effects on Brazilian Politics

For Brazil the expenses of this war against Paraguay mounted up to almost 60 million dollars a year. In all, the war cost Brazil more than 300 million dollars and over 50,000 lives. The emperor's involvement in it was subjected to severe criticism during the war by both Conservatives and Liberals. Brazilians concluded that they had borne the brunt and that their allies had reaped most of the benefits from it. All that Brazil appeared to have gained was the protection and slight territorial expansion of Matto Grosso and the right of unrestricted navigation of the Paraguay River. Uruguay remained independent under the joint protection of Brazil and Argentina. Paraguay also retained its independence in accordance with the assurances given by the allies at the beginning of the war. During the war Argentina was able to strengthen its national position and to expand its commerce while Brazilian troops and ships were engaged in hostilities. Even the opening up of the Paraguay River proved to be more beneficial to Buenos Aires and Montevideo than to Brazil.

This war, with its legacy of heavy taxation and its dubious advantage to Brazil, stimulated the republican movement in that country. The Brazilian monarchy was a unique phenomenon among the nations of the Americas, contrasting sharply with the surrounding republics, in which antimonarchical sentiment was strong. Liberal sentiment in Brazil had long been critical of the *poder moderado* vested in the emperor. During the Paraguayan war when the Liberal cabinet quarreled with the emperor over Brazil's involvement in the war and over his appointment of Caxias, he dismissed them. As a result the Liberals abstained from participation in the forthcoming elections in order to register their silent protest against monarchical absolutism. Their program included demands for curtailment of the emperor's authority and abolition of the system of slavery, which still survived in Brazil. They thus committed themselves to the cause of emancipation. In 1868 agitation began for an elective senate, rather than an appointive one as stipulated in the constitution of 1824, and a limited tenure of office rather than life terms for senators. Though the Liberals did not yet advocate the outright abolition of monarchy they favored a sovereign who would reign but not rule, and they wished to cut back the emperor's powers by transferring his *poder moderado* to the president of the cabinet of ministers. Political authority would be taken away from the council of state and given to the cabinet, which would thus be enabled in effect to exercise parliamentary government. The Liberals also advocated a decentralization of authority to the states, the extinction of monopolies, and the independence of the judiciary from imperial control. With these demands as a program, a Republican party was organized in December, 1870, and a republican press was established.

The emperor himself never opposed the republican movement. Indeed he characterized himself as the leading republican in Brazil. "Were I not a monarch," he declared on his visit to the United States in 1876, "I should be a republican." As a person Dom Pedro was not the object of republican criticism; his wholehearted, single-minded, and indefatigably skillful administration of affairs of state was not questioned. But the monarchical system under which he governed, with its implications of royal absolutism, was coming to be considered anachronistic. He tried to make concessions to the new liberal forces of the times without, however, fully comprehending them. One of the emperor's weaknesses, if weakness it was, was his indifference to the interests of his throne. He acted as if unconvinced that monarchy was necessary to the country. When the abolition of slavery was adopted as a program of the liberal movement in 1869 the emperor espoused it, being an abolitionist himself at heart. And when later the franchise was broadened and his own powers were curtailed he willingly accepted these liberal reforms without seeming to appreciate the personal consequences that were likely to flow from them. But by temporizing with the liberal principles of abolitionism, cabinet responsibility to the legislature, commercial *laissez faire,* and an increased measure of popular participation in government he was, perhaps unwittingly, undermining the social and economic groups that sustained him in power. Perhaps his only alternative was to establish an absolutist regime, which conceivably in the Brazilian milieu might have shortened his reign.

Dom Pedro, taught by his experience in the Paraguayan War, thereafter ceased to meddle with his neighbors and followed instead a policy of abstaining from intervention in their affairs. From the beginning of his reign he had sought to advertise his country in Europe and to enlist foreign capital for its economic development. He made trips to Europe for this purpose and became well known there as the hard-working ruler of a large and well-ordered country in South America rich in natural resources. By reason of his efforts thus to "sell" Brazil abroad and at the same time to maintain the internal order and stability which foreign capitalists considered necessary, Brazil became an increasingly attractive area for foreign investors. Regular steamship service was opened up between Brazil and Europe in 1850, and the first telegraph was introduced in 1852. The ports of Brazil flourished as outlets for growing exports of rubber, coffee, sugar, and minerals, and its trade with the outside world was stimulated by the opening of the Amazon River to the commerce of foreign nations in 1867—a result due largely to Dom Pedro's insistence upon the free navigation of interior rivers in the war against Paraguay and to his interest in Prof. Louis Agassiz's journey on the Amazon in 1865, which called attention to the large potentialities of that region. During his reign Brazil finally abandoned many of its colonial attributes and acquired some of the characteristics and institutions of a modern capitalist nation, including corporations and stock exchanges.

To stimulate the development of his country the emperor encouraged immigration. For German immigrants, who had begun to settle in Rio Grande do Sul in 1825, he founded a new colony at Blumenau in the state of Santa Catarina in 1851. He also welcomed several hundred Confederates from the United States after their defeat in the Civil War, offering land to them at from 22 to 40 cents an acre. One of these Confederate colonies, named Lizzieland after a favorite daughter of its New Orleans promoter, was located about 100 miles south of São Paulo on the Ribeira River. Nearby a second colony was established. A third was located some 300 miles north of Rio de Janeiro in Espirito Santo, and a fourth was set down in the heart of the equatorial jungle near the small town of Santarém, located some 600 miles up the Amazon River. The increase in Brazil's contacts with the foreign world, combined with the new immigration, tended to dilute or hybridize its hitherto predominantly Portuguese culture, which was now largely overwhelmed by influences from abroad, particularly from Paris. In addition the economic development of the country, signalized by the construction of new roads, the expansion of the railroad network, and the increased commercial interchange, hastened the breakdown of feudal power which had been dominant throughout most of the history of Brazil.

Brazil's prosperity suffered a severe setback as a result, first, of the Paraguayan War and, later, of the world-wide financial panic of 1873. Even the Viscount of Mauá went bankrupt two years later, though in justice to him it must be mentioned that through his own industry he subsequently paid off 90 per cent of his indebtedness. The depression generated new popular discontents and demands for a change. Encouraged by these developments Brazilian Liberals began to press their campaign on three fronts, advocating, first, a broadening of the base and responsiveness of the government through constitutional changes, second, abolition of Negro slavery, and, third, stimulation and rationalization of the economic life of the nation. As a result of their first demand, a law was enacted in 1881 which extended the franchise. It represented only a modest attempt at the broadening of the political base of the nation, and in the first election held under it only 142,000 citizens qualified as voters in a total population of perhaps 12 million. But it brought new middle-class groups into the political life of the nation and therefore presented the possibility of new restraints on arbitrary action by the government. This law, which was pushed through by Prime Minister José Antônio Saraiva, was not liked by the emperor but was loyally accepted by him. Thereafter he undertook to govern in accordance with parliamentary majorities. He chose no cabinet that was not supported by the majority of the lower house, and he assumed that the chamber of deputies was representative of the wishes of the nation. In effect Dom Pedro thus accepted the British parliamentary system, with its principle of executive responsibility to the legislature, and governed in accordance with it. He nevertheless became expert at contriving subtle ways of undermining the authority of members of his cabinet of whom he disapproved. He masterminded Brazilian politics for a generation. By the exercise of his moderating power, so thoroughly disliked by the Liberals, he, in reality, maintained the two-party system in Brazil and ensured the rotation of the parties in office. He was "a kind of 'cotton breakwater' against which the waves of partisan passions died down, harmlessly." [2]

[2] Erico Verissimo, *Brazilian Literature: an Outline*, The Macmillan Company, New York, 1945, p. 57.

Slavery and Emancipation

Slavery had existed in Brazil since earliest colonial times. In the north-eastern section slaves furnished almost all the labor used in the production of the staple exports, sugar, tobacco, and cotton. In the coastal settlements both north and south, slaves were often hired out by their owners as artisans or laborers for all types of menial work. They unloaded the casks and barrels from shipside to warehouse, dragged the heavy wagons or drays over deeply rutted streets, and carried bags of coffee or manioc on their heads in queues, chanting rhythmically as they jogged along. Sometimes they were shackled to their task with lock and chain. An auction of slaves in Rio de Janeiro in 1846 was thus described by an observer from the United States:

There were fifty-three males, most of whom ranged between eighteen and thirty years of age—carpenters, masons, smiths, and country hands. . . .

Of females, the oldest was twenty-six, and the youngest between seven and eight —washers, sewers, cooks, two dressmakers "muita prendada"—very accomplished.

They were of every shade, from deep Angola jet to white or nearly white, as one young woman facing me appeared. . . . The anguish with which she watched the proceedings, and waited her turn to be brought out, exposed, examined, and disposed of, was distressing. A little girl, I suppose her own, stood by her weeping, with one hand in her lap, obviously dreading to be torn away. This child did not cry out—that is not allowed—but tears chased each other down her cheeks, her little bosom panted violently, and such a look of alarm marked her face as she turned her large eyes on the proceedings, that I thought at one time she would have dropped. . . .

The auctioneer, a tall, black-whiskered man of thirty-five, was a master of his profession, if one might judge from his fluency and fervor. A hammer in his right hand, the forefinger of his left pointing to a plantation hand standing confused at his side, he pours out a flood of words. The poor fellow had on a canvas shirt, with sleeves ending at the elbows and trousers of the same, the legs of which he is told to roll above his knees. A bidder steps up, examines his lower limbs, then his mouth, breast and other parts. He is now told to walk toward the door and back, to show his gait. As he was returning, the hammer fell, and he was pushed back within the railing. . . .

The clerk next went behind the rails and brought forward a woman—a field hand. She was stout, and seemed older than reported in the catalogue. Dressed as sparely and plainly as the men, she too was examined, and told to walk to and fro. When near the door a bidder interrogated her, but on what I could not comprehend. His last remark was translated plainly by raising her skirt to expose her legs. They were much swollen. Two hundred and fifty milreis was the sum she brought.[3]

On the estates of a benevolent plantation owner the slaves might be treated well. An English visitor to a typical Brazilian *fazenda* reported that after breakfast one morning she "attended the weekly muster of all the

[3] Thomas Ewbank, *Life in Brazil* . . . , Harper & Brothers, New York, 1856, pp. 283–284.

Negroes of the *fazenda*. Clean shirts and trousers were given the men, and shifts and skirts to the women, of very coarse white cotton. . . . As each slave passed in review, some questions were asked concerning himself, his family, if he had one, or his work; and each received a portion of snuff or tobacco, according to his taste." Each slave's daily allowance of food consisted of flour, kidney beans, and dried beef, a fixed measure of each to every person. The Negroes and mulattoes, the visitor was told, "are the best artificers and artists. The orchestra of the opera-house is composed of at least one-third mulattoes. All decorative painting, carving, and inlaying is done by them; in short they excel in all ingenious mechanical arts."

As was natural in a predominantly agricultural society the pattern of life was set by the large landowners. At their plantation houses high officials of state and church and relatives and friends of the owner were welcomed and lavishly entertained at all times. Food and imported wines were served with prodigal hospitality. Guests were sometimes received also at the planter's house in town and were entertained by him at the local theater. The planter's conversation with his friends concerned principally his crops of cotton, sugar cane, or coffee and his slaves. Every man's standing was determined by the number of Negroes he owned. On his plantation, a small village in itself with its own herds, sawmills, carpentry shops, beehives, cane fields, coffee trees, and slave masters, the planter maintained the patriarchal economy of colonial times.

The example of earlier emancipation in the British colonies and in the United States and the growing world-wide agitation against Negro chattel slavery directed increasing attention toward the matter of the abolition of slavery in Brazil after the Paraguayan War. Under pressure from Great Britain the regency abolished the slave trade into Brazil in 1831 and prescribed that all slaves thereafter brought into the country should be free. But this law was not enforced; indeed, it could not be enforced because of Brazil's extensive coast. In 1850 by the Queiroz law the slave trade within the country was abolished, but by 1870 more than one-sixth of Brazil's population was held in legal bondage. The agitation on this question threw into sharp focus the conflict of interests—social, economic, and political—between the northeastern states, which were the traditional center of Brazil's plantation economy and exportable agricultural wealth, and the rising and ambitious states of Rio de Janeiro, São Paulo, and Minas Gerais in south central Brazil. With the intensification of coffee culture in these latter states the coffee *fazendeiros* met their increased labor needs by buying slaves from the north, thus intensifying the plight of the sugar industry. By the middle of the century the slave population of the southern states exceeded that of the north.

In 1871 while the emperor was in Europe the legislature, under the leadership of José Maria de Silva Paranhos, later the Viscount of Rio Branco, passed a law freeing all children thereafter born of slave mothers when they reached the age of twenty-one. Until they reached that age these so-called *ingênuos* remained bound to service as apprentices to their masters. This method of gradual emancipation proved quite effective, and under it the number of slaves was reduced from 1,584,000 in 1870 to only 743,000 in 1887. Since the Brazilian constitution recognized no distinction in civil rights on the basis of color, many of the freed Negroes soon achieved social rank.

But this law disrupted Rio Branco's Conservative party, the mainstay of the monarchy. It struck a severe blow at the plantation economy of the north, which had lost its political influence to Rio de Janeiro when the Portuguese court established its capital there in 1808 and which now seemed threatened with economic and social subordination to the growing southern metropolises of Rio de Janeiro and São Paulo. The patriarchal slave society of these sugar-growing states of the northeast was meeting with increasing competition from foreign sugars, from the new coffee economy of São Paulo based partly upon free immigrant labor, and from the rise of new and varied capitalist enterprises in the states to the south. The lines were becoming clearly drawn between, on the one hand, the *fazendeiros* who constituted the monarchical and titled class and, on the other, the new industrial class. The shift in economic power from the *fazendeiros* to the new industrial leaders and the resulting struggle between them for political power were not appreciated by the emperor. And yet, as it turned out, it was the former, including the majority of the nobility which in 1883 comprised 1 duke, 5 counts, 39 viscounts, and 268 barons, who sustained the imperial throne. They found it difficult to accept modern innovations in commerce and industry.

Typical of the new lords of banking and industry, who were gradually eclipsing the northern *fazendeiros,* was the Baron of Mauá, mentioned above. The *cariocas* and *Paulistas* in the south, reflecting the new industrial and commercial interests of the nation, resisted the continued influence of the northeast in government and politics and opposed slavery as a wasteful and anachronistic economic system. They desired a liberalized economic system, based on laissez-faire principles, and a decentralization of authority to the local units, which would, they hoped, lead to the aggrandizement of the influence of Rio de Janeiro, São Paulo, and Minas Gerais. The republican movement opened up this prospect to them, and accompanying it as companion movements pointing in the same direction were Freemasonry and the cult of Positivism.

A conflict over Freemasonry in 1872–1875, which developed into a kind of Brazilian *Kulturkampf,* widened the breach between conservatives and liberals, *fazendeiros* and republicans. Church and state had long been closely allied in Brazil. Saint Anthony of the eleventh century, who was especially venerated by pious Brazilians, was made a lieutenant colonel in the Brazilian army, and his monthly salary was paid to his monastery in Rio de Janeiro from the public treasury. But this close relationship became increasingly distasteful to liberals, many of whom actively criticized it in their Masonic societies. The emperor himself was a Roman Catholic but was not regarded as staunchly loyal to the church because he favored toleration of Protestant sects and was himself a Freemason. He refrained from sanctioning the circulation in Brazil of the encyclical of Pope Pius IX, issued in 1864, condemning Masonry, as was his right to do under the Brazilian constitution. His liberal views on religion antagonized devout churchmen in Brazil.

The conflict between the church and the state emerged into the open when two militant Catholic bishops in Pará and Olinda ordered the church brotherhoods or *irmandades* to expel their Masonic members on pain of losing the privilege of using the churches for their meetings. When the brotherhoods refused to comply, the bishops placed them under the interdict. The brotherhoods in turn then appealed to the crown. In response the council of state, after long sessions with the emperor, decided in favor of the brotherhoods and ordered the offending bishops to rescind the interdicts and allow the Masons to remain in the *irmandades*. When the bishops refused to yield they were tried in the civil courts and were given sentences of four years' imprisonment at hard labor, which, however, were promptly commuted by the emperor to simple imprisonment. Dom Pedro felt that strong governmental action was required to uphold the law of the land and to prevent future attempts at usurpation by the church, but in April, 1876, he was persuaded to sign a decree of amnesty for the imprisoned prelates. The imperial government was thus virtually obliged to surrender to the church, but it had lost the support of the clergy, most of whom sided with the bishops. The incident stirred deep feelings and revealed that the Princess Isabel, who was the eldest daughter of Dom Pedro and heir to the throne, was sympathetic with the imprisoned priests. The resulting reaction against the monarchy stimulated the republican movement.

These same movements were favored also by the widespread acceptance of the doctrine of Positivism by the intellectual classes in Brazil. Positivism, developed by the French founder of the science of sociology, Auguste Comte (1798–1857), rejected metaphysical social abstractions and proposed to apply to society the empirical and experimental methods, that is, the "positive" methods, of the natural sciences. Under this philosophy society would be directed by savants in accordance with the positive truths of science. It emphasized technical progress through social utilization of human skills and called for the application of the methods of science to the organization and control of the relationships of human society, still dominated in large measure by antiquated customs and traditions. It repudiated the old laissez-faire liberalism as a romantic conception and proposed to replace it with social planning. A coordinated effort of machines, finance capital, and human efficiency would create the material things that society needed. By these methods the forces of nature could be controlled for the sake of the commonweal.

This doctrine, which basically only proposed to apply to the social sciences the inductive methods of the natural sciences, suggested the need for social innovation and possibly even the remaking of living patterns. Comte believed these ends could be best achieved by a "dictatorial republic." His requirement of dictatorship (his own word) to govern his humanitarian state made an appeal to Latin Americans and reinforced the centralistic trend in liberalism. From his philosophy evolved a new cult of Positivism or religion of humanity. For Comte, humanity was the ultimate and only conceivable supreme being. For this reason and because his system condemned all theological explanations of phenomena, Positivism, both as a science of social and national development and as a religious cult, was generally repugnant to the Catholic Church, but it was viewed in a friendly light by the church in Brazil, which was already critical of the monarchy and sympathetic to republicanism. With the religio-scientific mysticism of Positivism church leaders in Brazil had little quarrel. Partly for this reason the movement, though it had a short career in Europe, took root and flourished in Brazil. It was welcomed as Catholicism without dogma. It would counteract the futility of Brazilian life under the old order that was subtly criticized by Machado de Assis in his *Memórias póstumas de Braz Cubas.*

Traces of the new cult appeared in the military academy at Rio de Janeiro as early as 1850. Its ablest and most ardent exponent was Lieut. Col. Benjamim Constant de Botelho Magalhães, a professor of mathematics in the military academy, who indoctrinated the younger officers of the army with Positivist ideas. These ideas carried many reformist and even revolutionary implications. They supported the growing movement for republicanism and were certain to be politically disruptive.

Brazil was one of the last nations in the Western world to abolish the system of human chattel slavery. The Negro leader Toussaint L'Ouverture had abolished it in St. Domingue in 1801, and one of his successors as ruler of Haiti, Alexandre Petión, who befriended Bolívar during his exile from Venezuela in 1815, extracted from the Liberator a promise that he would abolish slavery in the countries that he would conquer from Spain. Accordingly after Bolívar liberated the mainland countries of South America the first constitution of Gran Colombia, drawn up at Cúcuta in 1821, provided for the gradual abolition of slavery. But already in 1811 Chile had won the distinction of being the first country in the American hemisphere after Haiti to abolish Negro slavery and to provide for the gradual emancipation of its slaves. The Argentine national assembly followed suit in 1813. In 1842 Uruguay abolished slavery. In the 1850s Ecuador and Venezuela provided for compensated emancipation of those Negro slaves who were still held in bondage in violation of the Gran Colombian emancipation law of 1821. Even Paraguay freed its slaves in the early 1870s after its defeat in the war against the Triple Alliance. In Middle America Negro slavery was abolished in the Federation of Central America by decree in 1824, and in Mexico by a similar decree in 1829. After the emancipation of Negro slaves in the United States the Spanish government was persuaded to promise emancipation also in Cuba, and abolition of slavery was accomplished there by the middle of the 1880s.

But Brazil still maintained the institution of slavery. Even the church there accepted it and some wealthy Brazilian monasteries owned and worked thousands of slaves.

In the view of the Positivists the plantation economy of Brazil was marked by extravagance, reckless depletion of soil fertility, and inefficient utilization of labor. The abolition of slavery became a main objective of Brazilian liberals, led by Ruy Barbosa and Joaquim Nabuco and reinforced by the eloquent poetry of Antônio de Castro Alves. They were dissatisfied with gradual progress toward it and pressed for its immediate and complete extinction. To accomplish this purpose a few large Brazilian landowners and some states granted emancipation on a local basis, hoping thus to make as easy as possible for themselves the transition to the slave-free society which they foresaw. In 1884 the Liberal Dantas ministry introduced a bill freeing all slaves at the age of sixty. The defeat of this bill made slavery a truly national issue

Fig. 16-1. Machado de Assis as a young man. (*Courtesy of Noonday Press, Inc.*)

and tremendously stimulated the abolitionist agitation, even encouraging slave uprisings. But the antislavery movement was strongly resisted by the succeeding Conservative ministries, despite the increasing tempo of popular interest in it and the subtle influence for it exerted by the Count d'Eu, husband of the Princess Isabel and grandson of Louis Philippe of France. Finally in May, 1888, while the Emperor Dom Pedro was abroad convalescing from an illness and his daughter, Princess Isabel, was acting as regent for him, the speech from the throne called for absolute, immediate, and uncompensated emancipation of the slaves. Within eight days this revolutionary measure passed both houses and was signed into law by the Princess. By it nearly 750,000 slaves with a legal value of nearly 250 million dollars were given their freedom.

Downfall of the Monarchy

By this action emancipating the slaves without compensation to their owners the monarchy forfeited the support of the rural aristocracy. To the Princess Isabel after she had signed the measure into law one of her ministers said prophetically: "Your Highness has taken the trick but has lost the throne." From the standpoint of the preservation of the monarchy, the failure of the Princess to recommend an indemnity to the slaveholders was a fatal blunder, for it resulted in the impoverishment of many of them, alienated the conservatives, and further encouraged the republican movement. Already the monarchy had forfeited the support of the church. Its only remaining pillar of support was the army, which was becoming deeply permeated with Positivism and republicanism. The idea gained currency that the days of the monarchy were numbered. One unpopular act might cause its downfall. In the face of the rising republican sentiment the conservatives could no longer be depended upon to assist it and the liberals, who had long been appeased by the emperor, would furnish only weak support.

At about this time a visitor from the United States witnessed Dom Pedro's visit to a theater in Rio de Janeiro. The emperor was received with no shouts or applause and only about twenty persons in the large audience rose to their feet in tribute to him. "This was truly a democratic manner of receiving the head of a great empire," the visitor sarcastically wrote.[4] More probably it revealed an almost complete lack of popular enthusiasm for the monarchy. In this republican era the old emperor seemed to typify a discredited institution. The mass indifference toward him reinforced the open antagonism toward the monarchy on the part of the clerico-conservative *fazendeiro* class, the ambitious business and industrial interests in the south, and most important of all, the army, which was stirred by the intellectual ferment and ideas of progress generated by Positivism.

[4] Frank Vincent, *Around and about South America: Twenty Months of Quest and Query,* D. Appleton & Company, Inc., New York, 1890.

Dom Pedro, after his experiences in the Paraguayan War, developed pacifist inclinations and undertook to limit both the size and the prerogatives of Brazil's military establishment. That war gave a new impetus to militarism, which had never before been popular in Brazil. Accordingly, the Ouro Preto ministry, while trying to conciliate the military, undertook to cut it down to size. In a planned reorganization of the empire's defensive arm it proposed to divide the army into small detachments widely scattered through the nation and to enlarge and revitalize the national guard to serve as a kind of loyal counterpoise to the regular army. But this maneuver only pushed the army further along the road of republicanism. The younger officers of the army became highly sensitive about their professional and bureaucratic rights. They were apprehensive that they might lose their privileged positions and their influence in Brazilian political life. Moreover, as they were restive under the ennui of peacetime life in the slow years after the Paraguayan War they yearned for more active careers, possibly in politics.

The recognized leader and champion of the professional army was Marshal Manoel Deodoro da Fonseca, and when he was sent off to Matto Grosso in early 1889, his brother officers interpreted his assignment as a punishment. When he was finally allowed to return, Professor Constant openly threatened the Liberal ministry of Ouro Preto, which, it was assumed, was preparing the way for the succession of the emperor by Princess Isabel and her unpopular husband, Count d'Eu, scion of the Orleans family which had been banished from France. The discontent in the army was shrewdly exploited by the republican leader Ruy Barbosa to gain further strength for the antimonarchical movement. To resist this movement Ouro Preto submitted to Parliament a reform program which included removal of property qualifications for voting, full autonomy of the provinces and the municipalities, election of presidents of the provinces instead of their appointment, and abandonment of life tenure for senators. To carry out this program he proposed a coalition of the two parties supporting the monarchy—the liberal and the conservative—but he was unable to bring it about. The old parties were exposed as bankrupt of ideas. They were losing their controlling position in Brazilian politics.

Under the leadership of Deodoro and Professor Constant the army plotted to overthrow the monarchy. One of the conspirators, Floriano Peixoto, adjutant-general of the army, enjoyed the confidence of the prime minister and continued to assure him of the loyalty of the military leaders. In the early morning of November 15, 1889, while the emperor was vacationing in his summer palace at Petrópolis in the mountains some forty miles from Rio de Janeiro, Deodoro took command of the troops and demanded the resignation of the members of the cabinet. Their resignations were telegraphed to the emperor, and before he could reach Rio de Janeiro that afternoon the leaders of the uprising had organized a provisional government, named themselves as ministers, and issued a decree announcing that Brazil had become a federal republic. The emperor was deposed, and he and his family were respectfully required to leave the country within twenty-four hours. He did not insist upon retaining the throne against the popular will nor did he invoke any constitutional or prescriptive rights in his favor. Burdened with debts, he paid all of them by selling the furniture and jewels of his palace at public auction and left his library to the nation. With dignity Dom Pedro refused the ample pension which was offered him and retired to Europe where he died two years later. His body was brought back to Brazil and buried at Petrópolis in 1920 when the order of banishment against him and the entire Braganza family was rescinded.

Under the two monarchs, Pedro I and Pedro II, who had governed Brazil since independence, except during the period of the regency from 1831 to 1840, the country had enjoyed a considerable degree of stability and unity. The monarchy had established a climate of dignity, integrity, and aversion to violence. It had held the nation together and prevented it from succumbing to the regionalism, anarchy, and bankruptcy that had plagued many of Brazil's Spanish-speaking neighbors. Instead, Brazil under Dom Pedro II, the only purely Brazilian monarch that the country had had, enjoyed almost a half century of internal peace and a large measure of prosperity. The emperor was a limited monarch governing under the constitution of 1824, which served the country for sixty-five years. He was subject to the provisions of this basic law, and after 1881 Dom Pedro chose to make his administration subject also to the legislature, selecting cabinets which represented parliamentary majorities.

But even the adoption of this technique of administration did not enable him to make his policies sufficiently responsive to the modern currents of public opinion. "The Emperor," it was well said, "passed fifty years in maintaining the pretense that he ruled over a free people." His imperial system had been a patriarchal government operating under specious parliamentary forms. The immediate causes of its downfall were the abolition of slavery and the so-called "military question." In these two issues the fundamental inconsistency between the institution of monarchy itself and the growing republican movement, which even leaders of the army accepted, was highlighted. The army overthrew the empire "for the salvation of the country and the only possible means of restoring the army," as the leaders of the revolt declared. It was the only force in Brazil capable of moving effectively against the government, and it felt that it must displace the monarchy in order to maintain or regain its position. That its action was assisted by a minority of republicans and that it led eventually to the establishment of republican government was largely uncalculated and incidental.

The Brazilian Empire was thus brought to an end by what was essentially a military *coup d'état*. The new government was soon afterward characterized by one of the conspirators as purely military. "The work was theirs and theirs alone," he commented, "for the collaboration of the civilian element was almost *nil* and . . . the people stood by stupefied, dumbfounded, without an inkling of what it all meant. Many honestly believed they were beholding a parade." With the downfall of Pedro II a fundamental change in Brazilian life, like the break with Portugal in 1822, took place without bloodshed. In both events the people were only bystanders. As they had become accustomed in 1822 to a colonial status they woke up to discover that they were an independent empire. Now they suddenly became a republic.

Republican Brazil

The new government headed by Marshal Deodoro was received with popular enthusiasm, was accepted by the municipal council of Rio de Janeiro and by the provincial authorities, and was not confronted by any attempts at counter-revolution. Its members were not motivated by vindictiveness. They manifested no resentment toward the deposed emperor, nor did they take reprisals against the emperor's associates in government or confiscate their property. Brazil now became in fact a centralized military dictatorship, but the new government, which had assumed the responsibility of governing a nation of 17 million people, was committed to the forms and principles of republicanism. It rapidly replaced the old imperial bureaucracy with its own officials and in the appointment of new governors chose persons who were sympathetic with the republican movement. Benjamim Constant became the new minister of education, the first in Brazil's history. With the overthrow of the monarchy Brazil abandoned the British royal and parliamentary system which had previously served it as a model and turned to the presidential, federal, and republican system of the United States.

The provisional government, in order to embody this new federal republican system in law and also to consolidate its own political power, summoned an assembly to adopt a new constitution. The constitution promulgated in February, 1891, was based on a draft prepared by the minister of finance, Ruy Barbosa, on the model of the Constitution of the United States and was only slightly modified by the assembly. It declared Brazil to be a federal republic called the United States of Brazil. It provided for the three traditional branches of government—legislative, executive, and judicial. In the bicameral legislature the senators represented the twenty states and the federal district and were elected by direct vote for nine years, three being chosen from each state and one-third going out of office every three years. The imperial council of state and the old system of life tenure for senators were abolished. The deputies in the lower house represented the people of the states and were elected by popular vote for three-year terms. Suffrage was granted to all literate male citizens over twenty-one years of age except beggars, common soldiers of the regular army, and members of religious orders.

Under the new constitution the president and vice president were elected for four-year terms by direct popular vote—not by an electoral college as in the United States—and their powers were similar to those assigned to the president in the Constitution of the United States, except that the president was made ineligible for immediate reelection. As in the United States the president's cabinet was appointed by him and was responsible only to him. The judicial power was exercised by a supreme court and a hierarchy of other federal courts. The constitution forbade the government to engage in a war of conquest or to begin hostilities against any other nation without first resorting to arbitration. It abolished all titles of nobility, guaranteed freedom of worship, speech, and the press and trial by jury, and abolished the death penalty. It also provided for the separation of church and state, making Brazil one of the first of the Latin American nations to accept this principle.

The new constitution fell far short of establishing the centralized republic which the Positivists advocated. The federal system was to be assured by allowing each state to handle its own administration under its own governor with a minimum of legal restraints by the central government. In this constitution the powers of the states within the Brazilian federal system were so thoroughly respected that the states were even allowed to levy export duties. Under it the states of Brazil were almost sovereign and regarded the central government at Rio de Janeiro as only an entity of convenience set up to serve their interests. The inauguration of this federal system meant that henceforth the powers of the central government, in so far as they were exercised, would be controlled by the wealthiest and most populous states, namely, São Paulo and Minas Gerais, which together contained nearly one-third of the people of Brazil. Between these two states thereafter a kind of gentlemen's agreement was reached by which they alternated control over the most important positions in the federal government, including the presidency.

When this constitution was promulgated the provisional government came to an end after fourteen months in office. By a special article the first president was to be chosen by the Congress, and a regular constitutional government was now inaugurated with Marshall Deodoro da Fonseca as president and Marshal Floriano Peixoto as vice president. From being a centralized empire with a constitutional monarch and a *de facto* parliamentary form of government, Brazil thus transformed itself after a brief period of disorders into a federal republic with a presidential form of government. The republican movement, which had been first organized in 1871 with a program of liberal action, had triumphed after twenty years of effort.

Brazil, after its bourgeois revolution, entered upon an era of wild speculation, seeking to anticipate the twentieth century in its zeal for modernization. Every aspect of Brazilian life seemed anachronistic, and new industries, factories, coffee plantations, companies, banks, railways, and telegraph lines became the rage of the hour. Ruy Barbosa as minister of finance under the provisional government had already reorganized the financial system of the country by decentralizing the banks and authorizing them to issue enormous quantities of paper currency totaling, in United States equivalents, approximately 250 million dollars. Markets were flooded with money, and concessions of all sorts for banking, railroad, mining, and factory development were lavishly granted by both the federal and the state governments, each vying with the other to make concessions and to float new loans. Within a year Ruy Barbosa had to make a complete about-face and reestablish a centralized banking system, the Banco da República, with authority to issue paper currency only against gold. The government itself had begun to indulge in dubious extravagances and even frauds, and the instability of its financial policy had produced disillusionment. Moreover, the leaders of the republican movement in Brazil had not expected their movement to be inaugurated by the army, nor did they believe that continued military domination of the country augured its success. All these considerations created doubts about the stability of Brazil's federal, republican system. Whether Brazil, which had been accustomed for almost four centuries to the monarchical system, could successfully adjust itself to a system of popular self-government accompanied by a high degree of decentralization of authority remained to be seen.

The overthrow of the monarchy in Brazil signalized a shift in the center of gravity of Brazil's economic and political life which had been slowly taking place for many decades. The disruption of the old master-slave relationships stimulated a free labor system, made possible a greater mobility of population, and weakened the class structure of society. Power moved definitively from the old sugar-cane region of Bahía and Pernambuco in the northeast to the southern states of Rio de Janeiro, São Paulo, Minas Gerais, and Rio Grande do Sul, where the coffee industry now entered upon a boom period. Coffee was king, and coffee, unlike sugar, could survive without slaves, for the coffee of Brazil, unlike its sugar, fixed the world price of that commodity. Into the southern states came increasing numbers of free European laborers—mainly Italian—at the rate of 100,000 a year—and in smaller numbers Portuguese, Spaniards, and Germans—to perform the hand labor urgently needed in the burgeoning coffee industry. The establishment of republican government meant that power was transferred from the old imperial conservative class to a liberal group, representing new ideas, new economic interests, and new regions of the country.

Additional Reading

Barrett, William E.: *Woman on Horseback,* Doubleday & Company, Inc., New York, 1952. Biography of Eliza Lynch, the Irish mistress of Francisco Solano López, who is here dealt with sympathetically.

Benítez, Justo Pastor: *La Vida solitaria del Dr. José Gaspar de Francia, dictador del Paraguay,* El Ateneo, Buenos Aires, 1937.

Bernstein, Harry: *Modern and Contemporary Latin America,* J. B. Lippincott Company, Philadelphia, 1952, chap. 19.

Box, Pelham Horton: *Origins of the Paraguayan War,* University of Illinois, Urbana, Ill., 1930.

Calogeras, João Pandiá: *A History of Brazil,* trans. and ed. by Percy Alvin Martin, University of North Carolina Press, Chapel Hill, N.C., 1939, chaps. VIII–XIII.

Dambaugh, Luella N.: *The Coffee Frontier in Brazil,* University of Florida Press, Gainesville, 1959.

Hill, Lawrence F. (ed.): *Brazil,* University of California Press, Berkeley, Calif., 1947, chap. 1.

Keen, Benjamin: *Readings in Latin American Civilization: 1492 to the Present,* Houghton Mifflin Company, Boston, 1955, chap. XXVIII.

Marchant, Anyda: "A New Portrait of Mauá, the Banker: A Man of Business in Nineteenth-century Brazil," *Hispanic American Historical Review,* vol. 30, pp. [411]–431, 1950.

Martin, Percy A.: "Federalism in Brazil," *Hispanic American Historical Review,* vol. 18, pp. 143–163, 1938.

———: "Slavery and Abolition in Brazil," *Hispanic American Historical Review,* vol. 13, pp. 151–196, May, 1933.

———: "Causes of the Collapse of the Brazilian Empire," *Hispanic American Historical Review,* vol. 4, pp. 4–48, February, 1921.

Nabuco, Carolina: *The Life of Joachim Nabuco,* Ronald Hilton (ed.), Stanford University Press, Stanford, Calif., 1950.

O'Leary, Juan E.: *El Mariscal Solano López,* 2d ed., Imprenta de Felix Moliner, Madrid, 1925.

Sánchez Quell, H.: *Político internacional del Paraguay* (*La Junta de 1811, Francia y los López*), 2d ed., Editorial Tupa, Buenos Aires, 1945.

Stein, Stanley J.: *Brazilian Cotton Manufacture: Textile Enterprise in an Underdeveloped Area, 1850–1950,* Harvard University Press, Oxford, 1957.

Warren, Harris G.: *Paraguay: An Informal History,* University of Oklahoma Press, Norman, Okla., 1949.

XVII

The Consolidation of Liberalism

While the liberal forces were gaining ground in Brazil and organizing a movement which contributed to the final forcible overthrow of the monarchy, liberals in other countries of Latin America were consolidating their gains. In Chile the transition from conservatism to liberalism was accomplished not by the forcible transfer of power from one class to another but rather by the gradual amalgamation of the conservative and liberal forces. They moved to meet each other as members of the aristocratic, landowning class accepted the new ideas of liberalism and slowly absorbed the young liberals into their society. The fusing of these two forces in the latter half of the nineteenth century encouraged a spirit of nationalism and enabled new so-called "national parties" to emerge. Argentine liberalism, which was committed to a decentralized structure of government had crystallized in the constitution of 1853. It received a slow and grudging acceptance by the unitaries, and in the process liberalism itself was transformed into a new vested interest. In Mexico liberalism, embattled both at home and abroad, became a militant movement and found its hero champion in Benito Juárez. But under both domestic and foreign pressure it lost much of its fervor for decentralization in government.

In the philosophy of Positivism not only the Brazilians but also other Latin Americans found a means of achieving a new social and political order after 1875. They accepted the current ideas of science and progress in order to move from the anarchy and militarism of the past into a new industrial era. Latin America must move quickly into this era, admonished the Mexican Positivist Justo Sierra, because the giant nation to the north—the United States—"which grows mightier and comes nearer and nearer to us all the time by means of the industrial and agricultural development of its border states and the extension of its railroad network will absorb and extinguish us if it finds us weak." Under the stimulus of the new immigration and the ideas of Positivism these countries now began to place new emphasis upon the development of their own resources and the education of their citizens in the practical arts and sciences.

The influence of these new forces was all-pervasive in Latin America. Even before Comte set forth the principles of Positivism liberals in Latin America were prepared to receive it and were already preaching its doctrines of order and progress. The Argentines expected Positivism to eliminate political tyranny. The Chileans found in it a body of ideas which reinforced their evolutionary liberalism. In Uruguay it was hailed as a moral doctrine which would make further barracks revolutions unnecessary and would prevent corruption. Peru and Bolivia looked to it as a means of salvation after their defeat in the War of the Pacific. It provided revolutionary leaders in Cuba with new motives for independence from Spain. Almost everywhere in Latin America Positivism was seized upon as a means of discrediting old clerical and oligarchic regimes. Armed with this doctrine the nations of Latin America could meet the challenge of the modern industrial age and wealthy foreign nations.

Evolutionary Liberalism in Chile

In Chile liberalism was an upper-class movement. As the foreign commerce and industry of the nation expanded after 1845, intellectual leaders of liberal views and new business leaders gained prominence. They found their spokesman in José Victorino Lastarria, a teacher and writer, who was strongly influenced by French Positivism and who emphasized parliamentary methods as the means of moving Chile forward along the lines of technical progress. These leaders owed their position to the growing urban population in Santiago, Concepción, and Valparaíso, and they drew their wealth from Chile's growing trade and commerce and from the exploitation of its copper and nitrate resources. They found it convenient to form marriage alliances and business partnerships and to cooperate with Chile's landed oligarchy for common economic and political action.

But in this fusion of forces both groups were necessarily obliged to modify their views to some extent. The old landed aristocracy was thus slowly changed into a new aristocracy which was less dependent on the land and less averse to the liberal ideas of the nineteenth century. Indeed, they found that these ideas of individual initiative, local autonomy, and economic progress fitted in very well with their own interests. The old Chilean landed aristocracy, then, like the old Whig aristocracy of England, gave way to a new entrepreneurial aristocracy, but the governing power continued to be exercised by an aristocracy. In Chile, unlike in Brazil, liberalism did not remain the monopoly of a new social group, nor did it come to power by direct revolutionary action.

The gradual shift to a liberal political system began during the Montt administration. It was facilitated by a split in the ranks of the conservatives, as a result of which the ultraconservatives, distrusting Montt for his appeasement of the liberals, went into the opposition and eventually became an almost exclusively proclerical party. Montt and his principal minister, Antonio Varas, organized a new middle-of-the-road party, the *Partido Nacional,* which because it was largely based upon personal leadership was generally referred to as the Montt-Varista party. But the personal nature of their leadership and their blatant attempt to impose Varas on the country as the next president were so sharply criticized that in 1858 Montt forcibly moved against the *Club de la Unión* in Santiago which was a center of opposition, arresting more than 150 members, and eventually he declared the entire provinces of Santiago, Valparaíso, and Aconcagua to be in a state of siege. Indian insurrections in the south added to the disorder in the country. In addition, Chile's wheat was meeting with increasing competition in world markets, and her profitable trade with California was cut back by the opening of the Panama railroad. The general economic position of the country deteriorated in the economic crisis of 1857. For these various reasons Varas found it convenient to withdraw in 1861 as a candidate for the presidency, and in his place José Joaquín Pérez was selected as the official candidate of the Montt-Varistas.

Pérez, after being put into the presidency in 1861 by the Montt-Varistas, at first tried to govern by means of a coalition of all parties but soon broke with the Montt-Varistas and sought to maintain himself in power by a fusion of the extreme conservatives and the extreme liberals in which the so-called "young liberals" gradually gained the ascendancy. But his two terms, covering the decade 1861–1871, were in general an era of good feeling, orderly development, and respect for constitutional guaranties. His policy of political conciliation was fortuitously advanced by the outbreak of war with Spain in 1865, which emphasized the need for unity in defense of the country. In this war Chile went to the aid of Peru in opposing foreign intervention.

In the previous year Spain had begun efforts to force Peru, whose independence she had never recognized, to indemnify her for damages to Spanish lives and property, going back in some cases to the wars of independence. When the United States expressed concern about her intentions Spain assured Secretary of State Seward, as France had already done in 1861 before invading Mexico, that she had no intention of effecting a permanent occupation of Peruvian territory. But when Peru refused her demands, the Spanish fleet seized the Chincha Islands, rich in *guano* and a principal source of revenue for the Peruvian government. Spain also forced Peru, then headed by President Juan Antonio Pezet, to sign a treaty agreeing to pay Spain's claims and also the expenses of the naval expedition which had been sent against the country. At this juncture the Spanish minister in Washington was again warned by Seward that the United States could no longer be expected "to remain in their present attitude of neutrality between Spain and the Spanish-American republics," but again this warning was not followed up by the United States.

These acts of the Spaniards against Peru outraged Chile and inspired popular demonstrations against the Spanish legation in Santiago. Chile made common cause with Peru, addressing notes of protest to all the other South American governments and joining in a new alliance with Peru, Ecuador, and Bolivia to resist Spain. A Spanish fleet now appeared at Valparaíso, presented a claim for damages to the Chilean government, and demanded a salute within four days. When Chile rejected this ultimatum Spain proclaimed a blockade of the Chilean coast and bombarded the unfortified port city of Valparaíso, committing an estimated 14 million dollars worth of damages. It encountered only token resistance from the weak Chilean navy, which consisted of only one gunboat and two schooners reinforced by a captured Spanish frigate. The Spanish fleet then proceeded to Peru where it began a blockade of Callao, which was, unlike Valparaíso, fortified. There the Spanish fleet took a severe drubbing and was obliged to withdraw. The military operations, which were exclusively maritime, thus came to an end in 1868, and an armistice was concluded in Washington three years later. Not until a treaty of peace was signed in 1879, however, did Spain finally recognize the independence of Peru.

The growth of liberalism which slowly took place during the decade of the Pérez administration in Chile came to fruition in the administration of Pérez's successor, Federico Errázuriz Zañartú, who had served as minister of war during the conflict with Spain. Though a member of an aristocratic family, Errázuriz belonged to the liberal wing of the *Partido Nacional*. Taking office in 1871 at the age of forty-six he soon displayed the same energetic leadership as president that he had displayed as minister. Errázuriz chose to govern with a cabinet responsible to the majority of the legislature and so, though under no constitutional compulsion to do so, adopted the parliamentary form of government, which had already been partly followed by Pérez. In 1873 when a new congressional majority of Liberals took control of the legislature Errázuriz broke with his conservative supporters and formed a new political coalition, the *Alianza Liberal* which threw the old conservative coalition into an obscurity from which it never emerged. Liberalism now became the strongest political force in the nation.

The two dominant elements in the Liberal program were the curtailment of clerical influences and the alteration of the constitution of 1833 in such ways as to limit the powers of the executive. The Liberals complained that the Roman Catholic Church was hostile to republicanism. The church denied the fundamental principles of republicanism, explained Francisco Bilbao, namely, the sovereignty of the people and the rule of reason in every man, and instead emphasized authoritarianism and dogma. Already in 1865 the Pérez administration had liberalized the article in the constitution which established the Catholic Church as the state religion by passing a law which allowed Protestants to worship in their own homes. This was the first official step taken toward religious toleration. Again in 1873 the religious question came to the fore in a controversy over the issue of religious instruction in the schools, which resulted in another victory for the Liberals. The conservatives favored freedom of instruction and freedom of choice in textbooks for the private church schools. But Errázuriz supported government supervision and made this one of the objectives of the new *Alianza Liberal*.

The Liberals continued to take the offensive against the conservatives on church questions in 1874 and 1875 when they abolished ecclesiastical courts. For this act the members of the Chilean Congress were excommunicated by the archbishop. The Liberals also sought to legalize civil marriages, to place vital statistics under the complete control of the government, and to disestablish the church, but in these measures they failed during the Errázuriz administration. Not until 1884, when the church question came up again in Congress, were the Liberals able to push through new laws legalizing civil marriages, taking the control of vital statistics away from the parish churches and turning it over to government agencies, and in addition secularizing all cemeteries. But they failed again at that time to separate church and state, which indeed remained united in Chile until 1925. The Liberals made no effort to interfere with the large landholdings of the church.

With a president who shared their liberal views and who followed the parliamentary system, which made the executive responsible to the legislature, now predominantly Liberal, the Liberals necessarily contented themselves with only mild attempts at the limitation and supervision of executive authority. In 1871 a law was passed prohibiting the immediate reelection of a president and thus making impossible the ten-year spans of presidential power which had characterized Chile's political history since 1831. Three years later the constitution was amended to reduce the extraordinary powers which the president might use under a state of siege. On the congressional committee, the *comisión conservadora,* which sat as a permanent committee between legislative sessions to pass upon and exercise the legislative interest in acts of the president, was now placed a majority of members from the lower house. Similarly on the council of state, a court appointed by the president with advisory functions, the two houses of Congress were given the right to appoint a majority of the members. But the fact of a compliant president and the rapport which existed between him and the Liberal Congress seemed to make more drastic constitutional reform unnecessary. The principle and practice of large presidential authority was not seriously challenged by the Liberals. They had little reason to consider it a basic problem and had no recent examples of its abuse in Chilean political history to excite them. Besides, their substantial identification with the Chilean aristocracy made it undesirable for them to tamper overmuch with the constitution of 1833.

Meanwhile, as the Liberals consolidated their political position, Chile experienced the full force of the economic depression which broke over the entire Western world in 1873. In Chile it was aggravated by overspeculation in nitrate, copper, and other mining enterprises. Errázuriz passed on this depression in 1876 to his successor, Aníbal Pinto, a son of the Francisco Pinto who had served from 1826 to 1829 as the last Liberal president before the rise of Portales. Pinto had been minister of war and marine in the Errázuriz cabinet. Though he had not been active in politics he was selected as the official candidate and succeeded in defeating both of his opponents, Miguel Luis Amunátegui and Benjamín Vicuña Mackenna. His solution to Chile's economic crisis was increased taxation, but this did not remove the cause of the country's economic plight, which was, rather, due to its diminishing balance of payments. In an effort to improve Chile's balance-of-payments position Pinto adopted a policy of suspending specie payments in 1878. But this only depreciated the currency and eventually made it virtually inconvertible in foreign exchange.

War of the Pacific

During the Errázuriz administration much Chilean and British capital went into the northern nitrate provinces of Antofagasta and Tarapacá. The former province was claimed jointly by Chile and Bolivia, Chile's claim extending as far north as the 23d degree of latitude and Bolivia's as far south as the 27th. In 1866 as Chile and Bolivia prepared to make common cause with Peru against Spain, they concluded a treaty which fixed the 24th degree as the tentative boundary between them but provided that both of them would have equal rights to revenues derived from the exports of minerals, including nitrates, from the entire region between the 23d and 25th degrees. To the north the province of Tarapacá, rich in nitrates and other minerals, was incontestably Peruvian. Both of these provinces were openly coveted by Chile and were of great interest to Anglo-Chilean capitalists. To restrain this interest, Peru and Bolivia concluded a secret alliance in February, 1873, directed against Chile. Anglo-Chilean capital which invaded these provinces, therefore, placed itself at the mercy of the territorial governments.

Both Peru and Bolivia imposed restrictions upon the Chilean operations in their territories. Peru first established a monopoly of the distribution of nitrates and when this failed in 1875 expropriated the Chilean nitrate works in Tarapacá under the right of eminent domain, paying an indemnity which was regarded by Chile as inadequate. Meanwhile an energetic Chilean nitrate company had obtained a fifteen-year concession from the Melgarejo government of Bolivia to work the nitrate deposits of Antofagasta, and this concession remained in force after the southern boundary of the province was fixed permanently at the 24th degree in 1874. At the same time Chile gave up all claims to a share of the revenue received from exports north of the new permanent boundary, and Bolivia agreed not to increase for twenty-five years the taxes on Chilean companies operating there. But Peru, anxious undoubtedly to safeguard her own nitrate monopoly in Tarapacá against Chilean competition, pressed Bolivia to levy new taxes on Chilean nitrate exports from her territory. Bolivia succumbed to this pressure in 1878 when its Congress at the insistence of the Bolivian dictator, Hilarión Daza, imposed a tax of 10 *centavos* per hundredweight on nitrates sent out of Antofagasta by Chilean nitrate companies. When Chile protested, Bolivia seized the Chilean nitrate properties and announced that it would sell them on February 14, 1879, to pay taxes. It twice refused to arbitrate the dispute though arbitration was provided for in the treaty of 1874. On the date of the announced sale Chilean troops entered Antofagasta, occupied the Chilean properties, and raised the Chilean flag. Thus began the so-called "War of the Pacific," which was to result in a great enhancement of Chile's power and prestige.

Peru offered in apparent good faith to mediate the dispute and submitted the following terms: (1) that Chile should evacuate the Bolivian coastal area which she had seized, (2) that this area should be put under the administration of the three nations concerned, and (3) that the revenues derived from the area should be divided equally between Bolivia and Chile. But Chile, under pressure from British capital, was convinced that Peru was responsible for the tax reprisals against the nitrate companies and, having learned of the secret Peru-Bolivia treaty of 1873, concluded that Peru was not acting in good faith. She therefore rejected Peru's terms and instead presented an ultimatum requiring Peru to abrogate the treaty and declare its neutrality. When Peru's representative, José Antonio Lavalle, refused to do so, Chile declared war in April, 1879.

What began, therefore, as an apparently sincere attempt by Peru to prevent hostilities between her neighbors ended with her involvement in them. Indeed Peru was forced to bear the burden of the fighting almost alone, for the Bolivian government was ill-prepared for war and proved to be hopelessly inefficient. Chile, on the other hand, was spoiling for war and for a chance to use her new modern navy, including two ironclad vessels with revolving turrets and superior armament. The outcome of the war was really settled by the Chilean navy, for the topographical conditions in the disputed provinces and the difficulties of transport made land fighting impractical. With the support of the navy, Chilean forces quickly overran not only Antofagasta but also the Peruvian provinces of Tarapacá, Tacna, and Arica by the end of 1880. The defense of the Morro de Arica by the Peruvians under Col. Francisco Bolognesi, in which the last survivors made suicidal jumps over the cliff rather than surrender to the invading Chileans, was one of the most heroic episodes of the war and helped to turn foreign public opinion against Chile as responsible for a premeditated and brutal aggression.

This breach of the peace of the hemisphere now began to give considerable concern to the United States, particularly because its official representatives in Lima and Santiago each espoused the position of the government to which he was accredited. As a result the United States came to be cordially disliked by both sides in the fighting, but it nevertheless offered its good offices to end the hostilities. These were accepted, and an effort at mediation was made on a United States warship, the *Lackawanna,* in the harbor at Arica in October, 1880. But this effort came to nothing, as the Chileans plainly appeared to be bent upon further conquest and the complete subjugation of their enemies. Under these circumstances the United States mediator virtually encouraged Peru to continue the war, though without any prospect of assistance from the United States.

The fighting was now resumed, and 25,000 Chilean troops, led by Gen. Manuel Baquedano, occupied Lima in January, 1881, sacking and reducing it to anarchy. The priceless archives of Peru were carried off and scattered, and the national library was used as a stable. Chile pursued her aggressive course with ruthless thoroughness. By skillful diplomacy she kept Argentina from going to the aid of Peru and Bolivia. After two years of smashing military victories the Chileans were practically obliged to allow Gen. Miguel Iglesias to come to power in Peru in order to have a government with which they could treat. By the Treaty of Ancón concluded in 1883, they took outright possession of Peru's richest province, Tarapacá, and occupied Tacna and Arica for a period of ten years. At the end of that period, it was agreed, a plebiscite should be held to determine ownership and the loser of the plebiscite would receive an indemnity of 10 million *pesos* from the winner. This arrangement was regarded by Chile as only a postponed indemnity, for she realized that bankrupt Peru, now saddled with a debt of 50 million dollars, would be unable to pay her indemnity for many years to come.

Peru, in the decades after her defeat by Chile, experienced a strong resurgence of nationalism, guided by her intellectuals, Manuel González Prada, Mariano Cornejo, Javier Prado y Ugarteche, and Manuel Vicente Villarán. They attributed Peru's defeat and backwardness to the "dead hand" of the colonial past, the romanticism of the continuing Spanish tradition, and domination of the Roman Catholic Church. To counteract these influences they advocated a new and more scientific type of education which would deal realistically with Peru's problems, would enable the Peruvians to improve their social and economic levels, and would bring them forward into the modern age. Their country needed highways, railroads, docks, ships, machinery, factories, and all the other tools of an industrial nation. In the philosophy of Positivism these reformers found a useful tool to achieve their objective of a brave new Peruvian nationalism embracing all elements in the nation, particularly the oppressed Indian. To this latter element as well as to the nation as a whole they offered a positive program of order and progress.

Bolivia emerged from the war weakened by the loss of her seacoast province and disconsolate over her now landlocked status. Liberals there, like the liberals in Peru, sought to bring about a social and economic regeneration of their country, prostrate after its defeat in the War of the Pacific, by espousing the Positivist philosophy. The truce which Bolivia concluded in 1884 recognized Chile's occupation of her province of Antofagasta until a final treaty could be concluded. The peace treaty, which was finally signed in 1904, ceded all of Bolivia's seacoast outright to Chile in return for an indemnity of 300,000 pounds sterling and a promise that Chile would build a railroad at her own expense to connect Arica with La Paz, would allow Bolivia to transport goods over this railroad free of customs duties, and would turn over the Bolivian part of the railroad to Bolivia fifteen years after its completion. By this arrangement Bolivia secured a kind of outlet to the Pacific supplementing the outlet by way of Lake Titicaca to Mollendo which she

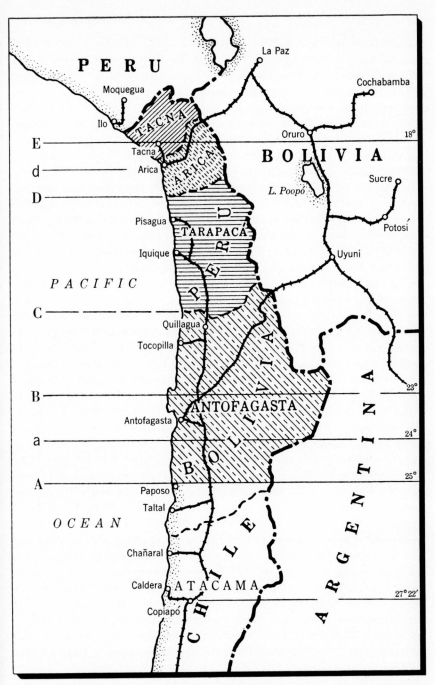

Chilean expansion northward. A. Original Chile-Bolivian boundary. B. Claimed by Chile in 1842. a. Established by treaty in 1866, but in A–B nitrate revenues were divided equally. C. Original Peru-Bolivian boundary. D. Boundary of Chile as a result of the War of the Pacific, 1883, with D–E to be occupied by Chile for ten years. d. Chile-Peruvian boundary by settlement of 1929. (*Reproduced from W. J. Dennis, Tacna and Arica, New Haven, 1931, courtesy of Yale University Press.*)

had already received from Peru. The railroad connecting Arica with La Paz was not finally completed until 1913, and the Bolivian portion was turned over to Bolivia in 1928.

The Chilean Liberals made political capital from their complete victory over Peru and Bolivia in the War of the Pacific. At first their power was challenged by a political boom, started by the conservatives, for General Baquedano, the captor of Lima and military hero of the war, as the next president, but this threat was ended with Baquedano's withdrawal as a candidate. The official candidate, Domingo Santa María, who had been minister of foreign relations and navy during the War of the Pacific, therefore easily won the election in 1881. The Liberal victory was now complete. With the aid of the troops returning from the war the government finally subjugated the rebellious Araucanian Indians and opened up the region between the Bío-Bío River and Valdivia to white settlement. The Santa María administration also made the changes in the laws regulating church activities mentioned above. As indicative of the nationalist attitude of the government in relation to the church, Santa María insisted upon the selection of an archbishop favorable to the government, even defying the Pope's special legate on this issue and eventually handing him his passports. These Liberal actions on the church question were matched by similar Liberal actions on political questions. Property qualifications for voting were removed in 1884, guaranties against arbitrary arrest were strengthened, and increased local autonomy was granted in minor matters.

But on these and other questions the line between Liberals and Conservatives was not clearly drawn. The Conservative party as such was no longer a major political factor, but government power, exercised by the official Liberal party, rested upon shifting coalitions of political groups in Congress. The machinery for governmental control of elections already existed; it had grown up under the constitution and had been customarily used in every campaign up to and through the election of Santa María in 1881. With the unofficial adoption of the system of ministerial responsibility to Congress the government found it more and more necessary to control elections in its own interest, for without majority support in the legislature it was impotent. In case of a deadlock between the executive and Congress, the executive, though operating under a parliamentary system, had no means, under the constitution, of dissolving Congress and appealing to the country. To the extent that government found it necessary to interfere in elections it failed to provide popular government. Even Liberal presidents, therefore, really represented the traditional ruling oligarchy; they did not prepare the way for genuinely popular government.

Chile's Civil War

The difficulties of keeping the Liberal factions together in a working majority to cooperate with a political cabinet operating under a system of ministerial responsibility to the legislature, particularly in the absence of a strong opposition, was demonstrated in the election of 1886. For lack of party discipline and cohesion the official candidate, José Manuel Balmaceda, was opposed as a candidate by a strong Liberal faction. Balmaceda was the outstanding leader of his party, a *hacendado* of inherited wealth, who began his career as a student for the priesthood. Later entering politics he was one of the founders of the Young Liberal party and achieved a distinguished career as an orator and a diplomat. He was credited with having kept Argentina neutral in the War of the Pacific. As a cabinet minister under Santa María he was identified with the liberal program of action of that administration. But he was unacceptable to a strong faction in the Liberal party and finally had to be put into office by the party machine. His own program, announced immediately after his election, called for improvement and expansion of education, religious freedom, increased local self-government, extension of the suffrage, and a national program of public works. But the Liberal opposition now tried to block approval of the government's budget and accepted it only after pressure was applied. The legislature was kept in session continuously four days beyond the end of the old year, and the budget was forced through.

Balmaceda failed to overcome this inauspicious beginning of his tenure of office. For the extravagances of his administration, which were indeed excessive, and for his failure to restore specie payments—a failure which benefited the exporting interests at the expense of the economy as a whole—he was severely criticized. Serious labor troubles, brought on by the currency question and by the increasing competition from the new immigrants, also occurred to plague the government for the first time in Chilean history. Under these circumstances all his efforts to promote political unity failed. He even tried to conciliate the conservatives by accepting a compromise archbishop, but to no avail. His parliamentary coalition deserted him, and between April, 1888, and October, 1889, he appointed and tried to govern with ten successive cabinets. Finally, unable to secure a majority or to organize a new bloc of support, he abandoned the system of parliamentary government. He thus attempted to return to the system of a strong executive provided for in the constitution of 1833, but he did so at a time when national sentiment was moving in the opposite direction. Eventually Balmaceda ignored the parliamentary majority altogether. To his Liberal opponents this meant only that the president intended to set up a dictatorship. Liberalism, as Francisco Bilbao had warned earlier, was making its peace with dictatorship. With the best of intentions it was using authoritarian methods for the purpose of promoting the public welfare. It was involving itself in the paradox of using despotism to promote liberty. On the other hand Balmaceda's defenders argued that he was seeking to return simply to the system prescribed in the constitution and was prevented from doing so by party factionalism. Was it not logical to suppose that a popularly elected president was better able to act in the national interest than party groups in Congress?

Chile now rapidly slid into civil war. A dangerous deadlock developed between the president and Congress when Balmaceda made plain that he was backing Enrique Sanfuentes as a candidate to succeed him. Sanfuentes was regarded by many Liberals as a man of small ability who as president would simply serve as a puppet for Balmaceda. They demanded a pledge that the president would not use official pressure in the election and tried to pass a law limiting the control of the minister of the interior over elections. But after Congress recessed in 1890 Balmaceda defiantly appointed a new ministry headed by Sanfuentes. A law which this new ministry prepared abolishing parliamentary government and restoring the presidential system was rejected by the new Congress, but the cabinet refused to resign. Congress, still exercising the power of the purse, thereupon refused to approve the budget for the next year starting on July 1. The deadlock was aggravated by the president's action in requiring officers of the army and navy to take oaths of allegiance to him and by the outbreaks of labor disturbances in Valparaíso and the nitrate districts. Finally Balmaceda was obliged to yield and appoint a new ministry, whereupon Congress passed a budget law that would run the government until the end of the calendar year.

But Balmaceda largely ignored the new ministry which had been forced upon him and when this ministry resigned in October, 1890, he appointed a personal ministry in its place. The new ministry dissolved Congress, which was meeting in special session and which had not yet passed the budget for the next year. Balmaceda himself then proclaimed the budget in effect without congressional approval on January 1, 1891. With this provocative and dictatorial act of the president, open hostilities began between the president and the army on the one side and the Congressionalists and the navy on the other. Seven days later he was formally deposed by Congress and replaced by a *junta* headed by Jorge Montt. Since the president kept the loyalty of most of the army he retained control of both Santiago and Valparaíso, but his enemies controlled the provinces. Once again a basic regional rivalry between urban and rural districts took the form of a conflict over the nature of the political organization of the nation. The basic conflict was between two systems of government—the presidential and the parliamentary. Opinion was divided also along the lines of foreign economic interests, the United States element, led by the Irish-born United States minister, Patrick Egan, favoring the Balmacedists and the Anglo-Chileans supporting the Congressionalists. During the next eight months of civil war—from January to August, 1891—Chile endured more suffering than during the entire War of the Pacific.

Balmaceda, under the exigencies of civil war, now became increasingly despotic, decreeing martial law, censoring and closing down the press, and arresting his critics. In the race which immediately began between the Balmacedists and the Congressionalists for the customs-houses in the north, with their revenues from nitrate exports, the Congressionalists with navy support had a decisive advantage and within a few weeks seized the ports in the north including Iquique, the chief port of Tarapacá, which they made their capital. There they mobilized an army equipped largely by filibustering operations, since they were unrecognized as a government by any foreign government, and organized by a German army officer, Gen. Emil Körner. As a conflict between the two armies approached, the diplomatic corps in Santiago sought to bring about peace, but in vain. Congressional forces numbering about 10,000 moved south and, landing at Quintero Bay north of Valparaíso in August, engaged the presidential forces numbering about 22,000. There on the battlefield of Concón and later at Placilla they severely defeated the president's forces, which were handicapped by singularly inept leadership. Eight days after landing, the Congressionalists captured Valparaíso and moved inland to occupy the capital, forcing Balmaceda to resign. The defeated ex-president found asylum in the Argentine legation, where on September 18, the very day when his term of office was legally scheduled to end, he committed suicide.

The victory of the Congressionalists in the civil war determined that Chile should be governed henceforth by the popular wing of the Liberal party at least nominally through congressional majorities in accordance with the parliamentary form of government. It repudiated the strong executive type of government which O'Higgins and Portales had earlier followed and which Balmaceda sought in vain to reintroduce. In this sense it represented a triumph of the liberal and federal principles of government which emphasized individual and local units rather than overriding central authority. Chilean nationalism would be embodied not in a strong dictator-president but in the local communities of the nation represented in the legislature. To the Congress rather than to the president the voters would look for programs of political action and national welfare. As a result interference by the national government in local elections ceased, and in 1892 the municipalities were given increased autonomy and the right to supervise their own elections both for local and for national officers.

But in many cases the result of this change was only to devolve power upon the local *hacendados* and political bosses, who simply replaced the national officials in regimenting the voters and controlling elections. A considerable part of the congressional opposition to Balmaceda came from the local oligarchs who did not want the central government to lead a liberal program of national action which would extend educational facilities, further curb the powers of the church, embark upon a national program of public works, or broaden the suffrage. In opposing the enactment of this program by a dictator-president they found themselves in alliance with the Liberals, who also favored the weakening of central authority. But the decentralizing of power, as it turned out, did not ensure free elections, eliminate corruption, or destroy the power of the economic and political oligarchy. Nevertheless the possibility of executive dictatorship was exorcised from Chile for more than a generation. This was the real significance of the Chilean civil war of 1891. Henceforth until 1925 Chilean political history was characterized by congressional supremacy and weak executive leadership.

The ferment generated by liberalism in both Brazil and Chile, therefore, brought experimentation in political methods, resulting in the abolition of monarchy in the former and of strong executive rule in the latter. The very concern of the liberals with political matters, their receptiveness to change, their aversion to privilege, and their belief in progress—particularly material progress—as an end in itself to be achieved through human effort made adjustments to their viewpoints necessary. In both countries the parliamentary system was experimented with, and in Chile it became firmly established after 1891. But attempts by the liberals, in so far as they were able to achieve political organization, thus to increase the responsiveness of government to the electorate were countered by the efforts of the traditional oligarchies to maintain their control over areas not only of political but also of social and economic action. The results achieved, therefore, appeared to be something less than the liberals desired and impelled them eventually to question not their objectives of progress and human betterment through popular action but the methods of gradualism, education, decentralization of authority, and weak executive leadership which they had used to reach these objectives.

Argentine Liberalism

In Argentina after the downfall of Rosas in 1852, native Argentine forces were weakened and the country increasingly succumbed to foreign influences. The creole era which had reached its zenith under Rosas ended and Argentina became more cosmopolitan. Political controversy continued to revolve mainly around the issue of centralization or decentralization of government. That issue appeared to have been definitely resolved in favor of decentralization by the adoption of the federal constitution in 1853. The forcible union of the independent Buenos Aires city and province with the federal republic in 1860 and Mitre's military victory at Pavón in 1861, though they strengthened the centralist element in Argentine politics and brought a *porteño*, Mitre, into the presidency, did not overthrow the federal system. Thereafter the rivalry over the political nature of the government involved mainly the issues of the role of Buenos Aires province in the federal union and the federalization of the port city of Buenos Aires as the capital of the country. If these issues did not directly call in question the constitutional character of the Argentine government they nevertheless involved the basic issue of the actual locus of power, which was more important in terms of political realities than were the clauses of the constitution.

During Mitre's administration a split developed in the Federalist party of Buenos Aires province between the faction that wanted to keep the province autonomous and the faction that wanted to federalize it. The former, which was the majority faction, was led by Adolfo Alsina, governor of Buenos Aires;

the latter, supported by President Mitre, was led by Rufino de Elizalde. The influence of this latter nationalist group in Buenos Aires declined as Mitre's popularity waned during the Paraguayan War, for Mitre's duties as commander in chief of the allied armies of Argentina, Brazil, and Uruguay distracted him from his duties as president of Argentina, and the war itself, as it dragged on year after year, became increasingly unpopular. This politi-

Fig. 17-1. Domingo Faustino Sarmiento. (*Courtesy of Pan American Union.*)

cal schism weakened the influence of Buenos Aires in the election of 1868 and made it possible for the provinces to elect as president Domingo Faustino Sarmiento, a native of San Juan, who though he had a provincial origin had been identified with the *porteños* and was acceptable to them. The election of Sarmiento was a revolutionary event in Argentine history, for it denoted the passing of power out of the hands of the *porteños;* the selection of Alsina as his vice president represented a concession to the autonomous or separatist faction of Buenos Aires.

Sarmiento, a vigorous, purposeful, and vehement leader, a very volcano of a man, had established his reputation in journalistic and educational work. An exile in Chile during the Rosas period he returned to Buenos Aires after the overthrow of Rosas and loyally accepted the federal constitution of 1853. At the time of his election to the presidency in 1868 he was serving as Argentine minister to the United States, where he had built many friendly connections with distinguished educators, including particularly Horace Mann. Believing profoundly in public education he made instruction available to all levels of the population—children, adults, soldiers, sailors, workers, and even convicts. He made strenuous efforts with public funds to reduce the 82 per cent illiteracy of the Argentine population which was revealed in the census of 1869. As a schoolmaster-president he declared that "to govern is to educate," and he made a profound imprint on Argentine education, giving it a cosmopolitan character. He was responsible for founding the first teacher-training school and for bringing a group of schoolteachers from the United States to improve the quality of Argentine teaching. This school became a center for the spread of Argentine liberalism overlaid with the doctrines of Positivism. Under his regime Argentina built its naval and military academies and its first astronomical observatory. In his prolific writings (his collected *Obras* fill fifty-two volumes) Sarmiento unceasingly emphasized Argentina's need for more and better education. His purpose, he said, was to *desasnar* the Argentine people, that is, to render them less stupid, less like a donkey.

A passionate champion of democracy and freedom Sarmiento believed that government under his energetic leadership should use its power to enforce both. His classic *Facundo,* first published in 1845, depicted with scathing disparagement the barbarities of *caudillismo.* When he became president *caudillismo* was still a serious problem in the provinces, as was to be expected under a federal system which recognized a large measure of provincial autonomy. He, perhaps somewhat naïvely, ascribed the persistence of this system of strong local leaders to the ignorance of the provincial populations and prescribed education as the remedy. The most serious threat from *caudillismo* in his administration occurred in the province of Entre Ríos where Urquiza, since his retirement from the presidency, remained not only as governor but also as a sort of feudal lord or patriarch with a well-trained provincial army of 15,000 men. Sarmiento went out of his way to conciliate Urquiza, with gratifying results. He had no trouble with this particular *caudillo,* but his expressions of friendliness for Urquiza unwittingly brought trouble to the latter. A strong faction arose in Entre Ríos, led by an ambitious army officer, Ricardo López Jordán, who opposed friendship with Buenos Aires and with the new federal administration. A band of assassins representing this group entered Urquiza's *estancia* on an April night in 1870 and murdered Governor Urquiza in the midst of his family. Three days later López Jordán was elected governor in his place by the compliant provincial legislature of Entre Ríos.

In the general rage and horror that followed this crime Sarmiento declared a federal intervention of Entre Ríos, as permitted by the constitution. In this move he was supported by public sentiment and by Congress. But López denied the power of the federal government to intervene on the ground that he had not appealed for an intervention. Instead, the federal intervention was directed against him. Entre Ríos was now placed under a state of siege, but nearly a year of hard fighting was required to defeat López and drive him into Brazil. He returned again in 1873 and in attempting to seize power held off the government forces again for several months. He was finally captured in the late 1870s and was assassinated in 1889 by the son of one of his victims. This episode, besides costing the Sarmiento administration nearly 10 million gold *pesos,* which was one-third of a European loan just obtained for internal improvements, demonstrated that *caudillismo* remained an acute problem both for the provinces and for the central Argentine government. Could it be dealt with adequately by expansion of public education, or was the application of force by the central government required? Sarmiento tried both methods. And how could the intervention of the federal government be resorted to without diminishing provincial autonomy and thus altering the federal system? These questions posed a serious dilemma for liberals who believed in local self-government and a weak central executive and at the same time supported nationalism.

When Sarmiento's term ended in 1874 the dominant Federalist party was able to perpetuate itself in power, aided by the continued schism in Buenos Aires between the autonomists, led by Alsina, and the nationalists or followers of Mitre. The official candidate, supported by Sarmiento, was Nicolás Avellaneda, the son of the Marco Avellaneda who had been beheaded after leading an anti-Rosas movement in Tucumán in 1841. Avellaneda was a provincial who had never been identified with the *porteños.* His candidacy was supported by most of the provincial governors, and with the backing of the governors and the Sarmiento administration he was elected after waging a vigorous campaign. His triumph represented another rebuff to the *porteños* and derogated from the effects of their military victory in 1861. Despite that victory it was apparent that the federalists were not going to allow Buenos Aires to dominate the country. By shrewd maneuvering and well-timed compromise they were gradually undoing the results of Pavón. But they were nevertheless confronted by die-hard opposition. In September, 1874, three months after Avellaneda's election but before his inauguration, a revolt, led by Mitre, broke out and spread through Buenos Aires and Córdoba. Sarmiento commissioned Gen. Julio A. Roca, who had participated in the war against Paraguay, to suppress the uprising. By December it was crushed, the leaders were imprisoned, and Mitre was given a sentence of six years of banishment, which, however, was not carried out.

The federal system embodied in the constitution of 1853 and triumphant both in politics and in battle, except in the brief period of *porteño* supremacy under Mitre, represented the liberal philosophy of the nineteenth century. It opposed tyranny, whether of a president-dictator or of a strong and wealthy federal capital city, and insisted that power should remain decentralized among the component political units of the nation. In Argentina this meant a recognition of the power of the provincial governors, their political machines, and the *estanciero* oligarchy which usually maintained them in office. Provincial autonomy was not synonymous with popular rule on a numerical basis. As in Chile, the federal system tended to strengthen the power of the landowning, provincial oligarchies. After their successes in the Sarmiento administration and particularly in the election of Avellaneda the provincial governors proceeded to consolidate their strength by organizing the so-called "Córdoba clique" which was able to bargain advantageously with the *porteños*. The Córdoba clique became the political agency of the provincial oligarchs, united to maintain their social and economic position against pressures from the capital. Their own class interests, therefore, which they thought could be best promoted by maximum local autonomy, determined their conception of Argentine nationalism. The central government operating under this conception could not, with good conscience, really move against *caudillismo* or undertake to supplant it with a national *caudillo*. And yet, in their view, the development of local strength in the provinces tied together under a cooperative federal arrangement meant a stronger Argentine nationality.

The federal government was dominated by the clique from Córdoba, and sometimes government leaders even met and transacted their business there. But the government party was not an exclusively provincial party, for from time to time dissident elements in the provinces who opposed the controlling provincial oligarchy joined forces with groups in Buenos Aires who were hostile to the provinces and their governments. Moreover, even the government clique received support from the federalist faction in Buenos Aires. But the political lines between provincials and *porteños* tended to be more sharply drawn as the question of the federalization of the capital became acute. Under the five-year compromise arrangement of 1862, the city of Buenos Aires remained as the capital of both the province and the nation. Though this arrangement was regularly renewed it became increasingly unsatisfactory to the provincial governors, who desired to federalize Buenos Aires, that is, virtually to capture it from the province of Buenos Aires and thus to bring it, the outstanding port city of the nation, under the exclusive control of the federal government, which they dominated.

This proposal, when advocated by Avellaneda in a message to Congress, aroused a storm of *porteño* opposition and drove the competing autonomous factions of Buenos Aires finally into fusion with the *Mitristas* in 1877 for a unified resistance to the government. Buenos Aires was not willing to surrender its provincial capital to the federal government or to allow the federal capital to be moved elsewhere. Preparing for a showdown on this question the *porteños* formed a military organization, the *Tiro Nacional,* and even mobilized the volunteer firemen or *bomberos* into military units. When Avellaneda countered by moving troops from the interior into Buenos Aires to protect the federal government the *Tiro* staged an immense demonstration for the purpose of overawing the government, which, they declared, was forcing it into rebellion. In this condition of incipient civil war over the question of the federalization of the capital, the election of 1880 was held.

In that election the official candidate was General Roca, fresh from new military triumphs against the Indians of the south. There since Rosas's time the territory of the Indians—descendants of the nomadic Tehuelche and Puelche of preconquest times—had been separated from the white settlements by a line of frontier forts, and the Indians had been kept pacified by government subsidies. For 100 leagues across the pampas between the forts a deep trench protected by barbed wire had been dug marking the northern limit of Indian territory. But the Indians, restive in their confinement, invaded territory wrested from them during the Rosas regime as far north as the Colorado River and along this extensive frontier made raids into the settlements of Buenos Aires province, murdering settlers and stealing cattle which they sold in Chile. Continued Indian occupation of this territory southwest of Buenos Aires was an element of weakness in Argentina's boundary claims against Chile, which were still undetermined. The purely defensive policy, which had been followed by successive Argentine governments, of simply holding the frontier against the Indians by the line of forts connected by barbed-wire fences was proving ineffective and inadequate.

At the mouth of the Chubut River a colony of Welsh were encouraged to settle as early as 1863, and there serving as shock troops for the white advance southward they established the first permanent settlement in Argentine Patagonia. After 1878 General Roca moved against the Indians with light-armed, mounted troops, who were instructed to kill or capture every Indian they could find. Within six months he and his forces pushed the Indians beyond the Río Negro, thus opening up all of Buenos Aires province to white settlement, making possible the establishment of a territorial *gobernación* over La Pampa, and strengthening his own claims to the presidency. The Indians who were captured were brought back and settled in the provinces of Santa Fe and Entre Ríos. Between 1879 and 1883 other armed expeditions were sent south of the Río Negro into the windy and gashed Patagonian plains. There they opened up new areas for settlement as far south as the Straits of Magellan. As a result Argentina's Indian population dwindled from an estimated 100,000 in 1852 to only 20,000 in 1914. Meanwhile the large Negro element in Argentina's population was being diluted by intermarriage with the new white immigrants from Spain, Italy, and Germany, and eventually disappeared.

The Argentine federal union in 1880 included fourteen provinces, the federal district of Buenos Aires, and several territories lying outside the recognized limits of the provinces. These latter had been declared in 1862 to be national territories. A basic law was adopted in 1884 for the government of nine of them, modeled after the territorial law of the United States. Under this law the governor of each territory was appointed by the president with the consent of the Senate. When the territory attained a population of 30,000 the inhabitants could elect a legislature and exercise local powers of self-government; on reaching a population of 60,000 it could be admitted into the federal union as a province. As the lands in the territories were wrested from the Indians they were granted in some cases to the soldiers who had helped to open them up to white settlement, and they were colonized in part by newcomers from Europe who came to Argentina through a national program of assisted immigration. The process of converting the territories into provinces coequal with the older provinces was not completed until the presidency of Juan Domingo Perón (1946–1955).

In the presidential campaign of 1880 the *porteños* realized that their candidate, Carlos Tejedor, could not possibly win. After the election but before the results were announced, they renewed their military preparations, indicating that they intended to carry through their resistance to the official candidate and to the absorption of their capital into the federal government. When the *Tiro* received a consignment of arms through customs, street fighting began in Buenos Aires under the direction of Tejedor. Avellaneda and his followers moved out of the capital to the federal garrison at Belgrano. The civil war continued for almost three weeks, culminating in two days of serious fighting on June 20 and 21, when a peace settlement was arranged through the mediation of the diplomatic corps. A general amnesty was granted, but the federal government disbanded the provincial government of Buenos Aires. When Congress assembled in August it passed a law, on the recommendation of Avellaneda, federalizing Buenos Aires. Under this law the federal government took over the buildings, railroads, and other property of the city of Buenos Aires as well as its municipal debt. The province of Buenos Aires was thus deprived of its capital, and in 1882 it selected a prairie site some 30 miles southeast of Buenos Aires, established a new capital there called La Plata, and attempted to construct a new port with the unattainable object of competing with Buenos Aires.

By 1880, therefore, sixty years after the victory of Cepeda, federalism achieved its ultimate triumph. The ancient capital of the viceroyalty of La Plata was finally integrated into the federal system. Its primary role as the instigator of the revolutionary movement in the early part of the century had been challenged by Artigas and his *caudillo* associates who refused to recognize it as the natural capital of the Argentine Confederation. Their antagonism to Buenos Aires, it must be admitted, was justified in part by the intransigent unitarism of the *porteños,* who, even after they were defeated in battle at Cepeda in 1820, had tried to impose their system upon the country under Rivadavia. The validity of federalism for Argentina was confirmed in the constitution of 1853, but it remained for Mitre and finally Avellaneda to incorporate Buenos Aires into the federal system and to make it the capital of a nation of federated provinces.

The struggle to vindicate Argentine federalism had been a slow, painful process, characterized by the tradition of violence which was a heritage of the wars of independence and limited by the principles of individualism, local autonomy, and decentralization which formed the core of nineteenth-century liberalism. In this process the liberal movement, struggling toward a federal system of cooperation among politically equal states, fell subject to new pressures and developed its own rigidities. The old liberalism became a new conservatism. The end result was to strengthen centralism. Government came to be monopolized by the landowning class, who rigged the elections in their favor, controlled the provincial and national legislatures, and showed little interest in stimulating party activity or increasing popular participation in government. The Córdoba clique, or the *Partido Nacional* as it came to be called after 1880, seemed to be preoccupied exclusively with maintaining the dominance of the large provincial landowning families. The liberal movement had been transformed into the party of the great *estancieros*. Party membership and even political activity were limited to the old patrician families, the new rich, and the relatively small group of middle-class intellectuals. Such was Argentine nationalism in the 1880s and 1890s.

Positivism in Mexico

In general, liberalism was so strongly committed to principles of *laissez faire*, local self-government, and decentralization of power that it did not promote a strong nationalism or create symbols of national power or even develop its own outstanding leaders to fix the character of the liberal movement. Nationalism could be and was better promoted by the conservatives, using traditional institutions and the agencies of centralized government for the advancement of their own interests, which to them seemed identical with the national interests. From their viewpoint the nation was contained in their own semifeudal, oligarchic pattern of life and was represented by a strong national leader who served their interests by maintaining order and stability without a too tender regard for civil liberties, constitutional prescriptions, and the wishes of either the legislature or the electorate. Such a leader was a protector of their own class interests and became the symbol of the nation. To the conservatives operating under such leaders, therefore, had generally gone the responsibility of reconciling regional differences and promoting national unity.

But Mexican liberalism became identified with *personalismo*—with the character of a personal leader—under Juárez in the 1850s, just as liberalism in Central America had earlier been identified with Morazán. In Mexico the emergence of such a leader was perhaps facilitated by the apparent necessity for liberalism to contend almost simultaneously with both a strongly entrenched clericalism and foreign invasion. It became a fighting movement personified in its leader, Juárez. Its principles were consecrated in the constitution of 1857 and vindicated in successful battles. These victories in war against the French-Austrian armies made Mexican liberalism a truly national movement and foreshadowed its future interest in national development.

When Juárez, after executing Maximilian in 1867, was inaugurated president for the third time, his government encouraged foreign capital to move into Mexico to promote the economic development of the country. Juárez and his advisers decided to push the military into the background and reconstruct Mexico along industrial lines in order not only to modernize its economy but also to create a strong nation which would be able to resist absorption by the United States. To promote this program of national strength Juárez opposed the limitation of Mexico's territorial jurisdiction which was implied in the proposal to create a so-called "free zone" along the Río Grande border in the north open to the commerce of the United States on equal terms with Mexico. The creation of such a zone, he objected, would not only reduce the revenues of the central government and encourage smuggling but would also be likely to weaken the allegiance of the residents there to the central government. Mexican liberals were thinking in terms of Mexico's national interests but were interpreting those interests more broadly than the conservatives.

In the efforts which the victorious liberals made to strengthen the nation, to consolidate the gains won in battle, and to facilitate the reconstruction of the country they could not make use of the traditional ruling classes, namely, the conservatives, the Roman Catholic Church, and the military, for these had supported the Maximilian empire. Their movement demanded a new ideology. Because of their hostility to the church they threw Mexico open to Protestant missionaries. And in another action almost equally repugnant to the Catholic Church they espoused the ideology of Positivism.

Under Juárez Positivism made its first official impact on Mexico. It was promoted intelligently and effectively by Gabino Barreda, who had studied in France under the founder of Positivism and who was made head of the newly created National Preparatory School in 1868. It was a counterrevolutionary doctrine which responded to the needs of a Mexico dissatisfied with stagnation and disorder. It was a philosophy that could be used to consolidate the ideals of the Reform. Comte himself had insisted that as politics evolved into the stage of a positive science requiring special knowledge, preparation, and expert judgment, its procedures ought not to be subjected to the decision of public opinion. To do so would condemn all superiors to "an arbitrary dependence upon the multitude of their inferiors" and would represent a transfer "to peoples of the divine right so much reproached to kings." This antirevolutionary doctrine coincided with the aspiration of the Mexican people and the Juárez government for a respite from anarchy and disorder.

The Positivists now gave liberalism a content which it had never before had for the Juárez liberals. From a fighting ideology they converted it into an ideology of order, peace, and material progress. Mexico, they insisted, could not pass from anarchy to true liberty without first establishing order.

In order to achieve these results the federal system would have to be modified to permit a regulated dictatorship operating in accordance with the positive principles of science. As in Brazil, Positivism stressed the need for a scientific analysis and treatment of the problems of society, but in Mexico it became almost exclusively economic. It relegated moral objectives to the background and while it purported to be a science it did not become a religion of humanity. This cult of progress soon became the basis for a new intellectual movement organized by the *científicos*, as the Mexican Positivists were called. They worked out elaborate programs for the rationalization of Mexican society along national lines with the aid of foreign technicians and foreign capital. In doing so they transformed Mexican liberalism into a purely technical movement and in effect made scientific progress a substitute for the liberal constitution of 1857.

To the Mexican Positivists it seemed clear that Juárez and his associates sinned against liberalism through their excessive idealism. The constitution of 1857 could only work in a utopia. The *Juaristas* had wished to give Mexico a government based on absolute laws conforming to their republican ideal, but for their system the Mexican people were not ready. They had not based their panaceas upon scientific study and inductive conclusions about the needs of a country of Mexicans. They had been hopelessly romantic and their philosophy of statecraft was no longer suited to an age of science. They had been limited by their ideals, which must now give way to a new concern for material welfare, for economic prosperity. To the Positivists the rights of man, for which the *Juaristas* contended, were only chimeras. They were not absolute nor did they have any permanent reality.

The leading figure in this movement was José Yves Limantour, who was later to achieve high political influence in Mexico as minister of finance under Gen. Porfirio Díaz. Positivism in Mexico, as in Brazil, was a highly intellectualized development. It represented a stirring among the elite and was a philosophy of education and statecraft for the privileged intellectuals. "The people," declared the *científicos*, "can only be considered as crazy people or as children." To them the Indians were inferior creatures without rights. The doctrines of the Positivists therefore made no appeal to the Indians and to the illiterate *mestizos*, who, however, would eventually be affected by it. It was a system which under the slogan "science and technology" proposed to deliver Mexico over to scientific experts—the nineteenth-century "technocrats"—but since many of these were foreign-trained, the *científicos* undertook to buy their services and the technological machinery which they needed to swing Mexico into the currents of the modern age. They admired and deliberately sought to imitate the material growth of the United States, and they aspired to create a Mexico strong in material things and better able to resist the growing danger from the north.

This program had scarcely been begun when Juárez died in 1872 while opposing a rebellion by Porfirio Díaz. In pursuance of the constitution the chief justice of the supreme court, Sebastián Lerdo de Tejada, succeeded Juárez as provisional president and in a special election held soon afterward was chosen president over Díaz. But Díaz refused to accept defeat, marched into Mexico City in November, 1876, forced Lerdo out of office and into exile, and had himself chosen president of Mexico.

Díaz, who was of mixed Spanish and Mixteca origin, was a native of Oaxaca, as Juárez had been. He had studied law under Juárez at the Institute of Oaxaca and had fought with him first against Santa Anna and later in the War of the Reform and against the French invaders. Though he thus identified himself with the liberal movement as led by Juárez and embodied in the constitution of 1857 his views were essentially conservative, favoring a strong, centralized executive government, which eventually became a military dictatorship. But at the expiration of his first term he formally followed the constitution by declining reelection and allowing Manuel González to be chosen president in his place. In 1884, however, he moved into the presidency again and had the constitution amended to permit him to be reelected. Thereafter he served continuously as president until 1911. In that long regime the gains which liberalism had made under Juárez were gradually lost and Mexico was delivered over to an elite class consisting of *científicos* or technocrats and a wealthy oligarchy rich in lands and industrial properties and largely controlled by foreign capital.

Nineteenth-century liberalism in Latin America, starting as a revolution of protest against entrenched privilege, autocratic government, and central authority, campaigned against the privileges of the Catholic Church, the monopoly of government by the conservative classes, the exercise of arbitrary authority whether by an emperor or by a constitutional president, and the concentration of power in the capital. During and after the wars of independence it appealed particularly to the creoles who had been excluded from the seats of power and to the new intellectual classes who challenged the traditional ways of doing things. This movement, spawned and supported by European romanticism, reached its cultural heights in the romantic art and literature of the period. In music it was represented by the republican composers Melesio Morales, Carlos Gomes, and Louis Moreau Gottschalk, who were animated by the faith that Americans could write good music, though in the European mode. The liberalism of the mid-nineteenth century, coinciding in time with new economic upsurges in Latin America, supported the interests of the groups who were ambitious for power and who espoused liberalism as a means of attaining it. But as they acquired governing responsibility in many countries after the middle of the century—by a military *golpe de estado* in Brazil, by a process of gradual infiltration and accretion in Chile and Argentina, through the inspiriting leadership of a national *caudillo* in Mexico, and by similar methods in several other countries—they accepted many of the very principles which they had been combatting. They developed their own privileged classes, established new centralized power, and even allowed their anticlericalism to become diluted.

Additional Reading

Bernstein, Harry: *Modern and Contemporary Latin America,* J. B. Lippincott Company, Philadelphia, 1952, chap. 28.

Bunkley, Allison Williams: *The Life of Sarmiento,* Princeton University Press, Princeton, N.J., 1952.

——— (ed.): *A Sarmiento Anthology,* Princeton University Press, Princeton, N.J., 1948.

Calderón de la Barca (Frances Erskine): *Life in Mexico during a Residence of Two Years in that Country,* E. P. Dutton & Co., Inc., New York, 1931, 1946.

Correas, Edmundo: *Sarmiento and the United States,* University of Florida Press, Gainesville, 1961.

Dennis, William J.: *Tacna and Arica: an Account of the Chile-Peru Boundary Dispute and of the Arbitrations by the United States,* Yale University Press, New Haven, 1931.

Edwards, Alberto: *El Gobierno de Don Manuel Montt, 1851–1861,* Editorial Nascimento, Santiago, Chile, 1932.

Galdames, Luis: *A History of Chile,* trans. and ed. by Isaac Joslin Cox, University of North Carolina Press, Chapel Hill, N.C., 1941, chaps. XIV–XVII.

Kiernan, V. G.: "Foreign Interests in the War of the Pacific," *Hispanic American Historical Review,* vol. 35, pp. [14]–36, 1955.

Knapp, Frank A.: *The Life of Sebastián Lerdo de Tejada, 1823–1889: A Study of Influence and Obscurity,* University of Texas Press, Austin, Tex., 1951.

Levene, Ricardo: *A History of Argentina,* trans. and ed. by William Spence Robertson, University of North Carolina Press, Chapel Hill, N.C., 1937, chaps. LV–LVIII.

McGann, T. F.: "The Generation of 'Eighty'," *Americas,* vol. 10, pp. 141–157, October, 1953.

Millington, Herbert: *American Diplomacy and the War of the Pacific,* Columbia University Press, New York, 1948.

Walford, A. J.: "Economic Aspects of the Argentine War of Secession (1852–1861)," *Inter-American Economic Affairs,* vol. 1, no. 2, pp. 70–96, 1947.

XVIII

Conservative Reaction

In the last decades of the nineteenth century, liberalism was largely subverted in several parts of Latin America not only by the weakening of its own principles but also by a conservative reaction which seemed to be required by the temper of the times. As mentioned above, liberalism itself became identified with oligarchy and privilege. Furthermore, not only in Mexico but in other countries as well, it depended upon a strong *caudillo* to maintain it in power, thus inconsistently undercutting its own principle of the decentralization of authority. In several countries it was destroyed by the heavy hand and the armed force of the traditional conservatives. In this plight liberalism could not appeal to the unfranchised working classes, the *mestizo* illiterates, the inarticulate *peones* and *rotos* for support, partly because nineteenth-century liberalism was not dedicated to popular government and partly because it had allowed itself either to absorb or to be absorbed by the forces of privilege which abhorred not only the working classes but even the new nascent middle classes. Under these circumstances and for these reasons the old liberalism lost ground.

Conservatism in Ecuador, Colombia, and Venezuela

This swing to conservatism was particularly apparent in the countries which had constituted Gran Colombia, beginning first in Ecuador. There the period of Liberal supremacy, which began in 1845 with the overthrow of the Conservative Juan José Flores, was marked by so much turmoil and anarchy that almost all national unity was lost and *caudillo* governments were set up in many parts of the country. In vain did Gen. José María Urbina, who seized the presidency by a *golpe de estado* in 1851, seek to carry out a liberal program of anticlericalism, abolition of slavery, expansion of the school system, and freedom of the press. Neither he nor his weak-willed associate and successor, Gen. Francisco Robles, was able to stem the growing opposition from the Conservatives, who represented the propertied classes and were dismayed by the disintegrating effects of liberalism. Finally in May, 1859, their leader, Gabriel García Moreno, backed by the exiled ex-president, Flores, overthrew the *caudillo* government at Guayaquil and making his way up a little-used mule trail over the Cordillera to Quito surprised the *Urbinistas* and established himself in power in Quito.

García Moreno was a native of Guayaquil of pure Castilian descent, educated in the natural sciences, mathematics, and law at the University of Quito. Through his marriage with the sister of the vice president, later president, Manuel Ascásubi of Ecuador (she was twelve years his senior), he acquired both money and political influence. While in practically forced exile in Europe in 1849 and again in 1855–1856 he acquired a complete abhorrence of liberalism and a strong predilection for both political and religious conservatism. After returning from Europe he engaged in journalism and university teaching in Quito, was elected mayor of Quito, and later became rector of the university there. He then entered the Senate where he outspokenly criticized the Liberal administration and sought legislation against the Masonic lodges which were now springing up in Ecuador for the first time as offshoots of the powerful lodge in Lima. After seizing control of the government he had a new constitution adopted under which he was chosen constitutional president. Believing that Roman Catholicism was the only basis on which society could develop, he made himself a clerical dictator and converted Ecuador into an apparent theocracy. "Civilization itself," he held, "is the fruit of Catholicism and degenerates whenever it departs from it." The new constitution made Catholicism the only religion of the country, and under it the church became dominant in Ecuador. García Moreno readmitted the Jesuits and in 1862 entered into a concordat with the Vatican which gave the Roman Catholic Church in Ecuador more power than it had exercised while Ecuador was a colony of Spain and more, perhaps, than it had enjoyed in any country of the Western world since the thirteenth century. It became virtually the supreme power, dominating and limiting the freedom of action of the legislature, the judiciary, and some of the executive agencies of the nation. It was exempted not only from control but also from interference by the civil authorities and was substantially given extraterritorial status. Papal bulls did not have to be inspected by the governmental authorities; the *Index* was to be observed by all schools, colleges, and universities; no organizations disapproved by the Holy See could exist; ecclesiastical courts were recognized as all-powerful in cases involving the church; education was solely entrusted to members of the clergy; and even the power of censorship was given to them.

García Moreno retired from the presidency at the end of his term in 1865, but when his successors proved unable to maintain order he resumed the presidency. In 1869 he had the constitution changed in such ways as greatly to increase the authority of the president, to extend his own term to six years, and to permit the reelection of the president. He gave Ecuador an honest administration, largely eliminating governmental corruption and improving the efficiency of the public service. The fiscal system of the country was modernized, a new mint was established, and the *sucre* rose to par with the dollar. A wagon road was begun in 1870 to take the place of the mule track which had previously been the only connecting route between Guayaquil and Quito. The eucalyptus tree was introduced from Australia and was planted on the mountain slopes to prevent erosion. Educational facilities were expanded at both the primary and secondary levels, though remaining in charge of the religious orders; and a polytechnic school, a medical school, an astronomical observatory, and an academy of fine arts were founded.

García Moreno thus carried out an ambitious program for the physical advancement of his country, holding that social and even religious progress were impossible without material progress. In this respect Ecuador made greater advances during the sixteen years of his rule than during all the rest of the nineteenth century, and his program of national development was later held up as an ideal for liberals. He devoted all his enormous resourcefulness and energy to his country's welfare as he conceived it, imposed on himself an eighteen-hour work day, and gave up his salary as president to the public service. But this program was accompanied by an intensification of his religious fervor and his clerical dictatorship. When the Italian armies captured the Holy City of Rome in 1870, carrying out their program of national unification, García Moreno sent a protest to the king of Italy thus acquiring a reputation throughout Europe as a champion of the Vatican. He deprived heretics of all civil rights, at his behest Congress voted gifts to the Pope from the public treasury, and in 1873 he induced Congress to change the name of Ecuador to the Republic of the Sacred Heart of Jesus.

But at the same time García Moreno kept the church in Ecuador subordinate to himself and often imposed his will upon it. As the temporal ruler of his country he sought to use the church as a force for righteousness, and to that end he undertook to improve the moral tone and quality of the religious orders. In doing so he ran afoul of the higher clergy in both Ecuador and Rome. Of course, his clerical program antagonized the Liberals and the Freemasons who conspired against him both inside and outside the country from their places of exile, particularly in Colombia and Peru. Of these none was more implacable or more eloquent than Juan Montalvo, an indefatigable champion of freedom. After García Moreno's reelection to the presidency in 1875 for another six-year term he was attacked on the steps of the government palace in Quito by an assassin armed with a machete and was hacked to pieces. Montalvo later boasted, "It was my pen that killed him."

Despite the murder of García Moreno the Conservatives, strongly inclined to clericalism, remained dominant in Ecuador for the next twenty years. The same conservative-clerical reaction occurred in Colombia, developing somewhat later than in Ecuador and lasting longer. There Conservative opposition to the dominant Liberal party was directed particularly against the so-called Ríonegro constitution by which the Liberals had consolidated their political position in 1863. Conservatives objected strongly both to the anticlerical and to the decentralizing features of that constitution, believing that both a

strong church-state and a strong state-church were essential to national prosperity, or at least to their own prosperity. This constitution served Colombia,
however, and kept the Liberals in power for twenty-three years. But it so
weakened the central government that during that period of Liberal rule the
maintenance of domestic peace and order became almost impossible. Since
the constitution was adopted without either the contributions or the concurrence of the Conservatives and since it could be amended only by unanimous
vote of the Senate, neither it nor the successive Liberal governments which
came to power under it could provide an administration that was adapted to
Colombia's changing needs.

During the two-year administration of the last Liberal president in this
period, Rafael Núñez, who had played a leading role in the preparation of
the Ríonegro constitution and who was first elected president in 1880, Colombia fell into a destructive civil war, which continued through the two-year
administration of his successor. During the period when Núñez was out of
the presidency, being unable under the constitution to serve an immediately
succeeding term, he resided in Europe and while there apparently decided to
swing over to a conservative-clerical position, being no more inhibited by
considerations of consistency than had been his predecessor Tomás Cipriano
de Mosquera, who, as mentioned above, had made an alternate shift from
conservatism to liberalism. Writing from Europe to the press of his native
city, Cartagena, Núñez suggested the need for a new party possessing a
different political outlook and dedicated to a reorientation of the country
along not only political but also moral and religious lines. Without making
clear that he now favored a conservative-clerical position he allowed the
Liberals to reelect him in 1884 while he was still in Europe. After taking office
he immediately began to organize a conservative-clerical party with the
object of establishing a thoroughly centralized government, eliminating the
federal system, restoring order and financial stability to the country, and
bringing the church back into politics and education. His program was very
similar to the program earlier carried out in Ecuador by Gabriel García
Moreno.

Núñez was now accepted as the leader of the Conservative party, but was
denounced as a traitor by the Liberals who charged him with abandoning his
lifetime principles in order to remain in power. They determinedly started
a serious revolution against him in 1885 which, however, was so completely
suppressed by Núñez that he was able thereafter to ignore the national
Congress and to govern by means only of a national council whose members
agreed with him on Colombia's need of a strong central government and who
were favorable to his program of action. This program included a new constitution, which the national council, after first confirming Núñez in the
presidency, proceeded to draw up. The national council which drafted it was
composed of eighteen men whom Núñez and his governors arbitrarily selected
from among his followers in the Conservative party without consulting public

opinion. Their intellectual leader was Miguel Antonio Caro, who was an eloquent crusader against the Ríonegro constitution. Caro was determined that, as he said, sovereignty should no longer be divided among "the individual, the province, and the nation," but that instead authority should be unitary and the nation should be one.

This so-called Caro constitution, which was promulgated by Núñez in August, 1886, entirely abandoned the earlier Ríonegro constitution and established a system of political centralization for Colombia. It provided for weak legislative powers but gave large powers to the president, who was to be elected for a six-year term and who was given the authority to supplement legislation by issuing decrees. The Roman Catholic Church was closely identified with the national government and was to be protected by it. The doctrines of the church were to form the basis of all public education. In this new constitution for the Republic of Colombia, changed from the "United States of Colombia," the states no longer counted for much; they were reduced to the status of departments headed by governors appointed by the president. For the better maintenance of order the army was given first priority on the budget.

Under this constitution Núñez served as president or virtual dictator of Colombia until his death in 1894, but because the high altitude of Bogotá did not agree with him he spent most of his time in Cartagena, leaving the nominal government in the hands of the vice president. In 1887 he signed a concordat with the Vatican which greatly strengthened the church in relation to the state and made it virtually a state within a state. The church was placed in charge of primary and secondary education and was given opportunities to take part in politics. The Jesuits were, of course, readmitted. But this concordat and the continued Conservative domination of the country encountered persistent opposition from the Liberals who had maintained almost uninterrupted control of the country for more than thirty years before Núñez and who were loath to give it up, particularly through such a fortuity as their president's conversion to conservatism. As a result the Conservatives experienced great difficulty in maintaining peace and order. In 1899 the Conservative-Liberal rivalry erupted in the most disastrous civil war in Colombian history—the so-called "War of 1,000 Days"—which was not brought to an end until November, 1902, in a peace settlement concluded on board the United States battleship *Wisconsin*. But the Conservatives survived even this civil war and continued in power until 1930, and the constitution of Caro under which they governed Colombia was not superseded until 1936.

In Venezuela, liberalism, in the nineteenth-century sense of the term, had a somewhat longer tenure of power than in the other two component parts of Gran Colombia already discussed. There it was maintained in power, as in Mexico, by a liberal *caudillo*. Antonio Guzmán Blanco was the son of the founder of the liberal *El Venezolano,* which vigorously assailed the old conservative Páez oligarchy. Liberal and federal principles of government had been adopted in the Venezuelan constitution of 1864, but the Liberal government was temporarily ousted from power four years later by the Conservatives. At this juncture Guzmán launched a revolution against the Conservatives and established himself in power in Caracas by force in 1870 at the age of forty-one, acting in the name of the liberal constitution. He remained, whether in the presidency or in private life, the supreme power in Venezuelan politics for the ensuing eighteen years and during that period carried out many phases of the liberal program, particularly its anticlericalism. A grand master of the Masonic order, he legalized civil marriages, required civil registration of births and deaths, granted toleration to Protestant sects, suppressed monastic orders, and confiscated church property. In general his administration was able and effective, emphasizing order, honest government, financial stability, and modernization of the country. Civil disturbances were reduced to a minimum, a new monetary system was established based on the *bolívar* as a unit of currency, the nation was put on a gold basis, public education was made free and compulsory, and a network of highways and railroads was constructed.

But the centralized, dictatorial nature of Guzmán Blanco's rule nullified the spirit if not the letter of the decentralized, federal constitution of 1864. A strong, able, and energetic president, though dedicated wholeheartedly to liberal principles, was nevertheless a liability to theoretical liberalism, because the methods which such a president found it expedient to use in advancing the liberal program—namely, the imposition of his authority, disregard of the wishes of the constituent states, and violation of civil rights—not only denied the practical validity of liberal principles but could be used against the liberals by the conservatives when they came to power. Such a president also, as Guzmán Blanco's career demonstrated, revealed that liberalism was not identical with popular government. In Venezuela the liberal program was carried out by the president-dictator in the interest of the country as he conceived it, but he employed the methods advocated by the conservatives in doing so. Liberalism was thus quietly and unwittingly betrayed by the very leaders who established it, yielding gradually to conservative methods and eventually conservative leaders. Liberals found that the methods which were necessary for effective administration were the very methods of centralized authority, disregard of minority rights, and respect for privilege and tradition which they deplored. Furthermore the liberals when in office naturally desired to perpetuate their own privileges and traditions and thus to make personal capital from the advantages which their tenure of office conferred.

Guzmán Blanco found that the office of the president could serve as a useful symbol of administration. He therefore had his statue erected in many plazas and public buildings as the leader who was the embodiment of the nation. He encouraged an idolatry of the presidency and of himself as president. When he had served seven years in the presidency he retired from office, turning his powers over to one of his associates, who, however, sought to remain in power beyond his constitutional term, the term having been limited to two years in 1874. Guzmán thereupon ousted him from power and resumed the presidency in 1879. At the expiration of his term in 1884, the president's tenure having again been changed—this time to five years—he surrendered the presidency to Joaquín Crespo. When Crespo's term ended in 1886 Guzmán Blanco again took over the administration, but soon afterward evidences of dissatisfaction with his rule began to appear. When he went abroad in 1888 he appreciated that Venezuelans were tiring of his arbitrary government, and he wisely decided not to return. In 1889 public demonstrations were staged against him by some of the people who had welcomed him back to power by noisy acclamation only three years before. His statues were torn down, and Congress declared against him.

More than any other Venezuelan ruler of the nineteenth century Guzmán Blanco deserved the gratitude of his country for his energetic, enlightened, and peaceful administration. He had given Venezuela almost two decades of orderly government and had paid off the foreign debt. But he had done little to prepare the country for self-government. His domination of Venezuela, extending from 1870 to 1889, was highly personalistic and worked to the advantage of the traditional oligarchy.

After the usual period of anarchy following the end of a strong rule the liberal oligarchy, now turned thoroughly conservative, reestablished its political control over Venezuela with the accession of Crespo to the presidency again in 1892. This military leader restored order and effective administration but was killed in battle in 1898 while trying to prevent the debacle and disorder which occurred under his mild-mannered successor. *Caudillismo,* exercised by strong leaders acting in the name of liberal principles but opposing change which would threaten the traditional oligarchic control, was the prevailing political system of Venezuela. It seemed well suited to the needs of the governing classes of that country. It had a minimum of ideological content but was the system which was dictated by considerations of practical politics.

Peru and Bolivia

In other politically unsophisticated countries of Latin America similar developments occurred after 1865: the principles of liberalism sometimes triumphed under liberal *caudillos* and then either were suppressed by a conservative reaction or were subverted by the liberal leaders themselves. *Caudillismo* was basically antithetical to the principles of nineteenth-century liberalism. And yet it seemed to be the only practicable system around which these countries could build their political life. The continued existence of the nation, which was considered synonymous with the perpetuation of the rule of existing oligarchies, was deemed to be dependent upon the maintenance of peace and order, which was possible only under strong-man rule. When liberal principles of a limited executive and the devolution of power from the capital outward seemed to be triumphant they were usually being undermined, either subtly or overtly, by the traditional privileged classes or by the inexorable prescriptions of political power. Political theories had to yield to political necessity, and party differences became indistinguishable.

In Peru sentiment favored a conservative, centralized government, partly because of the heritage of a strong monarchical tradition and partly because of the reaction against the anarchy which disfigured Peru's history in the years after independence. This type of government was provided in the constitution of 1860, but respect for constitutional arrangements of any sort was not strong enough to allow this constitution to mold Peru's future development. When President Ramón Castilla, who promulgated this constitution, retired from office in the following year Peru lapsed into a decade of anarchy. Constitutional provisions, it became apparent, were not adequate to provide stable government to a people who did not see the advantages of following any prescribed constitutional forms. Moreover, the physiographic divisions of Peru created regional particularisms and rivalries which made centralized government difficult.

A government dominated by civilians was tried in 1872 when Manuel Pardo came to power. It was his administration which, in an effort to secure additional national revenue to pay the approximately 12-million-dollar annual interest on Peru's foreign debt, made the exploitation and sale of nitrates a government monopoly in 1876, and then set in motion a chain of developments which led to the War of the Pacific. That war, which plunged Peru again into anarchy and bankrupted its treasury, fixed a military dictatorship upon Peru under Gen. Andrés Cáceres in 1886 and led to the mortgaging of many of its assets to foreign bondholders, mostly English. Not until 1895 did civilians again get control when Nicola de Pierola overthrew the government and made himself president. The authority of the *Civilista* party which thus came to power was directed toward preserving the interests of the small upper class of *hacendados* from whom its power was derived. The methods which members of this class used in extending their landed power at the expense of the Indian communities are dramatically described in the novel published in English under the title *Broad and Alien Is the World* by Ciro Alegría. The tradition of arbitrary, centralized government persisted in Peru into the twentieth century, resting upon the basis of the conservative constitution of 1860.

Bolivia, too, after her defeat in the War of the Pacific continued under conservative domination during the remainder of the nineteenth century. The constitution of 1880 provided for a centralized type of government and conferred large powers upon the president, whose term of office was fixed at four years. Congress, however, was permitted to pass measures over the president's veto by a two-thirds majority. Roman Catholicism continued to be established as the only religion of the country. Between 1825 and the end of the century Bolivia experienced over sixty revolutions and six presidents were assassinated.

Bolivian politics can be explained in terms not of theories and principles of government but only of personalities and regional rivalries. The tradition of rule by a military leader was strong and almost invariably prevailed in the selection of presidents down to 1899. The interests of the privileged few were the primary concern of government. Local interests of a conservative nature strongly entrenched in politics in Oruro, Cochabamba, and Sucre successfully opposed the nationalist and centralizing pressures exerted by the government in La Paz, which was the nominal capital of the country. They were so successful that the government itself was physically divided, the president and Congress having their headquarters in La Paz and the supreme court in Sucre.

Paraguay and Uruguay

Equally unstable and uninfluenced by considerations of liberal and conservative theory in the latter third of the century were the governments of Paraguay and Uruguay. The tragedy of Paraguay's defeat at the hands of Brazil, Argentina, and Uruguay in 1870, brought on by the arbitrary one-man rule of Francisco Solano López, inspired a governmental reorganization there which took form in the constitution of 1870. But this attempt at the establishment of constitutional government along liberal republican lines did not accord with the realities of Paraguayan politics and remained largely doctrinaire. Revolutions were chronic, and almost no president completed his term of office. But the alternation of political power among the leaders of the various groups in the capital, Asunción, calling themselves by various political names and representing the small upper class in this predominantly pastoral country, had little effect upon the life of the great majority of the Paraguayan population.

Uruguay's peaceful development was hampered not only by its insecure status as a buffer state between Argentina and Brazil but also by persistent party feuding between the almost equally divided *Blancos* and *Colorados*. As a result its career was turbulent and disorderly. Of its twenty-five presidents who served between 1830 and 1903 nine were forced out of office, two were assassinated, one was seriously injured, ten faced revolutionary situations, and only three completed quiet administrations. The *Colorados,* who were the urban party of the merchant and professional classes, came to power in 1865 under Venancio Flores with the aid of Brazil and continued in power throughout the remainder of the century, though their power was constantly challenged and often threatened by revolutionary uprisings by the *Blancos*. Their *Blanco* opponents, who drew their strength from the conservative rural population and the clerical elements, opposed Brazilian interference and represented themselves as the national party. But there was little ideological difference between the parties, politics being largely a vain struggle of the "outs" against the "ins." After the *Colorados* came to power they almost necessarily strengthened the central government, thus giving the *Blanco* opposition an opportunity to acquire a reputation as a liberal party opposing a strong central government and the dominance of the capital city, Montevideo.

In 1872 after two years of bloody civil war the *Colorados* bought off their *Blanco* adversaries to remain in power, granting a generous amnesty and permitting the *Blancos* to take over the administration of four of the fifteen territorial units or departments of the country. For a decade after 1876 the *Colorados* governed through a military despotism. They observed the letter of the constitution but ignored its spirit. Their opponents, thus deprived of many of their constitutional liberties, became almost fanatical in their opposition. Their guerrilla warfare against the *Colorados* was sympathetically described for English readers by the Victorian novelist W. H. Hudson in his classic *The Purple Land,* first issued in 1885. They entrenched themselves in military positions in the sparsely settled frontier regions of the country, sometimes using the territory of neighboring states as bases of operations against the *Colorado* government.

At the same time an Uruguayan intellectual, José Pedro Varela, determined upon another method of countering the successive dictatorship and anarchy that disfigured his country. Impressed by the educational system of the United States, which he had visited, he persuaded the current dictator, Col. Lorenzo Latorre, to allow him to draw up a law in 1877 establishing an educational system. His purpose was to change the social thinking of Uruguayans in order to make future dictatorship impossible. The school system thus established became a powerful center of rationalism, anticlericalism, and Positivism, working slowly to produce the social transformation that occurred in Uruguay in the twentieth century.

After the election of 1886 the new president, Gen. Máximo Tajes, began to weaken the military influence in the government and to give it a civilian complexion. But this was changed in 1897 when President Juan Idiarte Borda was assassinated and the executive power passed into the hands of the president of the Senate, Juan Lindolfo Cuestas. The new president, less partisan than his predecessor, made plans with the *Blanco* malcontents but then proceeded, as the dominant *Colorados* had done in the 1870s and 1880s, to establish dictatorial government. In order to carry out the program which he deemed necessary for Uruguay he arbitrarily dissolved Congress, which was obstructing his plans, and summoned a new one, which confirmed him in the presidency for a four-year term in 1899. He thus provided the political milieu of a centralized benevolent despotism in which the national socialism of his successor, José Batlle y Ordóñez, took root.

The Caribbean "Republics"

In Haiti and the Dominican Republic, which jointly occupied the old Spanish island of Española, theory and principle counted for little, partly because of the heritage of political turbulence and partly because of inexperience with the machinery of sophisticated government and even lack of interest in it. Government in those countries oscillated between strong military dictatorship and anarchy, the former generally providing the order and stability which brought prosperity to the privileged classes, the latter pointing toward social and economic change and accompanied by violence and destruction. Regardless of constitutional prescriptions, the volcanism of pent-up resentments among the "outs" erupted in violent action against the dictator, who was the symbol of oppression; but when the "outs" succeeded in overthrowing him, their own political inexperience made them easy captives of the same social and economic forces which had determined the character of the preceding dictatorship. The old oligarchy was only replaced by a new one, and the same pattern of executive absolutism, repression of dissident groups, and finally a harvest of blind resentment and destruction continued. The conservative forces were generally lined up on the side of the ruler, but the anti-conservatism of their opponents could not be described as liberalism. The only principle of political action which was apparent here was the principle of *caudillismo*, or as it is more properly called in these Caribbean countries, *caciquismo;* it had been the principal method of government before the conquest and it continued, unlimited by political theory, to be the dominant form of government there throughout the nineteenth century.

In Haiti the so-called "liberal" regime of the mulatto elite, which began in 1870, lasted for nine years, and an attempt was made during that period to follow the requirements of the constitution on division of powers between the executive and the legislative branches. The first liberal president, Nissage-Saget, refused to coerce the legislative body when it disagreed with him, saying that "each ass should bray in his own pasture." But the liberals, representing only a small minority, could not successfully govern the country in the interests of their own class under such loose constitutional arrangements. Moreover, their political organization was racked by factionalism, which so completely paralyzed party action in Congress that the last liberal president, Boisrond-Canal, resigned in disgust in 1879. The period of rule by the liberal elite thus came to an end, and they almost voluntarily allowed the government to pass by default into the hands of military chiefs—leaders of the black masses—who represented other areas of the country than Port-au-Prince. The first of these was Lysius Salomon, who had been chief adviser to Soulouque. His ruthless proscription of the elite combined with the death of the opposition liberal leader Boyer-Bazelais in 1883 almost entirely ended liberal resistance to his rule.

But the only principle upon which Haitian government was based under Salomon and his military successors to the end of the century was simply that of the personal leadership of a chief over his ignorant and mercurial followers. As the leader gained power through the fanatical devotion of his followers, usually a majority of the army, he later lost it as a result of an unpopular action. The army pulled the strings of government, and Congress was the constant prey of successful revolutionists. Under these circumstances the executive was controlled by a victorious political faction, and the maintenance of order and the steady advancement of the nation's prosperity were rendered difficult. Though the forces of conservatism seemed to have triumphed, nevertheless the Haitians were still tormented by the French revolutionary ideals of liberty, equality, and fraternity which had infused their early history as a nation.

The political development of the Dominican Republic in the last third of the nineteenth century also demonstrated nothing more than unabashed personalism in government. After the withdrawal of the Spanish forces of occupation in 1865 the rival chieftains, Buenaventura Báez and José María Cabral, alternated with each other in the presidency, vying in attempts to betray either the territory or the financial resources of the country to foreign interests. Negotiations were carried on for a ninety-nine-year lease of Samaná Bay, a large natural harbor in the northeastern corner of the island, to the United States, and also for the annexation of the entire country to the United States, but these arrangements ran afoul of political opposition in the United States and had to be abandoned temporarily. In 1869, the Báez government negotiated a loan with a London banker named Hartmont which was thoroughly disadvantageous to the Dominican government, practically mortgaging the finances and even some of the coal mines and forests of the country to the bankers and giving them virtual control over the two most important customs-houses of the country. Against this background of national betrayal, political power oscillated between the "reds," led by Báez, and the "blues," led by Gregorio Luperón, until the shrewd and unscrupulous Ulises Heureaux came to power in 1882.

Heureaux, a full-blooded Negro of illegitimate birth, self-educated, and possessed of a large popular following, dominated the Dominican government for the next seventeen years. But his government became increasingly despotic, and under it the country slid into bankruptcy. It was already burdened with a heavy debt—the consequence of Hartmont's failure to carry out the terms of the loan agreement of 1869—and Heureaux's solution was to make an almost equally disastrous arrangement with the Dutch firm of Westendorp. When this company became involved in financial difficulties it turned over its Dominican interests in 1892 to a United States firm, the San Domingo Improvement Company, which eventually found itself holding a virtual receivership of a bankrupt government. It not only collected the customs but supplied the Dominican government with funds, supervised and financed the construction of the Central Dominican Railway, and, after 1895, controlled the national bank of the country. With the funds which Heureaux himself received from these arrangements he was able to sustain himself in power through bribing and intimidating his critics, and he thus maintained order and the appearance of national prosperity. But the government's credit gradually declined, the public debt approached 30 million dollars, and four years after Heureaux's assassination in 1899 the annual service alone on the funded debt amounted to almost the entire income of the government.

Central America and Mexico

The same kind of arbitrary personal rule prevailed in the Central American countries, usually directed toward the preservation of the power of the conservative elite—but not always, for, as in Mexico, the example and tradition of strong past liberal leadership by a *caudillo* existed. Such leadersh'p had been provided by Francisco Morazán and had been associated with the union of all the Central American states centered in Guatemala City. After the destruction of the Central American Confederation in 1839 the Central American states in general were controlled by the Conservatives for a generation. Whenever Liberals came to power as they did at various times in El Salvador, Honduras, and Nicaragua they were forcibly overthrown by the intermeddling efforts of Rafael Carrera, president of Guatemala. By reason of his interventionism and the cooperation which he received from Conservatives in neighboring countries a Central American union existed, to all intents and purposes, under Conservative auspices and was used to suppress political action by the Liberals.

Six years after Carrera's death in 1865 the Liberals returned to power by concerted action in Guatemala, Honduras, and El Salvador and began to restrict the influence of the old clerical and landholding elements in those countries. In Guatemala the real leader of the Liberal party, Gen. Justo Rufino Barrios, became president in 1873. Under his government the religious orders and the leading aristocratic families were expelled from the country, their property was confiscated, religious freedom was granted, and the Catholic Church was disestablished. But his guiding idea was the reestablishment of the Central American union under Liberal auspices.

President Barrios was thus characterized by a perspicacious observer in the 1880s:

He was dramatic in the simplicity and frugality of his private life, as he was in the displays he was constantly making for the diversion of the people. In striking contrast with the customs of the country where the garments and the manners of men are the objects of the most fastidious attention, he was careless in his clothing, brusque in his manner, and frank in his declarations. ... He had no confidants, made his own plans without consulting any one, and when he was ready to announce them he used language that could not be misunderstood. In disposition he was sympathetic and affectionate, and when he liked a man he showered favors upon him; when he distrusted, he was cold and repelling; and when he hated, his vengeance was swift and sure. ... He was the most industrious man in Central

America; slept little, ate little, and never indulged in the *siesta* that is as much a part of the daily life of the people as breakfast and dinner.[1]

The failure of the various attempts which had been made in the 1840s and 1850s to reestablish Central American union by voluntary action convinced Barrios and other determined unionists that they could accomplish their purpose only by force. Barrios at first sought to persuade the presidents of the other Central American nations to agree voluntarily to unite in a federation, but he received noncommittal answers or no answers at all from them. Finally, convinced that the people of Central America themselves favored a union, he announced early in 1885 that he had assumed command of the military forces of the Central American Federation, and he invited the other states to send delegates to a constituent assembly which would meet in Guatemala City in May of the following year. To this invitation he received a favorable response only from Honduras but encountered opposition from all the rest. This soon took the form of armed opposition as Nicaragua, El Salvador, and Costa Rica raised armies to protect themselves against what they regarded as Barrios's efforts to coerce them into union and to make himself dictator of Central America. Barrios and his Guatemalan forces were defeated by a Salvadoran army at Chalchuapa in April, 1885, and Barrios himself was killed. With his death his plan of creating a Central American union by force collapsed.

Barrios's liberalism followed the nineteenth-century liberal tradition in certain respects; it was anticlerical and it sought to restrain privilege in the interest of national unity. But at the same time he was the prototype of a new liberalism suggestive of that of Morazán and Juárez. Inspired by a grandiose conception of what a liberal leader could accomplish in remolding society, effecting economic and educational improvements, and creating new national strengths by the methods of centralized power usually resorted to by the conservatives, Barrios's liberalism was centralistic, militant, and expansionist in character. But he lacked the funds needed to carry out his ambitious program in education, agriculture, commerce, and railroad construction, and as his expansionist program for the recreation of Central American union rested upon force it was defeated by superior force. His death in battle was followed by thirteen years of political turmoil and anarchy in Guatemala which ended only with the establishment of the Conservative dictatorship of Manuel Estrada Cabrera in 1898.

Costa Rica, after separating itself from the Central American Confederation in 1839, was dominated by a few Conservative families until 1870 when Gen. Tomás Guardia made himself president. Between 1870 and 1882 he overthrew the old governing aristocracy and confiscated their property. His Liberal administration promulgated a new constitution in 1871, which remained the basic law of the nation until 1917. It established a unicameral

---

[1] W. E. Curtis, *The Capitals of Spanish America,* Harper & Brothers, New York, 1888, pp. 100–104.

legislature, fixed the president's term of office at four years, and made him subject to the limiting authority of a council made up of department heads. The obvious suitability of this constitution to Costa Rica's political needs and Costa Rica's generally high levels of living and literacy made its successive governments strongly averse to absorption into any Central American union.

In Nicaragua the Liberal cause was discredited by its support of William Walker's filibustering operations in the 1850s. After Walker's death in 1860 the Conservatives gained power and kept it until 1893, holding power there more than twenty years longer than in any other Central American country. The Conservative-Liberal struggle in Nicaragua involved few ideological considerations but revolved mainly around the intense rivalry between the two leading cities of the country, León and Granada, often taking the form of internecine warfare. León, a city of small landowners and professional people, became a center of Liberal party activity, and Granada, a more wealthy and aristocratic city, became a Conservative stronghold. During the period of Conservative domination after 1860 the capital was located permanently in Managua in the Conservative section of the country.

Politics in Nicaragua, then, depended more upon local rivalries than upon ideological differences or class distinctions. Indeed party lines had little meaning except in terms of traditional regional interests. To the perennial struggle of rival leaders for power was added, therefore, the element of *localismo* as a disturbing factor in Nicaraguan politics.

Under Conservative rule Nicaragua was governed by a succession of presidents who were content to maintain existing conditions and to work closely with the Catholic Church. They governed the country efficiently and well until a schism in their party made a Liberal victory possible in 1893 with José Santos Zelaya as president. But the new president, who dominated the country for the next sixteen years, was Liberal in name only, for he established a cruel dictatorship, granted lavish monopolies to his friends, many of whom were wealthy Conservative *Granadinos,* violated civil rights, and tortured and exiled his political enemies. Perhaps his only policy which was consistent with liberalism was his attempt to organize a Central American union by the method of intermeddling in the affairs of his neighbors, which, if it was more subtle than the method of force which Barrios had tried, was equally unsuccessful.

By the close of the nineteenth century, throughout Central America liberal principles of government were professedly followed and were incorporated in existing constitutions, but in all these five nations, except possibly Costa Rica, they were honored in the breach rather than in the observance. The prevailing system of government was *caudillismo,* which was sometimes directed toward imposing liberal practices of government upon unready populations but was usually content to maintain existing practices. Politics was the servant of the prevailing social and economic pattern of life and seldom dared to attempt to impose a new pattern. The powers of government were customarily vested in a strong military ruler who, regardless of constitutional stipulations, would be kept in office as long as he maintained order and did not infringe upon the interests of the established oligarchy. Party lines almost entirely disappeared or ceased to have any distinctive meanings.

Caudillismo became strongly entrenched in Mexico also during the last quarter of the nineteenth century under José de la Cruz Porfirio Díaz, but it was not, at least in the beginning, dedicated exclusively to the perpetuation of the existing ways of Mexican life. The example of the liberal leadership of Juárez was too recent to allow an immediate and complete swing to conservatism. Under the long Díaz regime the plans of the Mexican Positivists, the *científicos*, were carried into action. Disgusted with the "infinity of laws which had produced nothing but misery and social discord" they now resolved to try "an honest tyranny" with the hope of producing better results. The execution of their program was facilitated by the internal peace and order which Díaz established and by the appeal which a peaceful and orderly Mexico, enjoying good credit standing and efficient administration, made to foreign investors. Monarchical sentiment, which had long been a divisive factor in Mexico, had died with Maximilian, and after the long civil war the Mexican people desired a breathing spell of peace. Internal order was promoted by Díaz's policy of eliminating brigandage through the use of the *guardias rurales*. He took advantage of the general prosperity of the country to make prompt payment of the installments due on Mexico's foreign debt, thus eliminating sources of friction with foreign countries. By almost miraculously and unexpectedly making the first payment of 300,000 *pesos* which fell due on Mexico's debt to the United States a few weeks after he claimed the presidency he proved that his new government was stable and was rewarded with diplomatic recognition by the United States. He then proceeded, in accordance with the plans of the *científicos*, to encourage foreigners to invest their money in Mexico, and with this capital, coming largely from England and the United States, he accelerated the economic development of the country. Almost 2 billion dollars flowed into Mexico from abroad—one-half of it from the United States—during the Díaz period to develop and exploit the resources of Mexico. Agricultural yields were increased by the introduction of the latest technical improvements, modern scientific methods of mineral extraction were applied, and Mexico's new petroleum industry was developed until by 1910 it was producing about 4 million barrels annually. The result was a tremendous expansion in Mexico's foreign trade.

The Díaz administration committed itself to large projects of national economic development. When Díaz took office the only railroad in Mexico was the line running from Veracruz over the Sierra Madre Oriental to Mexico City. This line tying the principal port with the capital city had been largely responsible for maintaining the axis of interests between them which had existed since colonial days and which had given them a dominant position in the political and economic life of the nation. But Díaz now made possible, largely with foreign capital, the construction of a railroad network, which opened up new areas of the country and incidentally tended to break down old regional rivalries. By the close of the Díaz regime Mexico's railroad mileage had increased from 447 to 16,000 and railroad connections had been established between Mexico City and most of the state capitals. In 1906 when the minister of the treasury, Limantour, recommended the nationalization of the railroads, the Díaz government proceeded to buy most of them from their foreign owners and to form them into a coordinated national system. The expansion of Mexico's railroad system was facilitated by the establishment of a nationally owned iron and steel industry at Monterrey, which operated necessarily under tariff protection. This industry, thus sponsored by the national government in accordance with the doctrines of Mexico's Positivist economists, was supplemented by industrial development in other fields, particularly beer, textiles, and paper.

Another work of national improvement undertaken and actively pushed by the Díaz regime was the construction of a drainage system that would relieve the valley of Mexico, in which the capital was located, of the menace of floods. An earlier drainage project, the canal of Huehuetoca, which had been built by the viceroys in the late eighteenth century, was proving inadequate to drain off the surplus water that accumulated in the valley during the rainy season. The new system when completed in 1903 consisted of a canal twenty-two miles long and a tunnel more than six miles long which emptied into the Pánuco River and thence into the Gulf of Mexico near Tampico. This and other projects of national development which bulked large in the plans of the Positivists for Mexico were carried through to completion under the active sponsorship of the central government. If the results would have pleased the Juárez liberals in expanding the facilities and promoting the economy of the nation, the means and the agency used would have been repugnant to them, for under Díaz the individual states were completely subordinated to the national government. In this era of peace and prosperity Mexican liberalism was undergoing a change. Foreign capital, not local effort, was regarded as the means and centralized executive power the agency by which national strength was to be promoted.

In fiscal matters also national unity was achieved at the expense of the independence of the states during the Díaz period. The principal cabinet minister, Limantour, was oriented toward the outside world. Regarding foreign commerce as the basis for the nation's prosperity, he made it his main object to expand Mexico's contacts with all the leading commercial nations. The national interest in the expansion of commerce was asserted in 1886 when internal customs levies were abolished by constitutional amendment and the central government alone was recognized as possessing the authority to collect customs. Already efforts had been begun to centralize Mexico's credit and banking facilities. In 1884 a central banking system was established under the Bank of Mexico. All currency emission was made the responsibility of this bank in 1896. In the following year the central government by law assumed the power to regulate all state banking. As a further centralizing move in the interest of promoting foreign commerce Limantour refused to support the silver-mining interests of Mexico, who wished to keep Mexico on the silver standard as a boon to their industry. Instead, in 1902 he put Mexico on the gold standard for the first time in its history. By all these actions of the central government the powers of the states were gradually whittled away so that by the end of the nineteenth century the federal system remained little more than a fiction.

Mexico's policies were being shaped primarily in terms of its interests as an exporting-importing nation and its need of foreign capital. By 1910 Díaz could boast that the value of all United States investments in his country approached 1 billion dollars. As Mexico deliberately made itself a virtual colony of foreign capital, imported principally from the United States, it became, as the saying went, "the mother of foreigners and the stepmother of Mexicans." In order to secure foreign capital Díaz alienated and dissipated a large part of the nation's resources. In 1884 he reversed the old Spanish law which separated subsoil and surface-soil concessions and secured legislation which gave ownership of the subsoil with the surface title. As this law was carried out it enabled foreign investors to get possession of a large part of Mexico's mineral wealth. Other legislation made it possible for Mexico's agricultural land to be bought up and monopolized in large estates, often by foreigners. A law passed in 1883 gave one-third of all unsurveyed lands to those who would survey them, and under this law twenty-nine individuals and companies acquired about 40 million acres of land in return for surveying them. The mines, the forests, and the land of Mexico, thus held as monopolies often by absentee foreign owners, were worked by Mexican *peones* and the profits were drained out of the country in the form of dividends for foreign stockholders. With these foreign interests Mexican bureaucrats of the Díaz regime cooperated, receiving bribes and other favors from foreign concessionaires and themselves becoming wealthy in the process.

In an effort to regularize the landholding system, Díaz in 1886 required all landholders to prove title to their land, but many of the residents of Indian villages were unable to establish ownership of the land which they and their forebears had been cultivating for centuries. The Indian system of land ownership from preconquest days often did not recognize title in severalty or in fee simple, and among the Indian settlements the prescriptive right which came from long occupation was customarily regarded as adequate. But this did not satisfy the *científicos,* and when the Indian farmers failed to produce documentary evidence of their title, the government expropriated their land and then often allowed it to pass into the hands of wealthy friends of the president or to be bought up by foreigners. The Indian system of communal landholdings (*ejidos*), which had persisted since preconquest times, was therefore largely destroyed. In its place the *hacienda* system came to dominate Mexican agriculture. By 1910 the soil of rural Mexico was almost entirely held in some 8,000 private estates, among which the largest, consisting of over 6 million acres, was owned by the governor of the state of Chihuahua. Ninety per cent of the rural population of the country owned no land. Mexico had become largely a feudal state in which the *peones* lived in a condition of debt slavery, tilling for the benefit of others the soil which had formerly been their own. Mexico's national patrimony was thus either monopolized by a few or was thrown wide open to foreign exploitation.

In this process Mexican nationality was diluted and the national economy was directed by a small elite segment of the population—the "frock-coated" intellectuals of the capital. The *científicos* repudiated the aptitudes of the Latin race in order to develop the strengths of the modern industrial nations, particularly the United States. Though they pretended to educate Mexicans in the methods of science and to encourage them to develop the riches of their own country they largely left the exploitation of these riches to foreigners. Members of a Díaz oligarchy closely allied with foreign capital dominated the country, largely in their own interests and without responsibility to the electorate. This oligarchy was divorced from the life of the country. Suffrage was severely limited and the possibility of effecting changes through elections disappeared as the ruling oligarchy firmly controlled the machinery of government, which it professed to operate in accordance with scientific principles. But these principles were used virtually to enslave a large part of the population. Under them Mexico traded material progress for freedom.

The oligarchy, needing a subservient peonage as a labor force, did not believe in education or promote its expansion. Under the Díaz regime the area and facilities of education for freedom were, therefore, severely limited, and illiteracy and ignorance were widespread. Though Mexico gave a superficial appearance of prosperity and soundness, in matters of national culture and in things of the spirit it was retrogressing. Mexico's national interests were too narrowly conceived. A regime too long in power was failing to meet the real needs of the Mexican people and to adjust the nation to the new requirements of the twentieth century. The pseudo liberalism of the *científicos* operating under the protective authoritarianism of the Díaz oligarchy had become a narrow conservatism, hidebound and repressive. In its preoccupation with scientific efficiency in government administration the oligarchy had become blind to the needs of all Mexico. It was using Positivism only to justify the social and political prerogatives of a class. The social scientists of the Díaz regime had become the prisoners of their own dogmas.

Chile

Less overt but no less effective was the domination which the Conservatives exercised over Chile under the system of congressional government that had triumphed there in the civil war of 1891. Government still operated under the conservative constitution of 1833, which had continued virtually unchanged during the period of control by the Liberal Alliance. But the engrafting of the system of responsible cabinet government onto it as a result of the congressional victory ensured that the power of the traditional oligarchy solidly entrenched in Congress would not be challenged by a strong president with liberal leanings. The very attempt by the Liberals to carry out their program through strong executive rule under Balmaceda had backfired against them and resulted in the restoration of power to the Conservatives and that remnant of the Liberal Alliance which opposed a strong presidency. As power was decentralized under the new system it was exercised by the local political bosses, the landowners, and even the local priests, operating, as before, through pressures applied to the members of Congress. It was not given the gloss of scientific principles, as in Mexico, but rested on the reality of power exercised by the agrarian and mercantile oligarchy centering in the Santiago-Valparaíso area. Chile continued to be governed by the old forces of conservatism and right-wing liberalism which had dominated it since their fusion in the 1870s.

The principle of leadership by a national *caudillo* was now denied, and the presidents who were put in office by these forces after 1891 were colorless mediocrities whose policies were subordinated to the wishes of congressional majorities. The first was the naval hero of the civil war, Jorge Montt, not related to former president Manuel Montt. Installed in the presidency by a conservative–right-wing-liberal coalition, he carried through a monetary policy which, though it stabilized the Chilean monetary system, worked chiefly to the advantage of the bankers and conservative propertied classes who supported his administration. All outstanding paper currency, which had been highly inflated by the desperate Balmaceda, was now redeemed at its face value to the benefit of Chile's international creditors and exporting interests. At the same time Chile adopted the gold standard, and to the dismay of the laboring and debtor classes, the Chilean *peso* was made redeemable not only at its face value but in gold. These measures stimulated a new prosperity, based largely on nitrate, copper, and agricultural exports, but this tended only to enrich the already wealthy governing classes and to widen the gap between them and the manual workers who toiled in the mines and on the *haciendas*. As the nineteenth century ended, Chilean politics degenerated into small-time bossism. It was a game played without regard to principles but always unquestioningly in the interest of the agrarian and exporting oligarchy which controlled the country through its power in the urban centers of Santiago, Valparaíso, and Concepción and which maintained close relations with foreign trade and banking circles.

In most parts of Latin America, then, in the closing decades of the nineteenth century the liberalism with which the century had started, growing largely out of the concepts of the French Revolution and the events of the Latin American wars of independence, was under eclipse. It had been transformed into an authoritarian and centralized political system similar in many respects to the system of imperial Spain against which Americans had rebelled. Ideas of personal liberty and local self-government, which had taken root during and after the revolutionary movement, had been subverted either by the wealthy creoles who had supported that movement or by the leaders of liberalism themselves who, when they came to power as they generally did in the middle third of the century, often adopted the methods of their conservative adversaries. Underlying the political contest between them were the perennial factors of a weak nationalism, geographical particularism making for local struggles for power and internecine conflicts, and certain social and economic rigidities.

These rigidities included the traditional power position of the Catholic Church, which was strongly influential not only in central governing circles but among the rural workers and the womenfolk, the need for a large military force which would maintain order, and the heritage of authoritarian government carried over from the times of the conquest if not before. Besides, there was the necessity of maintaining Latin America's export position, which was dependent upon agricultural production. Political power was generally associated with wealth in land, and although the *hacendados* and *estancieros* might sometimes call themselves liberal and might even find the doctrines of liberalism advantageous to their economic interests they had an essentially conservative outlook. As they took over power in the name of liberalism they in effect subverted it. To this class the maintenance of social stability, constantly threatened by those elements in the population who took seriously the doctrines of the French Revolution or who aspired to reach the seats of power themselves, was an overriding objective, and it sometimes had to be achieved by the violation of personal liberties, the strong-arm methods of the dictator, and the forcible suppression of disruptive elements in the population. These were the methods which *caudillos* such as Morazán, Guzmán Blanco, Juárez, Barrios, and Balmaceda also found necessary in imposing their liberal systems of government, foreshadowing the methods which would be used in the twentieth century to carry into execution a changed program of liberal action against the old combined conservative-liberal forces. But these latter were still generally dominant when the nineteenth century ended.

Additional Reading

Bernstein, Harry: *Modern and Contemporary Latin America*, J. B. Lippincott Company, Philadelphia, 1952, chaps. 6, 29, 35.

Burgess, Paul: *Justo Rufino Barrios: A Biography*, Dorrance & Company, Inc., Philadelphia, [1926].

Carrión, Benjamín: *García Moreno: El Santo del Patíbulo, Fondo de Cultura Económico*, Mexico and Buenos Aires, 1959.

Ford, Thomas R.: *Man and Land in Peru*, University of Florida Press, Gainesville, 1955.

Franklin, Albert B.: *Ecuador: Portrait of a People*, Doubleday & Company, Inc., New York, 1943.

Galdames, Luis: *A History of Chile*, trans. and ed. by Isaac Joslin Cox, University of North Carolina Press, Chapel Hill, N.C., 1939, chap. XVIII.

Hudson, W. H.: *The Purple Land* (Uruguay), London, 1855, reprinted by E. P. Dutton & Co., Inc., New York, 1927.

Osborne, Harold: *Bolivia, a Land Divided*, Royal Institute of International Affairs, London and New York, 1954.

Tischendorf, Alfred: *Great Britain and Mexico in the Era of Porfirio Díaz*, Duke University Press, Durham, N.C., 1961.

Wise, George S.: *Caudillo: A Portrait of Antonio Guzmán Blanco*, Columbia University Press, New York, 1951.

XIX

Latin America and the Imperialism of the United States

After 1860 the political relations of the Latin American countries with the outside world were increasingly determined by the principles of the Monroe Doctrine. These countries became objects of heightened interest and concern to the United States as their trade and commerce grew, as their contacts with the outside world multiplied, and as their rich natural resources were thrown open more generally to foreign exploitation. As they played a larger role in the world's economy they began to bulk larger also in international diplomacy. But here they exercised mainly a passive influence. Their importance was due to the fortuitous circumstances of their raw wealth and their geographical location. These countries were not the shapers and determiners of international relations or even, in many cases, of their own foreign relations. They were important rather as the recipients of attention from foreign governments, foreign investors, foreign engineers, and adventurers of all sorts. In turn, Latin Americans exerted on these foreign elements the influence which the whale exerts on his captors. That the Latin American countries were not strong enough by themselves to counter foreign aggression was demonstrated conclusively by the Maximilian affair. Henceforth their principal reliance in this sphere had to be placed upon mutual rivalry among potential aggressors or upon the Monroe Doctrine.

Chilean–United States Relations

The events of the Chilean civil war of 1891 worked to England's advantage. The Chilean navy, which had been first directed by the English admiral, Lord Cochrane, in the war of independence, remained under the influence of the British naval tradition. In the struggle of 1891 the Congressionalists were supported by the British-oriented Chilean navy and they generally won British sympathies. They were, from the British point of view, fighting for a responsible parliamentary form of government such as that of Britain against the pretensions of a strong executive operating or seeking to operate under a presidential system such as that of the United States. The news reports which were sent out of Chile during the civil war were controlled by the British. They generally gave a favorable interpretation to the Congressional cause, condemned the United States for supporting a despotic government, and accused it of seeking economic advantages for itself in Chile.

From the viewpoint of the United States, on the other hand, the Congressionalists were rebels against the legally recognized government of Chile and must be dealt with as such unless and until they could establish themselves in power. Members of the United States colony in Chile headed by the Irish-born minister of the Harrison administration, Patrick Egan, became convinced that President Balmaceda would succeed in suppressing the rebellion, and Egan supported the president, as it seemed to the rebels, over and beyond the call of duty. Egan had suffered what he regarded as several social snubs by the British, and his actions as the duly accredited representative of the United States were given the worst possible constructions by the British-controlled news. He was even accused of speculating in Chilean foreign exchange. The civil war in Chile, then, in its international aspects, disclosed bitter rivalry between England and the United States, in which the United States associated itself with the presidential forces and therefore played a losing role.

The worsening of relations between Chile and the United States occurred as a result of several unfortunate incidents. Since the Congressionalists had no status as belligerents they could not buy munitions of war in the open market. Their representatives succeeded, however, in making a surreptitious or colorable purchase of some 50,000 rifles and 2 million rounds of ammunition in New York and had them shipped to California. There a Congressional vessel, the *Itata*, received the consignment and seized with them the United States deputy marshal, Spaulding, who having been tipped off by the Balmaceda government, was attempting to prevent the delivery of the consignment to the Chilean Congressional party in violation of the neutrality laws of the United States. The *Itata* was pursued by the U.S.S. *Charleston* as far as Iquique, but it eluded capture. Meanwhile the leaders of the Congressional party at Iquique, the rebel capital, were persuaded by the United States commander in Peruvian waters, acting under instructions, to agree that they would surrender the arms consignment when it arrived there. The *Itata* was accordingly delivered and was escorted back to California where it was subjected to libel action. When the Congressional party finally triumphed over the Balmacedists they were able to have the libel action quashed and the *Itata* returned to them. But they remained resentful at what they regarded as an attempt by the United States to handicap their struggling cause.

In matters involving cable communications and the right of asylum the Congressional party saw additional evidence of United States hostility toward them. When Balmaceda demanded severance of the west coast cable lines connecting the rebels at Iquique with the outside world, the cables were cut under the protection of United States warships. But the rebels were not to be thus deterred. As they gathered their forces for an assault on the Balmacedists they made a secret landing at Quintero Bay and prepared to advance against Valparaíso. At this crucial time they saw the U.S.S. *San Francisco*, Admiral Brown, steam up the bay on what they concluded was a spying expedition. Soon afterward the presence of their forces became known to the Balmacedists, and whether rightly or wrongly, they blamed the *San Francisco* for divulging their whereabouts to the loyal forces in Valparaíso. Not until later was it learned that the *San Francisco* had simply sent a report to Washington by cipher cable and that the news of the rebel landing must have reached the Balmacedists from other sources.

When the victorious rebels finally marched into Santiago at the end of August, 1891, they were not favorably disposed toward either the United States minister or the country which he represented. As they set up their new government for Chile they stationed guards around the United States legation to make sure that none of the numerous Balmacedists who had taken asylum in the legation escaped. They made no attempt to violate the right of asylum, which under Latin American law and custom is regarded as a sacrosanct right of defeated presidents and their followers. When Egan, however, made the exceptional request for safe conduct for the refugees out of Chile, to which they were not entitled under international law, the revolutionary government refused his request and in turn asked for his recall. But this request was not granted by the United States, and in January, 1892, Egan himself conducted the refugee Balmacedists under his own personal protection out of his legation and put them safely on board the United States cruiser *Yorktown*. In the following April when a counterrevolutionary uprising occurred and was quickly suppressed by the government Egan granted asylum in his legation to the two leaders of the defeated movement and then obligingly allowed them to escape.

Already in October, 1891, a more serious incident affecting United States–Chilean relations had occurred. Sailors from the U.S.S. *Baltimore*, Cap. Winfield S. Schley, granted shore leave in Valparaíso and behaving as sailors are sometimes wont to do in a strange port, were attacked by a Chilean mob. They appear to have been given no protection by the local police authorities, with the result that one sailor was killed and several others were severely beaten and taken off to prison. This incident provided the Harrison administration, which was preparing for an election campaign, with an opportunity to whip up national patriotic sentiment. Egan presented vigorous demands for an apology and reparations but was unable to get any expression of regret from Chile. Finally Harrison in his annual message to Congress on December 9 reported that the new government of Chile was disinclined to treat courteously with friendly nations. When the Chilean foreign minister objected to this phrase in a note on December 11 both Secretary of State Blaine and President Montt of Chile seemed willing to end the dispute by referring it to arbitration. But on January 21, 1892, after a

United States naval board of inquiry reported out certain depositions on the incident which were damaging to Chile, Harrison presented Chile with an ultimatum requiring an apology for the foreign minister's note of December 11 and reparations for damages. He demanded a reply from Chile within four days, that is, by January 25 On that very day, before the expiration of the ultimatum period, Harrison delivered a war message to Congress. But the President had to eat his words, for later that day and well within the time limit prescribed, the United States received a note from Chile which met Harrison's demands and offered to allow the United States Supreme Court to settle the amount of damages. Six months later the United States received a payment of $75,000 in gold from Chile for distribution to the families of the sailors injured and killed in the *Baltimore* affair and accepted it as full payment for damages done, thus closing the matter.

These incidents left a legacy of ill will in Chile toward the United States. The animosity which the new Congressional government there might have been expected to show toward the defeated Balmacedists was diverted rather toward the United States. After a general amnesty was granted in 1892 the only bitterness that remained was bitterness toward the country of Patrick Egan and Benjamin Harrison. The success of the Congressional party brought new prominence to Col. Emil Körner, the German chief of staff of the Congressionalist forces, and at the invitation of the new government, Germany supplied a military mission to Chile. Though the members of this mission did not assume command positions they worked as staff officers and instructors in the military academy and exercised a great influence over the development of the Chilean army, almost completely Prussianizing it during the next decade. In the Chilean navy, however, British traditions and training methods continued strong into the twentieth century.

The pecuniary claims of the United States against Chile continued to be a source of discord between the two nations. Of these the most troublesome was the claim of the Allsop Company—a United States firm which was organized in 1870 and which operated under the auspices of the Bolivian government. In 1876 this company, possessing claims against the Bolivian government, was granted certain mining concessions and also a certain percentage of the customs collected at the Bolivian port of Arica. When Chile seized Arica and the territory involved in the Allsop's mining concession, the company presented Chile with claims for damages. The rightfulness of these claims was acknowledged by Chile and payment was repeatedly promised, but no payments were made. Meanwhile the claims of Chile's own citizens and of Chile's European creditors similarly circumstanced were promptly paid. Finally Chile offered to settle with the Allsops at about one-tenth the value of the claim, which amounted by that time to approximately 2.5 million dollars. Thereupon in the autumn of 1909 the United States minister to Chile demanded either immediate payment or arbitration of the claim. Chile agreed to arbitration by Great Britain, which in the following year validated approximately 1 million dollars of the claim. From this time onward, relations between the United States and Chile became more amicable.

"Cuba Libre"

Meanwhile the United States was sharpening up the Monroe Doctrine to prevent European interventions in the Western Hemisphere. In 1869 President Grant grafted on it the no-transfer principle prohibiting the transfer of the colonial territory of any European nation in the Western Hemisphere to another European nation. But the United States did not invoke this principle when eight years later Sweden sold her Caribbean island, St. Bartholomew, to France. In 1895, however, President Cleveland and his secretary of state, Richard Olney, brandished the Monroe Doctrine to prevent Britain's seizure of territory in dispute between British Guiana and Venezuela. "Today," bumptiously announced Secretary Olney, "the United States is practically sovereign on this continent, and its fiat is law upon the subjects to which it confines its interposition." The intervention of the United States in this boundary dispute involving claims to territory in the jungle of northern South America disclosed a new and perhaps ominous interest in Latin America. It had the effect of bringing the disputants together in an arbitration agreement, which produced, at least temporarily, an amicable settlement of the dispute.

The wars of Spanish American independence, climaxed by the victory at Ayacucho in 1824, were only one phase of Latin America's struggle for independence. The struggle did not end with Ayacucho but has continued intermittently ever since, waged against changing foes and seldom reaching the overt phase that it attained at the beginning of the nineteenth century. For political subservience was succeeded after independence by economic subservience and even by an occasional danger of a restoration of political subservience. And two areas of the American world, Cuba and Puerto Rico, continued to be subject to both the political and economic colonialism of the old mother country Spain. The weak revolutionary movements in those colonies which flamed up in 1812 and again in 1823 had been easily suppressed by Spain.

But Cuban revolutionists, from their places of exile in the United States and Mexico, continued to agitate for the independence of these two remaining Spanish colonies. Notable among them was the poet José María Heredia, whose ode "The Cuban Star," letter "To Emilia," sonnet to Don Tomás Boves, and "Hymn of the Exile"—all published in Mexico in the 1820s— evoked tremendous enthusiasm among the younger generation in Cuba. The independence movement was also stimulated by the liberalism of the time and by the contagion of European revolution. But the creole agitation for independence and the various efforts, both official and unofficial, of the

United States to bring these islands into the Federal Union only seemed to harden Spain's determination to retain them. Finally in 1868 the Cubans themselves rose in insurrection against Spain's rule under the leadership of Carlos Manuel de Céspedes.

This Cuban rebellion, or Ten Years' War as it is commonly called, waged at the very doorsill of the United States, threatened to involve the Grant administration, first, because of annexationist longings in the United States, second, because of the interventionist inclinations of President Grant himself, and finally because of the indiscretions of the Cuban insurgents. In the *Virginius* affair of 1873 the rebels flagrantly violated the neutrality of the United States and misused its flag. As the war continued into bloody extremes Grant's secretary of state, Hamilton Fish, in an effort to prevent further destruction of life and property on the island, proposed joint mediation by the United States, Great Britain, France, Germany, Italy, Russia, and Austria. But Cuba's fate was not to be settled by this method. The insurgents there were finally compelled to accept an unsatisfactory peace in the Treaty of Zanjón in 1878.

The agitation for independence continued. It was stimulated by the publication in 1879 of *Cecilia Valdés*, a romantic novel critical of both Spanish colonialism and slavery by a revolutionary writer Círilo Villaverde, which soon became a Cuban classic. In Cuba "all literature, all culture even," as Pedro Henríquez-Ureña has observed, "was a kind, at times a very subtle kind, of rebellion." The intellectual emancipation of Cubans from Spain was encouraged by the writings of José de la Luz y Caballero and Enrique José Varona, who undertook through education to make their countrymen think of themselves as Cubans and thus to be ready for independence. They were impressed by the teachings of Herbert Spencer showing how evolutionary change contributes to individual fulfillment, and they stressed resistance to intellectual dogmatism as an essential preliminary to political freedom. A Liberal party (*Partido Liberal*, later *Partido Autonomista*) was organized by Rafael Montoro to press for insular autonomy, a political status for Cuba within the Spanish Empire similar to that of Canada and Australia within the British Empire.

In accordance with the Treaty of Zanjón, laws for the gradual liberation of slaves in Cuba were passed in 1881, and at the end of five more years— in 1886—slavery was abolished throughout the island. But the pledges given by Spain to provide the Cubans with better government were evaded, and the administration of the island continued to be corrupt and inefficient. The Spanish promise to give the Cubans the same constitutional rights that Spaniards enjoyed was denied when the new governor general, who took the place of the old captain general, was given the same authority that the captain general had exercised, including the authority to appoint the Cuban members of the Spanish Cortes. Taxes remained oppressively high, and Cuban resentment against Spain's misrule continued scarcely unabated. It was aggravated by the economic depression of 1893 which brought Cuba's economy to the verge of collapse and by the Wilson-Gorman Tariff Act, enacted into law by the United States in 1894. This act, imposing a duty upon foreign sugars imported into the United States, virtually completed Cuba's economic ruin.

Meanwhile anti-Spanish agitation was being carried on by the brilliant Eugenio María Hostos, who dreamed of the independence of his native island, Puerto Rico, not as an isolated nation but as a unit in a Caribbean confederation which would include also Cuba and the Dominican Republic. Much of the plotting and planning for independence was carried on from New York City and later Haiti. In Cuba the cause was sustained by the emotion-charged speeches and writings of the poet-pamphleteer José Martí and the field commander Máximo Gómez. Their forces in the island waged a punishing guerrilla warfare against the Spaniards from their hideouts in the mountainous eastern provinces of Santiago de Cuba and Puerto Principe.

Fig. 19-1. José Martí, apostle of Cuban independence, photograph by Gonzalo de Quesada. (*Courtesy of Pan American Union.*)

While they were thus stalemated, fearful to risk their cause to the arbitrament of open warfare and unable to gain control of an island port, they received no encouragement or assistance from the government in Washington.

But their prolific propaganda industriously ground out by the insurgent *junta* in New York and the horror stories from Cuba sensationally circulated by Joseph Pulitzer's New York *World* and William Randolph Hearst's New York *Journal* stimulated the war spirit in the United States. The cause of "Cuba Libre" became a matter of passionate concern to the public. Anti-Spanish sentiment was aroused by the disclosure of an intercepted letter written by the Spanish minister in Washington, Dupuy de Lôme, characterizing President McKinley as "weak and a bidder for the admiration of the crowd, besides being a common politician who tries to leave a door open behind himself while keeping on good terms with the jingoes of his party." Then the U.S.S. *Maine* was blown up in Havana harbor. Soon afterward McKinley demanded of Spain the complete abandonment of its *reconcentrado* policy in Cuba, the granting of an armistice to the insurgents, and negotiations for peace. To these demands he received a conciliatory response on April 10, 1898, in which Spain agreed to grant an armistice to the Cubans and to submit the dispute to the mediation of the Pope, but on the following day the President sent a war message to Congress calling for armed intervention in Cuba and alluding in only the last two brief paragraphs to Spain's latest concessions. The grounds justifying intervention by the United States, he asserted, were the interests of humanity, the protection of the "commerce, trade, and business of our people," and the need to terminate a conflict that was "a constant menace to our peace."

In response to McKinley's message Congress immediately authorized the President to use force for the purpose of establishing the independence of Cuba, but it appended to this declaration of war the so-called "Teller resolution" declaring that the United States disclaimed any intention of exercising "sovereignty, jurisdiction, or control over said island, except for the pacification thereof, and asserts its determination when that is accomplished to leave the government and control of the island to its people." The war ended four months later in the expulsion of Spain from the Western Hemisphere. In the protocol which ended the fighting on August 12 Spain agreed to evacuate Cuba immediately and to abandon her sovereignty over the island, to cede Puerto Rico to the United States, and likewise to transfer certain of her territories in the Pacific area to the United States. In the final peace treaty, concluded on December 10, 1898, Spain was obliged to confirm these conditions and in addition to cede the whole of the Philippine Islands to the United States.

The reactions of Latin Americans to the war between Spain and the United States were mixed. Their antipathy to the mother country, carried over from the days of their own struggle for independence, impelled them toward sympathy with the Cubans and Puerto Ricans in their similar struggle for independence. At the same time their feelings of resentment against Spain had been quieted by the passage of time. The wars of independence had been the work of a minority, and the descendants of even this rebellious minority had come to realize during the intervening three-quarters of a century that they were, after all, descendants of the *conquistadores,* cousins-german of the once hated *peninsulares,* and with them heirs of Spanish culture. *La Leyenda Negra* or the Black Legend of Spain's unparalleled colonial iniquities had been reexamined and found inaccurate in many respects. Though Latin Americans therefore rejoiced that Cuba finally aspired to join their ranks as an independent Spanish-speaking nation they became apprehensive over the turn of events in 1898, which appeared to result simply in the substitution of the United States for Spain as a colonial power over Latin American peoples. The removal of Spain from the hemisphere led to a revival of interest in Spanish culture in Latin America and a new idealization of the Spanish tradition. It also aroused fears about the possible future course of the United States.

These fears appeared to be justified when the United States not only accepted Puerto Rico as a colony, obviously not destined for statehood in the Union, but established a protectorate over Cuba and made war against Spanish-speaking *independentistas* in the Philippine Islands, led by Emilio Aguinaldo. The United States, instead of acting only as a midwife of Latin American independence, had become a baby snatcher. When the United States terminated its military occupation of Cuba in 1902 it required the new, supposedly independent government there to agree in the Platt amendment not to enter into any treaty or other compact with a foreign power which would impair its independence or to contract any public debt which it could not service out of its current income. The United States also insisted upon its "right to intervene for the preservation of Cuban independence" and for "the maintenance of a government adequate for the protection of life, property, and individual liberty," and upon the right to purchase or lease certain lands in Cuba for coaling or naval stations. Cuban protests against this arrangement had no effect, but Cuba's feelings were mollified by tariff concessions by the United States in the following year which gave the island the advantage of a 20 per cent reduction on sugar and other agricultural products sent into the United States.

The Panama Canal

Meanwhile, interest in the possibilities of constructing a canal through the isthmus connecting North and South America was reviving. At various times for almost four hundred years projects for building such a canal as an aid to commerce had been broached. The Panama Railroad, completed in 1855 and financially profitable for its backers almost from the beginning, demonstrated the commercial advantages of transisthmian transportation.

Toward the end of the nineteenth century the strategic need of a canal was shown by the voyage of the U.S.S. *Oregon* around the southern tip of South America to join the rest of the United States fleet in operations against Spain in Caribbean waters. A canal through the American isthmus would have rendered the long voyage of the *Oregon* unnecessary and in the future would vastly increase the mobility of the United States fleet and, consequently, its ability to fight a two-ocean war. In 1901 the impediment of the Clayton-Bulwer Treaty to the construction of such a canal by the United States was removed by the conclusion of a new treaty, the Hay-Pauncefote Treaty, with Great Britain. The United States was now free to acquire a preponderant position in the Caribbean.

It now took up the transisthmian canal project in earnest. Of the four feasible routes, the Tehuantepec, Nicaragua, Panama, and Atrato River routes, named from north to south, the Nicaragua and Panama were judged the most eligible. After much debate the Panama route was finally adopted by the United States Congress, provided that satisfactory arrangements could be made with Colombia, of which Panama was a province, and also with the new Panama Canal Company, the residuary legatee of the old French company of Ferdinand de Lesseps, whose efforts to construct a canal across the Isthmus of Panama had ended in failure in 1880.

Satisfactory arrangements were made with the company, but the Colombian Senate, which had the constitutional right to pass upon the Hay-Herrán Treaty granting to the United States a canal leasehold through Panama, proved recalcitrant. When the Colombian Senate adjourned at the end of October, 1903, without approving the treaty, a group of revolutionists in Panama, instigated by agents of the Panama Canal Company, launched an insurrection against Colombia, with the foreknowledge of President Theodore Roosevelt. Their revolution was protected from Colombian reprisals by the United States gunboat *Nashville,* Commander Hubbard, which opportunely arrived at Colón and prevented Colombian troops from engaging in land operations against the insurgents. Thus safeguarded, the revolutionary government was able to establish itself in power on November 6; it received recognition from the United States three days later. This intervention by the United States in Panama to help that province revolt from Colombia was justified by Roosevelt under the Bidlack-Mallarino Treaty of 1846 in which the United States guaranteed to Colombia the neutrality of the Isthmus of Panama "with the view that the free transit from one to the other sea may not be interrupted or embarrassed in any future time." But in the same treaty the United States had also guaranteed, "the rights of sovereignty and property which New Granada [Colombia] has and possesses over the said territory" (Article XXV)! By this latter article the United States had committed itself to the prevention of revolution in Panama, but Roosevelt now reverted to the original policy of the United States of sympathizing with revolutions in Latin America.

A treaty was hastily concluded by Secretary of State John Hay with Philippe Bunau-Varilla, a representative of the New Panama Canal Company and Panama's new minister to the United States. By this treaty Panama gave the United States a perpetual leasehold on a strip of territory ten miles wide across the isthmus and all the necessary facilities therein for constructing a canal. Work on the canal was begun immediately by the United States and reached completion in 1914 when interoceanic traffic commenced to move through the artificial waterway. The canal proved to be a boon of considerable importance to Latin America, but the method by which the United States had acquired the right to build it rankled in Latin American minds and was hardly rectified by the gratuitous payment by the United States to Colombia in 1922 of 25 million dollars for the purpose of removing "all the misunderstandings growing out of the political events in Panama in November, 1903."

As a result of action by the United States the number of independent Latin American nations had increased to twenty between 1898 and 1903, but Cuba began its national career under military occupation of the United States and Panama was made a "protectorate" of the United States by the Hay–Bunau-Varilla Treaty. Thereafter, as canal construction proceeded, sponsored and financed by the United States government, successive administrations in Washington, whether Republican or Democratic, made it their dominant objective to strengthen the defenses of the canal in outlying areas of the Caribbean and to maintain political and economic stability there. To this end the United States gave a new construction to the Monroe Doctrine, established financial receiverships in several Caribbean countries, sent in Marine forces of occupation, and finally purchased additional territory in the Caribbean area. By all these actions it may have kept out foreign interlopers, promoted its own security, and ensured the stability of Middle America, but it also incurred the ill will of Latin Americans. No longer was the odium which Latin American debtors customarily feel distributed among many creditors. It was now focused almost solely upon the United States.

The Roosevelt Corollary

The so-called "Roosevelt Corollary" to the Monroe Doctrine, announced in the President's annual message of December 6, 1904, was provoked by a German-Anglo-Italo debt-collecting expedition sent against Venezuela in the winter of 1902–1903. If the purpose of the expedition, which established a "pacific blockade" of the Venezuelan coast, was to test the efficacy of the Monroe Doctrine it encountered no objections from the United States at the outset on this score. The intervening countries assured themselves in advance that the United States would not object to their use of force against the government of Cipriano Castro so long as it did not take the form of the acquisition of territory. When as a result Castro agreed to arbitration, the dispute was referred to the Hague Tribunal. In February, 1904, the court decided that Venezuela in discharging its debts must give preference to the claims of those nations which had used force against her. This decision put a premium upon the use of force by foreign creditors to collect debts owed them by an American state. It seemed to Roosevelt to jeopardize the Monroe Doctrine and to call for preventive action by the United States. In his message in the following December, therefore, he announced that "chronic wrongdoing, or an impotence which results in a general loosening of the ties of civilized society, may in America, as elsewhere, ultimately require intervention by some civilized nation, and in the Western Hemisphere, the adherence of the United States to the Monroe Doctrine may force the United States, however reluctantly, in flagrant cases of such wrongdoing or impotence, to the exercise of an international police power."

This Corollary was first applied by the United States in its relations with the Dominican Republic in the following year. In order to forestall possible intervention by the non-American creditors of that republic—Belgium, England, France, Germany, Italy, and Spain—and thus prevent a repetition of the Venezuelan incident, Roosevelt resolved to undertake the collection of Dominican customs revenues himself and with the proceeds to discharge the Dominican Republic's foreign obligations. He negotiated an agreement to this effect with the Dominican government and in submitting it to the Senate explained that "those who profit by the Monroe Doctrine must accept certain responsibilities along with the rights which it confers; and that the same statement applies to those who uphold the doctrine." It seemed to him "incompatible with international equity for the United States to refuse to allow other powers to take the only means at their disposal of satisfying the claims of their creditors and yet to refuse, itself, to take any such steps." But these "steps" which Roosevelt proposed to take in the Dominican Republic were not approved by the Senate. The customs-collecting features of the agreement were nevertheless put into effect by Roosevelt under a *modus vivendi,* and 45 per cent of the receipts were used to meet the current needs of the Dominican government and the remaining 55 per cent, less the expenses of the United States customs receivership, were applied to meet the demands of the Dominican Republic's foreign creditors. This arrangement, which was finally approved by the Senate in 1907 after substantial modifications by Roosevelt, made the United States the agent of the foreign creditors of the Dominican Republic.

To the delight of the European creditors of the Caribbean countries the United States now assumed the responsibility for maintaining the financial solvency, peace, and stability of this debtor area. When President Tomás Estrada Palma of Cuba, his vice president, and all the members of his cabinet resigned their offices in September, 1906, leaving no successor to the presidency, United States Secretary of War William Howard Taft, who had already been sent to Cuba by President Roosevelt, issued a proclamation establishing a United States provisional government over the island with himself as head. The United States continued to govern it until January, 1909. In the latter year it intervened to promote the success of a revolutionary movement in Nicaragua against President José Santos Zelaya. The execution of two United States citizens, Cannon and Groce, by the Zelaya government gave Secretary of State Philander C. Knox a pretext for declaring "that the revolution represents the ideals and the will of a majority of the Nicaraguan people more faithfully than does the Government of President Zelaya." This note, presented to the Nicaraguan *chargé d'affaires* in Washington, caused Zelaya's downfall and brought the rebel leader, Juan J. Estrada, to power. In 1912 the Taft administration responded to the importunate demands of a new administration in Nicaragua for support against a resurgence of the Zelaya forces by landing Marines and supporting the government there, as Secretary of State Knox explained, "for the benefit of the people of Nicaragua." Its position in that country was converted into one of quasi protector by the Bryan-Chamorro Treaty, signed in August, 1914, which authorized the United States "to take any measure necessary" in Nicaragua for the protection of both the Panama Canal and its rights acquired by the same treaty in a Nicaraguan canal. The United States, which had been responsible for establishing the Conservative party in power in Nicaragua, continued to maintain a legation guard of 100 Marines in Managua, and as the election of 1916 approached, the United States minister warned the Liberal party that his government would not recognize their candidate if he should be elected. The Liberals therefore abstained from participating in the election.

Many years earlier, in September, 1911, the Taft administration had landed 750 Marines in the Dominican Republic. Taft's representatives in the Republic forced the resignation of President Eladio Victoria on a threat that he would receive no further money from the United States–administered customs if he remained in power. In May, 1916, United States Marines entered Santo Domingo City to sustain the government of President Juan Isidro Jiménez against a rebel faction led by Desiderio Arias. They subsequently occupied other ports and several inland towns of the Republic. When later in that year Provisional President Dr. Francisco Henríquez y Carvajal issued a call for a new election which seemed certain to bring Arias to power Secretary of State Robert Lansing recommended immediate military occupation of the Republic. This recommendation was approved by President Woodrow Wilson, and Capt. Harry S. Knapp, commanding United States naval forces in Dominican waters, proclaimed "that the Republic of Santo Domingo is hereby placed in a state of Military occupation by the forces under my command." Dr. Henríquez left the country.

In the preceding year when President Guillaume Sam of Haiti was captured and torn to pieces by a mob, the Wilson administration had landed Marines at Port-au-Prince and assumed control of the country. It immediately concluded with the new president a ten-year treaty, later extended to twenty years, which established a financial receivership, subjected the local police to control by United States forces of occupation, required the government of Haiti, in terms reminiscent of the Platt amendment, not to surrender any part of its territory or "to enter into any treaty or contract with any foreign power or powers that will impair or tend to impair the independence of Haiti," and permitted the United States to "take such steps as may be necessary to insure the complete attainment of any of the objects comprehended in this treaty" including "the preservation of Haitian Independence and the maintenance of a government adequate for the protection of life, property and individual liberty."

By means of these arrangements the governments of several of the countries fronting on the Caribbean, operating either as protectorates of the United States or in close cooperation with it, were able to handle adequately the claims of their European creditors and to avoid intervention by non-American nations. As the international rivalries in Europe sharpened toward World War I, the Caribbean area was therefore saved from involvement in them. At the same time the area became increasingly interesting to private United States capital, which, encouraged by the government in Washington, moved in to replace non-American capital. Cuba, for example, though freed after 1909 from overt political control by the United States, became an economic dependency of railroad, mining, sugar, and tobacco interests centered in New York. Cuban land was sold to some of these interests at 10 cents per *caballería* (33½ acres), and Cuban peasants became dependent upon United States companies for their education, recreation, and food. A factor of the highest importance affecting the international relations of not only the Caribbean and Central American countries but also the Latin American countries generally was the increasing stake of the United States in their area. That stake was determined both by the strategic interests of the United States in the Panama Canal then nearing completion and by its financial penetration of the area. The political expression of its stake in the area was the new twentieth-century version of the Monroe Doctrine called the Roosevelt Corollary.

As a result, the Caribbean and Central American countries were largely dominated by non-Latin American peoples. Here more colonial territories belonging to foreign governments were found than in any other part of the hemisphere. Puerto Rico was governed as a territory of the United States, and it was rarely considered that she was being readied for statehood in the Union. The Danish West Indies, lying east of Puerto Rico, were purchased by the United States, mainly for strategic purposes, in 1916 for 25 million dollars and were governed as a territory under the name Virgin Islands. The Leeward and Windward Islands, which swept in a wide semicircle southeast from the Virgin Islands to Trinidad, were monopolized by the British, French, and Dutch and were governed by them as colonial dependencies. The island of Jamaica and the mainland area of Belize (British Honduras) were also controlled by Britain.

Under the Roosevelt Corollary to the Monroe Doctrine the island republics of the Caribbean area were safeguarded against financial and political control from Europe, but they continued to be dominated by the United States. During the Wilson administration all three of them were occupied successively by United States Marines—Haiti in 1915, the Dominican Republic in 1916, and Cuba in 1917—under the policy of protecting United States investments in the area, establishing stable regimes there, and preventing intervention by European governments. Among the isthmian nations Panama remained under the protection of the United States as provided in the treaty of 1903 and in pursuance of that treaty was forced by Secretary of State Charles Evans Hughes in 1921 to accept an arbitral award unfavorable to her involving Costa Rica's claim to the Coto region on the Pacific side of the isthmus. Nicaragua, which had been occupied by United States Marines in 1911, continued under their control. The refusal of the Wilson administration and of Nicaragua to accept the award of the Central American Court of Justice upholding the claims of Costa Rica and El Salvador under the Bryan-Chamorro Treaty of 1914 caused the death of the Court in 1918. Mexico was threatened with similar control by the United States in 1914 when the port city of Veracruz was seized by United States forces in an effort to prevent the landing of a cargo of German arms intended for the revolutionary government of President Huerta. After Huerta withdrew from the presidency, the government of Venustiano Carranza which succeeded him was recognized by the United States in late 1915.

The nationalism of all the Caribbean peoples was stimulated by the acts of intervention by the United States, but their resistance to pressures from outside was partially mollified by the abandonment by the United States of some of the more overt and objectionable features of its imperialism, as, for example, the withdrawal of United States forces from Cuba in 1922, from the Dominican Republic in 1924, and from Nicaragua in 1925. The continued intervention of the United States in Latin America appeared to be incompatible with the Monroe Doctrine, which had been newly characterized as a "regional understanding" in the Covenant of the League of Nations. But this characterization stemmed from a substantial amount of wishful thinking on Wilson's part. Since it obviously overlooked the fact that the existing degree of political stability in the Caribbean countries did not meet the requirements of either United States strategy or business interests, the United States soon reverted once again to the Roosevelt Corollary. The Platt amendment for Cuba was neither withdrawn nor modified, and United States Marines were sent back into Nicaragua in 1927 to restore order. Elections in Nicaragua continued to be supervised by the United States until 1933. Haiti continued to be occupied by United States Marines until 1934, Panama remained under a United States protectorate until 1936, and the Dominican Republic was a financial protectorate of the United States until 1941. These interventions produced strong resentment against the United States, particularly in the Caribbean area but also throughout the South American continent, encouraging sentiments of Hispanic-American solidarity and anticolonialist movements there.

The five Central American nations, in an effort to promote the peace and stability of their area, accepted an invitation of the Harding administration to a conference which met at Washington in 1922–1923. There they agreed among themselves to reconstitute the defunct Central American Court of Justice for the settlement of judicial disputes between them and not to recognize new governments which established themselves in power in their countries by revolutionary means. For the duration of the latter agreement, that is, until 1934, they received the support of the United States, which undertook to embargo arms shipments from its territory to revolutionary forces in those countries. This policy was applied for the benefit of the government of Honduras in 1924 and of Nicaragua in 1926, and was even applied gratuitously by the Franklin D. Roosevelt administration on behalf of the government of Cuba in 1934. But under this policy, established governments were in effect given substantial protection in the commission of whatever irresponsible acts they chose to take and were enabled to act arbitrarily without danger of being overthrown. In Nicaragua, for example, Adolfo Díaz, who was backed by the United States, thus maintained himself in the presidency from 1926 to 1929 against strong opposition from Dr. Juan B. Sacasa and Gen. Emiliano Chamorro, both of whom incurred Washington's displeasure. In Cuba Gen. Gerardo Machado was similarly able to retain the presidency from 1924 to 1933. But this policy aroused increasing bitterness against the United States not only in the countries in which it was applied but throughout Latin America.

Additional Reading

Adler, Selig: "Bryan and Wilsonian Caribbean Penetration," *Hispanic American Historical Review,* vol. 20, pp. 198–226, 1940.

Duval, Miles P., Jr.: *And the Mountains Will Move: The Story of the Building of the Panama Canal,* Stanford University Press, Stanford, Calif., 1947.

————: *Cadiz to Cathay: The Story of the Long Diplomatic Struggle for the Panama Canal,* 2d ed., Stanford University Press, Stanford, Calif., 1947.

Hill, Roscoe R.: *Fiscal Intervention in Nicaragua,* Paul Maisel, New York, 1933.

Hudson, Manley O.: "The Central American Court of Justice," *American Journal of International Law,* vol. 26, pp. 759–786, 1932.

Lindsell, Harold: *The Chilean-American Controversy of 1891–1892,* New York University Press, New York, 1943.

Livermore, S. W.: "Theodore Roosevelt, the American Navy, and the Venezuelan Crisis of 1902–1903," *American Historical Review,* vol. 51, pp. 452–471, April, 1946.

Mañach, Jorge: *Martí, Apostle of Freedom,* trans. by Coley Taylor, Devin-Adair Company, New York, 1950.

Millspaugh, Arthur C.: *Haiti under American Control, 1915–1930,* World Peace Foundation, Boston, 1931.

Munro, Dana G.: *The United States and the Caribbean Area,* World Peace Foundation, Boston, 1934.

Rodó, José Enrique: *Ariel,* first published 1900, 9th ed., Librería Cervantes de J. M. Serrano, Montevideo, 1911, Trans. by F. J. Stimson, Houghton Mifflin Company, Boston and New York, 1922.

XX

The New Liberalism

For reasons already suggested, the liberalism associated with such political figures as Santander and Mosquera in Colombia, Gómez Farías in Mexico, Errázuriz in Chile, and Sarmiento in Argentina became sterile and doctrinaire as the nineteenth century advanced and became indistinguishable in most respects from the conservatism which it theoretically opposed. Never much concerned with social problems it expended its energy in usually fruitless struggles over religious, constitutional, and legal matters. Liberals were primarily concerned with combatting the abuses of power by the conservatives rather than charting original programs of political action. Living by constitutions in force and exalting property rights over human rights, liberals substantially merged their interests with those of the conservatives to defend unwritten tradition and the prevailing social, economic, and political system. With this objective in view they emphasized the importance of constitutional forms, the sovereignty of law, and respect for the rights of property. They believed that national progress would come through gradual improvement of morality, laws, and education for citizenship. Never a revolutionary doctrine, liberalism as it came to power and cooperated with the forces of the *status quo* lost much of its fervor even for evolutionary change. The creed of the nineteenth-century liberals called for much liberty but little democracy. Even their humanitarianism was transmuted by Positivism into a demand for increased governmental intervention in the life of individuals. As liberalism became scientific it became authoritarian and doctrinaire. Everywhere the new Positivist liberalism exalted faith in progress and science. It influenced all aspects of life, from academic culture to economic activity.

Immigration to Latin America

Meanwhile, many parts of Latin America were taking on an increasingly international complexion because of immigration from the non-American world. During the latter part of the wars of independence the tide of European immigration had set in as enterprising British merchants and veterans of the Napoleonic Wars arrived. But the tide of European newcomers did not attain numerically sizable proportions until the important states of Argentina, Brazil, and Chile achieved a certain amount of stability around the middle of the century. As immigration swelled to a great stream after 1870 it not only accompanied but also contributed to the capital development of Latin America. Immigrants turned up simultaneously with the railroad, the refrigerator ship, the factory, and the power line.

The population of the area increased threefold or fourfold during the century, rising from an estimated 20 million in the early 1800s to a figure between 60 million and 80 million in 1900. Immigration accounted for about 13 million of the increase. Argentina received some 2 million Italians, 1 million Spaniards, and several hundred thousand Germans. To Brazil went about 1.3 million Italians and hundreds of thousands of Portuguese and Germans. Smaller but still considerable numbers of British merchants settled in Latin America's coastal cities, and French professional men moved into the capital cities of Rio de Janeiro, Buenos Aires, and Mexico City. These same foreign nationalities, though in smaller numbers, entered Chile, Uruguay, Venezuela, and Colombia. To Peru and Cuba came thousands of Chinese coolies, but they had a negligible cultural effect.

The newcomers preferred the countries which had temperate climates and an already large white population. Into the tropical countries, as for example, Bolivia and Ecuador, few immigrants went. The coming of large numbers of foreigners brought a fresh infiltration of European culture and ideologies, accentuating French, German, Italian, and even Spanish influences there, sometimes to the prejudice of the United States. European literary and artistic styles accounted for the rise of the modernist movement in Latin America beginning with José Martí's poem *Ismaelillo* in 1882 and continued with Rubén Darío's cosmopolitan *Azul*, first published in 1888. During the last two decades of the century literary currents in Latin America reflected, not nationalism, but the internationalism which was characteristic of the economy of the area. The imaginative writers "were as cosmopolitan in literature as their materialistic compatriots were cosmopolitan in business affairs." [1]

The new immigrants strengthened the white element in areas where the whites were already dominant, and as they tended to settle in the cities they swelled the urban proletarian class. With the English immigrants came new industrial techniques, new merchandising practices, and abundant capital. The Italians furnished much of the agricultural labor that transformed the Argentine provinces from grazing to wheat production for export and developed the coffee economy of São Paulo. The Germans, largely Lutheran in religion and industrious by nature, gave a new character to southern Brazil and south central Chile.

The France of Napoleon III having been discredited in the competition for Latin America by the outcome of the Maximilian affair, England and the United States remained as the principal rivals for position there. England, the

[1] Luis Monguió, "Nationalism and Social Discontent as Reflected in Spanish-American Literature," *Annals of the American Academy of Political and Social Science,* vol. 334, p. 67, March, 1961.

largest non-American occupant of lands in the area south of the United States, established also a commercial and financial preeminence in many parts of that area. English influence in the Argentine and the tide of English migration to that country had necessarily been checked during England's difficulties with Rosas, but after his overthrow the British government and British investors found the unitary *émigrés* who assumed positions of power in Buenos Aires quite cooperative. These unitaries, during their long residence abroad, had learned the advantages of material progress, and once in power they oriented Argentina toward the foreign world in order to share in the benefits of the Industrial Revolution.

As a result of foreign investment, the adoption of new types of agricultural machinery imported from both England and the United States, and the large influx of immigrant labor, Argentina experienced an agricultural revolution during the closing decades of the century. The city of Buenos Aires was modernized, new berthing facilities were built, streets were paved and gas lighting installed, and steamships were constructed for river traffic and for commerce with Montevideo across the estuary. With English capital, Argentina's railroad mileage was increased from only 460 miles in 1870 to 20,805 in 1913. The railroad out of Buenos Aires reached the Bolivian border in 1908 and Asunción in 1913. In 1909 the first transcontinental railroad connection was established between the capital of Argentina and the capital of Chile.

The new agricultural machinery introduced into Argentina included the thresher and the reaper; these together with imported barbed wire and windmills accelerated the opening up of the vast humid pampa. This level region surrounding Buenos Aires began to be converted from a grazing to a wheat area. As a result the area of land under cultivation in Argentina increased from 200,000 acres in 1862 to more than 60 million acres in 1914. Cereal production, in particular, began to assume new importance, and the exports of wheat exceeded imports for the first time in 1878 during Avellaneda's administration, foreshadowing an export trade that would later assume enormous proportions. But the expansion of cereal exports did not diminish the importance of Argentina's meat exports. The arrival of the first refrigerated ship at Buenos Aires in 1876 opened up new opportunities for meat exports, which increased in value from 11 million dollars in 1894 to over 90 million dollars in 1914. Argentina became one of the world's largest exporters of certain foodstuffs and raw materials, including sheep, cattle, flax, *quebracho*, cotton, wine, goats, beef, wool, wheat, oats, and corn.

For this extraordinary economic accomplishment foreigners supplied most of the capital and immigrants most of the skilled labor. Much of Argentina's export trade was produced by immigrant laborers who were induced to leave their European homelands by Argentine labor-recruiting agents and by the offer of generous transportation subsidies. "To govern is to populate," Alberdi had written in 1853 to encourage official support of immigration as a means of developing the economy of the country. So great was the influx of immi-grants into Argentina that one of her writers, Manuel Gálvez, paraphrasing Alberdi, sarcastically observed that "to govern is to Argentinize."

The contribution that immigrants made to Argentine life was well illus-trated by the ancestral background of Carlos Pellegrini, who moved into the presidency of the country in 1890. He was the son of an English mother and a French father, his grandparents were of Italian and other European origin, and he had not a drop of either Indian or Spanish blood in his veins. Be-tween 1869, when the first census was taken, and 1914 the population of Argentina made a more than fourfold gain, increasing from 1,737,000 to 7,885,000. In 1914 the capital city, Buenos Aires itself, contained almost as many people—1,571,614—as the whole country had contained forty-five years before. In this process of expansion Argentina became closely tied economically to England, largely because of the complementarity of its trade interests with that country, and came to be known as the "Fifth Dominion." But Argentina's cultural outlook was French, and social prominence was reserved only for those who had visited Paris.

In several of the Latin American nations into which the new immigrants came they constituted the basis for a new middle class gradually eclipsing the traditional middle class of intellectuals, artists, government employees, priests, and junior officers in the armed forces. In Argentina, Brazil, Chile, Mexico, and Uruguay they helped to bring about a technological awakening which stimulated industrial development and increased commercial inter-change with the foreign world. Settling largely in the cities, they not only accelerated urbanization but identified themselves more closely with the work-ing classes than the older elite had done. They therefore promoted in con-siderable part the movement for social welfare legislation, that is, for cen-tralization in the national government of the responsibility for the care of underprivileged elements in the population. This would eventually lead in some cases, as for example in Uruguay, to radical experiments in state capitalism.

In certain parts of Latin America the development of a strong national feeling and of centralized control was impeded by the continuing difficulties of transportation. In 1928 Brazil possessed only 19,796 miles of railroad. In Peru during the 1920s the trip from Lima across the Andes ranges to Iquitos, the principal outlet of Peru on the Amazon—a trip made by railroad, auto-mobile, pack mules, canoe, and finally a steamer for a total distance of 1,200 miles—required twenty-four days of hard travel. With luck a trip from the Colombian port of Barranquilla to the capital, Bogotá, by land, water, and railroad—a distance of 800 miles—could be accomplished in a little more than seven days. Venezuela had only 700 miles of railroad in the entire country. Many Latin Americans obviously had not yet felt the impact of the Industrial Revolution.

Social Stirrings in Chile

As the liberal forces fused with the forces of conservatism during the latter third of the nineteenth century in many parts of Latin America, they stressed cooperative party action as a step toward national unity. This was indicated even in the tendency to emphasize nationalism and unity in party nomenclature, as for example in the designation of the dominant party as the *Partido Unión Liberal* in Argentina after 1880 and the *Unión Liberal* in Mexico after 1892. But this united national action was narrowly construed. Nowhere was it based upon a full participation of all or even a majority of the national population in government. Government remained the monopoly of an oligarchy, which variously called itself liberal, conservative, or national, as required by local political exigencies. But this arrangement seemed unsatisfactory to certain nineteenth-century Latin Americans who conceived of both liberalism and nationalism in broader terms.

The basis for this new liberalism was laid in the closing decades of the century. Among the new liberals there was no reverence for institutions simply because they were long established, no unquestioning veneration for constitutional or even legal methods of achieving social goals deemed desirable, no intention of allowing vested property interests to eclipse the rights of persons either as human beings or as citizens. In the liberal movements headed by Morazán in Central America and Juárez in Mexico, and to a lesser extent in those led by Guzmán Blanco in Venezuela, Barrios in Guatemala, and Balmaceda in Chile, was foreshadowed a new type of liberalism, more broadly based in the people and dedicated to the French revolutionary principles of liberty, equality, and fraternity. These and other similar movements were influenced by radical theories of the rights of man and democratic equalitarianism, which were the heritage of the French Revolution. To them the processes of national action, strong executive authority, and power politics habitually employed by the conservatives and by liberal-conservative coalitions offered a fruitful means of obtaining their objectives. These new liberals deplored the fragmentation of the nation which domination by an oligarchy, whether conservative or liberal, had brought about, and they combined their advocacy of social and economic reform with a fervent nationalism. An integrated nation, broadly based upon a democratic public opinion which was thoroughly indoctrinated in the ideas of the new liberalism, was the goal of this movement.

But this remained merely an academic goal during the nineteenth century, unrealized in any Latin American country. Its appeal was limited to a small class of extremist intellectuals, but the basis for a much broader appeal existed in the prevailing social and economic milieu which was characterized by ignorance, illiteracy, poverty, and a social organization approaching almost a caste system. Within it was the possibility of social revolution. Genuine inversions of the social order rarely occurred in Latin America during the nineteenth century. Sarmiento, describing one phase of Argentina's revolutionary war against Spain, wrote contemptuously that "in less than 24 hours a fiddler had become a general, a lame cobbler was making laws, and a clown deciding the fate of a country." The movement for independence in Mexico passed through the same phase under Hidalgo, who as leader of undisciplined Indian masses was bent upon destroying the social order. A still better example was furnished by the War of the Reform in Mexico, fought to vindicate the socially revolutionary constitution of 1857 and led to a victorious conclusion by Juárez.

One of the pioneers of this new social liberalism was the Chilean, Francisco Bilbao. More concerned with the rights of human beings than with property, Bilbao began in the 1840s to advocate social democracy, opposing both the semifeudal organization of the Chilean society of his day and the evils of individualistic capitalism. He was much influenced by the contemporary utopian socialism of Western Europe and was a student of French revolutionary philosophy. The example of the revolutions of 1848 only stimulated his interest in organizing workingmen to bring about social reforms, and in 1850 he formed his *Sociedad de la Igualdad* for this purpose. Strenuously resisted by the Liberals, who were soon to take over power in Chile, this *Sociedad* became the progenitor of the Radical party, which was organized in 1859 by Pedro León Gallo, one of the rich mining magnates from the northern copper-nitrate region. The original program of the Radical party included demands for extension of the franchise, a fairer basis of representation in Congress, disestablishment of the Catholic Church, equality of all religious sects before the law, and secularization of education.

In addition, the Chilean Radical party was particularly concerned with social inequalities and injustice, and it advocated intervention by the state to prevent them through welfare legislation and social security. Its basic philosophy was therefore nationalistic, and it appealed not only to wage-earning elements but also to small businessmen and manufacturing interests who wanted tariff protection against foreign competition. Not being involved in any basic coalition with the Conservatives it was not hampered, as were the Liberals, by any timid inhibitions in speaking out on the problems of land monopoly and the plight of *hacienda* labor. In appealing for support from the copper miners, nitrate workers, and other wage earners in foreign-owned industry, Radicals attributed the almost intolerable living conditions in those industries to the evils of foreign ownership and exploitation. The Radical party therefore gathered strength from the increasing class consciousness and articulateness of labor after 1890 and also, unexpectedly, from the church which intensified its concern with social justice after the encyclical Rerum novarum of Leo XIII.

Even more radical methods than those of the Radical party were advanced for dealing with Chile's social problems after the new century opened. These included the proposals of the anarcho-syndicalists, who, influenced by European syndicalism, emphasized the solidarity of world labor and proposed the violent overturn of existing governments by means of the general strike and their replacement by governments operated by and responsive to the working classes. Their agitation, aggravated by inflation, the high cost of living, and financial depression, produced serious strikes in Santiago in 1905 and in Iquique in the nitrate zone in 1907. The plight of the Chilean miners was described with vivid realism by Baldomero Lillo in his short story "El Chiflón del Diablo" and other writings. At the same time the Marxian socialists, led by Luis Recabaren, were organizing the miners in the north and the industrial workers in central Chile. In 1912 Recabaren formed the Socialist Labor party. In the same year a master politician from Tarapacá, Arturo Alessandri, capitalizing on the labor unrest in the north, entered the Senate from Tarapacá as a Labor senator and began the political career which put him in the presidency in 1920 as "a man of the people."

The New Liberalism in Argentina

In Argentina an intellectual leader who moved into the vanguard of the new liberalism in the 1840s was Bilbao's Argentine contemporary Esteban Echeverría. One of the anti-Rosas exiles, Echeverría conceived that the logic of unitarism required not only national unity but also a high degree of social integration. His doctrines of social democracy, set forth in his *Dogma socialista* which was first published in 1839, expressed deep faith in the ability of the ordinary people of Argentina to cooperate for purposes of social action. A romantic poet of considerable distinction Echeverría was one of the earliest advocates of utopian socialism in Latin America. He stressed the supremacy of society over the individual and his interests. The *Asociación de Mayo*, a youth group which he organized, had many points in common with Bilbao's *Sociedad de la Igualdad*. Echeverría's doctrines and even his *Asociación* made little political impact on the Argentina of his day, but they formed the background for the political ferment which stirred Argentina toward the close of the century and prepared the way for the triumph of the new liberalism there in 1916. They were reinforced by the doctrines of Positivism which stimulated a vast educational movement in the 1880s emphasizing science and progress and centering in the Paraná Normal School. In the writings of Juan B. Justo and José Ingenieros the doctrines of Echeverría and of Comte merged in a new scientific socialism. The so-called "generation of '80" inspired an intellectual awakening in Argentina, which, under the guidance of Sarmiento and foreign intellectuals, created academies, literary institutes, and scientific centers where new ideas were freely discussed.

Meanwhile the politics and economy of Argentina were dominated by the *estanciero* oligarchy, the so-called "Córdoba clique," which after 1880 operated in politics as the *Partido Nacional*. The leaders of this clique maintained their extensive *latifundios* and their old patriarchal mode of life and refused to accommodate their politics to the nascent urban middle class of the new immigration which was flooding into Argentina. Because they refused to alter their landholding system in order to channel the new immigrants into the hinterland provinces, as the contemporary United States was doing through its homestead policy, they shortsightedly connived at the aggrandizement of the cities of the littoral, principally Buenos Aires, whose population, greatly augmented by immigrants, passed the 500,000 mark in 1889. Their politics rested on a cozy understanding among the "best" families, and the outcome of elections was determined in advance.

The nationalism of the *Partido Nacional* rested on a narrow basis, but the interests of this party happened to coincide, during the last two decades of the century, with Argentina's expanding agricultural and exporting interests. To advance these interests the Córdoba clique encouraged a centralization of power in the hands of the federal government. Quite paradoxically, the very elements which had fought for two generations to organize the Argentine government on a federal basis now cooperated to make it really unitary. The increase of national power at the expense of the provinces under the federal constitution of 1853 and under the auspices of the Córdoba clique proceeded apace after 1880. The *caudillo* tradition of strong personal power operating from Buenos Aires over the rest of the country became the basis of Argentine nationalism. As the provinces, lacking resources which they deemed necessary for expansion of their production and export trade, came to look to the federal government for subsidies they necessarily surrendered power to it. Besides they were subject to intervention by the Buenos Aires government, which did not hesitate to use this important agency of central power. Between 1883 and 1899 the federal government resorted to intervention twenty-four times. If, then, federalism was accepted as the established system of government for the Argentine it was nevertheless a strongly centralized federalism, and under it the provinces gradually lost much of their autonomy as the sphere of action of the national government was expanded. Local governments degenerated into mere puppets of the national executive. The theory of federalism was thus gradually supplanted by a practical unitarism.

This centralizing process both hastened and was hastened by the internal development of Argentina, which became especially marked after 1880. The general rapid expansion of the Argentine economy was stimulated by the importation of new agricultural machinery from England and the United States, the fencing in of the open range, the introduction of refrigerator ships, the subsidized influx of immigrants, particularly from Italy, Spain, and Germany, and the extension of the railroad network. It was also encouraged by large government borrowings abroad for the construction of new port works at Buenos Aires and for other internal improvements. In the speculative boom that ensued, Argentina's paper currency became depreciated, and the government, attempting to back it up, adopted a new bank-note law which required that banks of issue must acquire specified amounts of bonds as security for the paper money which they issued. The bank-note situation, nevertheless, got beyond control, partly because Argentina's gold supply which was the basis for its paper currency was inadequate. When an unfavorable balance of trade developed in 1884 the government suspended specie payments for three years, thus artificially creating conditions for a domestic boom, and at the same time it embarked upon an orgy of extravagance which was to precipitate a crisis in 1890.

When the term of President Roca expired in 1886 his brother-in-law, Miguel Juárez Celman, a former governor of Córdoba, was nominated by the clique as his successor. With official backing he was easily elected president over four other candidates, for the *Partido Nacional* completely controlled elections. After he was installed in the presidency Juárez Celman was not willing to be considered simply a lackey of his brother-in-law, and by following an independent course, he soon alienated Roca. He then attempted to build up a political following of his own. But he was vain and incapable and soon became a tool of the speculative interests. His administration became notorious for its unrestrained political corruption. The president did nothing to check the financial prodigality which affected not only the federal government and the state governments but almost all levels of Argentine life. When specie payments were scheduled to be resumed in 1888 Juárez Celman not only postponed resumption but allowed the currency to be further inflated by more issues of paper money. He thus encouraged the financial recklessness which plunged Argentina virtually into bankruptcy two years later.

As early as 1889 the opposition to Juárez Celman and the dominant *Partido Nacional* was organized in Buenos Aires in the house of the greatest Argentine orator of his day, Aristóbulo del Valle in the Jardín Florida. In a sense this new organization, which was called the *Unión Cívica,* represented a revival of the old *porteño* movement, because it opposed the provincial or Córdoba clique. But it was organized, not to espouse the now dead issue of unitarism, but rather for the purpose of opposing the carnival of extravagance in which the Juárez Celman government was an accomplice, and of demanding free and honest elections, which would, as the founders of the *Unión Cívica* knew, give the hitherto inarticulate small middle class a chance to gain control from the *estanciero* minority. This program appealed therefore to the politically excluded groups not only in Buenos Aires but also in the provinces where large numbers were kept from participation in government by the provincial oligarchies. The leaders of the new *Unión Cívica* included not only del Valle but also former President Mitre, Bernardo de Irigoyen, and Leandro N. Alem.

In this organization was soon concentrated all the Argentine opposition to the Juárez Celman administration, and as both the financial and the political situation deteriorated in 1890 the leaders of the *Unión Cívica* began to plan a campaign of violence against the administration. They finally launched a revolt on July 26, led by Gen. Manuel J. Campos and supported by several of the army garrisons and the fleet. The fighting went on for two days around La Plaza Lavalle and resulted in more than one thousand casualties. At the end of the fighting the rebels were forced to surrender and were granted amnesty. But though they were ostensibly defeated, their action so discredited the government that Juárez Celman was abandoned by his own followers in a desperate effort to save the party. "The revolution, Mr. President, is beaten," announced Dr. Manuel Pizarro in the Senate. "But the government is dead." Within a week Juárez Celman was forced to resign.

His place was taken by the vice president, Carlos Pellegrini, a conservative of great wealth and a social leader, who had been educated largely in England, was the founder of the influential Jockey Club, and had been one of the organizers of the *Partido Nacional*. Pellegrini had served as cabinet minister at various times under Avellaneda and Roca. But he was powerless to prevent Argentina from sliding into the abyss of bankruptcy. In order to preserve order he persuaded General Roca to become his minister of the interior, but repressive action could not avert the imminent financial crisis. The new minister of the treasury, Vicente Fidel López, only seemed to render the crisis inevitable by issuing more paper money and bringing the value of Argentine currency down to about one-fourth of its face value. But the event that brought financial disaster was the failure of Argentina's financial agent, Baring Brothers of London. As a result Argentina was unable to pay the interest on its foreign debt in January, 1891, and by March of that year was swept into a severe financial panic when the *Banco Nacional* and all the provincial banks were obliged to close. The only one remaining open was the London and River Plate Bank. From this debacle Argentina did not fully recover for nearly a decade.

Pellegrini was caught up in the whirlwind, and his party leaders in an effort to keep control made overtures to the *Unión Cívica* for a compromise, fearing that unless they agreed to a compromise they would be faced with violence. Their candidate, General Roca, therefore negotiated an agreement with Mitre, the candidate of the *Unión Cívica,* whereby the latter would become president while a representative of the *Partido Nacional* would become vice president. But this settlement was unacceptable to a faction in the *Unión Cívica* led by Leandro Alem and including del Valle, Bernardo de Irigoyen, Alem's nephew Hipólito Irigoyen, and Marcelo T. de Alvear, who refused to compromise. Calling themselves the *Unión Cívica Radical,* they named their own ticket in the first national political convention in the history of Argentina and prepared to use violence if necessary to put their candidates in office.

Their opponents—the *Partido Nacional* and the *Unión Cívica*—faced with the prospect of revolution now dropped Mitre and united in supporting Luis Sáenz Peña, a very respectable judge of the supreme court, whose lack of political experience ensured that although he might have no friends he would also have no enemies. But he was still not acceptable to the members of the

Radical Civic Union, who though they had no specific objections to him were determined to overthrow the political machine which made the election of officially supported candidates inevitable. They realized, however, that with that political machine operating their candidate for the presidency, Bernardo Irigoyen, could not possibly be elected. Since they planned to overthrow the machine by violence President Pellegrini declared martial law and deported the leaders of the Radical Civic Union, including Alem, until after the elections. With the opposition thus muzzled, the official candidate, Sáenz Peña, was elected. The Radical Civic Union was momentarily broken but not defeated, and after 1892 its members refrained from participating in elections until 1912, preferring rather to campaign against the dominant *Partido Nacional* by undercover and revolutionary methods.

The *Partido Nacional* continued in power but under unfavorable conditions. Sáenz Peña, having no personal following and no political experience, was unable to lead Congress or to prevent disaffection in the provinces. The ineffectiveness of his leadership was indicated by the recurring cabinet crises —as many as twenty-three in nine months. When the provincial governors refused their cooperation and when discontent in the provinces increased, stimulated by the agitation of the Radical Civic Union, Sáenz Peña turned from the *Partido Nacional* to the Civic Union for support and asked del Valle to form a cabinet. Del Valle agreed and from his own position as minister of the interior issued orders for the disarming of the provincial forces. But by September, 1893, three provinces—Santa Fe, Santiago del Estero, and Tucumán—rose in revolt against the federal government and were brought into line only after General Roca was put in command of an expedition against them. The Radicals, for their part in inspiring this rebellion, were again outlawed. Sáenz Peña's popularity still further declined, and in 1895 he resigned from the presidency.

Under the leadership of Sáenz Peña's vice president, José Evaristo Uriburu, who now succeeded him in the presidency, Argentina began to pull out of its depression, aided by several good harvests and the intelligent efforts of the federal government. Argentina's agricultural production rapidly grew to meet the increasing demand of industrial Europe for foodstuffs, and the resulting increase in its exports soon produced a favorable balance of trade. The federal government was able to resume interest payments on its foreign debt in 1897, and it strengthened the trend toward further centralization by assuming the foreign debts of the provinces, which it now funded in a single issue of national bonds. By a law of conversion passed in 1899 the *peso* was officially stabilized at 44 cents through the efforts of Pellegrini and Ernesto Tornquist, the leading Argentine banker. Thus the country returned to the gold standard, though with a devalorized currency.

As Argentina finally emerged from this financial depression and entered a new twentieth-century era of prosperity the official *Partido Nacional* regularly reelected its candidates to federal office. Revolutionary overturns of government seemed to be discredited, and none occurred after the unsuccessful revolutionary attempts of 1890 and 1892. Successive administrations governed Argentina in the interest largely of the landed aristocracy. The only real opposition came from the Radical Civic Union, which, however, continued to adhere to its policy of not participating in elections. After the leader of the party, Leandro Alem, returned from exile he committed suicide in 1896, and the leadership passed to his nephew, Hipólito Irigoyen, who was the political boss of Buenos Aires province. For Irigoyen, the only possibility of success lay not in elections but in armed rebellion against the oligarchy with the support of the rising labor and lower middle classes. The growth of these classes favored the movement which he led. With this backing and with the assistance of certain army officers in Buenos Aires the Radical party made a revolutionary attempt in 1905 which was quickly suppressed. Thereafter the leaders of the Radical Civic Union bided their time and stimulated the political drift toward more popular government which eventually brought them to power by legal means in 1916.

Meanwhile, for the first time in Argentine history a president was elected for a second term when General Roca, supported by Uriburu and the provincial governors, triumphed over Mitre in the election of 1898. Labor problems became vexatious during this second administration of General Roca, and the influence of labor, enlarged by the considerable influx of immigrants, began to loom up as a factor in politics. But it was unable to prevent the triumph of the oligarchy in the election of 1904, when Manuel Quintana was elected president. Both Quintana and, after his death in March, 1906, his vice president, José Figueroa Alcorta, who succeeded him in the presidency, tried to follow an independent course. The latter showed an antilabor bias by countenancing terroristic practices and assassinations of labor leaders, and he tried to break the hold of the opposition in the provinces by a series of federal interventions, replacing hostile provincial authorities with new officials loyal to him and thereby setting a precedent which was later used effectively against his party. Figueroa Alcorta also rode roughshod over Congress, going so far as to suspend Congress in January, 1908, and by an unconstitutional decree to declare the budget of the previous year in force. His successor, however, Roque Sáenz Peña, a son of the former president, who was elected as the official candidate in 1910, showed more concern for public opinion, and under his administration the franchise was so broadened as to make possible the triumph of the Radical Civic Union in the election of 1916. This came about in the following manner.

Sáenz Peña, though himself a member of the oligarchy, appreciated the growing strength of Irigoyen and his party and the danger that might result from their further exclusion from government. The degree of political control by the landed oligarchy was notorious and was becoming a threatening issue in politics. More than half the land in Argentina was held in parcels of over 12,500 acres, and the census of 1914 was to show that 506 landowners held a total of 725 million acres of land. The Argentine government had been long dominated by the beneficiaries of *latifundio* or land monopoly. They had developed efficient methods of assuring the outcome of elections by mobilizing the *peones* on their *estancieros* and the recently arrived immigrants to vote for their candidates. The extension of the franchise could be expected not only to broaden the base of Argentine political life but also to eliminate electoral evils and machine politics. With these purposes Sáenz Peña sympathized. He desired particularly to make possible the extension of Argentine citizenship to some two million immigrant aliens. Any politician could see profound political possibilities in such a move.

The task of drafting the new electoral law was entrusted to the minister of the interior, Dr. Indalecio Gómez, who had been Argentine minister to Germany and later a senator. As enacted into law it provided for the secret or Australian ballot, compulsory voting for all males over eighteen years of age, and effective minority representation. It was a landmark in Argentine history, for it assured all male citizens the right to express their opinions freely at the polls. The requirement of compulsory voting was not carried out, but when the secret ballot was first introduced, as it was in the congressional elections of 1912, the Radical Civic Union, after having abstained from participation in elections for twenty years, came out in the open, entered the campaign, and elected one-third of the members of the Chamber of Deputies. Soon afterward the Radical Civic Union won governerships in Santa Fe, Entre Ríos, and Córdoba. In the legislature and in the governorships appeared newcomers in politics, men who did not have aristocratic names and who did not belong to the best clubs. In 1916 in the first presidential election held under the Sáenz Peña law the long-time leader of the Radical Civic Union, Hipólito Irigoyen, was chosen president and his party gained control of the House of Representatives, though not of the Senate because of the staggered terms of senators. This triumph was looked upon as marking the overthrow of the *estanciero* oligarchy.

The Radical Civic Union, despite its name, was essentially dedicated to the nineteenth-century liberal program of extension of the suffrage, freedom of speech and the press, representative government, and respect for private property. It had originally included a socialist element, heirs of Echeverría and his *Dogma socialista*. Among them were Lisandro de la Torre of Santa Fe and Juan B. Justo, but they had defected from the Radical movement in 1895 to organize the Argentine Socialist party with *Vanguardia* as its journalistic organ. The only radical quality that remained to the Radical party was its concern for labor, and between 1912 and 1915 under Radical leadership much legislation beneficial to labor was adopted, including laws which prohibited Sunday labor for wages, fixed employers' liability for accidents to workmen in certain industries, established a national department of labor, set up employment agencies, provided inexpensive housing, and required pensions for railway employees. When Irigoyen became president he was represented as the friend of the workingman and his party as the party of the masses. His election was hailed as the triumph of a new liberalism dedicated to the establishment of more popular government than had previously existed. It also signalized the transition of Argentina from a pastoral to an agricultural economy and to the beginnings of an industrial economy. This revolution by consent was peacefully accomplished and marked the beginning of a new era for Argentina.

The Batlle Program

Similar forces were at work contemporaneously in Argentina's neighbor across the Río de la Plata, but there they took a more radical turn. The new orientation given to Uruguayan life and politics by Juan Cuestas, governing as a benevolent despot, was continued under his *Colorado* successor, José Batlle y Ordóñez, who became president in 1903. Chosen only by the legislature he could not interpret his election as a mandate for political reform.

After he was elected president he tried to form a coalition government with the *Blancos*. When they repulsed his efforts he defeated them in a decisive battle at Masoller on September 1, 1904, and thus became something of a war hero. Having consolidated his position, he proceeded to impose upon the country his solution of Uruguay's social and economic problems through a strong use of the executive power.

Batlle's ideas of government were learned in Europe where he was educated; they had little basis in the experience and realities of his native country. He did not base his program upon a labor movement, which was then too weak to give him much support; nor did he develop it as a middle-class program nor seek to exploit class antagonisms. By means of his presidential powers and the newspaper *El Día,* which he had founded in 1885, he himself created support for his program and practically remade the political and social thinking of Uruguay along national socialist lines. The system which he introduced into Uruguay was a partial or modified European socialism involving nationalization of certain resources and utilities. But he began moderately with a legislative program establishing an eight-hour day, abolishing capital punishment, and recognizing divorce. His system was further developed by his successor Claudio Williman, who became president in 1907. During Williman's administration Batlle ripened his political ideas by study and travel in Europe, and when he returned he announced his candidacy for a second term. Though the *Blancos* threatened to use violence to prevent his election Batlle ensured his victory by establishing wireless connections with all the military stations in the country, equipping the army to resist a *Blanco* uprising, and—perhaps most important of all—corralling all the horses, which in that plains country were indispensable in launching a successful revolution.

Batlle's purpose as president was to use the powers of government to reduce the gaps between the rich and the poor. For this reason he insisted that the state must regulate industry in order, as he said, "to make more happy the life of the masses." He also sought to diminish the large role that foreign capital played in the economy of Uruguay. In his second administration, which began in 1911, Uruguay established freedom of the press, provided for old-age pensions, began to levy inheritance taxes, expanded facilities for adult education, and took over the operation of several utilities as a public service. The government thus began the system of public ownership which later was expanded to include almost all the insurance business of the country, the manufacture and distribution of alcohol, petroleum, and cement, and ownership of the docks of Montevideo, banks, railroads, electric systems, telephone and telegraph companies, street railways, refrigeration and meat-packing facilities, and even hotels and theaters. Under Batlle's leadership Uruguay became one of the most completely socialized nations in the world. Its ventures in government ownership, particularly as they required expropriation of foreign-owned industries, were reprobated abroad as manifestations of antiforeignism.

Batlle, who had established this system, first, through the educational effort of his newspaper *El Día* and, later, through his quasi-dictatorial methods as president, perceived the danger of strong-man executive rule. While in Europe he made an intensive study of the government of Switzerland and became enamored of its collegiate system of a divided or plural executive. He broached this *colegiado* plan for Uruguay in *El Día* soon after he began his second administration and, in spite of strenuous opposition, summoned a constitutional convention to meet at the national university in 1917 and to incorporate this commission form of executive in a new constitution. The new constitution, when promulgated soon afterward, included many of Batlle's suggestions. It provided for a collegiate executive composed of a president and an executive council of nine, all of whom were to be elected directly by the people. The president, whose term was continued at four years, was given command over the military and police forces and was made the nation's spokesman in foreign affairs. His nine associates were elected for six years by direct popular vote, three being elected every two years. They, together with the president, constituted the national council of administration, and all the executive functions not assigned to the president were to be performed by the other members of the council. They were placed in charge of the various departments of the government, including finance, health, banking, industry, labor, public instruction, public works, and others and were given the privileges of sitting in Congress and debating but not voting. Members of the council were independent of the president and need not all act under his orders or even together.

This constitution of 1917, superseding Uruguay's only other constitution, which had served the country since 1830, virtually abolished the traditional balance between the executive, legislative, and judicial departments of the government. Like the Mexican constitution of the same year, to be discussed later, it also set a new constitutional pattern by including a comprehensive program of social legislation. It provided for old-age pensions, pensions for invalids, government officials, schoolteachers, workers on railroads and other public works, minimum wages of $18 per month for rural workers, and minimum salaries of $50 per month for workers in the government service and on public works. The minimum salary for such employment in Montevideo was fixed at $70 per month with an additional allowance of $10 per month for each child. The maximum workday was fixed at eight hours, nightwork in certain industries was prohibited, and workers were declared to be entitled to compensation for industrial accidents. To ensure the fulfillment of this detailed social program a galaxy of boards were set up, including separate boards to look after primary and secondary education, the university, the normal schools, industrial education, public health, the post and telegraph lines, and many others. The program of the board of public health, for example, was eventually to supply every resident of the nation with free medical service. For the first time in Uruguayan history, church and state were separated and the death penalty was abolished. The secret ballot was established, and an electoral court, composed of three neutral members, was given supervision over all elections.

Under the Batlle program as carried into practice after 1903 and embodied in this constitution Uruguay became the first welfare state in the Western Hemisphere. This was the new liberalism advocated by the doctrinaire socialists of Argentina from Echeverría onward and finally put into force by semi-autocratic methods in Uruguay. Its roots in Europe were obvious. The groundwork for it was prepared by Positivism, a European doctrine, and it responded originally neither to any indigenous nor to any existing system in Latin America. It was justified as a social welfare program undertaken on the responsibility of the national government for the benefit of the majority of the citizens. But this liberalism was the reverse of the nineteenth-century laissez-faire liberalism, which advocated curtailment of central authority and permitted individual citizens and local communities to exercise responsibility for correct social living.

Batlle, unlike many other Latin American *caudillos,* built up a political party which was able to retain power long after his death. His system greatly extended the area of central government action and intervention in the life of the citizens. It established the responsibility of government not only for their life but also for their good life. Under this system Uruguay, which among all the nations of Latin America had been one of the most amorphous throughout the nineteenth century, began to stand for something and in the process acquired a stability which it had not possessed before. But its new system was precariously maintained; the *Colorados* themselves divided into two factions on the question, among others, of government ownership of key industries, and the *Blancos* persistently opposed government ownership and most other features of the *Batllista* program. In deference to this opposition the *Batllistas* discreetly refrained from challenging the power of the great *estancieros* by redistributing the land or applying their social legislation to the rural workers. They thus recognized and indeed accentuated the traditional cleavage between the port city and the rural areas.

Social Revolution in Mexico

In Uruguay the new liberalism or system of national socialism was accepted peacefully, but in Mexico it became established only after a civil war which is one of the epics of twentieth-century Latin America. The causes of a movement as profound and momentous as the Mexican revolution cannot be summarized in capsule form, for they are as complicated as life itself. The upheaval which began in Mexico in 1910 resulted from all the grievances and frustrations that had accumulated during the long Díaz regime and from its failure, which became increasingly notorious, to meet the needs of the Mexican people. Díaz lingered too long on the Mexican stage, and his policies, which had originally matched the liberal post-Juárez era of the 1870s, came to be regarded as anachronistic and even positively detrimental to the real interests of the nation. The Liberal party continued to dominate the government, but the liberalism of the party of Juárez, with its emphasis upon individualism and representative government, was now being used to repress individual liberties and to provide strong executive government, which, behind a façade of scientific administration, was a ruthless and corrupt machine. Díaz was kept in office long beyond his time by a political machine which responded to the desires of those narrow interests which were well served by his continuance in the presidency. In that machine operation, no more than 4 per cent of the Mexican electorate were ever allowed to vote. According to credible estimates the controlling upper class in Mexico under Díaz amounted to less than 1½ per cent of the total population, and the voiceless lower class comprised over 90 per cent. To the Mexican Positivists the Indians were only a negative element.

As Díaz grew old his government was transformed into a personal dictatorship, with which the *científicos* were closely associated and for which they were held responsible. Mexico's political system was frozen

Fig. 20-1. Porfirio Díaz. (*Courtesy of Pan American Union.*)

into an immobile tyranny. Positivism, instead of being a philosophy of progress, had become an instrument of reaction. It was bankrupt of ideas and was left only with its formulas. Instead of supporting social evolution the *científicos* were obstructing it. They had undertaken to explain and perfect Mexican society, but they had failed in their purpose. They had not fulfilled their objective of strengthening, integrating, and homogenizing Mexican society. To them liberalism had become nothing but docks, bridges, and railroads. Their philosophy was too systematic, too logical. It lacked imagination and sentiment. It was only half a program for Mexico—material prosperity. The Positivists had betrayed liberalism. They expected men to live by public works rather than by faith in themselves. Either their society was too narrowly conceived or their science was faulty. Instead of offering definitive solutions to the problems of society, they were only creating problems. They had accented only the material element in life, considering it something permanent. The political order, established and maintained by Díaz, served only to make possible the personal enrichment of the small class of the Mexican *bourgeoisie*.

The failures of the Díaz regime seemed particularly glaring in the northern states of Mexico where the Indian population remained unintegrated into the national economy and the *hacienda* economy continued, as a consequence, to be notoriously unstable. In Mexico as a whole in 1910, government census reports showed, 70 per cent of the 15,150,369 Mexicans, or almost 11,000,000 persons, were illiterate. While the government was erecting magnificent public buildings, the *peones* lacked roads over which to move their crops to market, schools for the education of their children, and hospitals for the care of their sick. In protest against these conditions, which were identified with *Porfirismo,* a new humanism and a new nationalism arose, emphasizing the plight of the landless *peones* and calling in question the wisdom of foreign capital exploitation of the land of Mexico. Against the Díaz regime an undercover movement gathered momentum, centering in the Masonic lodges, the weak Socialist party, the inflammatory anarcho-syndicalist movement, and ambitious *caudillos,* of whom Francisco Madero proved to be the most important. A strong reaction set in against the pseudo science and crass materialism of Mexican Positivism, imported from France, in favor of a pattern developed from Mexico's own background and embodying traditional spiritual values. The underprivileged found a literary spokesman in Guillermo Prieto and a graphic artist in José Guadalupe Posada, whose folk drawings anticipated the later revolutionary art of Diego Rivera. "Democratic" party clubs were formed in many parts of Mexico in 1908, agitating for political liberties, free elections, and a new president. And at the same time radical labor agitators spread the revolutionary doctrines of Spanish syndicalism among the wretched *jornaleros.* The leaders of this new movement of protest, like the leaders of the Mexican revolution of a century earlier, came largely from the *mestizo* class, the mixed Indian and white, or *mestizaje*.

The movement against Díaz was at first directed toward political reform, but it eventually became a genuine social revolution, operating with a violence that was commensurate with the intransigence of the social and economic forces arrayed against it. The political opposition was particularly antagonized in 1904 when Díaz at the age of seventy-four had the presidential term extended to six years, had himself reelected, and secured the election of Ramón Corral, governor of Sonora, as vice president, presumably to succeed him. The creed of Positivism, as formulated by Comte, had deplored elections and insisted that public functionaries of all kinds should name their successors, subject only to the approbation of their superiors. Francisco Madero, a rival *caudillo,* with almost mystical powers of leadership, put himself in the forefront of the political opposition to this attempt by the Díaz regime to perpetuate itself in office. He was a member of a wealthy family of Coahuila and had been deeply and profitably involved in the industrial development and land monopoly of the Díaz period. He now provided the anti-Díaz movement with its slogan "Effective Suffrage—No Reelection"— but he was imprisoned by Díaz, who in 1910 had himself and Corral reelected for another six-year term. When Madero was released after the election, he fled to San Antonio, Texas, where he issued a call to revolt. In this pronouncement—the so-called "Plan of San Luis Potosí"—he demanded the overthrow of Díaz by revolutionary force and called for changes in the electoral system which would provide for effective suffrage and so destroy the Díaz machine. In it he also hinted vaguely at a restoration of lands to the Indians, which would restore Mexico's patrimony to the agrarian workers. The revolution thus launched gathered strength, and Díaz was forced to resign in May, 1911. He then retired to Paris where he died four years later.

Madero, short of stature and wearing a black goatee, was an intense idealist, kind and well intentioned. He became provisional president and in free elections held in October, 1911, was elected constitutional president on the slogan "Effective Suffrage—No Reelection," affirming the need for popular elections and a time limit on the tenure of the president. Around him gathered bands of peasants with their *jefes* (chiefs), armed with guns and machetes, with their own dreams of bread and land, of schools, of sovereignty over the nation's wealth, of a new role for Indians in Mexico's national life. But Madero had unleashed forces which he could not control, particularly in his appeal for restoration of lands to the landless *peones.* This was now taken up by Emiliano Zapata, a peasant leader in Morelos, and Felipe Carillo Puerto in Yucatan, who began campaigns of terrorism and destruction against landlords, particularly foreign ones. *Tierra y Libertad* (Land and Liberty) became the cry of the revolutionists. The earlier political objectives of the revolution yielded, under duress, to demands for agrarian reform and social welfare legislation by the national government.

The plight of the landless *peones* of Mexico had aroused the sympathy of humanitarian liberals ever since the struggle for independence and had inspired many programs of action. During the early movement for secession from Spain, a high church official in Michoacán, Manuel Abad y Queipo, had proposed in an *Informe sobre inmunidades del clero* (*Report on Clerical Immunities*) "the gratuitous division of all the lands of the Crown among the Indians and the half-castes" and "an agrarian law that will confer upon the people a right, equivalent to ownership, upon the uncultivated land of

Fig. 20-2. Emiliano Zapata, detail from a mural painting by José Clemente Orozco, Mexico. (*Courtesy of Pan American Union.*)

the great proprietors." In the conservative reaction which brought Iturbide to power the problem of land monopoly or *latifundio* was lost sight of. But in the Gómez Farías program, which was embodied in the "laws of '33" striking at privilege both of the church and the landed aristocracy, some redistribution of lands was implicit. Redistribution of some lands actually was accomplished by force in the ensuing Social War. Later Juárez, like Gómez Farías in his challenge to the power of the church, sought to make the land resources of Mexico available to those who could use them. This program was not so much abandoned as subverted during the long regime of Porfirio Díaz. The land of Mexico was made available to those who could develop it scientifically, namely the large companies and entrepreneurs, both domestic and foreign. Against this system protest had slowly smoldered among the landless to break out in revolutionary heat under Madero.

But Madero in power was content with laissez-faire liberalism which stressed individual rights and responsibilities. He refused to allow his government to back any threat to private property or to embark upon a program of social legislation. Having antagonized the Díaz group, who believed in law and order, by leading the revolution, Madero now alienated his revolutionary followers and became increasingly stubborn and petulant. He was content with political change and was not prepared to carry out the social and economic implications of the revolution.

The opposition to Madero was spearheaded by the commander of his armies, Victoriano Huerta, who now found it convenient, under prodding from the United States minister in Mexico City, Henry Lane Wilson, to change sides and turn against the president. Huerta had Madero and his vice president, Pino Suárez, arrested and killed under the *ley de fuga* (while attempting to escape), and then he himself assumed the presidency in February, 1913. But Huerta was a mere military *caudillo*, the tool of the interests which wished to restore the Díaz system. He was also supported by British petroleum interests which had large concessions in Mexico. He undertook to govern Mexico by dictatorial methods and arrested more than one hundred members of Congress. Against him the aroused middle class and peasants launched a guerrilla type of revolution, carried on from the backs of fast-moving Mexican ponies, from armored trains captured by the rebels from their *Huertista* foes, and from many a mesquite ambush. Mexico was seething with rebellion. The original movement of protest had swelled into a lusty, full-girthed revolution.

Both the manner of Huerta's accession to the presidency of Mexico and his methods of governing were so repugnant to the United States government that he was unable to secure recognition from the Woodrow Wilson administration in Washington. As a result his relations with the United States became strained, and the two nations came to the verge of war. In April, 1914, Huerta was confronted with a demand from Admiral Mayo, commander of the United States naval forces in Mexican waters, for reparation for the arrest by Tampico authorities of several United States sailors in a forbidden area in Tampico. The reparation which was demanded included release of the sailors, an apology for their arrest, and a salute of twenty-one guns. Huerta immediately released the men and granted the apology but saw in the demand for a salute to the United States flag an opportunity to win a following among Mexican patriots. He accordingly refused the salute. As a result, the Mexican port of Veracruz was forcibly occupied by United

States Marines, with the loss of eighteen marines and sixty Mexicans. This serious imbroglio between the two nations was ended by a mediation of Argentina, Brazil, and Chile—the so-called "ABC powers." Their recommendations, adopted in their meeting at Niagara Falls, Ontario, called for Huerta's abandonment of the presidency and the setting up of a provisional government "actually, avowedly, and sincerely in favor of the agrarian and political reforms" advocated by the Mexican revolutionists.

Meanwhile resistance to the dictator had been stirred up throughout the northern states of Mexico by Alvaro Obregón of Sonora and by Gen. Venustiano Carranza, who had been one of Madero's principal supporters and was now governor of Coahuila. After February, 1914, they were able to secure assistance from the United States when the Wilson administration lifted its embargo against the shipment of war supplies across the border to Mexican rebels. The revolutionary armies, thus reinforced, converged on Mexico City. As they did so, the terms proposed by the ABC mediators were announced in Mexico City. Under these pressures Huerta was forced to resign on July 15, 1914, whereupon he went into exile in Europe. His place in Mexico City was taken by Carranza, who was deemed acceptable to the United States. The Mexican revolution, which was as yet only slightly tinged with the elements of social upheaval, seemed to be guttering out in the struggle for power among rival *caudillos*.

Like Madero before him, Carranza desired to carry out the principles of liberal individualism embodied in the constitution of 1857 and opposed any program of expropriation or socialization. He himself was an *hacendado* and had been a Díaz senator. But he was gradually driven by public pressures to accept more radical programs. In the south, Zapata, heading a revolutionary Indianist movement, formulated demands for restoration of lands to the Indians in his Plan of Ayala and incited the Indians to seize sugar plantations in Morelos. In Yucatan, Carillo Puerto was advocating socialization of the land. Their counterpart in the north, Francisco or "Pancho" Villa, was using his guerrilla bands to seize monopoly lands and other property and turn them over to the landless *peones*. Aggrieved labor was also moving into a militantly revolutionary state of mind. The rumbling volcanism in the Mexican situation could not be overlooked even by the moderate Carranza.

These public pressures came to a focus in the constitutional convention which met at Querétaro in 1916. The constitution which the convention submitted to Carranza in the following year outran his expectations but was perforce accepted by him. Promulgated by him in 1917 this document, coinciding in time with the adoption of the Batlle constitution of Uruguay, which virtually made possible the socialization of that nation, represented the advance wave or the highwater mark of the new liberalism. It built upon the principles of the Gómez Farías legislation of 1833 and the Juárez constitution of 1857, particularly in its anticlericalism. Its individualism, however, was no longer a laissez-faire individualism but rather an individualism guaranteed by the federal government. This was not only a logical development from the centralization achieved by Díaz but, more significantly, a reflection of the new concern of that government with the living conditions of the rank and file of the Mexican people and of its determination to solve by coercive action the problems presented by those conditions. A strong reaction against the *científicos* and their materialistic brand of Positivism had set in, spearheaded by the writings of Mexico's nationalist philosophers, José Vasconcelos and Antonio Caso. The old social, economic, and political system which had seemed satisfactory to the Juárez liberals and to the Díaz *científicos* was now scrapped and a new system was adopted. Though it repudiated many of the elements in Mexico's past it represented a consummation of others and came at a time—in the midst of World War I—when many other nations also were placing reliance upon strong government as a means of promoting human welfare.

The innovations of the Mexican constitution of 1917 were primarily social and economic. That document legitimized the revolution and dedicated the authority of the Mexican government to the ultimate purpose of raising the living levels of the masses of small farmers and manual workers by eliminating land monopoly, peonage, and foreign control over the resources of the nation. Unlike many other Latin American constitutions the Mexican constitution was a secular document. Its provisions affecting the powers of the Catholic Church in Mexico reflected not only the strong nationalism of the Mexican revolution directed against the influence of the papacy in Mexican life but also a disposition to limit the exercise of the Catholic religion. Members of the clergy were limited to purely religious work and were deprived of participation in public primary education and in the work of public charitable institutions. All church buildings and all other religious establishments were declared to be the property of the nation, and religious ceremonials outside the churches were prohibited. Religious orders were abolished. All priests were required to register with the civil authorities; alien priests were banned; and the total number of priests who might serve within the jurisdiction of each state could be limited by the state. Under this constitution the Catholic Church operated in Mexico only at the sufferance of the government, both federal and state, and became largely subservient to it. The status of the church in relation to the state of Mexico after 1917 was reminiscent of its status in Spain during the reign of Ferdinand and Isabella, except that in Mexico the church was hampered by an anticlericalism which had not existed in Spain.

The constitution set forth a new conception of property rights, derogating from the traditional rights of private property in favor of the overriding authority of the state. In article 27 it declared that private property is subordinate to public welfare. The nation was declared to be the original owner of all lands and waters under its jurisdiction, and its right to expropriate private property for compensation was recognized. The ownership by the nation of its territorial waters and its subsoil resources could never be alienated, declared the constitution, though the right of the government to grant concessions for the development of such resources by individuals was acknowledged. The constitution thus separated the subsurface resources of the nation from its surface resources, reverting in this respect to the old Spanish customary law which had prevailed in Mexico until 1884. In addition the constitution recognized the prior and inalienable right of Indian communities (*comunes*) to their common property in land in the *ejidos,* annulled all alienations of *ejidos* under the *Ley Lerdo* of 1856, and declared the *ejidos* henceforth to be the communal property of the villages, susceptible of being divided into plots for the use of peasants but not subject to transfer in fee simple. No foreigners could acquire ownership of any lands or waters in Mexico unless they agreed not to invoke the protection of their governments in their behalf. These provisions went a long way toward laying a basis for the recovery of the patrimony of Mexico from the monopolists, both domestic and foreign, to whom it had been largely transferred and also for the restoration of the traditional communal village life of Mexico's Indian population. In these respects the constitution was therefore both nationalist and Indianist in its implications, reversing the trends of several previous decades.

The new Mexican constitution, like the contemporary Uruguayan constitution, also responded to the prevalent demand for social legislation by containing a long chapter on this subject, thus setting a new style in constitutions. The type of social program which had been embodied in legislation in the United States under Woodrow Wilson's New Freedom, which constituted the platform of Lloyd George's Liberal party in England, and which was advocated by the new liberals in many other countries was now incorporated in the basic charter of the Mexican government. Aiming to improve the living conditions of the masses of the Mexican people through governmental action backed by force and to prevent violations of human rights by abusive individuals, the constitution established an eight-hour day and a minimum wage, abolished child labor, and provided for profit sharing and for compensation for injuries and dismissals of workers. It gave a strong impetus to organized labor not only by imposing these requirements upon employers but also by recognizing the right of wage earners to belong to unions and to strike to obtain their demands. By virtue of these provisions the labor movement in Mexico, which had been assuming antigovernmental attitudes under the leadership of the anarcho-syndicalist Flores Magón, was, in effect, brought under the wing of the government, and the way was prepared for the organization of the *Confederación Regional Obrera Mexicana* (CROM) under Luis Morones, which was less radical and was content to be a virtual partner of government.

The Mexican revolution reached its legal consummation in the constitution of 1917. By that date the revolution had come to be dominated by leaders who represented, thought they represented, or aspired to represent the rural and industrial working class. The constitution which they drafted provided more than a frame of government; it was promulgated as a charter of human rights to be guaranteed by the federal government of Mexico. It was a product of the Mexican revolution, which was itself a product of the callousness of the Díaz regime toward the broad social and economic interests of the urban and rural working class. Reacting against the Díaz program, the writers of the new constitution enshrined the rights of labor in the organic law of Mexico, thus opening up new vistas of power for this class. Moreover, the constitution established a basis for a broader electorate and therefore a broader nationalism than had ever existed before in Mexico's history. In short, in this constitution the blind forces of social upheaval which first erupted in 1910 produced a new type of national socialism or statism which was not envisaged at the outset, except perhaps by Zapata and like-minded agitators, and which would have been as repugnant to Madero as to Díaz.

At the same time, the Mexican revolution, at least as it was eventually embodied in the constitution of 1917, represented a real triumph for Positivism, which after the revolution became more broadly based and was more generously construed than under Díaz. The leaders of the revolution seemed to assume that the philosophy of Positivism had been diluted and betrayed by the absolutism of *Porfirismo* and that all Mexico would profit from a truly scientific and expanded Positivism. They accepted the postulates of nineteenth-century liberalism and sought to carry those postulates to their logical conclusions. The revolutionary upheaval was therefore not a revolt against intellectualism and science but a demand for a greater measure of both. As the principles of Positivism were vindicated and strengthened in the revolution of 1910, Mexico moved into step with the social forces which were dominant in the United States under President Wilson, which overthrew the Romanovs in Russia in 1917, and which were stimulated and given direction by the propaganda of World War I.

And yet both the Mexican revolution and the constitution of 1917 were explicable almost entirely in terms of Mexico's own experience. They were not imported from abroad. The Mexican government after 1917 was controlled by a powerful workers' and peasants' coalition which undertook to carry out a revolutionary reconstruction of society but which was not affiliated with any international movement. The new liberalism, unlike that of Uruguay, appeared in Mexico largely as a nativist movement with revolutionary overtones sounded in the conflict between the ideas of Díaz and Zapata. It grew by reason of its appeal to both urban and rural labor, and its nativist and nationalist implications were demonstrated particularly in its appeal to the submerged Indian masses who saw in it opportunity for new political expression and economic relief. For them it represented a continuation of the struggle for political independence and economic freedom which had begun in the mass uprisings led by Hidalgo in the war of independence and had been continued by Juárez in the War of the Reform. To secure these rights the revolutionary constitution, though it preserved the fiction of Mexican federalism, vested enlarged powers in the president and gave the central government a preponderant position in relation to the states.

The liberalism of the nineteenth century was therefore evolving into a social democracy or national socialism which was a new force in Latin America. Or perhaps it was only a new method of achieving the objectives of the nineteenth-century liberals in a twentieth-century context. In certain countries, as for example in Mexico, it drew its strength from the Indian and *mestizo* elements, and in all of them from the idea of nationalism. From this latter idea or ideal, sometimes latent and sometimes overt, the new liberals sought to shape a coherent national unity, based on the heart and faith of a people. This unity was being promoted by the technological changes that were taking place. As highways and railroads were extended into remote interior regions, as telephone and telegraph networks were laid down, as new processes were introduced for agricultural and mineral production, these innovations of the Industrial Revolution created a stronger sense of nationalism. The new liberalism was deeply infused with romanticism, but with a romanticism that was supported by the urgent economic and social imperatives of Latin America. It grew out of the mass demands for change and responded to these demands with intellectualized and tentative blueprints for action—blueprints that would be operated by socially conscious *caudillos* backed by a willing and disciplined people.

Indianismo

Closely associated with the nationalist upsurge in Latin America was a newly awakened concern for the Indian. Nineteenth-century liberals had generally expressed contempt for the American aborigines. To them, in the later words of Alfonso Reyes, the Indian "was a burden, not yet a proud duty and a strong hope." To Sarmiento it was clear that Latin America's weakness was due to the mixture of the Spaniards with the inferior native race and with the Negroes. To him mestization was a disaster, for it had contaminated and diluted the pure Spanish element. But the new liberals became interested in the Indian as a racial phenomenon and as an object of humanitarian concern. They therefore sought to restore the Indian patrimony, to raise the level of living of the Indian, and to make him an integral part of the life of the nation. They were moved in this direction by the idealization of the Indian which had formed an important element in the romantic literature of the nineteenth century, particularly the writings of Juan León Mera of Ecuador, Gertrudis Gómez de Avellaneda of Cuba, and Clorinda Matto de Turner of Peru. *Indianismo* was viewed by some as a penance for the Spanish conquest and for the ensuing centuries of compounded oppression and neglect of the Indian. Many of the modern champions of the Indian subscribe to the Black Legend, blaming Spain's imperial policy and the white Spanish element in Latin America for the plight of the Indian. Others espoused the cause of the Indian in order to absorb him into the traditional Spanish culture, and still others consider *Indianismo* a necessary method of emphasizing and developing the autochthonous cultures of the Latin American peoples.

Indianismo, as it had been an important feature of the Mexican revolution since 1910, became especially important in Peru, Bolivia, and Ecuador after World War I. In those predominantly Indian countries the democratic principles of universal suffrage and government by the consent of the governed, which were stimulated by the war, created new demands for political rights by previously overlooked majorities. But these demands could not be gratified in any meaningful way without radical social and economic change. In these countries, despite liberal constitutional provisions, the Indians still lived in a feudal status, lacking lands of their own, working at the mercy of the *hacendados,* and deprived of the opportunity to improve their position in life. On the land of the *patrón* they worked three or four days a week without pay, and to the *patrón* all members of the Indian family owed many other obligations, including domestic service in the house of the *patrón,* tribute of firewood and wool, care of the livestock, and often a cash payment. The *peón,* like any other chattel, could be rented out by the

Fig. 20-3. A native dance in Guatemala. (*Courtesy of the Estate of Dorothy Reynolds.*)

patrón when he was not needed for work on the estate, and when the estate changed hands the *peón* and his family were transferred with it to the new owner. The sale value of an estate was often determined by the number of native tenants attached to it. Sometimes as many as a dozen Indian towns or *ayllus* were included within a single estate, whose Indian serfs were required to tend the flocks, work in the fields, and transport the crops of the owner to market. Those who were dispossessed of their lands and were not willing to accept servitude drifted to the cities or found employment in mining in the highlands or in rubber gathering in the *selva* or took to the roads to become bandits.

The leadership in the efforts to improve the lot of the Indians was taken, not as in colonial times by ecclesiastics, but by literary men, social actionists, and political revolutionaries. In Brazil the principal champion of the Indians was Gen. Cândido da Silva Rondon, himself of Indian ancestry, who was responsible for founding a government agency, the *Serviço de Proteças aos Indios,* for this purpose. In Mexico the leaders in the movement for appreciation of the indigenous race and the blending of its cultural elements into the national pattern were José Vasconcelos and Manuel Gamio, who served as director of the *Dirección de Estudios Arqueológicos y Etnográficos.* They hoped to find something magic in the primitive Indian culture. Ringing denunciations of the exploitation of the Indians in Peru by the *gamonales* or large landowners were made by Manuel González Prada and José Mariátegui. The harsh conditions of Indian life there were sympathetically depicted by Ciro Alegría in his moving novel *El Mundo es ancho y ajeno,* which has been translated into English under the title *Broad and Alien Is the World* and which may be considered the *Uncle Tom's Cabin* of the Peruvian Indian. The liberation of the Indian and his restoration to the land was essential, these writers argued, to create a modern bourgeois capitalist society and a healthy national economy, such as existed in modern democratic states. In addition they urged that the Indian be given the right to vote. Their literary effort contributed to the program of the *Alianza Popular Revolucionaria Americana* (APRA), which was organized after 1924 by the young Peruvian idealist, Víctor Raúl Haya de la Torre. But in some of these countries, particularly in the Andean countries where the Indian element numerically predominated, these efforts sometimes resulted in Indianizing the nation instead of nationalizing the Indians. The "bucolic" philosophers who espoused the cause of the Indians harked back to pre-Columbian times and recommended the system of collective effort which they considered to have been effective then; but at the same time they inconsistently aspired to move the Indian farmers forward into the mid-twentieth century. In their enthusiasm for the indigenous peoples they identified the Indians with the proletariat, as in the Mexican revolution.

The transition from the old to the new liberalism was well illustrated in the changing concept of federalism. The establishment of a federal rather than a unified structure of government in Argentina, Mexico, and Brazil had been regarded as a triumph for the liberals in those countries. Even the forms of federalism were preserved in Venezuela under Páez and Guzmán Blanco. But the liberal system of autonomous or largely autonomous local governing units had gradually yielded to increased centralization. *Autonomista* liberals were smothered by the new nationalist liberals. Their programs of social and economic action were absorbed and were put into effect on a larger scale by the emerging nationalist groups of the nineteenth century. The transition which liberalism slowly made from federalism to nationalism was finally consummated in the Mexican revolution. It was the fate of nineteenth-century liberals to win their victories through vigorous, forward-looking leaders who by reason of their leadership imposed upon the movements that they led the character of both personalism and nationalism. Before World War I in most countries of Latin America militant national socialist leaders with political intelligence and the means to achieve political power were lacking, and large Indian populations who might have formed the shock troops of such a national socialist movement either did not exist or, where they did exist, lacked both revolutionary experience and articulateness. New leadership and mass followings did not appear in those countries until after World War I.

Additional Reading

Alexander, Robert J.: "The Latin American Aprista Parties," *Political Quarterly,* vol. 20, pp. 236–247, 1949.

Bernstein, Harry: *Modern and Contemporary Latin America,* J. B. Lippincott Company, Philadelphia, 1952, chaps. 7, 37.

Cumberland, C. C.: *Mexican Revolution: Genesis under Madero,* University of Texas Press, Austin, Tex., 1952.

Fitzgibbon, Russell H.: *Uruguay, Portrait of a Democracy,* Rutgers University Press, New Brunswick, N.J., 1954.

Gálvez, Manuel: *Vida de Hipólito Yrigoyen: El hombre del misterio,* 2d ed., Talleres Gráficos, Kraft, Ltd., Buenos Aires, 1939.

Gómez, R. A.: "Intervention in Argentina, 1860–1930," *Inter-American Economic Affairs,* vol. 1, no. 3, pp. 55–73, 1947.

Hanson, Simon G.: *Utopia in Uruguay,* Oxford University Press, New York, 1938.

Kantor, Harry: *The Ideology and Program of the Peruvian Aprista Movement,* University of California Press, Berkeley, Calif., 1953.

Keen, Benjamin: *Readings in Latin American Civilization: 1492 to the Present,* Houghton Mifflin Company, Boston, 1955, chaps. XXIX, XXX, XXXIII, XXXIV.

Pinchon, Edgecumb: *Zapata, the Unconquerable,* Doubleday & Company, Inc., New York, 1941.

Quirk, Robert S.: *An Affair of Honor: Woodrow Wilson and the Occupation of Veracruz,* University of Kentucky Press, Lexington, 1962.

———: *The Mexican Revolution, 1914–1915: the Convention of Aguascalientes,* Indiana University Press, Bloomington, 1960.

Romanell, Patrick: *Making of the Mexican Mind,* University of Nebraska Press, Lincoln, Neb., 1952.

Ross, Stanley R.: *Francisco I. Madero: Apostle of Mexican Democracy,* Columbia University Press, New York, 1955.

Sanchez, George: *Mexico: A Revolution by Education,* The Viking Press, Inc., New York, 1936.

Torres-Ríoseco, Arturo: *The Epic of Latin American Literature,* University of California Press, Berkeley, Calif., 1959, chaps. 3, 5, 6.

Vanger, Milton: *José Batlle y Ordóñez: The Creator of His Times, 1902–1907,* Harvard University Press, 1962.

Vasconcelos, José, and Manuel Gamio: *Aspects of Mexican Civilization,* University of Chicago Press, Chicago, 1926.

Wilson, Irma: *Mexico: A Century of Educational Thought,* Hispanic Institute, New York, 1941.

Zea, Leopoldo: *Apogeo y decadencia del positivismo en México,* El Colegio de Mexico, Mexico, 1944.

———: *El Positivismo en México,* El Colegio de México, Mexico, 1943.

Zum Felde, Alberto: *Evolución histórico del Uruguay,* García, Montevideo, 1945.

———: *Proceso intelectual del Uruguay,* Editorial Claridad, Montevideo, 1941.

XXI

New International Complications

During the last third of the nineteenth century some of the Latin American nations found themselves involved in difficult international situations—with their neighbors, with European powers, and with the United States—which in part represented a legacy from their colonial past and in part resulted from unresolved problems from the early independence period and from the new industrialism and the new philosophical movements of the age. They were increasingly affected by the policies and interests of the United States, but their contacts with the non-American world also widened. After the stresses and strains of nation building their culture once more became cosmopolitan, as it had been in the eighteenth century. They settled many of the boundary disputes which they had inherited from the period before independence. Their sense of evolving statehood nourished Pan-Hispanism as a counteractant to the Pan-Americanism which was sponsored by the United States and accounted in part for their general abstention from involvement in World War I.

Boundary Settlements

In the two most serious continuing boundary controversies between Chile and Argentina, agreement was reached to submit them to arbitration, respectively, by the queen of England and a representative of the United States. In 1881 the two nations had agreed upon a boundary in the disputed Patagonian area. The major part of the area was assigned to Argentina, the Strait of Magellan was neutralized in perpetuity as between the two nations, Tierra del Fuego was divided between them, and the Andean boundary in the south was to run along "the most lofty peaks of the Andes which divide the waters." The difficulty in applying this agreement arose from the fact that the highest peaks did not always form the watershed. In 1896 the disputants agreed to submit this question to arbitration by the queen of England. Meanwhile a controversy had developed between Chile and Argentina over territory known as the Puna (plateau) of Atacama or the Territory of the Andes which Argentina had acquired from Bolivia. This dispute was referred to the arbitration of the United States minister in Buenos Aires,

William I. Buchanan. When he gave his award in 1899 assigning about two-thirds of the disputed territory to Argentina and the remainder to Chile it was not well received in either country but was finally accepted by them in 1903.

While a British commission was making a careful survey of the disputed area in the south to assist the new king of England in his arbitration and feelings were running high between Chile and Argentina, President Germán Riesco of Chile and President Julio A. Roca of Argentina concluded new treaties in 1902 in which they agreed to compulsory arbitration for ten years of all controversies that might arise between their countries of whatever nature or from whatever cause except those involving constitutional matters. In accordance with this so-called "Argentine formula," which set a new model for treaties of virtually unlimited compulsory arbitration in modern times, all such disputes between the two countries would be referred to arbitration by Great Britain. At the same time the two nations, equally concerned over the costly armaments race between them which had begun in 1895, agreed to a limitation of naval armaments, which was almost unique in modern history up to that time. In the Chilean-Argentine agreement, which was concluded in 1902 through the friendly offices of Great Britain, both contracting nations agreed to sell some of their warships and to disarm others in order to establish naval parity. They further agreed not to acquire any new war vessels for a period of five years without giving eighteen months' prior notice to the other and not to acquire any such vessels except by mutual consent.

When Edward VII of England announced his award in the dispute over the southern boundary between the two nations in 1902, awarding 15,450 square miles to Argentina and 20,850 to Chile, both disputants readily accepted it. To commemorate this peaceful settlement of a once acrimonious dispute they united in erecting the memorial statue "Christ of the Andes" in the high Andes in 1904, cast from melted cannon. Brazil's acceptance of the Argentine formula of compulsory arbitration in a treaty in 1905 brought that powerful nation into the South American peace system and laid the basis for the so-called ABC (Argentina-Brazil-Chile) entente which flourished until World War I.

Inherited from the War of the Triple Alliance was a boundary dispute between Argentina and Paraguay involving the claims of the former to territory in the Chaco. This dispute was referred to the decision of President Rutherford B. Hayes of the United States, who in 1878 awarded to Paraguay all the territory in dispute, namely, the region between the Pilcomayo and the Verde Rivers. Grateful Paraguay then changed the name of Villa Occidental in the territory awarded to her, calling it now Villa Hayes. A controversy between Nicaragua and Costa Rica over the validity of a treaty concluded by them in 1858 and involving, among other things, the ownership of the district of Nicoya and the status of the San Juan River as a boundary

Expansion of Brazil. (*Reproduced from Hutton Webster, History of Latin America, 1941. Courtesy of D. C. Heath and Company.*)

river was referred to the arbitration of President Grover Cleveland and was decided by him in 1888 substantially in favor of Costa Rica.

Near the end of the regime of Dom Pedro II and at his suggestion, the United States was asked to arbitrate a troublesome dispute between Brazil and Argentina involving the boundary line between the Brazilian state of Santa Catarina and the Argentine territory of Misiones. The Brazilians claimed that the boundary rivers were the Pepiry-Guaçû and the San Antônio whereas the Argentines claimed they were the two rivers called by Brazil the Chapecó and the Chopim or Jangada. Brazil's claims were presented by José Maria da Silva Paranhos, Baron of Rio Branco and son of the Viscount of Rio Branco who had sponsored the law of "free birth" in 1871. Upon the basis of the presentation of the cases by the two disputants President Cleveland rendered an award in February, 1895, supporting Brazil's claims to the 11,500 square miles of territory in dispute. His award, announced during the Prudente administration, was considered a triumph for Brazil and was accepted by both Brazil and Argentina. Its reception was indicative of the high prestige in which the United States was held in those two countries. In commemoration of the award Brazil established the town of Clevelandia in the formerly disputed area.

In the liquidation of long-standing boundary disputes among the Latin American nations which occurred toward the end of the nineteenth century and the early twentieth century, those nations turned increasingly to other governments than that of the United States for assistance. Under a treaty concluded in 1894 Honduras and Nicaragua submitted a boundary dispute to the king of Spain, who handed down his award in 1906 fixing the boundary mainly along the Segovia (Coco) River. Nicaragua refused to comply with this award, which would have transferred a considerable part of the Mosquito Coast to Honduras. The Organization of American States brought about an agreement between the disputants in 1957 to submit the case to the International Court of Justice, which in late 1960 ruled by a vote of 14 to 1 that Nicaragua was obligated to give effect to the award of Alfonso XIII. Both nations accepted this result.

Brazil agreed with France in 1897 to submit to the arbitration of the Swiss Federal Council a dispute involving the area of Amapá near the boundary of French Guiana. Brazil's case was presented by the Baron of Rio Branco, and in the final award in 1900 she received 30,000 square miles of the 31,000 square miles in dispute, populated with some 18,000 Indians, Negroes, and half-breeds. In the following year a controversy between Brazil and Great Britain over the boundary of British Guiana was submitted to the arbitration of the king of Italy. Brazil's claim, which was presented by Joaquim Nabuco and which was based largely upon prior discovery, was held insufficient by the arbitrator. He decided that Brazil had not permanently occupied the disputed territory and accordingly divided it between the disputants along the watershed. The Baron of Rio Branco, who was appointed foreign minister of Brazil by President Rodrígues Alves and who continued in that office under four presidents until his death in 1912, tackled another of Brazil's boundary problems—the delicate problem of the Acre territory, which had been ceded by Brazil to Bolivia in the 1850s and was later, in defiance of Bolivian jurisdiction, occupied by Brazilian rubber gatherers. These workers refused to recognize the Bolivian authorities and in July, 1899, proclaimed the independent state of Acre under a Spanish adventurer "President" Luís Gálvez Rodríguez de Arias.

Rio Branco arranged with Bolivia to settle this dispute without foreign assistance. In the Treaty of Petrópolis concluded between the two nations in November, 1903, Brazil acquired the Acre territory in exchange for 2 million pounds sterling and agreed to construct a railway around the 200 miles of falls on the Madeira River giving Bolivia access to the Amazon Valley and thence to the Atlantic Ocean. By these settlements Brazil, though her territory abuts every other state in South America except Chile, was able to settle all her boundary controversies without war.

In the final settlement of the troublesome Tacna-Arica boundary dispute, which came much later and which involved Chile, Peru, and eventually Bolivia, the disputants turned to the United States for help. Chile by reason of its victory over Peru and Bolivia in the War of the Pacific gained, in the Treaty of Ancón in 1883, ownership of the province of Tarapacá and control of the provinces of Tacna and Arica for a period of ten years. At the end of that time a plebiscite was to be taken in the last-named provinces to determine their permanent ownership. When the two nations tried in 1893 to make arrangements for the plebiscite, their negotiations broke down. Efforts to settle the ownership of Tacna and Arica were renewed in 1920 when the two nations agreed to submit the dispute to the arbitration of the President of the United States. According to the award which was announced by President Coolidge in early 1925 a plebiscite should be held and all natives of the disputed provinces, their lineal descendants, and all legal residents of two years' standing should be allowed to vote for union with either Chile or Peru. With Gen. John J. Pershing as the neutral member, a commission was set up to arrange for holding the plebiscite in accordance with Coolidge's award, but it simply provided a facility for continued bickering between the two parties in dispute and produced no constructive results. Finally at the urging of President Herbert Hoover, Chile and Peru concluded a treaty at Washington in 1929 by which Chile retained Arica and transferred Tacna to Peru.

Pan-Hispanism versus Pan-Americanism

Under the Roosevelt Corollary to the Monroe Doctrine the United States, with the pleased concurrence of Great Britain and other European states having interests in Latin America, voluntarily assumed the role of collector of debts and guarantor of stability in the Caribbean and Central American areas. It replaced Spain as a colonial power in Latin America by its victory in 1898 and then proceeded to follow up its victory by establishing protectorates and financial receiverships over countries in Middle America. Upon it, therefore, as the embodiment of all Latin America's foreign creditors and oppressors, was now vented the cumulative resentment which Latin America felt toward foreign control. As the Latin American nations accepted capital from foreign countries, particularly from the United States, in order to finance their railroads, hydraulic and public utility plants, port installations, and highways, they became concerned over the threats to their sovereignty implicit in their economic development. Foreign finance capital backed by the United States government and supported by its Marine Corps seemed to menace their security. They accordingly began to place a new emphasis upon their own culture and modes of life. This was the theme of the so-called "Generation of '98." They rediscovered the sense of Spanish American brotherhood which had motivated them during the earlier struggle for independence. They became convinced that the rich, Protestant, Anglo-American nation to the north menaced their culture and independence. Literature was re-Americanized.

The high priest of this new movement was the Uruguayan journalist José Enrique Rodó, whose brilliant and moving little 100-page essay, *Ariel*, first published in 1899, established the Caliban-Ariel images, respectively, for Latin America and the United States. Latin America, Rodó declared, was, through the mother countries, Spain, Portugal, and France, the heir of Greece and the participant in its joy, its springtime, its etherealness, whereas the people of the United States were heirs of the Hebrew tradition, descendants of the dour Puritans, and the modern incarnation of science and utilitarianism. While acknowledging the devotion of the people of the United States to liberty, to public education, to habits of industry, and to "health, sanity, and strength," Rodó felt that they were bumptious, impatient, devoid of respect for tradition, lacking in sensitivity, addicted to the cult of bigness, committed to religious practices which made no place for either holiness or heroism, and dominated by an elite plutocracy. "Today," he concluded, "they openly aspire to the primacy of the world's civilization, the direction of its ideas, and they consider themselves the creators of a type of civilization which will prevail." This was the nation which was making both a physical and a moral conquest of Latin America.

Rodó's answer to this conquest was to reject the United States as a worthy model for Latin America and to emphasize instead the uniqueness and the "personal genius" of Latin America. "Care for one's own independence, personality, judgment," he preached, "is a chief form of self-respect. . . . America needs to maintain its original duality. . . . And if one dimly foresees even a higher concord in the future, that will be due not to one-sided imitation of one race by the other, but to a reciprocity of influences and a skillful

harmonizing of those attributes which make the peculiar glory of each race."
His ringing injunction to his fellow Latin Americans was: "Be conscious
possessors of the blessed power you contain within yourselves." While maintaining their own cultural integrity and inborn strengths they should not
imitate Caliban but should rather make North American positivism and
utilitarianism "serve the cause of Ariel."

Against the increasing influence of the United States many Latin Americans raised their voices. As often in the past, they discovered a new unity

Fig. 21-1. José Enrique Rodó, 1872–1917, portrait in the Senate Chamber, Montevideo,
Uruguay.

in the face of a common threat. In the nineteenth century, mutual security
had been the objective of many attempts to organize a union of some or all
of the nations of America, beginning with Juan Egaña's *Projecto de una
reunión general* in 1811. As noted in an earlier chapter, representatives of
Spanish American nations had met and concerted measures for a common
resistance to foreign aggression at Lima in 1847 and at Santiago in 1856.
Again in 1865 at Lima, when the armies of Louis Napoleon were in control
of Mexico, several Spanish American governments signed a Treaty of Union
and Defensive Alliance which provided a mutual guaranty of independence
and territorial integrity, each ally being entitled, however, to decide for itself when the *casus foederis* had occurred. At that conference, which was
attended by all the Latin American nations except Brazil, Paraguay, and
Uruguay, proposals for the abolition of war, compulsory arbitration, and

peaceful settlement of boundary disputes were also discussed, but the treaties that embodied these proposals were never ratified.

In 1880 Colombia and Chile initiated another "continental treaty" providing that all controversies be settled by compulsory arbitration and that if the disputants could not agree upon the choice of an arbitrator their dispute be referred to the President of the United States. This proposal would have made compulsory arbitration the basis of the international relations and the public law of the American nations, with the United States as the

Fig. 21-2. Delegates to the First International Conference of American States (1889–1890) at South Bend, Indiana, on six-week tour of the United States. (*Courtesy of Pan American Union.*)

final arbiter. The prestige of the United States at that time in Latin America was high because of its recent abolition of slavery and its effective opposition to the Maximilian intervention in Mexico. But this proposal was presented at an inauspicious time, for Chile was then engaged in the War of the Pacific against Bolivia and Peru. It therefore did not receive favorable action, and the congress of Latin American states which was envisaged to deal with it never met. Three years later, in 1883, representatives of nine Latin American nations gathered in Caracas and formulated a protocol which established the obligation of reciprocal and joint aid among the signatory governments to maintain the integrity of their territories.

The suggestion of compulsory arbitration as a method for pacific settlement of disputes in the Americas was brought up and discussed at the first inter-American conference which met at Washington in 1889–1890 under the chairmanship of Secretary of State James G. Blaine. There a plan of obligatory arbitration was adopted requiring the signatory states to submit to arbitration all disputes except those affecting their national independence. But the treaty in which this plan was embodied was never ratified or put into effect. A similar proposal, limited this time, however, to compulsory arbitration of all pecuniary claims, was brought before the second inter-American conference at Mexico City in 1902 as Latin America's answer to the current debt-collecting operation of Britain, Italy, and Germany against Venezuela. This proposal was objected to by the United States but was accepted by all the Latin American delegations, was subsequently ratified by a majority of their governments, and continued in force for some ten years. In each case of arbitration under it a special agreement or *compromis* had to be drawn up and agreed to by the disputants fixing the kind of arbitral procedure to be followed and the terms of reference.

But the enthusiasm of Latin Americans for the Pan-American movement, which had been auspiciously launched in the first Pan-American conference at Washington in 1889, was dampened as they saw the new Pan-American organization fall under the domination of the United States. This movement, which had been promoted by the United States as a means of maintaining the peace of the American hemisphere and of stimulating commercial interchange between itself and the Latin American nations, resulted in the establishment in Washington of the Bureau of American Republics, whose name was changed to the Pan American Union in 1910. On the governing board of this new inter-American organization only those Latin American governments which were recognized by the United States were represented. Their spokesmen were their diplomatic agents accredited to the government in Washington, and over this organization the secretary of state of the United States presided as ex officio chairman.

After the establishment of the new United States–sponsored inter-American organization, Latin Americans were generally gratified by the adoption by the United States of a new policy of commercial reciprocity under which six nations—Brazil, the Dominican Republic, Guatemala, Honduras, Nicaragua, El Salvador—and several colonial areas in the Western Hemisphere, including Cuba, Puerto Rico, and British Guiana, were able to send a few of their exports to the United States at reduced tariff rates or free of duty. But under this system they found that they were still competing with themselves as before for the United States market; Brazilian sugar, for example, still faced competition with Cuban sugar in the United States. Even these limited reciprocity arrangements were terminated by the Wilson-Gorman Tariff Act, which was adopted by the United States in 1894.

As an outgrowth of the interest of the United States in the stability of the Caribbean area the presidents of El Salvador and Guatemala were persuaded by President Roosevelt in 1906 to conclude a peace settlement on board the U.S.S. *Marblehead* ending their hostilities. In the following year, at the suggestion of both President Roosevelt and President Díaz of Mexico, the five Central American governments sent representatives to a conference in Washington. There they concluded a ten-year treaty of peace and amity, provided for the neutralization of Honduras, declared against the recognition of revolutionary governments in Central America, and set up a Central American Court of Justice, to which all future disputes among them would be referred. This Court, after settling several disputes among Central American nations, became involved in 1916 in a case involving the United States, specifically the Bryan-Chamorro Treaty by which Nicaragua had undertaken to grant to the United States in perpetuity and free from taxation the exclusive rights necessary for the construction and operation of a canal by way of the San Juan River, to lease to the United States for ninety-nine years the Great Corn and Little Corn Islands, and to give the United States for the same period the right to establish a naval base on territory bordering on the Gulf of Fonseca. Costa Rica protested against the treaty on the ground that her treaty of 1858 with Nicaragua, which had been held valid by President Cleveland in an arbitration in 1888, gave her rights in the San Juan River and recognized her right to be consulted before any contract was entered into for the construction of a canal. Costa Rica therefore appealed to the Central American Court.

El Salvador also claimed the right to be consulted on arrangements involving the Bay of Fonseca, denied that Nicaragua could alienate territory bordering on it without her consent, and appealed to the Court. The Court, after declaring itself competent to adjudicate the case, proceeded to rule that Nicaragua, in signing the Bryan-Chamorro Treaty, had violated the rights of both Costa Rica and El Salvador and was under obligation to restore the legal status which existed prior to the treaty, though it admitted that it had no right to pass upon the validity of the treaty. This decision was not recognized by either Nicaragua or the United States. As a result of their attitude the convention establishing the Court was not renewed and the Court itself was formally dissolved in March, 1918.

In the inter-American conferences which were held down to World War I —at Mexico City in 1901–1902, at Rio de Janeiro in 1906, and at Buenos Aires in 1910—resolutions were adopted and procedures worked out for fuller cooperation among the American nations in matters involving an intercontinental railway, pecuniary claims, extradition, public and private international law, exchange of publications, protection of copyrights, patents, and trademarks, status of naturalized citizens, statistics, trade and commerce, and banking. But the discussion of political subjects was banned at these meetings, and Latin Americans were inhibited in their relations with the United States by their only partially suppressed resentment against the new construction which had been given to the Monroe Doctrine and to the new policies of the United States under it. Though those policies were securing the Caribbean area against European intervention they seemed at the same time to have substituted for it an even more menacing intervention. In consequence, the modern Hispanidad movement began and Pan-Hispanism was stressed by such intellectual leaders as Rubén Darío of Nicaragua, Rufino Blanco-Fombona of Venezuela, Manuel Ugarte of Argentina, José Vasconcelos of Mexico, and José Carlos Mariátegui of Peru. They emphasized the need for a collective destiny and a continental solidarity of Latin

Fig. 21-3. Rubén Darío, 1857–1916, Nicaraguan poet. (*Courtesy of Aguilar, S.A. de Ediciones, Madrid.*)

America in opposition to the "Colossus of the North." Because of the popular appeal of these ideas they became powerful talking points of aspiring Latin American politicians.

But efforts at the maintenance of peace, whether under the auspices of the United States or not, enlisted the sympathy and support of the Latin American nations. Mexico was the only one of these nations invited to the First International Peace Conference which met at The Hague in 1899, but all of them except one were represented at the Second International Peace Conference in 1907. As they were thus assigned a role of equality in international society they developed a new sense of responsibility, a new appearance of sobriety. At the second Hague Conference they had the satisfaction of subscribing to conventions, among others, providing for the pacific settlement of international disputes, defining the rights and duties of neutral powers, restricting the belligerent right of capture in naval war, and condemning the use of "armed force for the recovery of contract debts claimed from the Government of one country by the Government of another country as being due to its nationals."

This latter convention finally embodied in an international agreement the doctrine that had been first advanced by Luis M. Drago, foreign minister of Argentina, in December, 1902, at the time of the pacific blockade of Venezuela by the joint German, British, and Italian forces. Drago had observed that the capitalist who lends his money to a foreign government always takes into account the resources of the country and the chances of recovering his investment. He is entitled to repayment, but the summary and immediate collection at a given moment through the application of force by the investor's government might result in the destruction of the weaker nation as a sovereign entity. To prevent this result Drago proposed the adoption of the principle "that the public debt cannot occasion armed intervention nor the actual occupation of the territory of American nations by a European power." This proposal, which was unpalatable to the United States, was responsible in part for Roosevelt's enunciation of his corollary to the Monroe Doctrine two years later, and in modified form it was successfully pressed by the United States for adoption at the second Hague Conference in 1907 as the Porter resolution. For its adoption the nations of Latin America had been partially responsible. Their self-consciousness, achieved through their own efforts, was also increased by the role played by the ABC powers in international affairs between 1905 and World War I.

Latin America and World War I

When, despite all the pious professions of the nations and the availability of elaborate peace machinery, World War I broke out, the Latin American nations were confronted with the difficult problem of preserving their neutral status. Bound to the Allied Powers by strong ties of consanguinity and culture they were nevertheless subjected to a persistent pressure from the Central Powers. Almost all the individual American governments issued neutrality proclamations in accordance with the Hague conventions. At the same time they made several collective attempts to maintain the neutrality of the Western Hemisphere. As early as August, 1914, Peru suggested that the American nations agree upon a common policy for the protection of their commercial interests and declare that their commerce within the American hemisphere extending to a line equidistant from Europe, on the one hand, and Asia, on the other, should not be "subject to the contingencies of the present European War." In addition, Brazil wanted to draw a neutral zone around South America from which all warships would be barred.

The Pan American Union, taking all these proposals under consideration, appointed a Special Neutrality Commission of nine members headed by the United States secretary of state. After many meetings this Commission drew up a series of recommendations which sought to define the rights of neutrals and to protect neutral property at sea. But though the Commission continued to function until 1917 its proposals were never acted upon because, first, the destruction of Admiral von Spee's fleet by a British fleet off the Falkland Islands in December, 1914, appeared to remove at least the German menace from American waters and, second, the United States, as it veered more and more toward the Allied side, became increasingly apathetic toward the Commission's work.

Since for these reasons the Commission was patently failing to provide the leadership required for hemisphere neutrality, at least four of the Latin American governments—Argentina, Bolivia, Ecuador, and Mexico—attempted to secure concerted action by the Latin American republics alone to safeguard their neutrality. The first three suggested a conference of neutrals at Buenos Aires, which never met; and Mexico, whose relations with the United States were particularly bad, proposed that the American neutrals not only refuse all kinds of war implements to the belligerents but also suspend all commercial relations with them. These nations thus sought to organize Latin American neutral sentiment. Though no united Latin American neutral front was formed, all the Latin American nations, along with the United States, succeeded in remaining neutral for more than two and one-half years.

During the period of their neutrality the economies of the Latin American nations were seriously affected by the war in Europe. At the outbreak of war foreign shipping disappeared from the seas as if by magic. As a result Latin America's markets in Europe were closed and the flow of European capital to their countries was suspended. As the economies deteriorated the sources of government revenue dried up and governments were forced to resort to deficit spending. Argentina, in order to protect its diminishing gold reserve, forbade exports of gold and suspended specie payments in 1914. It was not able to resume such payments until 1927. The impact of the war upon Brazil was equally serious. Brazil's imports fell off in 1914 to only one-half their prewar value and the price of coffee and rubber, the staple exports of the country, declined alarmingly. This decline was accompanied by a corresponding reduction in the income of many of the Brazilian states, for they derived large parts of their revenues from taxes upon exports. The resulting currency inflation could not be checked until 1917 when Brazil finally succeeded in resuming regular specie payments.

After the United States entered the war against Germany and Austria-Hungary in April, 1917, eight Latin American countries either immediately or eventually declared war against the Central Powers. These were Brazil, Costa Rica, Cuba, Guatemala, Haiti, Honduras, Nicaragua, and Panama. Five severed relations with Germany: Bolivia, the Dominican Republic, Ecuador, Peru, and Uruguay. But seven Latin American governments remained neutral throughout the war; these were Argentina, Chile, Colombia, Mexico, Paraguay, El Salvador, and Venezuela. According to their own avowals, those Latin American nations which declared war against the Central Powers or severed relations with them did so because they admired President Wilson's leadership, they wished to preserve the solidarity of the Americas, they believed that the Central Powers had violated basic principles of international law, and they felt a cultural and ideological identity with the Allies.

In Brazil, despite the existence of sizable enclaves of German population in the southern states, sentiment for the Allies—France, Britain, and Italy —was strong, and Ruy Barbosa organized a Brazilian League for the Allies which carried on an effective propaganda campaign. Brazil had one of the largest merchant fleets in Latin America, and its operations and profits were seriously interfered with by the naval war. Brazil threw upon the German government full responsibility for the damages to both Brazilian life and property which might result from Germany's violations of the principles of international law. Her entry into the war was ostensibly due to Germany's resumption of unrestricted submarine warfare in January, 1917. In the following month a Brazilian steamer was sunk, and when a second one, the *Paraná,* was sunk off the coast of France without warning on April 5, Brazil broke off diplomatic relations with Germany. After the United States entered the war against Germany the Brazilian Congress declared its solidarity with its American neighbor to the north. Thus Brazil technically abandoned its neutrality at the time when the United States declared war. The sinking of another Brazilian vessel in May prompted President Wenceslau Braz Pereira Gomes, who had moved from the vice presidency to the presidency in 1914, to announce that his country was linked with the United States and to seize some 250,000 tons of German shipping in Brazilian waters. Not, however, until another Brazilian vessel, the *Macau* was torpedoed by a German submarine off the coast of Spain in October, 1917, did Brazil finally declare war.

Brazil's trade relations with the United States had traditionally been characterized by complementarity rather than competitiveness, and her foreign policy had tended to follow that of the United States. Her appreciation of her traditional solidarity with the United States and her conviction that her fate was bound up with that country's fate, as announced by President Braz in his address of May, 1917, explain her decision to enter the war. Moreover, she gambled on an Allied victory. But Brazil was not prepared

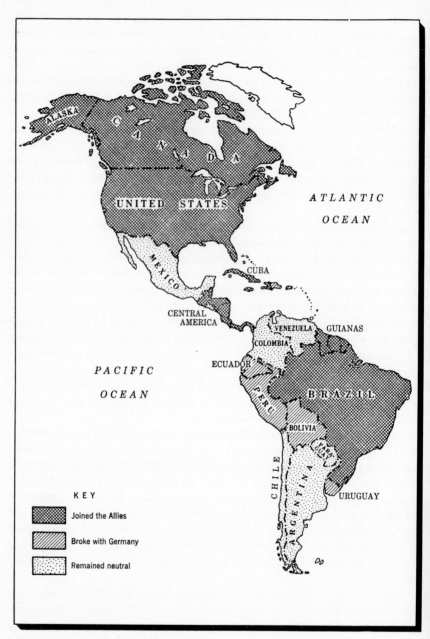

KEY

Joined the Allies

Broke with Germany

Remained neutral

The Western Hemisphere and World War I.

for active participation in the war. She supplied a few physicians and nurses to the war fronts in Europe, but in general she played an insignificant role in World War I. By 1917 the Brazilian navy was directed largely by armchair admirals whose experience in maneuvers was gained largely in the social clubs of Rio de Janeiro. Brazil nevertheless assumed partial responsibility for the South Atlantic patrol, but many of her ships were in such poor repair that they had to be reconditioned in the United States and they were not prepared for active duty until the war was over.

Brazil's military forces were augmented by a universal draft which brought 50,000 additional men into the army, but no Brazilian troops reached Europe before the end of the war because of shortages of supplies and transport facilities. They were therefore used at home to suppress domestic disorders, particularly among the German colonies in Paraná, Santa Catarina, and Rio Grande do Sul. In those states lived approximately 400,000 Germans, who were largely unassimilated into Brazilian life and who hoped and worked for a German victory up to the end of the war. In order to deal with their disruptive activities the Brazilian government, acting under war legislation passed in 1917, declared martial law not only in those three states but also in Rio de Janeiro, São Paulo, and the Federal District. It accordingly interned more than seven hundred Germans during the war, suppressed all newspapers printed in the German language, sequestered enemy property, and assumed control over German banks and commercial houses. At the end of the war the government promptly returned this property to its owners.

Brazil was the only country of South America which actually declared war, but others had as much provocation. Her entry into the war disrupted and finally terminated the ABC entente, for of her partners in that entente Argentina chose to remain neutral and Chile followed a course which was widely regarded as pro-German. Argentina's German population, numbering only around twenty thousand, was smaller than Brazil's, and German propaganda in the area of the Río de la Plata was more than counteracted by the strong French cultural tradition and by its long-standing and mutually profitable commercial ties with England. The sentiment of Argentines, so far as they expressed themselves, appeared to be predominantly pro-Allied. Their trade was seriously dislocated by Germany's naval blockade of the British Isles enforced on the high seas wherever British ships could be found, but after the first year of the war as the British navy regained control of the seas Argentine shipping returned to prewar levels. This renewal of trade with Britain, together with the expansion of trade with the United States, brought a new prosperity to Argentina, which enabled it to assume an attitude of indifference toward the war. War shortages of manufactured goods, which were needed elsewhere by the belligerents, compelled the development of new industry in Argentina, particularly in the light industries manufacturing boots and shoes, woolen goods and other textiles, and furniture, and this in turn contributed to Argentina's wartime prosperity and its resulting complacency toward the war.

All this conditioned the Argentine people and the government of President Hipólito Irigoyen to favor Argentine neutrality in the war. In March, 1917, Irigoyen placed an embargo on Argentine wheat exports, which were desperately needed by the Allies; he justified it as required by the rising wheat prices in Argentina. He had already formally protested Germany's resumption of unrestricted submarine warfare in January, 1917, and in April he sent a note to the United States recognizing the correctness of the Wilson administration's policy toward Germany. When several Argentine merchant vessels were sunk, Irigoyen again sent a protest to Germany in August. Even though Germany made amends, Argentine public opinion was so aroused that several assaults upon individual Germans took place. These anti-German demonstrations were countered by pro-German street parades and by pro-German propaganda in Spanish journals and newspapers in Argentina, particularly *La Gaceta de España,* for the peninsular Spaniards generally sympathized with the German cause. The influence ·of the Catholic Church in Argentina was also thrown in Germany's favor.

Argentine-German relations reached a crisis in September, 1917, when the United States published intercepted correspondence of Count von Luxburg, the German minister in Buenos Aires, dispatched to his government by way of the Swedish minister. In one of these dispatches von Luxburg recommended that certain small Argentine steamers, which he reported as being en route to Europe, either be spared or be *spurlos versenkt* (sunk without a trace). In another he characterized the Argentine foreign minister, Pueyrredón, as "a notorious ass." Though the Count's actions and sentiments were immediately disavowed by his government, Argentina's war spirit mounted. The Argentine government immediately handed the minister his passport, and both houses of the Argentine Congress passed resolutions demanding severance of relations with Germany. But neither Count von Luxburg's indiscretion nor the congressional resolutions moved President Irigoyen, who steadfastly refused to take Argentina into the war. He insisted that Argentina had been given no provocation for war and that Germany had made the *amende honorable.* Despite mounting criticism, particularly in the United States, that he was pro-German, the keynote of Irigoyen's policy continued to be neutrality. This seemed to him to be logically required in the interest of his nation.

Irigoyen's persistent adherence to neutrality could be justified solely in terms of Argentine interests as he conceived them. At the same time some of the Luxburg dispatches showed him to be sympathetic to the cause for which Germany was fighting, and certain members of the Argentine foreign office, though not the foreign minister, were known to be unfriendly to the United States. Irigoyen's policy may have seemed to him to be the policy best calculated to enable Argentina to assume a new and enlarged role in Latin America since both the United States and Brazil had allowed themselves to become entangled in the war.

Already in May, 1917, at a time when, perhaps coincidentally, the German submarine warfare was at the peak of its success, Irigoyen issued a call to all the Spanish American countries to meet and agree upon a common policy of neutrality. Argentina's initiative, which, coming when it did, was widely interpreted as an anti-United States move, was accepted by sixteen of the Spanish American governments, but the proposed conference never met. It aroused enthusiasm only in Mexico, whose President Carranza had his own reasons for being hostile to the United States. Meanwhile additional Latin American governments, whether under pressure from the United States or not, were aligning themselves against the Central Powers. As events showed, neutrality proved in fact to be the best policy for Argentina, for Irigoyen thus turned the war to the advantage of his country. From 1915 to 1919 Argentina enjoyed high prosperity, its industrial development got a good start through the shutting off of European imports for a period, and the Argentine *peso* was quoted higher than any other currency in the world.

In Chile the outbreak of World War I revealed a considerable public sentiment in favor of Germany. Chile might have been expected to support the Allies because of the strong British tradition in the Chilean navy, the prominent role which the British had played in developing the port of Valparaíso, the considerable British investment in the country, and the numerous marriages of Englishmen into high-ranking Chilean families. British support had also been thrown on the side of the triumphant Congressional forces in the Chilean civil war in 1891. In addition Chile's predilection for France was strong, for its culture, literature, and intellectual life had traditionally been determined by currents emanating from that country.

But these influences were counteracted by the large colonies of Germans whose coming had been encouraged by successive Chilean governments and who not only conserved but also propagandized German culture and German nationalism in Chile. They largely dominated the economic and social life of the southern part of the country. Both there and elsewhere in Chile, German methods and points of view were spread by teachers from Germany, many of whom had been brought over by Balmaceda for the purpose of improving the national educational system. As a result of the work of Colonel Körner, who became chief of the Chilean general staff in 1892 and of the German military mission which was called in soon afterward, the Chilean army was organized as a replica of the German army down to the last detail and its young officers went to Germany to complete their military training. Valparaíso became a regular port of call for German steamship lines and Chile developed close ties with German finance after the first German bank was established there in 1896. In the international rivalry of the prewar years for the trade of Latin America, Chilean commerce generally responded favorably to Germany's trade overtures and was diverted increasingly into the trade channels of that country. In that trade Chile was dependent upon German sea carriers, for she possessed only a few merchant ships of her own. However much Chilean social and intellectual circles might respect France as an *arbiter elegantiorum,* the Catholic Church in Chile considered French anticlericalism abhorrent and tended therefore to support the more Catholic Austria. These predilections in Chile for the cause of the Central Powers were reinforced by an active German propaganda which circulated in both the German and Spanish languages and which reached as far as Punta Arenas in the extreme south. Even the conservative and highly respectable *El Mercurio* of Santiago showed a pro-German bias.

The official Chilean attitude toward the belligerents in World War I, however, was one of studied neutrality—even of leaning over backward in order to give no offense to either side. The German merchant vessels which found themselves in the open roadstead at Valparaíso at the outbreak of the war were required to remain tied at their anchorages there for four years. Early in the war the Chilean authorities became convinced that Admiral von Spee, commanding the German naval squadron in the South Atlantic, was securing intelligence from Chilean bases, but they were unable to verify their suspicions. Chilean neutrality was violated when the Germans blew up an English vessel at Juan Fernández Island, but Chile demanded and received a prompt apology from Germany for this action. Later Chile joined her Latin American neighbors and the United States in protesting against Germany's resort to unrestricted submarine warfare. After the United States entered the war and the Allied and Associated Powers appeared to be winning, Chilean public opinion swung over to their side. *La Nación* was founded in 1917 as an avowedly pro-Allied newspaper. But Chile remained officially neutral up to the end of the war.

The Latin American nations played an inconsequential role in the actual hostilities and did little to support the Allied cause beyond supplying indispensable material for the winning of the war. But their participation in it moved them from the periphery of international politics toward its center. Eleven of these nations sent official delegations to the Peace Conference and signed the Treaty of Versailles. Seventeen of them—all except Mexico, the Dominican Republic, and Ecuador—immediately became members of the League of Nations, forming 36 per cent of its total membership. Brazil was given a nonpermanent seat on the Council, and she as well as many of the other Latin American states became deeply involved in the League's activities.

During the first two decades of the twentieth century, therefore, the Latin American nations, propelled by their own forces of nationalism and taking advantage of auspicious international developments, assumed increasing importance in world affairs. They were protected from European political pressures by the Roosevelt Corollary of the Monroe Doctrine, but many of them were now in turn subjected to political pressures from the United States.

All of them remained subject to economic pressures of various degrees from the outside world. Against these pressures Latin American nationalism developed an increasingly strong position, guided by Bolívar's ideal of a united Latin America which would be a counterpoise to other areas of the world. Latin Americans were stirred by a new vision of their potentialities as a fourth area of the world playing an enlarged role in world affairs. As they witnessed the philosophical, economic, and social disorder in postwar Europe they began to place new emphasis upon their own countries, their own land, their own people, their own problems, and their own future possibilities. In the literary field a new school of regionalism appeared, as evidenced, for example, in the novels of "Hugo Wast," Gustavo Martínez Zuviría, a native of Córdoba, which romantically depicted episodes of Argentine history and life. But the Latin American nations could not become a world area unless they developed, first, independent nationhood and, next, cooperative relationships with one another. In these new stirrings could be found the elements of both indigenous nationalism and Pan-Hispanism which are characteristic features of the history of Latin America in the twentieth century.

Additional Reading

Ferns, H. S.: "Investment and Trade between Britain and Argentina in the Nineteenth Century," *Economic History Review*, 2d series, vol. 3, pp. 203–218, 1950.

Frazer, R. W.: "The Role of the Lima Congress, 1864–1865, in the Development of Pan-Americanism," *Hispanic American Historical Review*, vol. 29, pp. 319–348, 1949.

Ganzert, F. W.: "The Baron do Rio Branco, Joaquim Nabuco, and the Growth of Brazilian-American Friendship, 1900–1910," *Hispanic American Historical Review*, vol. 22, pp. 432–451, 1942.

Ireland, Gordon: *Boundaries, Possessions, and Conflicts in Central and North America and the Caribbean*, Harvard University Press, Cambridge, Mass., 1941.

————: *Boundaries, Possessions, and Conflicts in South America*, Harvard University Press, Cambridge, Mass., 1938.

McGann, T. F.: *Argentina, the United States, and the Inter-American System, 1880–1914*, Harvard University Press, Cambridge, Mass., 1957.

Martin, Percy A.: *Latin America and the War*, Johns Hopkins Press, Baltimore, 1925.

Perkins, Dexter: *A History of the Monroe Doctrine*, rev. ed., Little, Brown, 1955.

Scott, James Brown: *The International Conferences of American States, 1889–1928*, Publications of the Carnegie Endowment for International Peace, Oxford University Press, New York, 1931.

Stokes, William S.: *Honduras: An Area Study in Government*, University of Wisconsin Press, 1950.

XXII

Limitations of Liberalism in the Twentieth Century

For the Latin American countries in their internal development the two decades between 1920 and 1940 were a period of strengthening nationalism, social change, and political innovation. Many of them, moved by the impetus given to nationalism by World War I, acquired a new self-consciousness, an increased awareness of their national being, and a determination to make their nationality meaningful. The principal obstacle to the realization of this goal seemed to be the economic control which was exerted over their destinies from abroad—primarily by business concerns, capitalists, and investors in New York, London, Paris, Berlin, and Rome. In the case of the Caribbean area the lines of control emanated from the United States; in most of the countries of South America they were directed from European centers of finance capital. When these lines collapsed in the world-wide economic debacle of 1929–1933 Latin Americans blamed the foreign industrialized, investing nations for their economic plight. Through the fall in the world demand for their raw materials and foodstuffs and the tapering off of foreign investment they were made overwhelmingly aware of their subordinate status in relation to the foreign world. The Depression brought home to them vividly the vulnerability of their economies to influences from abroad.

Latin Americans were therefore urgently required to find new local solutions to local problems which had become big with revolutionary potential. To them the adverse consequences of their involvement in the nexus of international economics and politics with which their destinies had been interwoven after 1919 seemed to be undeniably clear. As the nations of the foreign world introspectively and nationalistically grappled with their own problems of survival the Latin American peoples similarly tried to work out solutions which would meet their own local requirements. These efforts continued throughout the interwar period.

Republican Oligarchy in Brazil

In Brazil after the overthrow of the Emperor Dom Pedro II in 1889 the program of the Positivists was largely relegated to the background by the new rulers. Though they called themselves republican they primarily represented the interests of the military oligarchy and tended in their new role of responsibility to follow the same course as their predecessors. Despite the constitution the government remained a military dictatorship and no real autonomy was granted to the states. This situation aroused republican opposition, which became vocal in both houses of the first Congress soon after it met in June, 1891. President Deodoro da Fonseca immediately became involved in disputes with republican leaders and with Congress, which refused to pass any bills and which objected particularly to appropriation bills. As the tension between the president and Congress mounted, Fonseca issued a decree on November 3, 1891, dissolving Congress, declaring martial law, imposing strict censorship of the press, and conferring dictatorial powers upon himself. He alleged as justification for his act that his government had evidence of widespread monarchical plots to overthrow the republic by armed revolution, but whatever this evidence was, his action provoked strong resistance, particularly in the states of São Paulo and Rio Grande do Sul. His action also turned the army and the navy against him. Under threat from Adm. Custodio de Mello to bombard the capital, Rio de Janeiro, as a protest against his assumption of dictatorial powers, Fonseca resigned in favor of the vice president on November 23, 1891.

But Floriano Peixoto, too, was a military man, and his experience, outlook, and methods differed little from those of his predecessor. When he assumed the presidency the question was immediately raised whether a new election should be held or whether Floriano should serve until the end of Fonseca's constitutional term on November 15, 1894. The constitution stipulated that a new election should be held if the presidency became vacant during the first two years of a presidential term. Nevertheless Congress decided against a new election.

Floriano, however, shortsightedly chose to follow Fonseca's policies, favoring his military associates in matters of patronage and using his presidential authority to intervene in state and municipal affairs. He therefore incurred the increasing displeasure of not only the moderate republicans but also the conservatives and the imperialists, who compared his policies unfavorably with those of the displaced regime. An insurrection broke out in Rio Grande do Sul in August, 1893, and it was soon joined by a part of the navy which, under the lead of Admiral Custodio revolted, took command of the harbor of Rio de Janeiro, and demanded the resignation of President Peixoto. This rebellion soon took on the aspect of a struggle for power between the navy and the army, which had been responsible for the overthrow of the empire in 1889 and which had been its principal beneficiary. It also disclosed some features of an antirepublican movement, for monarchism was not yet dead in Brazil but lingered on among certain high officials of the navy. Admiral Custodio hesitated to bombard the capital city because it was full of sympathizers with the revolutionary movement, though still controlled by Floriano's government. His base of supplies therefore remained in the possession of the government.

Meanwhile Peixoto was making desperate and eventually successful efforts to purchase warships in Europe, and when these arrived, soon after Custodio had finally begun to bombard the capital city, the government established a blockade of the port, thus limiting Custodio's freedom of action and preventing him from maintaining contact with the insurgents in Rio Grande do Sul to the south. These latter, as they moved northward to catch Peixoto, found their plight so desperate that after reaching Paraná their leaders took asylum on some hospitable Portuguese men-of-war, which offered them protection. The commanders of these vessels, obviously sympathizing with the rebellion, refused Peixoto's demand for the delivery of the fugitive insurgents and instead delivered them to a safe place in Montevideo. This incident resulted in strained relations between Brazil and Portugal.

Meanwhile the United States minister to Brazil, Thomas S. Thompson, along with his European colleagues in the diplomatic corps, had refused to assist President Peixoto in measures to prevent the bombardment of Rio de Janeiro by the rebel ships. At the same time Thompson asked his government to send ships to the port of Rio de Janeiro in order to protect the lives and property of his fellow countrymen. The mere question of protection of their lives and property was involved here, for neither the United States nor other foreign governments accorded belligerent status to the Brazilian rebels during their eight months' campaign against the Peixoto government. But any aggressive action which Admiral Custodio might have taken against the government was now thwarted by the commanders of the naval forces of the United States, France, Italy, Great Britain, and Portugal, which were stationed in the harbor at Rio de Janeiro. These naval officers interceded in the revolution for the purpose of ending the threat to the lives and property of citizens of their countries. With the exception of the commander of the German warship in the harbor, who refused to cooperate with them, they informed Custodio that "they would oppose by force, if necessary, any enterprise against Rio de Janeiro," and at the same time they secured from Floriano a promise to remove the cannons from his shore batteries which were trained on the navy. Finally the United States commander, Vice Admiral Benham, refused to permit Custodio to establish a commercial blockade of the port and warned him that if he interfered with the loading or discharge of cargoes of vessels of the United States he would open fire on the Brazilian fleet. Since the United States squadron, consisting of five warships, outnumbered the Brazilian vessels, the revolt collapsed in March, 1894.

Simultaneously the revolt of Rio Grande do Sul which had been directed primarily against Floriano's representative there, the republican governor of the state, collapsed, and Floriano in both cases ruthlessly punished all who had cooperated with the rebels. He was able by these methods to remain in office until the end of his term. Meanwhile, two weeks before the surrender of Admiral Custodio's fleet, presidential elections, which were surprisingly free, were held. In those elections, equally surprisingly, Peixoto, instead of continuing a military dictatorship declined to be a candidate for reelection and selected a civilian as his successor. His candidate, Prudente de Morais Barros of São Paulo, had been one of the two republican deputies elected from that state to the national legislature in 1886 and had contended for the presidency as a republican candidate against Deodoro in 1891. His selection as the official candidate now marked the abandonment of military dictatorship, the recognition of the republic, and the final establishment of constitutional government.

Fig. 22-1. Euclides da Cunha, portrait by Belmiro de Almeida for the Brazilian Ministry of Foreign Relations. (*Courtesy of Pan American Union.*)

As had been anticipated by the states of both the north and the south at the time of the overthrow of the empire, power now definitely shifted to the latter. Rio de Janeiro and São Paulo became the business centers of the country. The opening up of new, fertile western areas in São Paulo and other southern states caused a further decline in the importance of the north. There in the isolated, drought-stricken back parts of the states of Bahía, Ceará, and Paraíba in 1896 there occurred a revolt of some five thousand benighted, highly emotional backwoodsmen (*sertanejos*) led by a religious zealot and mystic, Antônio Vicente Mendes Maciel, the *conselheiro* or counselor. This so-called "Canudos affair" was later dramatically portrayed by Euclides da Cunha, in what is probably Brazil's greatest literary work, *Os Sertões*. First published in 1902, it is Steinbeckian in its harsh realism and its sympathetic insights into the social and economic plight of these misled rebels. To suppress them the federal government sent more than thirteen thousand troops into the field and resorted to frightful massacres. The independent government which the rebels had set up was demolished, and by 1897 their last stronghold, Canudos, was captured and its defenders to the last man were killed. But the triumph of the Prudente government over these hapless backwoods fanatics in the Brazilian dustbowl of the north was a Pyrrhic victory. It provided no durable solution to the problems of this economically depressed area and cost the government so much money that it aggravated Brazil's already serious financial plight. The national debt, which stemmed from the Paraguayan War, had been pyramided by the spendthrift policies of the militarists, by financial corruption under the republic, and finally by the expenditures incurred by the civil wars. The government's solution was to issue large quantities of paper money.

By the mid-1890s Brazil was producing almost two-thirds of the world's supply of coffee. The high profits from this primary export crop stimulated an excessive expansion of coffee plantations and led to the diversion of large numbers of Italian immigrants from Argentina to work in the Brazilian coffee industry. When, as a consequence of the economic depression which swept over the Western world in the mid-1890s, the price of coffee declined, Brazil's foreign exchange also declined and its treasury receipts began to fall off. The financial condition of the government went from bad to worse. By 1898 Brazil's paper money was 21 per cent below par and the government was no longer able to continue payments on its foreign debts. President Prudente, as the last act of his administration, made an agreement with Brazil's foreign creditors to waive payment of interest for three years. At the same time he agreed that the government would reduce the volume of its paper currency and would establish a sinking fund to finance future interest payments. With this final fillip to a troubled and undistinguished administration Prudente turned over the presidency in 1898 to his elected successor, Brazil's second civilian president, Manoel Ferraz de Campos Salles.

As president-elect, Campos Salles went to London and there successfully concluded financial arrangements which averted the necessity of suspending Brazil's foreign debt payments. He negotiated a funding loan with the Rothschilds in June, 1898, which made possible the floating of a new issue of Brazilian bonds. They were issued at 5 per cent for a period of sixty-three years and were secured by Brazil's import duties. As a result of this funding arrangement and the skillful management of the minister of finance in the Campos Salles cabinet, Dr. Joaquim Murtinho, Brazil was able by 1901 to begin once more the payment of interest on its foreign debt. A new protective tariff law adopted in 1900 also contributed to national recovery by stimulating the development of industry.

As economic prosperity returned, liberalism in Brazil seemed to be inextricably identified both with republican forms of government and with a civilian executive. A third civilian president, Dr. Francisco de Paula Rodrigues Alves, like his two immediate predecessors a native of São Paulo, was virtually named to the presidency by the retiring president in 1902 and was duly elected. The effectiveness of the shift of power to the south was signalized during his administration by the emphasis given to the beautification of Rio de Janeiro. Under an engineer-mayor, Francisco

Pereira Passos, the business district of this city of 600,000 people was redesigned to facilitate its conduct of foreign trade, new port installations were constructed, and the shore attractions of this most beautiful harbor in the Western Hemisphere were developed. At the same time a strong campaign was launched under the guidance of Dr. Osvaldo Cruz, director of public health, to wipe out yellow fever and bubonic plague which were endemic in the capital. Inspired largely by the success of the United States in eliminating yellow fever from both Cuba and the Panama Canal Zone this campaign in Rio de Janeiro was equally successful.

São Paulo's seeming monopoly of the presidency was broken in 1906 when Dr. Affonso Augusto Moreira Penna of Minas Gerais, another civilian, was chosen president. As a signal accomplishment of his administration the national treasury appeared to have reached such a position of strength that it could redeem Brazil's outstanding paper currency. For this purpose a national bank, the *Caixa de Conversão*, was established in late 1906, and by this means much of Brazil's paper currency was soon redeemed. But a complete convertibility could not be accomplished, and consequently both gold and paper currency standards continued side by side. A complete return to the gold standard was prevented later by the outbreak of World War I, which necessitated the issuance of new unsecured paper currency and which accordingly drove the *Caixa* notes out of circulation.

In 1906 the Affonso Penna administration tried Brazil's first experiment with coffee valorization. In that year the coffee surplus over and above the world's total consumption requirements of approximately 12 million bags amounted to some 11 million bags. This surplus, combined with Brazil's prospect of a bumper crop estimated at an additional 20 million bags, appeared to spell disaster for Brazil's principal export and the basis for its foreign exchange. In order to save the coffee market the Brazilian government, therefore, leading from a position of strength as the world's principal coffee exporter, established a minimum price for coffee and borrowed money abroad to finance coffee exports, agreeing to meet the interest on the foreign loan from the export tax on coffee. With this foreign loan the government purchased some 8.5 million bags of coffee from private Brazilian producers, which it then sold abroad at the officially pegged price. This valorization or guaranteed-price experiment successfully averted a crisis in the coffee industry, but its continuance in the following year proved unnecessary since Brazilian production declined to only about 5 million bags. It was so successful, however, that in 1917, when Brazil again produced a bumper coffee crop, when coffee consumption was low because of the European war, and when export channels were dislocated, valorization was tried again. The government undertook to acquire enough of the current crop to enable it to dominate the world market and to obtain a price that would make a profit for Brazilian growers. Government purchases and sale of coffee at a pegged price again saved the coffee industry. These official actions were reinforced in the following year by a fortunate decline in coffee production, which rendered further government assistance unnecessary. But in both 1906 and 1917 the Brazilian government thus intervened and assumed a responsibility for maintaining the stability of Brazil's coffee export market.

Even before World War I the civilian influence in the Brazilian government began to wane. In 1908 the government, finding itself with only a single warship, and that obsolete, proceeded to augment its navy by purchasing vessels in England, thus starting a naval rearmament program which aroused the apprehensions of Argentina. Penna's death in 1909 brought another civilian, his vice president, Dr. Nilo Peçanha, into the presidential chair for the remaining year and one-half of his administration, but in the election of 1910 the militarists and the conservatives agreed upon a military candidate, Marshal Hermes da Fonseca, nephew of the first president of the republic. He was put forward for the presidency by a convention of the government party, the so-called "Republican Conservative party," largely through the maneuvering of the political boss of Rio Grande do Sul, Pinheiro Machado. He had served as minister of war under President Penna and was now supported by President Peçanha.

But this swing to the military was not supinely accepted by republican civilians, who gathered together their followers, particularly in the states of São Paulo, Minas Gerais, and Bahía, held a convention of their own, organized a *Civilista* party, rejected Fonseca's candidacy, and nominated the distinguished Ruy Barbosa of Bahía as their candidate. His campaign, which was carried straight to the people, was directed against overcentralization of power in the federal government at Rio de Janeiro, against the unresponsiveness of the federal government to the popular will, and particularly against its subordination to military influences. But Barbosa received only 126,292 popular votes to 233,882 for his military rival for the presidency. He and his associates charged that the election had been carried by fraud, but they were unable to prevent Fonseca from assuming the presidency. They carefully laid plans, however, for a continuation of their vigorous campaign against perversion of Brazil's republican government by the military.

The administration of Hermes da Fonseca, which controlled Brazil from 1910 to 1914, was itself largely controlled by the dominant military group. One of the costly failures of his administration was an attempt to support the rubber industry of the Amazon by subventions from the federal government when it was threatened with ruin not only by reckless mismanagement but also by destructive competition from the rubber plantations of the Far East. The heyday of the Brazilian rubber industry came in the years before World War I when increasing demands from industry, transportation, and medicine made it profitable to exploit the natural rubber resources of the Amazon Basin. The rubber trees growing as individual trees widely separated in the Amazon rain forest were tapped by experienced native tappers or *seringueiros*. The sap was regularly collected by them, was cured by being smoked over jungle fires, and was then carried in the form of large rolls of raw rubber, sometimes weighing as much as 150 pounds, to river ports on the backs of caravans of native carriers, both men and women. In 1903 exports of crude rubber from Brazil reached 32,000 tons. With the introduction of automobiles and the new use of rubber for tires the prospects for the industry seemed unlimited. The population of the principal rubber port, Pará, increased from 97,000 in 1900 to 236,000 in 1920. In 1912 Brazil exported the largest volume of rubber in her history, over 45,000 tons.

A step fatal to Brazil's large rubber industry was taken early in the century when some 70,000 seeds of the rubber tree, *Hevea brasiliensis,* were taken, in violation of Brazilian law, from the Amazon Basin, the natural habitat of the rubber tree, by a British planter to the British Royal Botanical Gardens at Kew. From there several thousand seedlings were shipped to Ceylon. Thence they were carried to Malaya, British Borneo, India, Burma, French Indo-China, and the Dutch East Indies. As the seedlings grew and thrived there under a plantation economy where labor was even cheaper than in Brazil, the rubber industry of Brazil entered into a permanent decline from which the federal-aid policy of the Fonseca administration failed to redeem it. In 1913 Brazil's rubber production totaled only 37,000 tons while that of the Far Eastern plantations reached more than 53,000 tons. By 1925 Brazilian production fell to less than 20,000 tons while shipments from the Far East rose to 400,000 tons.

As a result of this and other similar misadventures the Fonseca government was driven to currency inflation and issued a quantity of unsecured paper currency in 1914. It later successfully funded the national debt of Brazil by negotiating a large new loan in London. Brazil's financial system was further dislocated at this time by the outbreak of World War I which adversely affected its foreign trade by cutting off some of its European markets and European sources of manufactured goods.

At the end of the first quarter of a century of republican government, Brazil could point to an extraordinary record of material accomplishment. Its foreign trade had more than doubled, growing from 285 million dollars to 640 million; its railway mileage had also more than doubled, increasing from 6,000 to more than 15,000. By 1913 the country could boast 38,000 miles of telegraph line and 110,000 miles of telephone wire. The population had expanded from 14 million to 24 million. For this large population growth, foreign countries were partly responsible. Between 1891 and 1900 Brazil received 1,143,902 immigrants, and during the next decade the stream of foreigners continued, though at a slightly reduced rate, bringing 698,159 newcomers to the country. An estimated 80 per cent of the Brazilian population, however, still remained illiterate. Most of the backwardness in educational and cultural matters was found among the populations of the north and in the raw frontier areas which were peopled largely by Negroes and Indians. Black Africans, living largely in the north central states, especially in Bahía, were estimated at about one-tenth of the population of Brazil. The pure Indian element, largely confined to the Amazon Basin, was estimated at fewer than 100,000. Successive republican governments had done little to widen the basis of suffrage or to prepare the Brazilian people for the exercise of self-government. Oligarchic patterns of political action still prevailed, but they were now applied by new oligarchies.

Liberalism Aborted in Argentina

At the end of World War I Argentina seemed to be provided with a program of vital political action. Expectations of social and economic change which would benefit the middle and working classes were rife. The census of 1914 had disclosed a population of almost 7.9 million, of whom more than 30 per cent were foreigners, chiefly Italians, Spaniards, and Germans. As Argentina's urban centers in the littoral were growing faster than her rural population the political program of the Radical party when it came to power as a reform party in 1916 was directed especially toward amelioration of the condition of the city workers. This included legislation fixing hours of labor and minimum wages, regulating employment of women and children, providing for arbitration of industrial disputes, supervising the sale of drugs, and making homesteads available to settlers. Besides, Irigoyen's persistent adherence to a policy of neutrality in the war, dictated in part by the polyglot population, brought large material rewards to the nation and opened up radiant vistas of postwar prosperity for all classes.

Irigoyen's entire career had been spent in politics. And yet he never acquired the superficial arts and graces of the politician. He was remote and aloof and remained a behind-the-scenes operator, a party boss. Lacking the usual arts of the demagogue he nevertheless exerted a demagogic appeal. His name was magic to the great mass of the Argentines. He cared nothing for foreign decorations or for riches or for fiestas. Abstemious, austere, and mysterious, he became a legend during his presidency. "Introverted and fanatical, a man of very few ideas," concludes his Argentine biographer, "he was convinced that the country only needed free elections to be absolutely transformed." [1]

The Argentine people expected action from Irigoyen and his party, but they did not get it. Or rather they got a kind of action they did not expect. The Radical party in office proved to be not a radical party. The administration, it is true, represented a broader electorate than ever before in Argentine history. It spoke for the people, but its tones were muffled by

[1] Manuel Gálvez, *Vida de Hipólito Irigoyen,* 2d ed., Talleres Gráficos G. Kraft, Ltd., s.a., Buenos Aires, 1939, p. 241.

the ineptitude and inexperience of the new representatives of the people. The electorate generally approved Irigoyen's wholesale use of intervention in the provinces to unseat the old conservative oligarchs and to consolidate his party indubitably in power as the spokesman of the nation. The old Conservative party, it was confidently believed, would eventually disappear under the political impact of the new middle-class Argentine majority. But this creole elite, dismayed by the new political developments, simply bided their time on their landed estates and continued their old style of rural and patriarchal living. Finally they would be able to take advantage of the ideological bankruptcy of Irigoyen's party, of the disturbed postwar conditions, and of the schism that opened up in the Radical party under Irigoyen's leadership to retrieve their lost status and to win again a position of dominance in the 1930s.

As president, Irigoyen gave Argentina a highly personal administration. He obviously aspired to be a moderate reformer, like his contemporary, Woodrow Wilson, in the United States, but his good intentions were easily subverted. As they evaporated, his political following faded away. Generous and kind to a fault he often handed out public offices to the deserving poor without regard to merit. He did not hesitate to assume the role of dictator to advance democratic causes, but his conception of what were democratic causes in the postwar decade was, to say the least, somewhat cloudy. He curiously combined the qualities of both a Wilson and a Coolidge. He was the prototype of the twentieth-century Latin American *caudillo,* recognizing the political force of numbers, wooing the common people, and championing a program of political action on their behalf. But at the same time he rejected the extremist logic of the Radical program.

Paradoxically, despite Irigoyen's prolabor professions, his administration was disfigured by several serious strikes. Called "the father of the poor" he identified himself with the working classes and supplied them with reasons for making large demands. The Radical program encouraged labor to expect an equalization of income and so provoked strikes. Many of the strikes that occurred during Irigoyen's administration were caused, however, by wartime and postwar economic dislocations and the failure of wages to keep pace with rising prices. A railroad strike called in 1917 lasted about one month and finally succeeded in wringing from the companies a 10 per cent increase in wages, an eight-hour day, and recognition of trade unions. A general strike proclaimed in Buenos Aires in 1919 completely paralyzed the city and put the strikers virtually in control. Argentina's big dock strike in 1921 closed the port of Buenos Aires and forced vessels to load and discharge cargoes at Montevideo. In these crises Irigoyen was caught between the rising demands of the workers and the conflicting interests of the traditional Argentine oligarchy. In order to placate the latter he selected as his successor Marcelo T. de Alvear, who belonged to an aristocratic family and who was serving as Irigoyen's minister to France. With Irigoyen's backing and the support of the Radical machine Alvear was elected by an enormous majority.

Once established in the presidency Alvear showed his independence of Irigoyen. As a result the Radical party soon split into two almost equal factions—the *Personalistas,* who followed Irigoyen's leadership, and the *anti-Personalistas,* who, like Alvear, opposed Irigoyen. By reason of this schism the party sank into leaderless chaos and its legislative program was stalemated. But the name Irigoyen still had its old magic, and in 1928 his followers ran him again for the presidency against a candidate of the coalition of *anti-Personalistas* and Conservatives. Though Irigoyen made no speeches during the campaign and never even made a public appearance he won the election, carrying the country by almost 80 per cent of the total vote.

But the program of middle-class democracy which had carried the Radical party to victory under Irigoyen's leadership in 1916 and had elected him a second time in 1928 did not meet Argentina's needs in the depression years of 1929 and 1930. Alvear had stabilized Argentina's financial position in 1927 by resuming specie payments, which had been suspended since 1914, but the nation continued heavily dependent upon borrowed capital and foreign markets. As the sale of its wheat, meat products, and flax was increasingly blocked by foreign tariff walls, the prices of its exports declined on the world market and unemployment mounted. Irigoyen was now a tired administrator, unable to supply the vigorous leadership that the nation required. As he had gathered large powers into his own hands, he, like every absolutist ruler, had to bear the blame when things went wrong. He was therefore held responsible when the prices of Argentina's principal products, cattle and wheat, declined. Since he could not provide the panacea that would cure Argentina's economic ills his prestige sank. Finally in September, 1930, he lost the support of the navy and was presented with an ultimatum by a group of army officers, led by Gen. José F. Uriburu, demanding his resignation. Thus the Irigoyen regime collapsed, destroyed by its own inner contradictions and indecisiveness. Professing to be a party of the people the *Personalista* Radicals failed to implement their dogmas with action. They fell victim to their own demagogy.

In contrast the regime that now undertook to govern Argentina, headed by General Uriburu as provisional president, made no play for public support. Uriburu established a military dictatorship, supported and staffed largely by Conservatives. He persecuted the *Personalista* Radicals and even tried to secure the repeal of the Sáenz Peña law. He publicly denounced Irigoyen's minimum-wage law, condemned universal suffrage, and proposed the establishment of a corporative system similar to that which seemed to be flourishing in Mussolini's Italy. In the elections which he finally scheduled for November 8, 1931, he did not allow the *Personalistas* even to name a candidate. As a result of that election General Uriburu turned the presidency over to Gen. Augustín P. Justo, who was elected by a coalition of *anti-Personalista* Radicals, Conservatives, and provincial bosses. This coalition of parties, dominated by the Conservatives and calling itself the *Concordancia,* would govern Argentina until mid-1943.

Argentina had been a favorite investment outlet for British capitalists since the early part of the nineteenth century. As a result it had become closely linked with British banking and commercial interests. "The English dominated the country for many years with such skill and tact," explains an Argentine writer, "that their name is still attached to the best things— 'English punctuality,' 'an Englishman's word,' or 'English fashion.'" [2] In the Western Hemisphere, Argentina's status in relation to London was almost identical with that of Canada except that it lacked an organic connection with the British government. Its actual dependence upon London was clearly revealed in the Imperial Economic Conference held in Ottawa in 1932 when all the component parts of the British Commonwealth of Nations, consulting together on measures which they could take to overcome the economic depression, adopted a system of imperial preference in trade. Argentina was not entitled to share in this system, and without it her agricultural products could not compete with those of Australia and Canada, which were Argentina's principal competitors in the markets of the British Empire. As a result Argentine exports to England declined at the rate of 5 per cent per month. Argentina's loss of favor may have been attributable in part to the decline in the profits of British railroad and other investments in Argentina resulting from the Depression. The Fifth Dominion was obviously expendable in the British economy.

In this plight the Justo government was obliged to conclude an unfavorable commercial agreement with London—the so-called "Roca-Runciman agreement," which was negotiated by the Argentine vice president, Julio A. Roca, and the president of the Board of Trade in London, Walter Runciman. Argentina agreed to use her valuable pounds sterling to service her debt to the British, to give 85 per cent of her meat products to the British *frigoríficos* (meat-packing houses), to reduce her tariffs on British goods to the levels of 1930, and to give "benevolent treatment" to British public service enterprises operating in that country. In return the British agreed only not to reduce their takings of Argentine meat. This agreement was to run for three years from 1933, and upon its expiration in 1936 it was renewed for another three-year term. The government of President Justo seemed to have no alternative but to accept these humiliating terms, since the agreement assured a continued market for a considerable part of Argentina's meat, which accounted for 16 per cent of the country's total exports. The agreement bound Argentina to Britain more closely than ever before and furthermore bound her on the latter's own terms. Argentina, as she bought more from Britain,

[2] Luis Guillermo Piazza, "There'll Always Be a Córdoba," in Pan American Union, *Literature in Latin America,* Washington, 1950, p. 5.

was forced to buy less from the United States and even to impose quotas limiting her purchases from her Western Hemisphere neighbor in North America.

This agreement, combined with the repressive domestic policies of the Justo administration, made it highly unpopular with the Argentine people. Under the leadership of the minister of finance, Federico Pinedo, the government established controls over foreign exchange, crops, and prices and created a central bank to strengthen its control over banking. The opposition to Justo was spearheaded by the *Personalista* Radicals. When Irigoyen died in July, 1933, over 100,000 persons marched behind his funeral cortege. After his death the leadership of the party devolved upon Alvear, who was nominated as the party's candidate in the election of 1937. But the Radical party was divided and disorganized, and Alvear was defeated by Roberto M. Ortiz, a corporation lawyer, whose nomination was arranged by the *Concordancia* clique by means of fraud and intimidation. His election was accomplished by corrupt political methods and the support of the army.

But Ortiz, despite the method of his election, was an honest man and rose to the responsibilities of his new position. In an effort to eliminate corruption and ensure honesty in elections, he intervened the province of San Juan, annulled a demonstrably fraudulent vote there, and sent commissions to other provinces to investigate their voting. As a result when honest elections were held in 1940 the opposition Radicals gained a plurality in the Chamber over the *Concordancia* members, and a legislative stalemate developed between the Radical Chamber and the Conservative Senate.

To the horror of the wealthy *estanciero* class who controlled the *Concordancia,* Ortiz seemed to be delivering the country over to the Radicals. This landed oligarchy, owning much of the agricultural wealth of the country, through their mutually profitable alliance with the foreign owners of the *frigoríficos,* controlled the sinews of the nation's economic strength. Their monopoly of land was shown by the figures of land ownership for Buenos Aires province, where 272 individuals and companies owned 12.5 million acres or one-sixth of the entire province. This class, the descendants of the *porteños* of the early period of independence, had its journalistic spokesman in the Buenos Aires newspaper *La Prensa.* The interests of this class were best served by free trade with the foreign world, the continuation of a colonial economic status for Argentina, and the renewal of the Roca-Runciman pact. From the fate which Ortiz seemed to be preparing for them they were saved by his illness and the accession of the vice president, Ramón S. Castillo, to the executive power in July, 1940.

Under Castillo, who became president in fact upon the resignation of Ortiz two years later, further Radical gains were made impossible by Castillo's interventions of the provinces of Santa Fe, Mendoza, San Juan, and Buenos Aires and by his proclamation of a state of siege in late 1941. The Radicals were helpless and leaderless since Alvear had died, and they could not hope to effect any political change until they could gain the support of the army. But their efforts to win military backing to oust the Conservatives failed, and they would not condescend to woo the growing industrial urban middle and lower classes, which as a result of the expansion of Argentine industry since World War I offered a fruitful field for political exploitation. While the Conservative party, entrenched in power, maintained its traditional position in Argentine politics by force, the Radicals failed to provide effective opposition and hesitated to use the instrumentalities of mass appeal and mass support which alone would enable them to unseat the *Concordancia*. As the two leading Argentine parties became deadlocked, glowering at each other, both of them neglected the new industrial classes, particularly those in the building industry, flour milling, and textile manufacturing, who were not affiliated with the old *estanciero* class. From the point of view of the urban industrial classes, both management and workers, the Uriburu-Justo-Ortiz-Castillo regimes in the period from 1930 to 1943 represented a throwback to nineteenth-century conservatism and left them unrepresented and dissatisfied. They were ripe for new leadership. They would provide the basis for a new Argentine liberalism.

The traditional liberalism of Argentina, with which Irigoyen and the Radical party were identified, was of nineteenth-century origin. During the two decades after World War I it found no political expression and developed no ideology except the warmed-over milk-and-water formulas of Irigoyen, which were too weak to conquer the economic depression. Argentina remained ideologically and politically stalemated for twenty years as a curious case of arrested development, while unobtrusively a new economic and social orientation of classes was taking place which was big with future possibilities for Argentine liberalism conceived in the nationalist mold. A small group of dedicated socialists, who were disciples of Esteban Echeverría and his *Asociación de Mayo,* also carried on a nagging opposition, led by Dr. Alfredo Palacios. Their program calling for stronger governmental action and increased social welfare legislation pointed the way toward developments to come in Argentina.

The Alessandri Program in Chile

In the immediate years after World War I the hero of liberalism in Chile was the picturesque "Lion of Tarapacá," Arturo Alessandri, who was of Italian descent and who came from one of the most ill-favored of all the Chilean provinces. A powerful orator, clever politician, and magnetic personality, Alessandri ran for the presidency in 1920 as the candidate of the Liberal Alliance, a political coalition representing the middle and lower classes. His campaign presented a challenge to the landed oligarchy, which through its victory over Balmaceda and its resulting control of Congress had ruled Chile since 1891. The balloting was so close in 1920 that Congress was obliged to appoint a tribunal of honor to cast only one electoral vote deciding between Alessandri and his opponent, the candidate of the National Union. When Alessandri was declared the winner, the decision was accepted by the people.

Under Alessandri the Chilean political pendulum swung away from the parliamentary system of nineteenth-century liberalism, which had been installed after the victory of the Congressionalists in the Chilean civil war, and back to the Balmaceda system of a strong executive carrying through a presidential program of social betterment even, if necessary, in defiance of Congress. Balmaceda had pointed the way for the new liberals of the twentieth century. Alessandri, like Irigoyen in Argentina, was a *caudillo* in the nineteenth-century tradition, but a *caudillo* who under the changed conditions of the twentieth century found it politically necessary to appeal to a broadened electorate and to champion the interests of the rising and increasingly articulate class of manual workers. His victory therefore was very upsetting to Chilean "Whiggery," whose cozy little oligarchies were now thrown on the defensive by the specter of more popular participation in government and a program of governmental action aimed at the amelioration of the conditions of the manual workers.

Alessandri came into the presidency of Chile with the old Balmaceda program calling for a presidential system to replace the existing parliamentary system. He advocated an income tax, nationalization of banks and insurance companies, profit sharing by labor, increased public educational facilities, and the enactment of social legislation which would limit the hours of work, prohibit child labor, regulate the work of women, provide insurance against unemployment, accidents, disease, and old age, and guarantee retirement allowances. But his ambitious legislative program as well as his policies in foreign affairs ran into opposition from the conservative oligarchy which still controlled the upper house of the legislature. An executive-legislative deadlock developed similar to that of 1890. The Senate refused to enact an income tax law and forced the resignation of the cabinet; instead of passing the budget to provide operating expenses for the government, senators spent their time in discussing salary increases for themselves. They also opposed the protocol which Alessandri had concluded for the settlement of the long-pending Tacna-Arica dispute with Peru, which was a heritage of the War of the Pacific. Here was an exhibition of legislative bankruptcy similar to that in contemporary Italy and Spain, and it invited Alessandri to resort to the methods which were being used in those countries by Mussolini and Primo de Rivera, respectively. As in Italy and Spain, parliamentary government in Chile appeared to be breaking down.

As the chosen spokesman of the new Chile, Alessandri was willing to work under the parliamentary or congressional system if he could command the support of the Chilean Congress in his claims to national executive leadership. But this he could not obtain. To counter the willful obstructionism in the legislative body Alessandri appealed to the country to provide him with a Congress which would support his measures and would make his presidential leadership effective. At the same time he made ready to use the army and the national police in order to secure the kind of Congress he desired. His threats proved effective, and he now secured from his opponents, who were genuinely concerned that he might seek to accomplish his ends by dictatorial methods, a bargain by which they agreed to support his legislative program on condition that he refrain from using the army and the police in the election. Although as a result he was able to secure a favorable majority in both houses, his opponents now staged a military coup, following the pattern recently tried in Italy and Spain, and forced him to resign. Alessandri took refuge in the United States legation and departed from the country under the protection of the United States flag.

The army, whose support was essential to the stability of any Chilean regime, was divided in its attitude toward Alessandri. In his place a conservative military *junta,* representing the older officers and consisting of two generals and an admiral, installed itself in power in September, 1924. It dismissed Congress and identified itself closely with the National Union, which was the conservative opposition to Alessandri's Liberal Alliance. The system of parliamentary government which had been followed in Chile for thirty-three years thus came to an end and was replaced by an executive type of regime as a result of revolutionary action. Strong executive rule was a part of Alessandri's creed, but the establishment of such rule by a military *junta* was not included in his plans. Of this change when it occurred he was not the beneficiary.

But in less than five months this *junta* was overthrown by a group of younger officers who were favorable to Alessandri and were led by Maj. Carlos Ibáñez and Maj. Marmaduque Grove. When they invited Alessandri to return to the presidency he accepted their invitation. Upon his arrival in Chile he was received with a great popular demonstration. He now called a consultative commission which under his guidance drew up a new constitution for Chile replacing the conservative Portales constitution of 1833.

The new document declared that the parliamentary system which had been grafted onto Chile's constitutional system in 1891 had been a failure; in its place, the new constitution provided for a strong independent executive. He would be elected for a six-year term by a direct vote of the eligible voters and would be ineligible for immediate reelection. To him and not to Congress the members of the cabinet would thereafter be responsible. They would serve at his pleasure and could not be ousted by a congressional vote of censure. The president's budget could be put into effect without the sanction of the Congress. If it did not receive congressional approval within a specified time it would nevertheless go into operation. The constitution disestablished the Catholic Church, provided for a graduated income tax, and granted the suffrage to all literate males over the age of twenty-one. On the delicate subject of private property the constitution adopted a principle of eminent domain which was traditional in Spanish law, and made it subject to the "limitations ... necessary for the maintenance and progress of social order."

This constitution, the first in Chile's history since 1833, was approved in a popular plebiscite and went into force in 1925, establishing a new basis for stability and order. It became possible now for Chile to stabilize its *peso*, which had been irredeemable in gold since 1878. Meanwhile a gold fund had slowly been accumulated, which became large enough by 1925 to permit the stabilization of the *peso* at its real value, 12½ cents, instead of its face value of 36 cents, and to redeem all the paper money in circulation. In this financial reorganization Chile was assisted by a financial mission headed by Prof. Edwin W. Kemmerer of Princeton University.

A political tug of war now developed between the temperamental Alessandri and his minister of war, Carlos Ibáñez, which resulted in Alessandri's resignation a second time and his eventual replacement by Ibáñez. In the special presidential election which was held in May, 1927, Ibáñez received 222,139 votes out of a total of 230,211 votes cast. He established an efficient, executive type of government and carried into effect much of Alessandri's legislative program, sometimes by methods which appeared to violate civil liberties and minority rights. But like the governments of Irigoyen in Argentina and Leguía in Peru, the Ibáñez regime failed to survive the great deflation of 1929–1932. Chile was slow to feel the effects of the Depression, but its nitrate and copper industries, the keys to its economy, were especially hard hit. In an effort to strengthen nitrates Ibáñez organized the producers into a giant nitrate monopoly (*Compañía Salitre de Chile* or *Cosach*), but the industry nevertheless failed to show profits. Its decline, along with the reduction of United States capital investment in Chile, created an economic crisis and obliged Ibáñez to resign in July, 1931.

Chile now entered a decade of violent political oscillations. During the fifteen months after Ibáñez's downfall it had three different presidents. The weak government of Ibáñez's successor, Juan Esteban Montero, was as unable as the Ibáñez regime had been to make political capital out of the economic situation and was overthrown in June, 1932, by the Chilean air force which installed in power a *junta* composed of Col. Marmaduque Grove, Carlos Dávila, and Gen. Arturo Puga. Under the direction of Dávila, who made himself provisional president Chile became an outright "socialist republic" for one hundred days. But this attempt to make Chile over in the image of the national socialist states of Europe antagonized the army, which revolted and overthrew Dávila. The political situation disintegrated into anarchy. In Santiago, 160,000 unemployed Chileans, largely displaced from the nitrate industry, roamed the streets; other industries were paralyzed; and the national treasury was bankrupt, with a foreign debt of 3 million *pesos*.

In this grave national emergency Chile turned once more to the dramatic *caudillo,* Alessandri, putting him in the presidency again in the election of 1932. But Alessandri came back to power chastened by his political experience and cynical about the possibilities of democratic government. From the beginning his new administration followed a repressive course, putting the maintenance of public order and constitutional stability above human rights and freely using the militia and the police for this purpose. The early Alessandri, champion of popular rights, went over wholly to repression of popular rights. When he was confronted with a railroad strike early in 1936 he ordered the army to take over the railroads, declared a state of siege, dissolved Congress, closed down the opposition press, and banished popular leaders who criticized his government. The tragedy of a Latin American *caudillo,* well exemplified by Alessandri, is to allow his commendable social service impulses to be subverted or submerged by the implacable rigidities of his society. He is driven thus into either political martyrdom or one-man dictatorship. Alessandri chose the latter. As his candidate for the presidency in the election of 1938 he selected his minister of finance, Gustavo Ross, one of the wealthiest men in Chile. But his brutal punishment of his political opponents, who were charged with complicity in a plot to overthrow him during the campaign, reacted against Ross and gave the victory to the candidate of the opposition Popular Front, Pedro Aguirre Cerda.

The Chilean Popular Front, patterned after the contemporary Popular Fronts in Spain and France, provided a common rallying point for the Chilean Democrats, Radicals, Socialists, and Communists. In the election of 1938 it contrived to gain the support of ex-president Ibáñez, who was nominated as the candidate of the Popular Liberating Alliance, and of Gonzáles von Marees, leader of the Chilean Nazis. With their support it triumphed by a bare majority of 222,700 votes to 218,609 for Ross. Based on an unstable alliance of dissident political groups it sought in its program to be all things to all Chileans. It was "(1) Against oppression and for the restoration of democratic liberties, (2) Against imperialism and for the achievement of Chile for the Chileans, and (3) Against the material and intellectual misery of the people and for the realization of a modern socio-economic justice for the middle and working classes."

This program of generalities was a response to the continuing demand for action by the government to rehabilitate the still depressed Chilean economy and to satisfy the importunate needs of its underprivileged classes, the *rotos* and the *inquilinos.* It could be implemented along either radical or moderate lines but hardly along the repressive lines of the second Alessandri administration. Indeed the Popular Front came to power in Chile as a reaction against Alessandri's dictatorial methods but was, in effect, committed to carrying out a social welfare program similar to that of the earlier Alessandri, the Alessandri who had ridden to power in 1920 as the champion of the common people. Political leaders and political parties in order to gain power in the Depression-ridden 1930s found it expedient to emphasize the need for strong action by central government in the interest of the have-not elements in the population. Their liberalism was predominantly demagogic and nationalistic.

President Aguirre Cerda was himself a member of the conservative Radical party. That party supplied 55 per cent of the Popular Front's strength in Congress and held six of the eleven cabinet posts. One of the major accomplishments of the Popular Front government was to establish the Fomento Corporation, the forerunner of many such development corporations organized in Latin America during World War II, for economic planning, development, and financing of Chile's national resources. As the Chilean Socialists moved into key positions in the government and the Chilean Communists became increasingly influential in government circles Aguirre Cerda lost the support first of the Ibáñez party, then of von Marees's Nazis, and finally of the Radicals, led by Juan Antonio Ríos. The latter became convinced that the government was being infiltrated by Communists and was dominated by Communist ideology. In fact though the Communists held no cabinet posts, they made rapid progress, with the support of the government, in organizing and controlling Chilean labor unions; in the congressional elections in March, 1941, they made an extraordinary political showing, electing four senators and fourteen deputies to Congress. Because of their growing influence in government the Socialists, led by Marmaduque Grove and Oscar Schnake, finally deserted the Popular Front in January, 1941. The Chilean Popular Front then completely disintegrated and came to an end with the death of Aguirre Cerda in the following November, which necessitated a new election. In that election the anti-Communist candidate, Juan Antonio Ríos, who was backed by a coalition of conservative parties including the Agrarians, Democrats, Radicals, and the Chilean Falange (not to be confused with the Spanish Falange) was victorious over Ibáñez, now running as the candidate of the Liberals, Conservatives, and Nazis.

Liberal Action and Reaction in the Andean Countries

The cycle of political change that took place in Argentina and Chile during the two decades between 1920 and 1940 occurred in many of the remaining countries of Latin America. In general the first decade after World War I was characterized by moderate attempts at social improvement through legislation, but the liberalism of *laissez faire* remained dominant. This liberalism, however, was subsumed in a new militant, centralized liberalism after the great economic crisis of 1929–1932. That crisis established a pattern of economic, political, and social action in Latin America, as well as in the United States, which had been prefigured by the Mexican revolution and such movements as that of Batlle in Uruguay. The decade of the 1920s was the era of the traditionalists; the decade of the 1930s was the era of the social welfare *caudillos*.

This cycle was well exemplified by Colombia. There the Conservative party, which was the party of the army, the large landowners, the capitalists, and the Catholic clergy, controlled the central government continuously after 1884. But their monopoly was broken in 1930 by the election of a Liberal, Enrique Olaya Herrera. This accession of the Liberals to power was made possible by a split in the Conservative party, by popular dissatisfaction over corruption and graft in the government, by labor discontent with the government's repressive policy toward strikes, and, perhaps most important of all, by the economic depression which the Conservatives failed to grapple with courageously. The new administration immediately started a program of public works to furnish employment, made loans to coffee planters, and required that Colombians be given preference over foreigners in the petroleum industry. Through the combined efforts of both Liberal and Conservative parties the Olaya administration enacted legislation establishing social security, minimum wages, and maximum hours of labor. But Olaya lost the support of the Conservatives in the Leticia affair with Peru, which was settled by the League of Nations in 1933. His most intransigent opponent was Laureano Gómez, who now moved forward as the new Conservative leader. By 1934 the split between the two parties was so wide that the Conservatives refused to go to the polls.

The new Liberal president, Alfonso López, who, as a result of the Conservative boycott of the election, took office with an all-Liberal Senate and House, pushed through several constitutional changes in 1936. These made the state responsible not only for protecting the civil rights of the individual but also for assuring the fulfillment of both social rights and duties. They made the government the coordinator of the social and economic activities of the nation. They declared property to have a social function and correlative duties and authorized the government to expropriate private industries if necessary in order to discharge its duty of regulating production, distribution, and consumption and of protecting the workers from exploitation. All literacy and property qualifications for voting were removed, education was definitely made the responsibility of the state, and toleration was granted to all cults and religions which were not contrary to Christian morality. By these amendments, adopted under the grinding pressures of economic hardship and suffering, the central government was virtually enabled to impose economic democracy upon Colombia. But the amendments were not concurred in by the Catholic Church, which issued a manifesto against them, nor by the Conservative party, which denounced them as socialistic and as aiming at "the solution of social problems through the struggle of classes and the implementation of violence."

Much more avowedly national socialist was Bolivia in the 1930s. But the advent of national socialism there was delayed by the attempt of the ruling

Republican party to meet the Depression with unenlightened dictatorship
and also by the fact that Bolivia, as a result of the Chaco War with Paraguay, did not sink into the trough of depression until 1936. Her president-
dictators of the early 1930s, Hernando Siles and Daniel Salamanca, were
forced out of office. In the bloody war with Paraguay from 1932 to 1935
Bolivia lost a considerable part of her eastern lowlands, rich in petroleum
reserves. As the country plunged into an economic crisis and organized labor
demonstrated against the government, President José Luis Tejada Sórzano
was ousted by a bloodless coup directed by Lieut. Col. Germán Busch in
May, 1936. The head of the bipartisan *junta* which replaced him, Col.
David Toro, chief of staff of the army, then got himself elected as the
Socialist president and proceeded to put into effect a thoroughgoing program
of national socialism, suppressing monopolies and imposing new taxes upon
the wealthy, conscripting labor, and forcing all producers into labor unions
or syndicates. In this program he was supported by the National Socialist
party, which was composed largely of students and veterans of the Chaco
War. Toro's stated object was to "orient the nation toward a Socialistic
state." But the execution of his program was handicapped by the obstruc-
tionist tactics of the mineowners, and in July, 1937, Toro was forced to
resign and leave the country. His successor Germán Busch, now a general
and chief of the general staff, abandoned the experiment of state socialism
in name, but as the economic and political conditions in Bolivia deteriorated,
in April, 1939, he abolished constitutional guarantees, dismissed Congress,
and set up a totalitarian state. In Bolivia, then during the decade prior to
World War II, as often in Latin American politics, programs intended to
accomplish social and economic reforms in accordance with liberal preconceptions ended with dictatorship, imposed either by the advocates of these
reforms or by their embattled opponents.

In Peru and Venezuela also this evolution resulted in the establishment of
outright dictatorships, in the exaltation of the *caudillo*. In Peru this *caudillo*
was Agusto B. Leguía, who, after his first term as president from 1908 to
1912, swung over to the leadership of the middle and lower classes, like
Irigoyen in Argentina and Alessandri in Chile, in opposition to the vested
interests. His "Democratic Reform" party threw itself against the *Civilista*
party in which the *hacendados* or large landowners were entrenched. After
ousting President José Pardo by a *coup d'état* in July, 1919, Leguía seized
control and dominated the country until 1930. Though he had the Peruvian
constitution of 1920 amended along liberal lines and enacted a typical liberal program of legislation fixing maximum hours of labor and minimum
wages he kept himself in power by establishing a dictatorship—a form of
government which had not existed in Peru for many years.

Finally the strong man fell. In the small hours of the morning of August
25, 1930, Leguía came aboard one of his cruisers, the *Almirante Grau*.
Related one of the officers:

Haggard and nervous he came before us, a group of officers of the Peruvian Navy, at 4:30 in the morning, and told us of the dramatic incidents of the last few hours. His cabinet had been forced to resign. A group of army officers had urged a military cabinet in its place. Yielding, he appointed one and went to bed. Shortly they called him to his office and demanded changes. Inviting their suggestions, he appointed another and started to swear it in. Some one objected. The colonel at Arequipa, Sánchez Cerro, who had started the revolt in the army, should be in the cabinet. The President acceded. But there were further objections on the grounds that some of the appointees were not present, notably the colonel from Arequipa. Several spoke in a disrespectful manner, some were even intoxicated. Suddenly a lieutenant pushed his way in and with a revolver drawn demanded the immediate resignation of the Chief Executive. The entire group then flopped and joined in the demand. The resignation was penned and the President fled to the cruiser Almirante Grau. . . .

Immediately he sent for me, and there, as the first streak of dawn crept over the mountains, he complained that he was tired. He looked it—not only tired, but broken. His hands twitched. His eyes were sunken and blood-shot. . . . The power of decision was gone. Nearly 80 years of a vigorous and eventful life had exacted their toll. . . .

[He was] sent in disgrace first to the bleak island of San Lorenzo and later to the historic old prison in Lima, there to await the fate that has overtaken many another man in the stormy career of Peru, and, curiously enough, the fate he himself has meted out to scores of his enemies.[3]

Leguía's pattern of dictatorship was continued after his overthrow by his *Civilista* successor, Luis Sánchez Cerro, who was assassinated in April, 1933, and by his successor, Gen. Oscar Benavides. Both of these presidents moved ruthlessly against the opposition *Alianza Popular Revolucionaria Americana* (APRA) and had its candidates, including its leader, Víctor Raúl Haya de la Torre, who ran for the presidency in 1936, banned from the ballot. Peru's method of meeting the economic crisis of the 1930s then was the method of repressive *caudillismo,* upheld by the army.

The pattern of repressive, dictatorial rule, without benefit of any social welfare gloss, was also followed in Venezuela during the two interwar decades. It had been established by the rude cattleman president, Cipriano Castro, who governed the country until 1908, and was followed by his successor in the presidency, Juan Vicente Gómez, who dominated Venezuela until his death in 1935. A picturesque, lascivious military man of little education, Gómez was a conservative and a nationalist. The new constitution which he promulgated in 1914 extended his term to seven years, permitted reelection, and greatly increased presidential powers. During his first term, from 1915 to 1922, he never assumed the presidency but served instead as commander in chief of the army, showing by this action that the real power in Venezuela lay in the military establishment. When reelected in 1922 he

---

[3] A Peruvian naval officer quoted by Edward Tomlinson in the *Washington Evening Star,* Nov. 30, 1930, used by permission.

actually took office and served until 1929. He then allowed a figurehead president to succeed him but stepped into the presidency again in 1931 in order to quiet the restlessness resulting from the Depression. He continued to rule Venezuela almost as his own private estate until his death.

Using foreign capital invested in Venezuela as a hostage, Gómez made it contribute to the wealth and welfare of the country. He gave Venezuela high credit standing by meeting its financial obligations promptly, reducing its national debt, and maintaining a large gold reserve. Because of his careful management of Venezuela's economy and the country's large income from the foreign petroleum industry, Venezuela suffered perhaps fewer ill effects from the Depression of 1929 than any other Latin American country. But Gómez built up a cult around himself, replete with statues, portraits, and constant adulation of the president, and he maintained a cruel tyranny. His death was made an occasion for wild rejoicings by Venezuelans at their new liberation and for an orgy of reprisals against his family and followers. Under his successor, Gen. Eleazar López Contreras, a new constitution was adopted, the sixteenth in Venezuela's history, defining civil liberties and making possible the enactment of legislation for an eight-hour day, the organization of labor unions, and collective bargaining.

Gómez was the archetype of the Latin American *caudillo*-dictator during the interval between World Wars I and II. Others were Isidro Ayora in Ecuador, Jorge Ubico in Guatemala, Gerardo Machado in Cuba, Rafael Leonidas Trujillo Molina in the Dominican Republic, and Rafael Franco in Paraguay. Even Uruguay succumbed to dictatorship when in March, 1933, in the midst of threatening civil disturbances, President Gabriel Terra, with the support of the army, arrested his opponents in the government and expelled them from the country, imposed press censorship, disbanded the national administrative council, dissolved Congress, and established one-man rule. He then called a constitutional convention which drew up a constitution, the third in Uruguay's history. This constitution preserved many of the social features of the earlier Batllista constitution of 1917, including old-age pensions, state care of mothers, free medical service for the poor, workmen's accident insurance, an eight-hour workday, a six-day week, minimum wages, and recognition of the workers' right to strike and to form unions. But the constitution was largely window dressing for Terra's one-man rule, which continued until his voluntary relinquishment of the presidency in 1938.

Taking advantage of the restiveness, uncertainties, and ultimate economic collapse which followed World War I, leaders of this type often rode to power on programs which seemed to offer panaceas for the social and economic ills of their nations but which, once their leaders were established in the presidency, were quickly transformed into a defense of the *status quo* by methods of the police state.

These methods were explained by the inexorable necessity of maintaining political stability and, at the same time, advancing the economic interests of the Latin American peoples in a world of radical economic change. In some of the Latin American countries the new leaders sustained their social welfare programs after they got into office, particularly during the decade of the 1930s, and used their power to carry through programs of social amelioration. Driven by the dire economic plight of their peoples they acted along national socialist lines. For this purpose they took full advantage of the powers of the central government and on many occasions and in several countries stretched these powers to unprecedented lengths. By these means they could satisfy their own social impulses, could make a social conquest of the masses of their people, and could build up political followings which would keep them or at least their party in control of the national government. Almost totally submerged in this process was the nineteenth-century liberal ideology.

The positive state in Latin America in the 1930s, whether it was dominated by an old-type *caudillo* or by a socially conscious and experimentally minded *caudillo,* left little room for local self-determination or the exercise of decentralized responsibility. The central government acting in the interest of the numerical majority of the population assumed the role of guarantor of social and economic security for all. It resurrected the claims of the Spanish Hapsburgs of the sixteenth and seventeenth centuries to ultimate authority—claims which had been repudiated by the Latin Americans in their independence movements but which now reappeared in the guise of a new liberalism. Those Latin American countries which turned to the new liberalism under strong *caudillos* in the decade after the economic depression, it should be emphasized, simply followed the prevailing trend in many nations of Western Europe and in the United States.

Additional Reading

Bello, José Maria: *História da república, 1889–1930,* Edição da "Organizacão Simões," Rio de Janeiro, 1952.

Bernstein, Harry: *Modern and Contemporary Latin America,* J. B. Lippincott Company, Philadelphia, 1952, chaps. 15, 20, 30.

Burr, Robert N., and Roland D. Hussey: *Inter-American Cooperation,* 2 vols., University of Pennsylvania Press, Philadelphia, 1955.

Calogeras, João Pandiá: *A History of Brazil,* trans. and ed. by Percy Alvin Martin, University of North Carolina Press, Chapel Hill, N.C., 1939, chaps. XIV, XV.

Cunha, Euclides da: *Rebellion in the Backlands (Os Sertões),* trans. by Samuel Putnam, University of Chicago Press, Chicago, 1944.

Donoso, Ricardo: *Alessandri, agitador y demoledor: Cinquenta años de historia política de Chile,* Fondo de Cultura Económica, Mexico, 1952.

Ellsworth, Paul T.: *Chile, an Economy in Transition,* The Macmillan Company, 1945. An economic analysis of Chile's experience from the depression of 1929 to 1945.

Galbraith, William O.: *Colombia: A General Survey,* Oxford University Press, 1953.

Galdames, Luis: *A History of Chile,* trans. and ed. by Isaac Joslin Cox, University of North Carolina Press, Chapel Hill, N.C., 1941, chap. XIX.

Graham, R. B. Cunningham: *A Brazilian Mystic,* Dodd, Mead & Company, Inc., New York, 1925.

Hasbrouck, Alfred: "The Argentine Revolution of 1930," *Hispanic American Historical Review,* vol. 18, pp. 285–321, 1938.

Jefferson, Mark, S. W.: *Peopling the Argentina Pampa,* The American Geographical Society, New York, 1926.

Leonard, Olen E.: *Bolivia: Land, People, and Institutions,* Scarecrow Press, Washington, 1952.

Lieuwen, Edwin: *Petroleum in Venezuela, a History,* University of California Press, Berkeley, 1954.

Linke, Lilo: *Andean Adventure: A Social and Political Study of Colombia, Ecuador and Bolivia,* Hutchinson & Co., London, 1945.

————: *Ecuador, Country of Contrasts,* 3d ed., Oxford University Press, London and New York, 1960.

McClosky, M. B.: "The United States and the Brazilian Naval Revolt, 1893–1894," *Americas,* vol. 2, pp. 296–321, 1946.

Stevenson, J. R.: *The Chilean Popular Front,* University of Pennsylvania Press, Philadelphia, 1942.

Taylor, Carl C.: *Rural Life in Argentina,* University of Louisiana Press, Baton Rouge, 1948.

Turner, Charles W.: *Ruy Barbosa: Brazilian Crusader for the Essential Freedoms,* Abingdon Press, Nashville, Tenn., 1945.

Whetten, Nathan L.: *Guatemala: The Land and the People,* Yale University Press, New Haven, 1961.

Whitaker, Arthur: *The United States and Argentina,* Harvard University Press, Cambridge, 1954.

XXIII

Social Democracy versus National Socialism *

In the period after World War I the traditional ruling classes in many countries of Latin America fell into disrepute. They were numerically overwhelmed by the newly rising middle and working classes, they were held responsible as a class for the bad living conditions under which most Latin Americans lived, and they failed to accommodate their techniques of government to the requirements of the new era. In particular the Great Depression of 1929–1932 had a devastating impact upon the existing power structure. As a result, old aristocratic oligarchies, whose power position was based upon land, lost control to new leaders who represented urban, industrial majorities, who were susceptible to new political influences, and who had a larger conception of the potentialities of an integrated national society than the traditional ruling elite. The old way of life was equated with backward agricultural economies, concentration upon a single export commodity, a feudal social organization, and political dominance by privileged cliques. The new order would provide for better-balanced national economies through national planning, diversification and deemphasis of agriculture, industrialization, more social equality, universal voting rights, and majority rule. Latin American nationalism of the nineteenth century had an aristocratic basis. The great achievement of twentieth-century leaders has been to give Latin American nationalism a popular basis.

Latin America's new aspirations for self-consciousness and nationality found a tragic hero in Agusto Sandino, the "patriot" general who resisted the United States Marine occupation of Nicaragua. These aspirations were also revealed in the new self-assurance that characterized Latin American art, literature, music, and education. From a negative and defensive "anti-Yanqui" campaign, student, professional, and other intellectual groups in Latin America advanced to a positive program of Latin American cultural action. Such champions of this program as the Venezuelan novelist, Rómulo Gallagos, the Brazilian musical composer and conductor Heitor Villa-Lôbos, and the Mexican painters David Alfaro Siqueiros, Diego Rivera, and José Clemente Orozco began to emphasize with new fervor the rich local elements in Latin American life and the vital forces of their own soil. They ambi-

* The term "national socialism," as used in this book and spelled without capital letters, is not to be confused with Adolph Hitler's National Socialist Party in Germany.

507

tiously sought to weave local popular themes into a fabric of nationalism or into a larger *Americanismo cultural,* which, while containing elements of European culture, would nevertheless transcend it. They aspired to create artistic styles that would contain something unmistakably not European. Too long, they concluded, Latin America had only reflected foreign realities and had not known how to make them truly its own. For them art became a revolutionary tool, a means of social control.

At the same time Latin America's poets and novelists were using their literary talents to champion social and economic justice and to portray an imagined Latin America of the future freed from feudal servitudes and capitalistic exploitation. They belligerently appealed to the working classes to throw off the yoke of foreign, largely United States–controlled corporations, to oust local dictators, and to curb the power of the church and other local oligarchies. This revolutionary literature was proletarian, collectivist, nationalistic, and in the Andean countries and in Middle America, Indianist in character. The objective of these authors was a better Latin America, and the idealism of their writing should not be discounted. Meanwhile the university system of Latin America was thoroughly reorganized, following the pattern set in the *Reforma Universitaria* at the University of Córdoba in Argentina in 1918, for the purpose of converting the universities into instruments for the formation of a distinctive national culture and eventually a distinctive Indo-hispanic culture. This new sense of mission contained revolutionary implications, for it has stirred some of the Latin American universities from their passive nineteenth-century role to become instigators of social change.

The economic stresses and strains of the interwar period and the propaganda struggle between the United States and the totalitarian systems of Europe that shaped up after 1933 led to much political experimentation in Latin America. The pattern for social democracy had been set in the Uruguayan and Mexican constitutions, but the efficacy of this sytem was challenged by the more extreme socialism which was put into effect by Getúlio Vargas in Brazil. In the two systems thus exemplified was found the Latin American counterpart of the United States–Axis systems that would eventually involve the Western Hemisphere in World War II.

Revolution Institutionalized in Mexico

"The rich are always rich," bitterly observed one of the Indian villagers in Ciro Alegría's *Broad and Alien Is the World,* "and, for all its weight, money never comes down." To alter this perverse law of political gravity was one of the objectives of the Mexican revolution. The constitution of 1917, which vested the ownership of Mexico's subsoil resources in the nation in accordance with old Spanish law, stipulated that private property affected by it should not be expropriated except for adequate compensation. As this provision was put into execution protests were raised by the propertied classes against the methods of appraisal that were used in determining the value of the expropriated properties and also against the provision for payment in national bonds which had either no or only a very low current value. In 1918 President Carranza issued a decree which made the constitutional provision dealing with subsurface concessions retroactive in its effect. Thus foreign concessionaires, mainly citizens of the United States, who had previously acquired title to mines and oil wells and were operating them under their concessions, were required to pay additional royalties to the Mexican government. This decree gave rise to various diplomatic claims and protests by the United States.

But the new constitution as a whole was not enforced by Carranza; malfeasance and corruption by public officials became widespread, schools were closed for lack of funds, and lawlessness and disorder increased. In 1916 Carranza was confronted with an insurrection in the north led by Francisco Villa which caused the death of several citizens of the United States both in northern Mexico and in Villa's raid upon Columbus, New Mexico. Villa, a talented general in guerrilla-type operations and a natural leader of men, controlled a gang of cruel, tough hillmen. But he was a bandit whose swooping raids spread terror north and south of the Río Grande. One of his raids on an unnamed Mexican village was thus described by a member of his gang:

Shouting blood-curdling oaths, we galloped into the main street, and saw the frightened villagers dart terror-stricken into their houses.

"Pancho!" [Francisco!]

The cry went up on all sides. Women screamed it hysterically. Men shouted it, and swore. Children heard it, and cried. Doors were bolted. Shops and stores were hastily vacated, on the principle that the rifling of one's till or safe was better than the loss of one's life.

Villa seemed to know the geography of every village that we came to. We wanted food—he knew where we could get it. As we reined in our horses he barked instructions, and men darted into shops and stores to bring him what was needed. That was purely the business part of the raid, and foolish shopkeepers who tried to protect their goods were given short shrift.

It was after our immediate necessities had been provided for that the raids developed into orgies.... After the commercial possibilities of the village had been exhausted, the men were tacitly left to their own devices. Then it was that I saw sights that I would like to forget. Most of the bandits were half-breeds with a strain of Yoki Indian blood—the worst type of Indian—and they had no scruples whatsoever. As soon as they realized that the object of the raid had been achieved, and that they could enjoy themselves, they emitted whoops of animalistic delight, and went for the women.

The men-folk who tried to defend wives and daughters were shot without compunction, and the lust seemed to develop into a general lust for blood and damage. Rooms were pillaged and looted; old men were killed for no reason other than that they protested; and when the air resounded with the moaning of the dying and the weeping of the living, Pancho rode out with his men in triumph from the village.[1]

Since Carranza proved unable to capture Villa and to protect foreign lives and property, Mexico was invaded by United States troops under Gen. John J. Pershing in a costly and eventually futile attempt to capture Villa. The expedition cost the United States 130 million dollars and excited great alarm in Mexico. Villa was subsequently granted amnesty and pardon by the Carranza government.

During Carranza's administration a serious attempt at the new land-distribution program was begun, and approximately 450,000 acres of land were distributed by the government as *dotaciones* to some 48,000 families. In April, 1920, a revolt against Carranza was launched in Sonora headed by the vice president and national military hero, Alvaro Obregón. The insurgents enlisted the support of a large part of the army and organized the Liberal Constitutionalist party with "Effective Suffrage and No Reelection" as their slogan. They then fell upon Carranza as he was moving his government to Veracruz, attacked the twenty-one trains in his expedition to the coast, and forced him to flee. Soon afterward he was murdered. Obregón then entered the capital and was "elected" president in September at a very difficult time in Mexico's history.

Because of the grievances and claims of United States business and financial interests against the government of Mexico, President Obregón was denied recognition by the administrations of Wilson, Harding, and Coolidge. Finally the difficulties were straightened out in the Bucareli agreements which were arrived at in conferences in Mexico City in 1923. In these conferences the Mexican representatives, while not retreating from the claim of the Mexican government to control the subsurface resources of the nation, agreed to a liberal definition of the kind of "positive act" which was required to have been taken by foreign oil concessionaires in order to validate their concessions acquired before 1917. They agreed further that concessionaires who had not performed positive acts toward exploiting the subsurface resources of their concessions before 1917 would be given preferential rights to the renewal of the concessions. In the matter of expropriation of agrarian lands for *ejidos* for existing villages the agreements stipulated that in exchange for expropriations of lands up to 1,755 hectares (710 acres) United States owners would accept Mexican government bonds; for expropriations of larger acreages they would be paid in cash. As a result of the Bucareli settlement the Obregón government was recognized as the *de jure* government of Mexico by the United States in August, 1923, and after it negotiated similar claims settlements with Britain, France, and other foreign governments it was recognized also by them.

[1] Fred Walker, *Destination Unknown*, J. B. Lippincott Company, Philadelphia, 1955, pp. 131–132. Used by permission.

At the same time the labor, educational, and social program of President Obregón was threatened by a revolution headed by Obregón's former secretary of the treasury, Adolfo de la Huerta, which, though it assumed serious proportions, was eventually crushed at great expense and labor. The revolutionary spirit was meanwhile stimulated by a new class-conscious literature,

Fig. 23-1. Alfonso Reyes, 1889–1959, distinguished Mexican author. (*Courtesy of Universidad Nacional Autónoma de México.*)

of which the graphic novel *Los de abajo* by Mariano Azuela, translated into English as *The Under Dogs,* was noteworthy. Mexico's uniqueness as a mestizo culture in relation to other cultures was stressed by the philosopher Samuel Ramos, particularly in his *El Perfil del Hombre y la Cultura en Mexico.* The new literature represented the revolution of 1910–1917 as a basic repudiation of European culture and ideals and as the first systematic attempt in Mexico's history to Mexicanize the nation. The revolutionary spirit also inspired a renaissance in art, distinguished by the monumental didactic mural painting of Diego Rivera, José Clemente Orozco, and David Siqueiros. Their art, employing an art form of the Middle Ages resurrected in the twentieth century —became an expression of the power of moral indignation combined with monumental pathos.

During Obregón's presidency some 3 million acres of land were distributed among 624 villages. He encouraged unionization of workers but gave official protection only to the *Confederación Regional Obrera Mexicana* (CROM), which was first organized in 1918 under Luis Morones. The educational changes carried through by the Obregón administration were particularly notable. Under his secretary of education, José Vasconcelos, a leading nationalist ideologist, the Mexican educational system was oriented along the lines of the Mexican revolutionary movement, campaigns against illiteracy were organized, the traditionalist and Indianist elements in Mexico's cultural heritage were emphasized, and nearly a thousand rural schools were built. By methods such as these the Mexican revolutionary movement was gradually institutionalized and transformed into a monolithic national political system.

Obregón selected as his successor his secretary of *gobernación,* Plutarco Elías Calles, and saw him duly elected in 1924. As president, Calles made no significant deviations from the policies of his predecessor. He encouraged the organization of labor in CROM, extended the national educational system, stimulated sanitation and health projects, and continued the distribution of lands to the landless, which had become an essential element of the Mexican revolutionary program. In the four years of his administration he distributed 8 million acres to 1,500 villages and communities. In his church policies Calles went beyond Obregón. His attempt to enforce the anticlerical provisions of the constitution produced a bitter feud between church and state. When the archbishop officially announced in February, 1926, that the clergy could not and would not obey the constitution, the Calles administration countered with orders that the clergy must promptly register with the government and must abstain from the teaching of religion in the primary schools. In retaliation the Catholic clergy decreed a religious strike which began in August, 1926, but which was quite ineffective. During the strike the government forcibly kept the churches open and authorized laymen to perform certain sacraments. The feud between church and state was kept active by the *Cristeros,* on the one hand, who upheld the claims of the church, and, on the other, by the generals of the army, who were loyal to the constitution and to the government's anticlerical program.

Mexico's difficulties with the United States were reopened by the Mexican government's adoption of a retroactive interpretation of article 27 of the constitution. In 1925 the Mexican Congress violated the Bucareli understandings by enacting legislation which compelled all foreign owners of petroleum lands who had taken positive acts of exploitation prior to 1917 to convert their concessions into fifty-year licenses to exploit, which defined positive acts much more narrowly than the Bucareli agreements had done, and which required foreign licensees to subscribe to the Calvo clause, that is, to pledge in advance not to appeal to their governments for protection of their titles. All these new requirements had been successfully resisted by the United States in the Bucareli conferences two years earlier. Another law required foreign corporations owning lands in Mexico to sell the Mexican government a controlling interest in their corporations. These actions were sharply criticized by both President Coolidge and Secretary of State Frank Kellogg, who defended United States petroleum interests and insinuated that Mexico's oil policy was dictated by Moscow. President Calles indulged in recriminations in kind, but the United States Senate voted unanimously in January, 1927, in favor of arbitration of the controversy with Mexico.

To restore harmonious relations between the two nations Dwight W. Morrow, a personal friend of President Coolidge and a partner of J. P. Morgan and Company, was sent as United States ambassador to Mexico. He immediately established intimate personal relations with President Calles and began negotiations looking toward a termination of the controversy. As a result President Calles recommended, and the Mexican Congress enacted, certain changes in the oil legislation defining "positive act" in language identical with that of the Bucareli protocols, dropping the requirement of the Calvo clause, and responding in other ways to the United States position. They did not, however, renew the Bucareli promise to give preferential rights to owners of petroleum lands who had made no positive act of exploitation before 1917. They thus steadfastly adhered to the claim of successive revolutionary governments in Mexico that the emergency condition of the landless *peones* must override the rights already vested in holders of unused lands. The new legislative enactments were deemed satisfactory by the United States, which now agreed that future questions between the two nations would be settled directly through the Mexican administrative departments and courts.

Since ex-President Obregón was now eligible for reelection he was endorsed by Calles as his successor in the presidency. He was elected in July, 1928, but was assassinated before he could take office. Emilio Portes Gil was then chosen provisional president by Congress. When he took office Gil adopted a conciliatory policy toward the religious strike which was still in progress. In an effort to end the church-state feud he accepted the good offices of Ambassador Morrow and worked out a compromise settlement in June, 1929, allowing the church to appoint clergymen but requiring them after their appointment to register with the government. The settlement also permitted the clergy to teach religion "within the church confines" and granted clergymen the right to petition the government but not to vote. Under this settlement the long religious strike came to an end, but the underlying problem of the relationship between church and state remained to break out again in acute conflict in the 1930s.

Portes Gil was president of Mexico during a period of political reconciliation and regularization of revolutionary change. The revolution had developed its own social statics and its own vested interests of "millionaire socialists." The political party of the revolution was organized as the National Revolutionary party (*Partido Revolucionario Nacional* or PRN), which through the efforts of both Gil and Calles was broadened to include every important political group in the country. On the one hand, it crushed the power of the CROM as the spokesman of organized labor, and on the other, it moved against Communist and other extremist labor groups; it became increasingly middle class in outlook and was bent upon conserving and, as it were, institutionalizing the revolution. The ability of any single president while in office to follow through on such a program was limited by the constitutional prohibition against his immediate reelection, but the ban on *reeleccionismo* did not prevent a president from continuing to act after his retirement from the presidency as a powerful political force. This Calles did after his voluntary retirement from the presidency in 1928. He remained the political "boss" of Mexico and in the election of November, 1929, his candidate Pascual Ortiz Rubio of Michoacán was elected over José Vasconcelos, who had served as minister of education under Obregón. In September, 1932, when Calles forced the resignation of Ortiz Rubio, a subservient Congress chose Gen. Abelardo Rodríguez as provisional president. In the regular election which was held in July, 1933, another Calles candidate, Lázaro Cárdenas, governor of Michoacán, was elected for a six-year term.

The Cárdenas Regime

The compromise of 1929 between the church and the government had not achieved a permanently satisfactory relationship between them. Soon afterward the archbishop was fined for violating the law, and restrictions were imposed upon church activities by several of the states. When Veracruz limited the number of priests to thirteen for the entire state in 1931 and other states followed her example the church protested. In September, 1932, the Pope issued an encyclical which charged the Mexican government with persecuting the church. In response the Mexican government sent the papal delegate out of the country, compelled the archbishop to register as a priest with the civil authorities, and suppressed Catholic newspapers. Some of the states drove all priests out of their territories. When Cárdenas became president he followed a somewhat more conciliatory policy toward the church than Calles had taken, but he persisted in the revolutionary objective of keeping Mexico's educational system free of clerical influences. When his program of socializing or nationalizing education in accordance with the requirements of the constitution of 1917 was put into effect it was sabotaged by members of the clergy, who ordered parents not to send their children to school. The government then undertook to enforce the law requiring compulsory primary education and expelled all but a few hundred priests from the country. In 1935 all churches and church property in Mexico were nationalized.

Under the devastating effects of the Depression Mexico adopted a pro-

Fig. 23-2. Lázaro Cárdenas del Río, President of Mexico, 1934–1940. (*Courtesy of William Cameron Townsend and George Wahr Publishing Company.*)

gram of action very similar to the New Deal in the United States. The pace of revolutionary economic reform was accelerated. As the price of silver declined Mexico went off the gold standard in July, 1931. Already in the previous year it had declared the mineral industry to be a public utility and had required all foreigners who entered the industry to promise in advance to comply with article 27 of the constitution. In furtherance of its social welfare program, now seemingly made more urgent by the Great Depression, it also enacted a series of new labor laws. These established the eight-hour day, set a scale of minimum wages, recognized the right to strike, and provided for compulsory arbitration of worker-employer disputes. In December, 1933, the Calles administration, with the approval of the National Revolutionary party, adopted a Six-Year Plan of national development. As this plan was put into operation in 1935 Cárdenas made it serve as an instrument for socializing Mexican industry. Belonging to the radical wing of the party, he gave his administration a strong prolabor and profarmer orientation, but by doing so he broke with Calles. His policy of using government facilities in support of strikes was opposed by Calles but was endorsed by the Mexican Congress, by the laboring classes, and by the National Revolutionary party. As a result the administration considered it necessary to exile Calles to the United States.

Freed from the criticism of Calles, Cárdenas proceeded, in implementation of the Six-Year Plan, to distribute the land among the agricultural workers more generously than any of his revolutionary predecessors. "When the villages rest upon the land," he declared, "then the government will rest upon the villages." By September, 1937, he had allotted nearly 24 million acres of land as nonalienable *dotaciones* to 134,759 peasants, whereas all previous presidents had distributed only 21,250,000 acres. As a result the old *hacienda* system was largely broken up and land ownership became more widely diffused than at any previous time in Mexico's history. Many of the lands thus expropriated by the government were organized as *ejidos* or cooperative farms and the government provided agricultural credit for them by setting up a national *ejido* bank. In order to make this system of land distribution possible Cárdenas found it necessary, in pursuance of constitutional authority, to expropriate large landholdings of both Mexican and foreign concessionaires. At the same time the government also took over other private industries and began to expropriate the railroads of Mexico.

Cárdenas's political strength rested upon the *peón* class, the army, and labor, now organized principally in the *Confederación de Trabajadores de México* (CTM) under Vicente Lombardo Toledano. Cárdenas appreciated that Mexico needed foreign capital and technicians, but he was determined that their profits should not be excessive. When a strike broke out against United States and British oil companies in 1937 the Mexican government, after investigating the financial condition of the companies, ordered them to pay substantial wage increases and to promote Mexican citizens to responsible managerial positions. As the companies refused to comply, Cárdenas moved against them. "How many of the villages near the oilfields possess such things as hospitals, schools, social centers, water supply, or purification plants, or athletic fields, or electric plants, even if only fed by the untold millions of cubic feet of natural gas wasted in oil operations?" he asked the Mexican people in an address justifying his action. "What center of oil activities, on the other hand, is not provided with a company police force, designed to safeguard private interests, invariably selfish and occasionally unlawful? ... Who does not know, or is not acquainted with the irritating discrimination that governs construction and lay-out of company oil camps? Comforts of all kinds for the foreign staff; poor accommodation, misery and unhealthfulness for our nationals." The foreign companies, he charged, were not giving enough in exchange for the wealth they were drawing from the land of Mexico. Moreover, they were interfering in the politics of the nation. For these reasons he expelled the companies from Mexico, seized their properties in March, 1938, and set up a national agency, *Petroléos Mexicanos,* or *Pemex,* to exploit the newly acquired public oil reserves. Because *Pemex* was then boycotted by the expropriated companies the Mexican government was forced to conclude barter agreements with Germany, Italy, and Japan for the sale of its petroleum products. But officially its right to seize and nationalize the companies was recognized by the Roosevelt administration. Negotiations between the two governments over the amount of compensation due the companies continued down to 1941.

Cárdenas, like his predecessors Gómez Farías and Juárez in Mexican history and like his contemporaries Franklin D. Roosevelt in the United States, Getúlio Vargas in Brazil, and Alfonso López in Colombia, was a "liberal" in the national socialist sense, believing that the power of the national government should be used to bring about social justice. He continued the tradition of the strong executive dedicated to the improvement of the conditions of the manual workers and the rearrangement of the social and economic forces of the nation in accordance with the preconceived liberal program through the forcible intervention of the state. The role of Cárdenas in the positive state of Mexico was that of virtual dictator. But his manner was disarming, his living habits were simple, his opponents were allowed considerable liberty of criticism, and his administration was honest and vigorous. Central in his Six-Year Plan was an expansion of Mexico's national system of education. In 1936, 18 per cent of the national budget was allocated to education, the number of schools was greatly increased, and secondary education was made free. One of the aims of the educational system was to show the superiority of the cooperative plan over the competitive. During the Cárdenas administration more than five hundred cooperative enterprises were established. When his term expired in 1940 he threw his influence to Gen. Manuel Avila Camacho, who as the official candidate was elected and inaugurated in December of that year. The programs of radical social and economic change which had characterized the Cárdenas administration now were forced to yield priority to new programs of action made necessary by the outbreak of World War II.

The Mexican revolution after three decades had not yet accomplished all that its champions had hoped for. Banking credit provided by the government for the new *ejidos* to implement the land-distribution program had not been adequate nor had it been based on acceptable banking practices. Agricultural production on the *ejidos* was not efficient, and it continued generally on a mere subsistence basis, providing little for sale. The depletion of Mexico's soil resources was proceeding at an alarming rate. Moreover as the revolutionary movement had created its own vested interests—its own bureaucracy and its own wealthy class—revolutionary fervor had subsided, and after 1949 the influence of organized industrial labor declined. The economic paternalism and the political regimentation of successive "revolutionary" governments were almost indistinguishable in method from those of the earlier *científicos,* though they showed a broader social concern. Political life was dominated by a monolithic political party, the *Partido Revolucionario Institucional* (PRI), literally, the Institutional Revolutionary party or party of Revolutionary Institutions, which, though it permitted opposition parties, controlled the election machinery and always returned the official candidates with overwhelming majorities.

And yet the old system of land monopoly which had plagued Mexico since colonial times and which had come to be associated with *Porfirismo* had been broken. Large tracts of farmland had been redistributed, ranchland had been divided up and turned over to cultivators, and farmlands had been extended to include considerable areas of previously uncleared land. For the *hacienda* system had been substituted small individual freeholds and *ejidos* or communal landholdings. Agricultural methods were being modernized, and the federal government had undertaken a broad program of land reclamation and irrigation. The profits of labor were being more equitably distributed than before, and the resulting increase in generalized purchasing power had considerably stimulated business activity. The revolution had made the Indians of Mexico for the first time a consumer class and incorporated them in the economy of the nation. Under government encouragement and financing, educational facilities had been expanded, cultural missions sent to all parts of the country, and rural teachers given schooling in Mexico City. The proportion of illiteracy had been reduced from 70 per cent in 1910 to around 50 per cent. Human rights had been accorded a new dignity, and all Mexicans were permitted to enjoy a considerable measure of freedom of press, freedom of assembly, and freedom of speech.

Political Stalemate in Brazil

Whereas the new liberalism of Mexico was fully developed at the end of World War I and had only to be implemented by a series of strong executives and a monolithic political party during the ensuing two decades, Brazil entered the interwar period in an apathetic mood but shifted its course in 1930 to embark upon a genuinely revolutionary program. Here the new liberalism or national socialism, as it should more accurately be called, reached full cycle in the period between the two world wars.

In Brazil the dominant party was the Republican party, which had controlled the machinery of the federal government since the 1890s and which alternated the presidency with due regularity between the two wealthiest and most populous states, São Paulo and Minas Gerais. As long as these two states remained in agreement and cooperated in politics Brazil maintained a stable government. But illiteracy was so widespread, amounting to an estimated three-quarters of the population, that popular interest in elections was slight. The presidential candidate of the official party was nominated by a convention of representatives of the governors of the states, and the candidate thus selected was almost sure of election. The president being forbidden by the constitution of 1891 to succeed himself, President Wenceslau Braz was ineligible for reelection in 1918. The official candidate in that election was ex-President Rodrigues Alves. After his election he became too ill to take office, and his vice president, Delphim Moreira da Costa Ribeiro, served until the death of Alves in early 1919 when a special election was held in accordance with the constitution.

Under the new president, a former senator and supreme court justice from Paraíba, Dr. Epitácio da Silva Pessoa, the Republican party leadership was obliged to deal with the repercussions of the postwar economic depression. Currency became scarce, new issues of paper money failed to alleviate the financial crisis, and large sums were borrowed abroad, particularly from the United States. As a further remedy the president launched a moderate public works program, building storage dams at government expense in the drought areas of Rio Grande do Norte, Ceará, and Paraíba, the last his own home state, but for this action he was sharply criticized.

In science, education, art, music, and literature Brazil had been making rapid strides. In Alberto Santos-Dumont, born in Minas Gerais in 1873, she could claim a pioneer in air transportation, and she established the Brazilian Academy of Sciences in 1916. But much of the stimulus for achievement in these fields was supplied by foreigners, such as John Casper Branner of the United States in geology and L. L. Vauthier of France in architecture. Brazilian novelists, however, including particularly José Martiniano de Alencar, Bernardo Joaquim da Silva Guimarães, and Joaquim Maria Machado de Assis, though they wrote in the romantic tradition, were turning to Brazilian themes. Signs of a new Brazilian nationalism were beginning to appear. This nationalistic spirit was strengthened by World War I which enlisted the cooperation of the youth of all the states of Brazil in a common effort.

In the colloquia and exhibitions of Modern Art Week, held at São Paulo in 1922, Brazil's artists and intellectuals gave enthusiastic emphasis to the country's own cultural heritage and potentialities and started a Brazilian renaissance. In the diverse cultural milieu of the modern world they launched a movement to discover and vindicate Brazil's national culture, using modern techniques and daring experimental methods. Artists and intellectuals rejected stylized academic criteria and searched for new meanings and new beauties in their own native land, drawing their inspiration and strength from its soil. *Modernismo,* or the modernist school, thus originated, flowered in the work of Cândido Portinari in painting, Heitor Villa-Lôbos and Francisco Mignone in music, José Pereira da Graça Aranha and Erico Veríssimo in the novel, and Lúcio Costa, who designed Brazil's new interior capital, Brasília, in the late 1950s, in architecture. Their art is imbued with deep national emotion. In the prose fiction of José Lins do Rêgo, Jorge Amado, Graciliano Ramos, and Raquel de Queiroz the people and problems of the drought-afflicted northeastern states of Brazil were realistically presented for the first time since Euclides da Cunha.

Fed by this new literary and artistic nationalism, political discontent became so strong that after the election of the official candidate of the Republican party, Arturo da Silva Bernardes, governor of Minas Gerais, as Dr. Pessoa's successor in 1922 a dissident faction of the navy, led by Marshal Hermes da Fonseca and his son, Euclides, staged a rebellion to prevent Bernardes's inauguration. During their twenty-four-hour revolt they shelled Rio de Janeiro, but were soon suppressed by President Pessoa. Resentment smoldered in the military ranks, however, and broke into the open two years later when the garrison at São Paulo seized that city and held it for three weeks against federal troops. The revolt was presented as a political reform movement against the corrupt governing oligarchy. Military uprisings had already occurred in Rio Grande do Sul, and from 1924 to 1927 an officer in the Brazilian army, Capt. Luiz Carlos Prestes led a disciplined column of some eight hundred guerrilla fighters through the Brazilian back country, engaging in pitched battles with government troops, rallying opposition to the regime in Rio de Janeiro, and playing the role of Robin Hood to Brazil's forgotten folk. For his exploits Prestes gained wide fame as the "Cavalier of Hope." A state of siege was therefore maintained throughout the greater part of the country during most of Bernardes's term, and dissatisfaction with his administration became general. Later, in 1930, while Prestes was a refugee in Argentina, he became converted to communism and served thereafter as the personalist leader of the Brazilian Communist party, often in exile, often in prison.

The dissident *Paulistas* were mollified by the election of one of their number, Washington Luiz Pereira de Sousa, to the presidency in 1926. An experienced administrator he brought the regime of martial law to an end. Brazil had recovered from the depression which had immediately followed the war and now basked in a new prosperity. Since the war her railway mileage had increased by 30 per cent, her foreign trade had more than doubled, and her population had increased from 24 million to nearly 40 million. In 1924, when faced with a bumper coffee crop and resulting lower prices, Brazil did not resort to the valorization plan which the government had tried in 1906 and 1917. Instead, coffee growers formed an association and undertook to regulate the production, storage, and export of the crop, thus eliminating the brokers. This monopoly control, however, though it helped to raise price levels, stimulated foreign coffee growers to increase their coffee acreage.

Brazil's prosperity came to an end in 1929 when the economic depression knocked the bottom out of the market for coffee, which formed 70 per cent of Brazil's total exports, and caused a slump in the prices of sugar, cotton, rubber, and other Brazilian commodities. As depression stalked through the nation it caused a curtailment of public works, a rash of bankruptcies, mass unemployment, business decline, a falling off in public revenues, and finally revolution. Brazil had incurred an enormous foreign debt totaling 1,181 million dollars, three-fourths of which had been acquired by the federal government and was owed largely to United States bankers. The servicing of this debt alone required between 175 million and 200 million dollars annually, an amount much larger than Brazil's total export trade balance. As a result the Brazilian government was obliged to borrow in order to meet the annual service charges on its loans. This unhealthy economic situation was laid bare by the economic crisis of 1929. Moreover, at the very time when Brazil needed foreign credits the world market for coffee became glutted. By 1930 that country alone was producing a million bags more than the entire world consumption. As Brazil's sales of coffee abroad dwindled to a trickle, the confidence in the government of Washington Luiz declined. So serious was Brazil's plight that in September, 1931, under Washington Luiz's successor, Brazil joined the countries which were defaulting on their foreign loans.

Throughout the history of republican Brazil the states that composed the federal union enjoyed large powers, including the power to levy export taxes, to contract foreign loans, and to maintain state armies. Candidates for the presidency were chosen in a caucus or convention consisting of members of the national Congress who were creatures of the state administrators and who represented local oligarchic machines. But this system and the Republican party which had operated under it during their almost forty years of tenure of public office were brought into discredit by the economic debacle of 1929. In July of that year President Washington Luiz committed the strategic blunder of announcing his support of Dr. Júlio Prestes, governor of São Paulo, as his successor, thus defying the unwritten rule forbidding the election of two successive presidents from the same state and driving Minas Gerais into the opposition camp. The Republican party platform explained that the election of another *Paulista* was necessary as a "guaranty of the continuation of policies which during the present four-year administration have contributed to the greatness and glory of our institutions."

The principal opponent of the official candidate in the presidential election in 1930 was the candidate of the Liberal Alliance (*Aliança Liberal*) Getúlio

Dornelles Vargas, who was a member of an old *gaúcho* family of Brazil's southern frontier and president of its southernmost state, Rio Grande do Sul. When Prestes was declared elected with a majority of 1,089,949 votes to 735,032 for Vargas the opposition cried fraud, charging that the administration had used military force in Minas Gerais and Paraíba to secure the election of Prestes and that Congress, controlled by the president, had deprived those states of their representation in that body. Sharp lines of cleavage began to form between the politically influential sections of the country, Vargas being supported by his own state of Rio Grande do Sul, by Minas Gerais, and by the northern states of Paraíba and Pernambuco while the Republican administration was defended by São Paulo and Rio de Janeiro. To the grievances of the country against an administration which had shown itself bankrupt both ideologically and materially was added a strong sectional antagonism of the outlying states against the capital represented by the Rio de Janeiro–São Paulo axis of power. As Vargas launched a revolt and moved toward the capital the president's army deserted him and he was forced to resign in October, 1930.

The "Authoritarian Democracy" of Vargas

The military *junta* which replaced the Luiz government now offered the presidency to Vargas. His party had committed itself to many preelectoral promises, including the investigation of graft in the preceding administration, the punishment of those responsible for it, the creation of a department of labor, the liberalization of the franchise, greater protection to individuals, guaranties of the states against interference by the central government, breaking up of the large estates, and economy in government. But many of these promises were forgotten after Vargas assumed executive power. Both the method by which he acquired power and many of his actions as head of the provisional government for the next four years represented revolutionary departures from the familiar historical patterns of Brazil's republican era.

Under Vargas, Positivism finally came into its own in Brazil. The "dictatorial republic" of Auguste Comte found its almost perfect expression in Vargas's "authoritarian democracy." It had been thwarted by the revolution of 1890 and had been subverted at that time by the military who had engineered the overthrow of Dom Pedro II. The kind of national social planning which Positivism envisaged had not been possible under the loose confederation created by the republican constitution of 1891 nor had it been attempted on anything but a meager, partial scale by successive republican presidents. But Vargas, who was a Positivist by both training and conviction, now used the power which he acquired by the revolution of 1930 to put Positivism into effect. The "authoritarian democracy" which he established had Positivist objectives, that is, the rationalization of the economy and society of the nation. In carrying out this program Vargas demonstrated a keen intelligence, personal courage, deliberation in making decisions, and a lack of sentiment, either of hate or of affection, which guarded him against personal involvements that might have weakened his position. In him were joined an enormous personal ambition, an ardent Brazilian nationalism, and a fondness for direct action which was contemptuous of the normal processes of law and order and the delays incident to the functioning of democratic institutions. He exercised and enlarged the powers of the presidency to accomplish the ends which he considered desirable for Brazil. To secure these ends he often resorted to unscrupulous methods, and he was skillful and pragmatic in political manipulation.

The dire plight of the country seemed to Vargas to require drastic measures. He suspended the national Congress, the state legislatures, and the municipal councils, and intervened all the states, placing his own interventors in control. He governed by decree. By decree, for example, he abolished interstate duties. He limited the expansion of the coffee industry by decreeing in 1932 that no coffee trees should be planted for three years and that certain accumulated surpluses should be destroyed. He also sought to diversify Brazil's agriculture by encouraging the production of oranges and other citrus fruits, silk, and rubber. He made special efforts to improve the conditions of labor, to promote child welfare, to develop public works, and to eradicate disease, particularly leprosy.

But this action program was carried through without a Congress and simply by the decree law of the president aided by the members of the cabinet, the federal agents at the head of each state, and the prefects at the head of each municipality, all of whom were appointed by Vargas and were accountable only to him. In 1932 his rule was challenged by a serious revolt in São Paulo, a state which contributed one-third of the revenues of the federal government. All factions there formed a "united front" and carried on a rebellion against the federal government for almost three months, engaging the support of almost every man, woman, and child in the city. Their expectations of aid from Rio Grande do Sul and Minas Gerais were disappointed when the interventor in the former, Flores da Cunha, turned against them and the interventor in Minas Gerais followed his example. Finally the embattled *Paulistas* were overpowered, but they were granted amnesty by a magnanimous Vargas and their revolutionary debt was assumed by the federal government.

This *Paulista* uprising had a salutary effect, for it forced Vargas to return to constitutional methods and to call for the election of a constitutional convention. Both in the elections for members of the convention and in the constitution which they adopted on July 16, 1934, provision was made for functional representation, which was a new method of election in Latin America suggestive of the guild socialism which became prominent in England in the second decade of the twentieth century, of the APRA techniques of Víctor Raúl Haya de la Torre in Peru, of the political methods of Benito Mussolini's corporative state in Italy, and of the provisions of Antônio de Oliveira Salazar's constitution of 1933 for Portugal. Under this system, of the 254 delegates who assembled on November 15, 1933, in the Tiradentes Palace in Rio de Janeiro, 214 were chosen in the general election and the remaining 40 by labor, trade, and professional organizations.

The new constitution which emerged from the convention preserved the federal structure of the United States of Brazil and forbade the federal, state, and municipal governments to levy taxes or duties upon products moving from one state to another. It thus removed a hitherto serious barrier to domestic commerce. But it gave the federal government new power to direct national education and to legislate in matters affecting labor, production, and consumption. Especially significant were the social welfare clauses of the constitution. These nationalized the banking and insurance businesses outright and made it possible for the federal government acting in the public interest to nationalize other industries after giving full compensation to the owners. Authorization by the federal government was required before mines and water power, even when privately owned, could be exploited, and such authorization could be granted only to Brazilian citizens or to corporations having a majority of Brazilians on their boards of directors. Like the constitution of 1891, the new constitution made the president ineligible for immediate reelection, but Vargas was continued in the presidency for four years by act of the constitutional convention. Congress, as before, was composed of two houses, but the lower house included, besides deputies chosen by popular vote, representatives chosen by occupational groups. These groups were defined as (1) agriculture and stock raising, (2) industry, (3) commerce and transportation, and (4) the professions and government officials. Their total representation could not exceed one-fifth of the membership chosen by direct vote of the electorate. Suffrage was granted to all Brazilians, both men and women, over eighteen years of age, except illiterates, beggars, enlisted men in the army and navy, and persons deprived of their political rights.

But Vargas's constitutional government was soon challenged, as he declared, by both the Communists led by a former captain in the Brazilian army, Luiz Carlos Prestes, and by the *Integralistas* or green shirts, a paramilitary profascist political organization led by Plínio Salgado. In November, 1935, Vargas called for a campaign against the Communists, deported hundreds of them, suspended the constitution, placed the whole country under martial law, dissolved Congress, and announced that the presidential election scheduled for 1937 would not take place. Instead he promulgated a new constitution which frankly established a "corporative" state with himself as virtual dictator. By these actions, taken, as he said, in order to save the country from communism, he was able to carry out a policy of *continuismo* and to replace the *República Nova* with an *Estado Novo*. In all this he was supported by the armed forces, under Gen. Eurico Gaspar Dutra and Gen. Pedro Aurelio de Góes Monteiro, who were hostile to communism and impressed with the success of the Italian and German dictatorships.

Vargas's New State was an artificial creation. It looked toward a complete modification of Brazilian life at all levels. It was a doctrinaire innovation copied from Mussolini's Italy and Salazar's Portugal. Even the name *Estado Novo* was an importation from Portugal. It also owed much to the papal encyclicals Rerum novarum of 1891 and Quadragesimo anno of 1931, which defined the social responsibilities of the state and emphasized that social, cultural, and economic groupings form the fabric of national life. The new constitution, which was written by Dr. Francisco Campos, the minister of justice, extended the presidential term to six years, allowed the president to succeed himself indefinitely, and authorized him to govern by decree law. His right of intervention in local government was extended, and federal control over education was greatly increased. The powers of Congress were reduced, but in fact Congress was not allowed to meet for the next eight years during the remainder of Vargas's administration. Instead, a new national economic council was set up, similar to the Ministry of Corporations in Italy and the Corporative Chamber in Portugal, composed of representatives of the Brazilian agencies of national production and empowered to exercise legislative authority. The New State was a highly nationalistic organism. It subjected foreign nationals and foreign capital to strict regulation, demanded that two-thirds of the employees of every foreign company in each job category must be Brazilian, and required that prescribed amounts of Brazilian coal, Brazilian flour, Brazilian sugar, and other Brazilian products must be used by Brazilian industries. The press was subjected to censorship through advance scrutiny of news and editorials by the notorious *Departamento de Imprensa e Propaganda* (DIP) and through government control of newsprint. Vargas's position was made secure by a secret police which suppressed opponents of the government, including Communists, *Integralistas,* and later Nazis.

By such methods Vargas sought to win a mass following and in particular to gain the support of labor. To this end he inaugurated a comprehensive system of social security and labor benefits, including minimum wages and maximum hours of work. Under the auspices of the federal government, syndicates of workers and employers were organized, but workers were denied the right to strike. Arbitration of labor-employer disputes was made compulsory and was handled by special labor courts set up for this purpose. The benefits of education were made available to the masses of the Brazilian people on a scale unprecedented in the history of the country. During Vargas's first term of power, ending in 1945, both the number of elementary schools and the school enrollment more than doubled. The central government, following the educational patterns of Europe rather than the United States, took over control of education for the entire country.

526 LATIN AMERICA: AN INTERPRETIVE HISTORY

Brazil's political system from 1930 to 1945 under its shrewd, opportunistic, diminutive executive has been characterized as a dictatorship. Regardless of constitutional forms, Brazil was Vargas. His government was authoritarian in that it was thoroughly centralized, and it was unrepresentative, since it lacked a responsible cabinet and Congress. It was also intolerant of dissident viewpoints and un-Brazilian actions. But it was a democracy in the sense that it frankly sought to serve the interests of the majority of the Brazilian people and recognized the continuing importance of mass support. The president, Vargas, as the highest authority represented the nation in its various functional aspects, conceiving that democracy could be made real only if it dealt specifically with all the main activities of society. Like Cárdenas in Mexico, Vargas sought to carry out the social and economic program of the liberals by methods which sometimes seemed drastic and authoritarian but which were popular in the decade of the 1930s. The "democratic caesarism" of Vargas was no different in kind from the system of many of the so-called "democracies" after the Great Depression, though it employed perhaps too overtly the fascist trappings of corporativism. His government was concerned with institutional groupings and mass entities in Brazilian life rather than with the individual Brazilian. But Vargas was fundamentally a Brazilian *caudilho* who, having ridden to power on grievances engendered by the economic collapse, found it convenient to retain control by the methods of state power which seemed to be required during his era. His fascist-type constitution of 1937, like Bolívar's constitution for Bolivia, remains only a curious museum piece.

Additional Reading

Alexander, Robert J.: *Prophets of the Revolution,* The Macmillan Company, New York, 1962.

Azevedo, Fernando de: *Brazilian Culture: An Introduction to the Study of Culture in Brazil,* trans. by William Rex Crawford, The Macmillan Company, New York, 1950.

Bernstein, Harry: *Modern and Contemporary Latin America,* J. B. Lippincott Company, Philadelphia, 1952, chaps. 8, 9, 21, 22.

Clendenen, Clarence Clemens: *The United States and Pancho Villa: A Study in Unconventional Diplomacy,* Cornell University Press, Ithaca, New York, 1961.

Cline, Howard F.: "Mexico: A Matured Latin American Revolution, 1910–1960," *Annals of the American Academy of Political and Social Science,* pp. 84–94, March, 1961.

————: *The United States and Mexico,* Harvard University Press, Cambridge, 1953.

Cronon, E. David: *Josephus Daniels in Mexico,* University of Wisconsin Press, Madison, Wis., 1960.

Griffin, Charles C. (ed.): *Concerning Latin American Culture: Papers Read at Byrdcliffe, Woodstock, New York, August, 1939,* Columbia University Press, New York, 1940. A collection of essays by various specialists in Latin American subjects.

Helm, MacKinley: *Man of Fire: J. C. Orozco; An Interpretative Memoir,* Harcourt, Brace and Company, Inc., New York, 1953.

————: *Modern Mexican Painters,* Harper & Brothers, New York, 1941.

Keen, Benjamin: *Readings in Latin American Civilization: 1492 to the Present,* Houghton Mifflin Company, Boston, 1955, chap. XXXII.

Kneller, George F.: *The Education of the Mexican Nation,* Columbia University Press, New York, 1951.

Linné, Sigvald: *Treasures of Mexican Art: Two Thousand Years of Art and Art Handicraft,* Nordisk Rotogravyr, Stockholm, 1956.

Lipson, Leslie: "Government in Contemporary Brazil," *Canadian Journal of Economics and Political Science,* vol. 22, pp. 183–198, 1956.

Loewenstein, Karl: *Brazil under Vargas,* The Macmillan Company, New York, 1942.

Mosk, Sanford A.: *Industrial Revolution in Mexico,* University of California Press, Berkeley, Calif., 1950.

Poblete Troncoso, Moisés, and Ben G. Burnett: *The Rise of the Latin American Labor Movement,* Bookman Associates, New York, 1960.

Powell, J. Richard: *The Mexican Petroleum Industry, 1938–1950,* University of California Press, Berkeley, Calif., 1956.

Sánchez, George I.: *The Development of Higher Education in Mexico,* King's Crown Press, New York, 1944.

Schmeckebier, Laurence E.: *Modern Mexican Art,* University of Minnesota Press, Minneapolis, 1939.

Scott, Robert E.: *Mexican Government in Transition,* University of Illinois Press, Urbana, Ill., 1959.

Senior, Clarence: *Land Reform and Democracy,* University of Florida Press, Gainesville, Fla., 1958.

Simpson, Eyler N.: *The Ejido: Mexico's Way Out,* University of North Carolina Press, Chapel Hill, N.C., 1937.

Smith, T. Lynn: *Brazil: People and Institutions,* Louisiana State University Press, Baton Rouge, La., 1954.

—— and Alexander Marchant: *Brazil: Portrait of Half a Continent,* The Dryden Press, Inc., New York, 1951.

Tannenbaum, Frank: *Mexico: The Struggle for Peace and Bread,* Alfred A. Knopf, Inc., New York, 1950.

Townsend, William C.: *Lázaro Cárdenas, Mexican Democrat,* George Wahr Publishing Co., Ann Arbor, Mich., 1952.

Tucker, W. P.: *The Mexican Government Today,* University of Minnesota Press, Minneapolis, 1957.

Whetten, Nathan L.: *Rural Mexico,* University of Chicago Press, Chicago, 1948.

Whitaker, Arthur P.: *Nationalism in Latin America, Past and Present,* University of Florida Press, Gainesville, 1962.

Wolfe, Bertram D.: *Diego Rivera: His Life and Times,* Alfred A. Knopf, Inc., New York, 1943.

XXIV

War and Postwar Problems

The liberalism which was the dominant note in most parts of Latin America from the 1820s through the 1860s was a continuation of the struggle for freedom from governmental absolutism which was the rationale of the movement for independence at the beginning of the century. The triumph of this laissez-faire liberalism in the 1860s came as the logical fulfillment of independence. It marked the ultimate release of the individual from governmental oppression. It carried to completion the quest for freedom—both national and personal—which had been begun by Miranda, Bolívar, L'Ouverture, San Martín, Santander, and their colleagues.

The victory of liberalism brought new power to the liberals. It gave them control of government, and they now undertook to wield it for the welfare of the individual. But liberalism in power tended to reclaim for government the very authoritarianism against which liberalism had fought in the struggle for independence from Spain. The liberals might represent their government as the consummation of the struggle for individual freedom, as they repeatedly did, but their use of authoritarian methods necessarily drove true individualists into the opposition—into the camp of the conservatives. This was the inner meaning of the Chilean civil war in 1891, which was a struggle of the embattled laissez-faire liberals, called conservatives, against an aggressively liberal executive, determined to impose his program upon the country. This contest was repeated in country after country in Latin America during the latter years of the nineteenth century and the first half of the twentieth.

As liberals, professing a generous humanitarianism, enlarged the powers of government to carry their programs into effect, they ceased to be the heirs of the liberal patriots of the revolutionary period. They became instead the perpetrators of a new authoritarianism, which, though it called itself liberal, in fact betrayed the individualistic objectives of the romantic period. Against them therefore a new struggle for freedom was launched. The revolutionary idealism of the heroes of independence now demanded the overthrow of the usurping "liberals" who called themselves erroneously the heirs of the revolution. The roles of liberals and conservatives in the perennial struggle in Latin America for the rights of the individual were reversed. The new authoritarianism calling itself liberal had to be resisted by all true lovers of freedom. The new tyranny was the tyranny of the "liberal" state, which called itself democratic.

The political centralization that characterized Latin American societies in the two decades after World War I, particularly after 1930, was a product of basic social and economic conditions. The diminished trade, the fall in real wages, and the decline of large population groups to bare subsistence levels of living threw liberal democracy on the defensive in most of the Latin American countries. The conditions of economic hardship and social oppression which were either created or revealed in stark tragedy by the Depression destroyed confidence in the individualism and localism of the political system of the nineteenth century and led to power politics on a national scale as a means of solving the ills of society. This tendency was exemplified by the methods of Vargas in Brazil, Cárdenas in Mexico, and Aguirre Cerda in Chile. By means of New Deals imposed from above they and their less original imitators in other Latin American countries sought to remake the national economy, to achieve a more equitable distribution of the national income, to bring about social justice, and to start again the wheels of industry and trade. They also looked for ways of redeeming their countries from their virtually colonial dependence upon the demand situation for their few export products in foreign markets—a dependence which had been particularly disastrous to them during the years of the Depression.

A Hemisphere of Good Neighbors

Because of their necessitous condition the Latin American countries responded cordially to the new overtures for cooperation and friendship made by the United States after 1930. As the Hoover administration in Washington, finding the policy of military and fiscal intervention in the Central American and Caribbean countries expensive and unwarrantable in an era of deflation, prepared to liquidate the policy of imperialism, the Latin American countries once more became good neighbors of the United States. Hoover's good-will tour through South America as President-elect in 1928 prepared the way for the establishment of more cordial relations between the United States and Latin America. As President he declined to undertake military interventions in several Central American countries, withdrew the Marine forces of occupation from Nicaragua, and upon the recommendation of the Forbes Commission, which he appointed, prepared to evacuate United States forces of occupation from Haiti. But these gestures of good will were counteracted by the enactment of the Smoot-Hawley Tariff, which raised new tariff barriers around the United States against Latin American products. The Good Neighbor policy which was initiated by the Hoover administration was thus partly aborted by national industrial interests in the United States, who in the Depression period demanded and were given protection against foreign imports.

The Franklin Roosevelt administration implemented the Good Neighbor policy more effectively, mollifying the Latin American countries with long overdue concessions. The Platt amendment with Cuba was finally abrogated, the clause of the Gadsden Treaty of 1853 giving the United States rights of free transit across the Isthmus of Tehuantepec in Mexico was canceled, all United States Marines were finally withdrawn from Haiti, and a new treaty was negotiated with Panama increasing the annual rental which that country received from the United States for the use of the Canal Zone from $250,000 to $430,000. In addition, starting in 1934 the Roosevelt administration concluded trade agreements with ten Latin American governments as follows: Cuba in 1934; Brazil, Haiti, Colombia, and Honduras in 1935; Nicaragua, Guatemala, and Costa Rica in 1936; El Salvador in 1937; and Ecuador in 1938. By all these acts the United States manifested its intention to treat the Latin American countries as good neighbors.

The improvement of inter-American relations was also deemed to require the settlement of all boundary disputes and actual conflicts among the American nations. As a result of the suggestions made by President Hoover in 1929 for the solution of the Tacna-Arica dispute, Tacna was assigned to Peru and Arica to Chile. The controversy between Peru and Colombia over the Leticia area was settled in 1933 largely in Colombia's favor through the efforts of a League of Nations committee. In an attempt to end the hostilities which began in 1932 between Paraguay and Bolivia over the Chaco territory, the representatives of all the American nations sitting in Washington as a neutral commission summoned both belligerents to end the fighting and announced that their governments would not recognize any territorial acquisitions acquired by force of arms. President Roosevelt, acting under a joint resolution of Congress, which was intended to contribute to the restoration of peace in the Chaco, estopped the sale of arms and munitions of war to both belligerents by citizens of the United States. Finally through the good offices of the neutral commission and the mediating efforts of the League of Nations, Bolivia and Paraguay were persuaded to cease hostilities in the Chaco in 1935. Three years later they agreed by treaty to allow the presidents of Argentina, Brazil, Chile, Peru, Uruguay, and the United States to fix the boundary line between their countries in the Chaco.

The heart of the Good Neighbor policy of the Hoover and Roosevelt administrations was nonintervention by the United States in the affairs of its Western Hemisphere neighbors. At the seventh inter-American conference of American states at Montevideo in 1933 Secretary of State Cordell Hull along with delegates of all the other American nations signed a convention which declared, among other things, that "no state has the right to intervene in the internal or external affairs of another." The Roosevelt administration during the 1930s undertook to treat the twenty nations of Latin America as equals and to convert the inter-American system into a league of equals. This policy objective was furthered by Roosevelt's speeches disavowing all

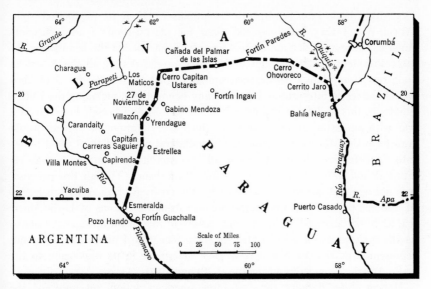

Boundary line between Bolivia and Paraguay fixed by the arbitral award of October 10, 1938.

meddling action by the United States in the Latin American countries, by the example of his own New Deal whose social welfare program strongly appealed to the economically underprivileged masses in Latin America, and by the efforts which both Roosevelt and Hull made at the Inter-American Conference for the Maintenance of Peace at Buenos Aires in 1936 and at the eighth inter-American conference at Lima in 1938 to court the Latin American nations. They were not able to achieve so complete a hemispheric solidarity as they deemed necessary to counter the mounting threats from the Axis allies, Germany, Italy, and Japan, but at the Buenos Aires conference they laid the groundwork for the procedure of consultation of the ministers of foreign affairs of the Americas which could be invoked whenever the peace of the hemisphere should be threatened. As the Roosevelt administration assumed an increasingly belligerent tone toward the Axis, it alienated some leaders of public opinion in Latin America who feared that Roosevelt was dragging their nations into a new world war, but by this policy Roosevelt won the enthusiastic support of large sectors of opinion in Latin America and came to be regarded by them as the world champion of democracy against the Axis challengers. The prescience of Roosevelt's leadership seemed to be vindicated when after the outbreak of the European war in September, 1939, Germany promptly overran the Netherlands, the Scandinavian countries, and finally France. The fate of all neutral countries seemed to be plunged into jeopardy.

In defense against the Axis threat, the United States and the Latin American nations, invoking the procedure of consultation of their foreign ministers, drew back into hemispheric isolationism. Often in the period since World War I they had broached plans for the creation of an exclusively American league of defense against assaults from outside the hemisphere. In 1921 President Baltasar Brum of Uruguay proposed that all the American countries "formulate a declaration, similar to that of Monroe, in which they would engage to intervene in behalf of any one of them, including the United States, if, in the defense of her rights, she should find herself involved in a war with an extracontinental nation." Such a declaration, he argued, would transform the Monroe Doctrine from a unilateral policy of the United States into "a defensive alliance between all the American countries ... with reciprocal obligations and advantages for all of them." Though this proposal was not adopted, agitation continued for the creation of an American league of nations, particularly among the Spanish-speaking nations of Latin America, as Brazil assumed an increasingly assertive role in the League at Geneva as the spokesman for all of Latin America. Since the United States was not represented at Geneva it generally gave first place in its diplomacy to the Latin American countries during the 1920s and 1930s.

During those decades common inter-American action not only for the defense of the American hemisphere but also for the preservation of the peace of the hemisphere was also emphasized, as, for example, in the suggestions for the creation of a distinctively American code of international public and private law and in the development of new peace machinery for the hemisphere in the so-called "Gondra Treaty" drawn up at the inter-American conference at Santiago in 1923, in the general convention of inter-American conciliation of 1929, and in the procedure of consultation worked out at the conferences at Buenos Aires in 1936 and at Lima in 1938. All these actions pointed toward the multilateralization or the continentalization of the Monroe Doctrine through the endorsement of its basic principles by all the American nations. They suggested the need for joint inter-American agreement (1) to oppose encroachments by any non-American nation upon the political independence of any nation of the Western Hemisphere and (2) to prevent the acquisition in any manner of territory in the Western Hemisphere by a non-American power.

Latin America and World War II

At the first meeting of consultation at Panama in September, 1939, the foreign ministers of all the American nations agreed to defend their common neutrality. They defined a maritime belt or zone of neutrality extending from the shores of the American nations to sea, in some cases as far as 300 miles, in which they agreed not to tolerate any belligerent action. But almost immediately this "chastity belt" was violated by the European belligerents when the German cruiser *Graf Von Spee* was pursued into Uruguayan waters by British and French warships and was finally scuttled by its crew off

Montevideo. The acting president of Panama spoke for all the American nations in protesting against this violation of the neutrality of the hemisphere, but his protest was not accepted as valid by any of the belligerents— England, Germany, or France. Hoping to avoid further involvement in the war, the Latin American nations adhered to their policy of neutrality, but they almost constantly received warnings both from Roosevelt and from other representatives of the pro-British viewpoint that Hitler and Mussolini intended to invade the Western Hemisphere. To these warnings the fall of France before the German war machine in June, 1940, gave new urgency.

A second meeting of foreign ministers was held immediately thereafter at Havana in June, 1940. There the official representatives of the American states, apprehensive that the victorious Hitler would take over French possessions in the Western Hemisphere including Martinique, Guadeloupe, French Guiana, St. Pierre, and Miquelon, agreed that their nations or any one of them should take them over in case of emergency in order to forestall German action and should administer them under trusteeship for the ultimate benefit of the people of the colonies. As it turned out, action of this sort did not have to be taken since Germany did not invade the Western Hemisphere. The various measures which the Roosevelt administration took to aid Britain, including the exchange of overage destroyers for island bases in December, 1940, and the enactment of the Lend-Lease legislation in March, 1941, aroused fears in the Latin American nations that they were being dragged into the war by Roosevelt, but on the other hand some of them saw clearly the incompatibility between the totalitarianism of the Axis nations and the American system. Presidents and foreign ministers of several Latin American nations assured Roosevelt that their governments would support the United States if it became involved in the war. The governmental centralization which they established in the 1930s to carry through social welfare programs and forestall revolution made it possible for these few national officials to speak authoritatively for their people. Some of these governments, particularly Colombia and Panama, became much concerned when Roosevelt in October, 1941, publicly exposed the existence of German air bases within a few hundred miles of the Panama Canal and reported that he had in his possession a German map showing that Hitler planned to partition the Latin American countries into five areas, each in charge of a *gauleiter*. This map was not made public at the time and has never since been found. But Roosevelt's announcement brought new support to his cause in Latin America.

Latin Americans were already favorably disposed toward the Roosevelt administration because of the Good Neighbor policy, which had largely accomplished its objectives of effecting a rapprochement among the nations of the Western Hemisphere. When the United States naval base at Pearl Harbor in the Hawaiian Islands was attacked by Japan in December, 1941, and the United States found itself openly at war with Japan, Germany, and

Italy, a third meeting of consultation of the foreign ministers of the American nations was hastily arranged to meet at Rio de Janeiro. "The shibboleth of classic neutrality in its narrow sense," the United States Undersecretary of State, Sumner Welles, told the foreign ministers, "can, in this tragic modern world, no longer be the ideal of any freedom-loving people of the Americas." In order to create the conditions of solidarity among the American nations which would enable them to meet the Axis danger, the United States, acting with Argentina, Brazil, and Chile, moved rapidly to settle an acrimonious boundary dispute between Peru and Ecuador which threatened to disrupt the peace of the hemisphere, and these four nations became guarantors of the settlement that was improvised at that time.

The reaction of the Latin American nations to the entry of the United States into the war was determined by their previous experience of the sincerity and beneficial effects of Roosevelt's Good Neighbor policy, by their estimate of the tangible benefits which they might hope to derive from military and economic collaboration with the United States in the war, and, most important of all, by the degree of their anxiety over a possible Axis invasion of the hemisphere. If the American hemisphere should be attacked they would have to seek protection behind the army, navy, and air power of the United States.

Within five days after the Japanese attack on Pearl Harbor nine Latin American nations—El Salvador, Guatemala, Haiti, Honduras, Cuba, Nicaragua, Costa Rica, the Dominican Republic, and Panama—declared war on Japan; and before the middle of December they similarly declared war against Germany and Italy. These same nine nations joined the United States, Great Britain, and their other allies in signing the United Nations Declaration on January 1, 1942, agreeing to employ their full resources against the Axis nations and not to make a separate armistice or peace with them. In addition to these Caribbean and Central American nations, Colombia and Mexico severed diplomatic relations with the Axis Powers; Ecuador, Paraguay, Peru, and Brazil declared their solidarity with the United States; and Uruguay, Argentina, Chile, Bolivia, and Venezuela offered to treat the United States as a nonbelligerent, exempting it from the limitations which they would otherwise have had to apply to it under their international obligations of neutrality. By the end of January, 1942, all the Latin American nations, except Argentina and Chile, had either declared war against the Axis Powers or had severed relations with them.

At the meeting of foreign ministers in Rio de Janeiro in January, 1942, the United States favored a resolution introduced by Colombia, Mexico, and Venezuela, which required all the American nations to break their political, commercial, and financial relations with Germany, Italy, and Japan. But it had to accept instead a resolution which merely recommended a rupture of relations with the Axis. An American hemisphere unanimously united against the Axis nations could not be achieved because of the opposition of

Legend:
- At war with axis
- Relations with axis broken
- Neutral

The Western Hemisphere and World War II, February 1, 1942. (*Courtesy of The New York Times.*)

Argentina and Chile. Those two nations refused cooperation largely for nationalistic and economic reasons. Influential groups in both countries, where British capital, British traders, and British diplomats had sometimes been offensively conspicuous, had developed anti-British prejudices. They were passionately committed to the preservation and defense of their own nationalism against all foreign threats from whatever source and were inclined toward the neutralism of Franco Spain. They could not abandon their admiration of Spain, which they regarded as the fountainhead of their cultures. In Argentina their national hero was Rosas, and as they admired him as a defender of Argentine nationality they depreciated Alberdi, Mitre, and Sarmiento, who, they felt, had unwisely subjected the country to foreign influences. Their point of view was represented in the highest circles of government by the foreign minister, Enrique Ruiz-Guiñazú.

The Argentine and Chilean nationalists were not convinced that their safety or the safety of the Western Hemisphere was threatened by the Axis victories in Europe and Asia nor did they think that Japan's attack on Pearl Harbor, situated beyond the limits of the Panama neutrality zone, constituted in the strict sense an attack on the Western Hemisphere which necessitated united American resistance. They were critical of Pan-Americanism, which they felt had been historically dominated by the United States and was now being exploited by it for the sake of its own security. Moreover, they desired to keep open their commercial channels with the Axis nations, particularly Germany and Italy, in order to reap the profits of neutral trade as they had done in World War I, and they looked forward to an enlargement of their trade with those nations after the war. Their governments were also responsive to the sentiments of the relatively large Axis elements in their national populations. Their remoteness from the existing theaters of war seemed to render highly improbable any reprisals against them by any of the belligerents.

But both Argentina and Chile, as they followed their independent courses of action, incurred the wrath of the Roosevelt administration. They were denied any share of the financial assistance and scarce commodities which the United States was doling out to its allies in the war. They were publicly denounced by Undersecretary Welles in a speech in October, 1942, for allowing "their brothers and neighbors of the Americas, engaged as they are in a life-and-death struggle to preserve the liberties and integrity of the New World, to be stabbed in the back by Axis emissaries." Chile finally succumbed to these pressures and broke diplomatic relations with the Axis nations in January, 1943. But its place as a standout against hemispheric solidarity in the waging of the war was taken by the government of Maj. Gualberto Villarroel which came to power in Bolivia by revolution in December, 1943. From the Villarroel regime, which was accused of being pro-Axis, the Roosevelt administration, acting ostensibly on the recommendation of the seven-man Emergency Advisory Committee for Political Defense at Montevideo, withheld recognition until that government severed relations with the Axis nations.

Under similarly strong pressures from the United States, Argentina finally broke relations with Germany and Japan in January, 1944, but because of this action the government of Pedro Pablo Ramírez, which had come to power there after the overthrow of President Castillo on June 5, 1943, was itself now overthrown. The government that replaced it, headed by Gen. Edelmiro J. Farrell but dominated by the minister of labor and social welfare, Juan Domingo Perón, showed the same disinclination as its predecessor to join with the other governments of the Americas in common action against the Axis nations. Though the new Argentine government failed to receive recognition from the United States it was immediately recognized by Chile, Paraguay, and Bolivia.

Meanwhile as a result of diplomatic negotiations and staff conversations with the United States starting as early as June, 1940, several of the Latin American governments had made their air and naval bases available to the United States. They were persuaded to expropriate Axis airlines operating in their countries, including AVIANCA, LATI, and CONDOR and, after the German conquest of France, Air France, and to take over other Axis-owned property. The Natal area of Brazil served as a station on an air thoroughfare for United States troops en route to all the fighting theaters of the world. Brazil herself was assigned responsibility under United States command for antisubmarine patrol in South Atlantic waters. Brazil and Mexico sent expeditionary forces to the fighting fronts in Italy and the Philippine Islands, respectively; and most important of all, all the Latin American countries supplied vitally needed war materials to their United Nations allies, particularly the United States. In return they were made equal sharers with the United States in the allocation of materials in short supply, though by reason of transportation shortages they seldom received delivery of all the materials allocated to them. Emergency relief had to be supplied to the Caribbean islands by the United States soon after Pearl Harbor when German submarines invaded the Western Hemisphere and cut off the essential food and drug imports of those islands. Their relief supplies were largely furnished under Lend-Lease and were allocated to the islands by the newly formed Anglo-American Caribbean Commission. The Good Neighbor policy was now abandoned in favor of the policy of the Good Partner, which, as President Roosevelt said, meant a policy of "one for all and all for one."

The declarations of war by the nine Central American and Caribbean governments against Japan and Germany immediately following the Japanese attack on Pearl Harbor satisfied the United States. The rest of the Latin American governments were neither encouraged nor required to come to its assistance with outright declarations of war. Their material assistance and their cooperation in eliminating Axis influences in their countries were deemed sufficient. At the meeting of foreign ministers at Rio de Janeiro in early 1942, therefore, the United States pressed the remaining Latin American governments only to sever relations with Japan and Germany. As noted above, all of them eventually did so, and Mexico, Brazil, and Bolivia went still further and declared war against both Germany and Japan in 1942 and 1943.

But in early 1945 as the war was approaching a victorious conclusion for the United Nations and plans were being drawn up by Roosevelt, Churchill, and Stalin for a postwar United Nations organization, the United States decided to press the seven South American nonbelligerents to issue declarations of war in order to qualify for membership in the postwar international collective security organization. As a result four governments—Paraguay, Peru, Uruguay, and Venezuela—declared war against both Germany and Japan, and two—Chile and Ecuador—declared war against Japan in February, 1945. A formula was then worked out at the Mexico City Conference on Problems of War and Peace by which Argentina might also declare war against the Axis nations and thus qualify for readmission to the American family of nations. Soon afterward Argentina accepted this formula and declared war against Germany and Japan. All the nations of the American hemisphere thus qualified for membership and participated in the San Francisco Conference of the United Nations in June, 1945, at which the new postwar international organization was born.

During World War II the Latin American allies of the United States became increasingly dependent upon it as their usual European markets and European sources of supply were cut off by enemy action. They were assiduously courted by the United States and became the targets of numberless good-will missions. To facilitate their military collaboration in the war, United States military, naval, and air missions which operated in several Latin American countries before Pearl Harbor were augmented and new ones were established in the Dominican Republic, Ecuador, Panama, Paraguay, and Venezuela. In addition the Latin American countries, except Argentina, were made the beneficiaries of the largess of the United States as after 1940 the Good Neighbor policy was transformed into a policy of financial assistance to Latin America. Under this new policy the United States made large dollar grants-in-aid for health and sanitation services, exchange of leaders, development of mineral resources, improvement of transportation, and many other projects in Latin America. The Lend-Lease aid which the Latin American countries received from the United States during the war totaled 475 million dollars. In addition they were given almost half as much more by the United States outside Lend-Lease channels for a grand total of 742 million dollars. The major recipients of this aid were Brazil, Mexico, Chile, and Peru, but all the Latin American countries except Argentina and Panama received some direct wartime financial aid from the United States.

This aid and the dislocation of normal trade resulting from the war seriously disrupted the economies of the Latin American countries. To meet the wartime needs of the United States, Latin Americans brought vast new areas of land under cultivation. They themselves suffered serious shortages of both foodstuffs and manufactures in order to meet their quotas required for the common war effort. Though they experienced acute wartime price inflation as the cost of living mounted they did not receive increased prices for the raw materials—meat, nitrates, coffee, vanadium, petroleum, copper, sugar, alcohol, balsa, and hundreds of other products—that they supplied to the United Nations war effort. For their prewar commercial dependence upon Europe was now substituted commercial dependence upon the United States. Between 1941 and 1945 the Latin American countries sent over 50 per cent of their exports to the United States and received back from it between 54 and 62 per cent of their imports. Both the inter-American policy of the United States and the exigencies of the war resulted in a closer relationship of dependence between Anglo-America and Latin America than had ever before existed.

Political Impact of the War

For this relationship the emphasis which Roosevelt's government placed upon the democratic system as opposed to the totalitarian system of the Axis nations was partly responsible. The propaganda of democracy made numberless converts in Latin America. Because the war of the United Nations was represented as a death struggle against the forces of tyranny, it received the enthusiastic support of the laboring classes in Latin America and stimulated the organization of those classes to support the war effort against the Axis. The wartime propaganda of democracy, emphasizing not individualistic democracy but rather social democracy, also caused an intensification of the social welfare programs of the Latin American governments. New attention was focused upon the underprivileged and upon the responsibility of government to alleviate their plight. But since little could be done to improve their situation during the war because of military priorities, plans were drawn up, with the encouragement of the United States, for ambitious social welfare programs to be put into operation after the war. The improvement of the condition of the large have-not classes in the Latin American countries, it was assumed, would become a shared responsibility of those countries and the United States, which by the generous policy of the Good Partner was showing concern for the welfare of her neighbors to the south. With the continued assistance of the United States into the postwar period, the Latin American governments would eliminate poverty among their peoples, would carry out large developmental programs along the lines of the Tennessee Valley Authority in the United States to create new sources of power, would bring in heavy industry to process their own mineral resources, would diversify their agriculture in order to improve diets and relieve themselves of their traditional dependence upon a few raw-materials exports, and would in general move their peoples forward out of the nineteenth century into the twentieth.

Starting with the Chilean Fomento Corporation created by the Aguirre Cerda administration in 1940, many developmental corporations were organized by Latin American governments and were given large responsibilities for planning and carrying out programs of national development. A project of an inter-American bank to finance these programs was worked out and was at first endorsed and later rejected by the United States. Some of the national planning agencies in the Latin American countries concentrated their efforts upon war-connected production and encouraged expansion into the field of heavy industry. Into the field of light industry, particularly textiles, beer, glass, and primary processing operations, Latin America had been drawn during World War I, but except for Mexico's iron industry at Monterrey, which was established with heavy government subsidies in 1900, Latin America had not ventured into the iron and steel industry before World War II. Much of the industrial expansion that was planned during World War II, including the construction of iron and steel mills, had to be postponed until after the war because of wartime shortages of both capital and equipment.

As World War II stimulated interest in the industrialization of the Latin American countries it also stimulated demands for increased popular

Fig. 24-1. Steel rolling mill at Volta Redonda, Brazil. (*Courtesy of Brazilian National Steel Company and Pan American Union.*)

participation in government and for a leveling or homogenization of their societies. Programs of social and economic change that had been put into operation by New Deal governments in the 1930s were given new momentum by the wartime propaganda in favor of democracy. The "people's war" against Hitler, Mussolini, and Tojo, as Roosevelt called it, seemed to render all irresponsible dictatorship obsolete. One-man rule became unpopular and the tenure of dictators unsteady. New popular leaders rode to power sometimes with the backing of organized labor, which made a phenomenal growth in many Latin American countries during the war. These new leaders responded to the democratic pressures of the time; they frankly recognized the need of mass support for effective political leadership; and like their *caudillo* prototypes during the previous century and a quarter they undertook to carry out their programs through strong personal leadership. The new *caudillos* now appeared in the guise of social reformers. They used the traditional centralist and authoritarian methods of the conservatives to advance the interests and welfare of the mass of their citizens and to gratify their aspirations for higher levels of living. As the principle of universal suffrage and the need for governments to rest upon mass support were increasingly recognized, several of the Latin American countries experienced revolution by consent.

A change of this sort occurred in Guatemala when the despotic Jorge Ubico was overthrown in 1944 and replaced in the following year by a social democratic government headed by Juan José Arévalo. Similarly in Costa Rica President Rafael Angel Calderón Guardia was forced out in 1944 and succeeded by a more social-minded president, Teodoro Picado. In El Salvador the one-man rule of Maximiliano Hernández Martínez came to an end in the same year. The same fate befell the regimes of Fulgencio Batista in Cuba and Carlos Arroyo del Río in Ecuador in 1944, and Isaías Medina Angarita in Venezuela and Getúlio Vargas in Brazil in 1945. In Peru the APRA, with its program of "democratic socialism," helped to put José Luis Bustamante y Rivero in the presidential chair. Old regimes which failed to respond to new popular pressures were toppled and in their places were set up governments which at least appeared to have a social, sometimes even a socialistic, outlook. Popular pressures for governments with such an outlook increased after the final victory of the United Nations over the surviving Axis nations, Germany and Japan, in 1945.

In the vanguard of the new socially conscious postwar regimes in Latin America were the governments of Teodoro Picado in Costa Rica, representing the *Vanguardia Popular;* Juan José Arévalo in Guatemala, governing for the Guatemalan Revolutionary party; and Rómulo Betancourt in Venezuela leading *Acción Democrática*. The programs of all these regimes were similar, calling for the utilization of the wealth of their countries for social ends in the interest of all or a majority of the people, a redress of the traditional imbalance between the haves and the have-nots, the subjugation of foreign investment to the welfare of the host nations, the curbing of land monopoly, and the enlargement of the powers of the central governments to encompass these objectives. They differed only in degree from the activist liberalism of the earlier twentieth-century Latin American political leaders— Batlle in Uruguay, Alessandri in Chile, Cárdenas in Mexico, Aguirre Cerda in Chile, and López in Colombia. Objecting to colonialism and imperialism in every form, they showed a detached attitude toward the developing schism between the United States and the Soviet Union, an attitude comparable to that of the neutralist nations of Western Europe and the Middle East. But they were primarily concerned with the social and economic problems of their own countries and with efforts to work them out through the instrumentality of centralized power. Theirs was the objective of the nineteenth-century utilitarians—the greatest good of the greatest number—and they invoked the full powers of the state to bring it about. Arévalo characterized his political program vaguely as "spiritual socialism."

Postwar Brazil

In Brazil even before the war, Vargas had shrewdly appraised the spirit of the times and concluded that the masses of the Brazilian people, awakened by industrialization and the prewar propaganda of ferment, were making social and economic demands that could only be met by an authoritarian government. But the democratic idealism of the war period, combined with dissatisfaction with wartime scarcities and inflated prices, generated a demand for more liberty in government. In early 1945 as the armies of the United Nations were clearly triumphing, Vargas acknowledged the force of the new public opinion by relaxing his control. He began by abandoning censorship and restoring full freedom to the press. Toward him was now directed a merciless criticism which prompted him to call for a national election in December, 1945, in which he ostensibly backed Gen. Eurico Gaspar Dutra for the presidency.

But Vargas himself remained a receptive candidate for the office which he had been filling for fifteen years and to which he had never been chosen by the Brazilian electorate. He became openly "populist" in his appeal to the Brazilian lower classes and began to mobilize a labor following by building up the *Partido Trabalhista Brasileiro* (Brazilian Workers' party or PTB) as his own party. This party emphasized the welfare of the laboring class and represented Vargas as "the little father of the poor." It demanded that the state assume a positive role as the planner, organizer, and operator of the national economy. By means of this new party Vargas sought a popular mandate for the kind of national planning or Positivism under the authority of the presidency which he had in fact been exercising for fifteen years. To strengthen his labor following, he liberated the leader of Brazilian communism, Luiz Carlos Prestes, from the prison in which he had long had him confined and legalized the Communist party. He probably convinced himself that his own continuance in the presidency was essential to the welfare of the Brazilian people, particularly the working classes. He therefore did nothing to check the organization of a pro-Vargas political movement, the *Queremistas,* who demanded that he continue in office, and he appointed one of the leaders of this movement, his own brother Benjamin of unsavory reputation, as chief of police in Rio de Janeiro. As a result the speculation became widespread that Vargas intended to cancel the scheduled election.

In this crisis the Brazilian armed forces turned against Vargas, threw him out of office, and installed the president of the supreme court, José Linhares, as temporary or acting president. The provisional government then held the election as planned in which the official candidate, General Dutra, heading the *Partido Social Democrático* (Social Democratic party or PSD) was elected with the backing of the conservatives, the remnants of Vargas's followers, and the Catholic Church. In this election, which was the first to be held since the franchise was broadened in the constitution of 1934, more than 7.5 million persons registered to vote. In this same election Vargas, who had retired to his ranch, was elected a senator from his native Rio Grande do Sul, and Communist leader Prestes, whose party polled 569,000 votes or 9.7 per cent of the total popular vote for president, was likewise chosen a senator.

The new constitution—Brazil's fifth—which was drawn up in 1946 by the new Congress sitting as a constitutional convention denied to the president the dictatorial prerogatives which Vargas had assumed in 1937 and sought to prevent a recurrence of presidential authoritarianism, without, however, abandoning the presidential system. It restored Brazil's federal form of government as it had existed under the constitutions of 1891 and 1934 and gave the president power to intervene the states only under certain conditions laid down in the constitution. It also provided for separation of the executive, legislative, and judicial branches of government. Under it the president would be elected by direct popular vote of the literate population for a five-year term and could not be reelected. He would be assisted by a cabinet appointed by himself and not responsible to Congress. Through the ministries of war, air, and marine, the president was entrusted with supreme command over the armed forces. He was also given the power to direct total or partial mobilization and to declare a state of siege, but he was required to obtain the consent of Congress to make war, declare peace, and permit foreign military forces to pass through Brazilian territory or in time of war remain in it.

The constitution also contained a declaration of civil rights guaranteeing inviolability of life and property, freedom of conscience and religion, freedom of the press, the right of assembly, association, and petition, and the right of habeas corpus. But it forbade "propaganda for war . . . [or] with the aim of subverting the political or social order, or [fomenting] race or class prejudices," and it banned political parties "whose program or action is contrary to a democratic regime." The Brazilian census of 1940 showed that 56.4 per cent of the population eighteen years of age and over could neither read nor write. These, along with enlisted soldiers of the lower ranks and persons who had lost their political rights, were the only persons excluded from voting. For all persons entitled to vote, registration and voting were made compulsory. Of the 7.5 million registered voters 22 per cent nevertheless failed to vote in the presidential elections of 1945. The general elections of 1950 brought out the largest vote ever cast in Brazil when nearly 70 per cent of the 11 million eligible voters went to the polls. After elections the nonvoters are regularly given a general pardon by the legislature for not performing their constitutional duty.

From the authoritarian constitution of 1937 the new Brazilian constitution of 1946 carried over certain social welfare and nationalistic provisions. It assured work for all and permitted the federal government to "promote" a fair distribution of property. It required the payment of a "minimum wage capable of satisfying, in accordance with the conditions of each region, the normal needs of the worker and his family," established an eight-hour day, and prohibited the employment of children under fourteen. In a significant nationalistic provision it required that concessions for the development and utilization of Brazil's resources could be made only to Brazilians or to Brazilian corporations.

According to the census of 1940, 95 per cent of the Brazilian people were Catholic, but the separation of church and state, which was effected in the constitution of 1891, was continued in all subsequent constitutions, including that of 1946. That constitution guaranteed freedom of worship and forbade federal and state authorities to subsidize any religion. It made education a lay responsibility, but in those parts of Brazil where public educational facilities were either inadequate or entirely lacking, education remained in the hands of the church. Cemeteries were secularized and civil marriage was made compulsory. Since Catholic priests were not prohibited from holding office by any legal or constitutional ban, several of them have won election to Congress and to other elective offices. Under Vargas the political influence of the church was somewhat curtailed, and in 1949 the church itself decided that members of the Catholic clergy should no longer be candidates for political office. Sporadic efforts have been made to establish a Brazilian national Catholic Church. As early as 1910 a movement in this direction led by Amorin Correa attracted thousands of followers, but the movement was abandoned after his death. Again in 1945 an Apostolic Brazilian Catholic Church was organized by an excommunicated priest, Carlos Duarte Costa.

The Dutra administration was plagued with many problems arising from the postwar economic distress. For them it tended to blame the Communists and to seek relief in loans from the United States for industrialization. When in the congressional elections of January, 1947, the Communists polled 450,000 votes and elected two senators, fourteen federal deputies, nearly forty-six deputies in the state legislatures, and the largest single party bloc of members in the city council of Rio de Janeiro, the Dutra administration moved against them. Pursuant to the constitution the supreme court ruled in May, 1947 that the *Partido Communista do Brasil* (Brazilian Communist party or PCB) was illegal since it was not in harmony with the democratic order and was not being financed and led by Brazilians. The police authorities therefore closed the party's offices, and in January, 1948, Dutra's party in Congress united with the representatives of Brazil's second largest party in Congress, the *União Democrática Nacional* (UDN), to expel Communist party members from both chambers of the legislature.

Beginning immediately after the overthrow of Vargas, political parties, which had been banned during his long administration, began to be organized. They experienced a phenomenal growth. Throughout the Dutra administration they directed their activities toward the election of 1950. Vargas, living on his ranch in Rio Grande do Sul and seldom attending to his duties as senator, built up an organized personal following in his party, the *Partido Trabalhista Brasileiro*. He received little support from the Catholic Church and the army, but appealed particularly to both the organized and unorganized labor forces of the country. Thoroughly socialistic in outlook this party demanded that capital should be subjected to the requirement of "social utility." Vargas was quoted in March, 1949, as favoring the socialization of "water-power resources, mineral deposits, electrical supply facilities, [and] means of transport—in short, the program that the British Labor party is carrying out."

The dominant political party, the *Partido Social Democrático,* also favored a substantial measure of governmental control over the economy of the country, government ownership of certain public utilities, imposition of restrictions upon foreign capital, and the enactment of social welfare legislation. The ideals of nineteenth-century liberalism were upheld only by the *União Democrática Nacional*, which opposed the centralization of power and the growth of the federal bureaucracy, and by the almost vestigial *Partido Re-públicano* (Republican party), headed by former president Artur Bernardes. In the election Vargas swept to victory with a plurality of almost 49 per cent of the popular vote. Together the candidates of the two parties, the PTB and the PSD, which had a centralizing and socialistic program polled almost 70 per cent of the total vote.

Vargas, now put into the presidency for the first time by popular vote, relied more and more upon the Brazilian working classes not only to maintain himself in power but also to bring about far-reaching institutional changes. He returned to govern, he said, "on the arms of the people." He may have been crushed by the embrace of those arms. Or as the self-anointed champion of the people he may have been destroyed by the enemies of the people, as he himself alleged. He courted the people, sometimes demagogically, in order to counter the growing antagonism of the elite and the armed forces upon whose support, he felt, he could no longer depend. As a "river of mud," to use his phrase, was discovered to be running through his presidential palace and his intimate political friends were shown to be responsible for graft, corruption, and even murder, Vargas was deposed by a group of army generals in August, 1954. Upon receiving the news he dramatically committed suicide. By his side after his death was found a palpitating farewell message, as follows:

Once more the forces and interests against the people are newly coordinated and raised against me. They do not accuse me, they insult me; they do not fight me, they slander me and do not give me the right of defense. They need to drown my voice and halt my actions so that I no longer continue to defend, as I always have defended, the people and principally the humble.

I follow the destiny that is imposed on me. After years of domination and looting by international economic and financial groups, I made myself chief of an unconquerable revolution. I began the work of liberation and I instituted a regime of social liberty. I had to resign. I returned to govern on the arms of the people.

A subterranean campaign of international groups joined with national groups revolting against the regime of workers' guarantees. The law of excess profits was stopped in Congress. Hatreds were unchanged against the justice of a revision of minimum wages.

I wished to create national liberty by developing our riches through Petrobras [government oil development company], and a wave of agitation clouded its beginnings. Electrobras [government hydroelectric development agency] was hindered almost to despair. They do not wish the workers to be free. They do not wish the people to be independent.

I assumed the government during an inflationary spiral that was destroying the value of work. Profits of foreign enterprises reached 500 per cent yearly. In declarations of goods that we import there existed frauds of more than $100,000,000.

I saw the coffee crisis increase the value of our principal product. We attempted to defend its price and the reply was a violent pressure upon our economy to the point of being obliged to surrender.

I have fought month to month, day to day, hour to hour, resisting a constant aggression, unceasingly bearing it all in silence, forgetting all and renouncing myself to defend the people that now fall abandoned. I cannot give you more than my blood. If the birds of prey wish the blood of anybody, they wish to continue sucking that of the Brazilian people.

I offer my life in the holocaust. I choose this means to be with you always. When they humiliate you, you will feel my soul suffering at your side. When hunger beats at your door, you will feel in your chests the energy for the fight for yourselves and your children. When they humiliate you, you will feel in my grief the force for reaction.

My sacrifice will maintain you united, and my name will be your battle flag. Each drop of my blood will be an immortal call to your conscience and will maintain a holy vibration for resistance.

To hatred, I respond with pardon. And to those who think they have defeated me, I reply with my victory. I was the slave of the people and today I free myself for eternal life. But this people, to which I was a slave, no longer will be a slave to anyone. My sacrifice will remain forever in your soul and my blood will be the price of your ransom.

I fought against the looting of Brazil. I fought against the looting of the people. I have fought bare-breasted. The hatred, infamy, and calumny did not beat down my spirit. I gave you my life. Now I offer my death. Nothing remains. Serenely I take the first step on the road to eternity and I leave life to enter history.[1]

Vargas at his death was trying to understand and control the new popular dynamism which was the fruit of the democratic propaganda and the social upthrusts of World War II. His successor in the presidency, Juscelino Kubitschek, elected in the poll of October, 1955, with the backing of both the PTB and the UDN, was faced with the same challenge. He made it one of his special objectives to establish a new inland capital, Brasília, replacing the cosmopolitan and sophisticated Rio de Janeiro which had served as capital since 1763. The date selected for the inauguration of Brasília, April 21, 1960, commemorated the execution of Brazil's patriot hero, Tiradentes, in 1789, and the name Brasília had been suggested by José Bonifácio in a memoir written in 1822.

The architecture of this new city, hewn out of the wilderness of the state of Goiás, is daringly conceived in the most *vanguardista* style by its architect, Lúcio Costa. As a modern example of town planning Brasília is designed along completely functional lines to provide architectural modes and facilities outstripping those of any other capital in the world and accommodating an ultimate population of 550,000 inhabitants. This deliberate transfer of the capital to a location far inland on the central plateau is intended to end the political cycle of the coastal region, to consummate the possession of the country, to encourage a new movement of population into the interior, to build up new population centers in the west—an area that comprises more than half the nation's territory but is almost devoid of population—and to change almost the entire economic and demographic character of the nation. Brasília may be considered one of the finest products of Brazil's new Positivism, symbolized in the name given to the new presidential residence, the Palace of the Dawn (*Palácio da Alvorada*).

But this and the huge program of national development launched by the Kubitschek administration brought serious economic consequences. At the expiration of Kubitschek's term in January, 1961, Brazil was burdened with a foreign debt of 3.8 billion dollars. The cost of living had increased 50 per cent in 1959, 30 per cent in 1960, and more than 800 per cent in the thirteen years after 1948. The problems of maintaining national financial solvency, curbing inflation, and meeting the demands of rebellious peasant groups in the northeast for land remained for his successor, Janio Quadros, former governor of the state of São Paulo, who became president of Brazil on January 31, 1961. When Quadros unexpectedly resigned in the following August, explaining that "terrible reactionary forces in Brazil and outside it made it impossible" for him to continue as president, leaders of the Brazilian armed forces quickly arranged to replace the presidential system with a parliamentary system before allowing vice president João Goulart to succeed to

[1] Doubts as to the authenticity of this message were summarized by J. V. D. Saunders, "The Death of Vargas," *The Mississippi Quarterly,* vol. IX, Spring 1956, [115]-131.

the presidency. In this crisis, a small military clique played the same role that General Deodoro da Fonseca and his associates had played in the constitutional crisis of 1889. In both cases the military intervened to establish limited, responsible, and decentralized government. The new president was a protégé of Getúlio Vargas and since 1956 had been vice president of the Brazilian Labor Party.

The Perón Era in Argentina

In Argentina popular ferments and social pressures were revealed in the overthrow of the Castillo government by the armed forces of the *Campo de Mayo* in June, 1943, and the gradual emergence of Juan Domingo Perón to prominence, first as minister of labor in the regime of Pedro P. Ramírez, then as vice president under Gen. Edelmiro Farrell, and finally as president by free choice of approximately 55 per cent of the Argentine voters in February, 1946. The serious interest which the Argentines showed in this election is indicated by the following eyewitness report of a preelection street battle between Perón's followers and the opposition *Democráticos:*

About five-thirty I heard the first shots, across the Plaza at the corner of Cevallos Street. . . . Democratic Union youths had linked arms, forming three solid human chains across Cevallos Street, and were holding back their enraged fellows who wanted to fight the gangs of *peronistas* a block away. . . . The shooting started when one Democratic youth who was being beaten broke away and ran toward the Plaza, followed by a shower of stones and by *peronistas.* Half a dozen *democráticos* broke through the chain and rushed to run interference for him. Before they returned to the corner, a few scattered shots came from the *peronistas,* answered by the *democráticos* with light pistol fire.

Suddenly, as if at a signal, the cordon vanished and no less than forty pistols appeared in the hands of the *democráticos,* directly below my balcony. They blazed away with heavy fire at the *peronistas,* who disappeared magically behind building corners a block away. I don't see how such volume of fire could have missed the tightly packed mob, but I saw none fall except a few who threw themselves down on the pavement to make a smaller target and immediately scrambled for safe spots.

The *democráticos* barricaded their end of Cevallos with park benches and with building tile from a construction job across the Plaza. They tore up other park benches for clubs. For the next two hours they fired at any male figure appearing at the other end of the block. The only exception was a peddler of ice cream suckers, who undoubtedly set the world's record for short bicycle sprints when he looked up the street and saw the barricades and the gleam of pistol barrels.

In general, the *democráticos'* fire was heavier than the *peronistas',* although the latter bounced enough bullets off surrounding buildings and steel shutters to keep everybody's head down. . . .

The battle finally wore itself out, and the defenders left the barricades just before dark.... The battle was over, but the atmosphere remained tense. The score was four killed and thirty-three wounded.[2]

Perón's triumph in the election marked the downfall of the old *estanciero* oligarchy, whose economic position had long been declining under the impact of the new industrialism of the twentieth century. In the previous half century the rural population of Argentina had declined from 57.2 per cent to only 31.8 per cent of the total population. The increasing mechanization of agriculture on the pampa and the exodus of farm labor to the cities of the littoral had diminished the political power of the landed aristocracy. The old regional conflict between the agricultural interior provinces and the urban littoral was accentuated, this time favoring the latter. Perón's election signalized the rise of the Argentine proletariat and brought new industrial and manufacturing interests into political power. They had already gained financial power, but having no champion in politics they had been denied political power by the *estanciero* oligarchy. Now, backed by the urban and rural proletariat whom Perón had mobilized for political action, they moved into government.

With their backing Perón engineered a social revolution. Not content, as some of his liberal predecessors in Argentina had been, merely with the free vote and universal suffrage as a means to the attainment of human welfare and the maintenance of social order, he became the knight of a new crusade, an authentic social revolutionary, a "state of mind of the working classes." In him and later in his dynamic and glamorous new wife, Eva Duarte Perón, was embodied the impatient liberalism of the twentieth century seeking to remake traditional institutions and to create a brave new world. For the industrial sector of Argentine life, both entrepreneurs and proletariat, Perón became an eloquent spokesman. To the frustrated and underprivileged working classes—the *descamisados* or "shirtless ones"—he and his wife were symbols of social justice. Under them the full powers of government were used to redistribute the wealth of the nation through a new tax system and a social welfare program. A powerful government agency, the Argentine Institute for the Promotion of Trade (IAPI), was set up to market Argentine products abroad in order to secure maximum profits for government and supposedly also maximum benefits for the nation. In two successive Five-Year Plans Perón promulgated blueprints for the development of the nation's economy and system of education along thoroughgoing Positivist or national socialist lines. And yet the *Peronistas* claimed to be only carrying to completion the changes begun by the Radical party under Irigoyen. They were merely transforming political democracy into social democracy and fixing upon the state the responsibility of ensuring the equality and the social benefits desired by the masses of the people. Argentine Positivism was made

[2] Scott Seegers, "Editor's Eye Witness Account," *The Inter-American*, January, 1946. Used by permission.

identical with national socialism. Perón was the ideological heir of Argentina's pioneer socialists, Echeverría, Juan B. Justo, and José Ingenieros. This program seemed to necessitate alterations in the constitution of 1853. When a new national constituent convention assembled in early 1949 Perón called for changes in more than half of the 110 articles of the old constitution. The dominant notes in the new constitution, which was adopted unanimously by the *Peronista* members, the Radical party members having withdrawn, were social justice and economic nationalism. Priority was given in the constitution to the social and economic doctrines of *Peronismo*. These were designed to appeal to the economically underprivileged, to the workers organized in the government-dominated labor unions, and to the rural *peones* working on the *estancias* of the rich. Part I repudiated the concept of private property contained in the constitution of 1853 and proclaimed instead that all property has a social function and exists for the general welfare. It placed capital "at the service of the national economy" with "social welfare as its principal object," and it authorized the federal government to intervene in the economy and to establish a monopoly over certain operations in order to protect the general welfare. An article suggestive of article 27 of the Mexican constitution reserved to the federal government control over the exploitation of all subsoil resources as the inviolable property of the nation. The constitution made all public services the primary responsibility of government and denied their use for private exploitation. "The state does not recognize the freedom to violate freedom," it proclaimed in article 15.

Though the new constitution of the *Peronistas* ostensibly preserved the federal structure of government for Argentina, it in fact deprived the provinces of their powers. To the federal government was given the authority to ensure national prosperity and to legislate on matters of health, morality, social security, culture, education, transportation, and industry. It was also empowered to break up the large estates which monopolized much of Argentina's 75 million acres of cultivated land. As a further step toward centralizing the powers of government, the constitution contained new clauses which provided for the direct election of a president by the people on a nationwide basis and permitted his immediate reelection, thus making possible the continuation of a popular president in office. As indicative of the extent to which the government limited provincial powers, it made the new constitution effective on publication without requiring or permitting ratification by the provinces.

Under this centralizing, social welfare constitution Perón exercised large powers in order to control the economy of the nation and to ensure a more homogeneous distribution of the national wealth. He threw the power of the state on the side of the underprivileged. By this means, despite disastrous drought conditions in 1950–1952 which administered a body blow to Argentine prosperity, Perón was reelected to the presidency in 1952 by approximately 67 per cent of the Argentine electorate. Like Vargas in Brazil he knew how to make populism and Positivism yield dividends in terms of votes.

Perón, though (perhaps because) he was a son of Italian immigrants, was above all an Argentine nationalist. The masses of his followers, consisting of the humblest classes and immigrants, came to share the creole spirit as an elemental tradition of the country, responded to its rhetoric, and appreciated its economic advantages for them. Perón welded the creole-immigrant conglomerate which was Argentina into a new political force. He rehabilitated as an Argentine nationalist hero Juan Manuel Rosas, some of whose policies he emulated and to whom he bore a striking physical resemblance. At the same time he depreciated Alberdi, Sarmiento, and the so-called "generation of 1880" who, he alleged, had failed to develop native Argentine culture but had instead looked abroad for their ideas and had introduced exotic systems into the nation. With their foreign outlook they had repudiated the *gaucho*. During Perón's second term as president he carried his nationalistic central-

Fig. 24-2. A busy street in the capital of Argentina. Calle Florida in Buenos Aires. (*Courtesy of Pan American Airways.*)

izing policy so far as to attempt to disestablish the Catholic Church, which had long been potent in Argentine politics and which had earlier supported him. In doing so, Perón ran into strong opposition from the ecclesiastical hierarchy, Argentine conservatives, and certain groups in the military. His nationalizing policies also antagonized British moneyed interests. He was supported, however, by the Argentine Jewish community, the largest in Latin America, which had found it advantageous to collaborate with him. Finally he was overthrown in September, 1955, by the military, which installed a governing *junta* in power under General Aramburu and arranged for new elections. These resulted in the triumph of the Radical party candidate, Arturo Frondizi, who was inaugurated in May, 1958, with a program which bore striking resemblances to Perón's. The "liberalism" of the positive state seemed to respond to the requirements of the Argentine people.

In several other countries of Latin America national socialism or Positivism with a centralistic, authoritarian basis showed a steady growth during World War II and burgeoned into strong national movements after the war. It was stimulated by the wartime propaganda of the United Nations, which sought to counter the Nazi-Fascist movement abroad by appeals for popular democratic action. The emphasis which the United Nations placed upon social and political equality as opposed to the elitism of the Nazi-Fascist nations had revolutionary implications for Latin America and denoted the course of political action for many aspiring political leaders after the war. Latin American nationalism was also nourished by the assurances that were given to Latin Americans of enlarged opportunities, improved living standards, and increased participation in world affairs after the war.

Whether denominated liberal or conservative all political leaders who came to power in postwar Latin America had to respond, if they wished to remain in power, to new postwar popular pressures for strong governmental action to achieve social justice, to level economic class distinctions, and to promote national development. These pressures gave unusual peremptoriness to the old objectives and methods of the revolutionary liberals, the Positivists. They accelerated the trend, already initiated by Batlle, Irigoyen, Alessandri, and Cárdenas toward the authoritarian government as the means of promoting the "liberal" program. One of the notable factors in the centralized power system was that the responsibility for decision making could be more clearly identified than before and government could be less manipulated by power elites. A centralized authority resting upon a popular consensus and acknowledging its mandate from the people is subject to more direct checks than were the old-fashioned conservative *caudillos*.

Additional Reading

Alexander, Robert J.: *The Perón Era,* Columbia University Press, New York, 1951.
Bernstein, Harry: *Modern and Contemporary Latin America,* J. B. Lippincott Company, Philadelphia, 1952, chaps. 16, 23, 31, 36.

Camacho, Jorge A.: *Brazil: an Interim Assessment,* 2d ed., Royal Institute of International Affairs, London, 1954.

Clark, J. Reuben: *Memorandum on the Monroe Doctrine,* Government Printing Office, Washington, 1930.

Cohen, Alvin: *Economic Change in Chile, 1929–1959,* University of Florida Press, Gainesville, 1960.

DeConde, Alexander: *Herbert Hoover's Latin American Policy,* Stanford University Press, Stanford, Calif., 1951.

Dozer, Donald M.: *Are We Good Neighbors: Three Decades of Inter-American Relations, 1930–1960,* University of Florida Press, Gainesville, Fla., 1959.

Goldwert, Marvin: *The Constabulary in the Dominican Republic and Nicaragua: Progeny and Legacy of United States Intervention,* University of Florida Press, Gainesville, 1962.

Griffin, Charles C.: *Concerning Latin American Culture,* Columbia University Press, New York, 1940.

Hughlett, Lloyd J., ed.: *Industrialization of Latin America,* McGraw-Hill Book Company, Inc., New York, 1946. A detailed treatment of various Latin-American industries.

Keen, Benjamin: *Readings in Latin American Civilization: 1492 to the Present,* Houghton Mifflin Company, Boston, 1955, chaps. XXXI, XXXV.

Kennedy, John J.: *Catholicism, Nationalism, and Democracy in Argentina,* University of Notre Dame Press, Notre Dame, Ind., 1958.

Mechan, J. Lloyd: *The United States and Inter-American Security, 1889–1960,* University of Texas Press, Austin, 1961.

Melo Franco, Afonso Arinos de: "The Tide of Government," *Atlantic Monthly,* vol. 197, 152–156 (February, 1956).

Palmer, Thomas W.: *Search for a Latin American Policy,* University of Florida Press, Gainesville, 1957.

Pike, Fredrick B. (ed.): *Freedom and Reform in Latin America,* University of Notre Dame Press, Notre Dame, Ind., 1959.

Ruiz-Guiñazû, Enrique: *La Política Argentina y el futuro de América,* Librería Huemel, Buenos Aires, 1944.

Schurz, William L.: *Brazil, the Infinite Country,* Dutton, New York, 1961.

Serxner, Stanley J.: *Acción Democrática of Venezuela: Its Origin and Development,* University of Florida Press, Gainesville, 1959.

Whitaker, Arthur A. (ed.): *Inter-American Affairs* (5 vols.), Columbia University Press, New York, 1942–1946.

Wood, Bryce, *The Making of the Good Neighbor Policy,* Columbia University Press, New York, 1961.

Zook, David H., Jr., *The Conduct of the Chaco War,* Twayne Publishers, Inc. (Bookman Associates), New York, 1960.

XXV

Latin America in the Contemporary World

Latin America, like other areas of the world, has been rousingly affected by the revolution of rising expectations generated by World War II. Since the wars of independence, revolutionary attitudes have been endemic in many of the Latin American countries. This area is often thought of as peculiarly susceptible to revolutions, though it may be doubted whether the loss of life and property suffered in a century and a half of Latin American political upheavals equals the costliness and devastation wrought by the Civil War in the United States. The Latin American peoples in general have made their adjustments to changing social, political, and economic conditions by means of a series of extralegal changes instead of by one gigantic cataclysmic revolution.

The revolutionary spirit was stimulated by the political ferments and the economic pressures that appeared in these countries after 1940. The propaganda for equalitarianism and for the rights of the have-not peoples that was released during World War II not only called the attention of the Latin Americans to their own underprivileged plight but also gave birth to new hope for an improvement in their economic condition after the war. Western technology has made a deliberate assault upon local social and economic structures in many of these countries causing serious dislocations and creating pressures for either a reorientation of certain elements in the traditional power structure or a defensive action against the effects of this external impact.

Postwar Latin America has been passing through a prolonged social revolution, the end of which is not yet in sight. The violence which accompanies it belies the *serenidad* or equanimity of spirit which Latin Americans continually laud but seldom exemplify. The aspirations of these people for a better life in terms of the standards achieved by the United States and other industrialized nations have come to be bound up with an ardent, even a fanatical nationalism. They are making their own governments the instruments by which they hope to achieve the better life. They are thinking big. They want to establish new industries in their countries, to produce all the shoes that their people need, to build enough schoolrooms to accommodate every child, to improve medical care, to eliminate illiteracy, and to expand recreational facilities. In short they want to control their own destinies.

Roots of Revolution

Factors making for a violent change in existing conditions are found almost everywhere in Latin America. "Millions of inhabitants" of these countries, declared Dr. Alberto Lleras Camargo, Secretary General of the Organization of American States, in 1948, are "without a home or an organized family life, without schools, without land, without even personal belongings. Their only risk in joining a revolutionary movement is the loss of the following day's wages." Many of them live constantly on the verge of starvation and in the shadow of death from disease. To earn sufficient wages to buy a loaf of bread an industrial worker in Brazil in 1946 had to work 52 minutes, in Guatemala 69 minutes, and in Colombia 80 minutes, as compared with only 4.4 minutes in the United States. To earn a pound of rice he had to work 77 minutes in Colombia and 96 minutes in Bolivia, as compared with less than 6 minutes in the United States. The average per capita income in Latin America is less than $275 as compared with $2,000 in the United States, and the highest per capita income in any Latin American country (Argentina) amounted to only $496 in 1950. Moreover, the rate of increase of real per capita income is so small that at the existing rate Latin Americans will require almost two and one-half centuries to reach one-third of the per capita income now enjoyed by citizens of the United States. Fidel Castro's estimate at an inter-American conference in late 1960 that Latin America will need 30 billion dollars to meet its capital needs is not wide of the mark.

By twentieth-century standards most of the Latin American peasants live in grinding poverty. Their only trade is the trade in merchandise carried on men's backs. They do not enter into the life of the countries in which they reside and in which their ancestors have resided for generations. They still live in a precapitalist economy and supply their needs largely through barter or by arrangements in which money, if it circulates at all, circulates only in the smallest denominations. After World War II their poverty was aggravated by runaway inflation which carried the prices of foodstuffs and other necessities to eight and even ten times their prewar levels. On a base of 1953 = 100 the cost of living at the end of 1960 ranged from 98 in the Dominican Republic to 622 in Argentina, 945 in Chile, and 2,398 in Bolivia, as compared with only 111 in the United States. During 1961 the figures steadily mounted, as is shown in Appendix II.

These conditions of hard living produce chronic social instability. To deal with problems of disease and injury Haiti has only 1 physician to 10,000 population, Brazil 2, and Uruguay 9, as compared with 13 in the United States. Life expectancy throughout Latin America therefore is much lower than in the United States; in Peru, for example, life expectancy is only 39 years as compared with almost 70 years in the United States. Illiteracy is widespread. Among persons 15 years of age and over, it was reliably estimated in 1956, more than 50 per cent were illiterate in Bolivia, Brazil, El Salvador, Guatemala, Honduras, Nicaragua, Paraguay, Peru, and the Dominican Republic, and this figure reached almost 90 per cent in Haiti. As most of them have nothing to lose from participating in a revolution against the constituted authorities, they readily follow leaders or *caudillos* who promise them a better way of life. These *caudillos* who provide the leadership for social revolution usually come from the middle class, and they attract a following both from their own class and from the lower classes.

Property in land has long been a status symbol in Latin America and had been monopolized by the wealthy. As a result Latin America is an area of land without men and of men without land. To give those who work the land ownership of the soil, the leaders of the Mexican revolution made redistribution of agricultural lands one of their objectives. Between 1916 and 1945 Mexican governments expropriated and made available to agricultural workers 15.5 per cent of the total area of the country or an area almost equal to all of New England and New York. Following Mexico's example, a few other countries have enacted similar programs. But land monopoly or *latifundio*, which had been a characteristic of the Latin American economy since the days of the *conquistadores*, has remained a favorite target of social revolutionaries. Where land redistribution has been undertaken it has often failed to create greatly improved living standards, important increases in production per hectare, or democratic institutions in rural society. In 1959 in nine countries of Latin America—Argentina, Brazil, Bolivia, Chile, the Dominican Republic, Mexico, Paraguay, Peru, and Uruguay—more than 50 per cent of the agricultural land was still held in parcels of more than 2,400 acres. Under the policy of the *Alianza para el Progreso* (Alliance for Progress) of the administration in Washington in 1961 the State Department is encouraging change in the ownership pattern of the land in Latin America and the supplying of supplementary facilities for the better utilization of the land. It expected this reform to be accomplished not by outright expropriation and redistribution of the land by Latin American governments but by tax reform measures.

Many Latin American revolutions headlined in the foreign press represent simple changes of administration. These palace revolutions, barracks uprisings, or *cuartelazos* as they are often called, usually accomplish a transfer of executive authority from one president to another with little bloodshed and no profound social and economic consequences, and they do not affect foreign business and investments. This has been the usual pattern of political revolution in Brazil. There change takes place without bloodshed. As Gilberto Freyre has pointed out, "No viceroy of Brazil, no king, no emperor, no president, no bishop has been assassinated in the history of the country."

Such a procedure is revolutionary only in a nominal sense. Under it a new administration when established in office often proceeds to consolidate its position by promulgating a new constitution and seeking to win majority approval of its policies. In this process the new president must assure himself of the continued support of the powers that established him in office. As a *caudillo* he must have all power or he has none. If his policies fail to satisfy public opinion or if they antagonize the powers that put him into the presidency or if he persists in remaining in power beyond the limit of his usefulness he will be ejected from office by a revolutionary coup and replaced by a new president or by a *junta* more acceptable to ruling oligarchies than the previous president. A new acting president or a governing *junta* thus assuming power provides an interim or caretaker administration until the new executive can restore constitutional procedures.

This process of administrative change is well exemplified in the history of Colombia. The Liberal party of Alfonso López disintegrated during his second administration, and when he resigned in July, 1945, in favor of Alberto Lleras Camargo, the extreme or national socialist liberals broke away to follow the leadership of Jorge Eliecer Gaitán. This split made possible the election of a Conservative president, Mariano Ospina Pérez, in 1946.

The Colombian Conservatives who controlled the presidency for the next twelve years, being a minority party and closely linked with the Roman Catholic hierarchy, were unable to prevent revolutionary action by the Liberal masses of the country, who were stirred by the postwar economic unrest. When their champion, Gaitán, was assassinated in April, 1948, during the meetings of the ninth international conference of American states in Bogotá, Colombia fell into anarchy and eventually civil war. The president's response to this so-called *"Bogotazo"* was to impose a state of siege throughout the country. He suspended Congress, all state legislatures, and all municipal councils and forbade all assemblies and public meetings throughout the nation. He ordered censorship of the press, radio, telegraph, and telephone, established curfew, conferred extraordinary powers on the departmental governors, and required that decisions on constitutional matters by the supreme court, which had a Liberal majority, must be made by a two-thirds majority. Against these actions the chief justice of the supreme court and eight justices protested to the president. Many Liberal leaders then retired to the *llanos* where they set up a guerrilla organization that defied the government. Their program called for the extension of social guaranties, protection of the working class by the state, and the strengthening of democratic institutions. But they refused to participate in elections, with the result that in the elections of November, 1949, an all-Conservative Congress was chosen and Laureano Gómez, who was cordially hated by the Liberals, was installed in the presidency.

Throughout the Gómez administration Colombia was racked by a civil war which cost the government more than 1 million *pesos* a day. Gómez determined to reform the constitution in order to strengthen the executive branch and render it no longer accountable either to Congress or to the supreme court. He proposed to set up administrative corporations under the control of the executive which would appoint the members of the Senate, as in the Portuguese constitution, but would allow the House of Representatives to continue to be political.

Against these proposals the Liberals directed bitter fire. They stressed the right of every citizen to participate in the management of national affairs. They insisted that the government, instead of depriving Colombians of their rights, should protect them in those rights, including the right to life, property, personal liberty, and freedom of thought and religion. They opposed the concentration of powers in a single person and emphasized that Congress must be able to act within its sphere independently of the president. Government, they contended, should assume social responsibilities and should ensure adequate medical services, food, shelter, and clothes for everyone.

But Gómez's actions had created a serious schism in his own party. On June 13, 1953, two days before the constitutional convention, composed entirely of Conservatives, was to convene, he was deposed by the chief of the army, Gen. Gustavo Rojas Pinilla, who seized control of the government by a sudden *coup d'état*. His accession to power was hailed with relief by both the moderate Conservatives and the Liberals, and the guerrilla warfare, which had continued for almost four years and was estimated to have cost 100,000 lives, was terminated by the granting of a general amnesty. But the Rojas Pinilla regime, which started auspiciously with promises of political liberty for all Colombians and social benefits for the workers, ended in repression and persecution and was ousted by another military coup in May, 1957. Liberals and Conservatives then worked out a bipartisan political scheme, unique in Latin America, by which they agreed that during the next twelve years the two parties would hold an equal number of cabinet posts and would have equal representation in Congress, the state legislatures, and the city councils. The presidency, it was agreed, would be assigned first to a Liberal for a four-year term and then to a Conservative for a four-year term. After this arrangement was approved in a national plebiscite on December 1, 1957, Liberal ex-President Lleras Camargo was installed as president with the concurrence of both parties. But civil disorders, which since 1948 were estimated to have taken a toll of 500,000 lives, continued and were aggravated during 1961 by unemployment and hard times in the sugar and coffee areas.

Every Latin American government is a government on trial. The revolutionary process illustrates the common Latin American belief that rotation in office is a good thing in itself. It provides mercurial Latin Americans with new faces, new names, and new policies and gives variety in government, though often at the expense of stability. It makes possible a transfer of executive power in more or less orderly fashion at a time when change is deemed essential. After such a revolution those who participated in it on the losing side customarily receive an *indulto* or pardon from the new executive allowing them to come out of hiding and return to their homes. The ousted president and members of his cabinet are usually permitted to seek asylum in a foreign embassy and eventually to go into exile. The Latin American aphorism *hoy por mi, mañana por ti* (today is mine, tomorrow yours) illustrates this genial custom.

This process emphasizes the Latin American requirement that the executive should be responsive to his constituents. If he ceases to be accountable for his policies and action he will not be permitted to continue in office to the end of his term. Regardless of constitutional prescriptions of a four- or five-year presidential term he becomes a lameduck executive as soon as he affronts his constituents or fails to satisfy their expectations, and according to the Latin American view a lameduck president cannot be allowed to remain in power.

The presidential system, taken over from the United States, has not worked in Latin America. If a president insists upon serving out his constitutional term and maintains himself in office by force—through martial law, armed bodyguards, suppression of freedom of the press, and decree law—he becomes a dictator. He sets aside the constitution and exercises personal rule beyond the constitutional limits of his term of office. This course may be followed either by a president who has been constitutionally elected to office or by one who has come to office by a *golpe de estado*. Many of the so-called "dictators" of Latin American countries, particularly those of the nineteenth century, remained in office in order primarily to serve the interests of wealthy oligarchic classes, such as large landowners, the church hierarchy, an entrenched military organization, or foreign business interests. This type of dictator still continues, but more typical in the twentieth century is the dictator who comes to power and maintains himself in power in order to satisfy the material aspirations of the mass of the population in his country. He responds to their importunate demands for economic relief and social justice, and he resorts to the methods of dictatorship and uses the enlarged powers of his office in order to crush out the traditional oligarchies who are held responsible for the plight of the masses. As the glamorous *caudillo* of the people he becomes the instrument for achieving a social revolution.

To counteract this perversion of the presidential system, several Latin American nations have experimented with the English parliamentary system, for example, Chile from 1891 to 1925, Cuba after 1941, and Brazil after the resignation of Janio Quadros in 1961. Under this system the president becomes only a decorative or ceremonial figure.

In general Latin America has achieved as much success with its legislative and judicial systems as has the United States, but it has not found a satisfactory pattern of executive leadership. The pattern of dictatorship was set in the nineteenth century by liberal executives who employed the methods of centralism to carry out liberal programs of action. They deemed that the end to be achieved justified the means employed to bring it about. The reprisals that a new regime in Latin America may take against its enemies can be excused in the reply that President Juárez gave to a visitor who asked him to pardon a rebel: "By pardoning a man of this kind who thinks that politics signifies disorders and barrack-room revolts, I am sentencing to death many hundreds of innocent people." So by this logic a new president justifies the ruthless proscription of his adversaries and even mass executions. He feels a patriotic and almost messianic mission to defend his revolution in the interest, as he conceives it, of the mass of his underprivileged followers. The nineteenth-century authoritarian presidents who accepted the goals of the democratic revolutionists laid the ground for the triumph of tyrannical majorities in the twentieth century, aspiring toward the liberty, equality, and fraternity which were promised by the French Revolution. Unlike most of the uprisings of the nineteenth-century modern revolutionary movements in Latin America have assumed the character of mass uprisings which aim at a fundamental reorganization of society and a redistribution of wealth. Unlike the *cuartelazo* they necessarily have a disruptive effect upon foreign business and investment. Latin Americans, faced with the rigors of making a living, possess a present-mindedness or future-mindedness which predisposes them to change—even radical and violent change.

This pattern of revolution has been starkly traced in postwar Bolivia. There the national socialist movement was organized as the *Movimiento Nacional Revolucionario* (National Revolutionary Movement or MNR) in 1941 by Víctor Paz Estenssoro. It collaborated in the government of Col. Gualberto Villarroel, who came to power in December, 1943. But he was overthrown in July, 1946, under circumstances reported as follows by the United States ambassador in La Paz:

Suddenly from my office windows we see civilians running down the streets with rifles and ammunition.

We learn immediately that the large MNR (official "National Revolutionary Movement") deposit of arms at the municipal headquarters has been left unguarded and that the people are willy-nilly arming themselves. At first we are not sure whether these are the MNR people or the students, but we soon discover that the Mayor—from spite, because the MNR has been thrown out of the government—withdrew the guards from the municipal headquarters with the intention of causing havoc.

This is not long in breaking loose—there is now anarchy in La Paz. Hundreds of students and their supporters, all armed with rifles, are already gathering outside the Embassy windows for an attack on the traffic-police headquarters, and still no representative of the law appears.

The traffic headquarters are soon taken, and part of the mob moves on to the prison and another part to the police school. These points are reduced, and now the whole group joins for an assault on the Presidential Palace.

The only persons in the Palace are the President, one aide-de-camp, one minor secretarial official, and some twenty-five heavily armed soldiers. For the first time the mob encounters resistance. . . .

But the mob is too much for the resisters. Although many are killed among the students, the firing is so heavy that the soldiers are overcome. Finally a tank is brought up by an army unit sympathetic to the students and the Palace doors are burst open.

The crowd enters. Not long after, the President and his two assistants are thrown to the pavement. They are all horribly mutilated, and are subsequently hanged to lamp posts.[1]

Villarroel's successors, Enrique Herzog (1947–1949) and Mamerto Urriolagoitia (1949–1951) demonstrated little ability to cope with Bolivia's economic problems. About 70 per cent of the nation's foreign exchange was derived from tin exports, and as these failed to find postwar purchasers in competition with Indonesian and Malayan supplies, Bolivia's economy sank into the doldrums. Only about 1 per cent of the country's agricultural land is cultivated, and half of Bolivia's population is therefore heavily dependent upon foreign exchange income for imports of foodstuffs and other necessities. In the election of 1951 the MNR candidate, Paz Estenssoro, won the largest number of votes, though not a simple majority required for outright election. Thereupon President Urriolagoitia, to prevent Paz Estenssoro's election, resigned in favor of a military *junta* which annulled the election. The *junta* then announced that it was making plans to hold an election, but it was overthrown in a three-day revolt which brought the MNR to power and established Paz Estenssoro as "constitutional president."

The MNR thus installed in power drew its strength from Bolivian labor, particularly the miners. Its program called for the utilization of the nation's mineral wealth for the benefit of the entire nation rather than merely the mineowning oligarchy, the diversification of the national economy, and the formation of a more homogeneous national community. In accordance with this program it nationalized the mining properties of the three big producers —Aramayo, Patiño, and Hochschild—in October, 1952, offering them in exchange what it considered reasonable compensation. It also undertook, with the help of the United Nations, to transfer some of its mining population from the *altiplano* to the jungle lowlands, but this experiment proved a fiasco. Since the MNR came to power Bolivia's economy has been largely sustained by the United States, which furnishes some 30 per cent of the government's income and in 1961 offered an additional 10 million dollars to build up the country's mining industry. Since 1954 Bolivia has received $185 million in direct aid from the United States government.

Pressure from organized Quechuan veterans of the Chaco War, reduced to their traditional *peón* status in the large estates of the Cochabamba Valleys,

---

[1] Joseph Flack, "Diary of a Successful Revolution, Official Despatch," Copyright © *Foreign Service Journal*, Washington, September, 1946. Used by permission.

forced the Paz Estenssoro government in 1953 reluctantly to issue a decree law inaugurating a program of land redistribution. This and other leveling practices of the revolutionary government since 1952 have resulted in the voluntary expatriation of many upper-class Bolivians and has caused a shortage of professional and administrative personnel and accentuated the trend toward a one-class society—a society in which status would have to be earned rather than inherited. The MNR has utilized its affiliation with the *campesinos* to preach a new integrated nationalism and has sought to carry out such a program despite the limitations imposed upon it by both the United States and the International Monetary Fund. Despite or perhaps because of these limitations Bolivia's political condition continues to be precarious. In mid-1961 the cost of living there rose to 3,470, taking 1953 as 100! But throughout gruelling political and economic vicissitudes Paz Estenssoro has maintained the independence of the Bolivian revolution from Soviet Communism. Though this MNR revolution has no roots in Bolivia's history it has proved acceptable to the masses of Bolivians because it produced results that were tangible and, at least in the short run, beneficial to them.

Revolutionary Methods and Objectives

Personal leadership or *caudillismo* continues to be the salient feature of Latin American politics, as it has been since the wars of independence. This is true not only in national politics but also in political life at all levels. "There are times," observed the Venezuelan publicist Mariano Picón-Salas, "when a bloody *caudillo* like Melgarejo or Pancho Villa says more to the frustrated and resentful multitude than the wise doctor who offers a civilizing solution." [2] In the face of this reality constitutional government is only a façade and the observance of the forms of representative democracy only a ruse designed to placate local visionaries or foreign public opinion. Above the constitution and above the law stands the *caudillo*. He embodies the constitution and the law. He is the source of all authority and all good. In short, as long as he exercises absolute power he is the nation, whether with or without the explicit sanction of the constitution of his predecessor, whether with or without the formality of an election. To ask therefore whether or not Latin America is becoming more democratic is to pose a question which is immaterial in the Latin American milieu.

In Uruguay an attempt has been made to depersonalize national leadership by a return to the *colegiado* or conciliar system of Batlle. That system had been relegated to limbo by the Terra dictatorship from 1931 to 1938, but it was adopted again by a national plebiscite in December, 1951. Under this system the president is chosen by other members of the executive coun-

[2] Mariano Picón-Salas, *De la conquista a la independencia: tres siglos de historia cultural hispanoameri*ɀ*ana,* Fondo de Cultura Económica, Mexico and Buenos Aires, 1950, p. 39.

cil, he serves for one year, and the office passes in rotation among the members of the council. Even the downfall in 1958 of the *Colorado* party, which had controlled the national government for ninety-three years, did not result in the abandonment of this form of government unique in Latin America.

As modern Latin American *caudillos* are forced by domestic pressures to champion social revolution their programs of action envisage the establishment of welfare government and the creation of a new integrated nationalism. Since the end of World War II governments have considered it their main problem to expand national production in such ways as to increase the real per capita income and to see that it is so distributed as to raise the general levels of living. The most urgent political force has been the social and economic pressure of the people for satisfaction of their basic human needs—food, clothing, and shelter. Latin American unrest in the postwar world has been caused mainly by pressure of population on the food supply, by the manipulation of the physical resources of these countries by uncontrolled capital, largely foreign, and by the exploitation of these grievances by both local agitators and foreign conspirators representing Soviet Russia and other Communist governments which seek to embarrass the United States in Latin America. Toward this kind of revolutionary program Latin American leaders are impelled by the precedents of the Mexican revolution and the *Batllista* program in Uruguay, by the examples of the New Deal and Fair Deal by which the Roosevelt and Truman administrations sought to deal with economic distress in the United States, and by the newly revitalized Positivist movement. Under the impact of these ideas civil rights in Latin America, which were traditionally construed as protecting individuals from encroachment by the central government, have come to be thought of as protecting certain classes of society from assault by other classes of society. The peasants and workers now are to be safeguarded by the state from exploitation by the capitalists.

The postulates and methods of Positivism, though not the cult, still exert large influence over the peoples of Latin America, and these have been accentuated by the emphasis placed upon science in the postwar period. The scientific absolutism which the Positivist philosophy offers seems to make man the master of his own fate and holds out the promise of a revolutionary regeneration of society. It accounts in part for Perón, for Vargas, and for Castro in Cuba.

One of the principal aims of modern revolutionary movements in Latin America is to unify and homogenize the society of the nation and at the same time to revitalize the national spirit. The achievement of an integrated society has seemed to require the division or *parcelación* of large landed properties among the landless following the pattern set by Mexican governments since 1916. Land ownership dispersed among citizens is considered to be a guaranty of social stability and personal independence. To the 42 million acres of land in Mexico that Cárdenas distributed between 1934 and 1940 his successors—Manuel Avila Camacho, Miguel Alemán Valdes, Adolfo Ruiz Cortines, and Adolfo López Mateos—added almost 40 million more between 1940 and 1961. Mexico's land distribution program since 1916 has accomplished a rather complete redistribution of farmland, much division of ranchland, and the extension of farms into large areas of previously uncleared land. It has destroyed the *hacienda* system as it existed before the Mexican Revolution.

The Mexican experience in land reform can be credited with many outstanding successful accomplishments, but in appraising it it must be noted that it has not adequately met the needs of a dynamic society with greatly increased needs for agricultural productivity. Since World War II Mexico has been forced to choose between a basic policy of agrarian reform involving the creation of communal and other small properties and increased harvests derived from large private farms. The systems of land tenure that have been tried under the reform program have failed, in large measure, to encourage the husbanding of the land entrusted to the new landholders and instead of yielding increased productivity have very often produced decreased harvests per hectare from fields of declining fertility. In many instances individual holdings have been too small to permit the economies of large-scale operations. As Mexicans say, "*latifundismo* has been exchanged for *minifundismo*." A free land policy in a nation in which 55 per cent of the labor force is still engaged in agriculture and where virgin lands in deserts and tropical forests can only with great difficulty be made arable has resulted in an excessive division of crop land. Many Mexican farmers are able to gain only a part of their income from their lands, and others have abandoned their small unproductive farms. Collective farming of large land units has proved successful in only a few places, and in others policy has been reversed as a result of successful petitions to parcelize collective *ejidos*.

Other difficulties have beset the Mexican land program. Many farmers have failed to receive adequate tools and training to make their farms serve family and nation well. Land redistribution is ineffective if cultural capital is not redistributed as well. Farms in the desert lands of Mexico are worthless without dams, wells, and irrigation canals, and if these are provided then drainage systems need to be installed to carry off waste irrigation waters. The agricultural credit system which was established to accompany land reform has proved deficient in several ways. Cooperative credit societies to which loans were originally exclusively made were modeled after those of nineteenth-century Europe, and in Mexico, where there had been little opportunity for the *peónes* to develop responsibility, millions of pesos were lost from defaulted loans. Funds available for crop loans have been inadequate. By 1960 at most only some 30 per cent of all *ejido* farmers, and a lower percentage of private farmers, were receiving credit from the government. Interest rates are high, and in many places money lenders have surreptitiously reestablished the ancient relationship of landlord and *peón* between themselves and the farmers.

Another difficulty encountered in agrarian reform in Mexico is the problem of making farmers into capitalists, that is, men who save to reinvest in order to produce more. In the long run it has not contributed to capital formation nor has it promoted land conservation because of insecurity of tenure. Members of collective *ejidos* show little desire to care for land that next year may be worked by others. On parcelized *ejidos* the plot of ground may pass out of the hands of one family to another. On private lands, even those which conform to the legal size limits prescribed by law, there is always the lingering threat of expropriation resulting from a change in the Agrarian Code or a new interpretation of it. The soil is sometimes carelessly "mined" not so much because the farmer lacks capital or ambition as because he does not know how much longer the land will be his.[3]

Despite these limitations the Mexican land program has been so politically successful as to have inspired imitative efforts in other Latin American countries. In Guatemala the distribution of lands was begun in mid-1952 by the legislature after President Jacobo Arbenz Guzmán explained to Congress that 22 families owned about 1,250,000 acres of land in Guatemala. Land-reform programs were also carried out modestly by Perón in Argentina and more extensively by Paz Estenssoro in Bolivia and Castro in Cuba. These programs, it is hoped, will incorporate hitherto neglected and oppressed sectors of the population in the economy of the nation. But these nationalist actions have sometimes seemed extreme to foreigners whose economic interests are adversely affected and to their governments which, in the oscillation of history, find themselves temporarily unsympathetic with nationalism abroad.

Since World War II the Latin American peoples have been trying impetuously to overtake the Industrial Revolution, skipping over epochs in their haste. That revolution, which swept over and transformed Europe and the United States during the nineteenth century, is now tearing apart the old settled ways of life in Latin America. In some of the countries it is making an impact for the first time; in others it is passing into an intermediate stage; but in all of them it is producing acute social stresses and strains. Construction has become a national anthem. By this means and by governmental action of a national socialist character Latin Americans hope to improve their actual living conditions and make them correspond more closely to their aspirations. The masses of the people aspire, probably in greater numbers than ever before, to till their own land, to express their views in politics,

[3] For the above paragraphs analyzing the Mexican land reform, acknowledgment is made to Prof. David A. Henderson, Department of Business and Public Administration, University of Arizona.

and to acquire the material paraphernalia of the good life which they know the privileged classes enjoy both in their own and in foreign countries. In the years since World War II they have lost their former docility and resignation both in relation to higher levels of living and in relation to those who already enjoy those higher levels.

In industrialization Latin Americans have been encouraged to hope they will find the solutions to their material needs, freedom from foreign controls, and fulfillment of their national selfhood. The Mexican revolution before World War II limited itself largely to agrarian operations, but after the retirement of Cárdenas it took industrialization as its objective and has come to be dominated by industrial leadership. It can point to results in the form of material improvements in rural and city life including better housing, more abundant food and clothing, improved medical services, and a multiplication of gadgets. Other twentieth-century revolutionary movements in Latin America, except APRA in Peru, have also undergone this change of direction. Leaders of these movements have become convinced that their countries have not been receiving their due share of the benefits of technical progress and that in order to move from the nineteenth into the twentieth century they must cease to be simply the suppliers of foodstuff and raw materials to the industrialized nations—Britain, France, Germany, the United States—and must manufacture increased quantities of goods from their own raw materials.

For this purpose several Latin American governments have concluded that foreign capital is indispensable. So they pay their respects to Dom Pedro II and Porfirio Díaz. As the Mexican revolution, for example, has become institutionalized, successive presidents of Mexico have sought to enlist the cooperation of foreign private capital in the economic development of their countries. But these neo-Positivists oppose absentee control of the resources of the nation and insist that foreign capital shall recognize the supreme responsibilities of the state and shall associate itself with local capital to achieve socially approved goals. Meanwhile some of them, as for example Mexico and Bolivia, through nationalization of industries deemed to be public utilities limit the area within which foreign private capital may operate.

By the middle of the twentieth century Latin America, in general, was some seventy or eighty years behind the rest of the Western world in industrialization. Approximately 61 per cent of its exports consisted of agricultural products, and of the total amount of such exports, valued at 4,280 million dollars, 90 per cent were accounted for by nine staples—coffee, sugar, cotton, wool, meat, wheat, bananas, timber, and cacao, in order of importance. Many of the Latin American countries were dedicated to the production of one or at best a few of these crops for export, thus sustaining a monocultural economy. And yet for only two of these crops—coffee and bananas—were they able to fix the world price. The prices of most of their other export commodities were determined by foreign monopolists. Because Cuba, for example, produced only about one-third of the world's sugar, the price of its principal export crop was determined by foreign purchasers. Its foreign exchange and therefore almost its entire economy were thus placed at the mercy of entrepreneurs who were outside Cuba—most of them Wall Street brokers. In the United States market, however, Cuban sugar enjoyed a privileged position. Under a reciprocity treaty concluded by the two nations in 1902 Cuban sugar was sold in the United States at 2 cents per pound above the world price, an arrangement which also had the not unintended result of conferring the same price benefit upon domestic producers of sugar in the United States.

As underdeveloped have-not nations in the postwar world, the Latin American countries needed and expected to receive sufficient material assistance to enable them to develop their national economies and improve the living standards of their peoples. These countries, declared one of their newspapers toward the end of the war, "will receive positive aid in improving their conditions and acquiring a high 'standard' which will enable them to produce, consume, and act like any European nation." They expected that the partner relationship that the United States had established with them during the war would continue into the postwar period and that together the twenty-one American nations would form a hemisphere of brothers. And yet from July, 1945, to July, 1950, while the Truman administration was pouring more than 20 billion dollars worth of aid into foreign countries, Latin Americans received only 514 million dollars, or 1.8 per cent of the total. They were repeatedly told by high officials of the United States—secretaries of state and many others—that they must solve their own problems in their own way without the help of the government in Washington. In dollar exchange Latin Americans have been losing 1,000 million dollars annually since 1951. And yet when their governments revived the project for an inter-American bank that would finance their developmental projects their plans were repeatedly frustrated by the United States. As a result they failed to find the means to produce the manufactured goods and even some of the foodstuffs that they required, they were denied the dollar credits that would enable them to acquire these commodities in the United States, and they saw their golden wartime hopes of a better life in the postwar world fade into the cold realities of business depression, unemployment, desperate want, and acute social maladjustments. These conditions aggravated, and were in turn aggravated by, the socioeconomic impact of the Industrial Revolution which went far toward replacing the traditional landowning oligarchy with a new financial and industrial oligarchy and supplanting the disorganized and submissive rural working class with a new organized and aggressive urban industrial proletariat.

Communism

The problem of achieving economic and social justice in Latin America through governmental action has been complicated by the strength of communism in the postwar world. The modern *caudillo* of the welfare state can support his conception of government by the Soviet example. In the constitution and policies of his government he will give the same high priority to the material needs of his people as do the Soviet rulers. Perón and Vargas, typical *caudillos* of the modern welfare state, sought and won the allegiance of the rural and urban proletariat in their countries with their programs of economic and social reform. By these programs they counteracted communism and so reduced its appeal to the masses of their people. The appeal of Soviet communism also is limited by the predominantly Catholic orientation of the majority of Latin Americans, though in many countries of Latin America the church, as in France and Italy, has accommodated itself to popular reform movements, even including communism, hoping in this way to exert moral and ethical influence upon them. Since World War II the church in many places has dissociated itself from the forces of conservatism. Quite apart from the effects of Catholicism upon the attitude of Latin Americans toward communism, the appeal that communism makes to them can often be measured by the virulence of their anti-Yankee sentiments and their reactions to the cold war between the Soviet Union and their Western Hemisphere ally, the United States.

In general the solutions offered by the Communists have not appeared attractive to Latin Americans, for Communist solutions are not indigenous solutions. Communist parties in Latin America ape European patterns of action which are not wanted in Latin America. Communism as an ideology does not appeal to traditional power elites and their bureaucracies. But as the failures of these governing elites became apparent Communism, which appears to have demonstrated its effectiveness in Soviet Russia, exerts a growing charm upon the technically trained younger generation who are, by virtue of their training in Western industrial processes, dissatisfied with structures that do not work and who are attracted to the managerial system of Communism.

All the American nations have a common stake in national independence and freedom from control by nations outside the Western Hemisphere. And yet the Positivism of the modern *caudillos* embodies so many features of centralism and national socialism that it almost inevitably shades into communism. The logic and example of this system, as well as its materialism, appeal to many intellectuals, even at the cost of individualism and freedom. In this direction they are also impelled by their humanitarian concern to eliminate the prevalent squalid living conditions. These conditions were not caused by communism, but they offer a fertile field for Communist propaganda and actions.

As Latin Americans have come to feel that their problems are not appreciated by the capitalist nations some of them have become increasingly impressed by the Soviet example as providing a method by which they may achieve material progress without capital and even without capitalism. A census of card-carrying Communists in the Latin American countries is not necessarily indicative of the extent of Communist influence, for a few active and trained agents in a revolutionary milieu can produce results incommensurate with their numbers. Furthermore, as revolutionary governments such as those of Arbenz in Guatemala from 1951 to 1954 and Castro in Cuba after 1959 were cold-shouldered by the United States and in turn accepted Soviet aid, their example encouraged other Latin American nationalists to do the same.

As Latin Americans were sharply rebuffed in their attempts to find solutions for their postwar economic and social problems within the framework of the inter-American system and as they were deliberately encouraged by the United States to look for aid to a Europe reconstructed with United States dollars, they turned away from the United States to look elsewhere for ways of achieving their national purposes and satisfying their basic requirements. Consequently the trade rivalry between the United States and Japan in Latin America has been resumed since the war. Europe's trade with Latin America has increased by as much as 62 per cent in a single year. The Soviet Union and its satellites in Eastern Europe are increasingly entering into the markets of Latin America as both buyers and suppliers. They are thus introducing a new factor, Russian trade rivalry, virtually nonexistent before World War II, into the competition for the trade of that area. This trade between the Communist countries and Latin America is carried on largely through barter arrangements—Russian machine tools, tractors, electric motors, oil, and pipe in exchange for Argentine wheat, meat and hides, Cuban sugar, and Colombian coffee—but it raises the possibility of the eventual establishment of a Soviet commercial bloc in Latin America to compete with the present dollar and sterling blocs in that area.

The Cuban revolutionary movement headed by Castro can—in its scope and implications not only for Cuba but for Latin America as a whole—be compared in scope and method to the Mexican revolution. It has undertaken to make a direct approach to the fundamental social and economic problems of Latin America. In this context the grievances which Cubans cite as justification for their revolution are more important than the factual record. They point out that after the liberation of their country from Spain in 1898 the United States government leased the 28,000-acre naval base at Guantánamo for an annual rental of only $2,000 in gold coin and since the devaluation of gold has paid the currency equivalent, $3,386.25, or only a little more than 12 cents per acre per year. This treaty of 1903 contains no provision for its termination. The reciprocity treaty of 1902 with the United States, Cubans complain, forced their agriculture into a disastrous concentration upon sugar and created an annual crisis of unemployment—the "dead season" between one sugar harvest and the next. In this one-crop economy rural Cubans lost control over their future. They labored all their lives for great foreign corporations which controlled their food, their education, and even their recreation. The apprehensions of Rafael Montoro and other leaders of the Cuban independence movement prior to the war with Spain had been realized; Cubans had escaped from one tyranny only to fall under the control of another nation. Even their sugar sales in the United States were determined by quotas fixed by the Congress and Department of Agriculture in Washington. During World War II the United States met 65 per cent of its sugar needs in Cuba, but after the war it chose to purchase only 28 per cent of its sugar there. Cuba's dependence upon the United States for its sugar income was shown when President Eisenhower slashed the United States quota of Cuban sugar by 700,000 tons in July, 1960, leaving Cuba a market for only 39,757 tons in the United States and causing a financial loss of 92.5 million dollars to the island government.

After Castro seized power by ousting President Fulgencio Batista in a *golpe de estado* on January 1, 1959, he launched a revolutionary program designed to complete Cuba's political emancipation of 1898 with economic emancipation of the island from foreign control. This program involved expropriation of large landholdings, the distribution of lands to the landless, and the nationalization of key industries in accordance with the familiar Latin American pattern—a pattern set by many previous Latin American governments, including, for example, those of Calles and Cárdenas in Mexico, Batlle in Uruguay, López in Colombia, Perón in Argentina, Arévalo and Arbenz in Guatemala, and Betancourt in Venezuela. Castro claimed to base his land program more specifically upon that which the United States imposed upon Japan after World War II, under which the United States provided for compensation of expropriated landowners with 24-year bonds at $3\frac{1}{2}$ per cent interest. Under the Agrarian Reform Law of June, 1959, in Cuba cattle ranches as large as 35,000 acres were reduced to a maximum size of 1,650 acres. On the lands taken over from foreign interests the government established a vast system of cooperatives. Its welfare program included the construction, at government expense, of new hospitals and housing developments, thousands of new classrooms, and public parks, playgrounds, and other recreational facilities. To this program Castro gave the name *Humanismo*. This revolution will never be stopped, he predicted, "because it has its roots in humanity." It aims, as Castro has said, at the creation of a single-class Cuban society.

On the other hand Castro carried out a purge of prominent *Batistianos* who had not left the country with Batista and who persisted in opposing his regime. This too followed a familiar Latin American pattern and was justified by the revolutionary government on the basis of precedents set not only by Batista but also by the United States in the war-crimes trials after World War II. He established rule by decree, rather than rule by law, severely limited the freedom of the press to criticize his policies, and dismissed uncooperative judges. He failed to provide the domestic and foreign owners of expropriated properties with "prompt, adequate, and effective" compensation for their properties. Deprived of markets in the United States, Cuba negotiated trade agreements to dispose of its sugar surpluses in Soviet Russia, China, and other Communist countries and in return received quantities of manufactured goods and scores of technicians from those countries. All this, together with the "anti-Yanqui" declamations of Castro and the Communist orientation of certain influential policy makers in the Cuban government, has been interpreted as proving the affinity of the Cuban revolution with communism. Moreover, his failure actually to implement his land reform program by giving land titles indicates that his objective is the establishment of a community of goods rather than a reparcelling of the soil. Finally in early December, 1961, Castro openly avowed himself a "Marxist-Leninist until the last day of my life."

Cuban public opinion was badly torn by the Castro program. The beneficiaries of his regime became his fanatical supporters, while his opponents, reacting against his policies with tense emotionalism, either exiled themselves to the United States and to sympathetic countries of Latin America or joined the anti-Castro guerrilla forces in the mountains of central and eastern Cuba. His policies have also been opposed by the Catholic hierarchy in Cuba, which is staffed largely by Spanish priests. But Castro's program during its first two years had accomplished such truly revolutionary results that, regardless of the fate of its leader, it seemed destined to have momentous consequences both for Cuba and for Latin America. Under its inspiration a land-reform program was launched in Venezuela in 1960; Peasant Leagues were organized in drought-ridden northeastern Brazil under the leadership of Francisco Julião preaching seizure of privately owned land; and the state of São Paulo adopted legislation, to become effective in late 1961, prescribing higher rates of taxes on unused than on used land. Where it is successful this Castro-type movement threatens the growing middle class or rather bids fair to create a new one-class society living at levels comparable to those of the present middle class.

Defense of the Western Hemisphere

The Communist threat to the Western Hemisphere has formed a serious topic of consideration at every inter-American conference since 1945. At the Conference on Problems of War and Peace which met at Mexico City in March, 1945, all twenty-one American governments declared that every attack upon the integrity, the inviolability, the sovereignty, or the political independence of an American state would be considered an act of aggression against all the American states and recommended in the so-called "Act of Chapultepec" that an inter-American treaty should be concluded which would establish procedures for meeting such acts of aggression. Such a Treaty of Reciprocal Assistance was signed at the inter-American conference at Rio de Janeiro in 1947 and was subsequently ratified by all the American governments. It declares that "an armed attack by any State against an American State shall be considered as an attack against all the American States" and pledges each one of them "to assist in meeting the attack." The obligation for the security of the hemisphere which President Monroe assumed for the United States in 1823 was thus accepted as the collective obligation of all the American nations. The basic policy of the Monroe Doctrine was thus "continentalized," though not by that name, and the doctrine as such continued to be also a unilateral policy of the United States.

Partly in response to the Soviet threat the inter-American system itself was strengthened and given a constitution in the Charter of the Organization of American States, which was adopted at the ninth inter-American conference at Bogotá in 1948. That conference condemned "the political activity of international communism" as a system "tending to suppress political and civil rights and liberties." A fourth meeting of foreign ministers was held in 1952 to strengthen "the common defense against the aggressive activities of international communism." The tenth inter-American conference, meeting at Caracas in 1954, went still further and under the guidance of Secretary of State John Foster Dulles declared that "the domination or control of the political institutions of any American state by the international communist movement, extending to this Hemisphere the political system of an extracontinental power, would constitute a threat to the sovereignty and political independence of the American States." These phrases, reminiscent of the original Monroe Doctrine, strengthened the bases for united Pan-American action against the international Communist movement as a non-American political and conspiratorial system. At the same time the Latin American delegates to the tenth inter-American conference, fearful of intervention by the United States in their affairs, insisted upon declaring "the inalienable right of each American State freely to choose its own form of government and economic system and to live its own social and cultural life." Even measures of collective defense, therefore, must not be allowed to interfere with the right of the people of an American nation to adopt the kind of economic and social system under which they wish to live.

Threats to the peace of the Western Hemisphere emanating mainly from the Castro government of Cuba led to the convoking of the fifth meeting of consultation of foreign ministers at Santiago, Chile, in August, 1959, and the adoption of a statement of principles of the democratic system "so as to permit national and international public opinion to gauge the degree to which political regimes and governments conform to that system." These principles included the separation of powers, free elections, limited terms of office, respect and protection for fundamental human rights, abolition of political proscription, freedom of information and expression, and the maintenance of just and humane living conditions.

While Venezuela, in accordance with these criteria, was eager to condemn Generalissimo Rafael Trujillo, the strong-man ruler of the Dominican Republic, as a disturber of the peace in the Caribbean, as a dictator, and as a violator of human rights, the United States and other governments were eager to condemn the Castro regime in Cuba as an agent of Soviet communism. Accordingly plans were made to hold the sixth and seventh meetings of the foreign ministers to deal with these two problems at San José, Costa Rica, in August, 1960. The meetings seemed to be rendered imperative when Soviet Premier Khrushchev made a gratuitous declaration in June that "in case of necessity Soviet artillerymen can support with rocket fire the Cuban people if aggressive forces in the Pentagon dare to start intervention against Cuba." This Soviet offer of protection was welcomed by Castro because, he insisted, the inter-American system would be unable to defend Cuba against the United States.

But Trujillo's regime was regarded as an ideological liability to the common democratic ideal professed by the nations of America, and Castro's regime was considered a beachhead for Soviet communism and hence a threat to the security of the Western Hemisphere. At the San José meetings the foreign ministers of the American governments "emphatically" condemned the Dominican Republic, called for a rupture of diplomatic relations with it, and banned trade with it "in arms and implements of war of every kind." With reference to Cuba a compromise resolution was adopted which, without mentioning Cuba or Castro by name, condemned intervention in the Western Hemisphere by an extracontinental power, reaffirmed the principle of nonintervention by any American state in the internal or external affairs of the other American states, and endorsed the principles of representative democracy. But these actions, prejudicial to two members of the inter-American system, had disruptive consequences. Peru, Venezuela, and Cuba refused to sign the latter resolution. The United States proceeded to sever diplomatic relations with both the Dominican Republic and Cuba, thus for the first time in forty years breaking its formal ties with another American nation. The realization of the Pan-American ideal, that is to say, the establishment of a close and reciprocally helpful relationship among all the nations of the Western Hemisphere, seemed to be indefinitely postponed.

The assassination of Trujillo in May, 1961, ending his thirty-one-year control of the Dominican Republic, and the subsequent introduction of democratic procedures there by the new regime made it possible for the United States and other American nations to end their boycott of the island republic.

But the threat posed by the Communist-oriented Castro government in Cuba seemed increasingly serious to the United States, Peru, and the Latin American nations bordering the Caribbean, particularly after the failure of the United States–sponsored invasion at the Bahía de Cochinos on the south coast of Cuba in April, 1961. Accordingly, at the eighth meeting of consultation of foreign ministers, held at Punta del Este in Uruguay in January, 1962, fourteen of these nations, constituting a bare two-thirds of the members of the Organization of American States, voted to exclude Cuba from participation in the inter-American system. But this action was not endorsed by the representatives of Argentina, Bolivia, Brazil, Chile, Ecuador, Mexico, nor, of course, Cuba, though all of them but Cuba joined in declaring that adherence of any member of the Organization of American States to Marxism-Leninism is incompatible with the inter-American system.

The postwar breakdown of understanding between the United States and Latin America can be explained only by a multiplicity of factors. It was hastened by the importunate demands of some Latin Americans that the United States should intervene in their countries to establish and maintain democratic governments and then by their charges of intervention when the United States saw fit to do so. Intervention by the United States even for praiseworthy objectives is odious to many Latin Americans, even to those who complain most bitterly against Latin American dictatorships. Their recollections of former interventions by the United States still rankle in their memories and histories. Like other peoples they do not like to be pushed around, and they view with pride the noninterventionist pledges which were made by all the American governments, including the United States, in the early days of Roosevelt's Good Neighbor policy. The United States has sometimes played the role of neighbor and partner with the Latin American peoples, but has also sometimes assumed the responsibilities of a guardian, with results harmful to hemispheric harmony. Realistically, one important deterrent to effective Pan-Americanism is the overwhelming power of the United States. In the inter-American system this colossal power, which supplies two-thirds of the budget of the Organization of American States, always looms as the ultimate reality. It is certain that in any kind of Pan-American regional military action the United States will be obliged to assume the major enforcement responsibilities.

The inter-American system, Dr. Alberto Lleras Camargo has declared, "has been built on the incredible premise that mighty nations and small ones have the same right to live together in peace—free from intervention in their domestic affairs, or from external pressure—that individuals enjoy in a democratic society." This principle has been embodied in the Charter of the Organization of American States which declares in article 15 that "no State or group of States has the right to intervene directly or indirectly, for any reason whatever, in the internal or external affairs of any other State." This principle, the article goes on to state, "prohibits not only armed force but also any other form of interference or attempted threat against the personality of the State or against its political, economic and cultural elements." In principle then, harmonious inter-American relations can only be based upon a realistic recognition of the differences that exist between the Latin Americans and the people of the United States—differences in governmental forms and practices, in history and culture, in race and creed, in attitudes toward social and economic justice, in standards of living and conceptions of the good life, yes, even in attitudes toward property rights—in all the factors that distinguish Anglo-America from Indo-Hispanic America and that give interest and uniqueness to each. Upon the reestablishment and maintenance of harmony between them the very existence of America may in the future depend.

Boundary disputes between the Latin American nations are no longer a major cause of discord, as they were during the nineteenth century, for boundary lines have generally become stabilized. But exceptions may be mentioned. Nicaragua has shown reluctance to accept a decision of the World Court handed down in November, 1960, affirming the earlier award of the queen of Spain in favor of the claim of Honduras to the Mosquitia area extending for some 150 miles along the Caribbean and 175 miles inland. Ecuador insists upon a revision of the boundary settlement with Peru which was negotiated, as she says under duress, at Rio de Janeiro in January, 1942, and guaranteed by Argentina, Brazil, Chile, and the United States. The area in dispute includes some 77,000 square miles of jungle territory giving access to the Amazon River system. Venezuela periodically reiterates her dissatisfaction with the arbitral award of 1899 in the matter of the boundary of British Guiana, and along with several other Latin American governments, she repeatedly denies the right of non-Latin American nations to own any territories in the Western Hemisphere. They thus call in question the title of Britain to British Guiana, Belize (British Honduras), and the Falkland Islands, of France to French Guiana, of the Netherlands to Dutch Guiana, and the claims of all these nations to islands in the Caribbean. In addition, both Argentina and Chile have asserted claims to lands in the so-called "American sector" of the Antarctic continent claimed by non-American nations.

Trends and Prospects

The lines of future development in Latin America are already prefigured. The ideal of republicanism which inspired the founders of nationhood in the early history of the new nations has been supplanted by the concept of democracy. But in the twentieth-century context this democracy has become only a brief and transitional phase of their ideological development leading into national socialism. All three of these systems—republicanism, democracy, and national socialism—have produced their own power elites and have been used to bring such elites to office and to keep them in office. The politics of Latin America, often chaotic and misunderstood, reflects the dilemma of traditional power elites as between a democratic and a national socialist system. Within the framework of a democratic ideology and while paying lip service to it, they conclude that they can only maintain their position by the techniques of socialism by which they hope to avert revolution and thus salvage at least part of their inheritance.

As the nineteenth century was a century of individualism, decentralization, and romantic liberalism, the twentieth century has become the century of collectivism, centralization, and welfare-state "liberalism." In this direction the Latin American peoples have been pushed by the proponents of state planning in both the United States and Europe. The scientific Positivism of the late nineteenth century was reinforced by the propaganda of the United Nations in World War II emphasizing universal suffrage and the social responsibilities of government and by the influence of Fabian socialism to produce a new national consciousness in most of the Latin American countries at the expense of localism. This change has been accompanied by a new emphasis upon elections and a significant extension of the franchise. As a result of the enfranchisement of women, reduction of the literacy requirements, lowering of the voting age, and the removal of property qualifications, the number of voters in Mexico, for example, increased by 300 per cent between 1940 and 1958 and in Brazil by 800 per cent between 1930 and 1960.

In the cycle of evolution from the old to the new, state controls have been enlarged and the restrictions upon personal liberty characteristic of the old *caudillismo* have often been intensified. Over the bridge of Positivism the new liberals advanced to power. The "liberal" leaders in Latin America today enforce a cult of progress conceived in materialistic terms, they exalt central government as the sole agency of progress and the redresser of wrongs, and they hope that by the methods of national socialism they may be able to thwart the appeal of communism to their frustrated peoples and to prevent the proletarianizing of their society. They would avert a revolutionary overturn, which they dread, by governmentally sponsored programs of social amelioration, and in many cases they show a frantic impatience to proceed with such programs. By these means they hope to realize their cultural autonomy and complete the political independence which they won in the nineteenth century.

Many of the problems of Latin America and many of the problems of the United States in Latin America arise from the maldistribution of wealth in that area, the continuance of archaic social institutions, the failure of economic expansion to keep pace with population increases, the disparities between import and export prices, low levels of living among large segments of the population, and chronic political instability. Poverty accounts for the low level of education and the poor health conditions, and these are aggravated by price inflation. Production in every field suffers from lack of skilled labor, capital investment, and credit. Fixed prices of most of the raw materials that Latin America produces limit the profits of the producers and inhibit the process of capital formation. At the same time the prices of the manufactured imports that Latin America needs continue to rise. Administrative incompetence and corruption are widespread.

To alleviate some of these conditions, faltering steps are being taken toward the development of a common market or a Latin American *Zollverein,* beginning with the formation of regional customs unions, as for example among the Central American states. In 1951 these states banded together in the Organization of Central American States (ODECA) to promote this as well as other common purposes, and their example was followed in February, 1960, by seven other Latin American nations—Argentina, Brazil, Chile, Mexico, Paraguay, Peru, and Uruguay—which concluded a free-trade pact at Montevideo looking toward an eventual common market and open to participation by other countries. It was subsequently signed also by Bolivia, Ecuador, and Colombia. When ratified, it is expected to eliminate, over a twelve-year period, all trade restrictions on at least 75 per cent of the commerce among the participating nations. The pact is based upon the theory that each of the member countries will specialize in the type of production for which it is best adapted and will find an outlet for its production not only within its own territory but also in neighboring countries. In a Central American customs union, for example, El Salvador, which might find it economically impractical to operate a shoe industry only for its own people, might profitably develop such an industry not only for its own people but also for customers in neighboring countries. By late 1961 less than 10 per cent of the previous tariff barriers between these countries remained, and by 1966 it is expected that Central America will be a completely free trade zone. Under this arrangement industry in these countries finds a market of not just one or two million consumers but more than eleven million. The formation of such regional economic groups has been advocated by Haya de la Torre's APRA since the 1920s and has been encouraged by the United Nations Economic Commission for Latin America. But such groupments, which are reminiscent of Bolívar's vision for Latin America, have been hindered by the varying effectiveness of the governments in meeting their own problems by their own national methods and by the general lack of a continental consciousness.

Analogous to the regional common market which includes several countries are the many projects currently under way for regional development in individual countries. Some of these are patterned after the Tennessee Valley Authority in the United States. Such, for example, is the *Corporación Autónoma Regional del Cauca* (CVC), a development authority established in the rich Cauca Valley of Colombia by the government in 1954 for purposes of flood control, reclamation, agricultural production, conservation, and the generation and distribution of electric power. Covering three departments, the CVC cuts across lines of local authority and has converted the entire valley into one of the most important industrial and agricultural regions of the country. A similar regional development agency has been created for a part of the mighty Magdalena, Colombia's longest river.

United States government aid funds have been made available for many of these projects, but nevertheless, the United States is widely criticized for having supported tyrannical unpopular regimes and the class of the wealthy, capital-exporting, cosmopolitan elite, thus thwarting the will of the majority of the people in these countries and blocking social reform. At the same time it is charged with exporting its own cultural image to Latin America and superimposing it upon the local Indo-Hispanic pattern of life. Its massive foreign aid program—the new dollar diplomacy—has vitiated its historic noninterventionist policy. These criticisms overlook the responsibility of the Latin Americans themselves for their underdeveloped economies and the inequitable distribution of wealth, but they are not limited to Communist organs of opinion nor do they necessarily imply an acceptance of the Communist way of life. But taken in the context of the prevailing social and economic discontent in many Latin American countries they create a climate favorable to revolution—a revolution similar to, and inspired by the example of, the Castro revolution in Cuba. This climate is especially apparent in Venezuela, Central America, and Mexico and is building up in many other countries. The alternatives confronting Latin Americans seem increasingly to be the United States or *Fidelismo*.

To many Latin Americans, however, the Communist affiliations of the Castro regime are repugnant. They would prefer a "third way" or a middle course between "imperialist capitalism" and "Communist dictatorship," a revolutionary way perhaps but one that would develop along lines more consonant with the spirit and history of the nation and independent of foreign influence. Supporting this view is the current shift in emphasis in Latin American art and literature away from concern with prevailing social conditions—characteristic of much Latin American thought for the past century—to a new concern with moral and spiritual values, without, however, much reference to the church. As the former generation of Latin American novelists, artists, and intellectuals were accustomed to ascribe the blame for the ills of their society to the social environment, the new school views these basic problems as psychological or, rather, philosophical. They emphasize the need for a drastic revision of both individual and social goals. They reject the sociological and class-conscious approach to Latin American society and do not expect change to result necessarily in social amelioration. Yet they are optimistic about the future of their countries.

The art and culture of this new school are existentialist with a Spanish imprint. In painting, for example, the Mexican mural school of revolutionary art with its repetitive rhythms and designs and its obsession with the triumph of material over spiritual forces has been cut off by the impact of international abstractionism. This trend is apparent in the modern literature of

Latin America, and architecture has become a design veneer or mere façade no longer expressing national individualism. This new development, which is still in its formative stages, represents a new flowering of the old and profound conviction of Latin Americans that human fellowship and community progress cannot be made dependent simply on the material welfare that people enjoy and on their economic productive efficiency. In this conviction may be hopefully discerned a repudiation of the materialism associated with Marxism, but it poses problems also for all nations, including the United States, that seek to build good relations with the Latin Americans on an exclusively economic basis. It confronts the Latin Americans with the dilemma whether they can reconcile their sought-after cultural autonomy with their aspiration for economic autonomy through industrialization.

Additional Reading

Alexander, Robert J.: *The Bolivian National Revolution,* Rutgers University Press, New Brunswick, N.J., 1958. A sympathetic study.
———: *Communism in Latin America,* Rutgers University Press, New Brunswick, N.J., 1957.
Allen, Robert L.: *Soviet Influence in Latin America: The Role of Economic Relations,* Public Affairs Press, Washington, 1959.
Cosío Villegas, Daniel: *Change in Latin America: The Mexican and Cuban Revolutions,* University of Nebraska, Lincoln, Neb., 1961.
Davis, Harold Eugene: "Revolutionary Cuba: Something Old and Something New," *World Affairs,* Spring, 1961, pp. [7]–11.
Lieuwen, Edwin: *Arms and Politics in Latin America,* rev. ed., Frederick A. Praeger, Inc., New York, 1961.
Nelson, Lowry: "Cuban Paradoxes," in A. Curtis Wilgus (ed.), *The Caribbean at Mid-century,* University of Florida Press, Gainesville, Fla., 1951.
———: *Rural Cuba,* University of Minnesota Press, Minneapolis, 1950.
Ortiz, Fernando: *Cuban Counterpoint: Tobacco and Sugar,* trans. by Harriet de Onís, Alfred A. Knopf, Inc., New York, 1947.
Ostria Gutiérrez, Alberto: *The Tragedy of Bolivia: A People Crucified,* The Devin-Adair Company, New York, 1958. A recital of Bolivian history from 1943 to 1958 from the anti-MNR viewpoint.
Pan American Union, Division of Economic Research: *The Foreign Trade of Latin America since 1913,* Washington, 1952.
Patch, Richard W.: "Bolivia: the Restrained Revolution," *Annals of the American Academy of Political and Social Science,* pp. 123–132, March, 1961.
Pike, Fredrick B. (ed.), *Freedom and Reform in Latin America,* University of Notre Dame Press, 1959.
Stokes, William S.: "The 'Cuban Revolution' and the Presidential Elections of 1948," *Hispanic American Historical Review,* vol. 31, pp. 37–79, 1951.
Taylor, P. B.: "The Guatemalan Affair: A Critique of United States Foreign Policy," *American Political Science Review,* vol. 50, pp. 787–806, 1956.
United Nations, Department of Economic and Social Affairs: *Foreign Capital in Latin America,* New York, 1955.
Whitaker, Arthur P.: *Argentine Upheaval: Perón's Fall and the New Regime,* Frederick A. Praeger, Inc., New York, 1956.

Appendix I

Latin American Fiction in English Translation

Alegría, Ciro: *The Golden Serpent* (*La Serpiente de oro*), trans. by Harriet de Onís, Holt, Rinehart and Winston, Inc., New York, 1943 (Peru).
————: *Broad and Alien Is the World* (*El Mundo es ancho y ajeno*), trans. by Harriet de Onís, Holt, Rinehart and Winston, Inc., New York, 1941 (Peru).
Alencar, José Martiniano de: *Iracema, the Honeylips: A Legend of Brazil,* trans. by N. Bidell, Rio de Janeiro, no date (Brazil).
Amado, Jorge: *The Violent Land* (*Terras do sem fim*), trans. by Samuel Putnam, Alfred A. Knopf, Inc., New York, 1945 (Brazil).
————: *Sea of the Dead: Yemanjá, Mistress of the Seas and the Sails,* in *Fiesta in November,* trans. by Dudley Poore, Houghton Mifflin Company, Boston, 1942.
Aranha, José Pereira da Graça: *Canaan,* trans. by Mariano Joaquín Lorente, Four Seas Company, Boston, 1920 (Brazil).
Arciniegas, Germán: *The Knight of El Dorado: The Tale of Don Gonzalo Jiménez de Quesada and His Conquest of New Granada,* The Viking Press, Inc., New York, 1942 (Colombia).
Assis, Joaquim Maria Machado de: *Philosopher or Dog* (*Quincas Borba*), trans. by Clotilde Wilson, Noonday Press, New York, 1954 (Brazil).
————: *Dom Casmurro* (*Dom Casmurro*), trans. by Helen Caldwell, Noonday Press, New York, 1953.
————: *Epitaph of a Small Winner, Posthumous Memoirs of Brás Cubas* (*Memórias póstumas de Brás Cubas*), trans. by William L. Grossman, Noonday Press, N.Y., 1952.
Azevedo, Aloísio Tancredo Gonçalves de: *A Brazilian Tenement* (*O Cortiço*), trans. by Harry W. Brown, Robert M. McBride Company, New York, 1926 (Brazil).
Azuela, Mariano: *Marcela, a Mexican Love Story* (*Mala yerba*), trans. by Anita Brenner, Holt, Rinehart and Winston, Inc., New York, 1932 (Mexico).
————: *The Under Dogs* (*Los de abajo*), trans. by E. Mungúia, Brentano's, New York, 1929.
Blanco Fombona, Rufino: *The Man of Gold* (*El Hombre de oro*), trans. by Isaac Goldberg, Brentano's, New York, 1920 (Venezuela).
Blest Gana, Alberto: *Martín Rivas,* trans. by G. A. Umphrey, D. C. Heath and Company, Boston, 1936 (Chile).
Bombal, María Luisa: *The Shrouded Woman,* Farrar, Straus and Cudahy, Inc., New York, 1948 (Chile).
————: *House of Mist,* Farrar, Straus and Cudahy, Inc., New York, 1947.
Carneiro, Cecílio J.: *The Bonfire* (*A Fogueira*), trans. by Dudley Poore, Holt, Rinehart and Winston, Inc., New York, 1944 (Brazil).
Costa du Nels, Adolfo: *Bewitched Lands* (*Tierras hechizados*), trans. by Stuart E. Grummon, Alfred A. Knopf, Inc., New York, 1945 (Bolivia).
Cruls, Gastão Luís: *The Mysterious Amazonia* (*Amazônia misteriosa*), trans. by J. T. W. Sadler, J. Olympio, Rio de Janeiro, 1944 (Brazil).
De Onís, Harriet (ed.): *The Golden Land: An Anthology of Latin American Folklore in Literature,* Alfred A. Knopf, Inc., New York, 1948.
Fernández de Lizardi, José Joaquín: *The Itching Parrot* (*El Periquillo sarniento*), trans. by Katherine Anne Porter, Doubleday & Company, Inc., New York, 1942 (Mexico).

Fernández Guardia, Ricardo: *Cuentos Ticos: Short Stories of Costa Rica,* trans. by Gray Casement, 3d ed., The Burrows Brothers Co., Cleveland, Ohio, 1925 (Costa Rica).

Flores, Angel (ed.): *Fiesta in November (Fiesta en Noviembre)* by Eduardo Mallea, and other novels and short stories, Houghton Mifflin Company, Boston, 1942.

Frank, Waldo (ed.): *Tales from the Argentine,* trans. by Anita Brenner, Holt, Rinehart and Winston, Inc., New York, 1930.

Gallegos, Rómulo: *Doña Barbara,* trans. by Robert Malloy, Cape and Smith, New York, 1931 (Venezuela).

Gálvez, Manuel: *Holy Wednesday (Miércoles santo),* trans. by Warre B. Wells, Appleton-Century-Crofts, Inc., New York, 1934 (Argentina).

―――: *Nocha Regules (Nocha regules),* trans. by Leo Ongley, E. P. Dutton & Co., Inc., New York, 1922.

García Calderón, Ventura: *The Lottery Ticket,* trans. by Richard Phibbs, Golden Cockerel Press, London, 1945 (Peru).

―――: *The White Llama (La Verganza del condor),* trans. by Richard Phibbs, Golden Cockerel Press, London, 1938.

Gil Gilbert, Enrique: *Our Daily Bread (Nuestro pan),* trans. by Dudley Poore, Holt, Rinehart and Winston, Inc., New York, 1943 (Ecuador).

Goldberg, Isaac (trans.): *Brazilian Tales,* Four Seas Company, Boston, 1921.

Güiraldes, Ricardo: *Don Segundo Sombra: Shadows on the Pampas,* trans. by Harriet de Onís, Holt, Rinehart and Winston, Inc., New York, 1935 (Argentina).

Guzmán, Martín Luis: *The Eagle and the Serpent (El Aguila y la serpiente),* trans. by Harriet de Onís, Alfred A. Knopf, Inc., New York, 1930 (Mexico).

Hernández, José: *Martin Fierro: The Argentine Gaucho Epic,* trans. by Henry Alfred Holmes, Hispanic Institute in the United States, New York, 1948.

Huidobro, Vicente: *Portrait of a Paladin,* trans. by Warre B. Wells, Liveright Publishing Corporation, New York, 1932 (Chile).

―――: *Mirror of a Mage (Cagliostro),* trans. by Warre B. Wells, Houghton Mifflin Company, Boston, 1931.

Isaacs, Jorge: *Maria, a South American Romance (María),* trans. by Thomas A. Janvier, Harper & Brothers, New York, 1925 (Colombia).

Lobato, José Bento Monteiro: *Brazilian Short Stories,* intro. by Isaac Goldberg, E. Haldeman-Julius, Girard, Kan., 1924(?) (Brazil).

López y Fuentes, Gregorio: *El Indio,* trans. by Anita Brenner, The Bobbs-Merrill Company, Inc., Indianapolis, 1937 (Mexico).

Magdaleno, Mauricio: *Sunburst (El Resplandor),* trans. by Anita Brenner, The Viking Press, Inc., New York, 1944 (Mexico).

Mallea, Eduardo: *The Bay of Silence (La Bahía de silencio),* trans. by Stuart Edgar Grummon, Alfred A. Knopf, Inc., New York, 1944 (Argentina).

Mármol, José: *Amalia, a Romance of the Argentine (Amalia),* trans. by Mary J. Serrano, E. P. Dutton & Co., Inc., New York, 1919 (Argentina).

Marroquín, Lorenzo: *Pax (Pax),* trans. by I. Goldberg and W. V. Schierbrand, Brentano's, New York, 1920 (Colombia).

Martínez Zuviría, Gustavo Adolfo ("Hugo Wast"): *Stone Desert (El Desierto de piedra),* trans. by Louis Imbert and Jacques Le Clercq, Longmans, Green & Co., Inc., New York, 1930 (Argentina).

―――: *The Strength of Lovers (Lucia Miranda),* trans. by Louis Imbert and Jacques Le Clercq, Longmans, Green & Co., Inc., New York, 1930.

―――: *Peach Blossom (Flor de durazno),* trans. by Herman Hespelt and Miriam Hespelt, Longmans, Green & Co., Inc., New York, 1929.

―――: *Black Valley, a Romance of the Argentine (Valle negro),* trans. by Herman Hespelt and Miriam Hespelt, Longmans, Green & Co., Inc., New York, 1928.

―――: *The House of the Ravens (La Casa de los cuervos),* trans. by Leonard Matters, Williams & Norgate, London, 1924.

Matto de Turner, Clorinda: *Birds without a Nest: A Story of Indian Life and Priestly Oppression in Peru (Aves sin nido),* trans. by J. G. J., C. J. Thyme, London, 1904 (Peru).

Menéndez, Miguel Angel: *Nayar* (*Nayar*), trans. by Angel Flores, Holt, Rinehart and Winston, Inc., New York, 1942 (Mexico).

Pan American Union: *Literature in Latin America* (Club and Study Fine Arts Series), [Washington, 1950].

Petit, Magdalena: *La Quintrala* (*La Quintrala*), trans. by Lulú Vargas Vila, The Macmillan Company, New York, 1942 (Chile).

Prieto, Jenaro: *The Partner* (*El Socio*), trans. by Blanca de Roig and Guy Dowler, Butterworth & Co. (Publishers) Ltd., London, 1931 (Chile).

Quiroga, Horacio: *South American Jungle Tales* (*Cuentos de la selva*), trans. by Arthur Livingston, Duffield, New York, 1922 (Uruguay).

Rivera, José Eustacio: *The Vortex* (*La Vorágine*), trans. by Earle K. James, G. P. Putnam's Sons, New York, 1935 (Colombia).

Setúbal, Paulo de Oliveira: *Domitila, The Romance of an Emperor's Mistress* (*A Marquesa de Santos*), trans. by Margaret Richardson, Coward-McCann, Inc., New York, 1930 (Brazil).

Spell, Jefferson Rea: *Contemporary Spanish-American Fiction,* University of North Carolina Press, Chapel Hill, N.C., 1944.

Spota, Luis: *Wounds of Hunger,* trans, and ed. by Barnaby Conrad, Houghton Mifflin Company, Boston, 1957.

Taunay, Alfredo Maria Adriano d'Escragnolle: *Inocência* (*Innocência*), trans. by Henriqueta Chamberlain, The Macmillan Company, New York, 1945 (Brazil).

Thoby-Marcelin, Philippe: *The Beast of the Haitian Hills* (*La Bête du Musseay*), trans. by Peter C. Rhodes, Rinehart and Company, Inc., New York, 1946 (Haiti).

———: *Canapé-Vert,* trans. by Edward Larocque Tinker, Rinehart and Company, New York, 1944.

Veríssimo, Érico: *Night* (*Noite*), trans. by L. L. Barrett, The Macmillan Company, New York, 1956 (Brazil).

———: *Time and the Wind* (*O tempo e o vento*), trans. by L. L. Barrett, The Macmillan Company, New York, 1951.

———: *Consider the Lilies of the Field* (*Olhai os lírios do campo*), trans. by Jean Neel Karnoff, The Macmillan Company, New York, 1947.

———: *The Rest Is Silence* (*O resto é silêncio*), trans. by L. C. Kaplan, The Macmillan Company, New York, 1946.

———: *Crossroads* (*Caminhos cruzados*), trans. by L. C. Kaplan, The Macmillan Company, New York, 1943.

Villaverde, Cirilo: *Cecilia Valdés* or *Angel's Hill: A Novel of Cuban Customs* (*Cecilia Valdés, o la loma del angel*), trans. by Sydney G. Gest, Vantage Press, New York, Washington, Hollywood, 1962 (Cuba).

Appendix II

Latin America—Basic Data

(Including United States for purposes of comparison. Latest official figures)

Country	Population (millions)	Area (thousands of square miles)	Population density	Largest city	Its population (thousands)	Cost of living (1953 = 100)	Gross national product (billions of dollars)
Argentina	20.9	1,073	18	Buenos Aires	5,617	656	7.23 (1959)
Bolivia	3.4	424	8	La Paz	321	3,470	*
Brazil	70.5	3,287	21	São Paulo	3,316	567	18.22 (1959)
Chile	7.6	286	26	Santiago	1,547	1,230	3.88 (1959)
Colombia	14.1	440	31	Bogotá	1,005	187	3.49 (1959)
Costa Rica	1.1	20	54	San José	212	116	.45 (1959)
Cuba	6.7	44	145	Havana	1,218	*	2.56 (1958)
Dominican Republic	2.9	19	148	Ciudad Trujillo	295	100	.66 (1959)
Ecuador	4.2	105	39	Guayaquil	290	107	.84 (1959)
El Salvador	2.6	8	316	San Salvador	204	105	.50 (1958)
Guatemala	3.7	42	83	Guatemala	284	102	.65 (1959)
Haiti	3.5	11	319	Port-au-Prince	196	104	.33 (1955)
Honduras	1.9	43	41	Tegucigalpa	100	111	.37 (1959)
Mexico	34.6	760	41	Mexico, D.F.	4,500	164	9.76 (1959)
Nicaragua	1.47	57	23	Managua	109	114	.15 (1950)
Panama	1.05	29	34	Panama	221	99	.37 (1958)
Paraguay	1.7	157	10	Asunción	219	317	.19 (1958)
Peru	10.8	496	21	Lima	1,405	171	1.34 (1958)
United States	180.5	3,615	57	New York	7,782	111	499.8 (1960)
Uruguay	2.7	72	36	Montevideo	845	392	*
Venezuela	6.7	352	18	Caracas	1,168	107	6.91 (1959)

* Not available.

Appendix III

Rulers of Spain, 1479-1875

Ferdinand and Isabella, 1479–1516; 1474–1504
Charles I (V), 1516–1556, Emperor, 1519–1556, died 1558
Philip II, 1556–1598
Philip III, 1598–1621
Philip IV, 1621–1665
Charles II, 1665–1700
Philip V, 1700–1746
Ferdinand VI, 1746–1759
Charles III, 1759–1788
Charles IV, 1788–1808
Joseph Bonaparte, 1808–1813
Ferdinand VII, 1813–1833
Isabella II, 1833–1868
Amadeo, 1870–1873
Republic, 1873–1875

Rulers of Portugal

John I (Avis), 1385–1433
Edward, 1433–1438
Affonso V, 1438–1481
John II, 1481–1495
Manoel I, 1495–1521
John III, 1521–1557
Sebastian, 1557–1578
Henry, Cardinal, 1578–1580
Philip II of Spain, 1580–1598
Philip III of Spain, 1598–1621
Philip IV of Spain, 1621–1640
John IV (Braganza), 1640–1656
Affonso VI, 1656–1683
Pedro II, 1683–1706
John V, 1706–1750
Joseph, 1750–1777
Maria I, 1777–1816
John VI, 1816–1826

Appendix IV

Latin American Chiefs of State

Argentina since 1810

Junta of Government

1810, May 25. The revolution of May 25 proclaims a provisional board of government consisting of nine members: president: Cornelio Saavedra; members: Juan José Castelli, Manuel Belgrano, Miguel Azcuenaga, Manuel Alberti, Domingo Matheu, Juan Larrea; secretaries: Juan José Passo, and Mariano Moreno.

1810, Dec. 18. Twelve members are added as deputies of the provinces.

First Triumvirate

1811, Sept. 23. Feliciano A. Chiclana, Juan José Passo, and Manuel de Sarratea. Secretary: Bernardino Rivadavia.

Second Triumvirate

1812, Oct. 8. Juan José Passo, Nicolás Rodríguez Peña, and Antonio Alvarez Jonte.

Supreme Directors

1814, Jan. 22. Gervasio Antonio Posadas.

1815, Jan. 9. Gen. Carlos María de Alvear.

1815, Apr. 21. Gen. José Rondeau.

1815, Apr. 21. Col. Ignacio Alvarez Thomas is provisionally appointed during absence of Rondeau.

1816, Apr. 16. Gen. Antonio González Balcarce.

1816, May 3. Gen. Juan Martín de Pueyrredón.

1819, June 9. Gen. José Rondeau.

Governors of Buenos Aires

1820, Feb. 18. Manuel de Sarratea.

1820, Mar. 6. Gen. Juan Ramón Balcarce.

1820, Mar. 12. Manuel de Sarratea.

1820, May 2. Ildefonso Ramos Mejía, acting governor, finally appointed on June 7.

1820, June 22. Gen. Miguel E. Soler.

1820, June 30. Gen. Marcos Balcarce.

1820, July 1. Gen. Carlos María de Alvear.

1820, July 4. Col. Manuel Dorrego, provisional appointment.

1820, Sept. 28. Gen. Martín Rodríguez.

1824, Apr. 2. Gen. Juan Gregorio de Las Heras.

Presidents of the Nation

1826, Feb. 7. Bernardino Rivadavia.

1827, July 7. Dr. Vicente López, provisional appointment.

Governors of Buenos Aires

1827, Aug. 13. Col. Manuel Dorrego.

1828, Dec. 1. Gen. Juan Lavalle.

1829, Aug. 26. Gen. Juan José Viamonte, provisional appointment.
1829, Dec. 8. Col. Juan Manuel de Rosas.
1832, Dec. 17. Gen. Juan Ramón Balcarce.
1833, Nov. 3. Gen. Juan José Viamonte.
1834, Oct. 1. Dr. Manuel Vicente Maza, provisional appointment.
1835, Mar. 7. Gen. Juan Manuel de Rosas.
1852, Feb. 5. Dr. Vicente López.
1852, May 31. Gen. Justo José de Urquiza.
1852, June 25. Dr. Vicente López, provisional appointment.
1852, July 26. Gen. Justo José de Urquiza.
1852, Sept. 4. Gen. José Miguel Galán, provisional appointment.
1852, Sept. 11. Gen. Manuel G. Pinto, provisional appointment.
1852, Oct. 31. Dr. Valentín Alsina.
1852, Dec. 7. Gen. Manuel G. Pinto.
1853, June 25. Dr. Lorenzo Torres, Dr. Francisco de las Carreras, and Gen. José María Paz, delegate governors.

Presidents of the Argentine Confederation

1854, Mar. 5. Gen. Justo José de Urquiza.
1860, Mar. 5. Dr. Santiago Derqui.

Governors of the State of Buenos Aires

1853, July 24. Dr. Pastor Obligado, provisionally appointed, and finally designated on Oct. 13.
1857, May 5. Dr. Valentín Alsina.
1859, Nov. 8. Felipe Llavallol, delegate.
1860, May 3. Gen. Bartolomé Mitre.

Presidents of the Argentine Republic

1861, Bartolomé Mitre, provisional, Nov. 5, 1861–Oct. 12, 1862.
1862, Bartolomé Mitre, Oct. 12, 1862–June 12, 1865.
1865, Marcos Paz, vice president, assumes the executive power during a journey of Bartolomé Mitre to the interior of the country, as general commander of the allied armies, June 12, 1865–Jan. 2, 1868.
1868, Bartolomé Mitre reassumes power, Jan. 2–Oct. 12, 1868.
1868, Domingo F. Sarmiento, Oct. 12, 1868–Oct. 12, 1874.
1874, Nicolas Avellaneda, Oct. 12, 1874–Oct. 12, 1880.
1880, Julio Argentino Roca, Oct. 12, 1880–Oct. 12, 1886.
1886, Miguel Juárez Celman, Oct. 12, 1886–Aug. 6, 1890.
1890, Carlos Pellegrini, vice president, assumes power after the resignation of the former, Aug. 6, 1890–Oct. 12, 1892.
1892, Luis Sáenz Peña, Oct. 12, 1892–Jan. 22, 1895.
1895, José E. Uriburu, vice president, assumes power after the resignation of the former, Jan. 22, 1895–Oct. 12, 1898.
1898, Julio Argentino Roca, Oct. 12, 1898–Oct. 12, 1904.
1904, Manuel Quintana, Oct. 12, 1904–Mar. 12, 1906.
1906, José Figueroa Alcorta, vice president, assumes power after the death of the former, Mar. 12, 1906–Oct. 12, 1910.
1910, Roque Sáenz Peña, Oct. 12, 1910–Oct. 6, 1913.
1913, Victorino de la Plaza, vice president, assumes the presidency during the illness of Roque Sáenz Peña, Oct. 6, 1913–Aug. 9, 1914.
1914, Victorino de la Plaza, vice president, assumes the presidency after the death of Roque Sáenz Peña, Aug. 9, 1914–Oct. 12, 1916.
1916, Hipólito Irigoyen, Oct. 12, 1916–Oct. 12, 1922.
1922, Marcelo Torcuato de Alvear, Oct. 12, 1922–Oct. 12, 1928.
1928, Hipólito Irigoyen, Oct. 12, 1928–Sept. 6, 1930.
1930, José Félix Uriburu, provisional president, Sept. 6, 1930–Feb. 20, 1932.
1932, Agustín P. Justo, Feb. 20, 1932–Feb. 20, 1938.

1938, Roberto M. Ortiz, Feb. 20, 1938–July 3, 1940.
1940, Ramón S. Castillo assumes the presidency during the illness of the former, July, 1940–July 7, 1942.
1942, Ramón S. Castillo assumes the presidency after the resignation of Roberto M. Ortiz, July 7, 1942–June 4, 1943.
1943, Gen. Arturo Rawson, June 5–7, 1943.
1943, Gen. Pedro P. Ramírez, June 7, 1943–Mar. 9, 1944.
1944, Gen. Edelmiro J. Farrell, Mar. 9, 1944–June 4, 1946.
1946, Gen. Juan Domingo Perón, June 4, 1946–June 4, 1952. Reelected in 1951 and overthrown, Sept. 19, 1955.
1955, Gen. Eduardo Lonardi, provisional, Sept. 23–Nov. 13, 1955.
1955, Gen. Pedro Eugenio Aramburu, Nov. 13, 1955–May 1, 1958.
1958, Arturo Frondizi, May 1, 1958–March 30, 1962. Overthrown by armed forces coup.
1962, José María Guido, Senate president, March 30, 1962—.

Bolivia since 1926

1926, Hernando Siles, Jan. 10, 1926–June 25, 1930.
1930, Carlos Blanco Galindo (acting), June 28, 1930–Mar. 5, 1931.
1931, Daniel Salamanca, Mar. 5, 1931–Nov. 27, 1934.
1934, José Luis Tejada Sorzano (acting), Nov. 27, 1934–May 17, 1936.
1936, José David Toro R., May 17, 1936–July 13, 1937.
1937, Germán Busch (provisional), July 13, 1937–May 28, 1938; (elected) May 28, 1938–Aug. 23, 1939.
1939, Carlos Quintanilla (provisional), Aug. 23, 1939–Apr. 15, 1940.
1940, Enrique Peñaranda del Castillo, Apr. 15, 1940–Dec. 20, 1943.
1943, Gualberto Villarroel, Dec. 20, 1943–July 21, 1946.
1946, Nestor Guillen (acting), July 21–Aug. 16, 1946.
1946, Tomás Monje Gutiérrez (provisional), Aug. 16, 1946–Mar. 10, 1947.
1947, Enrique Herzog, Mar. 10, 1947–May 7, 1949 (resigned Oct. 24, 1949).
1949, Mamerto Urriolagoitia (acting), May 7–Oct. 17, 1949; (president) Oct. 24, 1949–May 16, 1951 (resigned).
1951, Hugo Ballivián R., May 16, 1951–Apr. 9, 1952.
1952, Hernán Siles Zuazo (provisional), Apr. 9–16, 1952.
1952, Víctor Paz Estenssoro, Apr. 16, 1952–Aug. 6, 1956.
1956, Hernán Siles Zuazo, Aug. 6, 1956–Aug. 6, 1960.
1960, Víctor Paz Estenssoro, Aug. 6, 1960—

Brazil since 1889

1889, Manoel Deodoro da Fonseca, 1889–1891.
1891, Floriano Peixoto, 1891–1894.
1894, Prudente de Morais Barros, 1894–1898, São Paulo.
1898, Manoel Ferraz de Campos Salles, 1898–1902, São Paulo.
1902, Francisco de Paula Rodrigues Alves, 1902–1906, São Paulo.
1906, Affonso Augusto Moreira Penna, 1906–1909, Minas Gerais.
1909, Nilo Peçanha, vice president, 1909–1910.
1910, Hermes da Fonseca, 1910–1914, Rio Grande do Sul.
1914, Wenceslau Braz Pereira Gomes, 1914–1918, Minas Gerais.
1918, Francisco de Paula Rodrigues Alves, 1918.
1918, Delphim Moreira da Costa Ribeiro, vice president, 1918–1919.
1919, Epitácio da Silva Pessoa, 1919–1922, Paraíba.
1922, Arturo da Silva Bernardes, 1922–1926, Minas Gerais.
1926, Washington Luis Pereira de Sousa, Nov., 1926–Oct. 24, 1930, São Paulo.
1930, Provisional governing *junta*, Oct. 24–Nov. 3, 1930.
1934, Getúlio Dornelles Vargas (provisional), Nov. 3, 1930–July 20, 1934; (elected) July 20, 1934–Oct. 29, 1945, Rio Grande do Sul.
1945, José Linhares, chief justice of the supreme court (*ad interim*), Oct. 30, 1945–Jan. 31, 1946.

1946, Eurico Gaspar Dutra, Jan. 31, 1946–Jan. 31, 1951.
1951, Getúlio Dornelles Vargas, Jan. 31, 1951–Aug. 24, 1954.
1954, João Cafe Filho, vice president acting as president, Aug. 24, 1954–Nov. 8, 1955 (resigned).
1955, Carlos Luz, speaker of chamber of deputies, Nov. 8–11, 1955.
1955, Nereu Ramos (acting), Nov. 11, 1955–Jan. 31, 1956.
1956, Juscelino Kubitschek de Oliveira, Jan. 31, 1956–Jan. 31, 1961.
1961, Jânio Quadros, Jan. 31–Aug. 25, 1961 (rer'gned).
1961, Raniere Mazzilli, interim, Aug. 25–Sept. 8, 1961.
1961, João Goulart, Sept. 8, 1961—

Chile 1831–1891

1831, Gen. Joachím Prieto, 1831–1841.
1841, Gen. Manuel Bulnes, 1841–1851.
1851, Manuel Montt, 1851–1861.
1861, José Joachím Pérez, 1861–1871.
1871, Federico Errázuriz Zañartú, 1871–1876.
1876, Aníbal Pinto, 1876–1881.
1881, Domingo Santa María, 1881–1886.
1886, José Manuel Balmaceda, 1886–1891.

Chile since 1920

1920, Arturo Alessandri, Dec. 23, 1920–Sept. 8, 1924.
1924, Military *junta* headed by Gen. Luis Altamirano, Sept. 5, 1924–Jan. 23, 1925.
1925, Military *junta* led by Carlos Ibáñez del Campo, Jan. 23–Mar. 21, 1925.
1925, Arturo Alessandri, Mar. 21–Oct. 1, 1925.
1925, Luis Barros Borgoño (acting), Oct. 1–Dec. 1925.
1925, Emiliano Figueroa Larraín, Dec., 1925–May 4, 1927.
1927, Carlos Ibáñez del Campo, May 4, 1927–July 26, 1931.
1931, Pedro Opazo Letelier (acting), July 26–27, 1931.
1931, Juan Esteban Montero Rodríguez (acting), July 27–Aug. 18, 1931.
1931, Manuel Trucco Franzani (acting), Aug. 18–Nov. 15, 1931.
1931, Juan Esteban Montero Rodríguez, Nov. 15, 1931–June 4, 1932.
1932, Arturo Puga (acting), June 4–12, 1932.
1932, Marmaduque Grove (acting), June 12–16, 1932.
1932, Carlos Dávila Espinoza, June 17–Sept. 13, 1932.
1932, Bartolomé Blanche Espejo (acting), Sept. 13–Oct. 2, 1932.
1932, Abraham Oyanedel (acting), Oct. 2–Dec. 24, 1932.
1932, Arturo Alessandri Palma, Dec. 24, 1932–Dec. 24, 1938.
1938, Pedro Aguirre Cerda, Dec. 24, 1938–Nov. 10, 1941.
1941, Geronimo Méndez Arancibia (acting), Nov. 10, 1941–Apr. 2, 1942.
1942, Juan Antonio Ríos Morales, Apr. 2, 1942–June 27, 1946.
1946, Alfredo Duhalde Vázquez (acting), June 27–Oct. 17, 1946.
1946, Juan A. Irabarren (acting), Oct. 17–Nov. 3, 1946.
1946, Gabriel González Videla, Nov. 3, 1946–Nov. 3, 1952.
1952, Carlos Ibáñez del Campo, Nov. 3, 1952–Nov. 3, 1958.
1958, Jorge Alessandri Rodríguez, Nov. 3, 1958—

Colombia since 1926

1926, Miguel Abadía Méndez, Aug. 7, 1926–Aug. 7, 1930.
1930, Enrique Olaya Herrera, Aug. 7, 1930–Aug. 7, 1934.
1934, Alfonso López Pumarejo, Aug. 7, 1934–Aug. 7, 1938.
1938, Eduardo Santos, Aug. 7, 1938–Aug. 7, 1942.
1942, Alfonso López Pumarejo, Aug. 7, 1942–Aug. 7, 1945.
1945, Alberto Lleras Camargo, Aug. 7, 1945–Aug. 7, 1946.
1946, Mariano Ospina Pérez, Aug. 7, 1946–Aug. 7, 1950.

1950, Laureano Gómez, Aug. 7, 1950–June 13, 1953.
1951, Roberto Urdaneta Arbeláez (acting), Oct. 31, 1951–June 13, 1953.
1953, Gustavo Rojas Pinilla, seized power by *coup d'état* (provisional), June 13, 1953–Aug. 3, 1954; (elected) Aug. 3, 1954–May 10, 1957 (resigned).
1957, Military *junta,* May 10–Aug. 7, 1958.
1958, Alberto Lleras Camargo, Aug. 7, 1958–Aug. 7, 1962.
1962, Guillermo León Valencia, Aug. 7, 1962—.

Costa Rica since 1928

1928, Cleto Gonzáles Víquez, May 8, 1928–May 8, 1932.
1932, Ricardo Jiménez Oreamuno, May 8, 1932–May 8, 1936.
1936, León Cortés Castro, May 8, 1936–May 8, 1940.
1940, Rafael Angel Calderón Guardia, May 8, 1940–May 8, 1944.
1944, Teodoro Picardo Michalski, May 8, 1944–Apr. 19, 1948.
1948, Santos León Herrera (provisional), Apr. 19–May 8, 1948.
1948, José Figueres (provisional), May 8, 1948–Nov. 8, 1949.
1949, Otilio Ulate Blanco, Nov. 8, 1949–Nov. 8, 1953.
1953, José Figueres, Nov. 8, 1953–May 8, 1958.
1958, Mario Echandi Jiménez, May 8, 1958—

Cuba since 1925

1925, Gerardo Machado Morales, May 20, 1925–Aug. 12, 1933.
1933, Carlos Manuel de Céspedes (provisional), Aug. 12–Sept. 5, 1933.
1933, Council of Five, Sept. 5–10, 1933.
1933, Ramón Grau San Martín (provisional), Sept. 10, 1933–Jan. 15, 1934.
1934, Carlos Hevía (provisional), Jan. 15–18, 1934.
1934, Márquez Sterling (acting), Jan. 18, 1934.
1934, Carlos Mendieta Montefur (provisional), Jan. 18, 1934–Dec. 11, 1935.
1935, José A. Barnet y Vinageras, Dec. 11, 1935–May 20, 1936.
1936, Miguel Mariano Gómez Arias, May 20–Dec. 24, 1936.
1936, Federico Laredo Bru, Dec. 24, 1936–Oct. 10, 1940.
1940, Fulgencio Batista y Zaldivar, Oct. 10, 1940–Oct. 10, 1944.
1944, Ramón Grau San Martín, Oct. 10, 1944–Oct. 10, 1948.
1948, Carlos Prío Socarrás, Oct. 10, 1948–Mar. 10, 1952.
1952, Fulgencio Batista y Zaldivar, assumed power by *coup d'état,* Mar. 10, 1952–Feb. 24, 1955; (elected) Feb. 24, 1955–Jan. 1, 1959.
1959, Manuel Urrutia Lleo, appointed by revolutionary leader Fidel Castro, Jan. 2–July 17, 1959.
1959, Osvaldo Dórticos Torrado, July 18, 1959—

Dominican Republic since 1924

1924, Horacio Vásquez, July 12, 1924–Mar. 2, 1930.
1930, Rafael Estrella Ureña (acting), Mar. 3–Apr. 22, 1930.
1930, Jacinto Peynado (acting), Apr. 22–May 21, 1930.
1930, Rafael Estrella Ureña (acting), May 22–Aug. 16, 1930.
1930, Rafael Leonidas Trujillo Molina, Aug. 16, 1930–Aug. 16, 1938.
1938, Jacinto Peynado, Aug. 16, 1938–Feb. 24, 1940.
1940, Manuel de Jesús Troncoso de la Concha (acting), Feb. 24–Mar. 8, 1940; (constitutional) Mar. 8, 1940–May 18, 1942.
1942, Rafael Leonidas Trujillo Molina, May 18, 1942; reelected May 16, 1947–Aug. 16, 1952.
1951, Hector B. Trujillo Molina (acting), Mar. 1, 1951–Aug. 16, 1952; (elected) Aug. 16, 1952–Aug. 3, 1960.
1960, Joachín Balaguer, Aug. 3, 1960–Jan. 16, 1962 (resigned).
1962, Rafael Bonnelly, Jan. 16, 1962—. (Vice president assumes power after resignation of former.)

Ecuador since 1926

1926, Isidro Ayora, May 11, 1926–Aug. 24, 1931.
1931, Luis Larrea Alba (acting), Aug. 24–Oct. 15, 1931.
1931, Alfredo Baquerizo Moreno (acting), Oct. 15, 1931–Sept. 2, 1932.
1932, Alberto Guerrero Martínez (provisional), Sept. 2–Dec. 5, 1932.
1932, Juan de Díos Martínez Mera, Dec. 5, 1932–Oct. 18, 1933.
1933, Abelardo Montalvo (provisional), Oct. 18, 1933–Sept. 1, 1934.
1934, José María Velasco Ibarra, Sept. 1, 1934–Aug. 21, 1935.
1935, Antonio Pons (provisional), Aug. 21–Sept. 26, 1935.
1935, Federico Páez (provisional), Sept. 26, 1935–Oct. 23, 1937.
1937, G. Alberto Enríquez Gallo (provisional), Oct. 23, 1937–Aug. 10, 1938.
1938, Manuel M. Borrero, Aug. 10–Dec. 2, 1938.
1938, Aurelio Mosquera Narvaes, Dec. 2, 1938–Nov. 16, 1939.
1939, A. F. Córdova (provisional), Dec. 11, 1939–Aug. 17, 1940.
1940, Carlos Arroyo Del Río, Aug. 17, 1940–May 30, 1944.
1944, José María Velasco Ibarra, May 31, 1944–Aug. 24, 1947.
1947, Carlos Mancheno C., Aug. 24–Sept. 2, 1947.
1947, Mariano Suárez Veintimilla (acting), Sept. 2–16, 1947.
1947, Carlos Arosemena (acting), Sept. 16, 1947–Sept. 2, 1948.
1948, Galo Plaza Lasso, Aug. 31, 1948–Aug. 31, 1952.
1952, José María Velasco Ibarra, Sept. 1, 1952–Aug. 21, 1956.
1956, Camilo Ponce Enríquez, Aug. 21, 1956–Sept. 1, 1960.
1960, José María Velasco Ibarra, Sept. 1–Nov. 9, 1961.
1961, Carlos Julio Arosemena, vice president installed as president after air force coup, Nov. 9, 1961—

El Salvador since 1927

1927, Pío Romero Bosque, Mar. 1, 1927–Feb. 28, 1931.
1931, Arturo Araujo, Mar. 1–Dec. 4, 1931.
1931, Maximiliano Hernández Martínez (acting), Dec. 4, 1931–Aug. 29, 1934.
1934, Andrés Ignacio Menéndez, Aug. 29, 1934–Mar. 1, 1935.
1935, Maximiliano Hernández Martínez, Mar. 1, 1935–May 9, 1944.
1944, Andrés Ignacio Menéndez (provisional), May 9–Oct. 21, 1944.
1944, Osmín Aguirre y Salinas, Oct. 21, 1944–Mar. 1, 1945.
1945, Salvador Castañeda Castro, Mar. 1, 1945–Dec. 14, 1948.
1948, Manuel de J. Córdova (provisional), Dec. 15, 1948–Jan. 4, 1949.
1949, Oscar Osorio (provisional), Jan. 4–Oct. 22, 1949.
1949, Oscar Bolaños (provisional), Oct. 22, 1949–Sept. 14, 1950.
1950, Oscar Osorio, Sept. 14, 1950–Sept. 14, 1956.
1956, José María Lemus, Sept. 14, 1956–Oct. 26, 1960.
1960, Military junta, Oct. 26, 1960–Jan. 25, 1961.
1961, New military junta, Jan. 25, 1961–Jan. 25, 1962.
1962, Eusebio Rodolfo Cordón (provisional), Jan. 25, 1962—

Guatemala since 1926

1926, Lázaro Chacón (provisional), Sept. 26, 1926–Dec. 12, 1930.
1930, Baudilio Palma (provisional), Dec. 12–17, 1930.
1930, Manuel Orellana (acting), Dec. 17, 1930–Jan. 2, 1931.
1931, José María Reina Andrade (provisional), Jan. 2–Feb. 14, 1931.
1931, Jorge Ubico, Feb. 14, 1931–July 1, 1944.
1944, Military junta, July 1–4, 1944.
1944, Federico Ponce (provisional), July 4–Oct. 20, 1944.
1944, Triumvirate, Oct. 20, 1944–Mar. 15, 1945.

1945, Juan José Arévalo, Mar. 15, 1945–Mar. 15, 1951.
1951, Jacobo Arbenz Guzmán, Mar. 15, 1951–July 2, 1954.
1954, Carlos Castillo Armas, assumed power by revolutionary action; (elected) Oct. 10, 1954–July 26, 1957 (assassinated).
1957, Luis A. González López (provisional), July 26–Oct. 24, 1957.
1957, Military *junta*, Oct. 24–26, 1957.
1957, Guillermo Flores Avendaño (provisional), Oct. 26, 1957–Mar. 2, 1958.
1958, Miguel Ydígoras Fuentes, Mar. 2, 1958—

Haiti since 1922

1922, Louis Borno, May 15, 1922–May 15, 1930.
1930, Eugène Roy, May 15–Nov. 18, 1930.
1930, Stenio Vincent, Nov. 18, 1930–May 15, 1941.
1941, Elie Lescot, May 15, 1941–Jan. 11, 1946.
1946, Executive military committee, Jan. 11–Aug. 16, 1946: president: Frank Lavaud; members: Antoine Levelt and Paul E. Magloire.
1946, Dumersais Estimé, Aug. 16, 1946–May 10, 1950.
1950, Paul E. Magloire, president of Comité, May 10–Dec. 6, 1950; (elected) Dec. 6, 1950–Dec. 13, 1956 (resigned).
1956, Joseph Memours Pierre-Louis (provisional), Dec. 12, 1956–Feb., 1957.
1957, Léon Cantave, February, 1957.
1957, Franck Sylvain, February–April, 1957.
1957, Executive Council, April–May, 1957.
1957, Daniel Fignolé, May–June 14, 1957.
1957, A. T. Kebreau, June 14–Oct. 22, 1957.
1957, François Duvalier, Oct. 22, 1957—

Honduras since 1929

1929, Vicente Mejía Colindres, Feb. 1, 1929–Feb. 1, 1933.
1933, Tiburcio Carías Andino, Feb. 1, 1933–Jan. 1, 1949.
1949, Juan Manuel Gálvez, Jan. 1, 1949–Nov. 16, 1954.
1956, Julio Lozano Díaz (acting), Nov. 16, 1954–Oct. 21, 1956.
1956, Military *junta*, seized power by *coup d'état*, Oct. 21, 1956–Dec. 21, 1957.
1957, Ramón Villeda Morales, Dec. 21, 1957—

Mexico since 1876

1876, Porfirio Díaz, Dec. 23, 1876–1880.
1880, Manuel González, 1880–1884.
1884, Porfirio Díaz, 1884–May 25, 1911.
1911, Francisco León de la Barra (provisional), May 25–Nov. 6, 1911.
1911, Francisco Madero, Nov. 6, 1911–Feb. 18, 1913.
1913, Victoriano Huerta, Feb. 22, 1913–July 14, 1914.
1914, Venustiano Carranza, July 15, 1914–May 21, 1920.
1920, Adolfo de la Huerta (provisional), May 21–Dec. 1, 1920.
1920, Alvaro Obregón, Dec. 1, 1920–Dec. 1, 1924.
1924, Plutarco Elías Calles, Dec. 1, 1924–Dec. 1, 1928.
1928, Emilio Portes Gil (provisional), Dec. 1, 1928–Dec. 21, 1929.
1929, Pascual Ortiz Rubio, Dec. 21, 1929–Sept. 2, 1932.
1932, Abelardo L. Rodríguez (provisional), Sept. 4, 1932–Nov. 30, 1934.
1934, Lázaro Cárdenas, Nov. 30, 1934–Dec. 1, 1940.
1940, Manuel Avila Camacho, Dec. 1, 1940–Dec. 1, 1946.
1946, Miguel Alemán Valdes, Dec. 1, 1946–Dec. 1, 1952.
1952, Adolfo Ruiz Cortines, Dec. 1, 1952–Dec. 1, 1958.
1958, Adolfo López Mateos, Dec. 1, 1958—

Nicaragua since 1929

1929, José María Moncada, Jan. 1, 1929–Jan. 1, 1933.
1933, Juan Batista Sacasa, Jan. 1, 1933–May 31, 1936.
1936, Minister of gobernación, May 31–June 9, 1936.
1936, Carlos Alberto Brenes Jarquín (provisional), June 9–Dec. 31, 1936.
1937, Anastasio Somoza, Jan. 1, 1937–May 1, 1947.
1947, Leonardo Argüello, May 1–26, 1947.
1947, Benjamín Lacaya Sacasa (provisional), May 26–Aug. 15, 1947.
1947, Víctor Román y Reyes, Aug. 14, 1947–May 6, 1950.
1950, Anastasio Somoza (acting), May 7, 1950–May 1, 1951; (elected) May 1, 1951–Sept. 29, 1956 (assassinated).
1956, Luis Somoza Debayle (provisional), Sept. 29, 1956–May 1, 1957; (elected) May 1, 1957—

Panama since 1928

1928, Florencio Harmodio Arosemena, Oct. 1, 1928–Jan. 2, 1931.
1931, Harmodio Arias (provisional), Jan. 2–16, 1931.
1931, Ricardo J. Alfaro, Jan. 16, 1931–Oct. 1, 1932.
1932, Harmodio Arias, Oct. 1, 1932–Oct. 1, 1936.
1936, Juan Demóstenes Arosemena, Oct. 1, 1936–Dec. 16, 1939.
1939, Agusto S. Boyd, Dec. 18, 1939–Oct. 1, 1940.
1940, Arnulfo Arias, Oct. 1, 1940–Oct. 9, 1941.
1941, Ernesto Jaén Guardia, Oct. 9, 1941.
1941, Ricardo Adolfo de la Guardia, Oct. 9, 1941–June 15, 1945.
1945, Enrique Adolfo Jiménez, June 15, 1945–Oct. 1, 1948.
1948, Domingo Díaz Arosemena, Oct. 1, 1948–July 28, 1949.
1949, Daniel Chanis (acting), July 28–Nov. 20, 1949.
1949, Roberto Chiari, Nov. 20–25, 1949.
1949, Arnulfo Arias, assumed presidency by *coup d'état,* Nov. 24, 1949–May 10, 1951.
1951, Alcibíades Arosemena, May 9, 1951–Oct. 1, 1952.
1952, José Antonio Remón Cantera, Oct. 1, 1952–Jan. 3, 1955 (assassinated).
1955, José Ramón Guizado (acting), Jan. 3–15, 1955 (impeached).
1955, Ricardo M. Arias Espinosa (acting), Jan. 15, 1955–Oct. 1, 1956.
1956, Ernesto de la Guardia, Jr., Oct. 1, 1956–Oct. 1, 1960.
1960, Roberto F. Chiari, Oct. 1, 1960—

Paraguay since 1928

1928, José P. Guggiari, Aug. 15, 1928–Oct. 26, 1931.
1931, Emiliano González Navero (acting), Oct. 26, 1931–Jan. 28, 1932.
1932, José P. Guggiari, Jan. 28–Aug. 15, 1932.
1932, Eusebio Ayala, Aug. 15, 1932–Feb. 17, 1936.
1936, Rafael Franco (provisional), Feb. 18, 1936–Aug. 15, 1937.
1937, Félix Paiva (provisional), Aug. 15, 1937–Aug. 15, 1939.
1939, José Félix Estigarribia, Aug. 15, 1939–Sept. 7, 1940.
1940, Higinio Morinigo M. (provisional), Sept. 7, 1940–Aug. 15, 1943; (elected) Aug. 15, 1943–June 3, 1948.
1948, Juan Manuel Frutos (provisional), June 4–Aug. 15, 1948.
1948, Juan Natalicio González, Aug. 15, 1948–Jan. 30, 1949.
1949, Raimundo Rolón (provisional), Jan. 30–Feb. 26, 1949 (overthrown).
1949, Felipe Molas López (provisional), Feb. 26–May 14, 1949; (elected) May 14–Sept. 10, 1949 (resigned).
1949, Federico Chaves (provisional), Sept. 11, 1949–July 16, 1950; (elected) July 16, 1950–May 5, 1954 (deposed by army).
1954, Gen. Alfredo Stroessner, Aug. 15, 1954—

Peru since 1919

1919, Agusto B. Leguía (provisional), July 5–Oct. 12, 1919; (elected) Oct. 12, 1919–Aug. 25, 1930.
1930, Manuel Ponce (provisional), Aug. 25–27, 1930.
1930, Luis M. Sánchez Cerro, Aug. 27, 1930–Mar. 1, 1931.
1931, Ricardo Leoncio Elías (provisional), Mar. 1–5, 1931.
1931, Gustavo A. Jiménez (provisional), Mar. 5–11, 1931.
1931, David Sámanez Ocampo, Mar. 11–Dec. 8, 1931.
1931, Luis M. Sánchez Cerro, Dec. 8, 1931–Apr. 30, 1933.
1933, Oscar Raimundo Benavides, Apr. 30, 1933–Dec. 8, 1939.
1939, Manuel Prado y Ugarteche, Dec. 8, 1939–July 28, 1945.
1945, José Luis Bustamante y Rivero, July 28, 1945–Oct. 28, 1948.
1948, Zenón Noriega (acting), Oct. 29–30, 1948.
1948, Manuel A. Odría, Oct. 31, 1948–June 1, 1950.
1950, Zenón Noriega (acting), June 1–July 28, 1950.
1950, Manuel A. Odría, July 28, 1950–July 28, 1956.
1956, Manuel Prado y Ugarteche, July 28, 1956–July 19, 1962.
1962, Military *junta,* headed by Gen. Ricardo Pérez Godoy, July 19, 1962.

Uruguay since 1927

1927, Juan Campisteguy, Mar. 1, 1927–Mar. 1, 1931.
1931, Gabriel Terra, Mar. 1, 1931–June 19, 1938.
1938, Alfredo Baldomir, June 19–Aug. 9, 1938.
1938, César Charlone (acting), Aug. 9–15, 1938.
1938, Alfredo Baldomir, Aug. 15, 1938–Mar. 1, 1943.
1943, Juan José Amézaga, Mar. 1, 1943–Mar. 1, 1947.
1947, Tomás Berreta, Mar. 1–Aug. 2, 1947.
1947, Luis Batlle Berres, Aug. 2–31, 1948.
1948, César Mayo Gutiérrez (acting), Aug. 31–Sept. 14, 1948.
1948, Luis Batlle Berres, Sept. 14, 1948–Mar. 1, 1951.
1951, Andrés Martínez Trueba, Mar. 1, 1951–Mar. 1, 1952.
1952, Return to conciliar form of government, abolishing the office of president and setting up a federal council of nine members, six from the majority party and three from the minority.

Venezuela since 1899

1899, Cipriano Castro, 1899–1908.
1908, Juan Vicente Gómez, 1908–Apr. 22, 1929.
1929, Juan Bautista Pérez (provisional), Apr. 22, 1929–June 13, 1931.
1931, Juan Vicente Gómez, July 13, 1931–Dec. 7, 1935.
1935, Eleazar López Contreras, Dec. 18, 1935–May 5, 1941.
1941, Isaías Medina Angarita, May 5, 1941–Oct. 18, 1945.
1945, Rómulo Betancourt (provisional), Oct. 18, 1945–Feb. 15, 1948.
1948, Rómulo Gallegos, Feb. 15–Nov. 24, 1948.
1948, Carlos Delgado Chalbaud (provisional), Nov. 24, 1948–Nov. 13, 1950.
1950, Germán Suárez Flamerich (provisional), Nov. 27, 1950–Dec. 3, 1952.
1952, Marcos Pérez Jiménez, Dec. 3, 1952–Apr. 19, 1953; (constitutional) Apr. 19, 1953–Jan. 23, 1958.
1958, Military *junta,* Jan. 23, 1958–Feb. 13, 1959.
1959, Rómulo Betancourt, Feb. 13, 1959—

Index

595